I0312034

"Glory! Glory! Glory!"

Exploring Ellen White's Early Visions

WITH INSPIRING EYEWITNESS TESTIMONIES

by

Kevin L. Morgan

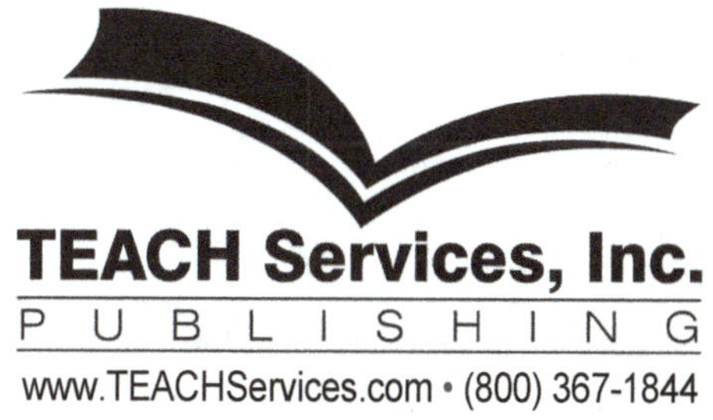

TEACH Services, Inc.
PUBLISHING
www.TEACHServices.com • (800) 367-1844

ISBN 978-1-4796-1815-6

The annotator, Kevin L. Morgan, M. A., studied homiletics, theology, biblical languages, and history. Among his books are *Sabbath Rest: Is There Something Missing in Your Busy Life; White Lie Soap: For Removal of Lingering Stains on Ellen White's Integrity as an Inspired Writer;* and *Journeying to the Same Heaven: Ellen G. White, the Civil War, and the Goal of Post-Racialism.*

Abbreviations

&c - etc. (et cetera)
1SG - *Spiritual Gifts*, volume 1
1BIO - *The Early Years, 1827–1862*
1EGWLM - *The Ellen G. White Letters and Manuscripts*, vol. 1
1T - *Testimonies for the Church*, volume 1
2SG - *Spiritual Gifts*, volume 2
10SDAC - *Seventh-day Adventist Bible Commentary*, vol. 10
11SDAC - *Seventh-day Adventist Bible Commentary*, vol. 11
AAR - *Australasian Record*
AHBA - *The Advent Harbinger and Bible Advocate*
AHSTR - *The Advent Herald and Signs of the Times Reporter*
AR - *The Advent Review*
Art. - Article
AUG - *Atlantic Union Gleaner*
BECOG - *Biographical Encyclopedia: Chronicling the History of the Church of God Abrahamic Faith 19th & 20th Centuries*, Jan Turner Stiles
Broadside1 - Broadside1, April 6, 1846, Ms. 1, Portland, ME
Broadside2 - Broadside2, Jan. 31, 1849, Ms. 4, Topsham, ME
Broadside3 - Broadside3, April 7, 1847
CAR - Center for Adventist Research
CUV - *Columbia Union Visitor*
EGW Estate DF - Ellen G. White Estate document file
DPF - *Divine Predictions of Mrs. Ellen G. White Fulfilled*, 1922, Frederick Carnes Gilbert
DS - *The Day-Star*
EGWEurope - *Ellen G. White in Europe*, Dwight Arthur Delafield
EGWE - *The Ellen G. White Encyclopedia*
ExV - *A Sketch of the Christian Experience and Views of Ellen G. White*
ExV54 - *Supplement to the Christian Experience and Views of Ellen G. White*
EW - *Early Writings*, 1882
FCC - Franklin Chauncey Castle
Footsteps - *In the Footsteps of the Pioneers*, 1990
Foy - *The Christian Experience of William E. Foy Together with the Two Visions He Received in the Months of January and February 1842*
GCB - *General Conference Bulletin*
GCDB - *General Conference Daily Bulletin*
GSAM - *The Great Second Advent Movement*, 1905, John Norton Loughborough
GT - *Girdle of Truth and Advent Review*
GV - *The Great Visions of Ellen G. White*, 1992, Roger W. Coon
HEVI - *Heavenly Visions*, John Norton Loughborough
HST - *The Signs of the Times and Expositor of Prophecy*, Joshua Vaughan Himes editor
HSAM - *History of the Second Advent Message*, Isaac C. Wellcome
inst. - "of this month"
JB - Joseph Bates
JNL - John N. Loughborough
JUBST - *The Jubilee Standard*
JW - James Springer White
L&EH - Leonard and Elvira Hastings
LEGW - *The Life of Ellen G. White*, Dudley Marvin Canright
LI - *Life Incidents*, James White
LS - *Life Sketches of Ellen G. White*, 1915
LS80 - *Life Sketches: Ancestry, Early Life, Christian Experience, and Extensive Labors, of Elder James White, and His Wife, Mrs. Ellen G. White*, 1880
LSMS - *Life Sketches Manuscript*
Lt. - Letter
LUH - *Lake Union Herald*
MGK- Dr. Merritt Gardner Kellogg
Ms. - Manuscript
MSC - Marion Stowell Crawford
MW - Mabel Workman
MOL - *Messenger of the Lord*, Herbert Douglass
MT - *The Messenger of Truth*
ONichols - Otis Nichols
née – literally "born," placed before a woman's maiden name after her married name
PCollins - Philip Collins
PFF4 - *The Prophetic Faith of Our Fathers*, vol. 4, LeRoy Edwin Froom
PGGC - *The Prophetic Gift in the Gospel Church*, 1911, John Norton Loughborough
PH016 - "To Brother J. N. Andrews and Sister H. N. Smith" June 1860
PrT - *The Present Truth*
PUR - *Pacific Union Recorder*
Robinson - *James White*, 1976, Virgil Robinson
RP - *The Rise and Progress of the Seventh-day Adventists*, 1892, John Norton Loughborough
RH - *The Advent Review and Sabbath Herald*
SHowland - Stockbridge Howland
SLG - *A Seal of the Living God*, 1849, Joseph Bates
SpM - Spaulding-Magan Collection
ST - *The Signs of the Times*
T04 - Testimony for the Church, no. 4
UCR - *Union Conference Record*
US - Uriah Smith
WCW - William Clarence White
WMiller - William Miller
WLF - "A Word to the 'Little Flock,' " May 30, 1847
YI - *The Youth's Instructor*

DEDICATION AND ACKNOWLEDGEMENTS

To John T. Richards, my brother-in-law, who supported me in my research of Ellen White's writings and who served as a literature evangelist in Rochester, New York, introducing truth-filled books into homes in the city where Ellen White's second book was published. His affirming words and optimism touched the lives of many.

I would also like to acknowledge several people who contributed to the production of this book since my research began in September 2020—

- My wife, Susan, for her help with genealogical tools on the Internet and her assistance in finding information about Joseph Turner and in identifying Elizabeth Haines, Ezra Stowell Eastman, and William M. Jordan
- Bob Pickle, for his historical sleuthing in helping to identify Sister Durben; Samuel, Mary, and Dorcas Moody; Dr. Lorenzo Dow Fleming; Dr. David H. Lord; Elizabeth Olcott; Nathaniel Pease; Louisa M. Divoll, née Morton; and Jacob Weston (in *online* **EXHIBIT-7**)
- Richard Bart, for resources to identify Nathaniel Pease
- Ron Graybill, for his collaboration in the discovery of the spiritualistic lecturer John S. Brown in Albion, Michigan, a long-standing mystery resolved
- Kevin Burton, for the identification of George Williams and John Thomas, witnesses to William Foy's visions
- Bruce Weaver (1952–2024), for the identification of Nicholas G. Reed and for his help in identifying William and Sarah Jordan and for locating the picture of John Megquier
- Stanley D. Hickerson (1952–2016), for his helpful annotation in *The Ellen G. White Letters and Manuscripts*, vol. 1, and for his many tantalizing historical clues on ancestry.com
- David Trim, for the insight about Jules-Etienne Dietschy
- Jessica Bessiere, Directrice bibliothèque Alfred Vaucher, for finding the death notice of Jules-Etienne Dietschy and to Benjamin Calmant, a graduate student at Adventist University of France–Collonges, for confirming the death date for Jules-Henri Guenin
- Dennis Kaiser, for the explanation of the 1882 republication of Ellen White's early writings
- Merlin Burt, for the identification of John Mason Avery and for allowing me to adapt his article on Ellen White's conversion
- Michael Campbell, for his work on the Evangelistic Conferences of 1848–1851
- Tim Poirier for assistance with many other resources from the Ellen G. White Estate
- Mystery Scoop, of London, for collaborating on the enhancement of the 1864 photograph of Ellen White used on the book's cover, which was further enhanced by the author using Krea.ai software
- Douglas F. Morgan, Jud Lake, and Ronald D. Graybill, for reviewing the early manuscript
- Joshua Knapp, for his suggestions in graphic design
- Mark Gutman and Brian Strayer, for copyediting the earlier manuscript
- Daniel Winters at www.earlysda.com, for his online transcription of the original text and his careful scrutiny of the later book manuscript, index, and *online* **EXHIBIT-7**
- Timothy Hullquist, at TEACH Services, Inc., for taking on the publishing of the book.

TABLE OF CONTENTS

https://www.academia.edu/115653485/Early_Adventist_Letters_and_Recollections

INTRODUCTION

"GLORY! GLORY! GLORY!" are words Ellen White often exuberantly uttered as she went into vision as she received wondrous *glimpses of glory*.[2] But what was the source of the visions?[3] Five general explanations have been offered, but only one of these fits all the evidence. We will consider their merits and limitations below.

The *first* explanation is that Ellen White's visions were "religious reveries" based on her previous thought and study.[4] Logical as this explanation may seem, it does not explain how she knew people before meeting them, nor does it explain her insights into people's hidden actions. On this point, Daniel T. Bourdeau, who translated for Mrs. White while she was in Europe, wrote:

> How interesting and wonderful it was to hear Sr. White correctly delineate the peculiarities of different fields she had seen only as the Lord had shown them to her, and show how they should be met; to hear her describe case after case of persons she had never seen with her natural vision, and either point out their errors or show important relations they sustained to the cause, and how they should connect with it to better serve its interests! As I had a fair chance to test the matter, having been on the ground, and knowing that no one had informed Sr. White of these things, while serving as an interpreter, I could not help exclaiming, "It is enough. I want no further evidence of its genuineness."[5]

Daniel T. Bourdeau

The *second* explanation is that her visions were the result of "mesmerism" (now called hypnotism) or some other form of altered consciousness.[6] Some who originally urged this explanation were present when Ellen White experienced a vision and were able to test their hypothesis. Dr. Merritt Gardner Kellogg described one such instance in 1853.

V132. *Pretensions of Holiness Vision, May 29, 1853*

> Sister White was in vision about twenty minutes or half an hour. As she went into vision every one present seemed to feel the power and presence of God, and some of us did indeed feel the Spirit of God resting upon us mightily. We were engaged in a prayer and social meeting Sabbath morning at about nine o'clock. Brother White, my father, and Sister White had prayed, and I was praying at the time. There had been no excitement, no demonstrations. We did plead earnestly with God, however, that he would bless the meeting with his presence, and that he would bless the work in Michigan. As Sister White gave that triumphant shout of "Glory! g-l-o-r-y-! g-l-o-r-y-!" which you have heard her give so often as she goes into vision, Brother White arose and informed the

Merritt G. Kellogg

> audience that his wife was in vision. After stating the manner of her visions, and that she did not breathe while in vision, he invited any one who wished to do so to come forward and examine her. Dr. Drummond, a physician, who was also a First-day Adventist preacher, who (before he saw her in vision) had declared her visions to be of mesmeric origin, and that he could give her a vision, stepped forward, and after a thorough examination, turned very pale, and remarked, "She doesn't breathe!"[7]

George I. Butler, whose father became an Adventist when George was but a child, summarized what many had witnessed during Ellen White's visions.

George I. Butler

> For nearly thirty years past these visions have been given with greater or less frequency, and have been witnessed by many, oftentimes by unbelievers as well as those believing them. They generally, but not always, occur in the midst of earnest sessions of religious interest while the Spirit of God is specially present, if those can tell who are in attendance. The time Mrs. White is in this condition has varied from fifteen minutes to one hundred and eighty. During this time the heart and pulse continue to beat, the eyes are always wide open, and seem to be gazing at some far-distant object, and are never fixed on any person or thing in the room. They are always directed upward. They exhibit a pleasant expression. There is no ghastly look or any resemblance of fainting. The brightest light may be suddenly brought near her eyes, or feints made as if to thrust something into the eye, and there is never the slightest wink or change of expression on that account; and it is sometimes hours and even days after she comes out of this condition before she recovers her natural sight. She says it seems to her that she comes back into a dark world, yet her eyesight is in no wise injured by her visions. . . .
>
> In this condition she often speaks words and short sentences, yet not the slightest breath escapes. When she goes into this condition, there is no appearance of swooning or faintness, her face remains its natural color, and the blood circulates as usual. Often she loses her strength temporarily and reclines or sits; but at other times she stands up. She moves her arms gracefully, and often her face is lighted up with radiance as though the glory of heaven rested upon her. She is utterly unconscious of every thing going on around her while she is in vision, having no knowledge whatever of what is said and done in her presence. A person may pinch her flesh, and do things which would cause great and sudden pain in her ordinary condition, and she will not notice it by the slightest tremor.
>
> There are none of the disgusting grimaces or contortions which usually attend spiritualist mediums, but calm, dignified, and impressive, her very appearance strikes the beholder with reverence and solemnity. There is nothing fanatical in her appearance. When she comes out of this condition she speaks and writes from time to time what she has seen while in vision; and the supernatural character of these visions is seen even more clearly in what she thus reveals than in her appearance and condition while in vision,

> for many things have thus been related which it was impossible for her to know in any other way.[8]

A hypnotic trance does not explain these phenomena. Some have suggested that she may have experienced what others have experienced in a deathlike state. However, unlike those described as being in a deathlike state, Ellen White was not motionless, with clammy skin and deathly pale coloring. Rather, her eyes were "open, not with a glassy appearance, or a vacant st8are, but with a look more like that of one looking intently at a distant object." She also sometimes arose, in vision, and moved around in the room, and sometimes she spoke in short sentences that were transcribed by someone present.[9]

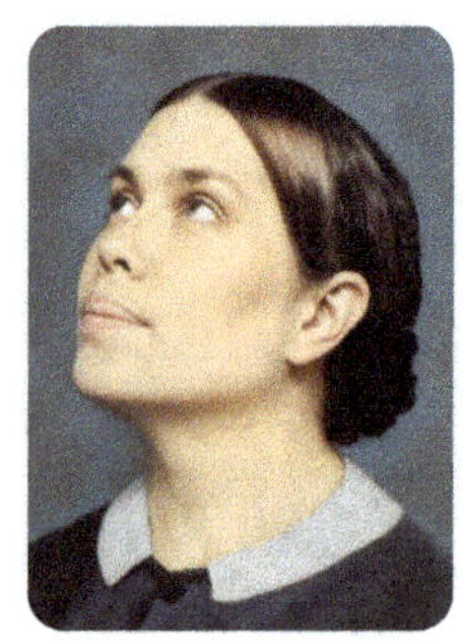

Ellen G. White

The *third* explanation, which has more recently circulated, is that what she experienced was "frontal lobe epilepsy." The notion is based on vague similarities between frontal lobe epilepsy and descriptions of Ellen White in vision, under the assumption that she suffered brain damage when she was hit by a rock in the face as a child or by her exposure to mercury chloride while shaping hats for her father the hatter. The proponents of this view note that people with this type of epilepsy often repeat words, and Ellen White did often say, "glory, glory," as she went into vision, and "dark, dark," as she came out, though she also said many non-repetitive things as well. Conversely, those with frontal lobe epilepsy often repeat nonsense and experience terrible hallucinations. Ellen White's visions made sense, and she had no apparent hallucinations. Moreover, the experiences of frontal lobe epilepsy are often characterized by fear, pleasure, depression, eroticism, or anger—emotions that are unlike what Ellen White experienced. We should note that, when epileptics are successful in their careers, it is *in spite of* their epilepsy and not because of it.

The *fourth* explanation is not naturalistic. It is the notion that Ellen White's visionary experiences, which gave evidence of supernatural power, were the result of spirit possession. In light of what her visions accomplished, Jesus' statement about attributing to the devil that which gives glory to God simply because it does not accord with one's theological assumptions is relevant. He said: "Every kingdom divided against itself is brought to desolation; . . . And if Satan cast out Satan, he is divided against himself; how shall then his kingdom stand?" (Matt. 12:25, 26).

Thus, we see that each of these first four explanations falls short. To simplistically explain the visions to be the result of a malfunctioning brain or previously ingested information or a self- or demonically-induced altered mental state does not align with the evidence, nor does it explain the foresight and insight from the visions or their biblical consistency. Could it not be that the visions were what Ellen White claimed for them—God-given messages of comfort, correction, and instruction? (See 1 Cor. 14:3.)

The dual emphasis of Ellen White's writings

Looking back over the years, Marion Concordia Stowell Crawford, a friend of Ellen White since their adolescence, explained to Mrs. White why people believed her when she came to share her first vision—it was because "it agreed with the Bible."[10] Indeed, Ellen White constantly pointed to God's Word as the standard of faith and practice, as she wrote at the close of her first book:

> I recommend to you, dear reader, the word of God as the rule of your faith and practice. . . . God has, in that Word, promised to give visions in the "LAST DAYS;" not for a new rule of faith, but for the comfort of his people, and to correct those who err from Bible truth.

The second emphasis were the *glimpses of glory* that inspired those who first heard the visions. Glimpses of God's *past* glory inspired them with awe over God's guidance and provision; glimpses of the *present* glory of Jesus shining through their lives inspired them to be better people; glimpses of *future* glory, when Christ returns and takes the redeemed home to glory, inspired them with hope to keep on the heavenly pathway and share the truth with others. Ellen's sister Sarah once wrote:

> I feel that we are growing stronger and stronger, and the path grows brighter and brighter. Praise the Lord! I know we are almost home, and sometimes it seems as though I could see the end of the way, and it is a glorious end. It seems sometimes just as though I should be there, that I, even I, should be on the new earth to behold its glories and feast with delight on its never-fading beauties, and, above all, to see Jesus—Him who gave His precious life for us, the Just for the unjust, that He might bring us to God.[11]

Throughout these early books are expressions pointing to visions—expressions such as "I had a vision/view," "the Lord gave me a vision/view," "I was shown," "I saw," "I was taken off in vision," "I was wrapt up in a vision," "I was carried," "I was pointed," "in my vision," "in vision," "in the night season," "the angel said," and "said the angel." That many of her visions were a "deep plunge in the glory" is indicated by her frequent use of "glory" and similar words in describing what she saw.[12] I sincerely hope that you are blessed, as was I, by Ellen White's **glimpses of glory** and by the eyewitness accounts of those who saw her in vision.

Book preview

Before the annotated text of Ellen White's two earliest books is a three-part essay on her preparation for her lifework, her early ministry, and the publishing work in Saratoga Springs and Rochester, New York. There is also **CHART-1**, a listing of Ellen White's visions, tagged by number, name, and date. Some vision names have long been established, while others have been taken from the heading provided by Ellen White, the location where the vision took place, or the main message of the vision. You will notice in the chart that the visions are not always presented in chronological order and that not all visions were published and that some were only delivered orally. You will also notice that many visions came during prayer. After the annotated text are eyewitness accounts of Ellen White in vision, comparisons of her first visions with other writings, and **CHART-2**, a "Timeline of Events in Ellen White's Early Life."

The published visions deal with subjects that were intended to encourage Adventist believers waiting for Christ's return, with many visions dealing with Bible prophecy. Among these were: the "sealing" or mark of authenticity of God's faithful commandment keepers, God's great love for His people, the biblical sign of the shaking of the powers of heaven before Christ's return, the open door and shut door of the heavenly sanctuary and the work of God's people while Christ ministers in heaven, an appeal to sacrifice personal means to share God's closing message with the world, the timeline of judgment in the thousand years of Revelation, the deceptive nature of Spiritualism, the qualifications of the messengers, or traveling ministers, who encouraged the Advent believers, the holiness of God, and the dangers in spiritualizing the return of Christ. Readers of this book will find answers to questions about the "shut door" and Ellen White's visions (pp. 28, 65, 211); what kept officers from arresting Israel Dammon (p. 30; *n76*); Ellen White's view of the personhood of God (p. 120), the divinity of Christ (*n476*), and the nature of the Godhead (p. 221); why people either accepted or rejected Ellen White's ministry (p. 171); Ellen White's use of 2 Esdras (p. 173); and whether Ellen White's first vision derived from others (pp. 177, 180).

In the marking of the text, green colorization draws attention to Scripture, showing the biblical nature of the visions, while red colorization draws attention to instances in vision in which Ellen White did not breathe, held a Bible, or shouted "glory!"[13] Also, each paragraph is referenced to the earlier compositions from which it was drawn (for example, {ExV 3.1; RH, July 21, 1851}). Such referencing illustrates how, from the start, Ellen White drew from her earlier materials in producing her books.[14] The endnotes identify people mentioned in the accounts and provide a treasure-trove of other background information, grounding these early stories in documentable facts.

Supplemental resources, which were originally part of the book manuscript and provide background on Ellen White's visions and early Adventist history, are available online via the QR code or URL link at the end of the table of contents. These include **EXHIBIT-7**, which is a collection of letters and recollections of James White and others, and CHART-3, "Evangelistic Conferences, 1848–1851."

In the introduction to Ellen White's third book, Roswell Fenner Cottrell observed: "Since a *special work* of the Spirit was necessary to *prepare* a people for the first Advent of Christ, how much more so for the second; especially, since the last days were to be perilous beyond all precedent . . . !"[15] It is not hard to comprehend why such a work of the Spirit would still be needed. Keep that in mind as you read about Ellen White's own preparation for her lifework in the following essay.

Roswell F. Cottrell

PREPARATION FOR HER LIFEWORK AND EARLY LABORS

So who was Ellen White? What was her background, and how did she begin receiving visions? Ellen White's life sketch in her first book is scant on details, so the following account of her early life fills in more of her background, giving readers a glimpse of the events that led young Ellen to find a trusting relationship with God.[16]

Early Life

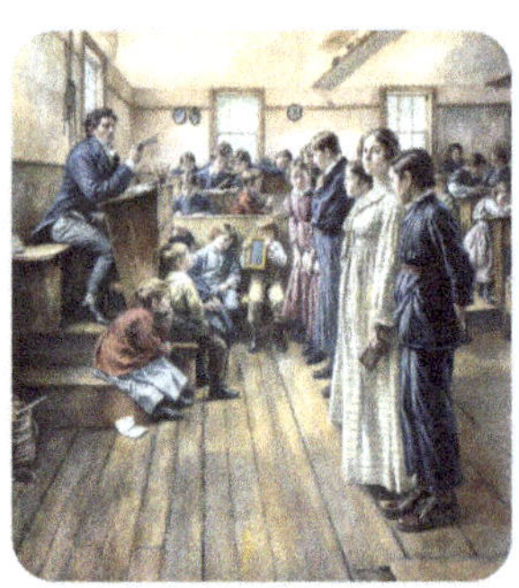

Typical school house scene

Ellen and her twin sister Elizabeth were born in 1827 in Gorham, Maine, the youngest of Robert and Eunice Harmon's eight children. Their parents were devout Methodists, and their father, a hatter by trade, was a lay exhorter, which means that he would rise in church to appeal to the people to respond to sermons. He also led out in meetings held in homes. Ellen enjoyed school and was often "called downstairs to the primary room" to read the little children their lessons. However, Ellen's plans for an education were radically altered by an event that occurred in **1836** when she was nine years old, as she, her twin sister, and a schoolmate were headed home, walking across a public common in Portland, Maine, while attempting to escape an angry older schoolmate. Ellen wrote, "I turned my head to see how far she was behind me, and as I did so, she threw the stone and it hit me on the nose. A blinding, stunning sensation overpowered me; I fell senseless."[17]

When Ellen finally regained consciousness, she found herself inside a merchant's store, her clothing covered in blood. A stranger offered her a ride home, but she turned it down, not wishing to soil his carriage with her blood. She attempted to walk home, but, as she later wrote, "after walking only a few rods, I grew faint and dizzy.[18] My twin sister and my schoolmate carried me home."[19]

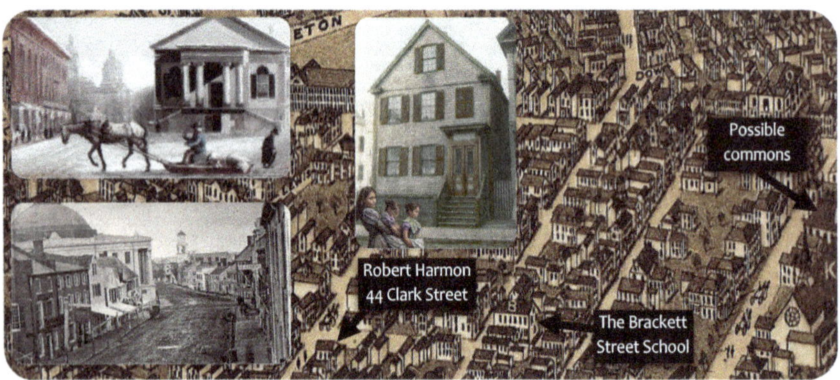

1876 map of Ward 7 of Portland, Maine, with several "commons," or empty lots, remaining; top left inset is Market Street (1869) ; bottom left is Middle Street (1850); other inset is the three girls in front of house once thought to be Harmons'

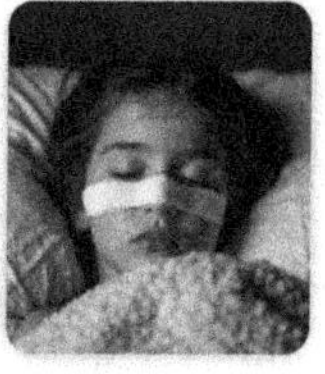

For the next three weeks, Ellen went in and out of consciousness.[20] In one lucid moment, she found herself resting in a "great cradle." Later, when she was allowed to see herself in a mirror, she saw that "every feature of my face seemed altered. The bone of my nose had been broken, and had to be removed; this caused the disfigurement. . . . Physicians thought that a silver wire might be put in my nose to hold it in shape. . . . I was reduced almost to a skeleton." Her father had been away on a business trip to Georgia. When he came home and greeted the children, he did not recognize her. "It was hard for him to believe that I was his little Ellen whom he had left only a few months before, a healthy, happy child."[21] Overhearing a visiting neighbor offer to buy a burial robe for her, Ellen realized just how close to death she was. Her mother turned the offer down, believing that her daughter would live. Confessing her sins in simple faith, Ellen found peace with God, and the fear of death left her.[22]

From **1836** to **1838**, through her prolonged illness, Ellen attended school sporadically due to a chronic cough, difficulty breathing, and poor concentration. In **1839**, Ellen made a final attempt to go back to school, attending a seminary for young women in Portland.[23] However, still not keeping up and finding the environment inhospitable to her relationship with God, she dropped out. Later she wrote, "I did not attend school after I was twelve years old."[24]

Westbrook Seminary and Female College

With the dashing of her hopes of preparing for a career in writing, she wrote, "I was unreconciled to my lot, and at times murmured against the providence of God in thus afflicting me."[25] But her resentment against God afflicted her tender conscience, and her peace and confidence in the acceptance of Jesus left her.[26] She concluded that God must be angry with her for her complaints, yet she kept it all to herself. Later she would write: "No one conversed with me on the subject of my soul's salvation, and no one prayed with me. So I locked my secret agony within my heart, and did not seek the advice of experienced Christians as I should have done."[27]

Guilt and fear of eternal damnation haunted Ellen's early adolescence leading to depression and hopelessness. She also learned how easily her young companions could turn away from her because her looks had been marred. Her painful experience made her more sympathetic to the suffering of others and heightened her desire for a closer relationship with God, equipping her, in the coming years, to better serve as a messenger for the Lord, though it was a heavy burden to bear in her youth.

The Chestnut Street Methodist Episcopal Church had a number of books on godly living, written for children. Some of these, ironically, featured a role-model named Ellen.[28] These books caught young Ellen Harmon's interest. She described her response: "I had conceived a great admiration for the paragons of perfection there represented. But far from encouraging me in my efforts to become a Christian, these books were as stumbling-blocks to my feet; for I despaired of ever attaining to the perfection of the youthful characters in those stories, who lived the lives of saints, and were free from all the doubts and sins and weaknesses under which I staggered. . . . The similarity of these avowedly true histories seemed to point the fact to my youthful mind that they really presented a correct picture of a child's Christian life. I repeated to myself again and again, 'If that is true, I can never be a Christian. I can never hope to be like those children.' This thought drove me almost to despair."[29]

During this same period of inner struggle, William Miller visited Portland, Maine, where he lectured on the second coming of Jesus from **March 11–23, 1840** in the Christian Connexion church. Ellen attended the meetings with many others. She later described the meetings' tenor: "No wild excitement attended the meetings, but a deep solemnity pervaded the minds of those who heard. Not only was a great interest manifested in the city, but the country people flocked in day after day, bringing their lunch baskets, and remaining from morning until the close of the evening meeting."[30]

Miller's lectures spurred a general awakening among Christians of different denominations. Special meetings for sinners to prepare for Jesus' return were linked with the lectures, and sinners were invited to come forward to the "anxious seat." Hundreds responded, and Ellen was one of them. Despite her intense internal desire for acceptance with God, she could find no peace. Her tortured conscience still obscured the Saviour. "I regarded it a great thing to be a Christian," she later wrote of this time, "and felt that it required some peculiar effort on my part."[31] For about 18 months more she lived with this thought until she attended a Methodist meeting in which she grasped the meaning of righteousness by faith.

William Miller, 1841

Experiencing Righteousness by Faith

The breakthrough occurred in August or early **September 1841** when Ellen and her parents attended the Methodist camp meeting in Buxton, Maine. It was in these meetings that a minister spoke on righteousness by faith, with his text being the words of Esther, "I will go in unto the king, . . . and if I perish, I perish" (Esther 4:16). He used these words to encourage his audience to go before King Jesus and receive pardon. He told them that they must avoid the fatal mistake of "waiting to make themselves more worthy of divine favor before they ventured to claim the promises of God."[32] The sermon gave Ellen hope, and she determined to find assurance with God.

A Methodist Camp Meeting, 1837

Yet one thing stood in the way. Ellen heard others loudly and frequently proclaim that they had received the "witness of the Spirit" of God's acceptance. Therefore, Ellen believed that she needed to experience spiritual ecstasy to affirm that she had been accepted by God. Years later, she reflected on this time: "How much I needed instruction concerning the simplicity of faith!"[33]

As she bowed at the altar with others seeking the Lord, Ellen experienced blessed relief: "I felt my needy, helpless condition as never before. But suddenly, as I prayed, my burden left me, and my heart was light. . . . I can never forget this precious assurance of the pitying tenderness of Jesus toward one so unworthy of His notice. . . . Again and again I said to myself, 'Can this be religion? Am I not mistaken?' . . . I felt that the Saviour had blessed me and pardoned my sins."[34]

For the first time in two years since her struggle had begun, she found sweet peace with God. Thus, in Buxton, Maine, Ellen finally realized Jesus' acceptance and the forgiveness of her sins. Righteousness before God was through faith in the merits of Jesus, not by her own merits and worthiness!

Ellen returned from the camp meeting a changed person. Everything was new and beautiful. Men in the streets seemed to be praising God. As she described her perceptions, her mother listened with tear-dimmed eyes, recalling her own experience of conversion.

Church records show that, on **September 20, 1841,** Ellen was recommended for the customary six-month probationary period before baptism, and, on **May 23, 1842**, she was recommended for baptism itself.

Ellen's desire for holiness before God intensified during William Miller's second course of lectures in Portland two weeks before her baptism. Miller at first calculated the 2300-day prophecy to end some time in the Jewish year of 1843, and Ellen had the strongest desire to be certain of her salvation. On **June 26, 1842**, a group gathered on the shore of the old baptizing beach of Portland to witness Pastor John Hobart baptize young Ellen and eleven others in the cold, choppy waters of Casco Bay.[35] Of that momentous day she later wrote: "Finally the day was appointed for us to receive this solemn ordinance. Although usually enjoying, at this time, great peace, I frequently feared that I was not a true Christian, and was harassed by perplexing doubts as to my conversion. It was a windy day when we, twelve in number, were baptized, walking down into the sea. The waves ran high and dashed upon the shore, but in taking up this heavy cross, my peace was like a river. When I arose from the water, my strength was nearly gone, for the power of the Lord rested upon me." That afternoon she and another sister were received into full membership in the Chestnut Street Methodist Episcopal Church.[36]

The "Old Baptising Shore"

Following William Miller's meetings and her baptism, Ellen entered a second period of severe mental struggle. Of the period just after her fifteenth birthday, in **November 1842**, she wrote: "For some time I felt a constant dissatisfaction with myself and my Christian attainments and did not continually realize a lively sense of the mercy and love of God."[37]

While Ellen had grasped the truth of being accepted with God and justified by faith, she did not yet grasp the reality that forgiveness and acceptance do not keep a believer from sinning. As she attended the continuing Adventist meetings in Portland's Beethoven Hall, she wrote, "my mind constantly dwelt upon the subject of holiness of heart. I longed above all things to obtain this great blessing, and feel that I was entirely accepted by God."[38]

Confused about the relationship between justification and sanctification, she sought insight from many sources. She wrote: "These two states [of justification and sanctification] were presented to my mind as separate and distinct from each other; yet I failed to comprehend the difference or understand the meaning of the terms, and all the explanations of the preachers increased my difficulties. . . . I felt that I could claim only what they called justification. In the Word of God I read that without holiness no man should see God. Then there was some higher attainment that I must reach before I could be sure of eternal life. I studied over the subject continually; for I believed that Christ was soon to come, and feared He would find me unprepared to meet Him."[39]

Ellen's fears and doubts were intensified by her misunderstanding hell and the state of the dead. She had a vivid imagination that brought terror to her heart as she heard ministers describing the fires of hell. "I feared that I should be lost, and that I should live throughout eternity suffering a living death. . . . The frightful descriptions that I had heard of souls in perdition sank deep into my mind. . . . While listening to these terrible descriptions, my imagination would be so wrought upon that the perspiration would start, and it was difficult to suppress a cry of anguish, for I seemed already to feel the pains of perdition."[40]

Believers seeking sanctification at the "anxious seat"

Shy and retiring, Ellen was reluctant to share her spiritual turmoil with others, and it finally came to a head. "Despair overwhelmed me," she wrote, "and for three long weeks no ray of light pierced the gloom that encompassed me."[41]

Dreams that Changed Her View of God

It was under this sense of gloom that Ellen had two impressive dreams. One dream was of entering a temple where she saw a bleeding lamb and happy people who received the lamb and then left her behind in darkness as a trumpet sounded. The dream gave her great concern that she was not right with God and that He had left her. But then she had another dream in which a beautiful, kind person led her up a steep stairway to a door, where she was instructed to leave all the treasured belongings she had brought with her. Then, passing through the open door, she looked over to see One she recognized as Jesus. She wrote: "There was no mistaking that beautiful countenance; that expression of benevolence and majesty could belong to no other. As His gaze rested upon me, I knew at once that He was acquainted with every circumstance of my life and all my inner thoughts and feelings. I tried to shield myself from His gaze, feeling unable to endure His searching eyes; but He drew near with a smile, and laying His hand upon my head, said, 'Fear not.' The sound of His sweet voice thrilled my heart with happiness it had never before experienced. I was too joyful to utter a word, but, overcome with emotion,

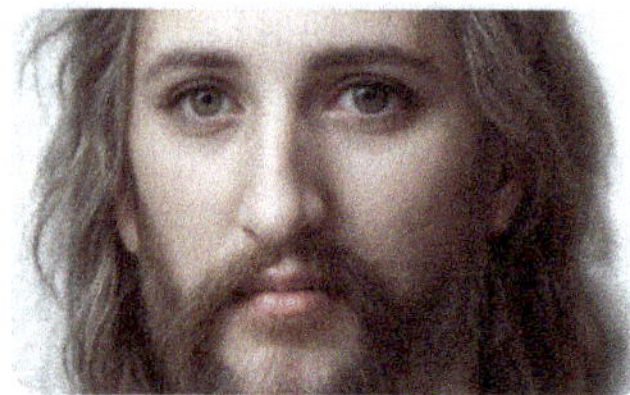

sank prostrate at His feet." In leaving the room, she wrote, "the loving eyes of Jesus were still upon me, and His smile filled my soul with gladness. His presence awoke in me a holy reverence and an inexpressible love."[42] This latter dream gave her peace and hope.

After the dreams, she opened her heart to her devoted mother, revealing her questions and pain. Her mother recommended that she share her concerns with Elder Levi Stockman, a beloved Adventist preacher of about thirty years of age living in Portland. A husband and a father of three children all under the age of ten, he was dying of tuberculosis. Ellen later wrote of him: "I had great confidence in him, for he was a devoted servant of Christ." As the beloved minister listened, he affectionately placed his hand upon her head and, with tears in his eyes, gently said: " 'Ellen, you are only a child. Yours is a most singular experience for one of your tender age. Jesus must be *preparing* you for some *special work.*' "[43]

Stockman's fatherly demeanor and wise counsel helped her to see God differently, as she later wrote: "My views of the Father were changed. I now looked upon Him as a kind and tender parent, rather than a stern tyrant compelling men to a blind obedience. My heart went out toward Him in a deep and fervent love. Obedience to His will seemed a joy; it was a pleasure to be in His service."[44]

Stockman offered for her a heart-felt prayer, and Ellen left the interview comforted and encouraged. She could now see that God was like her own kind parents—committed to helping her, even when she failed and made a mistake. When He disciplined her, He did not reject her for her failures. In the future, understanding the difference between loving discipline and punishment would play a key role in her attitude toward the failings of others. Following this interview with Stockman, she was able to pray publicly for the first time and, for six months, not a shadow clouded her mind, nor did she neglect a single known duty.[45]

Expelled from the Methodist Church

When a new pastor came to the Chestnut Street Methodist Episcopal Church, he was not at all favorable to the Millerite views of the members who held them. According to church records, the Harmon family was the first of the Advent believers in the church to be examined. On **February 6, 1843,** the church formed the first of five committees to address the "anti-Methodist conduct" of the Harmons. However, their remonstrances with Robert Harmon proved ineffective against his faith in the Advent. So, in **August**, the Harmons were expelled from the church. Despite Robert Harmon's appeal at the quarterly meeting on **September 2, 1843**, the session members voted to uphold the earlier church action.[46]

Chestnut Street Methodist Episcopal Church

Expulsion from the Methodist Church just over a year after her acceptance into it hit 15-year-old Ellen hard. That her father stood courageously for what he believed about Christ's return must have been an anchor for Ellen's faith, as the Harmons had now cast their lot fully with the Advent message.

The six months between the **autumn of 1843** and **March-April 1844**, were a time of expectation and personal witness. Of this period Ellen wrote: "I longed to tell the story of Jesus' love, but felt no disposition to engage in common conversation with anyone. My heart was so filled with love to God and the peace that passeth understanding that I loved to meditate and to pray."[47]

During this period, Ellen testified publicly at least twice regarding her new assurance. She was asked to give her testimony at a meeting held in the Christian Chapel on Temple Street, and, as she expressed her love for Jesus with a humble heart and moist eyes, the "melting power of the Lord came upon the assembled people. Many were weeping and others praising God."[48] When a leader called for sinners to arise for prayer, the people responded without hesitation.

Dreaming about Laboring for Souls

In the ensuing months, Ellen shared her faith with her friends and acquaintances—some considerably older than she was and a few who were even married—appealing to them to yield their lives to God. She prayed earnestly about each person and reported that all but one of them had been converted. Night after night she dreamed of laboring for the salvation of souls. "At such times," she wrote, "special cases were presented to my mind; these I afterward sought out and prayed with."[49] Some felt she was too zealous and tried to get her to moderate her active faith. Yet, Jesus and His soon return filled young Ellen's thoughts and gave her great joy, as she later described 1844 as "the happiest year of my life."[50]

Yet, Ellen's health was precarious. She was weak, and she coughed up so much blood that she had to sleep in a sitting position to keep from choking. The doctors did not give her long to live. Ellen described a conversation she had with one doctor.

"The physicians have said, 'You cannot live over three months, the lungs are so affected, raising blood,' and if you let me mesmerize you, I think that I can relieve you some of the pain that is in your body."

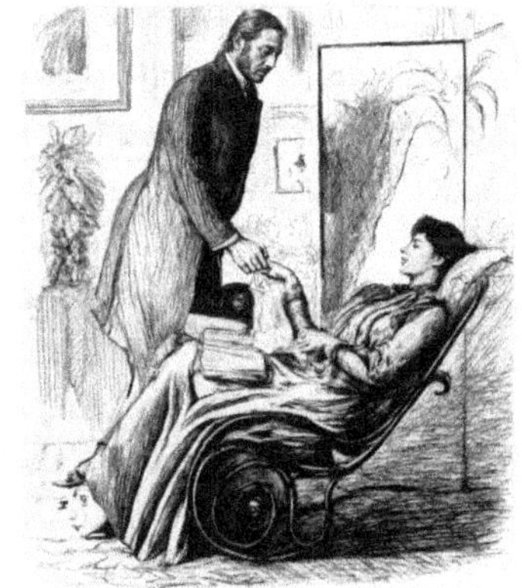

Said I, "You cannot mesmerize me, Doctor."

"Will you let me try?"

"You may try."

Well, he tried two hours, and he could not make the least impression upon me at all. Said he, "I don't understand it, I don't understand."[51]

With the passing of the expected time of Christ's return in October 1844, several of the Adventist families in Portland, Maine, continued meeting in various homes to encourage one another to remain faithful until Jesus did return.[52] As a help to Mrs. Harmon, Ellen would sometimes stay with Benjamin and Elizabeth Haines who had two small sons at home—John, who was nine years old, and Horace, who was just a baby.[53] It was at their house in **December of 1844** that Ellen had her first vision while praying with four other women.[54]

V1. *Midnight Cry Vision, Dec. 1844*

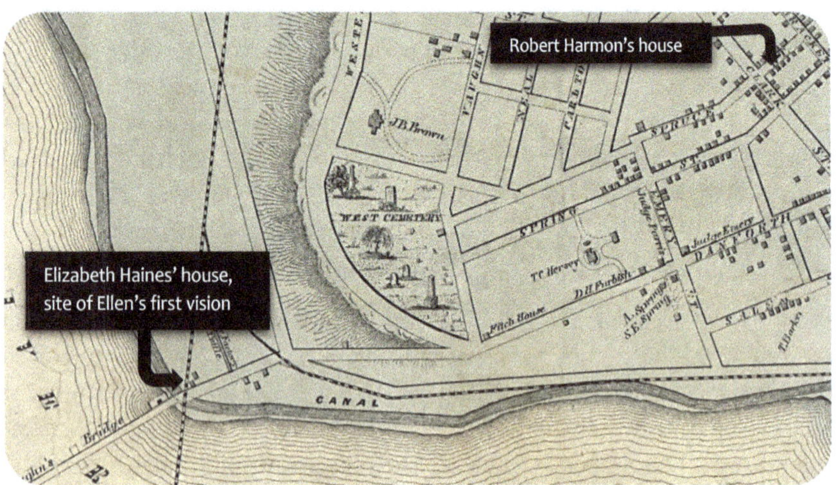

Western Portland, Maine, 1844, marked for the homes of Robert Harmon and Elizabeth Haines, the latter on Danforth Street (formerly Bridge Road), next to the Vaughn Bridge, which extended across the Fore River into South Portland

At the time that Ellen received the vision, most of the Adventists had given up their belief in the significance of the Midnight Cry, which pointed to the fulfillment of Daniel 8 in October 1844, and she had too. Yet, what she saw in that vision changed her thinking. Their general abandonment of the Midnight Cry left her reticent to share the vision with the others, yet, with God's urging and reassurance, she began sharing it with the scattered bands of believers in New England. By year's end, she also had written out the vision in detail in a letter to the editor of *The Day-Star*. Her written description in that letter linked the first vision with a later vision containing related content, which she had had by the time she wrote in December 1845.

Her account of these visions of **glory** was adapted and included in her first book (which you will find beginning on page 82 of this book). As you read on, you will hear—in Ellen's own voice—the encouragements God used to convince her to share her vision with the other Adventists in Portland and then with other groups of Adventists throughout New England. The reconstruction that follows comes from her own accounts, with the sources listed after each paragraph. It begins with Ellen White's recollections of what occurred as she gained consciousness immediately after coming out of the vision.

Early Ministry

They thought that I was dead, and there they watched and cried and prayed so long. But to me it was heaven—it was life—and then the world was spread out before me, and I saw darkness like the pall of death. When my breath came again to my body, after I came out of vision, I could not hear anything, oh! how dark this world looked to me. I could not discern the brightest light. It was thought that my eyesight was gone, but when I again became accustomed to the things of this world, I could see again. Everything looked changed, a gloom was spread over all I beheld. The light and glory that my eyes had rested upon had eclipsed the light, and thus it was for many hours. Then gradually I began to recognize the light, and I asked where I was. "You are right here in my house," said the owner of the house [***Elizabeth Haines***]. "What, here? I [am] here? Do you not know about it [the vision]?" Then it all came back to me. *Is this to be my home? Have I come here again?* Oh, the weight and the burden which came upon my soul. But then grace was given to me, and since that time nothing has cut off the glory that I could behold in Jesus Christ. My eyes have seen Him as much as human eyes could see Him. God had taken me away to behold His glory. I want you to know that that very sight made me strong so that nothing in the earth or in human beings would lead me to place my hopes in the earth or in human beings. I could see that Jesus was our only hope, and that to Him we can trust everything. He will never leave or forsake us.[55] {ExV 5.4; 2SG 35.1; Ms6a-1886; Ms16-1894.19-21}

At the time I had the vision of the "Midnight Cry," I had given it up in the past and thought it future as also most of the band had. I know not what time Joseph Turner got out his paper [*The Advent Mirror*]. I knew he had one out [*The Hope of Israel Extra*], and one was in the house, but I knew not what was in it, for I did not read a word in it.[56] I had been, and still was very sick. I took no interest in reading, for it injured my head and made me nervous. After I had the vision and God gave me light, He bade me deliver it to the band, but I shrank from it. I was young, and I thought they would not receive it from me. I disobeyed the Lord, and instead of remaining at home, where the meeting was to be that night, I got in a sleigh in the morning and rode three or four miles and there I found Joseph Turner. He merely inquired how I was and if I was in the way of my duty. I said nothing, for I knew I was not. I passed up chamber and did not see him again for two hours, when he came up, [he] asked if I was to be at meeting that night.[57] I told him, no. He said he wanted to hear my vision and thought it duty for me to go home. I told

THE ADVENT MIRROR. 1.

"Write, Blessed are they which are called to the marriage supper of the Lamb."

VOL. I.—NO. 1. BOSTON, JANUARY, 1845. A. HALE & J. TURNER, EDS.

Has not the Savior come as the Bridegroom?

Parable of the ten virgins . Matthew xxv.

V.1. "Then shall the kingdom of heaven be likened unto ten virgins, which took their lamps, and went forth to meet the bridegroom." Then—at the time when the faithful and the wise servants, having

answer:—"And there came unto me one of the seven angels, which had the seven vials full of the seven last plagues, and talked with me, saying, 'Come hither, I will shew thee the bride, the Lamb's wife.' And he carried me away in the Spirit to a great and high mountain, and shewed me *that great city, the holy Jerusalem*, descending out of heaven from God, having the glory of God:

6. When does the marriage of the Lamb take place—*before* or *after* he comes, as the King of glory, to make his people immortal? Now let us keep in mind these different parts of the scene, and it may not be so difficult to settle this question as might be at first supposed, viz., the coming of the Bridegroom "*to* the marriage," the marriage itself, and the marriage supper. It must be evident

him I should not. He said no more but went away. I thought, and told those around me, if I went I should have to come out against his views, thinking he believed with the rest. I had not told any of them what God had shown me, and I did not tell them in what I should cut across his track.[58] {2SG 35.1; Lt3-1847.3}

Winter travel by sleigh just outside of Portland, Maine

All that day I suffered much in body and mind. It seemed that God had forsaken me entirely. I prayed the Lord, if He would give me strength to ride home that night, the first opportunity I would deliver the message He had given me. He did give me strength, and I rode home that night. Meeting had been done some time, and not a word was said by any of the family about the meeting. {Lt3-1847.4}

Very early next morning Joseph Turner called, said he was in haste going out of the city in a short time, and wanted I should tell him all that God had shown me in vision.[59] It was with fear and trembling I told him all. After I had got through he said he had told out the same last evening. I was rejoiced, for I expected he was coming out against me, for all the while I had not heard anyone say what he believed. He said the Lord had sent him to hear me talk the evening before, but as I would not, He meant His children should have the light in some way, so He took him. There were but few out when he talked, so the next meeting I told my vision, and the band, believing my vision from God, received what God bade me to deliver to them.[60] It was a powerful time. The Spirit of the Lord attended the testimony, and the solemnity of eternity rested upon us. An unspeakable awe filled me, that I, so young and feeble, should be chosen as the instrument by which God would give light to His people. While under the power of the Lord, I was filled with joy, seeming to be surrounded by holy angels in the glorious courts of heaven, where all is peace and gladness, and it was a sad and bitter change to wake up to the realities of mortal life. {Lt3-1847.5; ExV 5.4; 2SG 35.1; 1T 62}

A Call to Travel

V2. Make Known to Others Vision, Jan. 1845

About one week after this, the Lord gave me another view and showed me the trials I must pass through, that I must go and relate to others what he had revealed to me. It was shown me that my labors would meet with great opposition, and that my heart would be rent with anguish, but said the angel, "The grace of God is sufficient for you; He will sustain you."[61] {ExV 5.4; 2SG 35.1; 1T 62; LSMS 90.1}

There were five sisters of us in our house, praying, and while we were praying, the power of God came upon me, and there I was taken off in vision. And what did I see? I saw a world with all the blackness of midnight upon it, the wickedness that was presented. And I said, "Is there no more coming here?" And then there was like a little chain, a thread of light from the heaven where I was, fastened to persons in that dense darkness. Then the instruction was given that these had the light from heaven and must let that light shine forth upon others, they must take Christ as their Example, and work as Christ worked, with all the self-denial and self-sacrifice; and if they win heaven at last, it is through Christ. . . . "I bid you go and give the message; I command you." "Why, I cannot speak a loud word," I said. "But go" was the message. {Ms190-1903}

The teaching of this vision troubled me exceedingly, for it pointed out my duty to go out among the people and present the truth. My health was so poor that I was in constant bodily suffering, and, to all appearance, had but a short time to live, and I was only seventeen years old, small and frail, unused to society, and naturally so timid and retiring that it was painful for me to meet strangers. I knew that many had fallen through exaltation and that, if I in any way became exalted, the Lord would leave me, and I should surely be lost. I went to the Lord in prayer and prayed earnestly for several days and far into the night, that the burden might be removed from me and laid upon someone more capable of bearing it. I lay upon my face a long time, and all the light of duty did not change [as] the words of the angel sounded continually in my ears: "Make known to others what I have revealed to you." {ExV 6.1; 2SG 36.1; 1T 62}

I was unreconciled to go out into the world and dreaded to meet its sneers and opposition. I had naturally but little self-confidence. Hitherto when the Spirit of God had urged me to duty, I had risen above myself, forgetting all fear and timidity in the thought of Jesus' love and the wonderful work He had done for me. The constant assurance that all was right between me and God and that I was fulfilling my duty, and obeying the will of the Lord gave me confidence that surprised me. At such times, I felt willing to do or suffer anything in order to help others into the light and peace of Jesus; and relying upon the strength of God could declare the testimony without fear. But the work seemed impossible for me to perform; to attempt it seemed certain failure. The trials attending it appeared severe—more than I could endure. How could I, a child in years, go forth from place to place, unfolding to the people the holy truths of God? The idea of a female traveling from place to place caused me to draw back. My brother Robert, but two years older than myself, could not accompany me, for he was feeble in health and his timidity greater than mine; nothing could have induced him to take such a step. My father had a family to support and could not leave his business; but he assured me that if God had called me to labor in other places, He would not fail to open the way for me. But these words of encouragement brought little comfort to my desponding heart; the path before me seemed hedged in with difficulties that I was unable to overcome. I coveted death as a release from the responsibilities that were crowding upon me. {2SG 36.1; 1T 62; LSMS 91.4}

At length the Lord hid his face from me. The sweet peace I had so long enjoyed left me, and darkness and despair again pressed upon my soul. I feared that He had forsaken me because I was unwilling to go and do His will. My prayers all seemed vain, and my faith was gone. The company of believers in Portland were ignorant concerning the exercises of my mind that had brought me into this state of despondency; but they knew that for some reason my mind had become depressed, and they felt that this was sinful on my part, considering the gracious manner in which the Lord had manifested Himself to me. While some sought to comfort me, others were faithful in warning me of my danger. I was afraid I had grieved the Spirit of the Lord from me forever and thought, if He would reveal himself to me again, I would obey him and would go anywhere. How small the opposition and frowns of men appeared to me then, compared with the frown of God! As I thought of the light that had formerly blessed my soul, it seemed doubly precious in contrast with the darkness that now enveloped me. {2SG 36.2; 1T 63}

The meetings were held at my father's house; but my distress of mind was so great that I absented myself from the meetings for some time. This did not relieve me from the burden which grew heavier until the agony of my spirit seemed more than I could bear, and again I was induced to attend one of the meetings in my own home. The church all united in earnest prayer for me. The church made my case a special subject of prayer. Father Pearson, who in my earlier experience had opposed the manifestations of the power of God upon me, now prayed earnestly for me and counseled me to surrender my will to the will of the Lord.[62] Like a tender father he tried to encourage and comfort me, bidding me believe I was not forsaken by the Friend of sinners. I felt too weak and despondent to make any special effort for myself, but my heart united with the petitions of my friends. I cared little now for the opposition of the world and felt willing to make every sacrifice and to be used to His glory if only the favor of God might be restored to me. Once more I consecrated myself to the Lord. {2SG 37.1; 1T 64; LSMS 92.2}

Father Pearson's Testimony

V3. Ball of Fire Vision, 1845

While prayer was offered for me that the Lord would give me strength and courage to bear the message, the thick darkness that had enveloped me rolled back, and a sudden bright light, something that seemed to me like a ball of fire, came towards me, struck me right over the heart, and, as it fell upon me, my strength was taken away and I fell to the floor. I seemed to be in the presence of Jesus and of angels. One of these holy beings again repeated the words: "Make known to others what I have revealed to you." {2SG 37.1; 1T 64; LSMS 92.3}

Father Pearson, who could not kneel on account of his rheumatism, witnessed this occurrence.[63] He heard a stir like hard breathing, and I had fallen on the floor, and he saw, and others saw it too, just like I saw it, like a ball of fire that struck me right over the heart. When I revived sufficiently to see and hear; he rose from his chair, and said, "I have seen a sight such as I never expected to see. A ball of fire came down from heaven, and struck Sister Ellen Harmon right on the heart. I saw it! I saw it! I can never forget it. It has changed my whole being. Sister Ellen, have courage in the Lord. After this night I will never doubt again. We will help you henceforth, and not discourage you."[64] {Ms131-1906; LSMS 93.1}

Fear of Self-exaltation

One great fear that oppressed me was that if I obeyed the call of duty and went out declaring myself to be one favored of the Most High with visions and revelations for the people, I might yield to sinful exaltation and be lifted above the station that was right for me to occupy, bring upon myself the displeasure of God, and lose my own soul. I had before me several cases, and my heart shrank from the trying ordeal. I now earnestly entreated that, if I must go and relate what the Lord had shown me, that I might be kept from undue exaltation. Said the angel: "Your prayers are heard and shall be answered." If I should be in danger of exaltation, His hand should be laid upon me, and I should be afflicted with sickness. Said the angel: "By affliction He will draw you to Himself and preserve your humility. If you deliver the messages faithfully and endure unto the end, you shall eat of the fruit of the tree of life and drink of the water of life."[65] {ExV 6.2; 2SG 37.1; 1T 64, 65; LSMS 93.2}

After recovering consciousness of earthly things, I committed myself to the Lord, ready to do his bidding, whatever that might be. {LSMS 94.1}

Travels in Maine

Samuel Hoyt Foss

I had had three visions and was then bidden to relate these to others. Providentially the way opened for me to go with my brother-in-law [***Samuel Foss***] to my sisters' in Poland [***Mary and Harriet***], thirty miles from my home. I there had opportunity to bear my testimony. Mr. Foss came to our house in Portland in a sleigh and said that Mary was anxious that Ellen should visit her. I thought that this was an opening from the Lord. I was in feeble health, my lungs were diseased; I was spitting blood. As I could not bear the cold air, I sat in the bottom of the sleigh with the buffalo robe over my head. {2SG 38.1; Lt37-1890.3; 1T 65; LSMS 94.2}

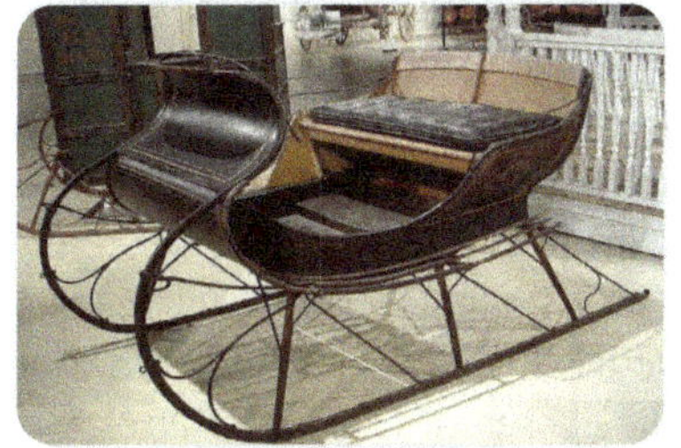
The "Portland Cutter," developed in Portland, Maine, was one of the most popular one-horse open sleighs.

The Lord gave me strength. I had been able to talk but little for about three months. My lungs and throat were very sore. It was with the greatest difficulty that I could speak aloud in a low, husky tone. {2SG 38.1; LSM 94.2}

Mary Plummer Foss

After I arrived at **Poland**, [my sister Mary Foss] said that there was to be a meeting at Megquier's Hill and asked me to go.[66] I went with [her] and [her] husband. I stood up in meeting to relate the testimony given me of God. I said, "Lord, I will stand on my feet," although I could not talk—I had no voice to talk, and [I] commenced speaking in a whisper and labored to speak for about five minutes, then everything broke away and the soreness and obstruction seemed to leave my throat and lungs, and my voice was clear and strong, and I could talk with perfect ease and freedom for nearly two hours. When my message was ended, my voice was gone until I stood before the people again, when the same singular restoration was repeated. I felt a constant assurance that I was doing the will of God and saw marked results attending my efforts. I frequently spoke over two hours. I knew nothing of the experience Hazen Foss had been passing through. In this meeting the power of the Lord came upon me and upon the people. {2SG 38.1; 1T 65; Ms190-1903; Lt37-1890.5, 6; LSMS 94.2}

Hazen Foss

The next day, I had related to me the exercises of Hazen Foss. I was told by one, in the presence of a roomful, that they had urged Hazen Foss to tell them the things which the Lord had shown him. He had been greatly disappointed that the Lord did not come in '44. He said that he had been deceived, and he refused to obey the promptings of the Spirit of God. After having plainly declared that he would not go from place to place and relate the visions God had given him, very strange feelings came to him, and a voice said, "You have grieved away the Spirit of the Lord." {Lt37-1890.7}

He was horrified at his stubbornness and rebellion and told the Lord that he would relate the vision. The Lord had told him that if he refused, He would give the light to someone else, and when he attempted to relate the vision, his mind could not grasp it. He tried and tried to relate it, but he said, "It is gone from me; I can say nothing, and the Spirit of the Lord has left me." Those who gave a description of that meeting said it was the most terrible meeting they were ever in. {Lt37-1890.8}

Next morning I met Hazen Foss. Said he, "Ellen, I want to speak with you. The Lord gave me a message to bear to His people, and I refused after being told the consequences; I was proud; I was unreconciled to the disappointment. I murmured against God and wished myself dead. Then I felt a strange feeling come over me. I shall be henceforth as one dead to spiritual things. I heard you talk last night; I believe the visions are taken from me, and given to you. Do not refuse to obey God, for it will be at the peril of your soul. I am a lost man. You are chosen of God; be faithful in doing your work, and the crown I might have had, you will receive." {Lt37-1890.9}

Map of Poland, Maine, marked for the properties of J. Megguire [*Meguier*], W. McAnn, and S. Foss around Tripp Pond

Arrest in Poland, Maine

I never was shut up. I never had a man's hand laid on me to harm me, and the promise was [that] it never should be. They tried once. They tried to hold me, and the brethren felt terrible. The officers of justice got hold of me, and said I, "Brethren, do not worry about me. The light has come to me that no man's hand should be laid upon me to hurt me, and so you need not have any fears."[67] Then these men would turn white, and the very men that they were trying to get hold of, they could not hold them. The power of God was upon His people and evidence of it was given. {Ms131a-1906.20}

Millerism.—The proceedings of the professors of this belief have been such, that the officers of this and some other towns in the vicinity have felt it their duty to put a stop to them.

Mr. George W. Brown, of Orrington, who has been for some weeks in this town and vicinity, was arrested on Tuesday by our selectmen, examined before Mr. Barton, and sentenced to the county jail for twenty days.

On Wednesday one of the leaders, well known as Joe Turner, another named Harmon, with one or two others, were arrested at the house of Mr. Megquier, in Poland, by the selectmen of that town, as was reported.—*Norway (Me.) Advertiser.*

Her arrest without incarceration was reported in the *Norway Advertiser*, April 25, 1845

Journey Northeast to Central Maine

Providentially the way opened for me to go to the central part of Maine. Thus I journeyed for three months. Brother William Jordan was obliged to go to Orrington on business, and his sister [***Sarah Jordan***] accompanied him, and I was urged to go with them and relate my visions.[68] It caused me some trial to go, but as I had promised the Lord that if he would open the way before me, I would walk in it; I dared not refuse. The Spirit of the Lord attended the message I bore, and the desponding were encouraged to renew their faith, and made to hope. {2SG 38.2; 1T 65; LSMS 94.3}

James White

At **Orrington** I met Elder James White, and learned that Brother Jordan had come for the purpose of taking to him his horse and sleigh.[69] James was acquainted with my friends and was himself engaged in the work for the salvation of souls. {2SG 38.3; 1T 65; LSMS 94.3}

At **Garland** a large number collected from different quarters to hear my message. But my heart was very heavy. I had just received a letter from my mother, begging me to return home, for false reports were being circulated concerning me. This was an unexpected blow. My name had always been free from the shadow of reproach, and my reputation was very dear to me. My cup of sorrow was full. I also felt grieved that my mother should suffer on my account. Her heart was bound up in her children, and she was very sensitive in regard to them. If there had been any opportunity, I should have returned immediately home and by my presence contradicted these lying reports.[70] But this was impossible. {2SG 39.1; 1T 65; LSMS 95.2}

My sorrow was so great that I felt too depressed to speak that night. My friends urged me to trust in the Lord, but [I] could not be comforted. At length, the brethren engaged in prayer for me, and the blessing of the Lord soon rested upon me, and I bore my testimony that evening with great freedom. I felt that an angel of God was standing by my side to strengthen me. Sweet heart-felt shouts of glory and victory went up from that house, the presence of Jesus was felt in our midst, and our hearts burned with his love. {2SG 39.1; 1T 65}

Soon after this I went to **Exeter**, a small village not far from Garland. At Exeter a heavy burden rested upon me, which I could not be free from until I related what I had been shown concerning some fanatical persons present, who were exalted by the spirit of Satan.[71] I mentioned that I must soon return home and that I had seen that these fanatical persons were anxious to visit Portland; but they had no work to do there; that they would injure the cause if they went, by carrying things to extremes; that they were deceived in regard to the Spirit they possessed. This seemed to cause some great trial. Then they all wanted to go to Portland with us, and I got right up, [and said,] "The Spirit of God does not want any of you there. Fanaticism is rooted in you right now, and if you go there, you will blaze it all out.[72] God forbids you to go." My testimony cut directly across their anticipated course but seemed to have little effect except to make these persons of extreme views jealous of me, and [they] secretly held bitter feelings against me. But they went. And the fanatical work took such a course, of men and women together, that it broke it all up. Our people saw where it was going. {2SG 39.1, 2; 1T 65; LS80 201; LSMS 95.2, 3; Ms131a-1906.15}

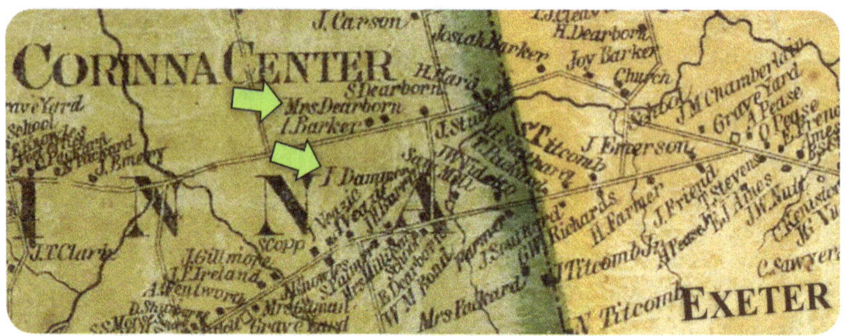

An 1859 map of Corinna and Exeter, Maine, marked for the residences of "Mrs. Dearborn" and "I Dammon"

Ellen Receives Light on the "Shut Door"

V5. Bridegroom Vision, Feb. 1845

The vision of events commencing with the Midnight Cry about the bridegroom's coming I had about the middle of February 1845, while in Exeter, Maine, in meeting with Israel Dammon, James, and many others. Many of them did not believe in a "shut door." I suffered much at the commencement of the meeting. Unbelief seemed to be on every hand. There was one sister there that was called very spiritual. She had traveled and been a powerful preacher the most of the time for twenty years. She had been truly a mother in Israel. But a division had risen in the band on the "shut door." She had great sympathy and could not believe the door was shut. (I had known nothing of their differences.) Sister Duerben [***Dearborn***] got up to talk.[73] I felt very, very sad. At length, my soul seemed to be in an agony, and, while she was talking, I fell from my chair to the floor. It was then I had a view of Jesus rising from His mediatorial throne and going to the holiest as Bridegroom to receive His kingdom.[74] {Lt3-1847.6, 7}

Israel Dammon

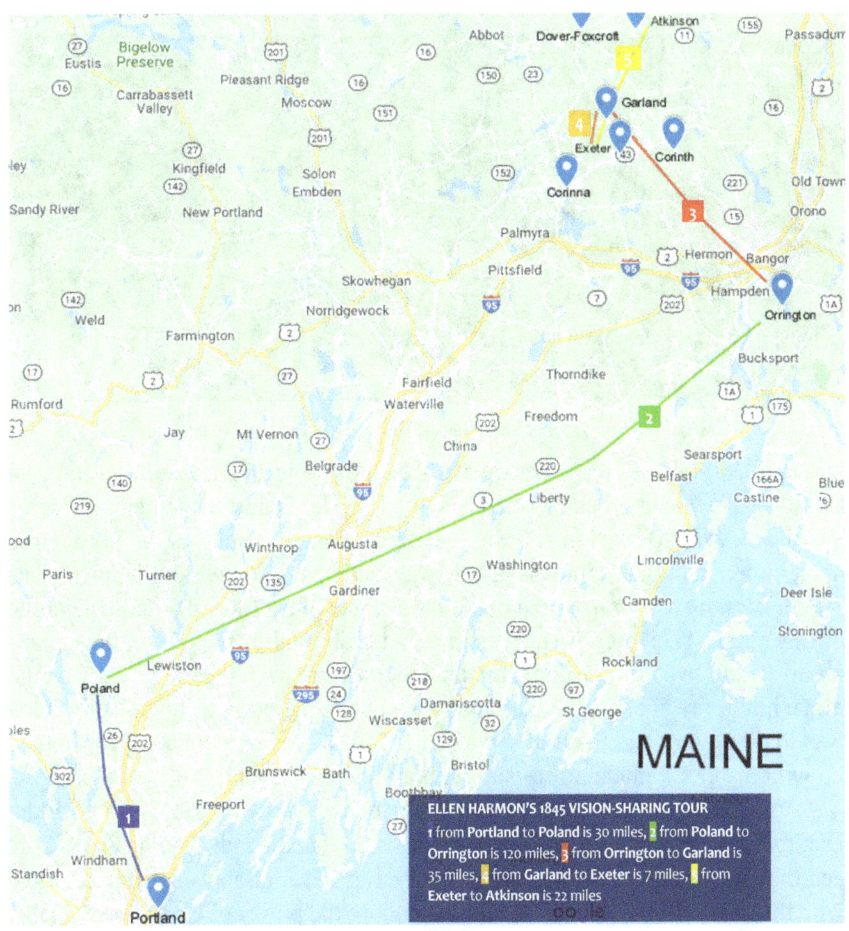

They were all deeply interested in the view. They all said it was entirely new to them. The Lord worked in mighty power, setting the truth home to their hearts. Sister Durben [***Dearborn***] knew what the power of the Lord was, for she had felt it many times, and, a short time after I fell, she was struck down and fell to the floor, crying to God to have mercy on her. When I came out of vision, my [ears] were saluted with Sis. Durbun's [***Dearborn's***] singing and shouting with a loud voice. Most of them received the vision and were settled upon the shut door. Previous to this I had no light on the coming of the Bridegroom but had expected Him to this earth to deliver His people on the tenth day of the seventh month. I did not hear a lecture or a word in any way relating to the Bridegroom's going to the holiest. {Lt3-1847.7}

Arrest of Israel Dammon

V6. *Atkinson Trial of Faith Vision,* Feb. 14, 1845

From Exeter we went to **Atkinson**. One night I was shown something that I did not understand. It was to this effect, that we were to have a trial of our faith. The next day, which was the first day of the week, while I was speaking, two men looked into the window where

Aerial view of James Ayer's property in Atkinson, Maine, where the meeting took place

we were assembled. We were satisfied of their object. They were coming to arrest us. They entered and rushed past me to Elder Dammon. When they came into the meeting to take him, he was kneeling down. The Spirit of the Lord rested upon him, and his strength was taken away, and he fell to the floor helpless. The officer [***Joseph Moulton***] cried out, "In the name of the State of Maine, lay hold of this man." Then they would rush up and grab hold of him. Two men seized his arms, and two his feet, and attempted to drag him from the room. They would move him a few inches only and then rush out of the house. The power of God was in that room, and the true servants of God, with their countenances lighted up with his glory, made no resistance, but all began to sing, "*We left old mystic Babylon, To sound the jubilee*," and the men who had taken hold of Elder Dammon were unable to carry out their design.[75] Their hands would slip off him, and they would start up. The efforts to take Elder Dammon were often repeated with the same effect. The men could not endure the power of God present in that room, and it was a relief to them to rush out of the house. Their number increased to twelve, still Elder Dammon was held by the power of God about forty minutes. There he lay on the floor, for three-quarters of an hour, and not all the combined strength of all those men could move him from the floor where he lay helpless. Now [when] they came up to him and began to take hold of him, they did not want me in the room. They wanted me to go out of the room. They said it was I that was keeping him. I stepped right out of the room, and I said, "Elder Dammon, the Lord will have you go with these men to this trial." Then, at the same moment, we all felt that Elder Dammon must go, that God had manifested His power for His glory, and that the name of the Lord would be further glorified in suffering him to be taken from our midst. And those men took him up as easily as they would take up a helpless child and carried him out.[76] {2SG 40.1; Ms131a-1906.23; DF 733-c, Dec. 12, 1906; LSMS 95.4}

After Elder Dammon was taken from our midst he was imprisoned in a hotel and guarded by a man who did not like the duty. He said that Elder Dammon was singing, and praying, and praising the Lord all night, so that he could not sleep, and he would not watch over such a man. No one else wished the duty of guarding him, and he was left to go about the village as he pleased, after promising that he would appear for trial. Kind friends invited him to share their

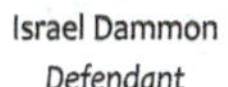
Israel Dammon
Defendant

Charles P. Chandler
Prosecuting attorney

James Stewart Holmes
Defense attorney

William C. Crosby, Esq.
Prosecution Witness

Joel Doore, Jr.
Defense Witness

hospitalities. At the hour appointed for the trial, Elder Dammon was present. The charge brought against Elder Dammon was that he was a disturber of the peace. A lawyer [***James Stuart Holmes***] offered his services.[77] Many witnesses were brought forward to sustain the charge, but they were at once broken down by the testimony of Elder Dammon's acquaintances present, who were called to the stand. There was much curiosity to know what Elder Dammon and his friends believed, and he was asked to give them a synopsis of his faith. He then told them in a clear manner, for he was a forcible speaker, his belief from the Scriptures. It was also suggested that Adventists sang curious hymns, and he was asked to sing one: "Now sing some of your hymns; I hear you have odd hymns." There were quite a number of strong brethren present, who had stood by him in the trial, who had excellent voices, and they joined with him in singing, "*When I was down in Egypt's land, I heard my Saviour was at hand. . . . We left old mystic Babylon to sound the Jubilee*," and they would tell them how the Lord was coming with power and great glory.[78] {2SG 41.1; Ms131a-1906.21; LSMS 96.3-97.3}

Elder Dammon was asked if he had a spiritual wife. Yes, he told them, he had a lawful wife, and he could thank God that she had been a very spiritual woman, ever since his acquaintance with her. "I have got a splendid wife who fears God and keeps His commandments. I have lived with her; so many years [six] we have lived together."[79] Then they would ask him similar questions about what he was preaching. Said he, "I do not know as you could know." Somebody said, "Get up and tell them." He got right up and gave them a discourse right there. {2SG 42.1; LSMS 97.4; Ms131a-1906.21}

Piscataquis County Courthouse, Dover, Maine, built in 1844

"Well, supposing you pray."

"Oh, certainly. We do not pray to you, though; we will pray to God." They would offer up a prayer there, and the tears would trickle down the faces of these men. The cost of court, I think, was thrown upon him, and he was released.[80] {Ms131a-1906.22; 2SG 42.2}

Sound the Jubilee.

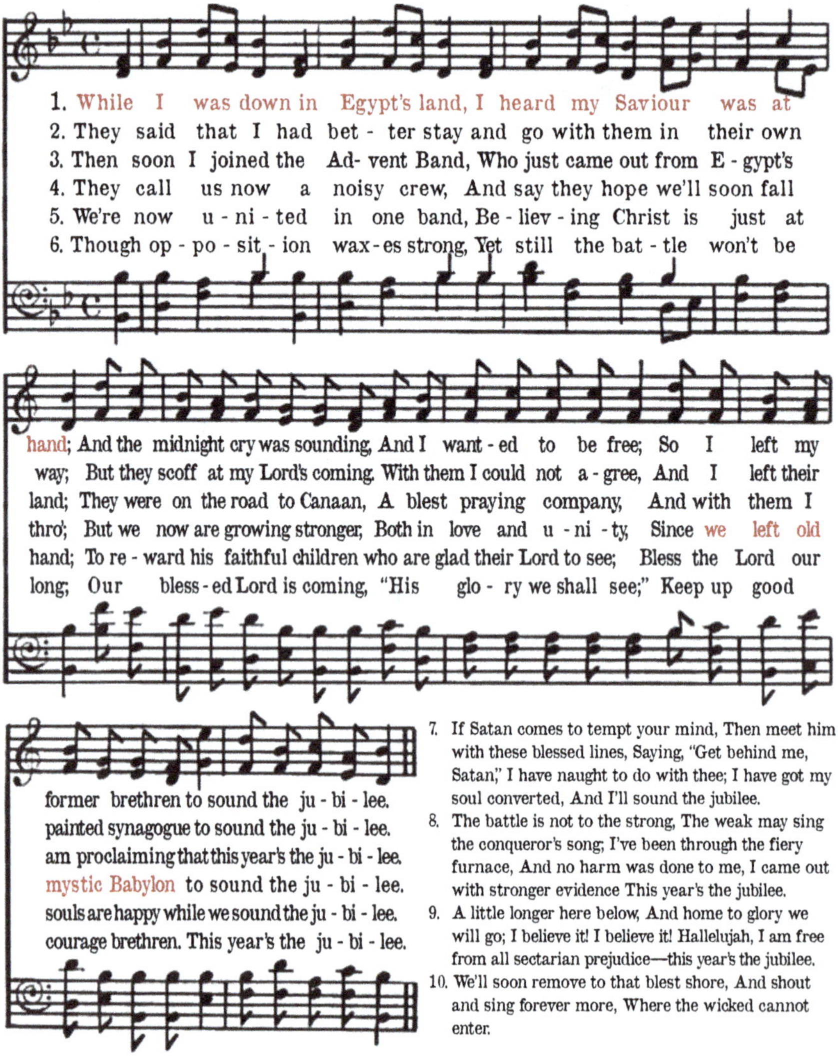

1. While I was down in Egypt's land, I heard my Saviour was at hand; And the midnight cry was sounding, And I want - ed to be free; So I left my former brethren to sound the ju - bi - lee.
2. They said that I had bet - ter stay and go with them in their own way; But they scoff at my Lord's coming. With them I could not a - gree, And I left their painted synagogue to sound the ju - bi - lee.
3. Then soon I joined the Ad- vent Band, Who just came out from E - gypt's land; They were on the road to Canaan, A blest praying company, And with them I am proclaiming that this year's the ju - bi - lee.
4. They call us now a noisy crew, And say they hope we'll soon fall thro'; But we now are growing stronger, Both in love and u - ni - ty, Since we left old mystic Babylon to sound the ju - bi - lee.
5. We're now u - ni - ted in one band, Be - liev - ing Christ is just at hand; To re - ward his faithful children who are glad their Lord to see; Bless the Lord our souls are happy while we sound the ju - bi - lee.
6. Though op - po - sit - ion wax - es strong, Yet still the bat - tle won't be long; Our bless - ed Lord is coming, "His glo - ry we shall see;" Keep up good courage brethren. This year's the ju - bi - lee.
7. If Satan comes to tempt your mind, Then meet him with these blessed lines, Saying, "Get behind me, Satan," I have naught to do with thee; I have got my soul converted, And I'll sound the jubilee.
8. The battle is not to the strong, The weak may sing the conqueror's song; I've been through the fiery furnace, And no harm was done to me, I came out with stronger evidence This year's the jubilee.
9. A little longer here below, And home to glory we will go; I believe it! I believe it! Hallelujah, I am free from all sectarian prejudice—this year's the jubilee.
10. We'll soon remove to that blest shore, And shout and sing forever more, Where the wicked cannot enter.

The words sung in Atkinson do not appear with a musical score in any hymnal. So, the reconstructed hymn above combines, for the first time in print, the words of the hymn "Sound the Jubilee," written by John Craig and published in *The Piscataquis Farmer*, with the tune "The Jubilee" (published in the 1880 hymnal, *Salvation Army Music*). That the words of John Craig were sung by this tune came to mind after discovering a common stanza shared by both hymns, which begins with the words, "A little longer here below, and home to glory we will go."[81]

Answers to Prayer

In the spring of 1845, I visited Topsham, Maine. On one occasion quite a number of us were assembled at the house of Brother Stockbridge Howland. His eldest daughter, Miss Frances Howland, a very dear friend of mine, was very sick with rheumatic fever.[82] She was under the doctor's care. Her hands were so badly swollen that we could not see the joints. As we sat together speaking of her case, Brother Howland was asked if he had faith that Frances could be healed in answer to prayer. He answered that he would try to believe that she might. "I will believe." Again he was asked, "Do you believe?" He answered that he did believe it possible. "I do." Then we all knelt in earnest prayer to God in her behalf. We claimed the promise, "Ask, and ye shall receive" (John 16:24). {2SG 42.4; LSMS 98.1, 2}

Stockbridge Howland's house

Sister Frances was in the chamber above. She had not stood on her feet for two weeks. The Spirit of the Lord indited prayer. The blessing of God attended our prayers, and we had the assurance of God's willingness to heal the afflicted one. Elder Dammon cried out in the Spirit and power of God, "Is there some sister here who has faith enough to go and take her by the hand, and bid her arise in the name of the Lord?" Sister Curtis [***Mercy A. Curtis***] was on her way as the words were spoken. She ascended the stairs with the Spirit of the Lord upon her, and took Frances by the hand, saying, "Sister Frances, in the name of the Lord arise and be whole." New life shot through the veins of the sick girl, a holy faith took possession of her, and obeying its impulse, Sister Frances rose from her bed and stood upon her feet and walked the room praising the Lord that she was healed. She was soon dressed and came down into the room where we were assembled, her countenance lighted up with unspeakable joy and gratitude [for] the blessing of God. {2SG 42.4; LSMS 98.3}

The next morning sister Frances sat at the breakfast table with us. And as Brother White was reading for family worship, from James, chapter 5, the doctor came into the entry hall, and as usual ascended the stairs to visit his patient. But he could not find her. He hurried down, opened the door leading into the large kitchen where we were sitting, his patient with us. He gazed upon her with astonishment, and, at length, said, "So Frances is better!" Brother Howland answered, "The Lord has healed her," and Brother White resumed his reading, which had been interrupted, "Is any sick among you? let him call for the elders of the church; and let them pray for him," &c. (James 5:14). The doctor listened with a curious expression of mingled wonder and incredulity upon his face, nodded, and hastily left the room. The same day Sister Frances rode three miles, returning home in the evening, and, although it was rainy, she sustained no injury and continued to improve rapidly in health. A few days after, at her request, she was led down into the water and baptized.[83] {2SG 43.1; LSMS 99.1, 2}

William Henry Hyde

There were Miss Ayres, an intelligent woman, William Hyde, and Mrs. Ayres, and another.[84] At this time Brother William Henry Hyde was very sick with the bloody dysentery. His symptoms were alarming. A physician said that unless he received help in a short time, his case was hopeless. He was dying. There was much unbelief and darkness in the place where he was staying, and we wished to get him away where there was more faith. [He] sent for us, and we visited him and prayed for him around the bedside, that the Lord would raise him up and give him strength to leave that place. But he had come under the influence of certain fanatical persons, who were bringing dishonor upon our cause. I went in, [and said,] "Now, Brother Hyde, you have sent for us to come and pray for you as a last resort. I want to tell you that we cannot do anything of this kind unless you shall give up all this great fanaticism of the enemy. God has nothing to do with it. *You have no right to lie on the bed, women and men together.* If you will receive the message that God gives you and turn right around, then the Spirit of the Lord will come in, but the Spirit of the Lord cannot come in [while you cling to this fanatical teaching.] You have been praying here, and you have been trying to do all that you can, but there is something for you to do, and that is to give up your error, and unless you do, fanaticism will be all through this vicinity, and God does not want it." {2SG 44.1; LSMS 100.1; Ms131a-1906.1}

We wished to remove him from among them and petitioned the Lord to give him strength to leave that place. Said he, "I will if you will pray for me." He had then been sick for two weeks, and he came right out. The fanaticism and errors into which he had fallen through an evil influence seemed to hinder the exercise of his faith, but he gratefully received the plain testimony borne him, made humble confession of his fault, and took his position firmly for the truth. Said he, "I take my position. I will have none of this work of familiarity that we have had going on; we will have none of it anymore." He just broke all down and asked the Lord to pardon him, and we could not ask him to do any more, and he was raised right straight up. He was blessed and strengthened and rode four miles to the house of Brother Patten, but, after arriving, he grew worse and seemed to be sinking every hour.[85] {2SG 44.1; LSMS 100.1; Ms131a-1906.2}

Some things had hindered faith in his case. Faithful testimony was borne to him, and humble confessions were made on his part, where he had erred, and only a few who were strong in faith were permitted to enter the sickroom. The fanatics whose influence over him had been so injurious, and who had persistently followed him to Brother Patten's, were positively forbidden to come into his presence, while we prayed fervently for his restoration to health. Our earnest, fervent prayers went up to God, that the progress of disease might be stayed, and then faith grasped still more, immediate restoration. He was healed; the Spirit of the Lord worked in that way. God's children seemed to groan in spirit. Such a reaching out after God and a searching out to claim the promises of God, I have seldom witnessed. The salvation of the Holy Spirit was revealed. Power from on high rested upon our sick brother and upon all those in the room. Brother Hyde called for his clothes, arose and immediately dressed himself, and walked out of the room, praising God, with the light of heaven shining in his countenance. His recovery was complete and permanent. A farmer's dinner was ready. Said Brother Hyde, "If I was well I should partake of this food, and I believe God has healed me, and shall act out my faith." Dinner was ready, and he sat right down and ate a hearty dinner, and it did not hurt him. He had not dared to eat anything for days. [It was] dysentery; it was all around in that section of the country. Then we came to this place, Topsham, Maine. He was about six miles from Topsham, and he rode down—or ate his dinner and then rode down—and we held a most wonderful meeting, and the blessing of the Lord came down. {2SG 44.1; LSMS 100.3, 4; Ms131a-1906.2}

Meeting Fanaticism

From Topsham we returned to Portland, and quite a number of our faith from the east were there, some of the very individuals to whom I had borne my testimony in Exeter, that it was not their duty to visit Portland. We trembled for the church, for they were in danger through these fanatical spirits. Some of these persons had laid aside reason and judgment and trusted every impression of their excitable and over-wrought minds. Their demonstrative exercises, which they claimed were the result of the working of the Spirit of God, were unworthy of their exalted profession. My heart ached for God's people. Oh, must they be thus deceived, and led away by this false enthusiasm? I faithfully pronounced the warnings given me of the Lord; but they seemed to have had but little effect, except to make those warned of extreme views jealous of me. {2SG 45.1; LSMS 101.1}

There were some who professed great humility and advocated creeping on the floor like children, as an evidence of their humility. They claimed that the words of Christ in Matthew 18:1–6 must have a literal fulfillment at this period, when they were looking for their Saviour to return. They would creep around their houses, on the street, over bridges, and in the church itself. {LSMS 101.2}

I told them plainly that this was not required; that the humility which God looked for in His people was to be shown by a Christ-like life, not by creeping on the floor. All spiritual things are to be treated with sacred dignity. Humility and meekness are in accordance with the life of Christ, but they are to be shown in a dignified way. {LSMS 101.3}

An old gentleman, who had heard me speak, made a request for an interview with me. During our talk he said, "Miss Harmon, do you advocate the creeping position?" I said, "I do not. I have plainly stated that this action is a dishonor to God. A Christian reveals true humility by showing the gentleness of Christ, by being always ready to help others, by speaking kind words and performing unselfish acts, which elevate and ennoble the most sacred message that has come to our world." {LSMS 102.1}

During this interview, a sister whom I loved as a Christian came into the room on her knees. Said the old gentleman in clear, distinct tones,

"If man was made to walk erect,
The serpent made to crawl,
Why imitate the odious thing
That introduced the fall?" {LSMS 102.3}

The false burdens and impressions of these fanatics might have turned me away from duty had not the Lord previously shown me my duty where to go and what to do, and, although so young and inexperienced, preserved me from falling into the snare of the enemy through the mercy of God by giving me special instructions whom to fear and whom to trust. Had it not been for this protection, I now can see many times when I might have been led from the path of duty. {2SG 45.2; LSMS 102.4}

Labors in New Hampshire

V9. *Visit New Hampshire Vision, spring 1844*

About this time I was shown that it was my duty to visit our people in New Hampshire. My constant and faithful companion at this time was Sister Louisa Foss, a sister of Samuel Foss, the husband of my sister Mary. I can never forget her kind and sisterly attention to me in my journeys. She was faithful to me, kind and attentive, ever ready with the care of a sister to sympathize with me in all my trials, and to cheer me in my despondency and gloom.[86] We were also accompanied by Brother Files and his wife, who were old and valued friends of my family, and by Brother Ralph Haskins and Elder James White.[87] There were about six persons that went in other sleighs. We all went in company. {2SG 46.1; LSMS 104.1; Ms131-1906.4}

A distracted state of things existed in New Hampshire, yet the Lord often manifested his power there. It was in New Hampshire that we had our first experience in relation to what is termed "spiritual magnetism."[88] We were cordially received by our friends in New Hampshire, but there were wrongs existing in that field which burdened me much. We had to meet a spirit of self-righteousness that was very depressing. I had previously been shown the pride and exaltation of certain ones whom we visited, but I had not the courage to meet them with my testimony. Had I done so, the Lord would have sustained me in doing my duty. {2SG 46.1; LSMS 104.2}

We visited **Claremont, New Hampshire**, and inquired for Adventists. We were told that there were two parties, one holding fast their past advent experience, the other had denied it. We stated that we wished to find those who had not denied their past experience and were directed to Elders John Garnsey Bennett and Albert Merritt Billings whom they said believed as we did. They had so much to say against these two men that we concluded that they were "persecuted for righteousness' sake."[89] We called on them and were received and treated kindly; yet a depression came upon me, and I felt that all was not right. {2SG 46.2; LSMS 116.1; Ms10-1859.2}

Albert M. Billings

Elder Bennett had the appearance of being a very holy man. He spoke upon the subject of faith, and said "that all we had to do was to believe, and what we asked of God would be given." He also had much to say upon charity. Brother White answered, "Blessings are promised on conditions," and quoted John 15:7, " 'If ye abide in me, and my words abide in you, ye shall ask what ye will, and it shall be done unto you.' Your theory of faith is empty as a flour barrel with both heads out. True charity is a very delicate personage, never stepping her foot out of the path of Bible truth." {2SG 46.3; LSMS 117.4; Ms10-1859.3}

In the afternoon we called at Brother Charles Sterne Collier's. We were to have a meeting that night at his house and supposed they were in union with Elder Bennett. We questioned them about him, but could get no information. Said Brother Collier, "If the Lord has sent you here, you will find them out and tell us." {2SG 47.1; Ms10-1859.4}

That evening as I was praying and reaching up by faith to claim the blessing of the Lord, Bennet and Billings began to groan and cry out, "Amen! Amen!" and threw their sympathy and influence in with my prayer. Brother White was much distressed. He arose and cried out, "I resist this spirit in the name of the Lord." When I got up to bear my testimony, they commenced groaning and crying out, "Amen! Amen!" I had no union with them, did not say a word until they had finished, for their amens chilled me. Brother White felt their influence upon him again, and arose and in the name of the Lord rebuked their wicked spirit, and they were bound. They could not rise again that night. {2SG 47.2; Ms10-1859.5; Ms46-1904}

After the meeting closed, Brother White said, "Brother Collier, now I can tell you about those two men. They are dealing in a satanic influence and are calling it the Spirit of the Lord." Said Brother C, "I believe that the Lord has sent you. We have called their influence mesmerism, and we do not generally have meetings here because we have no union with their spirit. They rise above us, manifest much feeling, but they leave an influence darker than Egypt. I never saw them checked or tied up before tonight." {2SG 47.2; LSMS 119.4; Ms10-1859.6}

V11. *Spiritual Magnetism Vision, spring 1845*

While at family prayer that night, the Spirit of the Lord rested upon me and I was taken off in vision. A curtain was lifted, and I was shown the case of these men, and a few others in union with them; that they were practicing deception upon the flock of God, while professing to be the chosen holy servants of God. I saw darkness and iniquity covered up with a pious garb over their dark designs and deeds, disclosing iniquities that some had scarcely dreamed of, and that God would rend off that false covering and expose hidden things that some have scarcely thought of. {2SG 48.1; Ms10-1859.7}

V12. *Voice of God—Time of Jacob's Trouble Vision, spring 1845*

We returned to **Grantham**.[90] On our way I fell from the wagon and so injured my side that I had to be carried into the house. That night I suffered great pain. Sister [***Louisa***] Foss prayed for me, and I united in pleading with God for His blessing and relief from pain. About midnight the blessing of the Lord rested upon me, and those in the house were awakened by hearing my voice while in vision. This was the first time I had a view of the voice of God in connection with the time of trouble. In the same vision, I was shown that great reproach was being brought upon the precious cause of God in Maine, and it was springing up in other states, and that His children were disheartened and scattered by a fanatical spirit, and that Joseph Turner and John Howell, whom we had placed confidence in, were scattering the flock, and under a cloak of godliness were casting fear among the trembling, conscientious ones.[91] I saw that we must go back to Maine and there bear the testimony God would give me for those who were in error. I related what I had seen to those present. I was shown the course some were pursuing whom I had previously had great confidence in as ministers of righteousness. The dangers that were shown me and the evils which would extend in consequence of these errors burdened me, and my grief was so great I could not rest. {2SG 48.1; LSMS 125.3, 4; Ms10-1859.8; Lt2-1874.11}

Again I was shown the cause of God was suffering, souls were in danger, and Satan was triumphing, that the truth of God was covered with reproach by men who professed to love the truth. Some men and women had acted out their natural temperament, were harsh and denunciatory, overbearing, and self-confident. They had by their inconsistent, fanatical course caused unbelievers to hate them, and those who bore the Advent name were brought into disrepute. The innocent suffered with the guilty. I was shown that some were thrown into prison, and severe measures were being pursued by those who had authority to prevent the evils they saw which were increasing. The hatred of many of the world against the preaching of the time of Christ's coming was increased as they saw the inconsistencies of those who had believed in the time. They exulted in the wisdom and prudence which they thought they had in opposing the preaching of the time. {Lt2-1874.12}

Again I saw that God was grieved, that His frown was upon the existing errors of some of His professed people. Said the angel, "Go and tell them the things which you have seen, and My spirit shall attend your testimony whether they will hear or reject. You must not withhold the message I give you to bear." {Lt2-1874.13}

I was shown that God had a work for me to do amid dangers and perils, but I must not shrink. I must go to the very places where fanaticism had done the most evil, and bear my messages of reproof to some of those who were influencing others; while I should give comfort and encouragement to those who were timid and conscientious, but deceived by those they thought were more righteous than they. I saw that we would be in danger of imprisonment and abuse. Although I should have no sympathy with the deceived, fanatical ones, no difference would be made, for anyone bearing the name of Adventist would have no consideration shown them. {Lt2-1874.14}

I was young and timid, and felt great sadness in regard to visiting the field where fanaticism had reigned. I pleaded with God to spare me from this—to send by some other one. The Spirit of the Lord again came upon me, and I was shown my faith would be tested, my courage and obedience tried. I must go. God would give me words to speak at the right time. And if I should wait upon Him, and have faith in His promises, I should escape both imprisonment and abuse; for He would restrain those who would do me harm. If I would look to God with humble confidence and faith, no man's hand should be laid upon me to do me harm. An angel of heaven would be by my side and direct me when and where to go. {Lt2-1874.15}

I waited no longer, but went trusting in God. I saw most of the brethren and sisters. As I warned them of their dangers, some were rejoiced that God had sent me; others refused to listen to my testimony as soon as they learned that I was not in union with their spirit. They said I was going back to the world, that we must be so straight and so plain and so full of glory, as they called their shouting and hallooing, that the world would hate and persecute us. Our brethren had hardly faith enough to let us go. They thought we were presumptuous to place ourselves in the way of an excited and wrathful community. We did not listen to their suggestions, but followed the Lord's bidding. {Lt2-1874.16}

Return to Portland

Having traveled and labored for three months, bearing the testimony that God had given me and experiencing His approbation at every step, I returned to Portland and found the brethren in great discouragement and confusion and indeed a fearful state of things. Some were refraining wholly from labor, and were full of censure for those opposed to their fanatical views. A meeting was appointed at the house of Sister Haines that I might have an opportunity to relate what had been shown me. We met with a few of the brethren and sisters and [there was a] sister [with] two daughters that she thought a great deal of. She whispered to me the first part of the meeting, "I wish you would talk with my daughter." Joe Turner was there. Then we had a praying season. While imploring the Lord for strength to discharge this painful duty the Spirit of the Lord came upon me and I was taken off in vision, and in the presence of Joseph Turner was again shown his ungodly course [and] the individual cases of some present. Joseph Turner and John Howell were among the number presented before me, and this Joe Turner was just as full of unholy thoughts and mischief as he could be. {2SG 49.2; LSMS 97.6; 126.1-127.2; Ms10-1859.9; Lt2-1874.13; Ms131-1906.20}

Elizabeth Haines' house in Portland, Maine

V13. *Joseph Turner's Ungodly Course Vision, spring 1845*

He said, "That is of the Lord," and he knew that that was of the Lord. And finally the words began to be spoken. Those present said I talked it out before him. They said a frown came over my face, and [I said] that he was not true, that he was not keeping the commandments of God, but was transgressing the commandments, giving attention to other women, and his wife suffering under the great strain that was upon her. {2SG 49.2; LSMS 127.2; Ms10-1859.9; Ms131-1906.21}

As soon as I could get strengthened after I came out of vision, I felt terrible because I came right out and said so and so before him. I related what I had seen, which was confirmed that same day by his wife, and brethren and sisters who were acquainted with his sinful course. Turner said that I was under a wrong influence, that a part of the vision was right and a part was wrong; that it would take a critical spiritual observer to detect the difference; that this was the same spirit that had always pursued him to crush him, etc. "There," said he, "I can tell that. The first part is of the Lord, and this last part, that is a kind of mesmerism." Well, who gave the mesmerism? There was nobody there but him. Well, he carried it through in that line. {2SG 49.2; LSMS 127.4; Ms10-1859.9; Lt2-1874.13; Ms131-1906.21}

He could take a child and set it on his hand, and so mesmerize the child that it would stay there if he took his hand away. I never saw that done, but that is what he said he could do. The mother of this girl whispered to me and said, "Go right up and speak to my daughter." So I hurried upstairs, and told her, "If he has not ruined you, he will, and now, do not have a word of conversation with him or see him alone because he will mesmerize you." It was hypnotism, but we did not know then what it was. {LSMS 128.1; Ms131-1906.23}

They took me in a carriage to where his wife and family had been for some time. They had had meetings there. Sarah Jordan and her brother [***William M. Jordan***] were [the ones] with me when I first went down to Orrington.[92] [Joe Turner] was hovering right over her all the time, and giving her mesmeric passes, and she was having these so-called "visions," and it was all mesmerism, and that was what I had to tell. He did not know that I had left the house. {Ms131-1906.24}

With anguish of spirit I left the meeting, for I had a message for Joseph Turner's wife.[93] I rode to their house [and] hurried right up to where his wife was, and knocked. She opened the door. This was where the meetings had been held, and where I had been staying. She looked most discouraged. She was a beautiful-looking woman. I put my arms around her back, and [she] cried like a baby. She was weeping as though her heart would break. Said she, "Sister Ellen, my heart is breaking." {2SG 49.2; LSMS 128.2; Ms10-1859.10; Ms9-1859.2; Ms131-1906.25}

She told how her husband and this Sarah Jordan—he was all the time right with her half of the night, and sometimes all night, giving her "visions"—that is what he was doing apparently. Said she [***Jane Barnard Turner***], "Because I cannot receive these things, she [***Sarah Jordan***] tells them things to do. It is not a bit like what you have; she tells them things to do that are contrary to reason and judgment, and that she must go with Turner. Because his wife has a family on her hands, she must take the place of his wife, and go and give the message." Then I bore my testimony to Sister Turner, which was to comfort her poor, sore heart. I told her that the Lord was not in it, that the Lord's arm was around her, and [He] would give her strength, and not to be too much discouraged. She confirmed that same day the vision which I related to her. {LSMS 128.2; Ms10-1859.10; Ms9-1859.2; Lt2-1874.13; Ms131-1906.26}

Then I told this Sarah Jordan just what she was doing. Said I, "God is not with you nor with Turner." {Ms131-1906.27}

We learned from united testimony that honest, precious souls had been set aside and told that they were rejected of God, and that these fanatical persons had flocked to my father's house and made that their stopping place. Joseph Turner and John Howell were leaders in this rank fanaticism. They followed impressions and burdens which led to corruption instead of purity and holiness. {2SG 49.2; Ms10-1859.10; LSMS 128.2; Ms9-1859.2}

Our parents were disgusted as they saw reason and judgment laid aside by them. They protested against the hypocrisy they witnessed, and as they could not get rid of this company they closed their house and left the city for Poland, where my two married sisters were living.[94] This did not suit Joseph Turner, and he told me when we arrived at Portland that my father was a doomed man; that my mother and sisters might be saved, but my father would be lost. The only reason he offered was because he did not give him possession of his house. When he left Portland his denunciations were bitter. We visited Poland, where my parents were, and as we listened to the recital of their trials and of incidents which had occurred, the vision given in [Claremont] New Hampshire was confirmed. {2SG 50.1; Ms10-1859.11; LSMS 129.1; Ms9-1859.3}

I had been shown that they needed help in Orrington, and that we must go there, for fanaticism had done its work there also; that fanatical spirits had rushed on without judgment until unbelievers became disgusted with their course, bringing reproach upon the cause of God. These fanatical ones seemed to think that religion consisted in great excitement, making a noise, being boisterous, rough, and talking in such a manner as to irritate and cause unbelievers to hate them and the doctrines that they taught, and then they would rejoice that they suffered persecution. Unbelievers were enraged. They could see no consistency in this wild spirit and they made stringent rules that no advent believer should come into town. The innocent here suffered with the guilty. The brethren in some places were prevented from assembling for meetings to encourage one another, for even the citizens of the place who were believers were denied this privilege. Sentinels were on the watch to hinder all who should attempt to enter the town. Yet the Lord bade me go. Naturally timid, I would gladly have been excused, but dared not take my own course. My life was not my own. {2SG 50.2; Ms9-1859.4; LSMS 130.1; 1T 66}

We first visited Brother S.'s family in Orrington.[95] They heartily welcomed us to their home and hearts. Every moment was precious to these hungry children, and we sat up till a late hour recounting the trials we had passed through and the refreshing seasons we had enjoyed; and we deplored together the sad state of the cause. I bore a sad and aching heart. It seemed so cruel that the cause of Christ should be injured by the course of these injudicious men. Not only were the men injuring their own souls but placing a stigma, a fearful stain, upon the cause of God which would not be easily wiped away [and] would cleave to the name of "Adventist" like the leprosy. Satan was willing to have it so, for this reproach would cause many precious souls to fear to have any connection with Adventists. It suited well his satanic majesty to see the truth mixed with error and then altogether trampled in the dust. He looked with hellish triumph upon the confused, scattered state of God's children. All that had been done wrong would be exaggerated, and would lose nothing by passing from one to the other. Jesus was crucified afresh and put to open shame by His professed followers.[96] The anguish of my spirit could not be described. My tears and prayers went up to God for His bleeding, suffering cause. I could see nothing that I could do to help those who refused to be helped. {2SG 50.2; LSMS 130.2; Ms9-1859.5; 1T 66, 67; Lt2-1874.28}

Next morning as we were in the front room two men entered the door leading into the kitchen. Sister S. as she opened the front room door looked pale and motioned to us.[97] We had no baggage. We put on our bonnets and stepped out of the front door. Just then there was quite a gathering at a meetinghouse nearby, for it was fast day. We passed on with the people and were not discovered. {Ms9-1859.6}

The meetinghouse was in the direction of Brother Brown's house, where we wished to call.[98] Gladly were we received. We prayed and wept together. Brother Brown said we need not fear being troubled in his house, for no one dared to dictate to him about who he should have in his family and who he should not. He had quite a war spirit against the course the citizens were pursuing. He was only partially in union with our people, but a portion of his family were fully with us. {Ms9-1859.7}

We visited many of the brethren from place to place, fanaticism raging, and brethren believing the truth were not permitted to visit one another, but were imprisoned and beaten. But we rode through these very places in broad daylight, visited from house to house, held meetings, and bore our testimony, showing them how God regarded their errors. We were hunted for, but the Lord always directed us out of their way to a place of safety, that, too, without the least effort on our part to conceal ourselves. We would start out, and we would say, "Shall we go this road?" We knew they were lying in wait, the men were, when we would go from these meetings. "Shall we go this road?" Just as distinctly [we would hear:] "Take another road." And they were left. They were there in that road; we found out decidedly that they were there in the other road, and they were all waiting to take us and shut us up. We were engaged in doing the will of God, going from house to house to visit His tried children.[99] We comforted the fearing and desponding, and rebuked those who were pressing their fanatical errors upon others. We had very precious seasons, and many showed their gratitude to God by weeping and rejoicing that relief had been sent to them. Others stubbornly refused to listen to the warnings and reproofs given. This class went on from bad to worse until their shame was made manifest to all. God gave them over to their own ways to be filled with their own doings. {Ms9-1859.8; Lt2-1874.24; Ms131a-1906.19}

At one house we found them much afflicted. Their children were sick with measles. We prayed for them and the power of God rested upon us. We passed on to Brother W's [***White's***], and then we rode two miles farther to visit a family in affliction.[100] Sickness was in their dwelling. We prayed with them and the Lord again met with us and comforted us with His love. {Ms9-1859.9}

As we rode to the last place we were noticed by several individuals, but we trusted ourselves in the hands of God. We had interviews with several families at the same time, who were brought together in a most wonderful manner. Many having no knowledge of the meeting, but were moved by an earnest desire to go to a certain brother's house, came, and the rooms were well filled. This occurred at three different points, giving me opportunity to bear my message to them. Through the earnest entreaty of a few brethren we visited a family that was in great error. A few months before they were standing in the clear light of truth, and we took sweet counsel together.[101] At one house in Orrington, the door was closed upon me as they saw me coming. Phebe Knapp, a young woman, was with them professing to have "visions" of God, yet teaching the grossest errors—that the resurrection of the dead had taken place already—and she warned the family she was with not to receive us into their house for we would oppose the truth, referring to the resurrection being past. She taught numerous other absurd errors. {Ms9-1859.10; Lt2-1874.17}

As the family saw Sister Foss and myself coming they fastened the door against us. But, in the name of the Lord, I opened it, for the door was insecurely fastened. We entered the dwelling in the name of the Lord. Immediately Phebe Knapp fell to the floor in great apparent agony, crying out in a most pitiful manner to the family, warning against me, "You are in danger, danger, danger."[102] {Ms9-1859.11}

I then went into the room where Phebe Knapp was groaning and crying out. They said [she] was in "vision." I bowed in their midst, knelt by her side, and asked my heavenly Father to hear me and for His own glory manifest Himself to these poor, deceived souls, and to show them that we had come to do them good, and to convince them of error, and give them evidence that this was a false burden, and rebuke the spirit which was upon her. Phebe Knapp's burden left her immediately. I then addressed those who were present in the name of the Lord [in] a few moments of calm conversation with the family. I reasoned with them, and rebuked their fanatical spirit, and showed them the inconsistency of their course. I told them they refused to speak with me, and feared if they looked upon me I should so affect them—that God would be displeased with them. {Ms9-1859.12; Lt2-1874.17}

I asked them why they showed me so much coldness. "Am I not the same as when I came to you with the power of God resting upon me a few months since? I hold the same views as when we parted in union, love, and Christian fellowship. Who has changed since that time?" They had not seen me since, but I was the same; I believed just as I did. They had changed and not us. They had been influenced by the spirit of error. "You have changed. You believe the dead are raised. You have been baptized in the faith of the resurrection of the dead. I know this is all a delusion. Satan has been trying to deceive you. When Christ the great Lifegiver shall come in the clouds of heaven, to raise the dead, there will be a terrible earthquake.[103] The trump of God will be heard resounding through earth's remotest bounds, and the voice of Jesus will call forth the dead from their graves to immortal life.[104] {Ms9-1859.11; Lt2-1874.17, 18}

"You have not seen Christ coming with power and great glory which shall illuminate the earth from east to west, from north to south, like the lightning's flash.[105] God has sent me to tell you that you are doing great injury to His cause. You take a blind, unreasonable position, and create hatred and prejudice by your fanaticism and inconsistencies. You call forth persecution and create prejudice unnecessarily, and then feel that you are suffering with Christ." {Lt2-1874.19}

Before I left, the delusive spirit of Satan was checked. They seemed softened and said God loved me and that I was right. After exhorting them faithfully and declaring to them their errors, we left them. I was free. I had performed a disagreeable task and the Lord had sustained me. {Ms9-1859.12; Lt2-1874.20}

As Sister Foss and I walked back, we rejoiced in the Lord. The brethren and sisters had not ventured to meet together for some time, but nearly all came together and there was quite a company assembled. It was a time of solemnity, of rejoicing, and weeping. It is impossible to describe such a meeting. There was no noisy shouting, but a solemnity rested upon all. We were suspected of holding a meeting somewhere, and we afterwards learned that persons were sent to Brother W's [***White's***] house to see if we were there, or if there was a meeting. At the time these two men came we were all bowed before God. There was no noise but a peaceful weeping spirit rested upon us. The windows were high so that none of us were noticed from the outside. The men went away satisfied that we were not there. {Ms9-1859.13}

Sudden Departure for Home

V14. *Leave by Daybreak Vision, spring 1845*

The last meeting we held there was especially solemn. The poor souls who had not the privileges of meeting for a long time were greatly refreshed. While we were praying and weeping before God that night, I was taken off in vision and shown that our work was done in Orrington, that we must leave by daybreak the next morning, for men would come to take us and we should suffer abuse. I had not refused obedience to the Spirit of God, His hand had been with me, and His angel had accompanied us and hid us from the people so that they did not know we were in the place. But our work was done; we could go; the emissaries of Satan were on our track, and we would fare no better than those who had been fanatical and wrong, and suffered the consequences of their inconsistent, unreasonable course by abuse and imprisonment. {Ms9-1859.14; Lt2-1874.21}

There was but little sleeping that night, for we wished to speak encouragingly to each other as long as we could, for we knew not when we should meet again on earth. Some did not close their eyes that night, and early the next morning we were on our way. Two brethren took us in a small rowboat to Belfast [and on] to Camden, about five miles. We stepped on board the large steamboat and were soon safely on our way over the water to Portland. We had been visiting two weeks among those who had been cursed with the fanatical course of men who were practicing "voluntary humility." The few who assembled on Sunday, the last meeting we had, were enabled to avoid the vigilance of the jealous citizens, and God was worshiped without boisterous noise and confusion, but with calm dignity. The melting Spirit of God subdued hearts, many tears were shed and penitent confessions made. As we left, we felt that we had done all we could in reproving, warning, comforting, and encouraging. We were free "from the blood of all" in that place (Acts 20:26). At our meeting, one of the enemy's agents, who had been an Adventist, informed the citizens that we were holding meetings in Orrington. {Ms9-1859.14; Lt2-1874.22}

We soon received a letter from Brother W. [***White***] [in] Orrington stating that, when these brethren who had taken us to the steamboat returned, soon after daylight, they were met by a number of exasperated citizens, who had come early to his house to find those who had dared to hold meetings in Orrington, and [they] were very angry when they searched in vain for us [in] the house where we had tarried and were greatly disappointed because they could not find us.[106] Our brethren informed these angry men that we were not in Orrington, but far away. They whipped and abused them, but their testimony was [that] they scarcely felt the stripes. {Ms9-1859.14; Lt2-1874.23}

We were sent to **Garland**, Maine, where we met Elder Dammon and many others in meeting and bore our testimony, that they were in error and delusion in believing that the dead had been raised. I told them that God had shown me that Satan had been introducing fanatical errors, that he might deceive and destroy their souls. When Christ should raise the dead there would be no small stir. He would ride forth "with power and great glory" (Matt. 24:30), escorted by the heavenly angels, with songs of triumph and victory. "For the Lord Himself shall descend from heaven, with a shout, with the voice of the archangel and with the trump of God; and the dead in Christ shall rise first." "Then" (not weeks, nor months, nor years, afterward, but then at that very time) "we which are alive and remain shall be caught up together with them in the clouds, to meet the Lord in the air: and so shall we ever be with the Lord" (1 Thess. 4:16, 17). {Lt2-1874.25}

V15. *Fanatics Unwanted in Portland Vision, spring 1845*

While I was repeating this Scripture, Elder Dammon arose and began to leap up and down, crying out, "The dead are raised and gone up; glory to God! Glory, glory, hallelujah!"[107] Others followed his example. Elder Dammon said, "Don't be tried, Brother White. I cannot sit still. The spirit and power of the resurrection is stirring my very soul. The dead are raised, the dead are raised, and gone up, gone up." {Lt2-1874.26}

Our testimony was rejected, and they clung tenaciously to their errors. Elder Dammon and several others were baptized many times and frequently by the hand of a woman, Mrs. Ayers, a female preacher who had drunk deep of fanaticism.[108] {Lt2-1874.27}

We had done our duty, and, with hearts filled with sorrow, we turned from these our brethren that we had loved, reluctant to leave them in error and delusion. These souls that I had warned turned from me because I had told them they were in error and in darkness. Many of this company went on farther and farther in delusion and deception, following impressions and impulse rather than the Word of God until they became disgusted with their own wicked course. {Lt2-1874.27}

Distracting influences have separated Elder Dammon from his friends who believe the third message; but we hope the time is not far distant when he and many others in Maine will joyfully receive the message.[109] {2SG 42.3}

As I returned to Portland, evidences increased of the desolating effects of fanaticism in Maine. Joseph Turner labored with some success to turn my friends and even my relatives against me. And what was all this for? It was because I had faithfully told them what had been shown me concerning his fanatical course. And to justify himself he circulated falsehoods to destroy my influence. My lot seemed hard to bear. I sank in discouragement, and the condition of God's people so filled me with anguish that my mind wandered for two weeks and I was prostrated with sickness.[110] My relatives thought I could not live. But the brethren and sisters who sympathized with me in this affliction met together to pray for me. I was sensible to their earnest, effectual prayers. The power of the strong foe was broken, and I was released from his grasp and was immediately taken off in vision. {2SG 50.2; LSMS 130.1; Ms9-1859.15}

Vision of the New Earth

V16. New Earth Vision, spring 1845

In this view I saw that the opposition of man and a human influence should never afflict me again. If I felt a human influence affecting my testimony I was to cry to God, wherever I should be, for another angel, and an angel would be sent to my rescue. I already had one angel guarding me continually, but, when necessary, the Lord would send another to raise me above the power of every earthly influence. I saw then for the first time the glory of the new earth.[111] {2SG 51.1; LSMS 131.1; Ms9-1859.16}

Brother William Henry Hyde, who was present during this vision, composed the following verses, which have gone the rounds of the religious papers, and have found a place in several hymn books.[112] Those who have published, read, and sung them have little thought that they originated from a vision of a girl, persecuted for her humble testimony. {2SG 55.1; LS80 218.1}

The Better Land

We have heard from the bright, the holy land,
We have heard, and our hearts are glad;
For we were a lonely pilgrim band,
And weary and worn and sad.

They tell us the pilgrims have a dwelling there-
No longer are homeless ones;
And we know that the goodly land is fair,
Where life's pure river runs. {2SG 56.1}

They say green fields are waving there,
That never a blight shall know;
And the deserts wild are blooming fair,
And the roses of Sharon grow.

There are lovely birds in the bowers green—
Their songs are blithe and sweet;
And their warblings gushing ever new
The angel's harpings greet. {2SG 56.2}

We have heard of the palms, the robes, the crowns,
And the silvery band in white;
Of the city fair with pearly gates,
All radiant with light.

We have heard of the angels there, and saints,
With their harps of gold, how they sing;
Of the mount, with the fruitful tree of life,
Of the leaves that healing bring. {2SG 56.3}

The King of that country, he is fair,
He's the joy and the light of the place;
In his beauty we shall behold him there,
And bask in his smiling face,

We'll be there, we'll be there in a little while;
We'll join the pure and the blest;
We'll have the palm, the robe, the crown,
And forever be at rest. {2SG 56.4}

The Burden of Pointing Out Wrongs

About this time I was subjected to a severe trial. If the Spirit of the Lord rested upon a brother or sister in meeting, and they glorified God by praising him, some raised the cry of mesmerism. {2SG 57.1; cf. ExV 6.4}

At this time visions were given me to correct the errors of those who had taken the extreme view of some texts of Scripture. {2SG 58.1; cf. ExV 7.1, 2}

V18. *No Work Doctrine Vision*

V19. *Time of Trouble Before the Advent Vision*

Up to this time I could not write. My trembling hand was unable to hold my pen steadily. While in vision I was commanded by an angel to write the vision. I attempted it, and wrote readily. My nerves were strengthened, and my hand became steady. {2SG 60.1; LSMS 138.4}

It was a great cross for me to relate to individuals what I had been shown concerning their wrongs. It caused me great distress to see others troubled or grieved. And when obliged to declare the messages, I often softened them down and related what I had seen as favorable for the individual as I could, and then would go by myself and weep in agony of spirit. I looked upon those who had only their own souls to care for, and thought if I were in their condition I would not murmur. How could I relate the plain, cutting testimonies given me of God? I anxiously watched the result, and if the individual reproved, rose up against it, and afterwards opposed the truth, these queries would arise in my mind. Did I deliver the message just as I should? Oh, God! could there not have been some way to save them? And then such distress hung upon my soul, I often felt that death would be a welcome messenger, and the grave a sweet resting-place. {2SG 60.2; cf. ExV 63.1, 2}

Another Conflict with Mesmerism

V22. *Attend Meeting in Poland Vision 1845*

While visiting my sisters in Poland, I was afflicted with sickness. There Joe Turner became my enemy, and he would raid out against me.[113] We had to have our meetings in private houses. Those present united in prayer in my behalf, and the disease was rebuked. Angels seemed to be in the room, and all was light and glory. I was again taken off in vision, and shown that I must go about three miles to a meeting, and when there should learn what the Lord would have me do. We went and found quite a large gathering of the brethren and sisters. None had known of any special meeting. Joseph Turner was there. He had boasted that he understood the art of mesmerism, and that he could mesmerize me; that he could prevent me from having a vision, or telling a vision in his presence.[114] There were many present who had heard this boast. I arose in the congregation. My visions came up fresh before me, and I commenced relating them, when I felt a human influence being exerted against me. I looked at Joseph Turner. He had his hand up to his face, and was looking through his fingers, his eyes intently fixed upon me—like snakes' eyes, evil. His lips were compressed, and a low groan now and then escaped him. In a moment I remembered the promise which the Lord had given me, and turned to him and related what the Lord had shown me in Portland; that if I was in danger of being affected by a human influence, I was to look up and call upon God for another angel, who would be sent to protect me. I turned and looked right around. I then raised my hands to heaven and earnestly cried, "Another angel, Father! another angel!"[115] I knew that my request was granted. The Spirit and power of God came upon me, and I felt shielded by the strong Spirit of the Lord, and was borne above every earthly influence, and

with freedom finished my testimony. The saints were comforted, and rejoiced in the Lord. Joseph Turner was asked why he had not stopped my relating the vision. "Well, why don't you stop it?" they said. "You said you could stop it." He answered, "Oh, some of you would have her talk." With strong confidence, rejoicing in God, we returned to my sister's. He never wanted to be in a meeting where I was after that. {2SG 62.1; Ms131-1906.31, 32; LSMS 142.2, 4}

Meeting Fanaticism in Paris, Maine

Some in Paris, Me., believed that it was sin to work. Jesse Stevens was leader in this error, and exerted a strong influence over others.[116] Stevens [believed] if you saw a carriage, and persons in it, and they broke down right in the road, you were not to go near them. You just let the Lord work with them, etc. He had been a Methodist preacher and was considered a faithful christian. He had won the confidence of many by his zeal for the truth, and apparent holy living, which caused some to believe him especially directed of the Lord. He rejected every evidence which the Lord gave to convince him of his error, and was firm to take nothing back in his course. He followed impressions and went weary journeys, walking great distances, where he would only receive abuse, and considered that he was suffering for Christ's sake. {2SG 63.1; LSMS 143.4; Ms131a-1906.12}

V23. Meet Fanaticism in Paris Vision April 1845

The Lord gave me faithful messages for this man, and I was sent long distances to warn the people of God against the errors he was urging upon them. At one time I was shown that I must go to Paris, for there was a meeting appointed which I must attend. I followed the directions given me, and we went where Brother Stevens' people lived, and Brother Andrews, and there learned that Jesse Stevens had notified the brethren that there was to be a great meeting the next day at the house of Brother C. [***Thomas or Sibley Chase***], and he urged all to attend.[117] {2SG 64.1; LSMS 144.1; Ms131a-1906.3}

V24. Jesse Stevens' Errors Vision July/Aug. 1845

The next morning we went to the place appointed for meeting. When Jesse Stevens came in and saw us present he seemed troubled. The meeting commenced with prayer. Then as I tried to pray, the blessing of the Lord rested upon me, and I was taken off in vision. Jesse Stevens had declared that he would listen to nothing but Bible. I was shown what the Bible taught in contrast with his errors. I then saw that the frown of God was upon him; that he was leading astray honest, conscientious souls. The Lord gave me a reproof for him—that he was going contrary to the Word of God in abstaining from labor and urging his errors upon others, denouncing all who did not receive them. They feared to differ with him. Yet they saw inconsistencies in his faith, and their judgment told them he was wrong. His object in appointing that meeting was to make an effort to strengthen the cords of error with which he had bound these souls. I saw that God would work for the salvation of his people; that Jesse Stevens would soon fully manifest himself, and all the honest would see that it was not a right spirit which actuated him, and that his career would soon close. {2SG 64.2; LSMS 144.2}

Stevens said, "I feel tempted to take that clock down." They laughed at him. He just had that clock down and all to pieces right there. Such things as that—fanatical. {Ms131a-1906.4}

I was told by those present that he would hear no more, and took his hat and left the house. Soon after this the snare was broken, and he could have but little influence over souls. He denounced the visions as being of the Devil, and continued to follow his impressions, until Satan seemed to take the full control of his mind. His friends at length were obliged to confine him, where, at last, he made a rope of some of his bed clothing with which he hung himself. Thus ended his career. {2SG 64.2; LSMS 145.1}

I had still another affair to deal with. On this occasion, when we were in Paris, Maine, with the Stowells, a talented minister came to me and said he would accompany me to Portsmouth, New Hampshire, for he wanted my message to be given there.[118] It was a great house, and he wanted me to go. He said he had a beautiful conveyance, and he would convey me right to different places where I wanted to go, around by Vermont, and then around by Massachusetts. He was one of those who were indulging fanatical fancies, and I had been warned to be afraid of all such ones.[119] I told him that I could not go with him. "No, sir. You cannot do that." He said the Lord had told him he must. "No," said I, "He has not. I have had my special orders." I had had strict instruction that there were men that would come to me and have a great burden, urging that I should go with them to this place and that place, but that I was not to go. At the same time it was presented to me that I could trust Elder James White, that he would guard me and that with him I would be in no danger. This man wanted to get some power over me. But he did not get it because I would not ride a rod with him. {LSMS 102.5; Ms131-1906.20, 28, 29}

An Evidence of God's Care

V26. Go to Portsmouth Vision

At my father's house in Portland, I was shown that I must go to Portsmouth the next day and bear my testimony there. My sister Sarah traveled with me, and Brother White was to accompany us. I had no means to pay my fare, but prepared to go, trusting in the Lord to open the way. The first car bell was ringing, as I put on my bonnet. I looked out of the window, and saw a good brother driving very fast up to the gate. His horse was reeking with sweat. He quickly entered the house, and asked, "Is there any one here who needs means? I was impressed that some one here needed money." We hastily related that we were going to Portsmouth at the Lord's bidding, and had nothing to go with, but resolved to start, trusting in the providence of God to open the way. The brother handed us fifteen dollars, enough to carry us to Portsmouth and back, [and] said, "Take a seat in my wagon, and I will carry you to the depot." On the way to the cars he told us that, while on the road to my father's, he could not hold his horse, he would come with great speed the whole distance of twelve miles. We had just taken our seats when the train started. Here the Lord tested and proved us, and strengthened our faith as we were brought into a very straight place, and were carried through by the manifestation of his providence. I had freedom in bearing my testimony in Portsmouth. {2SG 65.1; LSMS 146.2-147.3; Ms19-1885}

Labors in Massachusetts

V27. Visit Massachusetts Vision, Aug. 1845

Not long after our visit to Portsmouth, I was shown that I must visit Massachusetts, and there bear my testimony. This was in the summer of 1845. My sister Sarah accompanied me. When we reached Boston, we learned that Joseph Turner, who opposed me in Maine [and] whose course caused so much trouble, had arrived in Boston a few hours before us. We considered our being sent to Massachusetts, just at that time, was to save God's people from falling under his influence. {2SG 67.1; LSMS 148.1}

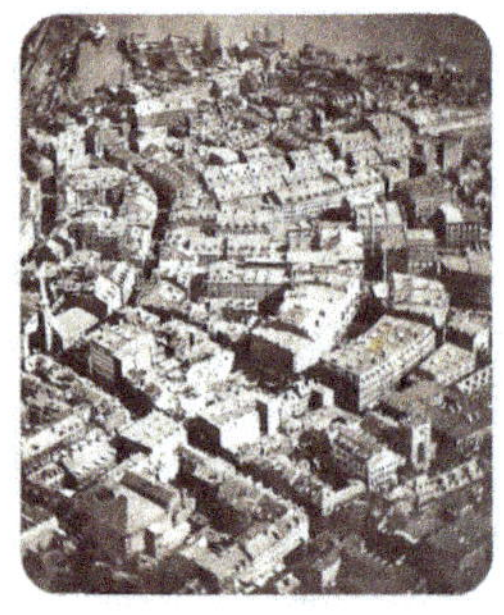

Aerial view of Boston, 1860

Meeting in Roxbury

It was arranged that I should go to Roxbury and there relate my message. I found a large company gathered in a private house. I felt the opposition that existed in the hearts of some of my brethren and sisters, yet in the strength of the Lord I delivered my unpopular message. As I was speaking, a sister who had been opposed to my work, arose and interrupted me. She grasped my hand, saying, "I said that the Devil sent you, but I can doubt your message no longer." Then she declared to those present that she believed I was a child of God, and that He had sent me. All in the meeting were greatly blessed. The power of the Lord attended the testimony, and many testified that they were comforted and refreshed. Thomas Waldo Haskins who had usually led in their meetings, arose with his countenance beaming with joy and said, "The same power attends this message that attended the truth in 1844. I do not expect to find another so green a spot this side of our deliverance." {2SG 67.2; LSMS 148.3-4}

Visit in Dorchester

From Roxbury, we next visited Brother Nichols' family in Dorchester, and had a meeting there of the deepest interest. Again, Thomas [***Waldo***] Haskins, the leader of the company at Roxbury, testified that the Lord had abundantly blessed him and said that he could go forty days on the strength he there received. But Joseph Turner was exerting his influence to discourage the brethren and to close up my way by spreading lying reports concerning my work. Howell, who had been made so happy as he received my testimony, fell under the influence of Joseph Turner, and as his mind turned, he became unsettled, then unstable. It was evident that he was rejecting "the counsel of God against" himself (Luke 7:30). He seemed unhappy, and finally took up the spiritualistic view of the second advent and received the grossest errors—that men and women could live above all sin—neglected his family, took a spiritual wife [***Rebecca Love Eaton***], and his lawful wife [***Mary Ann Haskins, née Soren***] died of a broken heart.[120] {2SG 67.2; LSMS 148.2-149.2; Ms46-1904}

The Hospitality of Brother and Sister Nichols

I next visited Randolph, New Bedford, and Carver. The Lord gave me liberty in all these places to bear my testimony, which was generally received, and the desponding and weak were strengthened. Brother and Sister Nichols invited Sarah and me to make their house our home. This kindness was gladly accepted. They were ever ready with words of encouragement to comfort me, and, when in trial, often their prayers ascended to heaven in my behalf, until the clouds were dispersed, and the light of heaven again cheered me. Nor did their kindness end here. They were attentive to all our wants, and generously supplied me with means to travel. They were reproached because they took a stand in favor of my visions, and on account of this they were obliged to be in almost constant conflict, for many were anxious to turn them against me. A faithful record is kept of their acts of love and benevolence. They will not lose their reward. He who seeth in secret and is acquainted with every kind and generous act, will reward them openly. {2SG 68.1; 149.3-150.2}

Otis R. Nichols and his wife, Mary Bird Nichols

Opposition in Carver

Soon John Howell, who had opposed me in Maine, came in great haste to Massachusetts with a document to destroy my influence. I have never had the privilege of reading it, or hearing it read, and have not been able to obtain a copy of it to this day. This document was read in my absence, when I could not answer for myself. As near as I can learn, John Howell got up the document, then urged a sister [***Elizabeth Haines***], who was occasionally with me during the two weeks of my extreme sickness, when my mind wandered, as stated on [2SG] page 51, to sign it. She was then on a sick bed, suffering great confusion of mind, and to get rid of John Howell, consented to have him sign her name to the document. At a later period this sister confessed to me in tears her regret that her name was ever attached to the document. She is not a Sabbath-keeper, yet has since cheerfully given her name to a certificate on another page which kills the slanderous document. May the Lord lead this sister to embrace the third message, and may we again enjoy sweet union as when at her altar of prayer, I had my first vision. {2SG 69.1}

We learned from one who had heard the document read in Boston and Roxbury, that John Howell had gone to Carver to read it there. At first I felt distressed. I could not see why God should suffer me thus to be reproached. I had to suffer anguish of spirit for others, and now my character was attacked. For a short time I sunk in discouragement. But as I went before the Lord with this severe trial, he gave me grace to bear it. His strong arm supported me. I was not suffering as an evil-doer, but for Christ's sake, and how many had suffered the same before me, even Jesus, the Saviour of the world, was reproached and falsely accused, and these words seemed ever before me, "Are ye able to drink of the cup?" Can ye "be baptized with the baptism?" (Matt. 20:22, 23). I felt, as I was bowed before the Lord, that I could say, Let me know the fellowship of Christ's sufferings. I knew what was reported as being in that document was false, and Jesus knew it, then why should I be troubled? I fully believed that Jesus was soon to come, and then my name, which was handled so maliciously here, would be justified. I there consecrated myself, my name and all, to God, and with reconciliation could say, Only let my poor name be "written in the Lamb's book of life" (Rev. 21:27), and men may handle it just as God suffers them. Let me suffer with Christ that I may reign with him. {2SG 70.1}

My sister had previously gone to Carver, expecting Brother Nichols to bring me in a few days. She was present at the reading of that document. She suffered on my account. John Howell said in the morning that he had been in a horror of darkness all night. No wonder. He feared my sister would expose him in his past fanatical course; but she would not condescend to mention those groveling acts of fanaticism in that portion of his career that she was acquainted with. {2SG 71.1}

I bear no ill will to those who used me thus. In a little from this the slanderer and the liar will receive their reward. That which they have sown they shall also reap. I could look up and rejoice from the depths of my heart, that there was a living God, Judge over all, who is acquainted with every heart, and to him I committed my cause. {2SG 71.2}

A Girl Cured of Fits

In a few weeks I visited Carver [***Oct. 1845***], and found that a few had been influenced by false reports of my enemies. But in many instances where the way had been previously closed against my testimony, it was now opened for me to bear it, and I had more friends than I had before. In the house where we tarried, there was a young sister who was subject to fits, and she was afflicted with a most distressing attack while we were there.[121] All seemed to be alarmed. {2SG 71.3; LSMS 150.3, 4}

Some said, "Go for the doctor;" others, "Put on the tea-kettle for hot water." I felt the spirit of prayer. We prayed to the Lord to deliver the afflicted. In the name and strength of Jesus I put my arms around her, and lifted her up from the bed, and rebuked the power of Satan, bidding her, "Go free." She was instantly brought out of the fit, and praised the Lord with us. We had a solemn, refreshing season in this place. We told the brethren and sisters that we had not come to defend character, nor to expose the wickedness of men who were laboring to destroy our influence, but to do our Master's will. We said that God would take care of the results of the efforts made by designing men. Our hearts were strengthened and the church encouraged. {2SG 71.3; LSMS 150.4}

Spiritualistic View of the Second Advent

About this time sister Clorinda S. Minor came from Philadelphia to her home in Roxbury, and we met in Boston.[122] She had recently made a trip to Jerusalem, Palestine, and was advocating some of the sentimental spiritualistic views that were coming in like a flood to ruin the faith of the Adventist people. Different errors were affecting the Advent people. The spiritual view of Christ's coming was ensnaring many. This great deception of Satan led many sophistries and corrupting errors. I could not understand the spiritualistic theories presented, but the Lord gave me a message to bear, which cut its way through the entangling sophistries, and we were often obliged, through a sense of duty in the fear of God, to bear a strong testimony against it. Many accepted the evidence that God was working through a humble instrument, and laid aside their fanciful theories. Sister Minor's influence went in favor of spiritualism, although she felt unwilling to acknowledge it. Those who would stand clear from this influence were obliged to be decided, and have nothing to do with it. With them the controversy was at an end. {2SG 72.1; LSMS 152.2}

THE

ADVENT MESSAGE

TO THE

DAUGHTERS OF ZION.

VOL. I BOSTON, MAY, 1844. NO. I.

AN APPEAL TO THE WOMEN OF OUR BELOVED COUNTRY.

The periodical edited by Clorinda S. Minor

At Roxbury we met a company over whom it seemed impossible to break the spell. The words of Scripture seemed to have no influence on them. They were bound by hypnotic influence. {LSMS 152.3}

I was invited to attend a meeting in Roxbury, and relate what the Lord had shown me. Brother Nichols took my sister and me to the meeting, where we found twenty persons assembled. Among them were brethren and sisters whom I dearly loved. They had acted a noble part in the advent movement, but they had been led astray by spiritualistic theories and fanciful doctrines, which led on and on, till they calumniated in lovesick sentimentalism and rank fanaticism. {LSMS 152.4}

As we were about to journey to New Bedford, a special message came to me from Sister Minor to come and relate what the Lord had shown me. Brother Nichols took my sister and me to the house where quite a number were collected. There were individuals present whom I had been shown were strong fanatics. They dealt in a human or satanic influence, and called it the Spirit of God. I had not seen them before with my natural eyes, yet, as I looked upon them, their countenances were familiar to me; for their course of life, their errors and corrupting influence had been shown me, and I felt forbidden to relate my vision in such a company. There were some present that we loved; but they had been led away in this deception. The leading ones considering this a favorable opportunity to exert their influence over me, and cause me to yield to their views, urged me to relate the visions. {2SG 72.2; LSMS 152.4, 5}

I was impressed that their only object was to mangle the truths presented in the visions and spiritualize away their literal meaning. I felt that they would endeavor to throw a Satanic influence upon me, and call it the power of God. Sister Minor addressed me, urging me to relate the visions. I respected her, but knew she was deceived in regard to that company. I felt forbidden to relate my visions to this company, and I refused to tell them anything except the part which related to them. They flattered; but it had no effect. Then they tried to terrify me, commanding me. They said it was my duty to tell them the visions. We told them we had no fellowship with their spirit, and in the name of God would resist it. I faithfully warned those whom I believed to be honest, and begged them to renounce their errors, and leave the company that was leading them astray. I told them that the views that they had accepted were but the Alpha of a great deception. {2SG 73.1; LSMS 153.1, 2}

Those were troublous times. If we had not stood firmly then, we should have made shipwreck of our faith. Some said we were stubborn; but we were obliged to set our faces as a flint, and turn not to the right hand nor to the left.[123] Those who believed in the spiritual coming of Christ were insinuating like the great serpent in the garden. When it suited their purposes, they would show such a mild, meek spirit, that we had to be on our guard, strengthened on every side with scripture testimony concerning the literal, personal appearing of our Saviour. I left them, free from their influence and spirit. In a few weeks, a portion of that company were left to run into the basest fanaticism. {2SG 74.1, 73.1; LSMS 153.3}

Second Visit To Massachusetts

Soon after our meeting in Roxbury, Sarah and I returned to Portland. Later, by invitation of Brother and Sister Nichols, we returned to Massachusetts, and for a time made their house our home. {2SG 75.1; LSMS 157.1}

No Work Theory Again

At this time there was in Boston and vicinity a large company of fanatical persons who held that it was a sin to labor. Their principal message was, "Sell that ye have, and give alms" (Luke 12:33). They said we were in the Jubilee, that the land should rest, and that the poor must be supported without labor. Sargent and Robbins were among the leaders in this fanaticism.[124] They denounced my visions as being of the devil because I had reproved their errors. They were severe upon all who did not believe with them. {2SG 75.1; LSMS 157.2}

While we were visiting at the house of Brother Nichols, Robbins and Sargent came from Boston to ask a favor of Brother Nichols and said that they had come to have a visit and tarry overnight with him. Brother Nichols replied that he was glad they had come, for Sisters Sarah and Ellen Harmon were in the house, and he wished them to become acquainted with us. They at once changed their minds and could not even be persuaded to come into the house. Brother Nichols asked if I might relate my message in Boston, and if they would hear and then judge, should I go there. "Yes," said they. "Come to Boston next Sabbath; we would like the privilege of hearing her." {LSMS 157.3}

Accordingly we planned to visit Boston, but in the evening, at the commencement of the Sabbath, while engaged in prayer, I was shown in vision that we must not go to Boston, but in the opposite direction, to Randolph, because the Lord had a work for us to do there.[125] {LSMS 158.1}

V31. Dorchester Vision, spring 1846

Surprise Meeting in Randolph

We went to Randolph, and found a large room full of people who had gathered for a meeting, and among them were the very men who said they would be pleased to hear my message in Boston. As we entered, Robbins and Sargent looked at each other in surprise, and began to groan. They had promised to meet me in Boston, but thought they would disappoint us by going to Randolph, and, while we were in Boston, would warn the brethren there against us. In the forenoon meeting, they did not have much freedom. During intermission one of them remarked that good matter would be brought out in the afternoon. Sister Nichols answered, "I believe it." Robbins told my sister that I could not have a vision where he was. {2SG 76.1; LSMS 158.2}

V32. *Randolph Vision, spring 1846*

In the afternoon, while we were pleading with God in prayer, the blessing of the Lord rested on me, and I was taken off in vision. I was again shown the errors of these deceived men, Robbins and Sargent, and others united with them. I saw that they could not prosper, that their errors would confuse and distract; that some would be deceived by them, but that truth would triumph in the end, and error be brought down. I was shown that they were not honest. {2SG 76.2; LSMS 158.3}

Then the future was opened before me, and I saw something of the course they would pursue, that they would continue to despise the teachings of the Lord, that they would reject reproof and resist God's Spirit until their folly should be manifest to all, and they would finally be left in total darkness. A chain of truth was presented to me from the Scriptures, in contrast with their errors. {2SG 76.2; LSMS 158.4}

When I came out of vision, candles were burning. I had been in vision nearly four hours. As I was unconscious of all that transpired around me while in vision, I will copy from Brother Nichols' description of that meeting. {2SG 76.2; LSMS 159.1}

"Sister Ellen was taken off in vision with extraordinary manifestations, and continued talking in vision with a clear voice, which could be distinctly understood by all present, until about sundown. S., R. and F. [***Sargent, Robbins, and French***] were much exasperated, as well as excited, to hear sister E. [***Ellen***] talk in vision, which they declared was of the Devil; they exhausted all their influence, and bodily strength, to destroy the effect of the vision. They would unite in singing very loud; and then alternately would talk and read from the Bible in a loud voice, in order that E. [***Ellen***] might not be heard, until their strength was exhausted, and their hands would shake so they could not read from the Bible. But amidst all this confusion and noise, E.'s [***Ellen's***] clear and shrill voice, as she talked in vision, was distinctly heard by all present. The opposition of these men continued as long as they could talk and sing, notwithstanding some of their own friends rebuked them, and requested them to stop. But says R [***Robbins***], 'You are bowed to an idol; you are worshiping a golden calf.' {2SG 77.2}

"Mr. [***Zaccheus***] Thayer, the owner of the house, was not fully satisfied that her vision was of the Devil, as R. [***Robbins***] declared it to be.[126] He wanted it tested in some way. He had heard that visions of satanic power were arrested by opening the Bible and laying it on the person in vision, and asked S. [***Sargent***] if he would test it in this way, which he declined to do. Then Thayer took a heavy, large quarto family Bible which was laying on the table, and seldom used, opened it, and laid it open upon the breast of E. [***Ellen***] while in vision, as she was then inclined backward against the wall in the corner of the room. Immediately after the Bible was laid upon her, she arose upon her feet, and walked into the middle of the room, with the Bible open in one hand, and lifted up as high as she could reach, and with her eyes steadily looking upward, declared in a solemn manner, 'The inspired testimony from God,' or words of the same import. And then she continued for a long time, while the Bible was extended in one hand, and her eyes looking upwards, and not on the Bible, to turn over the leaves with her other hand, and place her finger upon certain passages, and correctly utter their words with a solemn voice. Many present looked at the passages where her finger was pointed, to see if she spoke them correctly, for her eyes at the same time were looking upwards. Some of the passages referred to were judgments against the wicked and blasphemers; and others were admonitions and instructions relative to our present condition. {2SG 78.1}

"In this state she continued all the afternoon until near sunset, when she came out of vision. When E. [***Ellen***] arose in vision upon her feet, with the heavy open Bible in her hand, and walked the room, uttering the passages of scripture, S., R. and F. [***Sargent, Robbins, and French***] were silenced. For the remainder of the time they were troubled, with many others; but they shut their eyes and braved it out without making any acknowledgement of their feelings." {2SG 79.1}

Strange Experiences in Portland

Returning from our visit in Massachusetts, we passed through strange experiences in Portland [as] opposition to our faith increased. {2SG 79.2; LSMS 161.1}

One evening as we were engaged in prayer, the window was broken in just above my head, and the glass came down upon me. I continued praying. One man in his blind rage was cursing and swearing while we continued to plead with God that when His indignation should come upon the shelterless head of the poor sinner, we might be hid in the secret of His pavilion.[127] The man's voice hushed, and he was seen hastening from the place. He could not endure the sound of prayer or the thought of judgment. {2SG 79.2; LSMS 161.2}

Visit of the Police Officer

About this time Bro. Nichols visited us. Some of our wicked, profane neighbors complained that they were disturbed by our frequent praying, and we were several times interrupted by them. One afternoon we had a season of prayer. While bowed before the Lord, two of our most wicked, profane neighbors, entered the door, and broke in upon our worship, saying, "Up! and off your knees! for in fifteen minutes the work-house-cart will be after you." We did not heed the interruption, but continued in prayer. In a few moments they entered again, repeating nearly the same words. A number of times we were thus broken in upon by these poor, wicked men. {2SG 80.1}

The same afternoon an officer was sent to visit us, while some of our neighbors raised their windows to hear the result. Father was away at his business, and mother stepped to the door. He told her that complaints had reached him that we disturbed the peace of the neighborhood by noisily praying, and sometimes by praying in the night, and he was requested to attend to the matter. {2SG 80.2; LSMS 161.3}

Mother answered that we prayed morning and night, and sometimes at noon, and should continue to do so; that Daniel prayed to his God three times a day, notwithstanding the king's decree. {2SG 80.2; LSMS 162.1}

He said he had no objection to prayer; if there was more of it in the neighborhood it would be better. "But," said he, "they complain of your praying in the night." He was told that if any of the family were sick, or in distress of mind in the night, it was our custom to call upon God for help, and we found relief. {2SG 80.2; LSMS 162.2, 3}

He was referred by our neighbor who used strong drink. His voice was often heard cursing and blaspheming God. "Why did not the neighbors send you to him," my mother said, "to still the disturbances he causes in the neighborhood? He serves his master; we serve the Lord our God. Why is it that his curses and blasphemy seem not to disturb the neighbors, while the voice of prayer greatly troubles them?" {2SG 80.2; LSMS 162.4}

"Well," said the officer, "what shall I tell them that you will do?"

My mother replied, "Serve God, let the consequences be what they may."

The officer left, and we had no further trouble from that quarter. {2SG 80.2; LSMS 162.5-7}

Anger of Young Men

A few days after, while our family was quietly engaged in evening prayer, some young men, imitating the example of their parents, began making noise around the house. At length they ran for an officer. He came, and the boys told him to listen. Said he, "Is this what you have called me for? That family is doing what every family ought to do. They are making no disturbance; and if you call me out for this purpose again, I will put you in the lock-up, for disturbing a peaceable family while attending to their religious duties." After this we were not molested. {2SG 81.1; LSMS 162.8}

Fear of Thunder

That summer the neighbors were terrified by frequent thunder and lightning. A number were killed instantly; and if there was an appearance of a thunderstorm, some of the parents would send their children to our house to invite one of the family to visit them, and stay until the storm was over. The children innocently told the whole story: "For Ma says the lightning will not strike a house where the advent people are." {2SG 81.2; LSMS 163.1}

One night there was a fearful storm. The heavens presented a continual sheet of lightning. A few rushed from their beds into the street, calling upon God for mercy, crying, "The judgment day has come!" {2SG 81.2; LSMS 163.2}

My brother Robert, who was a devoted Christian, was very happy. He went out of the house and walked to the head of the street, praising the Lord. He said he never prized the hope of the Christian as he did that night, as he saw the terror and insecure position of those who had no hope in Christ. {2SG 81.2; LSMS 163.3}

During the latter part of 1845 and the beginning of 1846, I suffered great feebleness. At times I was called out to labor in various places, and was given strength to bear my testimony to the people. And although often wonderfully sustained during these labors, I afterward found myself weak and full of suffering. {LSMS 164.1}

Initial Resistance to the Sabbath

Joseph Bates

While on a visit to New Bedford, MA, in 1846, I became acquainted with Elder Joseph Bates. He had early embraced the advent faith, and was an active laborer in the cause. I found him to be a true Christian gentleman, courteous and kind. He treated me tenderly as though I were his own child. The first time he heard me speak, he manifested great interest. After I ceased speaking, he arose and said, "I am a doubting Thomas. I do not believe in visions. But if I could believe the testimony the sister related tonight was indeed the voice of God to us, I would be the happiest man alive. My heart is deeply moved. I believe the speaker to be sincere, but cannot explain in regard to her being shown the wonderful things she has related to us." {LSMS 164.2}

Elder Bates rested upon Saturday, the seventh day of the week, and he urged it upon our attention as the true Sabbath. I did not feel its importance, and thought that he erred in dwelling upon the fourth commandment more than the other nine. {2SG 82.1; LSMS 164.3}

The Sanctuary and the Sabbath

V45. Fairhaven Halo Vision, March 6, 1847

But the Lord gave me a view of the heavenly sanctuary [in early 1847]. I was conducted to the second vail. The temple of God was open in heaven, and I was shown the ark of God covered with the mercy-seat. Two angels stood one at either end of the ark, with their wings spread over the mercy-seat, and their faces turned toward it. This my accompanying angel informed me represented all the heavenly host looking with reverential awe toward the law of God, which had been written by the finger of God. {2SG 82.1; LSMS 165.1}

Jesus raised the cover of the ark, and I beheld the tables of stone on which the Ten Commandments were written. I was amazed as I saw the fourth commandment in the very center of the ten precepts, with a soft halo of light all around it. Said the angel, "It is the only one of the ten which defines the living God who created the heavens and the earth and all things therein." {2SG 82.1; LSMS 165.2; cf. V46, in ExV 16.1; RH, July 21, 1851; WLF; Broadside3; Lt. 1, 1847}

City of Portland — Clerk's Office Aug 15 1846
Aug. 16 Mr. James S. White of Palmyra, and Miss Ellen G. Harmon of Portland, enter their intentions of marriage — Attest W. Boyd, City Clerk
Cert: Aug 30th

August 16, 1846, intention of marriage for James S. White and Miss Ellen G. Harmon

Marriage and First View of Other Planets

V42. *Opening Heavens Vision,* November 1846

August 30th, 1846 I was married to Elder James White. In a few months we attended a conference in Topsham, Maine. Bro. J. Bates was present. He did not then fully believe that my visions were of God. It was a meeting of much interest. But I was suddenly taken ill and fainted. The brethren prayed for me, and I was restored to consciousness. The Spirit of God rested upon us in Bro. C.'s [***Robert G. Curtis's***] humble dwelling, and I was wrapt in a vision of God's glory, and for the first time had a view of other planets. After I came out of vision I related what I had seen. Bro. Bates asked if I had studied astronomy. I told him I had no recollection of ever looking into an "astronomy." Said he, "This is of the Lord." {2SG 83.1}

Between 1847 and 1851, James and Ellen White attended many conferences throughout New York and New England to share the Sabbath truth with scattered "bands" of Adventists (see *online* **CHART-3**). On November 18, 1848, Ellen received the "Like the Rising of the Sun Vision" (**V57**), in which she was shown that James should spread the Sabbath truth through a paper that could reach places they could not go. James decided to wait until the next summer to earn the money for printing by mowing hay. In **June 1849**, as he drove up to where they were staying, Ellen fainted. They united in prayer for her recovery, and she received the "Angels with Rods Vision" (**V74**), with reproof for James' delay and encouragement for him to "write, write, write."[128] Acting on this direction in July, James began publishing *The Present Truth,* in Middletown, Connecticut. Because the believers also needed reminding of their Adventist roots, the Whites moved to Centerport, New York, in August, staying with William and Lydia Harris to be able to publish *The Advent Review* in Auburn, New York. The paper cited Adventist writers who laid out the basis for the significance of the Midnight Cry, and rehearsing the 1844 position of early Adventist writers, showed who had departed from the earlier platform. In November, the Whites moved to Oswego, where James continued publishing *The Present Truth.* The following November, they moved to Paris, Maine, and combined the missions of the two papers in the *Second Advent Review and Sabbath Herald.* We pick up the story in mid-1851, as James and Ellen were attending conferences in New York.

Publishing in Saratoga Springs and Rochester, New York

During a conference at the home of Horace Cushman, in West Milton, New York, from June 27–29, 1851, Ellen received a vision not to return to Paris, Maine.[129] So, with the encouragement of the brethren, she and James, still both in their twenties, decided to move the publishing work to the bustling town of Saratoga Springs, New York, known for its many mineral springs and seasonal visitors and an area where many Adventist families then lived.[130] This would be the third move of their publishing homebase within a three-year period. James had begun publishing a regular paper in response to a vision given Ellen. She told him, "Begin to print a little paper and send it out to the people. Let it be small at first; but as the people read, they will send you means with which to print, and it will be a success from the first." Reflecting on the vision, she later added, "From this small beginning it was shown to me to be like streams of light that went clear around the world."[131] That paper was first published in Middletown, Connecticut, in July 1849, under the title *The Present Truth*. That same year, they moved their homebase to Oswego, New York, where they rented a house and the paper was published until May 1850. The paper's major object was to promote the biblical Sabbath, with the inclusion of an occasional vision of Ellen White to reinforce their biblical discoveries.[132] In early 1850, as James was going through a particularly discouraging period, Ellen "saw that God did not want James to stop yet, but he must *write, write, write, write*, and speed the message and let it go. I saw that it would go where God's servants cannot go."[133] Before the last issue of *The Present Truth* was published in November, in Paris, Maine, the Adventists had begun publishing *The Advent Review* in August 1850 in Auburn, New York. It had no articles written by Ellen White, for that wasn't its purpose.[134] Its articles were on the veracity of the Advent movement to encourage Adventists to stay on the Advent path to the City of God, and it included notes of travel regarding meetings in New England and New York planned for the same purpose. In November, James began publishing in Paris, Maine, *The Advent Review and Sabbath Herald*, a paper that merged the missions of the earlier papers. During this time, James would take on part-time work—hauling stone, chopping cordwood, and cutting hay to earn money for travel and living expenses. Travel was difficult for James and Ellen, particularly with harsh New England winters, unhealthy conditions on trains, and two small children in tow.

James and Ellen White, c. 1857

At great personal sacrifice in not being able to stay in one place to raise their boys themselves, James and Ellen White left their two small sons with consecrated

Adventist families during this time as they were duty-bound to travel from one town to another, boarding with other Adventist families and encouraging the "little flock."[135] In moving to Saratoga Springs, they would find accommodations in which they could reunite with their younger son. While looking for a suitable house to rent in Saratoga Springs, they stayed with Jesse Thompson and his wife and three daughters. Thompson was a farmer and Christian minister who had traveled with William Miller in the early 1840s.[136] His house and farm were two miles from Ballston Spa, New York, and nine miles from Saratoga Springs. James contracted the printing of the second volume of *The Advent Review and Sabbath Herald* with the steam press of Gideon M. Davison.[137]

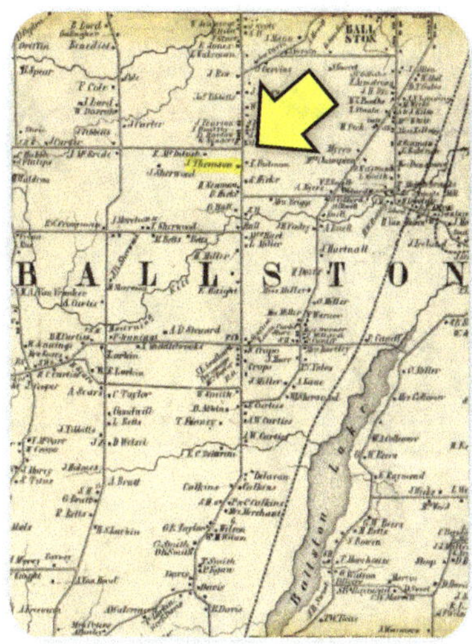

Ballston Spa home of Jesse Thompson

Previously, James White had published some of Ellen's visions in broadside format, which was on one side of a page.[138] Nonetheless, Adventists in Saratoga County and elsewhere had difficulty knowing what to make of her visions.[139] It was to better educate these believers with the visions' role that James published several of his wife's visions in July in an "Extra" of the *Second Advent Review and Sabbath Herald*. He explained his rationale for publishing the visions in this way:

> We do not design this extra for so general circulation as the regular paper, for the reason that strong prejudice exists in many minds against a portion of its contents. . . . Says Paul, "Despise not prophesyings, prove all things, hold fast that which is good." [I] Thess. v, 20, 21. We believe that God is unchangeable, that he is "the same yesterday, and to-day, and for ever." And that it is his will and purpose to teach his tried people, at this the most important period in the history of God's people, in the same manner as in past time. But as many are prejudiced against visions, we think that at present not to insert anything of the kind in the regular paper. We will therefore publish the visions by themselves for the benefit of those who believe that God can fulfil his word and give visions "in the last days." . . .[140]

He also announced plans to publish Ellen's visions as a separate pamphlet.

> We have concluded to publish the article entitled "Experience and Views," with other matter of the same nature, in a small, neat pamphlet, which will be ready as soon as possible. This we have been urged to do by a number of the brethren, who have offered to pay the expense.[141]

Saratoga Springs, New York, 1850

Residents of Saratoga Springs rented out houses that were sometimes hard to secure. In late summer 1851, James White was able to find one for rent on the corner of Circular and Phila Streets.[142] It was large enough to accommodate James and Ellen White, their son Edson, Stephen and Sarah Belden, Clarissa Bonfoey, Annie R. Smith, and, at times, John N. Andrews, "Aunt Rachel" Cushing, Marion Stowell, and other guests.[143] Moving day, August 5, 1851, was a busy day for James and Ellen White. Besides moving, James picked up the first regular number of Volume 2 of *The Advent Review and Sabbath Herald* from Davison's printing establishment. James also performed a marriage service for Stephen Belden and Sarah Harmon. With minimal furniture, which they had borrowed, they had to use a board atop a sink for a place to fold and wrap the freshly printed papers. Then, when Sabbath, August 9, came, Ellen had a vision in that house of "the exceeding loveliness and glory of Jesus."[144] The next month, James published, through the Davison printing establishment, the 64-page "pamphlet" that is considered Ellen White's first book, with its autobiographical account of her early Christian experience and her early visions, or "views."[145]

Stephen and Sarah Belden

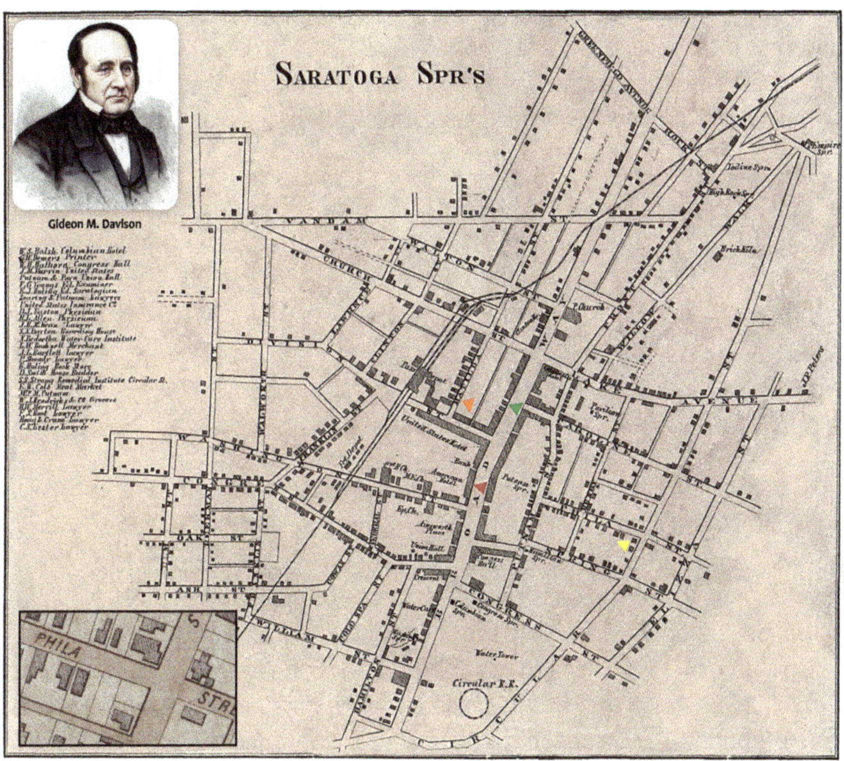

1856 Samuel Geil map of Saratoga Springs: 1 Davison's printing office on Long Alley, 2 his house on Broadway, 3 the post office in the basement of the American Hotel, 4 the Whites' rental on the corner of Circular and Phila. **Insets:** Gideon M. Davison; John Bevan map (c. 1850) showing the houses on the corner of Phila and Circular Streets

During the nine months they resided at Saratoga Springs, James and Ellen did more than publish periodicals and her first book. They continued traveling in New England, attending conferences in Medford, Massachusetts; Washington, New Hampshire; and East Bethel, Johnson, and Vergennes, Vermont, from October 23 to November 18. While away, Ellen White received visions that helped resolve difficulties among the various groups of believers. From December 22 to February 13, they attended conferences in Camden and Oswego, New York. Then, from March 12–15, 1852, the Whites led out in an organizing conference at the home of Jesse Thompson. Besides the Whites and the Thompsons, the attendees at the organizing conference included Joseph Bates, Samuel W. Rhodes, George W. Holt, Frederick Wheeler, John C. Day, Joseph Baker, William S. Ingraham, Ira Wyman, Heman Churchill, Washington Morse, Hiram Edson, Ezra A. Poole, Lebbeus Drew, and John N. Andrews.[146] In prayerful discussion, the attendees recognized "the disadvantages of having" the paper "published as it has been," and they determined to purchase a printing press of their own and move operations to Rochester, New York.[147]

When the little company left Saratoga Springs in April, Luman V. Masten, a 24-year-old foreman at Davison's printing office, went with them to set up and operate the Washington hand printing press as soon as it was shipped from New York City to their new location at 124 Mount Hope Avenue, Rochester, New York.[148] The press arrived, and the little company went quickly to work, with the first issue of volume 3 of *The Advent Review and Sabbath Herald* coming off the press on May 6.

124 Mount Hope Avenue, Rochester, New York; Washington hand printing press used in Rochester

In December 1853, James published a 52-page supplement to the first book, with explanatory notes and additional visions.[149] In 1855, publishing of Ellen White's "views" took another form, as the Battle Creek church voted to print Ellen White's 1855 testimony to them as a pamphlet. Other pamphlet testimonies would be subsequently published at an average of one or two per year.[150]

On March 14, 1858, Ellen White had her "Great Controversy Vision" in Lovett's Grove, Ohio, a vision that was the major source for her next book, *Spiritual Gifts*, vol. 1, subtitled *The Great Controversy Between Christ and His Angels, and Satan and His Angels.*[151] In 1860, she published her autobiographical work, "My Christian Experience, Views and Labor" (*Spiritual Gifts*, vol. 2). The two volumes were bound together for sale in 1864, with volumes 3 and 4 being published separately later that year.[152] In the 1870s, the portions of the four volumes dealing with the "great controversy" were expanded into the *Spirit of Prophecy* series, and the earlier books went out of print.

Spiritual Gifts, volumes 1, 2, 3, and 4

Republication of Ellen White's Earliest Books

B. F. Snook, 1896

There were those who surmised that the disappearance of the early books meant a cover-up. Dissident Adventists in Marion, Iowa, led by former Adventist minister Benjamin Franklin Snook, alleged that Seventh-day Adventists were suppressing Ellen White's early writings (which had gone out of print) because they had repudiated her "shut door" teaching that salvation supposedly closed in 1844 for all but Adventists who still believed in the 1844 fulfilment of Daniel 8:14.[153] To demonstrate the church's transparency in the matter, General Conference President George I. Butler arranged, in 1882, for the reprinting of her three earliest books in edited form—*Experience and Views* with its *Supplement* and the early *Great Controversy*, declaring all her early writings to be once again available. The combined form went through many editions and is still published to this day.[154] The Marion Party reacted, accusing him of deception for not also reprinting the 1847 pamphlet "A Word to the Little Flock," of which Butler was then unfamiliar.[155] Contacting John N. Andrews, who directed him to Joseph H. Waggoner, Butler got a copy of the pamphlet and had it reproduced in 1883.[156]

Butler also issued a ten-part series in *The Advent Review and Sabbath Herald* to rebut the charge that Adventists were hiding their early "shut door" teaching.[157] The series demonstrated that the view of early Sabbatarian Adventists agreed with that of other Adventist leaders immediately after the 1844 disappointment, including William Miller, George Needham, and John Ball Cook, among others.[158] Butler quoted from William Miller's letter to Joshua V. Himes: "We have done our work in warning sinners and in trying to awaken a formal church. God in his providence has shut the door. We can only stir one another up to be patient and to be diligent to make our calling and election sure." Yet, as time passed without Christ's returning, Adventists changed their thinking. Many Adventists abandoned belief in any significance for the 1844 fulfillment of prophecy and, to stir sinners to repentance, continued setting and announcing new dates for Christ's return. The Adventists who continued believing there was an 1844 fulfillment of Daniel 8:14 and maintained belief in the "shut door," recognized that the Old Testament types pointed to two phases in the atonement. In other words, they believed one door of the sanctuary had shut while another had opened. Though they continued to believe that the rejectors of the 1844 prophecy had shut themselves off from God, they also recognized that others besides the original 50,000 Adventists were responding to the final call for salvation.[159] They held that there were children and others who had not rejected the message. Regarding working for these two groups, Ira Abbey of North Brookfield, New York, attested: "Between 1846 and 1850, Brother and Sister White came to our house, and were very zealous for the children and those that had not rejected the truth."[160] One of these had married a Millerite wife in May of 1844 without any public profession of religion until 1845, yet the man was embraced by the Sabbatarian Adventists in 1850 after Ellen White had a message of hope for him, quieting the misgivings of any who had confidence in her visions.[161] While some had viewed other Christians as unconvertable, the visions changed their perspective. Ellen White wrote: "For a time after the disappointment in 1844, I did hold in common with the advent body that the door of mercy was then forever closed to the world. This position was taken before my first vision was given me. It was the light given me of God that corrected our error and enabled us to see the true position."[162] Biblically, that the saints were a literal 144,000 in number, as shown her in her first vision, meant that even 50,000 was far short of the goal. Her fifth vision explained more about the meaning of the shut door, preparing the way for acceptance of new people into their fellowship.

The chart on the following pages—for the first time in print—lists all of Ellen White's known visions for the first ten years of her prophetic ministry.[163]

CHART-1. Ellen White's Recorded Visions from 1844 to 1854

No. date	Location	*Vision Name.* Description, type of guidance: GENERAL, SPECIFIC, PERSONAL. An asterisk (*) before a **Vision Name** marks a sanctuary vision.	References
V1. 1844 last of Dec	Portland, ME, Elizabeth Haines', while praying	*Midnight Cry Vision.* "The travels of the Advent people to the Holy City," with Jesus' return and the heavenly city with the tree of life; talked with Charles Fitch and Levi Stockman; the 7th month movement was of divine direction. *Four other women were present with her praying. In Ms16-1894, she mentions breathing again after the vision.* (G)	JW, DS 6 Sep 1845; DS 17 Jan 1846; ONichols to WMiller, 20 Apr 1846 (EXH-7:26); Lt3-1847, 13 Jul; WLF 14-18; RH 21 Jul 1851; ExV 9-13; MT v1n3:4; 2SG 30-35; 1T 58; LS80 327; Ms16-1894, 3 Feb; RP 92; LS 64-68
V2. 1845 Jan, next week night	Portland, Robert Harmon's, while praying for her	*Make Known to Others Vision.* Instructed that she was to share what had been revealed; shown trials she would pass through; promised God's grace to sustain her and that God would preserve her humility through affliction. *Five women present.* (P)	ONichols to WMiller, 20 Apr 1846; RH 21 Jul 1851; ExV 5; 2SG 35; 1T 62; Ms190-1903, 11 Jul; GSAM 211; LSMS 923; LS 69
V3.	Portland, Robert Harmon's, as the church prayed	*Ball of Fire Vision.* "Make known to others what I have revealed to you"; mesmerism is from the devil; promised illness to keep her from self-exaltation. *John Pearson, Sr., saw the ball of fire; Ellen held up the family folio Bible, containing the Apocrypha; Noah Lunt was present.* (P)	ExV 6; 2SG 37; 1T 64, 65; GCDB 18 Mar 1891, 145; RP 103; GSAM 236; RH 28 Jan 1902, 63; Ms131-1906, 13 Aug; LS 71; WCW to S Peck,[164] 2 Apr 1919, DF 732a
V4.	Portland	*Three Steps Vision. Only mentioned by Loughborough as a contrast to the vision of William Foy, which he didn't understand the vision and which Hazen Foss rejected.* (G)	GSAM 146; see Ms131-1906, 13 Aug
V5. mid-Feb	Exeter, ME	**Bridegroom Vision.* Begins with Midnight Cry; Jesus goes to the Father in the Holy of Holies to receive the kingdom as in the wedding parable; events after the 2300 days parallel the earthly sanctuary; Father and Son have a form; Crosier was right about sanctuary parallels. *No indication mercy for the world closed.* (G)	Lt1-1846, 15 Feb; DS 14 Mar 1846; Ms1-1846, 6 Apr; Lt2-1847, 21 Apr; Lt3-1847, 13 Jul; ExV 43; LS 104
V6. Feb 14 FRI night	Atkinson, ME, James Ayer, Jr.'s	*Atkinson Trial of Faith Vision.* Advent believers would have a trial of their faith. *Israel Dammon was arrested at a meeting that Ellen attended the next day.* (P)	2SG 40; LS 98
V7. Feb 15	Atkinson, James Ayer, Jr.'s	*Cases of Believers Vision. Loton Lambert, William C. Crosby, Joel Doore, and George S. Woodbury reported that Ellen delivered specific and accurate descriptions of believers.* (S)	*Piscataquis Farmer*, 7 Mar 1845
V8. spring	Topsham, ME, Robert G. Curtis's[165]	*Topsham Vision. Held up a family folio Bible and quoted appropriate scriptures in a vision lasting two hours, witnessed by the Howlands and Marion Stowell.* (S)	GCDB 18 Mar 1891, 145; RP 107; MSC, FHL, LH, RHW; GSAM 237, 238; EGW Record Book 2, 18; AUG 24 Feb 1937, 3
V9. spring	Portland	*Visit New Hampshire Vision.* Needed to confront "spiritual magnetism." (P)	2SG 46; ST 4 May 1876; LS 77
V10. spring	Corinth, VT, W. Morse's, praying	*Encouragement for Washington Morse Vision.* Help for his bewilderment over the 1844 disappointment.[166] (S)	ST 4 May 1876; LS 77-78
V11. spring	Claremont, NH, Charles Colliers', praying[167]	*Spiritual Magnetism Vision.* John Garnsey Bennett and Albert Merritt Billings were practicing deception and teaching the erroneous concept of the "cannot-sin" theory.[168] (S)	Ms10-1859; 2SG 48; ST 11 May 1876; LS 83; 1EGWLM 761, n3
V12. spring	Grantham, NH, praying for relief with Louisa Foss	*Voice of God–Time of Jacob's Trouble Vision.* Joseph Turner and John Howell's fanaticism about the return of Christ and following impressions was wounding God's cause and leading to corruption; to return to Maine. *Her voice awakened those in the house.* (S)	Ms10-1859; Ms9-1859; 2SG 48-50
V13. spring	Portland, Elizabeth Haines', praying	*Joseph Turner's Ungodly Course Vision. Ellen White reproved Turner for his attention to women that were not his wife. Turner claimed the revelation was mesmerism.* (S)	Ms9-1859; Ms10-1859; 2SG 49; LS80 213, 214
V14. spring	Orrington, ME praying	*Leave by Daybreak Vision. Escaped by boat, bound for Portland.* (P)	Ms9-1859; Lt2-1874, 24 Aug
V15. spring	Garland, ME[169]	*Fanatics Unwanted in Portland Vision.* Reproof of "no mercy for sinners" doctrine. Fanatics would injure the cause in Portland. (S)	Lt2-1874, 24 Aug; 1T 66; RP 106; DPF 81
V16. spring	Portland, Elizabeth Haines', while others prayed	*New Earth Vision.* First view of the glory of the New Earth and New Jerusalem after the 1000 years, countering the spiritualizing view of the New Jerusalem, with literal trees, animals, and food; promised *another angel* to guard her whenever needed. *The vision came after two weeks of mind wandering* (G)(P)	Lt1-1845, Dec. 20; DS 24 Jan 1846; WLF 16, 17; AR Nov 1850; RH 21 Jul 1851; ExV 13; MT v1n1:2; Ms9-1859; 2SG 52-55; 1T 67-70; LSMS 131

V17.	Portland, prayer in the woods	Visions in the Woods. *She went alone in the woods or some retired place where God would sometimes give her a vision.* (P)	RH 21 Jul 1851; ExV 6; 2SG 57; 1T 71; LS 88
V18. night	Portland	No Work Doctrine Vision. Error of refraining from all labor. (S)	ExV 7; 2SG 58; 1T 72; LS 88
V19.	Portland	Time of Trouble Before the Advent Vision. Time setters would be disappointed. (S)	ExV 7; 2SG 58; 1T 72; LSMS 137
V20.	Portland, Robert Harmon's, at family prayer	Fifty Texts Vision. Write out Bible texts written in gold letters on a card to address fanaticism. *She looked up verses, her first writing of a vision. As she went into vision, she questioned if it were mesmerism and was struck dumb until the next morning.*[170] (S)	Lt3-1847, 13 Jul; RH 21 Jul 1851, Art. A; ExV 7; 2SG 59-60; LSMS 138; LS 89
V21. night	Unknown	Jesus' Disapproving Frown Vision. Softening the messages, she felt Jesus' disapproval and saw a company with blood-stained clothes. (S)	ExV 63; 2SG 61-62; 1T 74; LS 90
V22.	Poland, ME, Mary Foss's, while praying for her[171]	Attend Meeting in Poland Vision. Was instructed to go three miles to a meeting. *The next morning, Joseph Turner attempted to mesmerize her, but she prayed, "Another angel, Father! Another angel!" and was shielded from Turner's control.* (P)	2SG 62; ST 30 May 1878, 162; LS80 223.3; LSMS 143; Ms131-1906, 13 Aug
V23. Apr	Poland, John Megquier's, while praying[172]	Meet Fanaticism in Paris Vision. Was shown that she should go to Paris, Maine, and that, if Marion Stowell accepted the fanaticism and then saw her mistake, she would leave the Adventists forever. (P)	2SG 64; RP 114; Miles Grant, *The True Sabbath*, 70; MSC to EGW, 9 Oct 1908 (EXH-7:124); LS 86
V24.	Paris, ME, Bro. C.'s [**Thomas or Sibley Chase's**], while praying	Jesse Stevens' Errors Vision. God's work for His people's salvation; Bible teaching versus Jesse Stevens' errors, including not working;[173] he had the frown of God upon him and would soon manifest himself. *He hanged himself on Oct. 13, 1847.* (S)	2SG 64, 65; ST 30 May 1878, 162; LS80 225; MSC to EGW, 9 Oct 1908 (EXH-7:124); LSMS 144-145; LS 86-87
V25. Jul-Aug	Paris, Lewis Stowell's	Vision at Home of Lewis Stowell. *Mentioned by Marion Crawford, née Stowell.* (?)	MSC, 17 Aug 1875 (EXH-7:9)
V26. night	Portland, R. Harmon's, entering gate (?)	Go to Portsmouth Vision. (May have been while walking with friends and discussing the glories of the kingdom of God and passing through the gate.) *Man pays their way when they have no money.* (P)	2SG 65; LS80 226; Ms14-1885, 21 Sep; Ms19-1885, 21 Sep; (LI 272, regarding gate at her father's house
V27. Aug	Portland	Visit Massachusetts Vision. *With Joseph Turner's arrival ahead of them, they realized the visit was to stay his influence.* (P)	2SG 67; LS80 227; LSMS 148
V28. Aug	Randolph, MA	Visit New Bedford, Dartmouth, and Carver Vision. (P)	ONichols 1859 Account (EXH-7:20)
V29. mid-Oct	Carver, MA	*Time of Trouble Vision. Saints yet to pass through "time of Jacob's trouble." *Declaring that the date would pass by, the vision averted disappointment when James White and Otis Nichols had anticipated Jesus' return would be in Oct. 1845.* (G)	DS 14 Mar 1846 (Lt1-1846, 15 Feb); GT 20 Jan 1848, 27; Broadside1 (Ms1-1846, 6 Apr); JW, WLF 22; 1BIO 100.7
V30. **1846** after Mar 14	Unknown	Personhood of God Vision. Desolating effects of Enoch Jacobs' spiritual view of God; Jesus is a person, and Jesus said the Father "had a form like himself." (S)(G)	ExV 64; 2SG 74; LS80 230; LSMS 156
V31. spring, SAT night	Dorchester, MA, Otis Nichols'	Dorchester Vision. Instructed to go to Randolph. *Sargent and Robbins deceptively went to Randolph rather than Boston, as they had agreed to do when they visited Otis Nichols.* (S)	ONichols 1859 account; 2SG 76; ST 6 Jun 1878; RH 12 Sep 1899, 582; RP 116, 117; LS80 231
V32. spring, SUN	Randolph, MA, Z. Thayer's, praying	Randolph Vision. Shown the errors of Sargent and Robbins. *Ellen held up a large quarto Bible in the longest recorded vision—almost four hours.* (S)	ONichols 1859 account; 2SG 76-79; RH 12 Sep 1899, 582; RP 117, 118; GV 25
V33. spring	New Bedford, MA, carriage	Reproving of Faults Vision. *Correction of faults among the bands in the Boston area. Convinced Heman Gurney of the divine inspiration of the visions. Bates saw her in vision.* (S)	HGurney to CGurney, 12 Apr 1896 (EXH-7:33); GCDB 18 Mar 1891, 145
V34. summer	Fairhaven, MA, Sailing to West Island in storm	Protection in Storm Vision. During storm in the ocean, assured those in the sailboat would not die. *With her were Heman Gurney, Melora Ashley, and Sarah Harmon. Refuted prevailing accusation that her visions came only under mesmerism.* (P)	ExV 8; RH 15 Aug 1893, 516; HGurney to CGurney, 12 Apr 1896
V35.	Boston, MA	Agony of Spirit Vision. Shown wrongs of Boston company who separated from others as they waited for Christ's return without working. *Speaking of the wrongs of that company, she clinched her fingers in her hair, pulling it out.* (S)	HGurney to CGurney, 12 Apr 1896
V36.	Paris	Door of Mercy Not Closed Vision. A response to a lady who said that churches were all rejected with the "shut door."[174] (G)	MSC, 27 Jan 1891 (EXH-7:34)

V37.	Unknown	Visit Western New York Vision. In the future she would go to New York. (P)	2SG 93; (1T 85); LS 108
V38. Aug	Portland	Portland Vision. *Ellen had written James about a vision in Nichols' presence.* (P)	JW to PCollins, 26 Aug 1846 (EXH-7:35)
V39. fall	New Bedford	Sabbath Warning Vision. Responding to it, many would embrace the Sabbath. (G)	LS80 236; 1T 77
V40. fall	Unknown	Rebaptism Vision. *Immediately after raised, "she was in vision."*	LI 273; 1BIO 121; Robinson 41
V41.	Maine	High and Holy Path Vision. If Israel Dammon and Nicholas Gilman Reed faithfully traveled on to the end of the narrow path, they would receive the crown of immortality. (S)	Ms7-1876; Lt2c-1874, 24 Aug
V42. Nov	Topsham, Robert G. Curtis's, praying for her	Opening Heavens Vision. First vision of planets, the handiwork of God; shown that they would have trial of their faith on their return to Gorham. *Joseph Bates was convicted of the value of the visions.*[175] (G)(P)	WLF 22; 2SG 83; 1T 79; RH 30 Nov 1886, 745; RP 125, 126; GCDB 18 Mar 1891, 145; GSAM 258; MSC, Jan 27, 1891, in GSAM 260
V43. Nov	Topsham	Affliction and Trial in Gorham Vision. *It was awaiting her upon her return to Gorham.* (P)	2SG 83; LS 98
V44. fall	Travelling to Poland	Wild Colt Tamed Vision. *A wild colt stays calm as Ellen, in vision, walked behind it, described the beauties of the new earth, and got back up. Bates and Dammon traveled with the Whites.* (G)	RP 129; RH 5 Sep 1899, 566; PGGC 55, 56; RH 5 Jul 1923, 5; WCW to MW, 23 Jul 1937
V45. **1847** Mar 6 SAB	Fairhaven	*Fairhaven Halo Vision. Similar to the Sabbath Halo Vision (see below). *Joseph Bates wrote down the vision, but the transcription is lost, though Ellen White described it in 2SG.* (G)	Broadside3, 1847; WLF 21; 2SG 82; 1T 76; CET 85-87
V46. Apr 3 SAB	Topsham, Stockbridge Howland's, praying	*Sabbath Halo Vision. View of the heavenly sanctuary and the papal attempt to change the Sabbath; halo of glory on the fourth commandment; time of trouble and the Second Advent; God has children who have not seen the Sabbath (RP 147); starting the Sabbath at sunrise is wrong. (G)	Lt1-1847, 7 Aug; Broadside3, 1847; JW to E Hastings, 21 May 1847 (EXH-7:39); WLF 18-20; RH 21 Jul 1851; ExV 15-18; MT v1n5:1; 1SG 209; JW, RH 25 Feb 1868, 168; 23 June 1868, 9; RP 133; LS 100; GV 39; 1EGWLM 112
V47.	Unknown	*Millennium Vision. Two literal resurrections, 1,000 years apart; then the wicked are raised, Satan destroyed, the earth new. (G)	Lt2-1847, 21 Apr; WLF 11
V48. Aug	Gorham, ME	Go West Vision. To go west before the Lord comes; her work for the little flock was not complete. *The vision encouraged James that her sickness wasn't to death.* (P)	JW to E Hastings, 22 Aug 1847 (EXH-7:37)
V49. **1848**	Topsham, S. Howland's	Trying for Our Good Vision. God was trying James and Ellen for their good through trials, preparing them to labor for others. (P)	2SG 89; 1T 83; LS 106; LS80 242
V50. Jul 2 SUN	Berlin, CT, Richard Ralph's(?)	Go Further West Vision. Before returning to Maine, they were to go further west, and Bates was to go with them. (P)	JW to SHowland, 2 Jul 1848 (EXH-7:49); JB to L&EH, 7 Aug 1848 (EXH-7:51)
V51. Aug 18 FRI evening V52.	Volney, NY, David Arnold's carriage house, while others prayed	Error Versus Truth Vision. Her accompanying angel presented errors of attendees in contrast to the truth. *"Ellen had* ***two visions*** *at the meeting." She held up an ordinary-sized family Bible (probably a quarto), pointing without; looking to verses refuting the error of David Arnold that the thousand years had passed, that the 144,000 were raised when Christ arose, and that communion was only to be celebrated at Passover.* (S)	JW to Howlands, 26 Aug 1848 (EXH-7:53); RH 31 Dec 1857, 61; 2SG 98; LI 274, 275; 1T 86; RH 3 Mar 1885, 138; GCDB 27 Jan 1893, 3; RP 138; GSAM 268; LS 111
V53. Aug 26 SAB morning	Hannibal, NY, Isaac Cook Snow's house	Large Bible in Hand Vision. *Ellen arose in vision, took up a large Bible, talked from it, and gave it to a man undecided regarding the Sabbath. The vision lasted 1½ hours, during which time she did not breathe (first written mention of her not breathing).* (S)	JW to Leonard and Elvira Hastings, 26 Aug 1848 (EXH-7:53); LS 112
V54. Aug 28 MON	Port Gibson, NY, Hiram Edson's barn	Brethren to Lay Aside Differences Vision. "The Lord wrought for us in power before the close of that meeting." Again shown importance of laying aside differences. (S)	2SG 99; 1T 86; LS 112-113
V55. fall	Unknown	Filthy Weed Vision. Dangers of the "filthy weed" (tobacco), tea, and coffee; "God has shown several times by visions that He disapproves it in every way." (G)	Bates, SLG 67; Lt5-1851, 14 Dec; JW, RH 8 Nov 1870, 165
V56. Nov 18 SAB	Dorchester, Otis Nichols'	J. B. Cook Vision. *A response to John Ball Cook's repudiation of the Sabbath. Joseph Bates transcribed the words Ellen White spoke in vision.* (S)	Ms1-1848, 18/19 Nov; Bates, SLG 32; RH 31 Oct 1899, 698; HEVI 41

V57. Nov 19 SUN	Dorchester, Otis Nichols'	*Like the Rising of the Sun Vision.* Sabbath light increasing like the rising sun; publishing would take the message like "streams of light that went clear round the world"; angels are holding the four winds because the saints are not all sealed; therefore, a sealing work is required before Christ's return. *Joseph Bates transcribed the words Ellen White spoke in vision.* (G)(P)	JW to Howlands, 19 Nov 1848 (EXH-7:55); Ms1-1848, 18/19 Nov; Bates, SLG 24-26 (EXH-7:56); RH 31 Oct 1899, 698; LS 125
V58. Dec 16 SAB	Rocky Hill, CT, Albert Belden's (?)	*Shaking of the Powers of Heaven Vision.* Shaking of Matt. 24:29; Mark 13:25; Luke 21:26 not of European powers but of the sun, moon, and the stars in heaven; Holy City to descend through the open space in Orion. (G)	Lt2-1848, 18 Dec; JW to L&EH, 25 Jan 1849 (EXH-7:57); Ms4-1849, 31 Jan; PrT Aug 1849; ExV 23-24
V59. **1849** Jan 5 FRI	Rocky Hill, Albert Belden's, engaged in prayer	**Sealing Vision.* Jesus is interceding in the Most Holy Place; four angels are holding the four winds of strife; Michael had not stood up nor had the time of trouble such as never was commenced; the 144,000 triumph; angels sent to encourage the saints present a golden card after mission; attending angel said an explanation would later be given. (G)	Ms2-1849, 17 Jan; Ms4-1849, 31 Jan; Ms7-1849, 11 Mar; PrT Aug 1849; JCBowles, PrT Dec 1849, 40; ExV 19; MT v1n5:1; LS 116-118; CET 100
V60. Jan 6 SAB	Rocky Hill, Albert Belden's, praying for sick	*Final Events Vision.* Jesus calls on the four angels to hold the winds of strife until God's servants are sealed; rejecting visions means rejecting God's means of correcting those who have erred from Bible truth; attending angel gave the explanation. (G)	Ms2-1849, 17 Jan; PrT Aug 1849; ExV 20-21; GSAM 229; LS 118-119
V61. Jan 18 THU	Topsham	*Duty in View of the Time of Trouble Vision.* It is contrary to the Bible to make temporal provision for the time of trouble. *Shown repeatedly over two years.* (G)	JW to L&EH, 25 Jan 1849 (EXH-7:57); Ms3-1849, 18 Jan; Ms4-1849, 31 Jan; ExV 44-46
V62. Jan, one week later	Topsham	*Houses and Lands No Use in Time of Trouble Vision.* Should dispose of property as the need should arise; food and water will be sure. (G)	Ms3-1849, 18 Jan
V63. Jan	*Unknown*	*God's Love for His People Vision.* Angels' ministry on behalf of God's people; mentions a golden card. (G)	Ms4-1849, 18 Jan; PrT Aug 1849; ExV 21-22
V64. Jan	*Unknown*	*Other Worlds Vision.* Two trees like in Eden; a world with seven moons and inhabitants of all sizes; Enoch visiting; if faithful, she with the 144,000 would visit all the worlds. (G)	Ms4-1849, 31 Jan; PrT Aug 1849; ExV 22
V65. before Feb 8	Topsham, Stockbridge Howland's, at family prayer	*Go to Dartmouth Vision. After Ellen received a vision to go to Dartmouth, James received a letter from Philip Collins, urging them to come and pray for his son who had whooping cough.* (P)	2SG 108; LS 121; CET 121
V66. Feb	Fairhaven, James M. Hall's	*West Island Vision. Content unknown, mentioned in James' letter.* (?)	JW to L&EH, 25 Feb 1849 (EXH-7:61)
V67. Mar 3 SAB	Fairhaven, J. Bates (?)	*Tearing Down and Building Up Vision.* Confession of wrongs to prepare for the seal of the living God; activity of Spiritualism. (G)	Lt2-1849, c. 6 Mar
V68. Mar 11 SUN	New Ipswich, NH, L. Hastings',[176] praying for Elvira	*Power Over Elvira Hastings' Afflictions Vision.* Saw that an angel from God had hovered over Elvira and strengthened her or life would have departed from her. (S)	Ms7-1849, 11 Mar; 2SG 112 (testimony of L. Hastings)
V69. Mar 24 SAB	Topsham, Stockbridge Howland's	**Open and Shut Door Vision.* Jesus' ministry in the holiest; the commandments and the shut door cannot be separated; Satan seeking to deceive through mesmerism, false revivals, and the "mysterious knocking" of spiritualism; visit Lewis Stowell; those who are not called of God do not have a travail of soul for sinners. (G)(S)	Ms1-1849, 24 Mar; Lt5-1849, 21 Apr; PrT Aug 1849; ExV 24-27; RP 144; LS 123; GCDB 29 Jan 1893, 35; GSAM 229; GV 50 (calls it the "Rappings Vision")
V70. Mar 31 SAB	Paris	*Second Paris Vision.* Comfort of believers in Paris, ME. (*The first Paris Vision was* V24.) (G)	Lt5-1849, 21 Apr; ExV 25; LS 123, m
V71. Mar 31 SAB	Paris	*Third Paris Vision. Established Lewis Stowell in the shut door and present truth.* (S)	Lt5-1849, 21 Apr; LS 123, m
V72. May 27 SUN	Berlin, CT, Richard Ralph's, praying	*James to Strengthen Souls in Paris Vision.* James was to attend a meeting in Paris, Maine, not New York, to strengthen souls. *Richard and Abby Ralph laid prostrate.*[177] (S)(P)	Lt8-1849, 29 May/1 Jun
V73. May 31 THU	Portland, CT, George Penfield's[178]	*Earthly Physicians Vision.* God's willingness to heal; beauty, glory, and majesty of Jesus; seemed she "could plunge in the glory." *She shouted while in vision, and the doctor would not enter; Polly Penfield was healed.* (G)	Lt8-1849, 29 May/1 Jun

V74. Jun 30 SAB	Rocky Hill, Albert Belden's, as prayer was offered for her	*Angels with Rods Vision.* A large company of angels with rods as part of the time of trouble; four angels ready to go, probation almost finished; idols to be let go; urgent call for unity, sacrifice, and proclamation; the Lord had strengthened James to "write, write, write" and "speed the messengers." (G)(P)	Ms6-1849, 30 Jun; the "company of angels" was five angels, JW, AR Aug 1850, 16; 2SG 115; LS80 259; 1T 88; LS 125; RH 18 Sep 1924, 13
V75. Aug	Unknown	*Trial of Our Faith Vision.* Bitter cup to purify and cleanse. (G)	PrT Sep 1849; ExV 27-29
V76. Sep 15 SAB	North Paris, ME	*Speed the Swift Messengers Vision.* At each conference, she heard in vision: "The cry from the holy City is 'Speed the messengers.'" (S)	PrT Sep 1849; JB to L&EH, 25 Sep 1849 (EXH-7:70); JW to LH, 18 Mar 1850
V77. Sep 23 SUN	Topsham, Stockbridge Howland's	******Bible Applied Vision.* Holy life in view of impending crisis; seal of the living God, angels waiting, writing in scrolls, Christ's heavenly ministry; value of the Apocrypha; visited planet with beings of all sizes; meeting every Sabbath, which the pope changed on earth. *Opened Bibles of different sizes, placing them on three people.* (G)	Ms5-1849, Sep 23; JB to L&EH, 25 Sep 1849 (EXH-7:70); AR Aug 1850, 16; EGW Record Book 2, 18; MSC to EGW, 9 Oct 1908 (EXH-7:130)
V78. Oct	Topsham,	*Truth and Spirit Vision.* Melting, uniting power of truth and the Holy Spirit were but a drop; those not denying Jesus' new name as "King" would rise to never fall again. (G)	JW to Br Bowles, 17 Oct 1849 (EXH-7:71) and 8 Nov 1849 (EXH-7:72)
V79.	Unknown	*Refreshing before Michael Stands Vision.* Those keeping God's Word are rising to never fall again and are to have a refreshing before Michael stands. (G)	JW to Br Bowles, 8 Nov 1849 (EXH-7:72)
V80. Nov 3 SAB	Oswego, NY	*Dividing Spirit Vision.* Both parties wrong; David Arnold and James White to write on the gift of prophecy and Christ's heavenly ministry; rich not to support the able poor. (S)	JW to S Howland, 13 Nov 1849 (EXH-7:73); JW to L&EH, 3 Jan 1850 (EXH-7:74); 2SG 120
V81. Nov 18 SUN	Centerport, NY, Wm. Harris's,[179] praying	*Brother Rhodes in Thick Darkness Vision.* Bros. Hiram Edson and Richard Ralph to go after Bro. Samuel W. Rhodes, who was in thick darkness. *The vision was contrary to her former opinion.* (S)	Hiram Edson, PrT Dec 1849
V82. **1850** Jan 9 WED	Scriba, Oswego County, NY, Bezalell C. Storrs'	*Speed the Message Vision.* The *Present Truth* needed; James to write, write, write, write; the paper able to go "where God's servants cannot go." (G)(P)	JW to L Hastings, 10 Jan 1850 (EXH-7:75); Lt18-1850, 11 Jan; PrT Mar 1850
V83. Jan 10 THU	Oswego	*Work for the Honestly Deceived Vision.* The honestly deceived would see they had been deceived by some they trusted regarding a specific time for Christ's return. (P)	Lt18-1850, 11 Jan; 2SG 122
V84. winter	Oswego	*Dishonesty of the Revivalist Vision.* Message about "Bro. M," who was identified as being dishonest with public funds based on Hosea 5:6, 7; gave Hiram Patch and his wife Sarah confidence to accept the Adventist message.[180] (S)	RH 24 Feb 1885; Ms5-1885, 7 Mar; RP 154; GCDB 29 Jan 1893, 35 (has Hiram and Sarah's conversion in 1848); RP 152; GSAM 230 (cf. 2SG 123-124)
V85. Jan 12 SAB night	Oswego	*Message for a Returning Brother Vision.* "I think he will take the truth." James commented: "Her vision was interesting, but not much new." Ellen saw again that she needed to write the truth and "speed the third angel's message." (S)	JW to L Hastings, 11 Jan 1850 (EXH-7:75)
V86. Jan	Oswego	*Date for Second Coming Would Pass Vision.* The time for Christ's return, as predicted by the "Watchman" (published by John C. Bywater and Jonas Wendell), of Oswego, NY, who had removed the landmarks, would pass by. (S)	PrT Mar 1850; 2SG 122
V87. Jan 26 SAB	Oswego	*Perishing Souls Vision.* Destruction coming for God's "stupid and dormant" people; souls dying for want of the present truth; some unwilling to give up worldly goods; Redeemer who left glory calls for self-sacrifice; mighty shaking has commenced; Adam and Eve ate of the forbidden tree; God's judgments coming; saints reign 1,000 years in Holy City; immortality conditional; Apocrypha's value. (G)	Ms4-1850, 28 Jan; PrT Apr 1850; ExV 29-32; ExV54 10.3; CET 106
V88. Mar 16 SAB	Oswego	*Comfort for Hastings Vision.* With the death of his wife Elvira (Feb. 28, 1850), assurance that she was sealed. (S)	Lt10-1850, 18 Mar; JW to L Hastings, 18 Mar 1850 (EXH-7:80); AR Aug 1850, 14
V89. before May 15	Oswego	*Hypocritical Woman Vision.* Warnings about a hypocritical, adulteress woman—Emma Loretta (Pauling) Payne, née Prior—in Camden.[181] (S)	2SG 124; RH 24 Mar 1885; GCB 31 Jan 1893; GSAM 233, 322, 545
V90. May	Camden, NY, during earnest prayer	*Hypocritical Woman Follow-up Vision.* Frown of Jesus on Emma Payne, who feigned travail of soul for sinners while hiding wrong in her own heart, and on her husband, William Henry Payne. (S)	PrT May 1850, 80; 2SG 125; RP 157, 158; GSAM 233; LS 129; CET 132

V91. Jun 27 THU	Possibly New Ipswich, NH (PT Aug 1850, 14)	*Mark of the Beast Vision.* Rather than learning truth over years, as the earliest Adventists had done, newcomers would do so "in a few months," suffering for Christ's sake; seven last plagues are soon to be poured out; the pope is responsible for changing the day of rest; plagues to fall on Sabbath violators; glories of heaven. (G)	ExV 52-55; RH 26 Jun 1866, 25; EW 64-67
V92. before Jul 21	East Hamilton, NY, as the brethren prayed	*Publish The Advent Review Vision.* Opposition to the Sabbath coming from many Adventist papers. Publish the testimonies of John Ball Cook, William Miller, Freeman G. Brown, Oel Ray Fassett, Isaiah H. Shipman, John J. Porter, Apollos Hale. (P)	JW to LHastings, 21 Jul 1850 (EXH-7:82); Lt8-1850, 4 Aug; Lt12-1850, 15 Aug; Lt14-1850, 1 Sep
V93. Jul 22 MON	East Hamilton	*Vanquish Evil by Giving Praise to God Vision.* She saw that they were "dying, dying" and must "go free, go free" by singing and praising God to drive out the enemy. *Lydia Rhodes (Rhoda Abbey's mother) claimed revelations from God and spoke against shouting in worship and praising God through singing.* (S)	Lt8-1850, 4 Aug; Ms5a-1850, Jul; Sarah Belden to P. D. Lawrence, 29 Jul 1850 (EXH-7:83)
V94. Jul 29 MON	Oswego, Henry Lillis, Jr.'s,[182] praying	*Enchanted Ground Vision.* Some among God's people at the Oswego conference not right and languishing with lack of power because of doubt; must hold on in faith and look to Jesus; singing can drive back darkness; Satan's power rising through Spiritualism; rebaptism for those who formerly broke the commandments; four angels to let go; Brother Gorsline had wounded God's people; Brother R. R. Chapin rescued.[183] (S)	Ms5-1850, 29 Jul; Ms5a-1850, Jul; Lt8-1850, 4 Aug; ExV 60; MT v1n1; MT v1n3[184]
V95. Aug 24 SAB	Centerport, William Harris's, family prayer	*Mysterious Rapping Vision.* Spiritualism and church order; the paper "would help build up God's people in the most holy faith"; Satan's efforts to hinder the paper by afflicting Hiram Edson White with sickness; sending for Brother Samuel W. Rhodes saved Edson. (G)(P)	Ms7-1850, 24 Aug; Ms7a-1850, 24 Aug; SpM 3, 4; ExV 47-48; RH 7 Nov 1899, 715; CET 168
V96. Sep 7 SAB	Oswego	*Great Work for God's People Vision.* Eyes of formerly deceived opened; Sabbath opposers unable to biblically defend their position; Adventists must do so. (G)	ExV 57
V97. Sep 26-29 THU-SUN	Sutton, VT, conference	**Sutton Vision.* Sell property to spread the truth; weaknesses in Joseph Bates' teaching and practice on final events; loveliness of Jesus; mutual love of angels; mistake to pray for healing before unbelievers; seven last plagues poured out after Jesus leaves the heavenly sanctuary; voice of God delivers saints; judgment begins after the saints are caught up, during the 1000 years; the rebellious are destroyed; who the shepherds should consult. (G)(S)	Ms14-1850, Sep; AR Nov 1850; ExV 33-35; 49-51; MT v1n5:3
V98. Oct 23 WED	Dorchester, Otis Nichols'	**Gathering Time Vision.* Greater efforts in the "gathering time" to recover the remnant; need of paper and prophetic chart "truth ... made plain upon tables; God covered a mistake in the 1843 chart then uncovered it; "sacrifice" after "daily" (Dan. 8:11; 12:11) "added by man's wisdom"; time will never again a test; false visions of Clorinda S. Minor in saints going to Old Jerusalem; nominal Adventists to betray faithful Adventists to the Catholics for disregarding Sunday; Jesus' heavenly ministry almost done.[185] (G)(S)	Ms15-1850, 23 Oct; Lt26-1850, 1 Nov; Lt28-1850, 27 Nov; AR Nov 1850; SpM 1, 2; ExV 61-62; MT v1n4:2 (see https://ellenwhite.org/correspondence/259297); GSAM 505
V99. Nov 23 SAB	Paris, while Orrin Hewitt prayed	*Message for Brother Hewitt Vision.* Errors in Orrin Hewitt's prophetic interpretation. *Had little effect until God's presence and a vision impressed him to change his view.*[186] (S)	Lt28-1850, 27 Nov; Ms131a-1906
V100. Dec 24 TUE	Paris, while praying	*Holiness in Worship Vision.* Caution vs. "unhealthy and unnecessary excitement" in worship; order of heaven; papers to bring truth to many; hope for Gurney and Sally Chase.[187] (G)(S)(P)	Ms10-1850, 24 Dec; Ms11-1850, 25 Dec
V101. **1851** Jan 19 SUN	Waterbury, VT, at family prayer	*Cruel Oppressive Work Vision.* Underhanded treatment of the Whites through Nelson A. Hollis. (S)	2SG 146; RH Feb 1851, 45; LS80 280
V102. Jan	Paris, at family prayer	*James Not to Give Up the Paper Vision.* Encouragement to James as support for the paper was lacking. (P)	2SG 148; LS80 281; LS80 281; 1T 89; LS 140
V103. Mar 23 SUN	Paris, at family prayer	*Accusations of Brother Hollis Vision.* Satan working in the accusations of Brother Nelson A. Hollis; Brother Samuel W. Rhodes to intervene in Vermont. (S)	JW to Reuben and Belinda Loveland, 1 Apr 1851 (EXH-7:95); Lt6-1851, 1 Apr

V104. Apr 27 SUN	Paris	*Jesus' Mediation Almost Finished Vision.* Get ready for the refreshing; gain strength through humility and prayer. *Notes taken by an unidentified observer.* (G)	*unauthenticated* Ms3-1851, 27 Apr (1EGWLM 915), similar to Ms2-1852, 14 Mar
V105. May 14 WED	Paris	**Holiness of God Vision.* Beauty of Jesus; the blind leading the blind—opposers of the Sabbath self-contradictory; counsel for J. N. Andrews, Jesse Stevens, Samuel Rhodes. (G)(S)	Ms5-1851, 18 May; Lt10-1851, 18/19 May; Ms9-1851, Jun ?; ExV 55-56, 58
V106. Jun 21 SAB	Camden, C. Preston's[188]	*Time Never Again a Test Vision (Camden Vision).* The third angel's message doesn't need time to strengthen it. (G)	Ms1-1851, Jun 21; RH 21 Jul 1851; ExV 48; RH 22 Mar 1892
V107. Jun 23 MON	Camden, Abbeys', praying	*Disfellowshipping with Insufficient Cause Vision.* Through the influence of dreams and impressions, they had rejected Elmira Preston without due cause.[189] (S)	Ms2-1851, 23 Jun; Ms2a-1851, 23 Jun; 2SG 150, 151
V108. Jun 29 SUN	West Milton, NY, Horace Cushman's	*Not to Return to Paris Vision.* James to "lay his hand to the work" and, if circumstances open, they should remain; those in Paris were prideful and self-absorbed, not heeding the visions God gave them. She saw the "exceeding loveliness and glory of Jesus." (P)	Lt4-1851, 21 Jul; Lt3-1851, 11 Aug; (*unauthenticated* "Camden Vision," 29 Jun, https://ellenwhite.org/correspondence/259300)
V109. Aug 9 SAB	Saratoga Springs, NY	*Exceeding Loveliness of Jesus Vision.* Glories of heaven; angels singing and playing harps; importance of the Sabbath. (G)	Lt3-1851, 11 Aug
V110. Oct	Saratoga Springs	*Deceiving Woman in Vergennes, Vermont, Vision.* She is identified as "Mrs. C."[190] (S)	2SG 157
V111. Oct 25 SAB	W. Medford, MA, Paul Folsom's[191]	*Frown of God Vision.* God disapproved of the Adventists because they did not confront the errors of Henry Allen and Stephen Smith; must withdraw fellowship from them.[192] (S)	JW to Brethren in Christ, 11 Nov 1851 (EXH-7:105)
V112. Nov 1 SAB	Washington, NH, John Stowell's,[193] while in prayer	*Church Order Vision.* Church must bring order by disfellowshipping Stephen Smith and Henry Allen, for their own good. (G)	JB to Dartmouth church, 7 Nov 1851 (EXH-7:104); JW, 11 Nov 1851; Lt8-1851, 12 Nov; R Griffin, RH 23 Dec 1851, 67
V113. Nov 1 SAB	Washington, NH, John Stowell's	*Smith-Allen Vision.* The errors of Stephen Smith and Henry Allen were revealed. *The vision impressed Ezra P. Butler (though he remembered it being at Stowe, VT; see RH 7 Apr 1853, 151). The church voted to break fellowship with Smith and Allen.* (S)	JB to Dartmouth, 7 Nov 1851 (EXH-7:104); JW, 11 Nov 1851 (EXH-7:105); W. Morse, RH 23 Oct 1888, 658 (EXH-7:107); R Griffin, RH 23 Dec 1851, 67
V114. Nov 6 THU	Royalton, VT, W. Morse's, praying	*Hart-Wright-Baker-Butler Vision.* Errors of Josiah Rice Hart and John S. Wright about the "age to come" teaching; encouragement for Joseph Baker and Ezra P. Butler. (S)	JW, 11 Nov 1851 (EXH-7:105); Lt8-1851, 12 Nov; W. Morse, RH 23 Oct 1888, 658
V115. Nov 10 MON	Johnson, VT, Reuben Loveland's	*Feed the Sheep Not the Dogs Vision.* Brothers Baker and Ingraham should not get discouraged, for they were to feed God's sheep and not the dogs. (S)	JW, 11 Nov 1851; Lt8-1851, 12 Nov; W. Morse, RH 23 Oct 1888, 658
V116. Nov 15 SAB	New Haven, VT, Elon Everts', praying	*Age to Come Vision.* Brother Elon Everts to give up "age to come"; believers to put out errors of Henry Allen, one of which was spiritual union. (S)	Lt8-1851, 12 Nov
V117. Nov 16 SUN	Vergennes, VT, Henry Allen's, praying	*Woman in Vergennes Vision.* Again shown the deceiving woman, "Mrs. C." who was traveling with Henry Allen when she had a husband. (S)	2SG 158; RH 25 Nov 1851, 52
V118. Dec	Paris, Cyprian Stevens'	*Go, Go, Go Vision.* The angel instructed Ellen that Marion Stowell was to accompany them back from Maine to New York; gave details about the trip, including a "meeting in a private family" where James would speak. *Fulfilled in every detail.* (P)	MSC to EGW, 9 Oct 1908 (EXH-7:130)
V119. **1852** Feb	Oswego, NY	*Repeat Go, Go, Go Vision.* The angel said, "Go, go, go." (S)	MSC to EGW, 9 Oct 1908 (EXH-7:130)
V120. Mar 14 WED	Ballston Spa, NY Jesse Thompson's	*The Nations Vision.* Slackening of European conflict would catch people off guard; impending crisis to come when four angels let go; every sin of Israel must be confessed. *Words spoken in vision.* (G)	Ms2-1852, 14 Mar (1EGWLM 325, m); Ms1-1852, 18 Mar; SpM 2, 3; GCDB 26 Mar 1893, 518
V121. late May	Rochester, NY	*Brothers Bowles and Case Need Humility Vision.* In the Jackson church, John C. Bowles found fault over small things.[194] Hiram S. Case had moved injudiciously. (S)	Lt2-1852, 2 Jun; Lt5-1853, 5 Jul
V122. Aug 26 THU	Potsdam, NY, John Byington's[195]	*Sabbath Vision.* The value of the Sabbath and a great work for John N. Andrews to do (author of the book *History of the Sabbath and First Day of the Week*). (S)	RH 19 Aug 1852; RH 18 May 1944; HEVI 123

V123. Sep 3 FRI	Wolcott, VT, public	Wolcott Vision. *Samuel Benson "believed the vision he witnessed to be the power of God, and was affected by it. He fully embraced the truth."*[196] (S)	RH 19 Aug 1852; 2SG 168; ST 19 Sep 1878, 275; LS80 294
V124. Sep 10 FRI	Washington, NH	Getting Lord's Coming Too Far Off Vision. Believers in Washington, NH, putting the Second Coming too far off. (S)	Ms4-1852, Sep; RH 14 Oct 1852, 96; 1EGWLM 332, m
V125. Sep 30 THU	Dorchester, Otis Nichols'	Gospel Order Vision. Church organization based on Scripture; message for messengers in Boston who brought deficiencies to the cause: Ezra L. H. Chamberlain, Richard Ralph, David Chase, Joseph Baker, William S. Ingraham, Eri Barr, Howard Lothrop. (G)(S)	JW, 30 Sep 1852 (EXH-7:113); Lt4-1852, 25 Oct; ExV54 15-20; MT v1n3:2, 4
V126. Oct 1 FRI	Panton, VT, while in meeting	Panton Vision. Comforting message for Sister Almira Pierce, who was struggling with despair.[197] (S)	RH 14 Oct 1852; RH 16 Sep 1852; 2SG 169, 170; LS80 293, 4
V127. Oct 9 SAB	Rochester, NY, 124 Mt. Hope Ave., praying for Lewis Oswald Stowell	Thou Art the Man Vision. Encouragement for Loughborough to preach the Sabbath; how Elizabeth Riggs could escape the torment of the devil; secret sin of Christopher D. Riggs, away at the time. *An 80-minute vision. Ellen White did not breathe.*[198] (S)	JW, RH 14 Oct 1852; JNL, RH 25 Dec 1866; RH 4 Mar 1884; RP 171; GSAM 318-320; PUR, 12 Aug 1915
V128. Nov SAB	Rochester, NY, praying	Preach the Message and God Will Open the Way Vision. "Brother Loughborough [was] holding back from his duty to preach the message, trying to get means for his support."[199] (S)	RP 178; DPF 26; MML 22.2
V129. Dec 18 SAB	Rochester, NY, praying	Burdens God Did Not Require Vision. Two-part message: should not increase their family to gratify the wishes of any; Loughborough's decision to preach the truth was correct. (P)	2SG 173; Loughborough, RH 25 Mar 1884, 202; MML 23
V130. **1853** Mar 1 TUE	Rochester, NY	Character of the Ministers Vision. Purity in conversation and actions; warning against tobacco and an appeal for cleanliness. (G)	Ms2-1853, 1 Mar; ExV54 21; FCC, RH 30 Mar 1897
V131. May 7 or 8 SAB or SUN	Milan, OH	Sister Loughborough to Travel West Vision. *Only John Baptiste Bezzo reported this vision. Mary Loughborough (portrait, p. 264) relented, after much crying, and went west with the Whites to Jackson.* (S)	MT v1n3; RH 28 Apr 1853, 200.30
V132. May 29 SUN	Tyrone, Livingston County, MI, in William Dawson's barn	Pretensions of Holiness Vision. Described situations in Michigan; one was Mrs. Olcott's pretensions of holiness in Vergennes, Kent County, Michigan. *Traveling across the state to Vergennes, Ellen White confronted Olcott, who responded, "The Lord knows my heart." As Dr. Francis Pinkney Drummond examined her in vision, Ellen White did not breathe.*[200] (S)	JW, RH 7 Jul 1853, 28; JNL, RH 15 Jan 1867, 62; RH 6 May 1884, 299; RP 95; MGK, GCDB 31 Jan 1893, 59, 80; GCCP 61; GSAM 206, 322; RH 27 Jun 1935; MML 28-30
V133. Jun 3 FRI	Jackson, MI, Daniel R. Palmer's, at family prayer[201]	Jackson Vision. The excitability of Samuel Rhodes; not to dispose of property for traveling preachers with no message from God but to do so for the suffering cause; Hiram S. Case injured by support that should have gone to others; Abigail Palmer reproved for her wrong spirit and speaking harshly to her neighbor. *Case and Russell gloated over the rebuke. Ellen White did not breathe in vision. Also, Case tested her by putting his finger in her eye, and she did not flinch.* (S)	Ms1-1853, 2 Jun; Lt3-1853, 29 Jun; ExV54 11, 21; RH 4 Jul 1854, 173; 2SG 181; LS80 302; RH 25 Mar 1884; George States, RH 2 Aug 1906, 10; GSAM 558
V134. Jun 3 FRI	Jackson, MI, Cyrenius Smith's, while praying[202]	Case and Russell Vision. Revealed the character of Case and Russell, with reproof for their unmerciful course toward Sister Abigail Palmer. (S)	RH 7 Aug 1856, 110; RH 4 Jul 1854, 378; RH 22 Jul 1884, 472; 2SG 181
V135. Jun 11 SAB	Vergennes, MI, while praying after she fainted	Woman's Tongues Gibberish Vision. Revealed that the tongues of Mrs. Olcott was merely gibberish. *The vision lasted about thirty minutes.* (S)	RH 10 Jun 1884, 378; MML 31
V136. Jul 2 SAB	Rochester, NY	Commandment Keepers Vision. To increase paper from bi-weekly to weekly; lack of power in Jackson, especially due to Charles P. Russell; proper government of children; efforts to save them by correcting faults and encouraging their well-doing; looking on the dark side too much, James had become discouraged, but God was dealing in mercy and compassion.[203] (P)(S)	Ms3-1853, 2 Jul; Ms4-1853, 2 Jul; Ms5-1853, Jul; Lt4-1853, 30 Jun; Lt5-1853, 5 Jul; Lt6-1853, 3 Aug; ExV54 14, 22, 34, 35, 38, 45
V137. Aug	Unknown	False Shepherds Vision. Leading away from the Sabbath. (G)	RH 11 Aug 1853; ExV54 43-46
V138. Sep 12 MON	Stowe, VT	To Those of Little Experience Vision. Humility of new believers; must "Get ready! for the fierce anger of the Lord is soon to come." Some too fast and some too slow—Lothrop, John R.	Lt11-1853, 3 Dec; ExV54 39-42; GSAM 207

		Towle, and Ezra Stowell Eastman. *Examined by a physician, according to F. C. Castle, and Ellen White did not breathe.* (G)	
V139. Oct 28 or 29 FRI SAB	New Haven, VT, schoolhouse, "last conference"	*Testimonies in Meeting Vision.* Should not be timid about sharing testimony—even if there is repetition; nominal churches had fallen; harmony would come if following the Spirit of God; foot washing and Lord's supper to keep members humble; men not to wash women's feet; love of God in giving his only beloved Son. (G)	Lt9-1853, Dec 6; ExV54 35-37; 46-48
V140.	Unknown	*Self-Denial Vision.* Better use of means than the "filthy weed" tobacco. (G)	ExV54 42
V141.	Unknown	*Reverence for God Vision.* Use God's name with holy awe. (G)	ExV54 43
V142.	Unknown	*Love of God in Giving His Son Vision.* The earliest great controversy vision; describes the council between the Father and the Son. (G)	ExV54 46; 2SG 270; LS 162 (links it to ten years before Lovett's Grove)
V143. **1854** Feb 5 SUN	Oswego	*Early Health Vision.* Message for Oswego, Caughdenoy, and Roosevelt, NY; reproof for adultery and neglect of children; cleanliness, temperance, and rich foods; three were jerking with "spiritual magnetism" (one was Bro. Thompson); message for Bro. Ross. (S)(G)	Ms1-1854, 12 Feb; Ms3-1854, 12 Feb; 1BIO 291, 292
V144. Feb 18 SAB	Lincklaen, NY	*Courtesy and Kindness Vision.* Shortness of time; negative influence of Samuel W. Rhodes. (S)(G)	Ms6-1854, 19 Feb
V145. Apr	Rochester, NY	*Opposition to the Visions among Leadership Vision.* A testimony for David Henry Lamson, Jonathan T. Orton, John N. Andrews, and the Stevens family. (S)	Ms4-1854, Apr
V146. May 13 SAB	Sylvan, MI, Charles S. Glover's	*Sylvan Vision.* The work in the West and the importance of visiting Wisconsin; instruction, reproof, and counsel; cautions on severe church discipline. (P)(S)	Lt7-1854, May 13; RH 23 May 1854 142; Ms1-1855; RH 27 Jan 1885, 57; RP 199
V147. Jun 18 SUN	Sylvan, MI	*Child's Character Vision.* Parents responsible for discipline of their children; cautions on severe church discipline. (G)	Ms5-1854, Jun; Ms7-1854, c. Jun; cf. 1T 118-119; 4bSG 6, 7
V148. Jun 26 MON	Grand Rapids, MI, Lemon Fitch's, in prayer	*Evangelistic Tent Vision.* Counsel for Grand Rapids believers, tents in evangelism; warning against improper familiarity; weaknesses of Sealey Hungerford; an appeal for self-denial in Bedford, MI. (S)	Lt3-1854, 12 Jul; Lt7-1854, Jul; RH 24 Feb 1885, 122; RP 203; PUR 14 Apr 1910, 2
V149. Jul	Rochester, NY, The Whites'	*Triumph of the Saints Vision. Examined by two physicians, Ellen White did not breathe.* (G)	GCB1893-03, 60; RH 8 Aug 1899, 502; GSAM 207, 208; PCGC 45; CET 253; 1BIO 302
V150. Aug	Grand Rapids, MI	*Familiarity Vision. Alford Pearsall engaged in improper familiarity in giving the sisters the holy kiss.* (S)	Lt3-1854, 12 Jul; 7MR 208
V151. winter	Camden	*Georgianna Prior Vision.* A lack of judgment on the part of the Camden believers in the case of Sr. Prior in giving their influence against her obtaining medical aid. (S)	2SG 134
V152. winter	Unknown	*Encouragement for Brother Loughborough Vision. An appeal to Mary Loughborough to be fully supportive of her husband in his traveling ministry.* (S)	Lt6-1854, winter

Paul wrote that one who prophesies "speaketh unto men to edification, and exhortation, and comfort" (1 Cor. 14:3). This listing of Ellen White's visions reveals a pattern of guidance, correction, and encouragement for the early Adventists, preparing them to overcome disappointment, fanaticism, and indifference to faithfully proclaim their blessed hope in Jesus' return. They point to the Scriptures as the standard of faith and practice, *confirming* what they learned from careful Bible study regarding the heavenly ministry of Christ, the perpetuity of the law of God, the chronology of the millennium, and the personhood of God. They also warn against date setting for Christ's return and provide direction in spreading the Advent message. We also see what James White observed—that his wife frequently received a vision while praying.[204] She also described receiving visions under other circumstances.

> In the morn, we united in prayer for [Sister Penfield] again. The power came down like a mighty, rushing wind, the room was filled with the glory of God, and I was swallowed up in the glory and was taken off in vision.
>
> As I was led to speak upon the coming of CHRIST and the resurrection and the cheering hope of the Christian, my soul triumphed in GOD. I drank in rich draughts of salvation. Heaven, sweet heaven, was the magnet to draw my soul upward, and I was wrapt in a vision of GOD's glory.

We turn next to the annotated and illustrated text of Ellen White's first two books.

A SKETCH

OF THE

CHRISTIAN EXPERIENCE

AND

VIEWS

OF

ELLEN G. WHITE

SARATOGA SPRINGS, N. Y.
PUBLISHED BY JAMES WHITE.
1851.

PREFACE.

We are well aware that many honest seekers after truth and Bible holiness are prejudiced against visions. Two great causes have created this prejudice. First, fanaticism, accompanied by false visions and exercises, has existed more or less, almost everywhere. This has led many of the sincere to doubt anything of the kind. Second, the exhibition of mesmerism, etc., and what is commonly called the "mysterious rappings," are perfectly calculated to deceive, and create unbelief relative to the gifts and operations of the Spirit of God. {ExV 2.1}

But God is unchangeable. His work through Moses in the presence of Pharaoh was perfect, notwithstanding "Jannes and Jambres" were permitted to perform miracles by the power of Satan, that resembled the miracles wrought by Moses.[205] The counterfeit also appeared in the days of the apostles, yet the gifts of the Spirit were manifested in the followers of Christ. And it is not the purpose of God to leave his people in this age of almost unbounded deception, without the gifts and manifestations of his Spirit. {ExV 2.2}

The design of a counterfeit is to imitate an existing reality. Therefore the present manifestation of the spirit of error is proof that God manifests Himself to His children by the power of the Holy Spirit, and that He is about to fulfil His word gloriously. {ExV 2.3}

"And it shall come to pass in the LAST DAYS, saith God, I will pour out of My Spirit upon all flesh; and your sons and your daughters shall *prophesy*, and your young men shall see visions, and your old men shall dream dreams, etc." Acts ii, 17; Joel ii, 28. {ExV 2.4}

As for mesmerism we have ever considered it dangerous, therefore have had nothing to do with it. We never even saw a person in a mesmeric sleep, and know nothing by experience of the art.[206] {ExV 2.5}

We send out this little work with the hope that it will comfort the saints. {ExV 2.6}

James White.
Saratoga Springs, N. Y., August, 1851.

James White

EXPERIENCE AND VIEWS.

By the request of dear friends I have consented to give a brief sketch of my experience and views, with the hope that it will cheer and strengthen the humble, trusting children of the Lord. {ExV 3.1; RH, July 21, 1851}

At the age of eleven years I was converted, and when twelve years old was baptized, and joined the Methodist Church. At the age of thirteen I heard Bro. Miller deliver his second course of lectures in Portland, Me. I then felt that I was not holy, not ready to see Jesus. And when the invitation was given for church members and sinners to come forward for prayers, I embraced the first opportunity, for I knew that I must have a great work done for me to fit me for Heaven. My soul was thirsting for full and free salvation, but knew not how to obtain it. {ExV 3.2; RH, July 21, 1851}

In 1842 I constantly attended the Second Advent meetings in Portland, Me., and fully believed the Lord was coming. I was hungering and thirsting for full salvation, and an entire conformity to the will of God. Day and night I was struggling to obtain this priceless treasure, that all the riches of earth could not purchase. As I was bowed before God praying for this blessing the duty to go and pray in a public prayer-meeting was presented before me. I had never prayed vocally in meeting, and drew back from the duty, fearing that if I should attempt to pray I should be confounded. Every time I went before the Lord in secret prayer this unfulfilled duty presented itself, until I ceased to pray, and settled down in a melancholy state, and finally in deep despair. {ExV 3.3; RH, July 21, 1851}

In this state of mind I remained for three weeks, with not one ray of light to pierce the thick clouds of

4

darkness around me. I then had two dreams which gave me a faint ray of light and hope. After that I opened my mind to my devoted mother. She told me that I was not lost, and advised me to go and see Bro. Stockman, who then preached to the Advent people in Portland.[207] I had great confidence in him, for he was a devoted and beloved servant of Christ. His words affected me and led me to hope. I returned home, and again went before the Lord, and promised that I would do and suffer any thing if I could have the smiles of Jesus. The same duty was presented. There was to be a prayer meeting that evening which I attended, and when others knelt to pray I bowed with them trembling, and after two or three had prayed, I opened my mouth in prayer before I was aware of it, and the promises of God looked to me like so many precious pearls that were to be received by only asking for them. As I prayed the burden and agony of soul that I had so long felt left me, and the blessing of God came upon me like the gentle dew, and I gave glory to God for what I felt, but I longed for more. I could not be satisfied till I was filled with the fullness of God. Inexpressible love for Jesus filled my soul. Wave after wave of glory rolled over me until my body grew stiff. Everything was shut out from me but Jesus and glory, and I knew nothing of what was passing around me. {ExV 3.4; RH, July 21, 1851}

I remained in this state of body and mind a long time, and when I realized what was around me, everything seemed changed. Every thing looked glorious and new, as if smiling and praising God. I was then willing to confess Jesus everywhere. For six months not a cloud of darkness passed over my mind. My soul was daily drinking rich draughts of salvation. I thought that those who loved Jesus would love his coming, so went to the class-meeting and told them what Jesus had done for me, and what a fullness I enjoyed through believing that the Lord

5

was coming. The class-leader interrupted me saying, "Through Methodism," but I could not give the glory to Methodism, when it was Christ and the hope of his soon coming that had made me free. {ExV 4.1; RH, July 21, 1851}

Robert Harmon, Ellen White's father

My father's family were most all full believers in the Advent, and for bearing testimony to this glorious doctrine, seven of us were at one time cast out of the Methodist Church.[208] At this time the words of the Prophet were exceedingly precious to us. {ExV 5.1; RH, July 21, 1851}

"Your brethren that hated you, that cast you out for my name's sake, said, Let the Lord be glorified; but he shall appear to your joy, and they shall be ashamed." Isa. lxvi, 5. {ExV 5.2; RH, July 21, 1851}

V1. *Midnight Cry Vision, Dec. 1844*

From this time, up to December, 1844, my joys, trials and disappointments were like those of my dear Advent friends around me. At this time I visited one of our Advent sisters, and in the morning we bowed around the family altar. It was not an exciting occasion, and there were but five of us present, all females.[209] While praying the power of God came upon me as I never had felt it before, and I was wrapt up in a vision of God's glory, and seemed to be rising higher and higher from the earth, and was shown something of the travels of the Advent people to the Holy City, as will be seen in the vision hereafter.[210] {ExV 5.3; RH, July 21, 1851}

Ellen White's first vision at the home of Elizabeth Haines

After I came out of vision everything looked changed, a gloom was spread over all that I beheld. O, how dark this world looked to me.[211] I wept when I found myself here, and felt homesick. I had seen a better world, and it had spoiled this for me. I told the view to our little band in Portland, who then fully believed it to be of God.[212] It was a powerful time. The solemnity of eternity rested upon us. About one week after this the Lord gave me another view, and shewed me the trials I must pass through, and that I must go and relate to others what he had revealed to me, and that I should meet with great opposition, and suffer anguish of spirit by going.

V2. *Make Known to Others Vision, Jan. 1845*

6

But said the angel "The grace of God is sufficient for you: he will hold you up."[213] {ExV 5.4; RH, July 21, 1851}

After I came out of this vision I was exceedingly troubled. My health was very poor, and I was but seventeen years old.[214] I knew that many had fallen through

exaltation, and I knew that if I in any way became exalted that God would leave me, and I should surely be lost. I went to the Lord in prayer and begged him to lay the burden on some one else. It seemed to me that I could not bear it. I lay upon my face a long time, and all the light I could get was "Make known to others what I have revealed to you." {ExV 6.1; RH, July 21, 1851}

V3. *Ball of Fire Vision, 1845*

In my next vision I earnestly begged of the Lord, that if I must go and relate what he had shown me, to keep me from exaltation. Then he shewed me that my prayer was answered, and if I should be in danger of exaltation his hand should be laid upon me, and I should be afflicted with sickness. Said the angel, If you deliver the messages faithfully, and endure unto the end, you shall eat of the fruit of the tree of life, and drink of the water of the river of life.[215] {ExV 6.2; RH, July 21, 1851}

Soon it was reported all around that the visions were the result of mesmerism, and many Adventists were ready to believe, and circulate the report. A physician, who was a celebrated mesmerizer, told me that my views were mesmerism, and that I was a very easy subject, and that he could mesmerize me and give me a vision. I told him that the Lord had shown me in vision that mesmerism was from the Devil, from the bottomless pit, and that it would soon go there, with those who continued to use it.[216] I then gave him liberty to mesmerize me if he could. He tried for more than half an hour, resorting to different operations, and then gave it up. By faith in God I was able to resist his influence, so that it did not affect me in the least. {ExV 6.3; RH, July 21, 1851}

If I had a vision in meeting many would say that it was excitement, and that some one mesmerized me. Then I would go away alone in the woods,

7

V17. *Vision in the Woods*

where no eye could see, or ear hear but God's, and pray to him, and he would sometimes give me a vision there. I then rejoiced, and told them what God had revealed to me alone, where no mortal could influence me. But I was told by some that I mesmerized myself. O, thought I, has it come to this that those who honestly go to God alone to plead his promises, and to claim his salvation, are to be charged with being under the foul and soul-damning influence of mesmerism? Do we ask our kind Father in Heaven for "bread," only to receive a "stone," or a "scorpion?"[217] These things wounded my spirit, and wrung my soul in keen anguish, well nigh to despair, while many would have me believe that there was no Holy Ghost, and that all the exercises that holy men of God have experienced were only mesmerism, or the deceptions of Satan. {ExV 6.4; RH, July 21, 1851}

V18. *No Work Doctrine Vision, 1845*

At this time there was fanaticism in Maine. Some refrained wholly from labor, and disfellowshipped all those who would not receive their views on this point, and some other things which they held to be religious duties. God revealed these errors to me in vision, and sent me to his erring children to declare them; but many of them wholly rejected the message, and charged me with conforming to the world. On the other hand, the Nominal Adventists charged me with fanaticism, and I was falsely, and by some wickedly represented as being the leader of the fanaticism that I was actually laboring to do away.[218] Different times were repeatedly set for the Lord to come, and were urged upon the brethren.—But the Lord shewed me that they would all pass by, for the time of trouble must come before the coming of Christ, and that every time that was set, and passed by, would only weaken the faith of God's people.[219] For this I was charged with being with the evil servant, that said in his heart, "My Lord delayeth his coming."[220] {ExV 7.1; RH, July 21, 1851}

All these things weighed heavily upon my spirits,

8

V12. *Voice of God—Time of Jacob's Trouble Vision, spring 1845*

and in the confusion I was sometimes tempted to doubt my own experience. And while at family prayers one morning, the power of God began to rest upon me, and the thought rushed into my mind that it was mesmerism, and I resisted it. Immediately I was struck dumb, and for a few moments was lost to everything around me. I then saw my sin in doubting the power of God, and that for so doing I was struck dumb, and that my tongue should be loosed in less than twenty-four hours. A card was held up before me, on which was written in gold letters the chapter and verse of fifty texts of Scripture.[221] After I came out of vision, I beckoned for the slate, and wrote upon it that I was dumb, also what I had seen, and that I wished the large Bible. I took the Bible and readily turned to all the texts that I had seen upon the card. I was unable to speak all day. Early the next morning my soul was filled with joy, and my tongue was loosed to shout the high praises of God.[222] After that I dared not doubt, or for a moment resist the power of God, however others might think of me. {ExV 7.2; RH, July 21, 1851}

V20. *Fifty Texts Vision, 1845*

Sarah Harmon

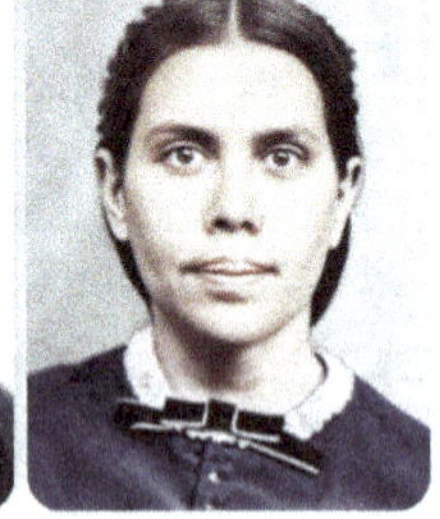

Ellen Harmon

In 1846, while at Fairhaven, Mass., my sister [***Sarah Harmon***], (who usually accompanied me at that time,) sister A. [***Melora Ashley***] and brother G. [***Heman Gurney***] and myself started in a sail-boat to visit a family on West's Island.[223] It was almost night when we started. We had gone but a short distance when a sudden storm arose. It thundered and lightened and the rain came in torrents upon us. It seemed plain that we must be lost, unless God should deliver. {ExV 8.1; RH, July 21, 1851}

I knelt down in the boat, and began to cry to God to deliver us. And there upon the tossing billows, while the water washed over the top of the boat upon us, the rain descended as I never saw it before, the lightnings flashed and the thunders rolled, I was taken off in vision,

V34. *Protection in Storm Vision, 1845*

and saw that sooner would every drop of water in the ocean be dried up than we should perish, for I saw that my work had but just

9

begun. After I came out of the vision all my fears were gone, and we sung and praised God, and our little boat was to us a floating Bethel. The editor of the "Advent Herald" has said that my visions were known to be "the result of mesmeric operations."[224] But I ask, what chance was there for mesmeric operations in such a time as that? {ExV 8.2; RH, July 21, 1851}

Bro. G. had more than he could well attend to, to manage the boat. He tried to anchor, but the anchor dragged. Our little boat was tossed upon the waves, and driven by the wind, while it was so dark that we could not see from one end of the boat to the other. {ExV 9.1; RH, July 21, 1851}

Originally owned by Stephen West, "West's Island" (shortened to "West Island") is marked for the later property owners: R. Anthony and J. Taber.

Soon the anchor held, and Bro. G. called for help. There were but two houses on the Island, and it proved that we were near one of them, but not the one where we wished to go.[225] All the family had retired to rest except a little child, who providentially heard the call for help upon the water. Her father soon came to our relief, and in a small boat, took us to the shore. We spent the most of that night in thanksgiving and praise to God, for his wonderful goodness unto us. {ExV 9.2; RH, July 21, 1851}

Here I will give the view that was first published in 1846. In this view I saw only a very few of the events of the future. More recent views have been more full. I shall therefore leave out a portion and prevent repetition.[226] {ExV 9.3; RH, July 21, 1851}

To the Remnant Scattered Abroad.

As God has shown me the travels of the Advent people to the Holy City, and the rich reward to be given those who wait the return of their Lord from the wedding, it may be my duty to give you a short sketch of what God has revealed to me.[227] The dear saints have got many trials to pass through. But our light afflictions, which are but for a moment, worketh for us a far more exceeding and eternal

10

weight of glory—while we look not at the things which are seen, for the things which are seen are temporal, but the things which are not seen are eternal.[228] I have tried to bring back a good report, and a few grapes from the heavenly Canaan, for which many would stone me, as the congregation bade stone Caleb and Joshua for their report, (Num. xiv, 10.) But I declare to you, my brethren and sisters in the Lord, it is a goodly land, and we are well able to go up and possess it.[229] {ExV 9.4; RH, July 21, 1851; WLF; GT Extra, Jan. 20, 1848; Broadside1, April 6, 1846; DS, Jan. 24, 1846 (Lt.1, 1845, Dec. 20)}

V1. *Midnight Cry Vision, Dec. 1844*

While praying at the family altar, the Holy Ghost fell upon me, and I seemed to be rising higher and higher, far above the dark world. I turned to look for the Advent people in the world, but could not find them—when a voice said to me, "Look again, and look a little higher." At this I raised my eyes and saw a straight and narrow path, cast up high above the world.[230] On this path the Advent people were traveling to the City, which was at the farther end of the path. They had a bright light set up behind them at the first end of the path, which an angel told me was the Midnight Cry.[231] This light shone all along the path, and gave light for their feet so they might not stumble. And if they kept their eyes fixed on Jesus, who was just before them, leading them to the City, they were safe. But soon some grew weary, and they said the City was a great way off, and they expected to have entered it before. Then Jesus would encourage them by raising his glorious right arm, and from his arm came a glorious light which waved over the Advent band, and they shouted Hallelujah! Others rashly denied the light behind them, and said that it was not God that had led them out so far. The light behind them went out leaving their feet in perfect darkness, and they stumbled and got their eyes off the mark, and lost sight of Jesus, and fell off the path down in the dark and wicked world below.[232] Soon we heard the voice of God like many waters, which gave us the day and

11

hour of Jesus' coming.[233] The living saints, 144,000, in number, knew and understood the voice, while the wicked thought it was thunder and an earthquake.[234] When God spake the time, he poured on us the Holy Ghost, and our faces began to light up and shine with the glory of God as Moses' did when he came down from Mount Sinai.[235] {ExV 10.1; RH, July 21, 1851; WLF; GT Extra, Jan. 20, 1848; Broadside1; DS, Jan. 24, 1846 (Lt.1, 1845, Dec. 20)}

The 144,000 were all sealed and perfectly united. On their foreheads was written, God, New Jerusalem, and a glorious Star containing Jesus' new name.[236] At our happy, holy state the wicked were enraged, and would rush violently up to lay hands on us to thrust us in prison, when we would stretch forth the hand in the name of the Lord, and the wicked would fall helpless to the ground.[237] Then it was that the synagogue of Satan knew that God had loved us who could wash one another's feet, and salute the holy brethren with a holy kiss, and they worshipped at our feet.[238] Soon our eyes were drawn to the East, for a small black cloud had appeared about half as large as a man's hand, which we all knew was the Sign of the Son of Man.[239] We all in solemn silence gazed on the cloud as it drew nearer, and became lighter, glorious, and still more glorious, till it was a great white cloud.[240] The bottom appeared like fire, a rainbow was over it, around the cloud were ten thousand angels singing a most lovely song.[241] And on it sat the Son of Man, on his head were crowns, his hair was white and curly and lay on his shoulders.[242] His feet had the appearance of fire, in his right hand was a sharp sickle, in his left a silver trumpet.[243] His eyes were as a flame of fire, which searched his children through and through.[244] Then all faces gathered paleness, and those that God had rejected gathered blackness. Then we all cried out, who shall be able to stand? Is my robe spotless?[245] Then the angels ceased to sing, and there was some time of awful silence, when Jesus spoke.[246] Those who have clean hands and a pure heart shall be able to stand, my

12

grace is sufficient for you.[247] At this, our faces lighted up, and joy filled every heart. And the angels struck a note higher and sung again while the cloud drew still nearer the earth. Then Jesus' silver trumpet sounded, as he descended on the cloud, wrapped in flames of fire.[248] He gazed on the graves of the sleeping saints, then raised his eyes and hands to heaven and cried, Awake! Awake! Awake! ye that sleep in the dust and arise.[249] Then there was a mighty earthquake.[250] The graves opened, and the dead came up clothed with immortality.[251] The 144,000 shouted, Hallelujah![252] as they recognized their friends who had been torn from them by death, and in the same moment we were changed and caught up together with them to meet the Lord in the air.[253] We all entered the cloud together, and were seven days ascending to the sea of glass, when Jesus brought along the crowns and with his own right hand placed them on our heads.[254] He gave us harps of gold and palms of victory.[255] Here on the sea of glass the 144,000 stood in a perfect square.[256] Some of them had very bright crowns, others not so bright. Some crowns appeared heavy with stars, while others had but few. All were perfectly satisfied with their crowns. And they were all clothed with a glorious white mantle from their shoulders to their feet.[257] Angels were all about us as we marched over the sea of glass to the gate of the City.[258] Jesus raised his mighty glorious arm, laid hold of the pearly gate and swung it back on its glittering hinges, and said to us, You have washed your robes in my blood, stood stiffly for my truth, enter in. We all marched in and felt we had a perfect right in

the City.[259] Here we saw the tree of life and the throne of God.[260] Out of the throne came a pure river of water, and on either side of the river was the tree of life.[261] On one side of the river was a trunk of a tree, and a trunk on the other side of the river, both of pure transparent gold.[262] {ExV 11.1; RH, July 21, 1851; GT Extra, Jan. 20, 1848; WLF; Broadside1; DS, Jan. 24, 1846 (Lt.1, 1845, Dec. 20)}

13

At first I thought I saw two trees. I looked again and saw they were united at the top in one tree.—So it was the tree of life, on either side of the river of life. Its branches bowed to the place where we stood; and the fruit was glorious, which looked like gold mixed with silver.[263] We all went under the tree, and sat down to look at the glory of the place, when brothers Fitch and Stockman, who had preached the gospel of the kingdom, and whom God had laid in the grave to save them, came up to us and asked us what we had passed through while they were sleeping.[264] We tried to call up our greatest trials, but they looked so small compared with the far more exceeding and eternal weight of glory that surrounded us, that we could not speak them out, and we all cried out Alleluia, heaven is cheap enough, and we touched our glorious harps and made heaven's arches ring.[265] {ExV 13.1; RH, July 21, 1851; GT Extra, Jan. 20, 1848; WLF; Broadside1; DS, Jan. 24, 1846 (Lt.1, 1845, Dec. 20)}

Charles Fitch

V16. New Earth Vision, spring 1845

With Jesus at our head we all descended from the City down to this earth, on a great and mighty mountain, which could not bear Jesus up, and it parted asunder, and there was a mighty plain.[266] Then we looked up and saw the Great City, with twelve foundations, twelve gates, three on each side, and an angel at each gate. We all cried out "The City, the Great City, it's coming, it's coming down from God out of heaven;" and it came and settled on the place where we stood.[267] Then we began to look at the glorious things outside of the City. There I saw most glorious houses, that had the appearance of silver, supported by four pillars, set with pearls, most glorious to behold, which were to be inhabited by the saints, and in them was a golden shelf. I saw many of the saints go into the houses, take off their glittering crowns and lay them on the shelf, then go out into the field by the houses to do something with the earth; not as we have to do with the earth here; no, no.[268] A glorious light shone all about their heads

14

and they were continually shouting and offering praises to God.[269] {ExV 13.2; RH, July 21, 1851; GT Extra, Jan. 20, 1848; WLF; Broadside1; DS, Jan. 24, 1846; 1SG 213.1}

And I saw another field full of all kinds of flowers, and as I plucked them, I cried out, They will never fade. Next I saw a field of tall grass, most glorious to behold; it was living green, and had a reflection of silver and gold, as it waved proudly to the glory of King Jesus. Then we entered a field full of all kinds of beasts—the lion, the

lamb, the leopard and the wolf, altogether in perfect union.[270] We passed through the midst of them, and they followed on peaceably after. Then we entered a wood, not like the dark woods we have here, no, no; but light, and all over glorious; the branches of the trees waved to and fro, and we all cried out, "We will dwell safely in the wilderness and sleep in the woods."[271] We passed through the woods, for we were on our way to Mount Zion. As we were traveling along, we met a company who were also gazing at the glories of the place. I noticed red as a border on their garments; their crowns were brilliant; their robes were pure white. As we greeted them, I asked Jesus who they were. He said they were martyrs that had been slain for him. With them was an innumerable company of little ones; they had a hem of red on their garments also.[272] Mount Zion was just before us, and on the Mount was a glorious temple, and about it were seven other mountains, on which grew roses and lilies.[273] And I saw the little ones climb, or if they chose, use their little wings and fly to the top of the mountains, and pluck the never fading flowers.—There were all kinds of trees around the temple to beautify the place; the box, the pine, the fir, the oil, the myrtle, the pomegranate and the fig tree bowed down with the weight of its timely figs, that made the place all over glorious.[274] And as we were about to enter the holy temple, Jesus raised his lovely voice and said, Only the 144,000 enter this place, and we shouted Alleluia.[275] {ExV 14.1; RH, July 21, 1851; GT Extra, Jan. 20, 1848; WLF; Broadside1; DS, Jan. 24, 1846 (Lt.1, 1845, Dec. 20)}

15

This temple was supported by seven pillars, all of transparent gold, set with pearls most glorious. The glorious things I saw there, I cannot describe. Oh, that I could talk in the language of Canaan, then could I tell a little of the glory of the better world. I saw there tables of stone in which the names of the 144,000 were engraved in letters of gold. After we beheld the glory of the temple, we went out, and Jesus left us, and went to the City. Soon we heard his lovely voice again, saying, "Come, my people, you have come out of great tribulation, and done my will; suffered for me; come in to supper, for I will gird myself, and serve you."[276] We shouted Alleluia, glory, and entered into the City. And I saw a table of pure silver, it was many miles in length, yet our eyes could extend over it. I saw the fruit of the tree of life, the manna, almonds, figs, pomegranates, grapes, and many other kinds of fruit.[277] I asked Jesus to let me eat of the fruit. He said, Not now. Those who eat of the fruit of this land, go back to earth no more. But in a little while, if faithful, you shall both eat of the fruit of the tree of life, and drink of the water of the fountain.[278] And he said, You must go back to the earth again, and relate to others what I have revealed to you.[279] Then an angel bore me gently down to this dark world. Sometimes I think I can stay here no longer, all things of earth look so dreary. I feel very lonely here, for I have seen a better land. Oh, that I had

V46. Sabbath Halo Vision, April 3, 1847

wings like a dove, then would I fly away and be at rest.[280] {ExV 15.1; RH, July 21, 1851; GT Extra, Jan. 20, 1848; WLF; Broadside1; DS, Jan. 24, 1846; cf. 1T 58.4–61.2}

The Lord gave me the following view in 1847, while at Topsham, Me.[281] The brethren were assembled on the Sabbath. {ExV 15.2; RH, July 21, 1851; WLF}

We felt an unusual spirit of prayer. And as we prayed, the Holy Ghost fell upon us. We were very happy. Soon I was lost to earthly things, and was wrapped up in a vision of God's glory. I saw an

16

angel swiftly flying to me. He quickly carried me from the earth to the Holy City. In the City I saw a temple, which I entered. I passed through a door before I came to the first vail. This veil was raised, and I passed into the Holy Place. Here I saw the altar of incense, the candlestick with seven lamps, and the table on which was the shew-bread. After viewing the glory of the Holy, Jesus raised the second vail, and I passed into the Holy of Holies.[282] {ExV 15.3; RH, July 21, 1851; WLF; Broadside1; Lt. 1, 1847}

In the Holiest I saw an ark; on the top and sides of it was purest gold. On each end of the ark was a lovely cherub, with their wings spread out over it. Their faces were turned towards each other, and they looked downwards. Between the angels was a golden censer.[283] Above the ark, where the angels stood, was an exceeding bright glory, that appeared like a throne where God dwelt.[284] Jesus stood by the ark. And as the saints' prayers came up to Jesus, the incense in the censer would smoke, and he offered up the prayers of the saints with the smoke of the incense to his Father.[285] In the ark, was the golden pot of manna, Aaron's rod that budded, and the tables of stone which folded together like a book.[286] Jesus opened them, and I saw the ten commandments written on them with the finger of God.[287] On one table was four, and on the other six. The four on the first table shone brighter than the other six. But the fourth (the Sabbath commandment,) shone above them all; for the Sabbath was set apart to be kept in honor of God's holy name.[288] The Holy Sabbath looked glorious—a halo of glory was all around it. I saw that the Sabbath was not nailed to the cross. If it was, the other nine commandments were; and we are at liberty to go forth and break them all, as well as to break the fourth. I saw that God had not changed the Sabbath, for he never changes.[289] But the Pope had changed it from the seventh to the first day of the week; for he was to change times and laws.[290] {ExV 16.1; RH, July 21, 1851; WLF; Broadside3; Lt. 1, 1847}

17

And I saw that if God had changed the Sabbath, from the seventh to the first day, he would have changed the writing of the Sabbath commandment, written on the tables of stone, which are now in the ark, in the Most Holy Place of the Temple in heaven; and it would read thus: The first day is the Sabbath of the Lord thy God. But I saw that it read the same as when written on the tables of stone by the finger of God, and delivered to Moses in Sinai, "But the seventh day is the Sabbath of the Lord thy God."[291] I saw that the Holy Sabbath is, and will be, the separating wall between the true Israel of God and unbelievers; and that the Sabbath is the great question, to unite the hearts of God's dear waiting saints.[292] {ExV 17.1; RH, July 21, 1851; WLF; Broadside3; Lt. 1, 1847}

I saw that God had children, who do not see and keep the Sabbath. They had not rejected the light on it. And at the commencement of the time of trouble, we were filled with the Holy Ghost as we went forth and proclaimed the Sabbath more fully.[293] This enraged the churches, and nominal Adventists, as they could not refute the Sabbath truth. And at this time God's chosen all saw clearly that we had the truth, and they came out and endured the persecution with us. And I saw the sword, famine, pestilence and great confusion in the land.[294] The wicked thought that we had brought the judgments down on them. They rose up and took counsel to rid the earth of us, thinking that then the evil would be stayed.[295] {ExV 17.2; RH, July 21, 1851; WLF; Broadside3; Lt. 1, 1847}

In the time of trouble, we all fled from the cities and villages, but were pursued by the wicked, who entered the houses of the saints with the sword.[296] They raised the sword to kill us, but it broke, and fell as powerless as a straw.[297] Then we all cried day and night for deliverance, and the cry came up before God.[298] The sun came up, and the moon stood still.[299] The streams ceased to flow.[300] Dark heavy clouds came up, and clashed against each other.[301] But there was one clear place of settled glory, from whence

18

came the *voice of God* like many waters, which shook the heavens, and the earth.[302] The sky opened and shut, and was in commotion.[303] The mountains shook like a reed in the wind, and cast out ragged rocks all around. The sea boiled like a pot, and cast out stones upon the land.[304] And as God spake the day and hour of Jesus' coming, and delivered the everlasting covenant to his people, he spake one sentence, and then paused, while the words were rolling through the earth.[305] The Israel of God stood with their eyes fixed upwards, listening to the words as they came from the mouth of Jehovah, and rolled through the earth like peals of loudest thunder.[306] It was awfully solemn. At the end of every sentence, the saints shouted, Glory! Hallelujah! Their countenances were lighted up with the glory of God; and they shone with the glory as Moses' face did when he came down from Sinai.[307] The wicked could not look on them for the glory.[308] And when the never-ending blessing was pronounced on those who had honored God, in keeping his Sabbath holy, there was a mighty shout of victory over the Beast, and over his Image.[309] {ExV 17.3; RH, July 21, 1851; WLF; Broadside3; Lt. 1, 1847; 1SG 204.1; 205.1, 2, 3; cf. PrT, Aug. 1849}

Then commenced the jubilee, when the land should rest. I saw the pious slave rise in triumph and victory, and shake off the chains that bound him, while his wicked master was in confusion, and knew not what to do; for the wicked could not understand the words of the voice of God.[310] Soon appeared the great white cloud.[311] It looked more lovely than ever before. On it sat the Son of Man.[312] At first we did not see Jesus on the cloud, but as it drew near the earth, we could behold his lovely person. This cloud, when it first appeared, was the Sign of the Son of Man in

heaven.[313] The voice of the Son of God called forth the sleeping saints, clothed with a glorious immortality.[314] The living saints were changed in a moment, and were caught up with them in the cloudy chariot.[315] It looked all over glorious as it rolled upwards. On either side of the chariot were wings, and beneath it

19

wheels. And as the chariot rolled upwards, the wheels cried Holy, and the wings, as they moved, cried Holy, and the retinue of Holy Angels around the cloud cried Holy, Holy, Holy, Lord God Almighty.[316] And the saints in the cloud cried, Glory, Alleluia. And the chariot rolled upwards to the Holy City.[317] Jesus threw open the gates of the Golden City, and led us in.[318] Here we were made welcome, for we had kept the "*Commandments* of God," and had a "right to the tree of life."[319] {ExV 18.1; RH, July 21, 1851; WLF; Broadside3; Lt. 1, 1847; 1SG 206.1, 2; 207.1; 208.1}

The Sealing.

V59. Sealing Vision, Jan. 5, 1849

At the commencement of the Holy Sabbath, (Jan. 5th, 1849) we engaged in prayer with Bro. Belden's family at Rocky Hill, Con., and the Holy Ghost fell upon us.[320] I was taken off in vision to the Most Holy Place, where I saw Jesus still interceding for Israel. On the bottom of his garment was a bell and a pomegranate, a bell and a pomegranate.[321] Then I saw that Jesus would not leave the Most Holy Place until every case was decided either for salvation or destruction, and that the wrath of God could not come until Jesus had finished his work in the Most Holy Place, laid off his priestly attire and clothed himself with the garments of vengeance. Then Jesus will step out from between the Father and man, and God will keep silence no longer; but pour out his wrath on those who have rejected his truth. I saw that the anger of the nations, the wrath of God, and the time to judge the dead, were separate events, one following the other. I saw that Michael had not stood up, and that the time of trouble, such as never was, had not yet commenced.[322] The nations are now getting angry, but when our High Priest has finished his work in the Sanctuary, he will stand up, put on the garments of vengeance, and then the seven last plagues will be poured out.[323] I saw that the four angels would hold the four winds until Jesus' work was done in the Sanctuary, and then will come the

20

seven last plagues.[324] These plagues enraged the wicked against the righteous, and they thought that we had brought them down upon them, and if they could rid the earth of us, then the plagues would be stayed. A decree went forth to slay the saints, which caused them to cry day and night for deliverance. This was the time of Jacob's trouble.[325] Then all the saints cried out with anguish of spirit, and were delivered by the voice of God. Then the 144,000 triumphed. Their faces were lighted up with the glory of God. Then I was shown a company who were howling

in agony. On their garments was written in large characters, "Thou art weighed in the balance, and found wanting."[326] I asked who this company were. The angel said, "These are they who have once kept the Sabbath and have given it up." I heard them cry with a loud voice, "We have believed in thy coming, and taught it with energy." And while they were speaking, their eyes would fall upon their garments and see the writing, and then they would wail aloud. I saw that they had drunk of the deep waters, and fouled the residue with their feet—trodden the Sabbath under foot, and that is why they were weighed in the balance and found wanting.[327] Then my attending angel directed me to the City again, where I saw four angels winging their way to the gate of the City, and were just presenting the golden card to the angel at the gate.[328] Then I saw another angel swiftly flying from the direction of the most excellent glory, and crying with a loud voice to the other angels, and waving something up and down in his hand. I asked my attending angel for an explanation of what I saw. He told me that I could see no more then, but he would shortly show me what those things that I then saw meant. {ExV 19.1; PrT, Aug. 1849; Broadside2; JW to the Hastings, Jan. 25, 1849; Ms. 2, 1849, Jan. 17}

Sabbath afternoon one of our number was sick, and requested prayers that he might be healed. We all united in applying to the Physician that never lost a case, and while healing power came down,

21

V60. Final Events Vision, Jan. 6, 1849

and the sick was healed, the Spirit fell upon me and I was taken off in vision.[329] {ExV 20.1; PrT, Aug. 1849; Broadside2; JW to the Hastings, Jan. 25, 1849; Ms. 2, 1849, Jan. 17}

I saw four angels who had a work to do on the earth, and were on their way to accomplish it. Jesus was clothed with priestly garments. He gazed in pity on the remnant, then raised his hands upward, and with a voice of deep pity cried, "*My blood, Father, my blood, my blood, my blood.*"[330] Then I saw an exceeding bright light come from God, who sat upon the great white throne, and was shed all about Jesus. Then I saw an angel with a commission from Jesus, swiftly flying to the four angels who had a work to do on the earth, and waving something up and down in his hand, and crying with a loud voice, "*Hold! hold! hold! hold!* until the servants of God are sealed in their foreheads."[331] I asked my accompanying angel the meaning of what I heard, and what the four angels were about to do. He said to me that it was God that restrained the powers, and that he gave his angels charge over things on the earth, and that the four angels had power from God to hold the four winds, and that they were about to let them go, and while their hands were loosening, and the four winds were about to blow, the merciful eye of Jesus gazed on the remnant that were not sealed, then he raised his hands to the Father and plead[ed] with him that he had spilled his blood for them.[332] Then another angel was commissioned to fly swiftly to the four angels, and bid them hold, until the servants of God were sealed with the seal of the living God in their foreheads.[333] {ExV 21.1; PrT, Aug. 1849; Broadside2; JW to the Hastings, Jan. 25, 1849; Ms. 2, 1849, Jan. 17}

God's Love for His People.

V63. God's Love for His People Vision, Jan 1849

I have seen the tender love that God has for his people, and it is very great. I saw an angel over every saint, with their wings spread about them; and if the saints wept through discouragement, or were in danger, the angel that ever attended them would fly quickly upward to carry the tidings, and

22

the angels in the City would cease to sing. Then Jesus would commission another angel to descend to encourage, watch over and try to keep them from going out of the narrow path;[334] but if they did not take heed to the watchful care of these angels, and would not be comforted by them, and continued to go astray, the angels would look sad and weep. Then they would bear the tidings upward and all the angels in the City would weep, and then with a loud voice say, Amen. But if the saints fixed their eyes on the prize before them, and glorified God by praising him, then the angels would bear the glad tidings to the City, and the angels in the City would touch their golden harps and sing with a loud voice—Alleluia! and the heavenly arches would ring with their lovely songs. I will here state, that there is perfect order and harmony in the Holy City. {ExV 21.2; PrT, Aug. 1849; Broadside2}

All the angels that are commissioned to visit the earth hold a golden card, which they present to the angels at the gates of the City as they pass in and out.[335] Heaven is a good place. I long to be there, and behold my lovely Jesus, who gave his life for me, and be changed into his glorious image. Oh, for language to express the glory of the bright world to come. I thirst for the living streams that make glad the City of our God.[336] {ExV 22.1; PrT, Aug. 1849; Broadside2}

V64. Other Worlds Vision, 1849

The Lord has given me a view of other worlds. Wings were given me, and an angel attended me from the City to a place that was bright and glorious. The grass of the place was living green, and the birds there warbled a sweet song. The inhabitants of the place were of all sizes, they were noble, majestic and lovely. They bore the express image of Jesus, and their countenances beamed with holy joy, expressive of the freedom and happiness of the place, I asked one of them why they were so much more lovely than those on the earth. The reply was, "We have lived in strict obedience to the commandments of God, and have not fallen by disobedience,

23

like those on the earth."[337] Then I saw two trees, one looked much like the tree of life in the City. The fruit of both looked beautiful; but of one they could not eat. They had power to eat of both, but were forbidden to eat of one. Then my attending angel said to me, "None in this place have tasted of the forbidden tree; but if they should eat they would fall." Then I was taken to a world which had seven moons. There I saw good old Enoch, who had been translated.[338] On his right arm he bore a glorious palm, and on each leaf was written Victory. Around his head was a dazzling white wreath, and leaves on the wreath, and in the middle of each leaf was written Purity, and around the leaf were stones of various colors, that shone brighter than the stars, and cast a reflection upon the letters, and magnified them. On the back part of his head was a bow that confined the wreath, and upon the bow was written Holiness. Above the wreath was a lovely crown that shone brighter than the sun. I asked him if this was the place he was taken to from the earth. He said "It is not, the City is my home, and I have come to visit this place." He moved about the place as if perfectly at home. I begged of my attending angel to let me remain in that place. I could not bear the thought of coming back to this dark world again. Then the angel said, You must go back, and if you are faithful, you, with the 144,000 shall have the privilege of visiting all the worlds and viewing the handiworks of God. {ExV 22.2; PrT, Aug. 1849; Broadside2, Jan. 31, 1849}

Shaking of the powers of Heaven.

V58. Shaking of the Powers of Heaven Vision, Dec. 16, 1848

Dec. 16, 1848, the Lord gave me a view of the shaking of the powers of the heavens.[339] I saw that when the Lord said "heaven" (in giving the signs recorded by Matthew, Mark and Luke,) he meant heaven, and when he said "earth" he meant earth. The powers of heaven are the Sun, Moon and Stars. They rule in the heavens. The powers of earth are

24

those who bear rule on the earth. The powers of heaven will be shaken at the voice of God. Then the Sun, Moon and Stars will be moved out of their places.[340] They will not pass away, but be shaken by the voice of God. {ExV 23.1; PrT, Aug. 1849; Broadside2; JW to the Hastings, Jan. 25, 1849; Lt. 2, 1848, Dec. 18}

Dark, heavy clouds came up, and clashed against each other. The atmosphere parted and rolled back, then we could look up through the open space in Orion, from whence came the voice of God.[341] The Holy City will come down through that open space.[342] I saw that the powers of earth are now being shaken, and that events come in order. War, and rumors of war, sword, famine and pestilence, are first to shake the powers of earth, then the voice of God will shake the Sun, Moon and Stars, and this earth also. I saw that the shaking of the powers in Europe is not (as some teach) the shaking of the powers of heaven, but it is the shaking of the angry nations.[343] {ExV 24.1; PrT, Aug. 1849; Broadside2; Lt. 2, 1848, Dec. 18}

The open space in Orion

The Open and Shut Door.

V69. Open and Shut Door Vision, March 24, 1849 spring 1845

Sabbath, March 24th, 1849, we had a sweet and very interesting meeting with the brethren at Topsham, Me. The Holy Ghost was poured out upon us, and I was taken off in the Spirit to the City of the living God.[344] Then I was shown that the commandments of God, and the testimony of Jesus Christ, relating to the shut door, could not be separated, and that the time for the commandments of God to shine out, with all their importance, and for God's people to be tried on the Sabbath truth, was when the door was opened in the Most Holy Place of the Heavenly Sanctuary, where the Ark is, containing the ten commandments.[345] This door was not opened until the mediation of Jesus was finished in the Holy Place of the Sanctuary in 1844. Then, Jesus rose up and shut the door in the Holy Place, and opened the door in the Most Holy, and passed within the second vail, where he now stands by the Ark, and where the faith of Israel now reaches.[346] {ExV 24.2; PrT, Aug. 1849; Lt. 5, 1849, April 21; Ms. 1, 1849, March 24}

"AND THE TEMPLE OF GOD WAS OPENED IN HEAVEN, AND THERE WAS SEEN IN HIS TEMPLE THE ARK OF HIS TESTAMENT." REV. 11:19.

25

I saw that Jesus had shut the door in the Holy Place, and no man can open it: and that he had opened the door in the Most Holy, and no man can shut it; [Rev. iii, 7, 8.] and that since Jesus has opened the door in the Most Holy Place, which contains the Ark, the commandments have been shining out to God's people; and they are being tested on the Sabbath question.[347] {ExV 25.1; PrT, Aug. 1849; Lt. 5, 1849, April 21; Ms. 1, 1849}

"BEHOLD, I HAVE SET BEFORE THEE AN OPEN DOOR, AND NO MAN CAN SHUT IT." REV. 3:7.

I saw that the present test on the Sabbath could not come until the mediation of Jesus in the Holy Place was finished, and he had passed within the second vail; therefore, Christians who fell asleep before the door was opened in the Most Holy, when the midnight cry was finished, at the seventh month 1844, and had not kept the true Sabbath, now rest in hope, for they had not the light, and the test on the Sabbath, which we now have since that door was opened.[348] I saw that Satan was tempting some of God's people on this point. Because so many good Christians have fallen asleep in the triumphs of faith, and have not kept the true Sabbath, they were doubting about it being a test for us now. {ExV 25.2; PrT, Aug. 1849; Ms. 1, 1849}

The enemies of the present truth have been trying to open the door of the Holy Place, that Jesus has shut, and to close the door of the Most Holy Place, which he opened in 1844, where the Ark is, containing the two tables of stone, on which are written the ten commandments, by the finger of Jehovah.[349] {ExV 25.3; PrT, Aug. 1849; Lt. 5, 1849, April 21; Lt. 5, 1849, April 21; Ms. 1, 1849}

Satan is now using every device in this sealing time, to keep the minds of God's people from the present truth, and to cause them to waver. I saw a covering that God was drawing over his people to protect them in the time of trouble; and every soul that was decided on the truth, and was pure in heart, was to be covered with the covering of Almighty God.[350] {ExV 25.4; PrT, Aug. 1849; Lt. 5, 1849, April 21; Ms. 1, 1849}

Satan knew this, and was at work in mighty power to keep the minds of as many as he possibly could unsettled and wavering on the truth. I saw that the

26

mysterious knocking in N. Y. and other places, was the power of Satan, and that such things would be more and more common, clothed in a religious garb, to lull the deceived to more security, and to draw the minds of God's people, if possible, to those things and cause them to doubt the teachings, and power of the Holy Ghost. {ExV 25.5; PrT, Aug. 1849; Lt. 5, 1849, April 21; Ms. 1, 1849}

I saw that Satan was working through agents in a number of ways. He was at work through ministers who have rejected the truth, and are given over to strong delusions to believe a lie that they might be damned.[351] While they were preaching or praying some would fall prostrate and helpless; not by the power of the Holy Ghost, but by the power of Satan breathed upon these agents, and through them to the people. Some professed Adventists who had rejected the present truth, while preaching, praying or in conversation used mesmerism to gain adherents, and the people would rejoice in this influence, for they thought it was the Holy Ghost.[352] And even some that used it were so far in the darkness and deception of the Devil, that they thought it was the power of God, given them to exercise. They had made God altogether such an one as themselves, and had valued his power as a thing of naught.[353] {ExV 26.1; PrT, Aug. 1849; Lt. 5, 1849, April 21; Ms. 1, 1849}

Some of these agents of Satan were affecting the bodies of some of the saints; those that they could not deceive and draw away from the truth, by a Satanic influence. Oh, that all could get a view of it as God revealed it to me, that they might know more of the wiles of Satan, and be on their guard. I saw that Satan was at work in these ways to distract, deceive, and draw away God's people, just now in this sealing time. I saw some who were not standing stiffly for present truth.[354] Their knees were trembling, and their feet were sliding, because they were not firmly planted on the truth, and the covering of Almighty God could not be drawn over them while they were thus trembling. {ExV 26.2; PrT, Aug. 1849; Lt. 5, 1849, April 21; Ms. 1, 1849}

Hydesville, New York, home of the Fox sisters and the birthplace of modern Spiritualism

27

Satan was trying his every art to hold them where they were, until the sealing was past, and the covering drawn over God's people, and they left out, without a shelter from the burning wrath of God, in the seven last plagues.[355] {ExV 27.1; PrT, Aug. 1849; Lt. 5, 1849, April 21; Ms. 1, 1849}

God has begun to draw this covering over his people, and it will soon be drawn over all who are to have a shelter in the day of slaughter. God will work in power for his people; and Satan will be permitted to work also. {ExV 27.2; PrT, Aug. 1849; Lt. 5, 1849, April 21; Ms. 1, 1849}

I saw that the mysterious signs and wonders, and false reformations would increase, and spread.[356] The reformations that were shown me, were not reformations from error to truth. My accompanying angel bade me look for the travail of soul for sinners as used to be. I looked, but could not see it; for the time for their salvation is past.[357] {ExV 27.3; PrT, Aug. 1849; Lt. 5, 1849, April 21; Ms. 1, 1849}

The Trial of our Faith.

In this time of trial, we need to be encouraged and comforted by each other. The temptations of Satan are greater now than ever before, for he knows that his time is short, and that very soon every case will be decided, either for Life, or for Death. It is no time to sink down beneath discouragement, and trial now; but we must bear up under all our afflictions, and trust wholly in the mighty God of Jacob.[358] {ExV 27.4; PrT, Sept. 1849}

V75. *Trial of Our Faith Vision, Aug. 1849*

The Lord has shown me that his grace is sufficient for all our trials; and although they are greater than ever before, yet if we trust wholly in God, we can overcome every temptation, and through his grace come off victorious. {ExV 27.5; PrT, Sept. 1849; 2SG 289.2}

If we overcome our trials, and get victory over the temptations of Satan, then we endure the trial of our faith, which is much more precious than gold, and are stronger, and better prepared to meet the next.[359] But if we sink down, and give way to the temptations of Satan, we shall grow weaker and get no reward for the trial, and shall not be so well prepared

28

for the next. In this way we shall grow weaker, and weaker, until we are led captive by Satan, at his will. We must have on the whole armor of God, and be ready at any moment for a conflict with the powers of darkness. When temptations and trials rush in upon us, let us go to God, and agonize with him in prayer. He will not turn us away empty; but will give us grace and strength to overcome, and to break the power of the enemy.[360] Oh, that all could see these things in their true light, and endure hardness as good soldiers of Jesus. Then would Israel move forward strong in God, and in the power of his might. {ExV 27.6; PrT, Sept. 1849; 2SG 290.1}

Ellen White, 1864

God has shown me that he gave his people a bitter cup to drink to purify and cleanse them. It is a bitter draught, and they can make it still more bitter by murmuring, complaining, and repining. But those who receive it thus, must have another draught, for the first does not have its designed effect upon the heart. And if the second does not effect the work, then they must have another, and another, until it does have its designed effect, or they will be left filthy and impure in heart. I saw that this bitter cup can be sweetened by patience, endurance and prayer, and that it will have its designed effect upon the hearts of those who thus received it, and God will be honored and glorified. It is no small thing to be a Christian, and to be owned and approved of God. The Lord has shown me some who profess the present truth, whose lives do not correspond with their profession.[361] They have got the standard of piety altogether too low, and they come far short of Bible holiness. Some engage in vain and unbecoming conversation, and others give way to the risings of self. We must not expect to please ourselves, live and act like the world, have its pleasures, and enjoy the company of those who are of the world, and reign with Christ in glory. {ExV 28.1; PrT, Sept. 1849; 2SG 290.2}

We must be partakers of Christ's sufferings here,

29

if we would share in his glory hereafter. If we seek our own interest, how we can best please ourselves, instead of seeking to please God and advance his precious suffering cause, we shall dishonor God and the holy cause we profess to love. {ExV 28.2; PrT, Sept. 1849}

We have but a little space of time left to work for God. Nothing should be too dear to sacrifice for the salvation of the scattered and torn flock of Jesus. Those who make a covenant with God by sacrifice now, will soon be gathered home to share a rich reward, and possess the new kingdom forever and ever. {ExV 29.1; PrT, Sept. 1849}

O, let us live wholly for the Lord, and show by a well ordered life and godly conversation that we have been with Jesus, and are his meek and lowly followers. We must work while the day lasts, for when the dark night of trouble and anguish comes, it will be too late to work for God. Jesus is in his Holy Temple, and will now accept our sacrifices, our prayers, and our confessions of faults and sins, and will now pardon all the transgressions of Israel, that they may be blotted out before he leaves the Sanctuary.[362] When Jesus leaves the Sanctuary, then he that is holy and righteous, will be holy and righteous still; for all their sins will then be blotted out, and they will be sealed with the seal of the living God. But those that are unjust and filthy, will be unjust and filthy still; for then there will be no Priest in the Sanctuary to offer their sacrifices, their confessions, and their prayers before the Father's throne. Therefore, what is done to rescue souls from the coming storm of wrath, must be done before Jesus leaves the Most Holy Place of the Heavenly Sanctuary. {ExV 29.2; PrT, Sept. 1849}

"WHAT IS DONE TO RESCUE SOULS FROM THE COMING STORM OF WRATH, MUST BE DONE BEFORE JESUS LEAVES THE MOST HOLY PLACE OF THE HEAVENLY SANCTUARY MANIFESTATION."

To The "Little Flock."

V87. Perishing Souls Vision, Jan. 26, 1850

Dear Brethren.—The Lord gave me a view, January 26, 1850, which I will relate. I saw that some of the people of God were stupid and dormant, and were but half awake, and did not realize the time

30

we were now living in; and that the "man" with the "dirt-brush" [see Bro. Miller's dream,] had entered, and that some were in danger of being swept away. I begged of Jesus to save them, to spare them a little longer, and let them see their awful danger, that they might get ready before it should be forever too late. The angel said, "Destruction is coming like a mighty whirlwind."[363] I begged of the angel to pity, and to save those who loved this world, and were attached to their possessions, and were not willing to cut loose from them, and sacrifice to speed the messengers on their way to feed the hungry sheep, who were perishing for want of spiritual food. {ExV 29.3; Ms. 4, 1850, Jan. 28; PrT, April 1850}

He went away sorrowful.

As I viewed poor souls dying for want of the present truth, and some who professed to believe the truth were letting them die, by withholding the necessary means to carry forward the work of God, the sight was too painful, and I begged of the angel to remove it from me.[364] I saw that when the cause of God called for some of their property, like the young man who came to Jesus, [Matt. xix, 16–22,] they went away sorrowful; and that soon the overflowing scourge would pass over and sweep their possessions all away, and then it would be too late to sacrifice earthly goods, and lay up a treasure in heaven.[365] {ExV 30.1; Ms. 4, 1850, Jan. 28; PrT, April 1850}

I then saw the glorious Redeemer, beautiful and lovely, that he left the realms of glory, and came to this dark and lonely world, to give his precious life and die, the just for the unjust.[366] He bore the cruel mocking and scourging, and wore the platted crown of thorns, and sweat great drops of blood in the garden, while the burden of the sins of the whole world was upon him.[367] The angel asked "What for?" O, I saw and knew that it was for us; for our sins he suffered all this, that by his precious blood he might redeem us unto God. {ExV 30.2; Ms. 4, 1850, Jan. 28; PrT, April 1850}

Then again was held up before me those who were not willing to dispose of this world's goods to save perishing souls by sending them the truth, while Jesus

31

stands before the Father, pleading his blood, his sufferings and his death for them; and while God's messengers were waiting, ready to carry them the saving truth that they might be sealed with the seal of the living God. It was hard for some who professed to believe the present truth, to even do so little as to hand the messengers God's own money, that he had lent them to be stewards over.[368] {ExV 30.3; Ms. 4, 1850, Jan. 28; PrT, April 1850}

Then the suffering Jesus, his sacrifice and love so deep, as to give his life for them, was again held up before me; and then the lives of those who professed to be his followers, who had this world's goods, and considered it so great a thing to help the cause of salvation. The angel said, "Can such enter heaven?" Another angel answered, "No, never, never, never. Those who are not interested in the cause of

God on earth, can never sing the song of redeeming love above." {ExV 31.1; Ms. 4, 1850, Jan. 28; PrT, April 1850}

I saw that the quick work that God was doing on earth would soon be cut short in righteousness, and that the swift messengers must speed on their way to search out the scattered flock. An angel said, "Are all messengers?" Another answered, "No, no, God's messengers have a message." {ExV 31.2; Ms. 4, 1850, Jan. 28; PrT, April 1850}

I saw that the cause of God had been hindered, and dishonored by some traveling who had no message from God. Such will have to give an account to God for every dollar they have used in traveling where it was not their duty to go; for that money might have helped on the cause of God, and for the lack of it, souls have starved and died for the want of spiritual food that might have been given them by God's called and chosen messengers, if they had had the means. {ExV 31.3; Ms. 4, 1850, Jan. 28; PrT, April 1850}

The mighty shaking has commenced, and will go on, and all will be shaken out who are not willing to take a bold and unyielding stand for the truth, and sacrifice for God and his cause. The angel said, "Think ye that any will be compelled to sacrifice?

32

No, no. It must be a free will offering. It will take all to buy the field."[369] I cried to God to spare his people, some of whom were fainting and dying. {ExV 31.4; Ms. 4, 1850, Jan. 28; PrT, April 1850}

I saw that those who have strength to labor with their hands, and help sustain the cause, were as accountable for that strength, as others were for their property. {ExV 32.1; PrT, April 1850}

Then I saw that the judgments of Almighty God were speedily coming. I begged of the angel to speak in his language to the people. Said he, "All the thunders and lightnings of Mount Sinai would not move those who will not be moved by the plain truths of the word of God, neither would an angel's message awake them." {ExV 32.2; Ms. 4, 1850, Jan. 28; PrT, April 1850}

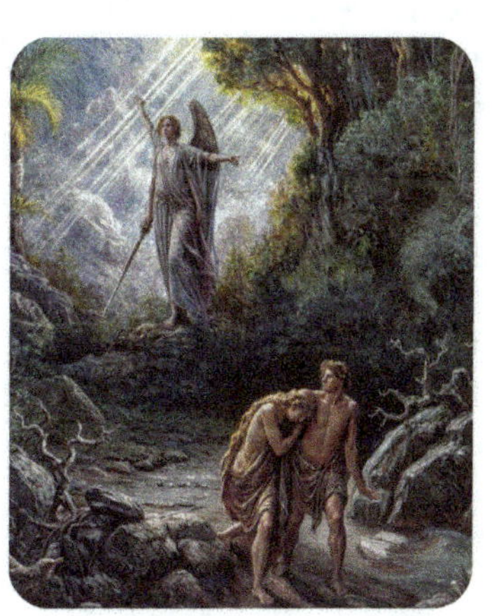

I then beheld the beauty and loveliness of Jesus. His robe was whiter than the whitest white. No language can describe his glory and exalted loveliness. All, all who keep the commandments of God, will enter in through the gates into the City, and have right to the tree of life, and ever be in the presence of the lovely Jesus, whose countenance shines brighter than the sun at noon-day.[370] {ExV 32.3; Ms. 4, 1850, Jan. 28; PrT, April 1850}

Then I was pointed to Adam and Eve in Eden. They partook of the forbidden tree, and then the flaming sword was placed around the tree of life, and they were driven from the Garden, lest they should partake of the tree of life, and be immortal sinners.

The tree of life was to perpetuate immortality. I heard an angel ask, "Who of the family of Adam have passed that flaming sword, and have partaken of the tree of life?"[371] I heard another angel answer, "Not one of the family of Adam have passed that flaming sword, and partaken of that tree; therefore there is not an immortal sinner. The soul that sinneth it shall die an everlasting death; a death that will last for ever, where there will be no hope of a resurrection; and then the wrath of God will be appeased."[372] {ExV 32.4; Ms. 4, 1850, Jan. 28; PrT, April 1850; 1SG 113.2}

I saw that the saints will rest in the Holy City,

33

and reign as kings and priests one thousand years; then Jesus will descend with the saints upon the mount of Olives, and the mount will part asunder, and become a mighty plain for the Paradise of God to rest upon.[373] The rest of the earth will not be cleansed until the wicked dead are raised (at the end of the one thousand years) and gather up around the City; for the feet of the wicked will never desecrate the earth made new. Then fire will come down from God out of heaven and devour them; burn them up root and branch.[374] Satan is the root, and his children are the branches. The same fire that will devour the wicked, will purify the earth. Yours in hope of immortality at the appearing of Jesus, E. G. W.[375] {ExV 32.5; Ms. 4, 1850, Jan. 28; PrT, April 1850}

The Last Plagues and the Judgment.

At the general conference of believers in the present truth, held at Sutton, (Vt.) September, 1850, I was shown that the seven last plagues will be poured out after Jesus leaves the Sanctuary.[376] Said the angel, It is the wrath of God and the Lamb that causes the destruction or death of the wicked.[377] At the voice of God the saints will be mighty and terrible as an army with banners; but they will not then execute the judgment written.[378] The execution of the judgment will be at the close of the 1000 years. {ExV 33.1; Ms. 14, 1850, Sept. 29; PrT, Nov. 1850}

V97. Sutton Vision, Sept. 26-29, 1850

After the saints are changed to immortality, and are caught up together, with Jesus, receive their harps, crowns, etc., and enter the City, Jesus and the saints sit in judgment.[379] The books are opened, the book of life and the book of death; the book of life contains the good deeds of the saints, and the book of death contains the evil deeds of the wicked.[380] These books were compared with the Statute book, the Bible, and according to that they were judged. The saints in unison with Jesus pass their judgment upon the wicked dead. Behold ye! said the angel, the saints sit in judgment, in unison with Jesus, and mete out to each of the wicked, according to the deeds

34

done in the body, and it is set off against their names, what they must receive at the execution of the judgment. This, I saw, was the work of the saints with Jesus, in the Holy City before it descends to the earth, through the 1000 years. Then at the close of the 1000 years, Jesus, and the angels, and all the saints with him, leaves the Holy

City, and while he is descending to the earth with them, the wicked dead are raised, and then the very men that "pierced him," being raised, will see him afar off in all his glory, the angels and saints with him, and will wail because of him. They will see the prints of the nails in his hands, and in his feet, and where they thrust the spear into his side. The prints of the nails and the spear will then be his glory. It is at the close of the 1000 years that Jesus stands upon the Mount of Olives, and the Mount parts asunder, and it becomes a mighty plain, and those who flee at that time are the wicked, that have just been raised. Then the Holy City comes down and settles on the plain. {ExV 33.2; Ms. 14, 1850, Sept. 29; PrT, Nov. 1850}

Then Satan imbues the wicked, that have been raised, with his spirit. He flatters them that the army in the City is small, and that his army is large, and that they can overcome the saints and take the City. While Satan was rallying his army, the saints were in the City, beholding the beauty and glory of the Paradise of God.[381] Jesus was at their head, leading them. All at once the lovely Saviour was gone from our

EVENTS OF THE MILLENNIUM BEFORE AND AFTER		
THE LAST DAYS	**THE 1000 YEARS** (The Millennium)	**ETERNITY**
Christ returns	The First Resurrection / The Second Resurrection	Christ and the city descend
Saints taken to heaven (the resurrected and the living)	Saints reign with Christ (in heaven) Review phase of judgment	Saints return with Christ
Living wicked slain (the wicked dead remain dead)		Wicked resurrected (with corruptible bodies)
Satan bound (confined to the earth)		Satan loosed (organizes attack on the holy city)
Investigative phase of judgment has ended		Executive phase of judgment; wicked slain by fire
Earth Desolated (via the last plagues, a great earthquake, and the second coming)		Earth renewed as the eternal home of the saints

Chart compiled by Kevin Morgan

company; but soon we heard his lovely voice, saying, "Come, ye blessed of my Father, inherit the kingdom prepared for you from the foundation of the world."[382] We gathered about Jesus, and just as he closed the gates of the City, the curse was pronounced upon the wicked. The gates were shut. Then the saints used their wings and mounted to the top of the wall of the City.[383] Jesus was also with them; his crown looked brilliant and glorious. It was a crown within a crown, seven in number. The crowns of the saints were of the most pure gold,

35

decked with stars. Their faces shone with glory, for they were in the express image of Jesus; and as they arose, and moved all together to the top of the City, I was enraptured with the sight. {ExV 34.1; Ms. 14, 1850, Sept. 29; PrT, Nov. 1850}

Then the wicked saw what they had lost; and fire was breathed from God upon them, and consumed them. This was the EXECUTION OF THE JUDGMENT. The wicked then received according as the saints in unison with Jesus had meted out to them during the 1000 years. The same fire from God that consumed the wicked, purified the whole earth. The broken ragged mountains melted with fervent heat, the atmosphere, also, and all the stubble was consumed. Then our inheritance opened before us, glorious and beautiful, and we inherited the whole earth made new. We all shouted with a loud voice, Glory, Alleluia.[384] {ExV 35.1; Ms. 14, 1850, Sept. 29; PrT, Nov. 1850}

V20. *Fifty Texts Vision, 1845*

TEXTS OF SCRIPTURE
REFERRED TO ON PAGE 8.[385]

[1.] And behold, thou shalt be dumb, and not able to speak, until the day that these things shall be performed, because thou believest not my words, which shall be fulfilled in their season. Luke i, 20. {ExV 35.2}

[2.] All things that the Father hath, are mine: therefore said I, that he shall take of mine, and shall shew it unto you. John xvi, 15. {ExV 35.3}

[3.] And they were all filled with the Holy Ghost, and began to speak with other tongues, as the Spirit gave them utterance. Acts ii, 4. {ExV 35.4}

[4.] And now, Lord, behold their threatenings, and grant unto thy servants that with all boldness they may speak thy word, {ExV 35.5}

By stretching forth thy hand to heal; and that signs and wonders may be done by the name of thy holy child Jesus. {ExV 35.6}

[5.] And when they had prayed, the place was shaken where they were assembled together; and they were all filled with the Holy Ghost: and they spake the word of God with boldness. Acts iv, 29–31. {ExV 35.7}

[6.] Give not that which is holy unto the dogs, neither cast ye your pearls before swine, lest they trample them under their feet, and turn again and rend you. {ExV 35.8}

36

[7.] Ask, and it shall be given you; seek, and ye shall find; knock, and it shall be opened unto you; {ExV 36.1}

For every one that asketh, receiveth; and he that seeketh, findeth; and to him that knocketh, it shall be opened. {ExV 36.2}

Or what man is there of you, whom if his son ask bread, will he give him a stone? {ExV 36.3}

Or if he ask a fish, will he give him a serpent? {ExV 36.4}

If ye then, being evil, know how to give good gifts unto your children, how much more shall your Father which is in heaven give good things to them that ask him? {ExV 36.5}

Therefore all things whatsoever ye would that men should do to you, do ye even so to them; for this is the law and the prophets. {ExV 36.6}

[8.] Beware of false prophets, which come to you in sheep's clothing, but inwardly they are ravening wolves. Matt. vii, 6–12, 15. {ExV 36.7}

[9.] For there shall arise false Christs, and false prophets, and shall shew great signs and wonders; insomuch that, if it were possible, they shall deceive the very elect. Mat. xxiv, 24. {ExV 36.8}

[10.] As ye have therefore received Christ Jesus the Lord, so walk ye in him; {ExV 36.9}

Rooted and built up in him, and established in the faith, as ye have been taught, abounding therein with thanksgiving. {ExV 36.10}

[11.] Beware lest any man spoil you through philosophy and vain deceit, after the tradition of men, after the rudiments of the world, and not after Christ. Col. ii, 6–8. {ExV 36.11}

[12.] Cast not away therefore your confidence, which hath great recompence of reward. {ExV 36.12}

For ye have need of patience, that, after ye have done the will of God, ye might receive the promise. {ExV 36.13}

For yet a little while, and he that shall come will come, and will not tarry. {ExV 36.14}

[13.] Now the just shall live by faith: but if any man draw back, my soul shall have no pleasure in him. {ExV 36.15}

But we are not of them who draw back unto perdition, but of them that believe to the saving of the soul. Heb. x, 35–39. {ExV 36.16}

[14.] For he that is entered into his rest, he also hath ceased from his own works, as God did from his. {ExV 36.17}

Let us labor therefore to enter into that rest, lest any man fall after the same example of unbelief. {ExV 36.18}

[15.] For the word of God is quick, and powerful, and sharper than any two-edged sword, piercing even to the dividing asunder of soul and spirit, and of the joints and marrow, and

37

is a discerner of the thoughts and intents of the heart. Heb. iv, 10–12. {ExV 36.19}

[16.] Being confident of this very thing, that he which hath begun a good work in you, will perform it until the day of Jesus Christ: {ExV 37.1}

[17.] Only let your conversation be as it becometh the gospel of Christ; that, whether I come and see you, or else be absent, I may hear of your affairs, that ye stand fast in one spirit, with one mind, striving together for the faith of the gospel; {ExV 37.2}

And in nothing terrified by your adversaries; which is to them an evident token of perdition, but to you of salvation, and that of God. {ExV 37.3}

For unto you it is given in the behalf of Christ, not only to believe on him, but also to suffer for his sake. Phil. i, 6, 27–29. {ExV 37.4}

[18.] For it is God which worketh in you, both to will and to do of his good pleasure. {ExV 37.5}

Do all things without murmurings and disputings, {ExV 37.6}

That ye may be blameless and harmless, the sons of God without rebuke, in the midst of a crooked and perverse nation, among whom ye shine as lights in the world. Phil. ii, 13–15. {ExV 37.7}

[19.] Finally, my brethren, be strong in the Lord, and in the power of his might. {ExV 37.8}

Put on the whole armor of God, that ye may be able to stand against the wiles of the devil. {ExV 37.9}

For we wrestle not against flesh and blood, but against principalities, against powers, against the rulers of the darkness of this world, against spiritual wickedness in high places. {ExV 37.10}

Wherefore take unto you the whole armor of God, that ye may be able to withstand in the evil day, and having done all, to stand. {ExV 37.11}

[20.] Stand therefore, having your loins girt about with truth, and having on the breast-plate of righteousness; {ExV 37.12}

And your feet shod with the preparation of the gospel of peace; {ExV 37.13}

Above all, taking the shield of faith, wherewith ye shall be able to quench all the fiery darts of the wicked. {ExV 37.14}

And take the helmet of salvation, and the sword of the Spirit, which is the word of God. {ExV 37.15}

Praying always with all prayer and supplication in the Spirit, and watching thereunto with all perseverance and supplication for all saints. Eph. vi, 10–18. {ExV 37.16}

[21.] And be ye kind one to another, tender-hearted, forgiving

38

one another, even as God for Christ's sake hath forgiven you. **Eph. iv, 32.** {ExV 37.17}

[22.] Seeing ye have purified your souls in obeying the truth through the Spirit unto unfeigned love of the brethren, see that ye love one another with a pure heart fervently. **1 Pet. i, 22.** {ExV 38.1}

[23.] A new commandment I give unto you, that ye love one another; as I have loved you, that ye also love one another. {ExV 38.2}

By this shall all men know that ye are my disciples, if ye have love one to another. **John xiii, 34, 35.** {ExV 38.3}

[24.] Examine yourselves, whether ye be in the faith; prove your own selves: know ye not your own selves, how that Jesus Christ is in you, except ye be reprobates? **2 Cor. xiii, 5.** {ExV 38.4}

[25.] According to the grace of God which is given unto me, as a wise master-builder I have laid the foundation, and another buildeth thereon. But let every man take heed how he buildeth thereupon: {ExV 38.5}

For other foundation can no man lay than that is laid, which is Jesus Christ. {ExV 38.6}

[26.] Now if any man build upon this foundation, gold, silver, precious stones, wood, hay, stubble; {ExV 38.7}

Every man's work shall be made manifest: for the day shall declare it, because it shall be revealed by fire: and the fire shall try every man's work, of what sort it is. **1 Cor. iii, 10–13.** {ExV 38.8}

[27.] Take heed, therefore, unto yourselves, and to all the flock over the which the Holy Ghost hath made you overseers, to feed the church of God, which he hath purchased with his own blood. {ExV 38.9}

For I know this, that after my departing, shall grievous wolves enter in among you, not sparing the flock. {ExV 38.10}

Also of your own selves shall men arise, speaking perverse things, to draw away disciples after them. **Acts xx, 28–30.** {ExV 38.11}

[28.] I marvel that ye are so soon removed from him that called you into the grace of Christ, unto another gospel: {ExV 38.12}

Which is not another: but there be some that trouble you, and would pervert the gospel of Christ. {ExV 38.13}

But though we, or an angel from heaven, preach any other gospel unto you than that which we have preached unto you, let him be accursed. {ExV 38.14}

As we said before, so say I now again, If any man preach any other gospel unto you than that ye have received, let him be accursed. **Gal. i, 6–9.** {ExV 38.15}

[29.] Therefore, whatsoever ye have spoken in darkness, shall

39

be heard in the light; and that which ye have spoken in the ear, in closets, shall be proclaimed upon the house-tops. {ExV 38.16}

And I say unto you, my friends, Be not afraid of them that kill the body, and after that have no more that they can do: {ExV 39.1}

But I will forewarn you whom ye shall fear: fear him, which, after he hath killed, hath power to cast into hell; yea, I say unto you, fear him. {ExV 39.2}

Are not five sparrows sold for two farthings? and not one of them is forgotten before God. {ExV 39.3}

But even the very hairs of your head are all numbered. Fear not, therefore; ye are of more value than many sparrows. **Luke xii, 3–7.** {ExV 39.4}

[30.] For it is written, He shall give his angels charge over thee, to keep thee; {ExV 39.5}

And in their hands they shall bear thee up, lest at any time thou dash thy foot against a stone. **Luke iv, 10, 11.** {ExV 39.6}

[31.] For God, who commanded the light to shine out of darkness, hath shined in our hearts, to give the light of the knowledge of the glory of God in the face of Jesus Christ. {ExV 39.7}

But we have this treasure in earthen vessels, that the excellency of the power may be of God, and not of us. {ExV 39.8}

We are troubled on every side, yet not distressed; we are perplexed, but not in despair; {ExV 39.9}

Persecuted, but not forsaken; cast down, but not destroyed. **2 Cor. iv, 6–9.** {ExV 39.10}

[32.] For our light affliction, which is but for a moment, worketh for us a far more exceeding and eternal weight of glory; {ExV 39.11}

While we look not at the things which are seen, but at the things which are not seen: for the things which are seen are temporal, but the things which are not seen are eternal. **Verses 17, 18.** {ExV 39.12}

[33.] Who are kept by the power of God through faith unto salvation, ready to be revealed in the last time. {ExV 39.13}

Wherein ye greatly rejoice, though now, for a season, if need be, ye are in heaviness through manifold temptations: {ExV 39.14}

That the trial of your faith, being much more precious than of gold that perisheth, though it be tried with fire, might be found unto praise and honor and glory at the appearing of Jesus Christ. **1 Pet. i, 5–7.** {ExV 39.15}

[34.] For now we live, if ye stand fast in the Lord. **1 Thess. iii, 8.** {ExV 39.16}

[35.] And these signs shall follow them that believe; in my

40

name shall they cast out devils; they shall speak with new tongues; {ExV 39.17}

They shall take up serpents; and if they drink any deadly thing, it shall not hurt them; they shall lay hands on the sick, and they shall recover. **Mark xvi, 17, 18.** {ExV 40.1}

[36.] His parents answered them, and said, We know that this is our son, and that he was born blind: {ExV 40.2}

But by what means he now seeth, we know not; or who hath opened his eyes, we know not: he is of age; ask him: he shall speak for himself. {ExV 40.3}

These words spake his parents, because they feared the Jews: for the Jews had agreed already, that if any man did confess that he was Christ, he should be put out of the synagogue. {ExV 40.4}

Therefore said his parents, He is of age, ask him. {ExV 40.5}

Then again called they the man that was blind, and said unto him, Give God the praise: we know that this man is a sinner. {ExV 40.6}

He answered and said, Whether he be a sinner or no, I know not: one thing I know, that whereas I was blind, now I see. {ExV 40.7}

Then said they to him again, What did he to thee? how opened he thine eyes? {ExV 40.8}

He answered them, I have told you already, and ye did not hear; wherefore would ye hear it again? will ye also be his disciples? **John ix, 20–27.** {ExV 40.9}

[37.] And whatsoever ye shall ask in my name, that will I do, that the Father may be glorified in the Son. {ExV 40.10}

If ye shall ask any thing in my name, I will do it. {ExV 40.11}

If ye love me, keep my commandments. **Chap. xiv, 13–15.** {ExV 40.12}

[38.] If ye abide in me, and my words abide in you, ye shall ask what ye will, and it shall be done unto you. {ExV 40.13}

Herein is my Father glorified, that ye bear much fruit; so shall ye be my disciples. **Chap. xv, 7, 8.** {ExV 40.14}

[39.] And there was in their synagogue a man with an unclean spirit; and he cried out, {ExV 40.15}

Saying, Let us alone; what have we to do with thee, thou Jesus of Nazareth? art thou come to destroy us? I know thee who thou art, the Holy One of God. {ExV 40.16}

And Jesus rebuked him, saying, Hold thy peace, and come out of him. **Mark i, 23–25.** {ExV 40.17}

[40.] For I am persuaded, that neither death, nor life, nor angels,

41

nor principalities, nor powers, nor things present, nor things to come, {ExV 40.18}

Nor height, nor depth, nor any other creature, shall be able to separate us from the love of God which is in Christ Jesus our Lord. **Rom. viii, 38, 39.** {ExV 41.1}

[41.] And to the angel of the church in Philadelphia write; These things saith he that is holy, he that is true, he that hath the key of David, he that openeth, and no man shutteth; and shutteth, and no man openeth; {ExV 41.2}

I know thy works: behold, I have set before thee an open door, and no man can shut it; for thou hast a little strength, and hast kept my word, and hast not denied my name. {ExV 41.3}

Behold, I will make them of the synagogue of Satan, which say they are Jews, and are not, but do lie; behold, I will make them to come and worship before thy feet, and to know that I have loved thee. {ExV 41.4}

Because thou hast kept the word of my patience, I also will keep thee from the hour of temptation, which shall come upon all the world, to try them that dwell upon the earth. {ExV 41.5}

Behold I come quickly: hold that fast which thou hast, that no man take thy crown. {ExV 41.6}

Him that overcometh will I make a pillar in the temple of my God, and he shall go no more out: and I will write upon him the name of my God, and the name of the city of my God, which is New Jerusalem, which cometh down out of heaven from my God: and I will write upon him my new name. {ExV 41.7}

He that hath an ear, let him hear what the Spirit saith unto the churches. Rev. iii, 7–13. {ExV 41.8}

[42.] These are they which were not defiled with women; for they are virgins: these are they which follow the Lamb whithersoever he goeth. These were redeemed from among men, being the first-fruits unto God and to the Lamb. {ExV 41.9}

And in their mouth was found no guile; for they are without fault before the throne of God. Rev. xiv, 4, 5. {ExV 41.10}

[43.] For our conversation is in heaven; from whence also we look for the Saviour, the Lord Jesus Christ. Phil. iii, 20. {ExV 41.11}

[44.] Be patient therefore, brethren, unto the coming of the Lord. Behold, the husbandman waiteth for the precious fruit of the earth, and hath long patience for it, until he receive the early and latter rain. {ExV 41.12}

Be ye also patient; stablish your hearts; for the coming of the Lord draweth nigh. James v, 7, 8. {ExV 41.13}

42

[45.] Who shall change our vile body, that it may be fashioned like unto his glorious body, according to the working whereby he is able even to subdue all things unto himself. Phil. iii, 21. {ExV 42.1}

[46.] And I looked, and behold a white cloud, and upon the cloud one sat like unto the Son of man, having on his head a golden crown, and in his hand a sharp sickle. {ExV 42.2}

And another angel came out of the temple, crying with a loud voice to him that sat on the cloud, Thrust in thy sickle and reap, for the time is come for thee to reap; for the harvest of the earth is ripe. {ExV 42.3}

And he that sat on the cloud thrust in his sickle on the earth, and the earth was reaped. {ExV 42.4}

And another angel came out of the temple which is in heaven, he also having a sharp sickle. Rev. xiv, 14–17. {ExV 42.5}

[47.] There remaineth therefore a rest to the people of God. Heb. iv, 9. {ExV 42.6}

[48.] And I John saw the holy city, new Jerusalem, coming down from God out of heaven, prepared as a bride adorned for her husband. Rev. xxi, 2. {ExV 42.7}

[49.] And I looked, and lo, a Lamb stood on the mount Sion, and with him an hundred forty and four thousand, having his Father's name written in their foreheads. Chap. xiv, 1. {ExV 42.8}

[50.] And he shewed me a pure river of water of life, clear as crystal, proceeding out of the throne of God and of the Lamb {ExV 42.9}

In the midst of the street of it, and on either side of the river, was there the tree of life, which bare twelve manner of fruits, and yielded her fruit every month; and the leaves of the tree were for the healing of the nations. {ExV 42.10}

And there shall be no more curse: but the throne of God and of the Lamb shall be in it; and his servants shall serve him. {ExV 42.11}

And they shall see his face; and his name shall be in their foreheads. {ExV 42.12}

And there shall be no night there: and they need no candle, neither light of the sun: for the Lord God giveth them light: and they shall reign for ever and ever. Chap. xxii, 1–5. {ExV 42.13}

43

A View of Events Occurring at the End of the 2300 Days.

V5. Bridegroom Vision, Feb. 1845

I saw a throne, and on it sat the Father and the Son. I gazed on Jesus' countenance and admired his lovely person. The Father's person I could not behold, for a cloud of glorious light covered him. I asked Jesus if his Father had a form like himself. He said he had, but I could not behold it, for said he, if you should once behold the glory of his person you would cease to exist.[386] Before the throne I saw the Advent people, the church and the world. I saw a company bowed down before the throne, deeply interested, while the most of them stood disinterested and careless. Those who were bowed before the throne would offer up their prayers and look to Jesus; then he would look to his Father, and appeared to be pleading with him. A light would come from the Father to the Son, and from the Son to the praying company. Then I saw an exceeding bright light come from the Father to the Son, and from the Son it waved over the people before the throne. But few would receive this great light; many came out from under it and immediately resisted it; others were careless and did not cherish the light, and it moved off from them. Some cherished it, and went and bowed down with the little praying company. This company all received the light, and rejoiced in it, as their countenances shone with its glory. And I saw the Father rise from the throne, and in a flaming chariot go into the Holy of Holies, within the vail, and did sit. Then Jesus rose up from the throne, and the most of those who were bowed down arose with him: and I did not see one ray of light pass from Jesus to the careless multitude after he arose, and they were left in perfect darkness. Those who rose up when Jesus did, kept their eyes fixed on him as he left the throne and led them out a little way. Then he raised his right arm and we heard his lovely

44

voice saying, "Wait here—I am going to my Father to receive the kingdom; keep your garments spotless, and in a little while I will return from the wedding and receive you to myself."[387] And I saw a cloudy chariot, with wheels like flaming fire, and angels were all around it as it came where Jesus was.[388] He stepped into the chariot and was borne to the Holiest where the Father sat.[389] There I beheld Jesus, standing before the Father, a great High Priest.[390] On the hem of his garment was a bell and a pomegranate, a bell and a pomegranate.[391] And I saw those who rose up with Jesus send up their faith to him in the Holiest, and pray—my Father give us thy Spirit.[392] Then Jesus would breathe upon them the Holy Ghost.[393] In the breath was light, power, and much love, joy and peace. Then I turned to look at the company who were still bowed before the throne; they did not know that Jesus had left it. Satan appeared to be by the throne, trying to carry on the work of God. I saw them look up to the throne and pray, Father give us thy Spirit; then

Satan would breathe upon them an unholy influence; in it there was light and much power, but no sweet love, joy and peace. Satan's object was to keep them deceived, and to draw back and deceive God's children.[394] {ExV 43.1; Broadside1; DS, March 14, 1846; Lt. 1, 1846, Feb. 15}

Duty in View of the Time of Trouble.

V61. Duty in View of the Time of Trouble Vision, Jan. 18, 1849

The Lord has shown me repeatedly, that it is contrary to the Bible to make any provision for our temporal wants in the time of trouble.[395] I saw that if the saints had food laid up by them, or in the fields, in the time of trouble, when sword, famine and pestilence are in the land, it would be taken from them by violent hands, and strangers would reap their fields. Then will be the time for us to trust wholly in God, and he will sustain us. I saw that our bread and water would be sure at that time, and we should not lack or suffer hunger; for God was able to spread a table for us in the wilderness. And if necessary, he

45

would send ravens to feed us as he did to feed Elijah, or rain manna from heaven, as he did for the Israelites. {ExV 44.1; Broadside2; JW to the Hastings, Jan. 25, 1849; Ms. 3, 1849, Jan. 18}

I saw that houses and lands would be of no use to the saints in the time of trouble, for they would then have to flee from their possessions, before infuriated mobs, and at that time they could not be disposed of to advance the cause of present truth.[396] I was shown that it was the will of God that the saints should cut loose from every encumbrance before the time of trouble comes, and make a covenant with God by sacrifice. If they have their property on the altar, and earnestly inquire of God for duty, he will teach them when to dispose of these things. Then they will be free in the time of trouble, and have no clogs to weigh them down. {ExV 45.1; Broadside2; JW to the Hastings, Jan. 25, 1849; Ms. 3, 1849}

V97. Sutton Vision, Sept. 26-29, 1850

I saw if any held on to their property, and did not inquire duty of the Lord, he would not make duty known, and they would be permitted to keep their property, and then in the time of trouble it would come up before them like a mountain to crush them, and they would try to dispose of it, but would not be able. I heard some mourn like this: "The cause was languishing, God's people were starving for the truth, and we made no effort to supply the lack, and now our property is useless. Oh! that we had let it go, and laid up treasure in heaven." I saw a *sacrifice* did not increase, but decrease, and was *consumed*.[397] I also saw that God had not required all of his people to dispose of their property at the same time, but in a time of need he would teach them, if they desired to be taught, when to sell and how much to sell, and that some had been required to dispose of their property in time past to sustain the Advent cause, while he permitted others to keep theirs until a time of need. Then as the cause needs it, their duty is to sell. {ExV 45.2; Broadside2; JW to the Hastings, Jan. 25, 1849; Ms. 3, 1849}

I saw that the message "sell that ye have and give alms," had not been given, by some, in its clear light, and that the object of the words of our Saviour

46

had not been clearly presented.[398] I saw that the object of selling was not to give to those who are able to labor and support themselves, but to spread the truth. It is a sin to support and indulge in idleness, those who are able to labor. Some have been zealous to attend all the meetings; not to glorify God, but for the "loaves and fishes." Such had much better been at home laboring with their hands, "the thing that is good," to supply the wants of their families, and to have something to give to sustain the precious cause of present truth.[399] {ExV 45.3; PrT, Nov. 1850; cf. Ms. 14, 1850, Sept. 29}

Now is the time to lay up treasure in heaven, and to set our hearts in order, ready for the time of trouble. Those only who have clean hands and a pure heart will stand that trying time.[400] Now is the time for the law of God to be in our minds (foreheads,) and written in our hearts. The Lord has shown me the danger of letting our minds be filled with worldly thoughts and cares. I saw that some minds were led away from present truth and a love of the Holy Bible, by reading other exciting books; and others were filled with perplexity and care for what they shall eat, drink and wear. I saw some, looking too far off for the coming of the Lord.[401] Time has continued on a few years longer than they expected, therefore they think it may continue a few years more, and in this way their minds are being led from present truth, out after the world. In these things I saw great danger; for if the mind is filled with other things, present truth is shut out, and there is no place in our foreheads for the seal of the living God.[402] I saw that the time for Jesus to be in the Most Holy Place was nearly finished, and that time cannot last but a very little longer; and what leisure time we have should be spent in searching the Bible, which is to judge us in the last day. {ExV 46.1; Broadside2}

My dear brethren and sisters—Let the commandments of God, and the testimony of Jesus Christ be in your minds continually, and let them crowd worldly

47

thoughts and cares from the mind.[403] When you lie down and when you rise up let them be your meditation. Live and act wholly in reference to the coming of the Son of man.[404] The sealing time is very short, and soon will be over. Now is the time to make our calling and election sure, while the four angels are holding the four winds.[405] {ExV 46.2; Broadside2}

Mysterious Rapping.

V95. Mysterious Rapping Vision, Aug. 24, 1850

August 24th, 1850. I saw that the *mysterious rapping* was the power of Satan; some of it was directly from him, and some indirectly, through his agents; but it all proceeded from Satan.[406] It was his work that he accomplished in different ways; yet many in the churches and the world were so enveloped in gross darkness that they thought, and held forth that it was the power of God. {ExV 47.1; Ms. 7 and 7a, 1850}

Said the angel, "Should not a people seek unto their God for the living to the dead? Should the living go to the dead for knowledge? The dead know not any thing. For the living God do ye go to the dead? [See Isa. viii, 19, 20.][407] They have departed from the living God to converse with the dead who know not any thing."[408] {ExV 47.2; Ms. 7 and 7a, 1850}

I saw that soon it would be considered blasphemy to speak against the rapping, and that it would spread more and more, and Satan's power would increase, and some of his devoted followers would have power to work miracles, and even to bring down fire from heaven in the sight of men. I was shown that these modern magicians would yet account for all the miracles wrought by our Lord Jesus Christ by the rapping and mesmerism, and many would believe that all the mighty works of the Son of God, when he was on the earth, were accomplished by this same power.[409] I was pointed back to the time of Moses, and saw the signs and wonders which God wrought through him before Pharaoh, most of which were imitated by the magicians of Egypt; and that just before the

48

final deliverance of the saints God would work powerfully for his people, and these modern magicians would be permitted to imitate the work of God. {ExV 47.3; Ms. 7 and 7a, 1850}

That time I saw would soon come, and we shall have to keep hold of the strong arm of Jehovah; for all these great signs and mighty wonders of the Devil were designed to deceive God's people and overthrow them. Our minds must be staid upon God, and we must not fear the fear of the wicked, that is, fear what they fear, and reverence what they reverence, but be bold and valiant for the truth.[410] {ExV 48.1; Ms. 7 and 7a, 1850}

Could our eyes be opened we should see forms of evil angels around us, trying to invent some new way to annoy and destroy us. And we should also see the angels of God guarding us from their power; for God's watchful eye is over Israel for good, and he will protect and save his people, if they put their trust in him.[411] And when the enemy shall come in like a flood, the Spirit of the Lord will lift up a standard against him.[412] {ExV 48.2; Ms. 7 and 7a, 1850}

Said the angel, "Remember, thou art on the enchanted ground." I saw that we must watch and have on the whole armor, and take the shield of faith, and then we should be able to stand, and the fiery darts of the wicked could not harm us.[413] {ExV 48.3; Ms. 7 and 7a, 1850}

Time not Connected with the Message of the Third Angel, Rev. xiv, 9–12.[414]

V106. *Time Never Again a Test Vision, June 21, 1851*

The Lord has shown me that the message of the third angel must go, and be proclaimed to the scattered children of the Lord, and that it should not be hung on time; for time never will be a test again. I saw that some were getting a false excitement arising from preaching time; that the third angel's message was stronger than time can be. I saw that this message can stand on

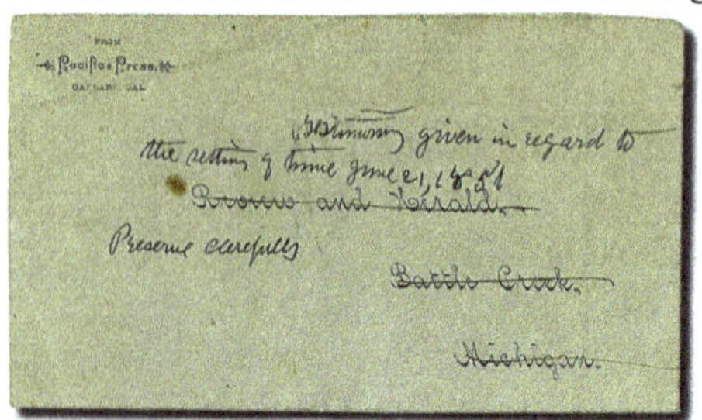

Envelope marked by Ellen White "Testimony given in regard to the setting of time June 21, 1851 Preserve carefully"

its own foundation, and that it needs not time to strengthen it, and that it will go in mighty power, and do its work, and will be cut short in righteousness. {ExV 48.4; RH, July 21, 1851; Ms. 1, 1851, June 21}

49

The Messengers.[415]

V97. Sutton Vision, Sep. 26-29, 1850

The Lord has often given me a view of the situation and wants of the scattered jewels who have not yet come to the light of the present truth, and that the messengers should speed their way to them as fast as possible, to give them the light.[416] Many, all around us, only need to have their prejudices removed, and the evidences of our present position spread out before them from the Word, and they will joyfully receive the present truth. The messengers should watch for souls as they that must give account.[417] I have seen that theirs must be a life of toil, and anguish of spirit, while the weight of the precious, but often-wounded cause of Christ rests upon them. They will have to lay aside worldly interests and comforts, and make it their first object to do all in their power to advance the cause of truth, and save perishing souls. {ExV 49.1}

They will also have a rich reward. In their crowns of rejoicing, those rescued by them and finally saved, will shine as stars for ever and ever.[418] And to all eternity they will enjoy the satisfaction of having done what they could in presenting the truth in its purity and beauty, so that souls fell in love with it, were sanctified through it, and availed themselves of the inestimable privilege of being made rich, and being washed in the blood of the Lamb, and redeemed unto God.[419] {ExV 49.2}

I saw that the shepherds should consult those in whom they have reason to have confidence, those who have been in all the messages, and are firm in all the present truth, before they advocate new points of importance, which they may think the Bible sustains.[420] Then the shepherds will be perfectly united, and the union of the shepherds will be felt by the church. Such a course I saw would prevent unhappy divisions, and then there would be no danger of the precious flock being divided, and the sheep scattered, without a shepherd. {ExV 49.3; Ms. 14, 1850, Sept. 29; PrT, Nov. 1850}

50

I also saw that God had messengers that he would use in his cause, but they were not ready. They were too light and trifling to exert a good influence over the flock, and did not feel the weight of the cause, and the worth of souls as God's messengers must feel in order to effect good. Said the angel, "*Be ye clean that bear the vessels of the Lord, Be ye clean that bear the vessels of the Lord.*"[421] They can accomplish but little good, unless they are wholly given up to God, and feel the importance and solemnity of the last message of mercy, that is now being given to the scattered flock. {ExV 50.1}

Some, that are not called of God, are very willing to go with the message. But if they felt the weight of the cause, and the responsibilities of such a station, they would feel to shrink back, and say with the Apostle, "Who is sufficient for these things?"[422] One reason why they are so willing to go is because God has not laid upon them the weight of the cause. {ExV 50.2}

Not every one that proclaimed the first and second angel's messages are to give the third, even after they fully embrace it, for some have been in many errors and delusions, (and they must have moved wrong in the first place, or God would not have given them up to such errors,) that they can but just save their own souls, and if they undertake to guide others, they will be the means of overthrowing them. But I saw that some who have formerly run deep into fanaticism would be the first now to run before God sends them, before they are purified from their past errors, and would have error mixed with the truth, and would feed the flock of God with it, and if suffered to go on, the flock would become sickly; and distraction and death would follow.[423] I saw that they would have to be sifted and sifted, until they were freed from all their errors, or they never could enter the kingdom. I saw that the messengers could not have that confidence in the judgment and discernment of those who have been in errors and

51

fanaticism, that they could in those who have been in the truth, and have not been into extravagant errors. Many, also, are too apt to urge out into the field some who have but just confessed the present truth, and have much to learn and much to do before they can be right in the sight of God themselves, instead of pointing out the way to others.[424] {ExV 50.3}

I saw the necessity of the messengers, especially, watching, and checking all fanaticism wherever they might see it arise. Satan is pressing in on every side, and unless we watch for him, and have our eyes open to his devises and snares, and have on the whole armor of God, the fiery darts of the wicked will hit us.[425] There are many precious truths, contained in the word of God, but it is "present truth" that the flock needs now.[426] I have seen the danger of the messengers running off from the important points of present truth, to dwell upon subjects that are not calculated to unite the flock, and sanctify the soul.[427] Satan will here take every possible advantage to injure the cause. {ExV 51.1}

But such subjects as the Sanctuary, in connection with the 2300 days, the commandments of God, and the faith of Jesus, are perfectly calculated to explain the past Advent movement, show what is our present position, and establish the faith of the doubting, and give certainty to the glorious future.[428] These, I have frequently seen, were the principal subjects on which the messengers should dwell. {ExV 51.2}

I saw that if the chosen messengers of the Lord waited for every obstacle to be moved out of their way, many never would go to search for the scattered sheep. Satan will present many objections in their way, to keep them from duty. But they will have to go out by faith, trusting in Him who has called them to his work, and the Lord will open their way before them, as far as it will be for their good and his glory. Jesus, the great teacher and pattern, had not where to lay his head.[429] His life was one of

52

toil, sorrow, and suffering; he then gave himself for us. Those who, in Christ's stead, beseech souls to be reconciled to God, and who hope to reign with Christ in glory, must expect to be partakers of his sufferings here. "They that sow in tears shall reap in joy. He that goeth forth and weepeth, bearing precious seed, shall doubtless come again with rejoicing, bringing his sheaves with him." Ps. cxxvi, 5, 6. {ExV 51.3}

A view given me June 27th.

V91. *Mark of the Beast Vision, June 27, 1850*

Said my accompanying angel, "Time is almost finished. Do ye reflect the lovely image of Jesus as ye should?" Then I was pointed to the earth, and saw that there would have to be a getting ready among those who have of late embraced the third angel's message. Said the angel, "Get ready, get ready, get ready. Ye will have to die a greater death to the world than ye have ever yet died." I saw that there was a great work to do for them, and but little time to do it in. {ExV 52.1; cf. Ms. 14, 1850, Sept. 29}

Then I saw that the seven last plagues were soon to be poured out upon those who have no shelter, yet the world regard them no more than they would so many drops of water that were about to fall. Then I was made capable to endure the awful sight of the seven last plagues, the wrath of God.[430] I saw that his anger was dreadful and terrible, and if he should stretch forth his hand, or lift it in anger, the inhabitants of the world would be as though they never had been, or would suffer the incurable sores and withering plagues that would come upon them, and they would find no deliverance, but be destroyed by them. {ExV 52.2}

Terror seized me, and I fell upon my face before the angel, and begged of him to cause the sight to be removed, to hide it from me, for the sight was too dreadful. Then I realized, as never before, the importance of searching the word of God carefully, to know

53

how to escape the plagues that are declared in that word shall come on all the ungodly who shall worship the beast and his image, and receive his mark in their foreheads or hands.[431] It was a great wonder to me that any one could transgress the law of God, and tread down his Holy Sabbath, when such awful threatenings and denunciations were against them. {ExV 52.3}

The Pope has changed the day of rest from the seventh to the first day, and has thought to change the very commandment that was given to cause man to remember his Creator, so that the nations might not forget God.[432] He has thought to change the greatest commandment in the decalogue, and thus make himself equal with God, or even exalt himself above God. I saw that God is unchangeable, therefore his law is immutable; but the Pope had exalted himself above God, in seeking to change his immutable precepts of holiness, justice and goodness. He has trampled under foot God's Sanctified Day, and put in its place one of the six laboring days, on his own authority. And the whole nation has

> **32]** They also refer to the example of the apostles, who commanded Christians not to eat blood and animals that had been strangled (Acts 15:29). **33]** They say that the Sabbath Day was changed into the Lord's Day, although this seems to be contrary to the Ten Commandments. There is no example they make so much of as this changing of the Sabbath Day. The power of the church is very great, they say, since it has done away with one of the Ten Commandments!

The Augsburg Confession about the papacy's claim of the change of the Sabbath

followed after the beast, and every week they "rob God" of his Holy Time. The Pope has made a breach in the holy law of God, but I saw that the time had fully come for this breach to be made up by the people of God, and the waste places built up.[433] {ExV 53.1}

I plead before the angel that God would save his people who had gone astray, to save them for his mercy's sake. I saw that those who continued to break the Holy Sabbath, when the plagues begin to fall, will not open their mouths to plead those excuses that they now make to get rid of it. Their mouths will be closed while the plagues are falling, and the great Law-giver is requiring justice of those who have had his holy law in derision, and have called it "a curse to man," "miserable," "rickety," etc. And when they feel the iron grasp of this law, taking hold of them, these expressions will appear before them in living characters, and they will then

54

realize the sin of having that law in derision, that the word of God calls, "*holy, just,* and *good*."[434] {ExV 53.2}

Then I was pointed to the glory of heaven, to the treasure laid up for the faithful. Every thing was lovely and glorious. The angels would sing a lovely song, then they would cease singing, and take their crowns from their heads and cast them glittering at the feet of the lovely Jesus, and with melodious voices cry, "Glory, Alleluia." I joined with them in their songs of praise and honor to the Lamb, and every time I opened my mouth to praise him, I felt an unutterable sense of glory that surrounded me. It was a far more, an exceeding and eternal weight of glory.[435] Said the angel, "The little remnant who love God and keep his commandments, and are faithful to the end, will enjoy this glory, and ever be in the presence of Jesus, and sing with the holy angels."[436] {ExV 54.1}

Then my eyes were taken from the glory, and I was pointed to the remnant on the earth. Said the angel to them, "Will ye shun the seven last plagues?[437] Will ye go to glory, and enjoy all that God has prepared for those that love him, and are willing to suffer for his sake?[438] If so, ye must die that ye may live. Get ready, get ready, get ready. Ye must have a greater preparation than ye now have, for the day of the Lord cometh, cruel both with wrath and fierce anger, to lay the land desolate, and to destroy the sinners thereof out of it.[439] Sacrifice all to God. Lay all upon his altar, self, property and all, a living sacrifice. It will take all

to enter glory. Lay up for yourselves treasure in heaven where no thief can approach or rust corrupt. Ye must be partakers of Christ's sufferings here, if ye would be partakers with him of his glory hereafter." {ExV 54.2}

Heaven will be cheap enough, if we obtain it through suffering. We must deny self all along the way, die to self daily, and have Jesus alone appear, and have his glory continually in view. I saw that those who of late have embraced the truth would

55

have to know what it was to suffer for Christ's sake. That they would have trials to pass through that would be keen and cutting, in order that they may be purified, and fitted through suffering to receive the seal of the living God, pass through the time of trouble, and see the King in his beauty, and dwell in the presence of God, and in the society of pure and holy angels.[440] {ExV 54.3}

As I saw what we must be to inherit glory, and then saw how much Jesus had suffered for us to obtain for us so rich an inheritance, I prayed that we might be baptized into Christ's sufferings, that we might not shrink at trials, but bear them with patience and joy, knowing what Jesus had suffered, that we might through his poverty and sufferings be made rich. Said the angel, "Deny self, ye must step fast." I saw that some of us have had time to get the truth, and to advance step by step, and every step we have taken has given us strength to take the next. But now time is almost finished, and what we have been years learning, they will have to learn in a few months. And they will have to unlearn much, and learn again. And those who will not receive the mark of the beast and his image, when the decree goes forth, must have decision *now* to say, *nay*, we will not regard the institution of the beast. {ExV 55.1}

The Blind leading the Blind.[441]

V105. *Holiness of God Vision, May 14, 1851*

I have seen how the blind guides were laboring to make souls as blind as themselves, and they little realize what is coming upon them. They are exalting themselves against the truth, and as the truth triumphs, many who have looked on these teachers as men of God, and have looked to them for light, are troubled. They inquire of these leaders relative to the Sabbath, who, with the object of getting rid of the fourth commandment, will answer them thereto. I saw that real honesty was not regarded in taking the many positions that were taken against the Sabbath.

56

The main object is to get around the Sabbath of the Lord, and observe another day than that sanctified and hallowed by Jehovah.[442] And if they were driven off from one position they would take an opposite one, even a position that they had but just before condemned as unsound. {ExV 55.2; cf. Ms. 5, 1851}

But God's people are coming into the unity of the faith, and those who observe the Sabbath of the Bible are united in their views of Bible truth.[443] But those who oppose the Sabbath among the Advent people are disunited, and strangely divided. One comes forward in opposition to the Sabbath, and declares it to be thus and so, and at the conclusion calls it settled. But as his effort does not put the question to rest, and as the Sabbath cause progresses, and the children of the Lord embrace it still, another comes forward to overthrow it. But in presenting his views to get round the Sabbath, he entirely tears down the arguments of him who made the first effort against the truth, and presents a theory as opposite to his, as to ours. So with the third and the fourth; but none of them will have it as it stands in the word of God. "The seventh day is the Sabbath of the Lord thy God."[444] {ExV 56.1; cf. Ms. 5, 1851}

Such, I saw, have the carnal mind, therefore, are not subject to the holy law of God.[445] They are not agreed among themselves, yet labor hard with their inferences, to wrest the scriptures to make a breach in God's law, to change, abolish, or do anything with the fourth commandment rather than to observe it.[446] They wish to silence the flock upon this question, therefore they get up something with the hope that it will quiet them, and many of their followers search their Bibles so little, that their leaders can easily make error appear like truth, and they receive it as such, not looking higher than their leaders. {ExV 56.2; cf. Ms. 5, 1851}

57

A view given me September 7th.

V96. *Great Work for God's People Vision, Sept. 7, 1850*

At Oswego, (N. Y.), the Lord shewed me that there must be a great work done for his people before they could stand in the battle in the day of the Lord.[447] I was pointed to those who claim to be Adventists, but reject the present truth, and saw that they were crumbling, and that the hand of the Lord was in their midst to divide and scatter them now in the gathering time, so that the precious jewels among them, that have formerly been deceived, may have their eyes opened to see their true state.[448] And now when the truth is presented to them by the Lord's messengers, they will be prepared to listen, and see its beauty and harmony, and leave their former associates, and errors, and embrace the precious truth, and stand where they can define their position. {ExV 57.1}

I saw that those who oppose the Sabbath of the Lord could not take the Bible and show that our position was incorrect, therefore they would slander those who believe and teach the truth, and would attack their characters.[449] And many who were once conscientious, and loved God and his word, have become so hardened by rejecting the light of truth that they will not hesitate to wickedly misrepresent and falsely accuse those who love the Holy Sabbath, if by so doing they can injure the influence of those who fearlessly declare the truth. But these things will not hinder the work of God. In fact, this course pursued by those who hate the truth, will be the very means of opening the eyes of some. Every jewel will be brought out and gathered, for the hand of the Lord is set to recover the remnant of his people, and he will accomplish the work gloriously.[450] {ExV 57.2}

I saw that we who believe the truth should be very careful and give no occasion for our good to be evil spoken of.[451] We should know that every step we take is in accordance with the Bible; for those who hate the commandments of God will triumph over our missteps and faults, as the wicked did in 1843. {ExV 57.3}

58

The Holiness of God.

V105. Holiness of God Vision, May 14, 1851

May 14th, 1851, I saw the beauty and loveliness of Jesus. As I beheld his glory the thought did not occur to me that I should ever be separated from his presence. I saw a light coming from the glory that encircled the Father, and as it approached near to me, my body trembled and shook like a leaf. I thought if it should come near to me I should be struck out of existence; but the light passed me. Then could I have some sense of the great and terrible God that we have to do with.[452] Then I saw what faint views some have of the holiness of God, and how much they take his holy and reverend name in vain, without realizing that it was God, the great and terrible God, they were speaking of. I have seen that many, while praying, used careless and irreverent expressions which grieved the tender Spirit of the Lord and caused their petitions to be shut out of heaven. {ExV 58.1; cf. Ms. 5, 1851}

I also saw that many did not realize what they must be in order to live in the sight of the Lord, without a High Priest in the Sanctuary, through the time of trouble. Those who receive the seal of the living God, and are protected in the time of trouble, must reflect the image of Jesus fully. {ExV 58.2}

I saw that many were neglecting the preparation so needful, and were looking to the time of the "refreshing" and "latter rain" to fit them to stand in the day of the Lord, and to live in his sight.[453] O, how many I saw in the time of trouble without a shelter! They had neglected the needful preparation, therefore they could not receive the refreshing that all must have to fit them to live in the sight of a holy God. Those who refuse to be hewed by the prophets, and do not purify their souls in obeying the whole truth, and are willing to believe that their condition is far better than it really is, will come up to the time of the falling of the plagues, and then see that they needed to be hewed and squared for the building.[454]

59

But there will be no time then to do it; and no Mediator to plead their cause before the Father. Before this time, the awfully solemn declaration has gone forth, "He that is unjust, let him be unjust still; and he which is filthy, let him be filthy still; and he that is righteous, let him be righteous still; and he that is holy, let him be holy still."[455] I saw that none could share the "refreshing," unless they obtain the victory over every besetment, all pride, selfishness, love of the world, and over every wrong word and action. We should, therefore, be drawing nearer and nearer to the Lord, and be earnestly seeking that preparation necessary to enable us to stand in the battle in the day of the Lord.[456] Let all remember that God is holy, and none but holy beings can ever dwell in his presence. {ExV 58.3}

Prayer and Faith.

I have frequently seen that the children of the Lord neglected prayer altogether too much, especially in secret; and that many do not exercise that faith which is their privilege and duty, and often wait for that feeling which faith alone can bring. Feeling is not faith, but the two are distinct. Faith is ours to exercise, but joyful feelings, and the blessing, is God's to give. The grace of God comes to the soul through the channel of living faith, and that faith it is our power to exercise. {ExV 59.1}

True faith lays hold of and claims the promised blessing before it is realized and felt. I have seen that we must send up our petitions in faith within the second vail, and have our faith take hold of the promised blessing, and claim it as ours. And we are then to believe that the blessing is ours, and that we receive it, because our faith has hold of it, and according to the Word it is ours. "What things soever ye desire when ye pray, believe that ye receive them, and ye shall have them."[457] Here is faith, naked faith, to believe that we receive the blessing, even

60

before we realize it. When the promised blessing is realized and enjoyed, faith is swallowed up. But many suppose they have much faith when sharing largely of the Holy Spirit, and that they cannot have faith unless they feel the power of the Spirit. Such confound faith with the blessing that comes through faith. The very time to exercise faith is when we feel destitute of the Spirit. When thick clouds of darkness seem to hover over the mind, then is the time to let living faith pierce the darkness, and scatter the clouds. True faith rests on the promises contained in the word of God, and those only who obey the Word, can claim the glorious promises contained in it. "If ye abide in me, and my words abide in you, ye shall ask what ye will, and it shall be done unto you." John xv, 7. "Whatsoever we ask we receive of him, because we keep his *commandments*, and do those things that are pleasing in his sight." 1 John iii, 22.[458] {ExV 59.2}

I have seen that we should be much in secret prayer.[459] Christ is the Vine, we are the branches.[460] And if we would grow and flourish in the Vine, we must continually draw sap and nourishment from the Living Vine, for without the Vine we have no strength. {ExV 60.1; Lt. 26, 1850, Nov. 1}

V94. Enchanted Ground Vision, July 29, 1850

I asked the angel why there was no more faith and power in Israel.[461] Said he, "Ye let go of the arm of the Lord too soon. Press your petitions to the throne, and hold on by strong faith. The promises are sure. Believe ye receive the things ye ask for, and ye shall have them." I was then pointed to Elijah. He was subject to like passions as we are, and he prayed earnestly. His faith endured the trial. Seven times he prayed before the Lord, and at last the cloud was seen.[462] I saw that we had doubted the sure promises, and wounded the Saviour by our lack of faith. Said the angel, gird the armor about thee, and above all take the shield of faith, for that will guard the heart, the very life from the fiery

61

darts of the wicked.[463] If the Enemy can get the desponding to take their eyes off from Jesus, to look to themselves, to dwell upon their own unworthiness, instead of dwelling upon the worthiness of Jesus, his love, his merits, and his great mercy, he will get away their shield of faith and gain his object, and they will be exposed to his fiery temptations.[464] Therefore, the weak should look to Jesus, and believe that they have faith, then they can exercise faith. {ExV 60.2; cf. Lt. 8, 1850, Aug. 4; Ms. 5, 1850}

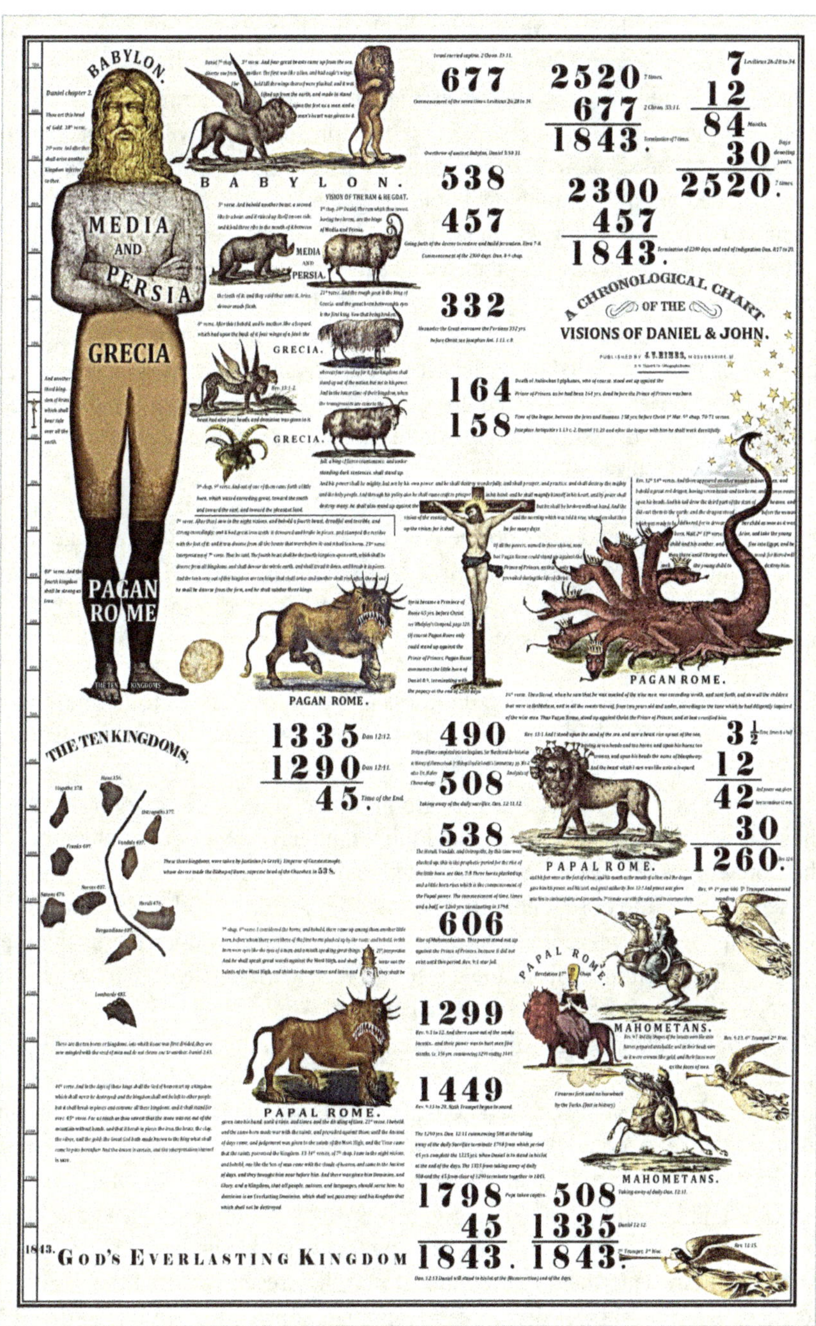

1843 prophecy chart

The Gathering Time.

V98. *Gathering Time Vision, Oct. 23, 1850*

September 23d, the Lord shewed me that he had stretched out his hand the second time to recover the remnant of his people, and that efforts must be redoubled in this gathering time.[465] In the scattering, Israel was smitten and torn; but now in the gathering time God will heal and bind up his people. In the scattering, efforts made to spread the truth had but little effect, accomplished but little or nothing; but in the gathering, when God has set his hand to gather his people, efforts to spread the truth will have their designed effect. All should be united and zealous in the work. I saw that it was wrong for any to refer to the scattering for examples to govern us now in the gathering; for if God does no more for us now than he did then, Israel would never be gathered. I have seen that the 1843 chart was directed by the hand of the Lord, and that it should not be altered; that the figures were as he wanted them. That his hand was over, and hid a mistake in some of the figures, so that none could see it, until his hand was removed.[466] {ExV 61.1; PrT, Nov. 1850; cf. Ms. 15, 1850}

Then I saw in relation to the "DAILY," that the word "SACRIFICE" was supplied by man's wisdom, and does not belong to the text; and that the Lord gave the correct view of it to those who gave the judgment hour cry.[467] When union existed, before 1844, nearly all were united on the correct view of the "DAILY;" but since 1844, in the confusion, other

62

views have been embraced, and darkness and confusion have followed. I have also seen that TIME had not been a test since 1844, and that time will never again be a test.[468] {ExV 61.2; PrT, Nov. 1850; cf. Ms. 15, 1850}

Then I was pointed to some who are in the great error of believing that it is their duty to go to Old Jerusalem, and think they have a work to do there before the Lord comes. Such a view is calculated to take the mind and interest from the present work of the Lord, under the message of the third angel.[469] For those who think that they are yet to go to Jerusalem, will have their minds there, and their means will be withheld from the cause of present truth, to get themselves and others to Jerusalem.[470] I saw that such a mission would accomplish no real good. That it would take a long while to make a very few of the Jews believe even in the first 'Advent of Christ,' much more, to believe in his second Advent. I saw that Satan had greatly deceived some in this thing, and that souls, all around them, in this land, could be helped by them, and led to keep the commandments of God; but they were leaving them to perish.[471] I also saw that Old Jerusalem never would be built up; and that Satan was doing his utmost to lead the minds of the children of the Lord into these things now, in the gathering time, to keep them from throwing their whole interest into the present work of the Lord, and to cause them to neglect the necessary preparation for the day of the Lord.[472] {ExV 62.1; PrT, Nov. 1850; cf. Ms. 15, 1850}

DEAR READER. A sense of duty to my brethren and sisters, and a desire that the blood of souls might not be found on my garments, has governed me in this little work. I am aware of the unbelief that exists in the minds of the multitude relative to visions, also, that many who profess to be looking for Christ, and teach that we are in the "last days," call them all of Satan. I expect much opposition from such, and had I not felt that the Lord required

63

it of me I should not have made my views thus public, which will probably call forth the hatred and derision of some. But I fear God more than man. {ExV 62.2}

Enhanced frontispiece from *The Coming King*, identified in White family tradition as "the most nearly correct" representation of Jesus as seen by Ellen White in vision

V21. *Jesus' Disapproving Frown Vision, 1845*

When the Lord first gave me messages to deliver to his people, it was hard for me to declare them. And I often softened them down, and made them as mild as possible for fear of grieving them. It was a great trial to declare the messages as the Lord gave them to me. I did not realize that I was so unfaithful, and did not see the danger and sin of such a course, until I was taken in vision into the presence of Jesus.[473] He looked upon me with a frown, and turned his face from me. It is not possible to describe the terror and agony I then felt. I fell upon my face before him, but had no power to utter a word. O, how I longed to be covered and hid from that dreadful frown. Then could I realize, in some degree what the feelings of the lost will be, when they cry, "Mountains and rocks, fall on us, and hide us from the face of him that sitteth on the throne, and from the wrath of the Lamb."[474] {ExV 63.1}

Presently an angel bid me rise, and the sight that met my eyes can hardly be described. A company was presented before me whose hair and garments were torn, and whose countenances were the very picture of despair and horror. They came close to me, and took their garments and rubbed them on mine, I looked at my garments, and saw that they were stained with blood, and that blood was eating holes in my garments. Again I fell like one dead, at the feet of my accompanying angel. I could not plead one excuse. My tongue refused all utterance, and I longed to be away from such a holy place. Again the angel stood me up on my feet, and said "This is not your case now, but this scene has passed before you, to let you know what your situation must be, if you neglect to declare to others what the Lord has revealed to you. But if you are faithful to the end, you shall eat of the tree of life, and shall drink

64

of the river of the water of life.[475] You will have to suffer much, but the grace of God is sufficient." I then felt willing to do all that the Lord might require me to do, that I might have his approbation, and not feel his dreadful frown. {ExV 63.2; 1T 74.1, 2}

I have frequently been falsely charged with teaching views peculiar to spiritualism. But, before the editor of the "Day-Star" run into that delusion, the Lord gave me a view of the sad and desolating effects that would be produced upon the flock, by him and others, in teaching the spiritual views. I have often seen the lovely Jesus, that he is a *person*. I asked him if his Father was a person, and had a form like himself. Said Jesus. "I am in the express *image* of my Father's PERSON."[476] {ExV 64.1}

V30. Personhood of God Vision, 1846

I have often seen that the spiritual view took away all the glory of heaven, and that in many minds the throne of David, and the lovely person of Jesus had been burned up in the fire of spiritualism. I have seen that some, who have been deceived, and led into this error, would be brought out into the light of truth, but it would be almost impossible for them to get entirely rid of the deceptive power of spiritualism. Such should make thorough work in confessing their errors, and leaving them forever. {ExV 64.2}

I recommend to you, dear reader, the word of God as the rule of your faith and practice. By that Word we are to be judged. God has, in that Word, promised to give visions in the "LAST DAYS;" not for a new rule of faith, but for the comfort of his people, and to correct those who err from Bible truth.[477] Thus God dealt with Peter when he was about to send him to preach to the Gentiles. Acts x. {ExV 64.3}

Ellen White continually held up the Bible as the standard of Christian faith and practice.

To those who may circulate this little work, I would say, that it is designed for the sincere only, and not for those who would ridicule the things of the Spirit of God.[478] {ExV 64.4}

*"And the **glory** of the LORD shall be revealed, and all flesh shall see it together: for the mouth of the LORD hath spoken it."*[479]

SUPPLEMENT

TO THE

CHRISTIAN EXPERIENCE

AND

VIEWS

OF

ELLEN G. WHITE.

Rochester, N. Y.

PUBLISHED BY JAMES WHITE.

1854.[480]

SUPPLEMENT.

DEAR CHRISTIAN FRIENDS:—As I have given a brief sketch of my experience and views, published in 1851, it seems to be my duty to notice some points in that little work; also, to give more recent views. {ExV54 3.1}

V46. Sabbath Halo Vision, April 3, 1847

1. On page 17, is as follows:—"I saw that the Holy Sabbath is, and will be, the separating wall between the true Israel of God and unbelievers; and that the Sabbath is the great question, to unite the hearts of God's dear, waiting saints. I saw that God had children, who do not see and keep the Sabbath. They had not rejected the light on it. And at the commencement of the time of trouble, we were filled with the Holy Ghost as we went forth and proclaimed the Sabbath more fully."[481] {ExV54 3.2; ExV 17.1, 2; RH, July 21, 1851}

This view was given in 1847, when there were but very few of the Advent brethren observing the Sabbath, and of these, but few supposed that its observance was of sufficient importance to draw a line between the people of God and unbelievers. Now, the fulfillment of that view is beginning to be seen. {ExV54 3.3}

"The commencement of the time of trouble," here mentioned, does not refer to the time when the plagues shall begin to be poured out; but to a short period just before they are poured out, while Christ is in the Sanctuary. At that time, while the work of salvation is closing, trouble will be coming on the earth, the nations will be angry, yet held in check,

4

so as not to prevent the work of the third angel. At that time the "latter rain," or refreshing from the presence of the Lord, will come, to give power to the loud voice of the third angel, and prepare the saints to stand in the period when the seven last plagues shall be poured out.[482] {ExV54 3.4}

V69. Open and Shut Door Vision, March 24, 1849

2. The view of the "Open and Shut Door," on pages 24–27, was given in 1849. The application of Rev. iii, 7, 8, to the Heavenly Sanctuary and Christ's ministry, was entirely new to me. I had never heard the idea advanced by any one. Now, as the subject of the Sanctuary is being clearly understood, the application is seen in its beauty and force. {ExV54 4.1}

3. The "false reformations" referred to on page 27, are yet to be more fully seen. This view relates more particularly to those who have heard and rejected the light of the Advent doctrine.[483] They are given over to strong delusions. Such will not have "the travail of soul for sinners" as formerly. Having rejected the Advent, and being given over to the delusions of Satan, "the time for their salvation is past." This does not, however, relate to those who have not heard and have not rejected the doctrine of the Second Advent. {ExV54 4.2}

4. The view that the Lord "had stretched out his hand the second time to recover the remnant of his people," on page 61, refers only to the union and strength once among those looking for Christ, and that he had begun to unite and raise up his people again.[484] {ExV54 4.3; ExV 61.2}

V98. Gathering Time Vision, Oct. 23, 1850

5. *Spirit Manifestations*. On pages 25, and 26, read as follows:—"I saw that the mysterious knocking in N. Y., and other places, was the power of Satan, and that such things would be more and

V69. *Open and Shut Door Vision, March 1849*

5

more common, clothed in a religious garb, to lull the deceived to more security, and to draw the minds of God's people, if possible, to those things and cause them to doubt the teachings, and power of the Holy Ghost." {ExV54 4.4; ExV 25.5; RH, Aug. 1849; Ms. 1, 1849}

This view was given in 1849, nearly five years since.[485] Then *spirit manifestations* were mostly confined to the city of Rochester, known as the "Rochester knockings." Since that time the heresy has spread beyond the expectations of any one. {ExV54 5.1}

Much of the view on page 47, headed, *Mysterious Rappings*, given August 1850, has since been fulfilled, and is now fulfilling.[486] Here is a portion of it: {ExV54 5.2}

"I saw that soon it would be considered blasphemy to speak against the rapping, and that it would spread more and more, and Satan's power would increase, and some of his devoted followers would have power to work miracles, and even to bring down fire from heaven in the sight of men.[487] I was shown that these modern magicians would yet account for all the miracles wrought by our Lord Jesus Christ by the rapping and mesmerism, and many would believe that all the mighty works of the Son of God, when he was on the earth, were accomplished by this same power." {ExV54 5.3; ExV 47.3; Ms. 7a, 1850}

V95. *Mysterious Rapping Vision, Aug. 24, 1850*

I saw the rapping delusion—what progress it was making, and if it were possible it would deceive the very elect.[488] Satan will have power to bring the appearance of a form before us purporting to be our relatives and friends that now sleep in Jesus. It will be made to appear as though they were present, the words they uttered while here, which we were familiar with, will be spoken, and the same tone of voice, which they had while living, will fall upon the ear.

6

All this is to deceive the saints, and ensnare them into the belief of this delusion.[489] {ExV54 5.4; 1SG 173.1}

I saw that the saints must get a thorough understanding of the present truth, which they will have to maintain from the Scriptures.[490] They must understand the state of the dead; for the spirits of devils will yet appear to them, professing to be beloved friends and relatives, who will declare to them that the Sabbath has been changed, and, also, other unscriptural doctrines. They will do all in their power to excite sympathy, and work miracles before them, to confirm what they declare.[491] The people of God must be prepared to withstand these spirits with the Bible truth, that the dead know not any thing, and that they are the spirits of devils.[492] Our minds must not be taken up with things around us, but must be occupied with the present truth, and a preparation to give a reason of our hope with meekness and fear.[493] We must seek wisdom from on high that we may stand in this day of error and delusion. {ExV54 6.1; 1SG 173.2}

I saw that we must examine well the foundation of our hope, for we shall have to give a reason for it from the scriptures; for we shall see this delusion spreading, and we shall have to contend with it face to face. And unless we are prepared for it, we shall be ensnared and overcome. But if we do what we can on our part to be ready for the conflict that is just before us, God will do his part, and his all-powerful arm will protect us. He would sooner send every angel out of glory to our relief, to make a hedge about faithful souls, rather than they should be deceived and led away by the lying wonders of Satan. {ExV54 6.2; 1SG 174.1}

I saw the rapidity with which this delusion was spreading. A train of cars was shown me, going

7

with the speed of lightning. The angel bade me look carefully. I fixed my eyes upon the train. It seemed that the whole world was on board; that there could not be one left. Said the angel: "They are binding in bundles ready to burn."[494] Then he shewed me the conductor, who looked like a stately fair person, which all the passengers looked up to and reverenced. I was perplexed, and asked my attending angel who it was. Said he, "It is Satan. He is the conductor in the form of an angel of light.[495] He has taken the world captive. They are given over to strong delusions, to believe a lie that they may be damned."[496] This agent, the next highest in order to him, is the engineer, and others of his agents are employed in different offices as he may need them, and they are all going with lightning speed to perdition. They are binding in bundles ready to burn.[497] I asked the angel if there were none left. He bade me look in an opposite direction, and I saw a little company traveling a narrow pathway.[498] All seemed to be firmly united, and bound together by the truth, in bundles, or companies. Said the angel, "The third angel is binding them (sealing them) in bundles for the heavenly garner."[499] {ExV54 6.3; 1SG 174.2}

This little company looked care-worn, as though they had passed through severe trials and conflicts. And it appeared as if the sun had just appeared from behind the cloud, and shone upon their countenances and caused them to look triumphant, as though their victories were nearly won. {ExV54 7.1; 1SG 175.1}

I saw that the Lord had given the world opportunity to discover the snare. This one thing was evidence enough for the Christian if there was no other.

8

There is no difference made between the precious and the vile.[500] {ExV54 7.2; 1SG 175.2}

Thomas Paine, whose body has now mouldered to dust, and who is to be called forth at the end of the 1000 years, at the second resurrection, to receive his reward, and suffer the second death, is purported by satan to be in heaven, and highly exalted there.[501] Satan used him on earth as long as he could, and now he is carrying on the same work through pretensions of having Thomas Paine so much exalted and honored; and as he taught on earth, satan is making it appear that he is teaching in heaven. And some on earth who have looked with horror at his life and death, and his corrupt teachings while living, now submit to be taught by him who was one of the vilest and most corrupt of men; one who despised God and his law.[502] {ExV54 8.1; 1SG 175.3}

He who is the father of lies, blinds and deceives the world by sending his angels forth to speak for the apostles, and make it appear that they contradict what they wrote when on earth, which was dictated by the Holy Ghost.[503] These lying angels make the apostles to corrupt their own teachings and declare them to be adulterated. By so doing he can throw professed Christians, who have a name to live and are dead, and all the world in uncertainty about the word of God; for that cuts directly across his track, and is likely to thwart his plans.[504] Therefore he gets them to doubt the divine origin of the Bible, and then sets up the infidel Thomas Paine, as though he was ushered into heaven when he died, and with the holy apostles whom he hated on earth, is united, and appears to be teaching the world.[505] {ExV54 8.2; 1SG 176.1}

9

Satan assigns each one of his angels their part to act. He enjoins upon them to be cunning, artful and sly. He instructs some of them to act the part of the apostles, and speak for them, while others are to act out infidels and wicked men who died cursing God, but now appear to be very religious. There is no difference made between the most holy apostles and the vilest infidel. They are both made to teach the same thing. It matters not who satan makes to speak, if his object is only accomplished. He was so intimately connected with Paine upon earth, and aided him, that it is an easy thing for him to know the very words he used, and the very hand-writing of one of his devoted children who served him so faithfully, and accomplished his purposes so well. Satan dictated much of his writings, and it is an easy thing for him to dictate sentiments through his angels now, and make it appear that it comes through Thomas Paine, who was his devoted servant while he lived. But this is the master-piece of satan. All this teaching purporting to be from apostles, and saints, and wicked men who have died, comes directly from his satanic majesty. {ExV54 9.1; 1SG 176.2}

This should be enough to remove the vail from every mind and discover unto them the dark, mysterious works of satan;—that he has got one whom he loved so well, and who hated God so perfectly, with the holy apostles and angels in glory: virtually saying to the world and infidels, No matter how wicked you are; no matter whether you believe in God or the Bible, or disbelieve; live as you please, heaven is your home;—for every one knows that if Thomas Paine is in heaven, and so exalted, they will surely get there. This is so glaring that all may see if they will.

Thomas Paine

10

Satan is doing now what he has been trying to do since his fall, through individuals like Thomas Paine. He is, through his power and lying wonders, tearing away the foundation of the Christian's hope, and putting out their sun that is to lighten them in the narrow way to heaven.[506] He is making the world believe that the Bible is no better than a story-book, uninspired, while he holds out something to take its place; namely, *Spiritual Manifestations!* {ExV54 9.2; 1SG 177.1}

Here is a channel wholly devoted to himself, under his control, and he can make the world believe what he will. The Book that is to judge him and his followers, he puts back in the shade, just where he wants it. The Saviour of the world he makes to be no more than a common man; and as the Roman guard that watched the tomb of Jesus, spread the false and lying report that the chief priests and elders put in their mouth, so will the poor, deluded followers of these pretended spiritual manifestations, repeat, and try to make it appear that there is nothing miraculous about our Saviour's birth, death and resurrection; and they put Jesus back, with the Bible, in the shade, where they want him, and then get the world looking to them and their lying wonders and miracles, which they declare far exceed the works of Christ.[507] {ExV54 10.1; 1SG 178.1}

Thus the world is taken in the snare, and lulled to security; not to find out their awful deception, until the seven last plagues are poured out. Satan laughs as he sees his plan succeed so well, and the whole world in the snare.[508] {ExV54 10.2; 1SG 178.1}

5.[6.] On pages 29–33, is a view given January, 1850.[509] That portion of this view, which relates to means being withheld from the messengers, more particularly applied to that time. Since that time friends of the

V87. *Perishing Souls Vision, Jan. 26, 1850*

11

cause of present truth have been raised up, who have watched for opportunity to do good with their means.[510] And some have handed out too freely, to the injury of the receivers. For above two years I have been shown more relative to a careless and too free use of the Lord's money, than a lack of means. {ExV54 10.3}

The following is from a view given me at Jackson, Mich., June 2d, 1853. It related mostly to the brethren in that place. "I saw that the brethren commenced to sacrifice their property, and handed it out without having the true object set before them—the suffering cause—and they handed out too freely, too much and too often. I saw that the teachers should have stood in a place to correct this error, and exert a good influence in the church. Money was made to be of little or no consequence; the sooner disposed of, the better. A bad example has been set by some [***Brethren Holt and Rhodes***] in accepting large donations, and not giving the least caution to those who had means not to use it too freely and carelessly. And by accepting so large an amount of means, without questioning whether God had made it their duty to bestow so largely, they sanctioned the brethren's giving too bountifully. {ExV54 11.1; adapted from Ms. 1, 1853, June 2}

V132. *Jackson Vision, June 2, 1853*

Those who gave, also erred, not being particular to inquire into the necessities of the case, whether there was actual need or not.[511] Those who had means were thrown into great perplexity. One brother was much hurt by too much means being put into his hands. He did not study economy; but lived extravagantly, and in his travels laid out money here and there to no profit. He spread a wrong influence by making such free use of the Lord's money, and would say to others, and in his own heart, There is means enough in Jackson, more than can be used before the Lord

12

comes. Some were very much injured by such a course, and came into the truth with wrong views, not realizing that it was the Lord's money they were using, and not feeling the worth of it. And I saw that these poor souls who have just embraced the third angel's message, and have had such an example set before them, will have much to learn, to deny self, and suffer for Christ's sake. They will have to learn to give up their ease, and cease studying their convenience and comfort, and bear in mind the worth of souls. Those who feel the "woe" upon them will not be for making great preparations and fixings outwardly, to travel in ease and comfort. Those who have no calling have been encouraged into the field. Others have been affected by these things, and have not felt the need of economy, of denying themselves, and putting into the treasury of the Lord. They would feel and say, "There are others who have means enough; they will give for the paper. I need not do anything. The paper will be supported without my help." {ExV54 11.2; adapted from Ms. 1, 1853, June 2}

It has been no small trial to me to see that some have taken that portion of my views which related to sacrificing property to sustain the cause, and make a wrong use of it, and use means extravagantly, while neglecting to carry out the principles of other portions. On page 31, read the following:—"I saw that the cause of God had been hindered, and dishonored by some traveling who had no message from God. Such will have to give an account to God for every dollar they have

V87. *Perishing Souls Vision, Jan. 26, 1850*

used in traveling where it was not their duty to go; for that money might have helped on the cause of God." Page 32.—"I saw that those who have strength to labor with their hands, and help

13

sustain the cause, were as accountable for that strength, as others were for their property." {ExV54 12.1; ExV 31.3; RH, April 1850}

V97. *Sutton Vision, Sept. 1850*

I would here call especial attention to the view of this subject given on pages 45, 46. Here is a short extract:—"The object of the words of our Saviour [Luke xii, 33] had not been clearly presented. I saw that the object of selling was not to give to those who are able to labor and support themselves, but to spread the truth. It is a sin to support and indulge in idleness, those who are able to labor. Some have been zealous to attend all the meetings; not to glorify God, but for the "loaves and fishes." Such had much better have been at home laboring with their hands, "the thing that is good," to supply the wants of their families, and to have something to give to sustain the precious cause."[512] {ExV54 13.1; ExV 45.3; RH, Nov. 1850; cf. Ms. 14, 1850, Sept. 29}

I have seen that it has been satan's design in times past to push out some with a hurried spirit to make a too free use of means, and influence the brethren to rashly dispose of their property, that means might be thrown out carelessly, and hastily disposed of, and souls injured and lost through an abundance of means, and now when the truth is to be spread more extensively, the lack might be felt. His design has in some degree been accomplished. {ExV54 13.2}

The Lord has shown me the error of many in looking to those only who have property to support the publication of the paper and tracts. *All* should act their part. Those who have strength to labor with their hands, and earn means to help sustain the cause, are as accountable for it as others are for their property.[513] Every child of God, who professes to believe the present truth, should be zealous to act his part in this cause.[514] {ExV54 13.3}

THE ADVENT REVIEW,

AND SABBATH HERALD.

"Here is the Patience of the Saints; Here are they that keep the Commandments of God and the Faith of Jesus."

VOL. IV. ROCHESTER, N. Y., FIFTH-DAY, JUNE 23, 1853. No. 3.

Before this vision, James had only published a bi-weekly edition of *The Advent Review.*

14

V135. Commandment Keepers Vision, July 2, 1853

July, 1853, I saw that it was not as it should be, that the paper, owned and approved of God, should come out so seldom. That the cause, in the time in which we are living, demands the paper weekly, and the publication of many more tracts to expose the increasing errors of this time; but the work was hindered for want of means. I saw that the truth must go, and that we must not be too fearful; that tracts and papers had better go to three where they were not needed, than to have one deprived of them who can be benefited, and who prized them. I saw that the last-day signs should be brought out and clearly shown; for the manifestations of satan are on the increase. Their publishing is increasing, their power is growing; and what we can do to get the truth before others, must be done quickly. {ExV54 14.1; cf. Ms. 3, 1853, July 2}

I was shown like this. The truth once got out now, will stand; for it is the truth for the last days, and it will live, and less need to be said upon the truth after it is out. Numberless words need not be put upon paper to justify what speaks for itself, and shines in its clearness. But it is not so with error. It is so winding and twisting that it needs a multitude of words to explain it in its crooked form. But truth is straight, plain, clear, and stands out boldly in its own defense. The cause of truth should not be hindered in its onward progress for want of means. {ExV54 14.2}

I saw that in some places all the light they had received came from the paper; and souls had received the truth in this way, and then talked it to others; and now in places where there are several, they had been raised up by this silent messenger. It was their only preacher. {ExV54 14.3}

15

GOSPEL ORDER.

V124. Gospel Order Vision, Sept. 30, 1852

THE Lord has shown me that gospel order has been too much neglected and feared.[515] That formality should be shunned; but in so doing, order should not be neglected. There is order in heaven. There was order in the church when Christ was upon earth; and after his departure, order was strictly observed among his apostles. And now in these last days, while God is bringing his children into the unity of the faith, there is more real need of order than ever before.[516] For as God is uniting his children, satan and his evil angels are very busy to prevent this unity, and to destroy it. Therefore men will be hurried into the field; men without wisdom, lacking judgment, perhaps not ruling well their own house, and not having order or government over the very few that God has given them charge of at home; yet they feel capable of having charge of the flock. They make many wrong moves, and all the messengers are thought, by those unacquainted with our faith, to be like these self-sent men; and the cause of God is reproached, and the truth shunned by many unbelievers, who would otherwise be candid, and anxious to inquire, Are these things so? {ExV54 15.1}

Men, I saw, whose lives are not holy, who are unqualified to teach the present truth, enter the field without being acknowledged by the church or brethren generally, and confusion and disunion is the result.[517] Some have a theory of the truth and can dwell upon argument, but lack spirituality, judgment and experience, and they fail in many things which is very necessary for one to possess before they can teach

16

the present truth to others.[518] Others have not the argument; but because a few brethren hear them pray well, and give an exciting exhortation now and then, press them into the field, to engage in a work that God has not qualified them for, and when they have not sufficient experience and judgment for the work. Spiritual pride comes in, and they are lifted up, and act under the deception of thinking that they are laborers. They do not know themselves. They lack sound judgment and patient reasoning. Talk boastingly of themselves, and assert many things which they cannot prove from the Word. God knoweth this, therefore he does not call such to labor in these perilous times. And brethren should be careful and not push out those into the field whom God has not called. {ExV54 15.2}

These men, who are not called of God, are generally the very ones that are the most confident that they are so called, and that their labors are very important. They go into the field, and do not exert a good influence generally, yet in some places they have a measure of success, which leads individuals to think that they are surely called of God. I saw that it was not a positive evidence that men are called of God, because they have some success; for now the angels of God are moving upon the hearts of his honest children to enlighten their understanding as to the present truth, that they may lay hold upon it and live.[519] And even if self-sent men put themselves where God does not put them, and profess to be teachers, and souls receive the truth by hearing them talk it, this is no evidence that they are called of God. The souls who receive the truth from them, receive it to be brought into trial and bondage, as they afterwards find that these men were not standing in the counsel of God.[520]

17

Even if wicked men talk the truth, some may receive it; but it does not bring those who talked it, into any more favor with God. Wicked men are wicked men still. And according to the deception they practised, and as they deceived those who were beloved of God, and brought confusion into the church, so will their punishment be greater, and their sins will not remain covered, but will be exposed in the day of God's fierce anger. {ExV54 16.1}

These self-sent messengers are a curse to the cause. Honest souls put confidence in them, think that they are moving in the counsel of God, that they are in union with the church, and suffer them to administer the ordinances, to lead them down into the water and baptize them, as duty is made plain that they must do their first works; and then when light comes as it surely will, and they are aware that these men are not what they understood them to be, God's called and chosen messengers, they are thrown into trial and doubt as to the truth they have received, and feel that they must learn it all over again, and are troubled, and perplexed by the enemy, about all their experience, whether God has led them or not, and are not satisfied until they are again baptized, and begin anew. And it is much more laborious, and wearing to the spirits of God's messengers, to go into such places where those have been, who have exerted this wrong influence. God's servants have to deal plainly, and not cover up wrongs, but act openly; for they are standing between the living and the dead, and must render an account of the faithfulness of their mission, and the influence they exert over the flock of which the Lord has made them overseers. {ExV54 17.1}

These jewels who received the truth and are brought into such trials, would have had the truth the same

18

if these men (who lack the qualifications they must have to be the Lord's messengers) had stayed away, and filled the humble place God designed for them. God's eye was upon his jewels, and he would direct his called and chosen messengers to them; men that would move understandingly, and the light of truth would shine and discover to these souls their true position, and they would receive the truth understandingly, and be satisfied with its beauty and clearness.[521] And as they feel the effects and power of the truth, will be strong and shed a holy influence. {ExV54 17.2}

Again: the danger of those traveling, whom God has not called, was shown me. If they do have some success, the qualifications that are lacking will be felt. Injudicious moves will be made, and some precious jewels may be driven off by a lack of wisdom, where they never can be reached.[522] I saw that the church should feel their responsibility, and should look carefully and attentively at the lives, qualifications, and general course of those who profess to be teachers. And if unmistakable evidence is not given that God has called them, and that the "woe" is upon them if they heed not this call, it is the duty of the church to act, and let it be known that they are not acknowledged teachers by the church. This is the only course the church can take in order to be clear in this matter; for the burden lays upon them. {ExV54 18.1}

I saw that this door that the enemy comes in at, to perplex and trouble the flock, can be shut. I inquired of the angel how this door could be closed. Said he, "The church must flee to God's word, and become established upon gospel order which has been overlooked and neglected." This is indispensably necessary to bring the church into the unity of the

19

faith.[523] I saw that they were in danger in the apostles' days of being imposed upon and deceived by false teachers; and men were chosen by the brethren, or church, who had given good evidence that they were capable of ruling well their own house, and preserving order in their own families; men that could enlighten those who were in darkness. Inquiry was made of God concerning them, and then, according to the mind of the church, and the Holy Ghost, they were set apart by the laying on of hands.[524] Having received their commission from God, and having the approbation of the church, they go forth baptizing in the name of the Father, Son and Holy Ghost, and to administer the ordinances of the Lord's house, often waiting upon the saints by presenting them the emblems of the broken body and spilt blood of the crucified Saviour, to keep fresh in the memory of God's beloved children, his sufferings and death. {ExV54 18.2}

I saw that we are no more secure from false teachers now than they were in the apostles' days; and if we do no more, we should take as special measures as they did to secure the peace, harmony and union of the flock. We have their example, and should follow it. Brethren of experience, and of a sound mind, should assemble, and follow the word of God, and with fervent prayer, and by the sanction of the Spirit of God, should lay hands upon those who have given full proof that they have received their commission of God, and set them apart to devote themselves entirely to the work.[525] And by this act show the approving voice of the church, in their going forth as messengers to carry the most solemn message ever given to men. {ExV54 19.1}

God will not intrust the care of his precious flock

20

to men whose minds and judgment have been weakened by former errors that they have been in, such as so-called perfectionism and spiritualism, and by their course, while in these errors, have brought reproach upon the cause of truth and disgraced themselves. And although they may now feel free from error, and competent to go forth to teach this last message, God will not accept them. He will not intrust precious souls to their care; for their judgment has been perverted while in error, and is now weakened. {ExV54 19.2}

The great and holy One is a jealous God, and he will have holy men to carry his truth.[526] The holy law, spoken by God from Sinai, is a part of himself, and holy men, who are its strict observers, will alone honor him by teaching it to others. {ExV54 20.1}

I saw that the servants of God who teach the truth should be men of judgment. They should be men that can bear opposition, and not get excited; for those who oppose the truth will pick those who teach it, and every objection that can be produced, in its worst form, will be brought to bear against the truth. And the servants of God, who bear the message, must be prepared, with calmness and meekness, to remove these objections by the light of truth. I saw that the opposers would often talk to ministers of God in a provoking manner, to call out something from them of the same nature, that they can make as much of as possible, and declare to others that the teachers of the commandments have a bitter spirit, and are harsh, as has been reported. I saw that we must be prepared for objections, and with patience, judgment and meekness let them have the weight they deserve, and not throw them away, and dispose of them by positive assertions, and bear down upon the

21

objector, and manifest a hard spirit towards him, but give the objections their weight, then bring forth the light and the power of the truth, and let it outweigh, and remove the errors; and then a good impression will be left, and they will acknowledge that they have been deceived, and that the commandment-keepers are not what they have been represented to be. {ExV54 20.2}

V132. *Jackson Vision, June 2, 1853*

Those who profess to be servants of the living God, must be willing to be servants of all, instead of being exalted above the brethren, and they must possess a kind courteous spirit. If they err, they should be ready to confess thoroughly. Honesty of intention cannot stand as an excuse for not confessing errors. Confession would not lessen the confidence of the church in the messenger, and he would set a good example, a spirit of confession would be encouraged in the church, and sweet union would be the result. I have seen that those who profess to be teachers, should be patterns of piety, meekness, and of great humility, possessing a kind spirit, to win souls to Jesus, and the truth of the Bible. A minister of Christ should be pure in conversation and in actions. He should ever bear in mind that he is handling words of inspiration, words of a holy God. He must bear in mind that the flock is entrusted to his care, and he is to bear their cases to Jesus, and plead for them as Jesus pleads for us to the Father. I was pointed back to the children of Israel anciently, and saw how pure and holy the ministers of the Sanctuary had to be, because they were brought by their work into a close connection with God. They that should minister, must be holy, pure and without blemish, or God would destroy them.[527] I saw that God had not

V129. *Character of the Ministers Vision, March 1, 1853*

22

changed. He was just as holy and pure, just as particular as ever he was. He changeth not![528] Those who profess to be the ministers of Jesus, should be men of experience and deep piety, and then at all times, and in all places they can shed a holy influence. {ExV54 21.1; Ms. 1, 1853, June 2 (**V132**); Ms. 2, 1853, March 1 (**V129**)}

V135. *Commandment Keepers Vision, July 2, 1853*

I have seen that it was now time for the messengers to move out wherever there was an opening, and God would go before them and would open the hearts of some to hear. New places must be entered, and when new places are visited it would be well to go two and two, so as to hold up each other's hands, wherever they can consistently, and not neglect other places.[529] It was shown me like this. It would be well for two brethren to start together, and travel in company together to the darkest places, where there is much opposition, and where they need the most labor, and with united efforts and strong faith set the truth before those in darkness. And then if they could accomplish more, by visiting many places, to go separately, but often meet while on the tour to encourage each other by their faith, and thereby strengthen and hold up each others hands. Also, consult upon the places opened for them, and decide which of their gifts will be the most needed, and in what way they can have the most success, and reach the heart. And then as they separate again their courage and energy will be renewed to meet the opposition and darkness, and to labor with feeling hearts to save perishing souls. {ExV54 22.1; Ms. 4, 1853, July 2}

I saw that the servants of God should not go over and over the same field of labor, but should be searching out souls in new places. Those who are already established in the truth should not demand so much

23

of their labor; for they ought to be able to stand alone, and strengthen others about them while the messengers of God are in the dark and lonely places setting the truth before those who are not now enlightened as to the present truth.[530] {ExV54 22.2; Ms. 4, 1853, July 2}

To the Saints Scattered Abroad.

[The following is from the *Review* of Aug. 11th, 1853.]

DEAR BRETHREN AND SISTERS:—As error is fast progressing, we should seek to be awake in the cause of God, and realize the time in which we live. Darkness is to cover the earth, and gross darkness the people.[531] And as nearly all around us are being enveloped in the thick darkness of error and delusion, it becomes us to shake off stupidity, and live near to God, where we can draw the divine rays of light and glory from the countenance of Jesus. As darkness thickens, and error increases, we should obtain a more thorough knowledge of the truth, and be prepared to maintain from the Scriptures the truth of our position. {ExV54 23.1; RH, Aug. 11, 1853}

We must be sanctified through the truth, be wholly consecrated to God, and live out our holy profession, so that he can shed increasing light upon us, that we may have light in his light, and be strengthened with his strength.[532] Every moment that we are not on our watch, we are liable to be beset by the enemy, and in great danger of being overcome by the powers of darkness. Satan has his angels, who are commissioned by him to be vigilant, and overthrow all they can; to find out the waywardness and besetting sins of those who profess the truth, and throw darkness around them, that they may cease to be watchful, and take a course that will dishonor the cause they profess to

24

love, bring sorrow upon the church, while daily the misguided, unwatchful souls are growing darker, and the light of heaven is fading from them. They cannot discover their besetting sins, and satan weaves his net about them, until they are taken in the snare. {ExV54 23.2; RH, Aug. 11, 1853}

God is our strength. We must look to him for wisdom and guidance, and with his glory in view, and the good of the church, and the salvation of our own souls, overcome our besetting sins. Each individual should seek to obtain new victory every day. We must learn to stand alone, and depend wholly upon God. The sooner we learn this the better. Let each one find out where he fails, and then faithfully watch, that his sins may not overcome him, but get the victory over his sins. Then can we have confidence towards God, and great trouble will be saved the church. {ExV54 24.1; RH, Aug. 11, 1853}

The messengers of God, as they leave their homes, to labor for the salvation of souls, spend much of their time in getting those right, and free from temptation, who have been in the truth for years, and still are weak, because they needlessly let loose the reins, cease watching over themselves, and, I sometimes think, tempt the enemy to tempt them. They get into some petty difficulty and trial, and the time of the servants of the Lord is spent to visit them. They are held hours and even days, and their souls grieved and wounded, to hear little difficulties and trials talked over. Each magnifying his own grievances to make them look as serious as possible, for fear the servants of God will think them too small an affair for them to notice. Instead of depending on the Lord's servants to help them out of these trials, they should break down before God, and fast and pray till the trials are removed. {ExV54 24.2; RH, Aug. 11, 1853}

25

Some seem to think that all God has called messengers into the field for, is to go at their bidding, and carry them in their arms. And that the most important part of their work is to settle their petty trials and difficulties, which they have brought upon themselves by injudicious moves, and by giving way to the enemy, and having an unyielding, fault-finding spirit with those around them, to ease their conscience. {ExV54 25.1; RH, Aug. 11, 1853}

But where are the hungry sheep at this time? Starving for the bread of life. Those who know the truth and have been established in it, but obey it not, (if they did they would be saved many of these trials,) are holding the messengers, and the very object for which God has called his servants into the field, is not accomplished. The servants of God are grieved, and their courage taken away by such things in the church, when all should strive not to add a feather's weight to their burden; but by cheering words and the prayer of faith, should help them.[533] How much more free would they be if all who profess the truth, would be looking about them and trying to help others, instead of claiming so much help themselves. And as the servants of God enter the dark places, where the truth has not yet been proclaimed, they have a wounded spirit caused by the needless trials of their brethren. In addition to all this, they have to meet the unbelief and prejudice of opposers and be trampled upon by some. {ExV54 25.2; RH, Aug. 11, 1853}

How much easier it would be for the servant of God to affect the heart, and how much more would God be glorified, if his servants were free from discouragement and trial, that they might labor for him more effectually, and with a free spirit, present the truth in its beauty. {ExV54 25.3; RH, Aug. 11, 1853}

26

Those who have been guilty of requiring so much labor of God's servants, and burdening them with trials, which belonged to themselves to settle, will have to give an account to God for all the time and means that has been spent to gratify themselves, thereby satisfying the enemy. They should be in a situation to help their brethren. They should never defer their trials and difficulties to burden a whole meeting, or wait until some of the messengers come to settle them. But get right before God, have the trials all out of the way, and be prepared to hold up the hands of the laborers, instead of weakening them.

E. G. W. {ExV54 26.1; RH, Aug. 11, 1853}

[The following is from the *Review* of June 10, 1852:]

As I have of late looked around to find the humble followers of the meek and lowly Jesus, my mind has been much exercised. {ExV54 26.2; RH, June 10, 1852}

Many who profess to be looking for the speedy coming of Christ, are becoming conformed to this world, and seek more earnestly the applause of those around them, than the approbation of God. They are cold and formal, like the nominal church, that they but a short time since separated from. The words addressed to the Laodicean Church, describe their present condition perfectly. See Rev. iii, 14–20. They are "*neither cold nor hot*," but "*lukewarm*." And unless they heed the counsel of the "faithful and True Witness," and zealously repent, and obtain "gold tried in the fire," "white raiment," and "eye-salve," he will spue them out of his mouth. {ExV54 26.3; RH, June 10, 1852}

The time has come when a large portion of those who once rejoiced, and shouted aloud for joy, in view

27

of the immediate coming of the Lord, are on the ground of the churches and world who once scoffed at, and derided them for believing that Jesus was coming, and circulated all manner of falsehoods to raise prejudice against them, and destroy their influence.[534] If any one longs after the living God, and hungers and thirsts for righteousness, and God gives them to feel his power, and satisfies their longing soul, by shedding abroad his love in their hearts, and if they glorify God by praising him, they are, by these professed believers in the soon coming of the Lord, often considered deluded, and charged with having mesmerism or some wicked spirit. {ExV54 26.4; RH, June 10, 1852; AR, Aug. 1850, 16}

Many of these professed Christians dress, talk and act like the world, and the only thing by which they may be known, is their profession. Though they profess to be looking for Christ, their conversation is not in heaven, but on worldly things. {ExV54 27.1; RH, June 10, 1852}

"What manner of persons" ought those to be "in all holy conversation and godliness," who profess to be "looking for, and hasting unto the day of God?" 2 Peter iii, 11. "Every man that hath this hope in him, purifieth himself, even as he is pure." 1 John iii, 3. But it is evident that many who bear the advent name, study more to decorate their bodies, and appear well in the eyes of the world, than they do the word of God, to learn how they may be approved of him. {ExV54 27.2; RH, June 10, 1852}

What if the lovely Jesus, our pattern, should make his appearance among them, and the professors of religion generally, as at his first Advent? He was born in a manger. Follow him along through his life and ministry. He was a man of sorrows and acquainted with grief.[535] These professed Christians would be

28

ashamed of the meek and lowly Saviour who wore a plain, seamless coat, and had not where to lay his head.[536] His spotless, self-denying life would condemn them; his holy solemnity would be a painful restraint upon their lightness and vain laughter; his guileless conversation would be a check to their worldly and covetous conversation; his declaring the unvarnished, cutting truth, would manifest their real character, and they would wish to get the meek Pattern, the lovely Jesus, out of the way as soon as possible.[537] They would be among the first to try to catch him in his words, and raise the cry, Crucify him! Crucify him![538] {ExV54 27.3; RH, June 10, 1852}

Let us follow Jesus as he so meekly rode into Jerusalem, when "the whole multitude of the disciples began to rejoice and praise God with a loud voice, * * * Saying, Blessed be the King that cometh in the name of the Lord. Peace in heaven, and glory in the highest. Some of the Pharisees from among the multitude said unto him, Master, rebuke thy disciples. And he answered and said unto them, I tell you, that if these should hold their peace the stones would immediately cry out."[539] A large portion of those who profess to be looking for Christ would be as forward as the Pharisees were, to have the disciples silenced, and they would doubtless raise the cry, Fanaticism! Mesmerism! Mesmerism! And the disciples, spreading their garments and branches of palm-trees in the way, would be thought extravagant and wild. {ExV54 28.1; RH, June 10, 1852}

But God will have a people on the earth that will not be so cold and dead but that they can praise and glorify him. He will receive glory from some people, and if his chosen people, who keep his

29

commandments should hold their peace the very stones would cry out.[540] {ExV54 28.2; RH, June 10, 1852}

Jesus is coming, but not as at his first Advent, a babe in Bethlehem, not as he rode into Jerusalem, when the disciples praised God with a loud voice and cried, Hosannah; but in the glory of the Father, and with all the retinue of holy angels with him, to escort him on his way to earth. All heaven will be emptied of the angels. While the waiting saints will be looking for him, and gazing into heaven, as were the "men of Galilee" when he ascended from the Mount of Olivet.[541] Then, those only who are holy, those who have followed fully the meek Pattern will, with rapturous joy, exclaim as they behold him, "Lo, this is our God, we have waited for him, and he will save us."[542] And they will be changed "in a moment, in the twinkling of an eye, at the last trump," that wakes the sleeping saints, and calls them forth from their dusty beds, clothed with glorious immortality, shouting, Victory! Victory! over death and the grave.[543] The changed saints are caught up together with them to meet the Lord in the air, never more to be separated from the object of their love.[544] {ExV54 29.1; RH, June 10, 1852}

With such a prospect as this before us, such a glorious hope, such a redemption that Christ has purchased for us by his own blood, shall we hold our peace? Shall we not praise God, even with a loud voice, as the disciples did when Jesus rode into Jerusalem? Is not our prospect far more glorious than theirs was? Who dare then forbid us glorifying God, even with a loud voice, when we have such a hope, big with immortality and full of glory? We have tasted of the powers of the world to come, and long for more.[545] My whole being cries out after the

30

living God, and I shall not be satisfied until I am filled with all his fullness.

E. G. W. {ExV54 29.2; RH, June 10, 1852}

[The following is from the *Review* of Feb. 17th, 1853.]

DEAR BRETHREN AND SISTERS:—Do we believe with all the heart that Christ is soon coming? And that we are now having the last message of mercy that is ever to be given to a guilty world? Is our example what it should be? And do we show to those around us, by our lives and holy conversation, that we are looking for the glorious appearing of our Lord and Saviour Jesus Christ, to change these vile bodies and fashion them like unto his glorious body?[546] I fear that we do not believe, and realize these things as we should. Those who believe the important truths that we profess to believe, should act out their faith, in the immediate coming of Christ. There is too much seeking amusements, and things to take up the mind here in this world; the mind is left too much to run upon pride of dress; and the tongue is engaged too often in light and trifling conversation, which gives the lie to our profession, for the conversation is not in heaven from whence we look for the Saviour.[547] {ExV54 30.1; RH, Feb. 17, 1853}

Angels are watching over us, to guard us; and we often grieve these angels by indulging in trifling conversation, jesting and joking, and also by sinking down in a careless, stupid state. And although we may make an effort now and then for the victory, and obtain it, yet if we do not keep it, but sink down in the same careless, indifferent state, unable to endure temptations, and to resist the enemy, it is not enduring the trial of our faith, that is much more precious than gold. It

31

is not suffering for Christ's sake, and glorying in tribulation.[548] {ExV54 30.2; RH, Feb. 17, 1853}

There is a great lack of christian fortitude, and serving God from principle. We should not seek to please and gratify self; but to honor and glorify God, and in all we do and say, have a single eye to his glory. If we would let our hearts be impressed with the following important words, and ever bear them in mind, we should not so easily fall into temptation; but our words would be few and well chosen. {ExV54 31.1; RH, Feb. 17, 1853}

"He was wounded for our transgressions, he was bruised for our iniquities; the chastisement of our peace was upon him; and with his stripes we are healed." "Every idle word that men shall speak, they shall give account thereof in the day of judgment." "Thou God seest me."[549] {ExV54 31.2; RH, Feb. 17, 1853}

We could not think of these important words, and call to mind the sufferings of Jesus for us sinners, that we might receive pardon from our sins and be redeemed unto God by his most precious blood, without feeling a holy restraint upon us, and an earnest desire to suffer for him, who suffered and endured so much for us. {ExV54 31.3; RH, Feb. 17, 1853}

If we dwell on these things, dear self, with its dignity, will be humbled; a child-like simplicity will take its place, which will bear reproof from others, and will not be easily provoked, and suffer a *self-willed* spirit to come in and rule the soul. The true christian's joys, and consolation, must and will be in heaven. {ExV54 31.4; RH, Feb. 17, 1853}

The longing souls of those who have tasted of the powers of the world to come, and have feasted on heavenly joys, will not be satisfied, or amused, with things of earth. Such will find enough to do in their

32

leisure moments. Their souls will be drawn out after God. Where the treasure is, there will be their heart, holding sweet communion with the God they love and worship. Their amusements will be in contemplating their treasure—the holy city—the earth made new—their eternal home. And while they dwell upon these things, which are lofty, pure and holy, heaven will be brought near, and they will feel the power of the Holy Spirit, which will tend to wean them from the world more and more, and cause their consolation and chief joy to be in the things of heaven, their sweet home. The power of attraction to God and heaven will be so great, that nothing can draw their mind from the great object of securing their soul's salvation, and honoring and glorifying God. {ExV54 31.5; RH, Feb. 17, 1853}

As I realize how much has been done for us, to keep us right, I am led to exclaim, O, what love! What wondrous love hath the Son of God for us poor sinners! Should we be stupid and careless, while every thing is being done for our salvation that can be done? All heaven is interested for us. We should be alive and awake, to honor, glorify and adore the High and Lofty One.[550] Our hearts should flow out in love and gratitude to him who has been so full of love and compassion to us. With our lives we should honor him, and with pure and holy conversation show that we are born from above; that this world is not our home, but that we are pilgrims and strangers here, traveling to a better country. {ExV54 32.1; RH, Feb. 17, 1853}

Many who profess the name of Christ, and profess to be looking for his speedy coming, know not what it is to suffer for Christ's sake. Their hearts are not subdued by grace, and they are not dead to self; but it often appears in various ways; and at the same

33

time, they are talking of having trials. But the principal cause of their trials, is an unsubdued heart, which makes self so sensitive, that it is often crossed. If such could realize what it is to be a humble follower of Christ, a true christian, they would begin to work in good earnest, and begin right. They would first die to self, then be instant in prayer, and check every passion of the heart. Give up your self-confidence, and self sufficiency, and follow the meek Pattern. Ever keep Jesus in your mind, that he is your example, and you must tread in his footsteps. Looking unto Jesus, the author and finisher of our faith; who, for the joy that was set before him, endured the cross, despising the shame. He endured the contradiction of sinners against himself. He for your sins, was once the meek slain lamb, wounded, bruised, smitten and afflicted.[551] {ExV54 32.2; RH, Feb. 17, 1853}

Let us, then, cheerfully suffer something for Jesus' sake, crucify self daily, be a partaker of Christ's sufferings here, that we may be made partakers with him of his glory, and be crowned with glory, honor, immortality and eternal life.

E. G. W. {ExV54 33.1; RH, Feb. 17, 1853}

Explanation.[552]

On page 43 of *Experience and Views*, I stated that a cloud of glorious light covered the Father, and that his person could not be seen. I also stated that I saw the Father rise from the throne. The Father was enshrouded with a body of light and glory, so that his person could not be seen, yet I knew that it was the Father, and that from his person, emanated this light and glory. When I saw this body of light and glory rise from the throne, I knew that the Father moved, which was the cause of the body of light and glory rising, therefore said, I saw the Father rise.

34

The glory, or excellency of his form, I never saw—no one could behold it; yet the body of light and glory that enshrouded his person, could be seen. {ExV54 33.2; RH, April 14, 1853}

I also stated that "satan *appeared* to be by the throne, trying to carry on the work of God." I will give another sentence from the same page. "Then I turned to look at the company who were still bowed before the throne." Now, this praying company was in this mortal state, on the earth, yet represented to me as bowed before the throne. I never had the idea that these individuals were actually in the New Jerusalem. Neither did I ever think that any mortal could suppose that I thought that Satan was actually in the New Jerusalem. {ExV54 34.1; RH, April 14, 1853}

But did not John see the great red dragon in heaven? Certainly. "And there appeared another wonder in heaven; and behold a great red dragon, having seven heads and ten horns." Rev. xii, 3. Here seems to be as good a chance for ridicule, as that which some have taken in my views. What a monster to be in heaven! {ExV54 34.2; RH, April 14, 1853}

Faithfulness.

V135. Commandment Keepers Vision, July 2, 1853

The Lord has shown me that great interest should be taken by Sabbath-keepers to keep up their meetings and make them interesting. There has been a lack of interest, and there is great necessity of more energy being manifested by the commandment-keepers in their meetings. All should have something to say for the Lord, and by so doing they would be blest. A book of remembrance is written of those who do not forsake the assembling of themselves together, and speak often one to another. {ExV54 34.3; cf. Ms. 3, 1853, July 2}

The remnant are to overcome by the blood of the

35

Lamb and the word of their testimony. Some expect to overcome alone by the blood of the Lamb, without making any special effort of their own. I saw that God had been merciful in giving us the power of speech. He had given us tongue and utterance, and we are accountable to him for it, and we should glorify God with our mouth, speaking in honor of his unbounded mercy, and of the truth, and overcome by the word of our testimony, through the blood of the Lamb.[553] {ExV54 34.4; cf. Ms. 3, 1853, July 2}

V139. Testimonies in Meeting Vision, Oct. 28, 1853

We should not come together to remain silent;[554] those only are remembered of the Lord, who come together to honor and glorify him, to speak of his glory, and tell of his power; and upon such the blessing of God will rest, and they will be refreshed. If all moved as I saw they should, no precious time would run to waste, and no reproofs would be needed for long prayers and exhortations; for all the time would be occupied by short, sweet testimonies, and prayers to the point. Ask, believe and receive. There is too much mocking God, too much praying that is no praying, and that wearies angels and displeases God. Too many vain, unmeaning petitions. First we should feel needy, and then ask God for the very things we need, and then believe he gives them to us, even while we ask; and then, I saw, that our faith would grow, all would be edified, the weak would be strengthened, the discouraged and desponding made to look up, and believe that God is a rewarder of all those who diligently seek him. {ExV54 35.1; cf. Ms. 3, 1853, July 2}

Some hold back in meetings because they have nothing new to say, and must repeat the same story if they speak. I saw that pride was at the bottom of this. That God and angels witnessed the testimonies

36

of the saints, and the Lord was well pleased, and was glorified by their testimonies repeated weekly. The Lord and his holy angels love simplicity and humility. I saw that God had been displeased, and angels grieved, that professed heirs of God, and joint heirs with Jesus, should suffer precious time to run to waste in their meetings.[555] {ExV54 35.2; Lt. 9, 1853, Dec. 5}

If the brethren and sisters were in the place they should be, they would not be at a loss to find something to say in honor of Jesus, who hung upon Calvary's cross for their sins. If they would cherish more of a realizing sense of the condescension of God in giving his only beloved Son to die, a sacrifice for our sins and transgressions, and the sufferings and anguish of Jesus to make a way of escape for guilty man, that he might receive pardon and live, they would be more ready to extol and magnify Jesus. They could not hold their peace; but with thankfulness and gratitude, would talk of his glory, and tell of his power. And blessings from God would rest upon them by so doing. Even if the same story was repeated, God would be glorified. {ExV54 36.1; Lt. 9, 1853, Dec. 5}

The Angel shewed me those who ceased not day nor night, crying, Holy, Holy, Lord, God Almighty.[556] "Continual repetition," said the Angel, "yet God is glorified by it." Although we may tell the same story over and over, it honors God, and shows that we are not unmindful of him and his goodness and mercies to us. {ExV54 36.2; Lt. 9, 1853, Dec. 5}

I saw that the nominal churches had fallen; that coldness and death reigns in their midst. If they would follow the Word it would humble them. But they get above the work of the Lord. It is too humbling for them to repeat the same simple story

37

of God's goodness when they meet together; and they try to get something new; something great, and study to have their words exact to the ear, and please man, and God's Spirit has left them. When we follow the humble, Bible way, we shall have the movings of the Spirit of God. All will be in sweet harmony, if we follow the humble channel of truth, depending wholly upon God, and there will be no danger of being affected by the evil angels. It is when souls get above the Spirit of God, moving in their own strength, that the angels cease watching over them, and they are left to the buffetings of satan. {ExV54 36.3; Lt. 9, 1853, Dec. 5}

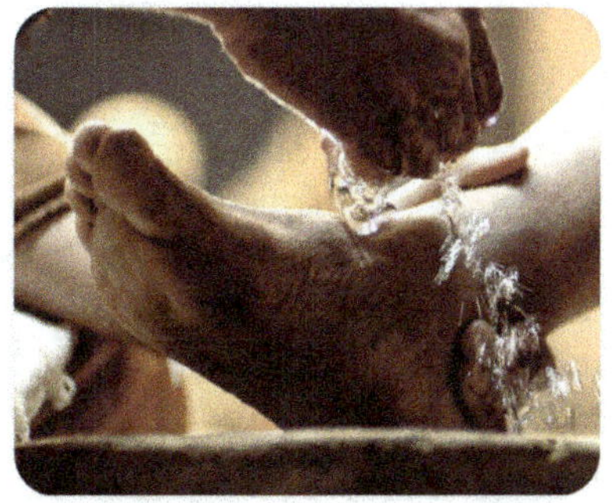

I saw that duties were laid down for us in God's word, to be performed to keep the people of God humble and separate from the world, and from backsliding, like the nominal churches. Washing feet, and the Lord's supper should be more frequently practiced. Jesus set us the example, and told us to do as he had done. I saw that the example of Christ should be as exactly followed as possible; yet brethren and sisters have not always moved as judiciously as they should in washing feet, and confusion has been caused.[557] It should be introduced into new places with carefulness and wisdom, especially where the people are not informed relative to the example and teachings of our Lord on this point, and where they have prejudice against it. Many honest souls are much prejudiced against this plain duty, through the influence of their former teachers in whom they had confidence; and the subject should be introduced to them in a proper time and manner. {ExV54 37.1; Lt. 9, 1853}

There is no example given in the Word for brethren to wash sisters' feet; but there is an example for sisters to wash the feet of brethren. Mary washed

38

the feet of Jesus with her tears, and wiped them with the hairs of her head.[558] Also see 1 Tim. v, 10. I saw that the Lord had moved upon sisters to wash the feet of brethren, and that it was according to gospel order. All should move understandingly, and not make the washing of feet a tedious ceremony. {ExV54 37.2; Lt. 9, 1853}

The holy salutation mentioned in the gospel of Jesus Christ as taught by the apostle Paul, should ever be regarded in its true character. *It is a holy kiss*.[559] It should be regarded as a sign of fellowship to Christian friends, when parting, and meeting again after a separation for weeks or months. In 1 Thess. v, 26, Paul says:—"Greet all the brethren with an holy kiss." And in the same chapter he says:—"Abstain from all appearance of evil." Verse 22. There can be no appearance of evil when the holy kiss is given at a proper time and place. {ExV54 38.1}

V135. *Commandment Keepers Vision, July 2, 1853*

I saw that the strong hand of the enemy is set against the work, and the help and strength of every one who loves the cause of truth, should be enlisted; and great interest manifested by them to uphold the hands of those who advocate the truth. And by steady watch-care, shut out the enemy. All should stand as one, united in this work. Every energy of their soul should be awake; for what is done must be done quickly. {ExV54 38.2; Ms. 3, 1853, July 2}

I then saw the third angel. Said my accompanying angel, "Fearful is his work. Awful is his mission. He is the angel that is to select the wheat from the tares, and seal or bind the wheat for the heavenly garner.[560] These things should engross the whole mind, the whole attention." {ExV54 38.3; Ms. 3, 1853, July 2}

39

To Those of Little Experience.

V138. *To Those of Little Experience Vision,* Sept. 1853

SOME, I saw, had not a realizing sense of the importance of the truth, or its effects, and often moved from the impulse of the moment, or from excitement, following their feelings, and disregarding church order, thinking that religion consists chiefly in making a noise. Some who have but just received the truth of the third angel's message, are ready to reprove and teach those who have been established in the truth for years, and have felt its sanctifying power, and have suffered for the truth's sake. Those who are so puffed up by the enemy will have to feel the sanctifying influence of the truth, and will have to have a realizing sense of where the truth found them, and *how;* that they were "wretched, miserable, and poor and blind and naked."[561] {ExV54 39.1}

When the truth begins to purify them and purge away their dross and tin, as it surely will when it is received, in the love of it, the one who has this great work done for him will not feel that he is rich and increased in goods, and has need of nothing. {ExV54 39.2}

Those who profess the truth, and before they have learned its first principles, think they know it all, and are forward to take the place of teachers, and reprove those who for years have stood stiffly for the truth, plainly show that they have no understanding of the truth, and know none of its effects; for if they knew any of its sanctifying power, they would yield the peaceable fruits of righteousness, and be humbled under its sweet, powerful influence.[562] They would bear fruit to the glory of God, and understand what the truth has done for them, and esteem others better than themselves. {ExV54 39.3}

I saw that the remnant were not prepared for what

40

is coming upon the earth. Stupidity, like the lethargy, seemed to hang upon the minds of most of those who profess to believe that we are having the last message.[563] My accompanying angel cried out with awful solemnity, "Get ready! get ready! get ready! for the fierce anger of the Lord is soon to come.[564] His wrath is to be poured out unmixed with mercy, and ye are not ready. Rend the heart, and not the garment. A great work must be done for the remnant. They are, many of them, dwelling upon little trials." Said the angel, "Legions of evil angels are around you, and are trying to press in their awful darkness, that ye may be ensnared and taken. Ye suffer your mind to be diverted too readily from the work of preparation, and the all-important truths for these last days. And ye dwell upon little trials, and go into minute particulars of little difficulties to explain them to the satisfaction of this one or that." Conversation has been protracted for hours between the parties concerned, and not only has their time been wasted, but the servants of God are held to listen to them, when the hearts of both parties are unsubdued by grace. If pride and selfishness were laid aside, five minutes would remove most difficulties. Hours have been spent in justifying self, which has grieved angels, and displeased God. I saw that God will not wait and bow down and listen to long justifications, and he did not want his servants to do so, and precious time be wasted, that should be spent in showing transgressors the error of their ways, and pulling souls out of the fire. {ExV54 39.4}

I saw that God's people were on the enchanted ground; and some have lost nearly all sense of the shortness of time, and the worth of the soul. Pride has crept in among Sabbath-keepers, pride of dress

41

and appearance. Said the angel, "Sabbath-keepers will have to die to self, die to pride and love of approbation." {ExV54 40.1; cf. Ms. 7a, 1850}

Truth, saving truth, must be given to the starving people, who are in darkness. I saw that many prayed for God to humble them; but if God answered their prayer, it would be by terrible things in righteousness.[565] It was their duty to humble themselves, I saw that if self-exaltation was suffered to come in, it would surely lead souls astray, and if not overcome, prove their ruin. When one begins to get lifted up in his own eyes, and thinks he can do something, the Spirit of God is withdrawn, and he goes on in his own strength until he is overthrown. One saint, I saw, could move the arm of God if he were right; but a multitude together, if they were wrong, would be weak, and could effect nothing. {ExV54 41.1}

I saw that many had unsubdued, unhumbled hearts, and were thinking more of their own little grievances and trials than the souls of sinners. If they had the glory of God in view, they would feel for perishing souls around them; and as they realized their perilous situation, would take hold with energy, exercising faith in God, and hold up the hands of his servants, that they may boldly, yet in love, declare the truth, and warn souls to lay hold upon it, before the sweet voice of mercy dies away. {ExV54 41.2}

Said the angel, "Those who profess his name are not ready." I saw the seven last plagues were coming upon the shelterless heads of the wicked; and then those who have stood in their way will hear the bitter reproaches of sinners, and their hearts will faint within them.[566] {ExV54 41.3}

42

Said the angel, "Ye have been picking at straws," (dwelling upon little trials,) and sinners must be lost. I saw that God was willing to work for us in our meetings, and it was his pleasure to work. Satan says, "I will hinder the work." His agents say, Amen. Professed believers in the truth dwell upon their petty trials and difficulties which Satan has magnified before them. Time that can never be recalled is wasted. The enemies of the truth have seen our weakness, God has been grieved, Christ wounded. Satan's object is accomplished, his plans have succeeded, and he triumphs! {ExV54 42.1}

Self Denial.

V140. *Self-Denial Vision, 1853*

I SAW that there was danger of the saints making too great preparations for conferences; that some were cumbered with too much serving; that the appetite must be denied. There is danger of some attending the meetings for the loaves and fishes. {ExV54 42.2; Ms. 14, 1850}

I saw all those who are indulging self by using the filthy weed, [tobacco,] should lay it aside, and put their means to a better use.[567] Those who deprive themselves of some gratification, and take the means they formerly used to gratify the appetite, and put it into the treasury of the Lord, sacrifice; and, like the widow's two mites, it will be noticed of God. The amount may be small; but if all will do this, it will tell in the treasury. And if all would study to be more economical in their articles of dress, and deprive themselves of some things which are not actually necessary, and lay aside such useless and injurious things as tea, etc., and give what they cost to the cause, they would receive more blessings here, and a reward in heaven. Many think, because God has

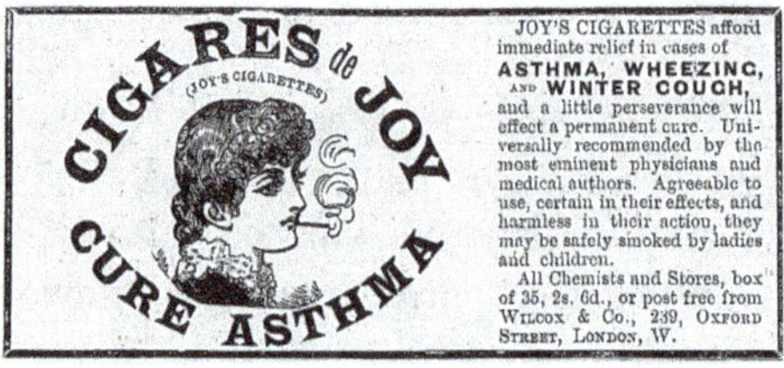

Tobacco was prescribed as a medicine during this era.

43

given them the means, they may live almost above want, can have rich food, and clothe themselves abundantly, and that it is no virtue to deny themselves when they have enough. Such do not sacrifice. If they would live a little poorer, and give to the cause of God, to help forward the truth, it would be a sacrifice on their part, and when God rewards every man according to their works, it will be remembered by him.[568] {ExV54 42.3}

Irreverence.

V141. *Reverence for God's Name Vision, 1853*

I SAW that God's Holy Name should be used with reverence, and awe. Said the angel, "Couple them not together; for fearful is His Name." I saw that God Almighty was coupled together, and used by some in meeting in a careless, thoughtless manner, which was displeasing to God. They have no realizing sense of God, or the truth; or they would not speak so irreverently of the great and dreadful God, who is soon to judge them in the last day. Those who realize the greatness and majesty of God, will take his name on their lips with holy awe. He dwelleth in light inapproachable; no man can see him and live.[569] I saw that these things would have to be understood and corrected where they exist, before the church can prosper. {ExV54 43.1}

False Shepherds.

V137. *False Shepherds Vision, 1853*

I HAVE been shown the false shepherds, that they were drunk, but not with wine; they stagger but not with strong drink.[570] The truth of God is sealed up to them; they cannot read it. When they are interrogated as to what the seventh-day Sabbath is, whether it is the true Sabbath of the Bible, they lead the mind to fables. I saw that the prophets were like

44

the foxes of the deserts. They have not gone up into the gaps, they have not made up the hedge, that the people of God may stand in the battle in the day of the Lord.[571] When these shepherds see the minds of any stirred up, and they begin to inquire of them about the truth, they take the easiest and best manner for themselves, to quiet their minds and effect their object, even to the changing of their own position. {ExV54 43.2}

Light has shone to many of these shepherds; but they would not acknowledge it, but have changed their position a number of times to evade the truth, and get away from conclusions that they must come to, if they continued in their former positions; while the power of truth tore up their foundation. And instead of yielding to the force of truth, they would get upon another platform, that they were not satisfied with themselves. {ExV54 44.1}

I saw that many of these shepherds had denied the past teachings of God; had denied and rejected the glorious truths which they once zealously advocated, and covered them with mesmerism, and all kinds of delusions. I saw they were drunken, but not with wine, they staggered but not with strong drink.[572] They were drunken with error, and were leading on their flock to death. {ExV54 44.2}

Many of the opposers of God's truth, devise mischief in their heads upon their beds, and in the day, they carry out their mischief and wicked devices, to put down the truth, and get something new to interest, and take the minds of their people, and divert them from the precious, all-important truth. I saw that the priests who are leading on their flock to death, are soon to be arrested in their dreadful career. The plagues of God are coming, and after one or two

45

has fallen, and they are tormented with the plagues, it is not enough; for all this, his hand is stretched out still, and will not be brought to himself again, until his purposes are fully accomplished, and they will be led to worship at the saints' feet, and acknowledge that God has loved them, because they held fast the truth, and kept God's commandments.[573] And his hand is stretched out still in wrath and justice, and he will not rest from his anger, until the hireling priests and all the unrighteous are destroyed from the earth.[574] {ExV54 44.3}

The different parties of professed Advent believers have a little truth, but God has given all that to his children who are being prepared for the day of God; also truths that neither of these parties know, and will not understand. Things which are sealed up to them, the Lord has opened to those who will see, and are ready to understand them. And if God has any new light to communicate, he will let his chosen and beloved understand it, without their going to hear those who are in error and darkness to have their minds enlightened. {ExV54 45.1; Ms. 3, 1853}

I was shown the necessity of those who believe we are having the last message of mercy, being separate from those who are daily imbibing new errors. I saw that young and old should not attend their assemblies; for it is wrong to encourage them by attending their meetings while they teach error that is poisonous, and death to the soul, and teach for doctrines the commandments of men.[575] And the influence is not good. If God has delivered us from such darkness and error, we should stand fast in the liberty wherewith he has set us free, and rejoice in the truth.[576] God is displeased with those who go to listen to error, when they are not obliged to; for unless he sends us to these

46

meetings, where error is forced home to the people by the power of the will, he will not keep us. The angels cease their watchful care over us, and we are left to the buffetings of the enemy, to be darkened and weakened by him, and the power of his evil angels; and the light around us becomes contaminated with the darkness. {ExV54 45.2; Ms. 3, 1853; Lt. 9, 1853; RH, Aug. 11, 1853}

I saw that we had no time to throw away in listening to fables. Our minds should not be thus diverted; but should be occupied with the present truth, and seeking wisdom that we may obtain a more thorough knowledge of our position; that with meekness we may give a reason of our hope from the Scriptures.[577] While the mind is occupied in hearing false doctrines, and dangerous error, pressed upon the hearers, it cannot be dwelling upon the truth which is to fit and prepare the house of Israel to stand in the day of the Lord.[578] {ExV54 46.1; RH, Aug. 11, 1853}

The Love of God in Giving his Son.

I HAVE been shown the great love and condescension of God in giving his Son to die that man might find pardon and live. {ExV54 46.2; Lt. 9, 1853}

V142. Love of God in Giving His Son Vision

I was shown Adam and Eve in the garden, privileged to behold its beauty and loveliness, and with permission to eat of all the trees in the garden except one. But the serpent tempted Eve, and she tempted her husband, and they both ate of the forbidden tree. They broke God's command, and became sinners. {ExV54 46.3; Ms. 4, 1850, Jan. 28}

The news spread through heaven, and every harp was hushed. The angels sorrowed, and feared lest they would put forth the hand and eat of the tree of life, and be immortal sinners. But God said he would

47

drive the transgressors from the garden of Eden, and by cherubims, and the flaming sword, guard the way of the tree of life, so that man could not approach unto it, and eat of its immortal fruit, which perpetuates immortality.[579] {ExV54 46.4; PrT, April 1850; 1SG 21.2}

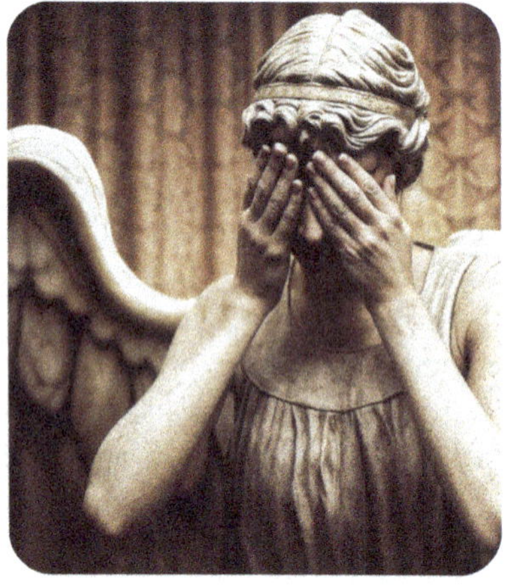

Sorrow filled heaven, as it was realized that man was lost, and the world that God created was to be filled with mortals doomed to misery, sickness and death, and there was no way of escape for the offender. The whole family of Adam must die. I saw the lovely Jesus, and beheld an expression of sympathy and sorrow upon his countenance. Soon I saw him approach the exceeding bright light which enshrouded the Father. Said my accompanying angel, "He is in close converse with his Father." The anxiety of the angels seemed to be intense while Jesus was communing with his Father. Three times he was shut in by the glorious light about the Father, and the third time he came from the Father we could see his person; and his countenance was calm, free from all perplexity and trouble, and shone with loveliness, such as words cannot express.[580] He then made known to the angelic choir that a way of escape had been made for lost man; that he had been pleading with his Father, and had obtained his consent to give his life a ransom, to bear their sins, and take the sentence of death upon himself to open a way that man might find pardon for transgressing God's command; that man, by taking hold of the merits of Christ's blood, could find pardon for past transgressions, keep God's law, and by their obedience be brought back to the garden from which our first parents were driven, and again have access to the glorious, immortal fruit of the tree of life that Adam

48

and Eve forfeited all right to.[581] Then joy, inexpressible joy, filled heaven, and the heavenly choir sung a song of praise and adoration. They touched their harps and sung a note higher than they had done before, for the great mercy and condescension of God in yielding up his dearly Beloved to die for a race of rebels, and praise and adoration was poured forth for the self-denial and sacrifice of Jesus; that he would consent to leave the bosom of his Father, and choose a life of suffering and anguish, and die an ignominious death to give life to others. {ExV54 47.1; 1SG 22.2; 26.1}

Said the angel, "Think ye that the Father yielded up his dearly beloved Son without a struggle? No, no." It was even a struggle with the God of heaven whether to let guilty man perish, or to give his darling Son to die for them.[582] Angels were so interested for man's salvation that there could be found among them those who would yield their glory and give their life for perishing man. But, said my accompanying angel, "That would avail nothing." The transgression was so great that an angel's life would not pay the debt. Nothing but the death and intercessions of his Son would pay the debt, and save lost man from hopeless sorrow and misery. {ExV54 48.1; 1SG 26.2}

But the work of the angels was assigned them, to ascend and descend, with strengthening balm from glory to soothe the Son of God in his life of sufferings. They administered unto Jesus. Also, their work would be to guard and keep the subjects of grace from the evil angels, and the darkness constantly thrown around them by satan. I saw that it was impossible for God to alter or change his law, to save lost, perishing man; therefore he suffered his darling Son to die for man's transgression.[583] {ExV54 48.2; 1SG 26.3}

"The Groaning Earth"

This groaning earth is too dark and drear,
 For the saints' eternal home;
But the King from heaven will soon appear,
We know that the moment is drawing near,
 When he in his glory shall come.
The gates of pearl we soon shall see,
 And the music we soon shall hear,
Joyous and bright our home shall be.
And we'll walk in the shadow of life's fair tree,
 With our Saviour for ever near.
We'll gladly exchange a world like this,
 Where death triumphant reigns,
For a beautiful home in that land of bliss,
Where all is happiness, joy and peace,
 And nothing can enter that pains:
There is no more sorrow and no more night;
 For the darkness shall flee away,
The crucified Lamb is its glorious light,
And the saints shall walk with him in white,
 In that happy, eternal day.

O there the loved of earth will meet
 Whom death has sundered here,
The Prophets and Patriarchs there we'll greet,
And all shall worship at Jesus' feet,
 No more separation to fear.
Though trials and grief await us here,
 The conflict will shortly be o'er,
This glorious hope our hearts doth cheer,
We know that our Saviour will soon appear,
 And then we shall grieve no more.

The original back cover of the *Supplement* included the poem above, which was a fitting bookend to both books' recurring theme of glory. The opening line derives from Romans 8:22: "For we know that the whole creation groaneth and travaileth in pain together until now," expressive of the yearning hope of the brighter future that God has in store for His people. The poem was written in 1851 by Annie R. Smith, the older sister of writer and editor Uriah Smith.[584] In November 1851, when the Whites were still in Saratoga Springs, New York, Annie came to work with them as a proof reader for the paper.[585] Sadly, Annie died in 1855 from tuberculosis, but the hope and glory of the future described in her poem remain.

This is believed to be a self-portrait of Annie R. Smith.

In 1852, while in Rochester, New York, James White published the words of the poem as supplemental hymn, number 6, in *Hymns for Second Advent Believers Who Observe the Sabbath of the Lord*. The words and musical score appeared under the title, "Restitution," in *The Advent Herald*, May 7, 1853, as taken from the *Advent Harp*.[586]

"For I reckon that the sufferings of this present time are not worthy to be compared with the glory which shall be revealed in us."[587]

EXHIBITS

Documenting these stories of faith helps us know that they are not "cunningly devised fables."

EXHIBIT-1. Eyewitness Accounts of Ellen White in Vision

The Whites once discussed writing a book that would "include particulars relative to Mrs. White's visions, her condition while in vision, and many circumstances connected with this whole matter" (LS 6). Though the book was never produced, its object is achieved in the accounts of Ellen White in "open vision" (1 Sam. 3:1). Visions after V152 are tentative and prefixed by ~.

1. Marion C. Stowell Truesdail—V8. "Topsham Vision," Robert G. Curtis' house, Topsham, ME, March 1845.[588]

I was fifteen years old in 1845, and was present at the time of Sister Harmon's first visit to Topsham, when she had the vision at the house of Brother Curtiss [***Robert G. Curtis***], where she took up the great family Bible and held it up in a position in which none of the others could hold a book on the hands without its slipping off at once.[589]

Sister Harmon was in vision over two hours. It was the most wonderful manifestation of the power of God I ever witnessed, and I have seen her in vision more than one dozen times. These were always occasions of deep solemnity and self-examination, but this exceeded them all. O! how we trembled as the Majesty of heaven instructed us through his feeble instrument; as she read to us passages so comforting and appropriate in our trying position; such as Heb. 2:2, 3; James 5:7, 8; Heb. 10:35, 39; 1 Peter 1:7; Luke 12:32–37, besides many others, holding the large family Bible so high that I was obliged to stand on a chair to read where she was pointing. I do not think Sister Harmon was over two inches the taller.

Heb. 2:2, 3. For if the word spoken by angels was stedfast, and every transgression and disobedience received a just recompence of reward; How shall we escape, if we neglect so great salvation; which at the first began to be spoken by the Lord, and was confirmed unto us by them that heard *him*.

James 5:7, 8. Be patient therefore, brethren, unto the coming of the Lord. Behold, the husbandman waiteth for the precious fruit of the earth, and hath long patience for it, until he receive the early and latter rain.

Heb. 10:35, 39. Cast not away therefore your confidence, which hath great recompence of reward. But we are not of them who draw back unto perdition; but of them that believe to the saving of the soul.

1 Peter 1:7. That the trial of your faith, being much more precious than of gold that perisheth, though it be tried with fire, might be found unto praise and honour and glory at the appearing of Jesus Christ.

Luke 12:32–37. Fear not, little flock; for it is your Father's good pleasure to give you the kingdom. Sell that ye have, and give alms; provide yourselves bags which wax not old, a treasure in the heavens that faileth not, where no thief approacheth, neither moth corrupteth. For where your treasure is, there will your heart be also. Let your loins be girded about, and *your* lights burning; And ye yourselves like unto men that wait for their lord, when he will return from the wedding; that when he cometh and knocketh, they may open unto him immediately. Blessed *are* those servants, whom the lord when he cometh shall find watching: verily I say unto you, that he shall gird himself, and make them to sit down to meat, and will come forth and serve them.

2. Frances Howland Lunt—the same vision (V8) as above.[590]

Frances H. Lunt

I, with my father's family, attended the meetings of Sister Harmon in Topsham, in 1845, and during these meetings she had a vision. It was the first time we ever saw her in vision. One of those old-fashioned Bibles was owned by Brother Curtiss [***Robert G. Curtis***]. This big Bible was taken from the bureau by Sister Harmon while in vision, and texts of Scripture were pointed out by her as she turned from leaf to leaf, while her eyes were looking upward, and away from the book. The texts she repeated were either words of instruction, encouragement, or reproof. Another peculiarity of the manifestation at that time was the position of the book. It was held on her open hand at an angle of forty-five degrees, and no one else was able to hold any book at a similar angle without its slipping at once from the hands; but Sister Harmon held this Bible at that angle for several minutes, as firmly as though it was stuck to her hand, she passing meanwhile from one to another in the room.

3. Louisa Howland, Rebekah Howland Winslow, Frances Howland Lunt,—the same vision (V8) as above.[591]

At a meeting held at Bro Curtis' in Topsham, Maine, she was taken off in vision, and arose to her feet, took the large family Bible from the table, and held it on her hand some time, at an angle of forty-five degrees, and said the hidden book was not there. When someone asked if the Apocrypha was not in the Bible, Bro Curtis remarked it was not. She talked some time about the hidden book. No one knew but Bro. Curtis' family that the Apocrypha was not there. —Mrs. S. Howland, Rebekah Howland Winslow, Frances Howland Lunt.

4. Abram Barnes and Samuel Whitmore Flanders—witnesses to several visions, Hartland, ME, 1845.[592]

I have been connected with the Advent people since 1844, was personally acquainted with those that was led into fanaticism. I was also acquainted with Sr. White and her father's family in Portland. I have seen her have a number of visions, have heard her relate them. I have compared them with the word of God, have found them to be in harmony with the Bible. I have perfect confidence in them. I knew Sr. White at that time to labor faithfully from place to place with a pointed testimony to those that had gone into fanaticism, showing them their wrong course and pointing out the errors that they had fallen into. Her labors was blessed and many rejoiced in the light that God had given them through her & any testimony that may be brought charging Sr. White as being in any wise connected with or countenancing in any degree those fanatical abominations practiced in Maine & elsewhere during the years 1844 to 1846 is utterly false. —Abram Barnes, S. W. Flanders.

5. Otis Nichols—V32. "Randolph Vision," Zaccheus Thayer's house, Randolph, MA, spring 1846.[593]

Sister Ellen was taken off in vision with extraordinary manifestations, and continued talking in vision with a shrill voice, which could be distinctly understood by all present, until about sundown. S., R. and F. [***Sargent, Robbins, and French***] were much exasperated, as well as excited, to hear sister E. [***Ellen***] talk in vision, which they declared was of the Devil; they exhausted all their influence, and bodily strength, to destroy the effect of the vision.[594] They would unite in singing very loud; and then alternately would talk and read from the Bible in a loud voice, in order that E. might not be heard, until their strength was exhausted, and their hands would shake so they could not read from the Bible. But amidst all this confusion and noise, E.'s clear and shrill voice, as she talked in vision, was distinctly heard by all present. The opposition of these men continued as long as they could talk and sing, notwithstanding some of their own friends rebuked them, and requested them to stop. But says R [***Robbins***], "You are bound to an idol; you are worshiping a golden calf."

Mr. Thayer, the owner of the house, was not fully satisfied that her vision was of the Devil, as R. declared it to be.[595] He wanted it tested in some way. He had heard that visions of satanic power were arrested by opening the Bible and laying it on the person in vision, and asked S. if he would test it in this way, which he declined to do. Then Thayer took a heavy, large quarto family Bible which was laying on the table, and seldom used, opened it, and laid it open upon the breast of E. while in vision, as she was then inclined backward against the wall in the corner of the room. Immediately after the Bible was laid upon her, she arose upon her feet, and walked into the middle of the room, with the Bible open in one hand, and lifted up as high as she could reach, and with her eyes steadily looking upward, declared in a solemn manner, "The inspired testimony from God," or words of the same import. And then she continued for a long time, while the Bible was extended in one hand, and her eyes looking upwards, and not on the Bible, to turn over the leaves with her other hand, and place her finger upon certain passages, and correctly utter their words with a solemn voice. Many present looked at the passages where her finger was pointed, to see if she spoke them correctly, for her eyes at the same time were looking upwards. Some of the passages referred to were judgments against the wicked and blasphemers; and others were admonitions and instructions relative to our present condition.

In this state she continued all the afternoon until near sunset, when she came out of vision. When E. arose in vision upon her feet, with the heavy open Bible in her hand, and walked the room, uttering the passages of scripture, S., R. and F. were silenced. For the remainder of the time they were troubled, with many others; but they shut their eyes and braved it out without making any acknowledgement of their feelings.

6. Joseph Bates to J. N. Loughborough—V44. "Wild Colt Tamed Vision," going to Poland, ME, fall 1846.[596]

In the fall of 1846 Brother and Sister White wished to go from Topsham to Poland, Me., a distance of about thirty miles. Brother White obtained the use of a partly broken colt, and a two-seated market-wagon [grocery delivery wagon], which was constructed without a dashboard. There was a step across the front of the wagon, and an iron step from the shafts. It was necessary that extreme care be taken in driving the colt; for if the lines or anything touched his flanks, he would instantly kick furiously; and he had to be held in continually with a "taut rein" to keep him from running. The owner of this colt lived in Poland. As Elder White had been used to managing unbroken colts, he thought he would have no serious trouble with this one. Had he known, however, that during its frantic demonstrations it had previously killed two men, one by crushing him against the rocks by the roadside, he might have been less confident.

Joseph Bates

Israel Dammon

On this occasion there were four persons in the wagon,—Elder White and his wife, on the front seat; and Elder Bates and Israel Dammon, on the back seat.[597] While Elder White was giving his utmost care to keep the horse under control, Sister White was conversing about the truth, when suddenly the power of God came down upon the company, and she was taken off in vision while seated in the wagon. The moment she shouted, "Glory!" as she went into vision, the colt stopped perfectly still, and dropped his head, looking like a sleepy old horse. At the same time, Sister White arose, and with her eyes turned upward, stepped over the front of the wagon, down onto the shafts, with her hand on the colt's haunches. Elder Bates called out to Elder White, "The colt will kick that woman to death." Elder White replied, "The Lord has the colt in charge now; I do not wish to interfere." The colt stood as quietly as an old horse. By the roadside was a bank about six feet high, and beyond, next the fence, was a grassy place. Brother Bates said that the bank was steeper than the roof of a house, and that they could not ascend it. Sister White, with her eyes still upward, not once looking down, went up the bank as readily as if she was going up a flight of stairs. She walked back and forth on the grass-plot for a few minutes, describing the beauties of the new earth. Then, with her eyes in the same posture, she came down the bank, and walking up to the wagon, stepped upon the step of the shafts, again laying her hand on the colt. She then stepped on the shafts, and into the wagon again. The moment she sat down upon the seat, she came out of vision; and that instant the horse, without any indication from the driver, started up, ready to go on his way.

While Mrs. White was out of the wagon, Elder White thought he would test the horse, and see if he were really tame. At first he just touched him with the whip; at other times the horse would have responded with a kick, but now he did not move. Elder White then struck him quite a blow, then harder, and still harder. The colt paid no attention whatever to the blows, but seemed as harmless as the lions whose mouths the angel shut the night Daniel spent in their den. "It was a solemn place," said Elder Bates, "and it was evident that the same power that produced the vision, for the time being subdued the wild nature of the colt."

7. Joseph Bates—V45. "Fairhaven Halo Vision," Fairhaven, MA, March 6, 1847.[598]

It is now about two years since I first saw the author, and heard her relate the substance of her visions as she has since published them in Portland (April 6, 1846). Although I could see nothing in them that militated against the word, yet I felt alarmed and tried exceedingly, and for a long time unwilling to believe that it was any thing more than what was produced by a protracted debilitated state of her body.

I therefore sought opportunities in presence of others, when her mind seemed freed from excitement, (out of meeting) to question, and cross question her, and her friends which accompanied her, especially her elder sister [***Sarah***], to get if possible at the truth. During the number of visits she has made to New Bedford and Fairhaven since, while at our meetings, I have seen her in vision a number of times, and also in Topsham, Me., and those who were present during some of these exciting scenes know well with what interest and intensity I listened to every word, and watched every move to detect deception, or mesmeric influence. And I thank God for the opportunity I have had with others to witness these things. I can now confidently speak for myself. I believe the work is of God, and is given to comfort and strengthen his "scattered," "torn," and "pealed people," since the closing up of our work for the world in October, 1844. The distracted state of lo, heres! and lo, theres! since that time has exceedingly perplexed God's honest, willing people, and made it exceedingly difficult for such as were not able to expound the many conflicting texts that have been presented to their view. I confess that I have received light and instruction on many passages that I could not before clearly distinguish. I believe her to be a self-sacrificing, honest, willing child of God, and saved, if at all, through her entire obedience to His will.

8. James White—V51. "Error Versus Truth Vision," David Arnold's carriage house, Volney, NY, Aug. 18, 1848.[599]

In the Spring of 1848, in company with Bro. Bates, we attended a Conference in Conn. There were probably twenty-five Sabbath-keepers present. Here we first saw Bro. Holt [***George W. Holt***]. We were all much encouraged at this meeting. Bro. Holt soon began to bear testimony for the truth. Bro. Bates began to labor more extensively as the way opened before him. At this time we had an invitation from Bro. Edson to visit Western New York, and hold a Conference with them. We were destitute of means; but with feeble health we entered the hayfield to earn the necessary means. And when fainting beneath the noon-day sun, we would bow before God in our swath, and cry to him for strength, rise refreshed and praise his holy name aloud, then mow on again. In five weeks we earned enough to bear our expenses with Mrs. W. to the Conference. Bro. Bates joined us at this meeting. The notice had been given to all in the Empire State who were in sympathy with our views, and there was a general rally, yet not over forty present.[600] And what a confusion of sentiments among this few! A spirit of discussion and contention for points not important prevailed, so that we who had come so far could hardly have chance to give our message, and the meeting would have proved a failure, and the good brethren would have separated in confusion and trial had not the Lord worked in a special manner. The Spirit of the Lord rested upon Mrs. W., and she was taken off in vision. The entire congregation believed that it was the work of God, and were deeply affected. She related to them what she had seen, which was given to correct some errors among them, and in melting strains exhorted them to leave their errors, and those points on which they had differed, and unite on the important truths of the Third Message.

Hiram Edson

And on that blessed evening, the brethren sacrificed their babel of sentiments, and united on the truth. And what was the result? Harmony began to prevail, and many came flocking to the standard of truth. Soon the Lord laid the case of our beloved Bro. Rhodes on Bro. Edson and others. He had labored faithfully and spent a good property in the first and second Messages, but being wounded by the backsliding and covetousness of professed Advent brethren, he left the flock in a state of despair, and sustained himself by hunting and fishing in an uninhabited part of the State of New York. Bro. Edson in company with others, visited him several times, with the design to induce him to come among the brethren, and in all traveled with his team near one thousand miles, and finally, with the special help of God, gained the object. When Bro. Rhodes first came among the brethren, despair was stamped upon every feature. But soon hope and faith revived, and he became a successful laborer in the cause.

9. Alexander Ross—the same vision (V51) as above.[601]

Sister White, while in vision, arose to her feet and took the family Bible upon her left hand; the book was one of ordinary size. While holding it open, high up, without looking toward it, with her right hand she would turn from text to text, and placing her finger on the scripture, would repeat the same. I looked at many of the texts to see if she was repeating the one to which she pointed. Myself or some of the company looked at them all. In every case she not only repeated the text to which she pointed, but she did so while her eyes were looking upward and in an opposite direction from the Bible. It was these scriptures which she repeated that overthrew the false theories of the Sabbath-keepers assembled at Volney, in August, 1848, and caused us to unite upon the truth.

10. James White—V53. "Large Bible in Hand Vision," Isaac Cook Snow's house, Hannibal, NY, Aug. 26, 1848.[602]

Ellen rose up in vision, took the large Bible, held it up before the Lord, talked from it, then carried it to this humble Brother who was not on the Sabbath and put it in his arms. He took it while tears were rolling down his bosom. Then Ellen came and sat down by me. She was in vision 1½ hours in which time she did not breathe at all. It was an affecting time.

11. Louisa Howland, Rebekah Winslow, Frances Lunt—V77. "Bible Applied Vision," Topsham, ME, Sept. 23, 1849.[603]

In the early history of this cause, we the undersigned have been witnesses of frequent special manifestations of the power of God upon Sister White while in vision. On one occasion while in meeting at our house in Topsham, Maine, she was taken off in vision, and soon rose to her feet and went to the table where there was a large number of books, and put her hand directly on the Bible, opened it, and went to a person in the room and laid it upon their breast, and then talked to them upon the text that they would find in the Bible where it was opened, which applied to their case. Then went and took another Bible, opened it, and placed it upon the breast of another, and talked to them upon scripture that applied to their case, and also did the same to a third person in the room. (All this time her eyes were opened and fixed upward,) and then went back and sat down in the place she arose from.

Louisa Howland

12. Marion Truesdail—the same vision (V77) as above.[604]

I was present when Sister White went to the table and picked up one Bible after another from among the books that were on the table, laying the Bible on the breast of the one for whom she had a text of Scripture. This was done while her eyes were uplifted toward heaven. On this occasion she held the Bible above her head while speaking to me; and then she placed it upon my breast. The passage given me was 2 Cor. 6:17.

13. Frances Lunt—the same vision (V77) as above.[605]

There was at the side of the room where the meetings were held, a table upon which were a number of books of various kinds, among which were several Bibles of ordinary size. While in vision, Mrs. White rose to her feet, went to the table, picked up a Bible without touching another book, and holding it open above her head with her left hand, with the index finger of the right hand pointed to the text of Scripture she was repeating as she stood before the person for whom it was designed, and then placed the open book on the chest of the person before whom she repeated the scripture. Returning to the table, she took another Bible, and in the same manner repeated another text of Scripture and placed the open Bible on the chest of the individual she was addressing. This act was repeated to about half a dozen persons; after which in a graceful manner, she took her seat in a chair, while her eyes were all the while looking upward and away from the book.

Marion and two of her siblings are mentioned in a manuscript that records Ellen White's words in vision:

(Putting the Bible on **Augusta Stowell**:) Study it, study it, take it, believe it, walk out on it, the Word of God, faith, the Book of books, the all-seeing eye![606] Tremble before the Lord of hosts. Look ye, the mind has been filled, it has been engrossed with trash. Cast it off, bear it away. Walk carefully before thy God. Keep thine eye steady upon thy God, faith, faith, faith, faith, faith. Take it as the man of thy counsel, take it as a hammer, a fire it will consume the dross, it will consume the tin, too much trash, cast it out.

(Taking the large Bible containing the Apocrypha:) Pure and undefiled, a part of it is consumed, holy, holy, walk carefully, tempted. The Word of God, take it (**Marion Stowell**), bind it long upon thine heart, pure and unadulterated. How lovely, how lovely, how lovely. My blood, My blood, My blood [quoting the words of Christ]. O the children of disobedience, reproved, reproved. Thy word, thy word, thy word, a part of it is burned unadulterated, a part of the hidden book, a part of it is burned (the Apocrypha).

Those that shall despitefully tread [treat?] that remnant would think that they are doing God service. Why? because they are led captive by Satan at his will. Hidden book, it is cast out. Bind it to the heart (4 times) bind it, bind it, bind it, (laying the Bible on **Oswald Stowell**) let not its pages be closed, read it carefully. Snares will beset on every side, take the strait truth bind it to the heart (3 times) let everything be cast out.[607]

14. Washington Morse—V113. "Smith-Allen Vision," Stowe, VT, Nov. 1, 1851.[608]

One meeting was held at Stowe, which we attended. Here, sister W. was given a vision of existing circumstances and conditions of much importance. As the meeting was a large one, and great interest was created by the incident of the vision, Bro. White called physicians to examine his wife while she was in vision. They were unable to account for her condition upon any other hypothesis than that of a supernatural manifestation; and such they believed it to be. They were much astonished and visibly affected by the solemnity of the occasion. The conviction fastened itself upon all, that the great God was, through the ministry of angels, communing with his servant. In relating what had been shown to her, which she did after regaining her natural condition and strength, sister White mentioned, among other things, that the angel had said to Eld. Joseph Baker, of Lebanon, N. H., 'Feed my sheep.'[609] This was repeated several times, and the statement was added, 'This you must do, if you would live,' or words of similar import. Bro. Baker arose and responded to the truthfulness of the testimony, so far as his convictions were concerned. Stepping to the chart, he pointed to the representation of the angel of Rev. 14:15–18, and said, with tears in his eyes, '*I never can go through.*' Sister W. arose, and with deep feeling encouraged him to go forward and do his duty. Her exhortation visibly affected the entire audience, and all felt that an angel had spoken through this servant of the Lord. It is a solemn fact that a short time after this, Eld. Baker gave up laboring, and went down to the grave. He was an efficient laborer in the Lord's vineyard, and no doubt had a very important work committed to his hands. But the burden seemed heavier than he could carry, and he was lost to the cause which was in such great need of his work.

Washington Morse

"THEY WERE UNABLE TO ACCOUNT FOR HER CONDITION UPON ANY OTHER HYPOTHESIS THAN THAT OF A SUPERNATURAL MANIFESTATION."

15. Martha Byington Amadon—V121. "Sabbath Vision," Potsdam, NY, Aug. 26, 1852.[610]

"We have heard from the bright, the holy land;
We have heard and our hearts are glad."[611]

Mrs. E. G. White was a woman very gifted in prayer, her voice clear, her words distinct and ringing; and it was almost always during one of these earnest seasons of prayer that she was taken off in vision. She also had important visions in public, usually an unexpected experience to those present.

Though many of her old friends and associates are passed away—Elders J. N. Loughborough, S. N. Haskell, G. W. Amadon, and others, yet there are people living today in various parts of the world who have seen her in vision from time to time, and what is here stated will doubtless be familiar to them.

George and Martha D. Amadon

As one who has frequently observed her in vision, knowing the company of people usually present, all deeply observant and believers in her exercises, I have often wondered why a more vivid description of the scenes which transpired has not been given.

In vision her eyes were open. There was no breath, but there were graceful movements of the shoulders, arms, and hands expressive of what she saw.[612] It was impossible for any one else to move her hands or arms. She often uttered words singly, and sometimes sentences which expressed to those about her the nature of the view she was having, either of heaven or of earth.

"I HAVE OFTEN WONDERED WHY A MORE VIVID DESCRIPTION OF THE SCENES WHICH TRANSPIRED HAS NOT BEEN GIVEN."

Her first word in vision was "Glory," sounding at first close by, and then dying away in the distance, seemingly far away. This was sometimes repeated. When beholding Jesus our Saviour, she would exclaim in musical tones, low and sweet, "Lovely, lovely, lovely," many times, always with the greatest affection. Looking upon the cloud which enveloped the Father, as she afterward explained, her shoulders would draw back, her hands lift in awe, and her lips would close. Sometimes she would cross her lips with her finger, meaning that she was not at that time to reveal what she saw, but later a message would perhaps go across the continent to save some individual or church from disaster. She said, "Words cannot express the beauties of heaven;" no more can they describe these scenes of which she was a part. Her visions seemed to bring you nearer heaven, and you longed to be there.

There was never an excitement among those present during a vision; nothing caused fear. It was a solemn, quiet scene, sometimes lasting an hour,—a scene, during which, like prophets of old, she saw so much of the vastness of God's work for His people, that it would be the principal subject of her writing for two or more years. When the vision was ended, and she lost sight of the heavenly light, as it were, coming back to the earth once more, she would exclaim with a long-drawn sigh as she took her first natural breath, "D-a-r-k." She was then limp and strengthless, and had to be assisted to her chair, her position in vision being a recumbent one. These impressive scenes encouraged and strengthened the faith of those present, not only in her work, but in the Word of God, which liveth and abideth forever.[613]

John Byington

The first time I ever saw her in vision was at my father's [***John Byington's***] house in Potsdam, New York.[614] I was a girl of twenty, and there were only a few Sabbath-keepers then anywhere, no church as yet having been organized. This was in the early fifties. Brother John Andrews accompanied Elder and Mrs. White to our place, my father having made an appointment for Sister White to speak at the Wesleyan Methodist church in Morley, two miles distant. Just as we were about to start for the meeting, a violent thunderstorm came up, lasting so long that we could not go.

But what I best remember of that evening nearly seventy-five years ago, was the occasion of our family worship, when Sister White was taken in vision. The subject of this vision was the Sabbath question, and, in connection with it, she saw that God had a great work for Brother Andrews to do. As she came out of vision she reached for the hand of a young woman near her, and, calling her by name, earnestly said, "Will you keep the Sabbath?" As the girl hesitated, Sister White repeated, "Will you keep the Sabbath? Will you?" She responded, "I will," and she always did to the day of her death. Sister White had had no acquaintance with this girl, a beautiful young woman about whom we had all been anxious, fearing that she would not take the right step concerning the Sabbath. The earnestness of the Lord's servant won her over, and it seemed that the Lord must have presented this case in the vision and impressed Sister White with what to say.

16. J. N. Loughborough—V126. "Thou Art the Man Vision," Rochester, NY, Oct. 9, 1852.[615]

I have seen Sister White in vision about fifty times.[616] The first time was about forty years ago, when Brother Oswald Stowell was very sick, and expected to die. It was on the Sabbath, the first Sabbath I ever kept. Brother Stowell wanted his case commended to God, and desired the brethren to pray for him. In answer to their prayers he was healed and went to work again two days later. Brother White, who was present at the time, said to me, "Ellen is in vision." I looked at her and saw her kneeling by the bed and looking up toward heaven, and she soon began to shout praises to God. Brother White said, "There is no breath in her body." Eyes open, no breath, yet her pulse beating naturally, and everything else in a normal condition! Her eyes seemed intently fixed upon something off at a great distance.

J. N. Loughborough

During this vision of Sr. White, which lasted one hour and twenty minutes, she did not breathe, as those present clearly proved, and as I have since that time seen tested and confirmed by physicians who have been present when she was in vision.[617] Her condition while thus deprived of breath was not that of one who has fainted. Instead of a deathly pallor to the countenance, its color was fresh and florid as usual. Her condition also agreed with that described in the vision of God given to Balaam: "Balaam the son of Beor hath said, and the man whose eyes are open hath said; he hath said, which heard the words of God, and knew the knowledge of the Most High, which saw the vision of the Almighty, falling into a trance, but having his eyes open." Num. 24:4, 15, 16. Her eyes were open, not with any ghastly or vacant stare, but a pleasant look, differing only from the natural in that she appeared to be looking intently at some object in the distance. Her eyes were raised upward, and she would turn them occasionally from side to side as though viewing different scenes. At the same time there were graceful movements of the arms and hands, either pointing to different objects shown her in vision, or clasping them together over her breast. Various tests were applied to show that she knew nothing of what was transpiring around her. For instance, a sheet of paper brought suddenly from behind and toward her eye would not produce even a wince, or the slightest movement on her part. Even the thrusting of the finger suddenly toward her eye, as though going to strike the sight (which of course would cause us to close the eye, or to dodge the anticipated attack), had no effect upon her. After using these various tests, we decided that these manifestations were something beyond human control, and that they were produced by some power superior to her own.

17. Franklin C. Castle—V129. "Character of the Ministers Vision," Rochester, NY, March 1, 1853.[618]

It is now forty-four years since my first introduction to the ADVENT REVIEW AND SABBATH HERALD, and to the office of publication, then in Rochester, N. Y. The paper was then printed on a hand-press. There I heard my first sermon on the Advent doctrine and formed a brief acquaintance with some of the early pioneers in the Advent movement. Many of them are sleeping, awaiting the Master's call at the morning of the glorious resurrection. I mention such names as Elder James White, Elder J. N. Andrews, and the sister of the Editor, Annie R. Smith, who, under trying circumstances, arose in the night, and composed the remarkable hymn beginning, "Be patient, be patient, no longer despairing." My soul has often been encouraged under its inspiring words. She, being dead, yet speaketh. I love the precious words so comforting to the heart of the pilgrim and stranger. It is No. 1182 in our hymn-book.

Franklin C. Castle

I might mention others who were connected with Brother White's family, as his house was the home of the workers connected with the office. I had traveled some eight hundred miles, hoping to find a chance to learn the printer's trade, but they had more help than work. The office seemed to be the most holy place that I had ever entered. There was a deep solemnity upon me as I went up those steps to find where the REVIEW was printed. As I became somewhat acquainted with the workers, I soon saw that they considered the work in which they were engaged as very sacred. The impressions that were made on my mind in the ten days I spent there have never been wholly effaced, though I have to acknowledge my unfaithfulness and a lack of humble devotion and consecration. But I am glad that the sweet voice of mercy is still extended to the straying and fallen ones of earth.

My heart wells up within me as I read the precious words of instruction that come from the pen of Sister White. One morning when I was at Brother White's, as worship was conducted in two rooms, a portion of the company being in the room where Brother Nathaniel White was sick with consumption, and praying for him, some one came into the room where we were, and said that Sister White was in vision. We all went into the room where she was, and there I saw the manifestation of God's power, and the means that he had chosen in his love to convey instruction especially to Christ's followers in the closing hours of probation.[619]

18. Merritt G. Kellogg—V131. "Pretensions of Holiness Vision," Tyrone, Livingston County, MI, May 29, 1853.[620]

I am quite certain that she did not breathe at that time while in vision, nor in any of several others which she had when I was present. The coming out of vision was as marked as her going into it. The first indication we had that the vision was ended, was in her again beginning to breathe. She drew her first breath deep, long, and full, in a manner showing that her lungs had been entirely empty of air. After drawing the first breath, several minutes passed before she drew the second, which filled the lungs precisely as did the first; then a pause of two minutes, and a third inhalation, after which the breathing became natural.

19. J. N. Loughborough—V132. "Jackson Vision"—V133. "Case and Russell Vision," Jackson, MI, June 3, 1853.[621]

Dan Palmer's house in Jackson

On June 3 a meeting was held in the house of Bro. P. [***Daniel R. Palmer***], when all the church of Jackson came together. In time of a praying season over the state of things in the Church, Sr. White had a vision. While she was in vision C. [***Hiram S. Case***] and R. [***Charles P. Russell***] came forward and examined her to see that she did not breathe, and that she knew nothing of what was taking place around her. Her eyes being open and uplifted to heaven, C. [***Case***] put his finger in her eye, to see if there would be any resistance, and then expressed himself as perfectly satisfied that the vision was something beyond her control.[622]

Daniel R. Palmer

Abigail Palmer

After she came out of the vision she related what she saw concerning Sr. P. [***Abigail Palmer***.] She spoke of the spirit she had manifested on the occasion referred to, saying that it was wrong, and that it was not right to have such a spirit even against our enemies. Having gone thus far, she said, "There is more that was shown me in this case, but it is not now distinctly before my mind." After she sat down, C. and R. got up, and each said it must now be evident to all that this vision was of God. They said that they were now perfectly satisfied, and that they could never doubt the visions any more. Then they bore down on Sr. P. in a most unmerciful manner, calling loudly to her to "confess! confess!" She did not confess the word they wanted her to, and so their indignation against her was aroused. In this state of things the meeting closed for that day.

Cyrenius Smith

On June 4 (Sabbath), we again met at the house of Bro. P., when Sr. White again bore testimony. On the evening of the 3d, as we were engaged in family worship at the house of Bro. Cyrenius Smith, in West Jackson, Sr. White was taken off in vision and shown the whole case again. On the 4th she related this vision. She delineated the character of C. and R., and reproved them for their unmerciful course toward Sr. P. Sr. White told them that although they had made such a great trial over the word Sr. P. had spoken, the Lord had shown her in vision that the word was never spoken by Sr. P.—that it was another word that sounded somewhat like it.[623] Then, for the first time since the trial began, Sr. P. told the word she did use. She confessed the wrong feelings and spirit she had manifested, and as far as she was concerned, the breach was healed. How was it with C. and R.? Did they confess? Not a bit of it. They complained bitterly of the reproof that had been administered to them. Their very spirit manifested in resisting the reproof was, however, of just the character that the testimony accused them, and so the more they talked, the more it was manifest to others that they had just the spirit the vision accused them of possessing. These two men who claimed the day before that they had such abundant evidence of the truthfulness of the visions that they could never doubt again, were now ready to give it all up, simply because their own sins had been set in order before them. On they went with their opposition, and in a few weeks, getting other disaffected spirits to join them, they commenced the publication of a sheet called *The Messenger of Truth*. The mission of the sheet and its conductors seemed to be to tear down and defame instead of building up.[624]

20. Franklin C. Castle—V138. "To Those of Little Experience Vision," Stowe, VT, Sept. 12, 1853.[625]

A physician was present, and made such examination of her as his wisdom and learning dictated, to find the cause of the manifestation. A lighted candle was held close to her eyes, which were wide open; not a muscle of the eye moved. He then examined her in regard to her pulse, and also in regard to her breathing, and there was no respiration. The result was that he was satisfied that it could not be accounted for on natural or scientific principles. Signed. F. C. Castle.

21. David H. Lamson—V149. "Triumph of the Saints Vision," James White's house, Rochester, NY, June 26, 1854.[626]

David Henry Lamson

[*Loughborough spoke*—] I want now to call before you a living witness here in this house. Brother Lampson [***David H. Lamson***], will you please step forward and relate to the audience what you saw during one of Sister White's visions where you were present?

It was in 1854, at the home of Brother White in Rochester. I was then seventeen years old. It seems to me I can almost hear those thrilling shouts of "G-l-o-r-y!" which she uttered. Then she sank back to the floor, not falling, but sinking gently, and was supported in the arms of an attendant. Two physicians came in, an old man and a young man. Brother White was anxious that they should examine Sister White closely, which they did. A small looking-glass was brought, and one of them held it over her mouth when she talked; but very soon they gave this up and said, She doesn't breathe. Then they closely examined her sides to try to find some evidence of deep breathing, but they did not find it. When the examination was over, she rose to her feet, and then had a view of some things connected with the seven last plagues. She put her hands up to her hair, and Brother White and Brother Andrews tried with all their might to keep her hands down, but they could not move them, nor keep her fingers from opening and closing, and she tore out locks of her hair. Then she saw the triumph of the saints, and her shouts of triumph I can seem to hear even now.

22. Drusilla Lamson—the same vision (V149) as above.[627]

Drusilla Orton Lamson

I remember the meeting when the trial was made, namely, to test what Brother White had frequently said, that Sister White did not breathe while in vision, but I cannot recall the name of the doctor who

was present. . . . It must have been Doctor Fleming [***Dr. Lorenzo Dow Fleming***], as he was the doctor called sometimes for counsel. He is, however, now dead. I can say this much, that the test was made, and no sign of breath was visible on the looking-glass.

23. David Seeley—the same vision (V149) as above.[628]

This is to certify that I have read the above testimonials of David Lamson and Mrs. Drusilla Lamson, concerning the physician's statement when examining Mrs. E. G. White while she was in vision, June

26, 1854. I was present at that meeting, and witnessed the examination. I agree with what is stated by Brother and Sister Lamson, and would say further that it was Doctor Fleming [***Dr. Lorenzo Dow Fleming***] and another younger physician [***Dr. David Abeel Baldwin***] who made the examination. After Mrs. White rose to her feet, as they have stated, quoting the texts of Scripture, Doctor Fleming called for a lighted candle. He held this candle as near her lips as possible without burning, and in direct line with her breath in case she breathed. There was not the slightest flicker of the blaze. The doctor then said, with emphasis, "That settles it forever, there is no breath in her body."[629]

24. Louisa M. Morton—V173. "Return Unto Me and I Will Return Unto You Vision," Hillsdale, MI, Feb. 15, 1857.[630]

The way opened for me to attend a conference at Hillsdale [Michigan, February 13–15, 1857]. There were two hundred Sabbath-keepers present; all firm believers in the Third Angel's Message. The messengers present were Brn. White, Holt, Waggoner and Cornell. I must say I was very much surprised when I heard the evidence presented in favor of present truth. They had Bible to prove every view they presented; and more than all, the Holy Spirit bore witness to the same. I realized more than ever the fulfillment of the Saviour's words, "It is expedient for you that I go away; for if I go not away the Comforter will not come unto you; but if I depart I will send him unto you"; again, "Howbeit, when he, the Spirit of truth, is come, he will guide you into all truth. . . . and he will show you things to come." [John 16:7, 13.] At the last meeting [Feb. 15, 1857] Sr. White was taken off in vision. It was the most solemn scene I ever witnessed. It has made an impression on my mind that can never be erased while reason and life remain. When she came out of vision she gave one of the most thrilling exhortations I ever heard. She repeated these words often: "Return unto me and I will return unto you, saith the Lord, and heal all your backslidings."[631] I am confident that no one could speak as she did without receiving instruction from that Teacher who spake as never man spake.

25. Mr. and Mrs. Archibald Franklin Fowler—the same vision (~V173) as above.[632]

We were present when (in February, 1857) Sister E. G. White had a vision in Waldron's Hall, Hillsdale. Dr. Lord [***David H. Lord, M.D.***] made an examination, and said, "Her heart beats, but there is no breath. There is life, but no action of the lungs; I cannot account for this condition."

26. Charles S. Glover—the same vision (~V173) as above.[633]

I was present when Sister White had the above named vision in Waldron's Hall, Hillsdale. In addition to the above statement, I heard the doctor say that Sister White's condition in vision was "beyond his knowledge." He also said, "There is something supernatural about that." Signed, "C. S. Glover, Battle Creek, Mich., Jan. 19, 1891."

Charles S. Glover

27. William R. and Eliza Carpenter—the same vision (~V173) as above.[634]

This is to certify that we were present in Waldron's Hall, Hillsdale, Mich., in February, 1857, when Mrs. E. G. White had a vision, and while in that condition was examined by Dr. Lord, and we heard his public statement respecting the case, as given above by Brother and Sister Fowler.

28. D. T. Bourdeau—~V176. "Buck's Bridge Vision," St. Lawrence County, NY, June 28, 1857.[635]

June 28, 1857, I saw Sister Ellen G. White in vision for the first time. I was an unbeliever in the visions; but one circumstance among others that I might mention convinced me that her visions were of God. To satisfy my mind as to whether she breathed or not, I first put my hand on her chest sufficiently long to know that there was no more heaving of the lungs than there would have been had she been a corpse. I then took my hand and placed it over her mouth, pinching her nostrils between my thumb and forefinger, so that it was impossible for her to exhale or inhale air, even if she had desired to do so. I held her thus with my hand about ten minutes, long enough for her to suffocate under ordinary circumstances; she was not in the least affected by this ordeal. Since witnessing this wonderful phenomenon, I have not once been inclined to doubt the divine origin of her visions.

"I HELD HER THUS WITH MY HAND ABOUT TEN MINUTES, LONG ENOUGH FOR HER TO SUFFOCATE UNDER ORDINARY CIRCUMSTANCES."

Daniel T. Bourdeau

Just two years after this, in a letter to Uriah Smith, Bourdeau contrasted Ellen White's appearance in vision with the appearance of a spiritualist from Morristown, Vermont.[636]

BRO. SMITH: A few days after my return from Jay, I attended a Spiritual meeting in this place, with the intention of being an eye-witness of the mysterious performances which are so much noised abroad in the land at the present time; and as my expectations were met, it may not be amiss for me to briefly relate what I saw and heard.

The principal speaker and performer in this meeting, was Mrs. Parker, from Morristown, Vt. A short time before the meeting commenced, she came into the room where the people were assembled, and sat down at a small distance from the congregation, while certain of my acquaintances were interrogating me in regard to the hell spoken of in the Bible. Hardly had Mrs. P. been seated five minutes before she fell into a trance. The eyes of the whole assembly were at once fastened upon her, and she commenced to perform. She rubbed her hands and face, twisted, and made such gestures as were calculated to captivate the attention of the congregation; and when she was perfectly under the control of the spirit of Doctor Franklin, she arose, with her eyes closed, drew near to me, and delivered me a lecture on the subject of universal salvation through Christ. And O, how she did extol Jesus; and how her remarks were calculated to charm and deceive the uninformed!

Here I could not help noticing how her views of the merits of Christ clashed with the sentiments of other Spiritualists, who trample under foot the Son of God, and say that his blood has no more virtue than the blood of any other man, and that the doctrine of atonement has the same tendency as the doctrine of indulgences. I was also led to contrast what I saw and heard, with what I have been permitted to witness since I joined the humble company who are keeping the commandments of God, and believe in the restoration of the gifts; and how plain it was to my mind that the spiritual manifestations of these last days are the spurious work.[637]

"WHILE THE POWER AND SPIRIT OF GOD RESTED UPON THOSE WHO WERE WITH HER, SHE WAS BREATHLESS."

On one hand I saw an individual [***Alvira Parker***], pale as death, and associated with such as make no difference between the holy and the vile, between light and darkness, with hellish looks, performing in such a manner as to gratify the desires of those who were imbued with the spirit she possessed, and overwhelm the timid and fearful, and create laughter in those of a trifling spirit. On the other hand was presented before me an unassuming and humble person [***Ellen White***], ardently striving to follow the meek and lowly Jesus, and willing to submit to the judgment of her brethren, (who prefer light to darkness, and righteousness to unrighteousness,) calmly and quietly raising her eyes toward heaven, while pouring her heart in supplication to the God of heaven; and while the power and Spirit of God rested upon those who were with her, she was breathless. Her countenance was bright and heavenly, and none of her actions were indecent and calculated to create laughter or fear. She was wrapped up in a heavenly vision, and had no knowledge of what transpired around her, occasionally moving her hands and uttering a few significant words, to indicate the scenes that passed before her and the things that she heard.[638]

Mrs. Alvira P. Parker

Mrs. Ellen G. White

On one hand was a Spiritualist [***Alvira Parker***], purporting to be under the direct influence of the spirit of a dead man, (while the Bible says, "The dead know not anything,") striking at the very foundation of the christian religion, and stating that men cannot and should not believe alike, and that a man's heaven or hell is in his own bosom, and that there is no Devil, thus fostering all kinds of sin—helping to swell the cry of peace and safety, and binding the wicked in bundles against the day of judgment and perdition of ungodly men.[639] On the other hand was a devoted christian [***Ellen White***], just out of vision, relating what the Lord had revealed unto her, reproving sin and sinners, strengthening and consoling the weak, teaching christians to love the Bible and live up to the doctrines therein contained, and to come up to the unity of the faith, that they might be strong in the Lord, fight the good fight, escape the wrath of God, and have a home in the kingdom soon to be ushered in. . . .[640]

DANIEL T. BOURDEAU.
West Enosburgh, Vt., Feb., 1859.

29. James White—V180. "Rich Young Man Vision," Monterey, MI, Oct. 8, 1857.[641]

From Caledonia we went to Monterey, where on the evening of the 8th inst. there was a meeting in the school-house near Bro. George Lay's, and an expectation to hear preaching.[642] We went to the house feeling that we had nothing for the people. We told brethren on the way that we could not decide on any subject, and wished them to select. We sung a hymn, and had great freedom in prayer; sung again, but felt perplexed as to duty. In this state of mind, knowing not what to do, we gave liberty to others to use the time, when Mrs. W. arose and spoke with much freedom.

"… HER VOICE CHANGED, AND THE DEEP, CLEAR SHOUTS OF GLORY! HALLELUJAH! THRILLED EVERY

The place was filled with the Spirit of the Lord. Some rejoiced, others wept. All felt that the Lord was drawing very near. How sacred the place. Those present will never forget that meeting. When seated, Mrs. W. began to praise the Lord, and continued rising higher and higher in perfect triumph in the Lord, till her voice changed, and the deep, clear shouts of Glory! Hallelujah! thrilled every heart. She was in vision.

Unknown to us there was a poor, discouraged brother present, who had thrown his armor down, in consequence, in part, at least, of neglect by his wealthy brethren, and was returning to strong habits which threatened the happiness of himself and family. A most touching and encouraging message was given for him. By the grace of God he raised his head that very evening, and he and his good wife are again happy in hope. Monterey church will never forget that evening. At least they never should.

30. William Rufus Hyde Avery—~V189. "Great Controversy Vision," Lovett's Grove, OH, March 14, 1858.[643]

The truth was preached here in Bowling Green, O[hio], in 1857, by G. W. Holdt.[644] Quite a number came out and commenced to keep the Sabbath. In the spring of 1858, Brother James White and wife came to our place and held a few meetings to encourage us in the faith. While they were here we lost a little boy [***John Avery***].[645] Brother White preached the funeral sermon, and during the service Sister White was taken off in vision. She was in this condition when we went to the grave. It was a solemn time. Quite a number of the congregation remained until she came out of the vision.

Lovett's Grove schoolhouse, location of Ellen White's "Great Controversy Vision" on the property of Oliver Mears

31. John N. Loughborough—~V214. "Great Distress Coming Vision," Parkville, MI, Jan. 12, 1861.[646]

When I first learned of the visions of sister White, some fifteen years ago, I was a firm unbeliever in anything like direct manifestations of the Spirit of God more than an ordinary blessing that might be felt in the heart in answer to prayer, without any outward manifestation attending it. So it will be readily seen that I would watch with carefulness anything that appeared of a different character. When I first heard of the visions of sister White I supposed them to be either pretensions or mesmerism. But it did not require any great length of time to satisfy myself that a person could not feign a state in which from fifteen minutes to two hours, breath is entirely suspended, the eyes are open, not with a glassy appearance, or a vacant stare, but with a look more like that of one looking intently at a distant object. And that, too, while in this condition, audible words were spoken without breath. (Were there one particle of breath it would produce steam on a looking-glass. But this test applied while she is in vision will detect no breath whatever.) Such were the appearance and facts relative to the first vision I saw her have, and the appearances have not changed in about fifty visions I have seen her have since that time.

Having become satisfied that the visions were not under the control of the instrument through whom they were given, next work was to prove, if possible, from what source they came. Having heard lectures on mesmerism, and seen persons in various states of mesmerism, I could see a marked difference between this and mesmerism. It is also a fact that many experienced mesmerizers have declared on witnessing her visions that it was not mesmerism, but was something with which they were unacquainted. I saw a noted Spiritualist and mesmerizer [***John S. Brown***] present once, when she had a vision at Parkville, Michigan. He had given out before she came that if she should have a vision there, as it was nothing but mesmerism, he could bring her out of it. When he saw her in vision he came forward where she was, but instead of trying to bring her out, he went staggering toward the door, saying to the congregation, "She don't breathe," and declaring that he did not know what it was, turned deadly pale and left the room.[647]

Parkville meetinghouse

Brown John S. clairvoyant and eclectic physician

Fort Wayne Directory, 1874–1875

32. William Clarence White—~V217. "Slavery and the War Vision," Roosevelt, NY, Aug. 3, 1861.[648]

"THAT MAN MIGHT KNOW BY PHYSICAL SENSE THAT THE VISIONS GIVEN TO HER WERE FROM GOD, SHE WAS GIVEN MANY VISIONS IN WHICH SHE WOULD . . . STOP BREATHING, AND YET HER HEART BEAT."

In order that man might know by physical sense that the visions given to her were from God, she was given many visions in which she would fall helpless to the floor, stop breathing, and yet her heart beat, and she would speak. Many times I have been present when she was thus in vision. I will mention only the first and the last that I remember.[649]

The first one I witnessed as a little boy in the meetinghouse at Roosevelt, New York. Father had given a short talk. Mother had given a short talk. Father prayed; Mother prayed; and as she was praying, I heard that shout, Glory. There is nothing like it—that musical, deep shout of "Glory." She fell backward. My father put his arm under her. In a little while her strength came to her. She stood up in an attitude of one seeing wonderful things in the distance, her face illuminated, sometimes bright and joyous. She would speak with that musical voice, making short comments upon what she was seeing. Then as she saw the darkness in the world, there were sad expressions as she spoke of what she saw. This continued ten or fifteen minutes. Then she caught her breath, breathed deeply several times, and then, after a little season of rest, probably five or ten minutes, during which time Father spoke to the people, she arose and related to the congregation some of the things that had been presented to her.

33. John N. Loughborough—V236. "Moses Hull Parleying with Satan Vision," Battle Creek, MI, Nov. 5, 1862.[650]

Locations of the SDA Church and James White's house in Battle Creek

At my house on Champion street, in this city, in the autumn of [1862] she had a vision. A brother was present, a stone mason [***John Daigneau***]. While she was in vision, kneeling, as her arms moved about seemingly in an easy manner, Elder White said to the man, "Brother, that looks like an easy motion, and as though you could readily bend her arm.[651] You can try it if you wish." This brother placed his knee in the bend of her arm, took hold of her extended hand with both his hands, and settled back with all his might. It made no impression. He said to Elder White, "I would as soon think of bending an iron bar as that arm." He had hardly spoken these words before her arm moved around the other way. As he tried to resist the pressure, he was slid along upon the floor.

34. Martha Amadon—V249. "Comprehensive Health Reform Vision," Otsego, MI, June 6, 1863.[652]

Martha D. Amadon

A vision was given to Sister White at Brother Aaron Hilliard's in Otsego.[653] This was in 1863. Brother White had been laboring under heavy discouragements. One Friday morning he invited some of his friends in Battle Creek to go with him to Otsego for a Sabbath meeting, for there was a tent effort at that place. Friday evening we found ourselves all assembled at Brother Hilliard's for family worship, about a dozen being present. A chapter was read and Sister White led in prayer, Brother White kneeling across the corner from her. Her burden in prayer was for him, and as she prayed, while still on her knees, she moved over to his side, laid her hands on his shoulders, and prayed until she was taken in vision. This lasted for about three quarters of an hour. At this time she was given light on the health reform. Brother White also was greatly blessed and encouraged, and he was relieved of the burden of discouragement that he had been carrying. … When she made her first visit to our old home in New York, she made a little appeal to our family. At first my brothers and sisters manifested some prejudice, and assembled in a room by themselves. As she ceased speaking to them I went to them and said, "It makes no difference how anyone feels, I know that she is a woman of God."

I am now nearly ninety-two years old and am the only living member of the first organized Seventh-day Adventist church in Buck's Bridge, New York, about a mile from father Byington's farm.

35. Edward Hilliard—~V254. "Blessed Jesus Vision," Aaron Hilliard's house, Otsego, MI, 1864.[654]

I shall never forget one visit that Elder White and his wife made. It was just prior to the close of the Civil War. I was then in my fourteenth year. Brother White gave a stirring discourse on Sabbath morning, and Sister White spoke in the afternoon with her usual power and freedom. At that time Elder White had a fine span of horses and a comfortable carriage for traveling about from church to church and meeting various appointments. After the services he and his wife drove to my father's farm [***Aaron Hilliard***], four miles from the church. Refreshments were served, and as the Sabbath was nearing its close we all gathered in our front room for worship. Brother White led in prayer, and after one or two other petitions had been offered, an oppressive silence seemed to rest upon the worshipers. This was broken by Brother White's saying, "My wife is in vision."

Aaron Hilliard

We all arose and resumed our seats, Brother White taking a chair just back of his wife, while she leaned against his knees. He placed his hands upon her breast to show that she did not breathe. There was not the slightest heaving of the chest. She then interlocked her fingers, and her husband, a man that would weigh at least 180 pounds, tried to raise one of them, but failed to make the least impression. Immediately releasing her hands, she would pass them to and fro while speaking of things that she was viewing in vision. At times she would say a few words about the glories of heaven. One expression I well remember was, "Blessed Jesus!"

Edward Hilliard

She was continually looking upward, her eyes moving to and fro as she turned her head this way and that, but not once winking or breathing at all during the time she was in vision, which, I should judge, was about twenty minutes. The last words I remember her saying were, "No, no!" Brother White then said, "She is coming out of vision." In a few seconds she was breathing as usual. She had a word of warning for us. She said, "A great responsibility rests upon the elder members of this family."

In those days we burned tallow candles. As the twilight had deepened into the shades of evening, mother lit a candle and placed it on the table a few feet from where Sister White was sitting. Realizing that Sister White was coming from the world of light back to this dark world, mother wondered if she could see, and asked, "Sister White, can you see?" She replied, "I can see a very dim light from the candle on the table."

Aaron Hilliard's house in Otsego, Michigan

During her vision she acted in a manner similar to the prophets of the Bible when in vision. For instance, the prophet Balaam, who "saw the vision of the Almighty, falling into a trance, but having his eyes open." Num. 24:3, 4. (See also verses 15, 16.) The prophet Daniel, when in vision, had no breath in him, and he was supernaturally strengthened. (See Dan. 10:16–18.) On some occasions Sister White remained in vision for more than an hour without breathing. Her physical powers were thoroughly tested, and she certainly proved to be supernaturally strengthened.

Incidentally, I have found myself a number of times in the presence of spirit mediums when in a trance. In every case their eyes were closed and they breathed more rapidly. This must be attributable to the fact that Satan, who controls his mediums, cannot take from them their breath and preserve their lives. But He who breathed into man the breath of life can take it away, retain life, and return it at His pleasure.

This test cannot be counterfeited. But as very few have had the privilege of seeing it, the best and most beneficial test is to read carefully the writings of the instrument that the Lord chose to guide, warn, reprove, and comfort His remnant people . . . These writings by no means take the place of the Bible, but they do shed light on, and are in harmony with, the sacred pages of God's Holy Word. . . . "Despise not prophesyings. Prove all things; hold fast that which is good." 1 Thess. 5:20, 21.

36. James White—~V259. "Rebuking One, He Designs to Correct Many Vision," Battle Creek, MI, June 12, 1868.[655]

Our meetings in this place have been deeply interesting. Sabbath evening a large congregation assembled. Mrs. W. spoke freely and very solemnly till near ten. She spoke to the young generally, and addressed several personally. And while speaking from the platform in front of the pulpit, in the most solemn and impressive manner, the power of God came upon her, and in an instant she fell upon the carpet in vision. Many witnessed this manifestation for the first time, with astonishment and perfect satisfaction that it was the work of God. The vision lasted twenty minutes. No one was expecting it. Mrs. W. has said more than twenty times since the Rochester vision, December, 1865, [~V255, the "Health Institution Vision"] upon which she has written several thousands of pages, that in view of the responsibilities of her work, if she could have her choice, to go into the grave or have another vision, she should choose the grave.

James White

Here I must introduce the part which the Spirit of God has led Mrs. W. to act in connection with this cause. I do this,

1. Because her experience and labors have been closely connected with its rise and progress.

2. Because of the spirit of prejudice and enmity existing against her calling and labors. This is manifested by those who are ignorant of the facts in the case, or if not wholly ignorant, are led by a spirit of frenzied persecution. The bearing which this has upon the cause is a sufficient reason for laying the facts as they are before the public.

3. Because of the importance of her work, in connection with this cause, as will be seen in the following pages.

It was but a few weeks after the passing of the time, in 1844, that she had her first vision [V1]. The circumstances of this manifestation are briefly stated by Mrs. W. as follows: "I visited sister H., [***Elizabeth Haines***] one of our Advent sisters, whose heart was knit with mine. In the morning we bowed at the family altar. It was not an exciting occasion. There were but five of us present, all females. While praying, the power of God came upon me, as I never had felt it before. I was surrounded with light, and was rising higher and higher from the earth," etc. (*Spir. Gifts*, vol. ii, p. 30.) Her condition in vision may be described as follows:

1. She is utterly unconscious of everything transpiring around her, as has been proved by the most rigid tests, but views herself as removed from this world, and in the presence of heavenly beings.

2. She does not breathe. During the entire period of her continuance in vision, which has at different times ranged from fifteen minutes to three hours, there is no breath, as has been repeatedly proved by pressing upon the chest, and by closing the mouth and nostrils.

3. Immediately on entering vision, her muscles become rigid, and joints fixed, so far as any external force can influence them. At the same time her movements and gestures, which are frequent, are free and graceful, and cannot be hindered nor controlled by the strongest person.

4. On coming out of vision, whether in the day-time or a well-lighted room at night, all is total darkness. Her power to distinguish even the most brilliant objects, held within a few inches of the eyes, returns but gradually, sometimes not being fully established for three hours. This has continued for the past twenty years; yet her eyesight is not in the least impaired, few persons having better than she now possesses.

"SHE HAS PROBABLY HAD, DURING THE PAST TWENTY-THREE YEARS, BETWEEN ONE AND TWO HUNDRED VISIONS."

She has probably had, during the past twenty-three years, between one and two hundred visions.[656] These have been given under almost every variety of circumstance, yet maintaining a wonderful similarity; the most apparent change being, that of late years they have grown less frequent, but more comprehensive. She has been taken off in vision most frequently when bowed in prayer. Several times, while earnestly addressing the congregation, unexpectedly to herself and to all around her, she has been instantly prostrated in vision. This was the case June 12, 1868, in the presence of not less than two hundred Sabbath-keepers, in the house of worship, in Battle Creek, Mich. On receiving baptism at my hands, at an early period of her experience, as I raised her up out of the water, immediately she was in vision [V40]. Several times, when prostrated by sickness, she has been relieved in answer to the prayer of faith, and taken off in vision. At such times her restoration to usual health has been wonderful. At another time, when walking with friends, in conversation upon the glories of the kingdom of God, as she was passing through the gate before her father's house, the Spirit of God came upon her, and she was instantly taken off in vision [perhaps V26]. And what may be important to those who think the visions the result of mesmerism, she has a number of times been taken off in vision, when in prayer alone in the grove or in the closet.

37. Uriah Smith—the same vision (~V259) as above.[657]

The church in Battle Creek have again been graciously favored with the presence of the Lord. Bro. and Sr. White returned from Monterey June 10, according to previous arrangement, to spend another Sabbath with this church. At the evening meeting commencing the Sabbath, a large congregation assembled at the house of worship. After some timely and close remarks by Bro. White, Sr. White arose to free her mind from a great burden resting upon it for this people. Wrongs were faithfully pointed out and reproved. Two personal testimonies for persons in the congregation were read, followed by most stirring appeals and exhortations. And while Sr. W. was thus speaking, reaching a point in her remarks of most intense solemnity, instantly, and unexpectedly to all present, she was taken off in vision, and fell to the floor.

Uriah Smith

Judging from her appearance and occasional expressions while in vision, scenes of a different character, some terrible to behold, and others of surpassing glory, passed before her. The scene was most impressive. Many were present who had never before had the privilege of witnessing a manifestation of this kind; and to these the privilege was given of coming forward and beholding for themselves the various phenomena attending it. Their testimony is that though they had before no occasion to doubt the visions, now they can look upon them as a reality. They see not how any one, witnessing the manner in which they are given, can for a moment doubt them to be the work of the Holy Spirit. People may talk of mesmerism, clairvoyants, and spirit mediums; but this has nothing in common with them. It is something else entirely, as different from any thing of that kind, as the heavens are higher than the earth; and those who attribute the visions to any of those sources, are only suffering the Devil to deceive them.[658]

"Many were present who had never before had the privilege of witnessing a manifestation of this kind; and to these the privilege was given of coming forward and beholding for themselves the various phenomena attending it."

The power of the Holy Spirit was present too manifestly to be mistaken. We doubt if there were many in the house, who did not feel that the Lord had drawn near for the especial instruction of his people. It was good to be there. What a privilege as well as necessity it is to be instructed from on high; for we are engaged in a work, not of building ourselves up in self-righteousness; but in trying to discover and put away our wrongs, and secure a moral preparation to enter, in a little from this, into the presence of the King of glory.

What has been shown will be made known to those whom it may concern as soon as possible. Meanwhile let us remember what a vast amount of labor is entailed upon Sr. White on account of the position she is called to occupy; and let us all endeavor to stay up her hands. All can do something in this respect, if in no other way, at least by holy living. . . . We shall look for good fruit from this meeting. Today, the 14th, Bro. White baptized twenty-five, most of whom have but recently commenced to live the Christian life.

[The visions] are not the effect of disease; for no disease has ever yet been known to have the effect of repeatedly suspending the functions of the lungs, muscles, and every bodily sense, from fifteen to one hundred and eighty minutes, while in obedience to some influence which evidently has supreme possession of the mind, and in obedience to that alone, the eyes would see, the lips speak, and the limbs move.

38. Nellie Sisley Starr—the same vision (~V259) as above.[659]

Nellie Sisley Starr

She walked back and forth and talked to us, and as she walked, she fell right down. She fell down gently. She went down as if an angel's hands were under her. . . . We thought she had fainted, but Brother White said, "Cause yourselves no alarm. Wife has not fainted, but has fallen in vision."

I wish I could describe the feeling that we all had. It was perfect quietness; even the children made no noise. . . . It seemed as though heaven was settling down upon us and closing us in. . . . Sister White lay perfectly quiet and unconscious. Oh, the feeling that was sensed in that building. Brother White said, "There may be some in the congregation that may have doubts in regard to my wife's inspiration. If there are any such we would be glad to have them come forward and try the physical tests given in the Bible. It may help some of you."

I knew my mother had some doubts. We had come over from England and she had come from the Church of England, and she could not quite understand it, so I said, "Mother, let us go right up and stand right by her head." In the meantime, Brother White had knelt down, and he raised Sister White's head and shoulders on his knees. Others came up, and there were two unusually large men [***Jotham M. Aldrich and Harrison Sherwood Woolsey***].[660] They stood one on each side of her shoulders. "Now," Brother White said, "we all saw Sister White fall; we know she lost her natural strength. Now we will see if she has supernatural strength." She was lying with her hands gently folded over her chest. She was lying quietly and looking up in the corner of the building. Her eyes were open, with a pleasant expression on her face. Nothing unnatural or unusual.

Jotham M. Aldrich

Harrison S. Woolsey

Brother White said to these large men, "Take her hands apart. You have two hands to her one. Just pull her hands apart." So they tried. They pulled and pulled till some of us got anxious that they would hurt her. Brother White said, "Don't be anxious; she is safe in God's keeping, and you can pull until you are perfectly satisfied." They said, "We are satisfied now. We don't need to pull anymore." He said, "Take up one finger at a time." That was impossible. They could not do so much as move a finger. It seemed like a block of granite. There was no change in appearance, but it just couldn't be moved. We looked to see if her eyes were closed and see if she was breathing. Then she took her hands apart and waved her hands. We said, "We will see when she comes out of vision that she has been flying." Brother White said to these men, "Now hold her." I think they thought they could. They grasped her by the wrists, but they could not retard the motion. It looked like any child could hold her, but she went on just the same.

"THEY GRASPED HER BY THE WRISTS, BUT THEY COULD NOT RETARD THE MOTION."

Rochester lamp

Elder White said, "Now we are satisfied with that. Now we must see if her eyelids will close." There was a large Rochester lamp close by on the stand. He removed the shade and put this light right in front of her eyes. We thought she would move her eyes to protect them. She didn't. She was perfectly unconscious. The expression of her countenance changed at times. Sometimes she looked pleased. At other times we could see that there was something distressing her, but the eyelids did not close.

"Now," Brother White said, "we must see if there is any breath in her body." There didn't seem to be any. Everything looked all right, only there was no breath. Brother White said, "Now we will send out and get a mirror, and we will test it." So someone went to the next door and got a mirror, and it was held close to her face, but no moisture gathered. So there was no breathing. . . . She spoke several sentences. I don't remember the words; in fact, I cannot give you the exact words for any part of it. I will express what she saw, but I must express it in my own language. It is all I have. When she came out of vision, Brother White said, "The congregation have been so interested, I know they will want to know something of what you have seen."

She said, "I will gladly tell them."

Brother White helped her up; then she talked for about half an hour. She answered a few questions, but mostly made her own statements. When she was taken into vision she seemed to be taken down the stream of time. She spoke about the new earth. She saw the people of God saved in their everlasting home. Then she said, "Oh, I wish I could describe it, tell even a little of it. I have no language to describe it. If you could have been there and have seen what I saw, you would never allow anything on earth to tempt you to live so that there would be danger of losing eternal life."

I suppose she saw the people of God, perhaps in their last struggles, passing through the closing scenes of this world's history and then down out of that into their peaceful home. She told us when she came out of vision that the scene was so glorious, so bright, that when she came back to earth she could see nothing. I have never forgotten her words in regard to that.

"Now," she said, "you may not understand why I could not see. But," she said, "you turn your face toward the sun for a while and then turn away. Heaven is brighter than the sun." While her eyesight was not impaired permanently, yet for a long time she could not see clearly after coming out of vision. We were pleased to know that.

She tried to describe it. . . . Oh, to be there, and what counsel she gave us in regard to preparation. "Now," she said, "there is another scene that passed before me that I would rather not tell, only that it may be a warning to you." She said, "I saw the great host of the lost. Oh, what a sight. The terror and agony of soul that was on those people. I looked upon them and I saw here and there all among them some of our own people, some of the Seventh-day Adventists scattered here and there."

I remember this, I remember that their agony was far greater than that of the others. They knew what they had lost and what they might have had had they been faithful. I wish I could tell you what she told us, but I cannot describe it as I would like to because I haven't language to. But it made an impression on my mind that I have never lost.

39. A. C. and D. T. Bourdeau—~V267. "As the Hand with the Body Vision," Bordoville, VT, Dec. 10, 1871.[661]

Lucinda Hall

Daniel T. Bourdeau

The meetings which were held in West Bolton, Dec. 7, and in Bordoville, Dec. 9 and 10 were very important to the cause in Vermont. Bro. James White did not attend these meetings on account of having a severe cold brought on by exposures in traveling. But sister White attended them, accompanied by Sr. Hall [***Lucinda Hall***].[662] Three meetings were held in West Bolton which were well attended, especially the one in the evening when the large school-house in which they were held was literally packed. There were about two hundred and fifty present. Sister W. spoke one full hour in each meeting—three times in one day. Her principal theme was the humble self-denying life of Christ upon which she dwelt with great clearness and power. Nearly all present seemed to feel the necessity of coming up more fully to the perfect pattern. How little we see in us to boast of! How deficient our labors, and poor our sacrifices, when we keep in view the disinterested and sacrificing life of Christ! The interest was intense. The truth was received with great eagerness, and never was the word spoken indorsed more generally by a promiscuous crowd.[663] We have reason to believe that whatever prejudice might have existed in regard to sister White was entirely removed. The friends generally expressed a strong desire to have Bro. and sister White spend at least two weeks with them in West Bolton the present winter. . . .

No regular meeting was held Sunday evening. The meetings closed at 3 P. M. But at 5 o'clock we realized what was more profitable to us and to the cause than a common meeting would have been. Sister White had spoken in the afternoon on the last days being like those of Noah, and was on the point of leaving for Berkshire to make sister Alida Kellogg who was on her dying bed a farewell call, when the two youngest sons of Bro. John Saxby—Brn. Parmenas W., and Arthur J., and sister Edna, wife of Bro. Parmenas—who had been in a backslidden state came to our house to bid sister White good bye.[664] At this point, sister White felt the real burden of their cases, and a special yearning after them for their salvation, and gave them rich instructions. She then kneeled down with them, and prayed for them with great earnestness faith and tenacity, that they might return unto the Lord. They yielded and prayed, promising to serve the Lord. The Spirit of the Lord drew nearer and nearer. Sister White was free, and soon, unexpectedly to all, she was in vision. She remained in this condition fifteen minutes. The news spread, and soon the house (Eld. A. C. Bourdeau's) was crowded. Sinners trembled, believers wept, and backsliders returned to God. The work was not confined to those present as we have since learned. Some who had remained at home were powerfully convicted. They saw themselves as they had never done before. The angel of God was shaking the place. The shortness of time, the terrors and nearness of coming judgments and the time of trouble, the worldly-mindedness of the church, their lack of brotherly love, and their state of unreadiness to meet the Lord, were strongly impressed upon the minds of all. A reform is started; hearty confessions are being made; brethren are coming together; and those who had assumed the stewardship of others are feeling measurably the responsibility resting upon them. Surely the Lord has wrought and he shall have all the praise. May the work deepen and widen until we are all prepared to stand in the Judgment. God keep us from the wiles of Satan, and help us to be thorough. . . .

Parmenas Saxby

Edna Saxby

Augustin C. Bourdeau

40. William Clarence White—-V272. "A World Work Vision," Battle Creek, MI, Jan. 3, 1875.[665]

James White brought Uriah Smith and J. H. Waggoner home to pray for Ellen White after she caught influenza. When Ellen attempted to pray, she received a vision about the expansion of the Adventist work throughout the world.

W. C. White, 1916

In a hoarse, labored voice, she uttered two or three sentences of petition. Suddenly her voice broke clear and musical, and we heard the ringing shout, "Glory to God!" We all looked up, and saw that she was in vision. Her hands were folded across her breast. Her eyes were directed intently upward, and her lips were closed. There was no breathing, although the heart continued its action. As she looked intently upward, an expression of anxiety came into her face. She threw aside her blankets, and, stepping forward, walked back and forth in the room. Wringing her hands, she moaned, "Dark! Dark! All dark! So dark!" Then after a few moments' silence, she exclaimed with emphasis, and a brightening of her countenance, "A light! A little light! More light! Much light!" . . .

Following her exclamatory remarks regarding the lights, she sat down in her chair. After a few minutes, she drew three long, deep breaths, and then resumed her natural breathing. Her eyes rested upon the company that had been assembled for prayer. Father, knowing that after a vision everything looked strange to her, knelt by her side, and spoke in her ear, saying, "Ellen, you have been in vision."

She indicated that she had seen many things but did not wish to share them just then. Her health restored, Mrs. White was able to attend the meeting that night. W. C. White continues:

In the next evening meeting she spoke about three quarters of an hour. In her remarks she spoke with great emphasis upon the necessity of our taking broader views regarding the work which God had given us to do. She dwelt upon the necessity of our laying much broader plans for the education of home and foreign workers. She said that our movements in sending workers to foreign fields were altogether too slow and inadequate. She told us that in vision she had seen, in different parts of the world, companies studying the Bible, finding there the promise of Christ's soon return to redeem His people, and also the facts regarding the sacredness of the seventh-day Sabbath. She saw little companies here and there keeping the Sabbath without knowing that there were any other Sabbathkeepers in the world; and she told us that as we heard of such companies, it would be our duty to send experienced ministers to labor among them, teaching them the way of truth more fully. Otherwise there would arise disagreements among them, and they would become discouraged and give up the faith.

Stephen N. Haskell recalled the effect of Ellen White's relating of the vision.

Stephen N. Haskell

When we came over to this country about fifteen years ago, there was not a Seventh-day Adventist in Australia. And now we can only say, See what God hath wrought. The message has been a success, and it will be a success. If the message could have failed, it would have failed years ago. We can only say, as expressed in the Bible, that the long-suffering of God is our salvation, and it is that the work may be accomplished in the world as God purposes it should. I am thankful to God that I had the privilege of coming to Australia. In a testimony given in 1874 by Sister White in the Battle Creek Church, she described the things that would take place in the message, and said the time had come that the truth should go to other countries, and that she had seen in other countries publications were issued and a great work was accomplished. Brother White asked her what countries. She thought for awhile and said, "I cannot think of but one name now, and I remember the angel said Australia." And it was no credit to us—we simply believed God, and then began to talk about Australia to our brethren, and they sent over some hundreds of papers every week.[666]

41. Ellen White's Perspective on Receiving and Writing Out Visions—1860, 1906.[667]

"After I come out of vision I do not at once remember all that I have seen . . ."

"As inquiries are frequently made as to my state in vision, and after I come out, I would say that when the Lord sees fit to give a vision, I am taken into the presence of Jesus and angels, and am entirely lost to earthly things. I can see no farther than the angel directs me. My attention is often directed to scenes transpiring upon earth. At times I am carried far ahead into the future and shown what is to take place. Then again I am shown things as they have occurred in the past. After I come out of vision I do not at once remember all that I have seen, and the matter is not so clear before me until I write, then the scene rises before me as was presented in vision, and I can write with freedom. Sometimes the things which I have seen are hid from me after I come out of vision, and I cannot call them to mind until I am brought before a company where that vision applies, then the things which I have seen come to my mind with force. I am just as dependent upon the Spirit of the Lord in relating or writing a vision, as in having the vision. It is impossible for me to call up things which have been shown me unless the Lord brings them before me at the time that he is pleased to have me relate or write them."

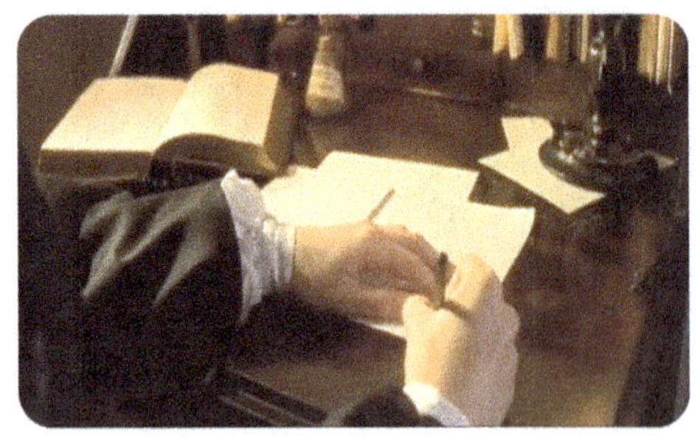

In 1906 she wrote: "These books that have been published are now immortalized in print. And there is throughout the whole a harmony with my present teaching. Some of the writings on these pages were given under circumstances so remarkable as to evidence the wonder-working power of God in behalf of His truth. Sometimes while I was in vision, my friends would approach me, and exclaim, 'Why, she does not breathe!'[668] Placing a mirror before my lips, they found that no moisture gathered on the glass. It was while there was no sign of any breathing, that I kept talking of the things that were being presented before me. These messages were thus given to substantiate the faith of all, that in these last days we might have confidence in the Spirit of Prophecy."

What to Do with the Evidence of the Eyewitness Accounts

Not all of Ellen White's visions had physical phenomena. Many came quietly in the night.[669] Yet, for those described as having physical phenomena, what stands out for you? The solemnity of the occasion? The exclamation "*Glory!*" or her holding up large Bibles and quoting verses while pointing to them without looking? Ellen White's uncanny physical strength in vision? The different ways investigators were able to tell that she was not breathing?[670] Did you wonder how she could speak under such circumstances? Several eyewitnesses described the timbre of her voice in vision. James White noted that, as she went into vision, "her voice changed, and the deep, clear shouts of Glory! Hallelujah! thrilled every heart." Otis Nichols mentioned "Ellen's clear and shrill voice, as she talked in vision." Heman S. Gurney said her voice would "ring out" clear.[671] Something supernatural was happening! A listing of the ways her visions were tested includes:

1. A burning candle held close to her open eyes or a piece of paper or a finger thrust toward or even touching her open eyes did not make her flinch.
2. The pricking of her hands with a needle did not cause a reaction.
3. A burning candle held close to her lips did not make the flame flicker.
4. A small mirror held in front of her mouth gathered no moisture.
4. A witness covering her mouth and nose for about ten minutes caused her no ill effects.
5. Observers could not make her move her arms or hands, nor could they keep her from moving.

Some accounts of Ellen White in vision were written right after the events, but most were written later, during a time of reflection. How deeply must the eyewitnesses have been impressed to remember years later what they saw! That there was often more than one eyewitness adds weight to the testimony, and knowing the religious bent of the examining physicians helps explain why they would have been interested in attending an Adventist meeting where Ellen White would speak and possibly have a vision.

Though skeptical at first, once **Heman Gurney** (in 1845), **Joseph Bates** (in 1846), **Ezra P. Butler** (in 1851), **John Norton Loughborough** (in 1852), **Daniel T. Bourdeau** (in 1857), and **Nellie Sisley Starr** (in 1868) saw Ellen White in vision, heard her insights, and observed the consistency of her life, they became convinced of the validity of her visions. In the 1870s, **Edith Brownsberger** was skeptical but came to accept Ellen White's gift after observing her speaking and the consistency of her life. In 1897, **Sarepta Myrenda Henry,** née Irish, a noted temperance reformer, also went from questioning to embracing Ellen White's visions.[672] Others did not require as much evidence, as Ellen White herself noted: "Some, I was shown, could receive the published visions, judging of the tree by its fruits. Others are like doubting Thomas; they cannot believe the published *Testimonies*, nor receive evidence through the testimony of others, but must see and have the evidence for themselves."[673]

But there were people who never saw her in vision (e.g., Joshua V. Himes and Isaac C. Wellcome) who rejected her visions based on someone else's own blind appraisal.[674] And there were those who were so biased that they even refused to believe after witnessing miraculous phenomena during a vision (e.g., Sargent, Robbins, French, John Megquier, and Ransom Hicks).[675] Similarly, there were those who saw the remarkable nature of her visions and acknowledged their insightfulness in revealing unspoken aspects of people's lives but ultimately rejected the visions because they were offended by a personal exhortation (e.g., Hiram Case, Charles P. Russell, Israel Dammon, and Elias Willets Shortridge).[676] Others rejected the visions because the visions did not measure up to a personal test (e.g., Henry E. Carver) or because they contradicted an interpretation of Scripture (e.g., William Sheldon and Abraham Cauffman Long) or a cherished belief (e.g., Barnet Matthias, James M. Stephenson, Dwight P. Hall, Benjamin Franklin Snook, and William Henry Brinkerhoff) or because they checked their impressions (e.g., Joseph Turner, Jesse Stevens, and John Howell and his wife Lucinda Burdick) or a life practice (e.g., Joseph Turner and Gilbert Cranmer).[677] Some of these, like the publishers of *The Messenger of Truth* and of *The Gathering Call*, made it their mission to gather complaints about Ellen White and her supporters.[678] One minister (Miles Grant) traveled where Ellen White was holding meetings to publicly undermine her influence.[679] On the other hand, there were others (e.g., John C. Day, Solomon Myers, Stephen Smith, Waterman Phelps, Elmore W. Waters, E. R. Seaman, and T. M. Steward) who, though at first sympathizing with the complainers and withdrawing their support, recognized the true nature of the complaints, quit nursing grudges against Ellen White and the brethren, and rejoined those who were blessed by the visions, remembering Paul's words: "Despise not prophesyings. Prove all things; hold fast that which is good" (1 Thess. 5:20, 21).[680] Thinking of the choices that each made, we wonder what good they might have each done had they not dismissed the positive evidence. And then, what about you? How will you respond?

PEOPLE WITH DIFFERENT RESPONSES TO ELLEN WHITE'S VISIONS

Heman Gurney  | Joseph Bates  | Ezra P. Butler  | J. N. Loughborough  | D. T. Bourdeau  | Nellie Sisley Starr

S. M. I. Henry  | Edith Brownsberger  | Horace L. Hastings  | Rachel Preston  | Worcester Ball  | John C. Day

Solomon Myers  | Stephen Smith  | T. M. Steward  | Philip Strong  | J. V. Himes  | Isaac Wellcome

Miles Grant  | John Megquier  | Israel Dammon  | B. F. Snook  | W. H. Brinkerhoff  | John B. Bezzo

Erastus Clark  | J. M. Stephenson  | Hiram V. Reed  | A. C. Long  | Gilbert Cranmer  | Henry C. Blanchard

Moses Hull  | D. M. Canright  | Albion Ballenger | Edward Ballenger | Elmer E. Franke | Ludwig R. Conradi

KEY TO COLORATION

Black - individuals who were hesitant at first to accept the validity of Ellen's gift but were ultimately convinced

Green - individuals who rejected the gift for a time but later reconsidered their view and returned to acceptance

Red - individuals who rejected the gift for a variety of reasons, with and without seeing Ellen White in vision

EXHIBIT-2. The Apocrypha in Ellen White's Early Writings

Because the Apocrypha is no longer used by most Protestants, it is a curiosity to find parallels to the Apocrypha in Ellen White's early writings.[681] Yet, had James White not footnoted them in "A Word to the 'Little Flock,'" we might never have noticed them. No doubt Ellen White saw value in understanding the Apocrypha, though she distinguished its authority from that of the Bible as a separate book: "I saw that *the Apocrypha* was *the hidden book*, and that the wise of these last days *should understand it*. I saw that *the Bible* was *the standard book, that will judge us* at the last day."[682] She also described the Apocrypha as "cast out," and she never quoted from it directly.[683] Her allusions to it are almost exclusively from 2 Esdras, a book used by other Adventists.[684] In the exhibit below, vision numbers are in the left column, words parallel to the Apocrypha are **boldfaced**; that are parallel to Scripture are colorized green. Entries not referenced by James White are in gray boxes and comments are in light brown.

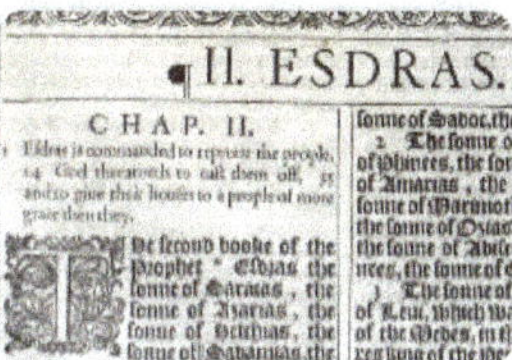
II. ESDRAS.

CHAP. II.

	"A Word to the 'Little Flock.'"	Apocrypha
1. V1.	We all entered the cloud together, and were **seven days** ascending to the sea of glass, when **Jesus** brought along the **crowns** and with his own right hand placed them on our **heads.**[(v)] {WLF 15; 2 Esdras 2:43 is footnoted}	[43] And in the midst of them there was a young man of a high stature, taller than all the rest, and upon every one of their **heads** he sets **crowns**, and more exalted which I marvelled greatly. . . .[46] Then said I to the angel, What the young person is it that crowneth them, and giveth them palms in their hands? [47] So he answered and said unto me, It is **the Son of God**, whom they have confessed in the world. (2 Esdras 2:43, 46, 47)
	Whether Ellen White drew from 2 Esdras is made less certain when we note that Jesus promised that he will give the faithful a crown: "Be thou faithful unto death, and **I** will give thee a crown of life" (Rev. 2:10), and a crown is worn on the "head" (Rev. 4:4). Paul also referred to receiving a "crown of righteousness" (2 Tim. 4:8). 2 Esdras 7:31 also uses **seven days** differently, after which the world "shall be raised up."	
2. V16.	Mount Zion was just before us, and on the Mount sat a glorious temple, and about it were **seven** other **mountains**, on which **grew roses and lilies,**[(ll)] and I saw the **little ones** climb, or if they chose, use their little wings and fly to the top of the mountains, and pluck the never fading flowers. {WLF 17; 2 Esdras 2:19 is footnoted}	And as many fountains flowing with milk and honey, and **seven** mighty **mountains**, whereupon there **grow roses and lilies**, whereby I will fill thy **children** with joy. (2 Esdras 2:19)
Comment	Ellen White described these seven mountains as being *in addition to* Mount Zion. Though Esdras mentions children, Ellen White describes seeing the little ones climbing or flying and then plucking flowers.	
3. V16.	And he said, You must **go** back to the earth again, **and relate to others what** I have revealed to you. {WLF 17; not in the footnotes}	then the angel said unto me, **Go** thy way, **and tell my people what** manner of things, and how great wonders of the Lord thy God, thou hast seen." (2 Esdras 2:42)
Comment	The difference in the command to go and tell is that the instructor in Ellen White's vision is Jesus while, in 2 Esdras, it is an angel.	
4. V46.	And I saw the sword, famine, pestilence, and great confusion **in the land.**[(m)] {WLF 19}	[5] Behold, saith the Lord, I will bring plagues **upon the world**; the sword, famine, death, and destruction. [6] For wickedness hath exceedingly polluted the whole earth, and their hurtful works are fulfilled. [7] Therefore saith the Lord, [8] I will hold my tongue no more as touching their wickedness, which they profanely commit, neither will I suffer them in those things in which they wickedly exercise themselves: behold, the innocent and righteous blood crieth unto me, and the souls of the just complain continually. [9] And therefore, saith the Lord, I will surely avenge them, and receive unto me all the innocent blood from among them. [10] Behold, my people is led as a flock to the slaughter: I will not suffer them now to dwell in the land of Egypt: [11] But I will bring them with a mighty hand and a stretched out arm, and smite Egypt with plagues, as before, and will destroy all the land

		thereof. 12 Egypt shall mourn, and the foundation of it shall be smitten with the plague and punishment that God shall bring upon it. 13 They that till the ground shall mourn: for their seeds shall fail through the blasting and hail, and with a fearful constellation. 14 Wo to the world, and them that dwell therein! 15 For the sword and their destruction draweth nigh, and one people shall stand up to fight against another, and swords in their hands. 16 For there shall be sedition among men, and invading one another; they shalt not regard their kings nor princes, and the course of their actions shall stand in their power. 17 A man shall desire to go into a city, and shall not be able. 18 For because of their pride the cities shall be troubled, the houses shall be destroyed, and men shall be afraid. 19 A man shall have no pity upon his neighbour, but shall destroy their houses with the sword, and spoil their goods, because of the lack of bread, and for great tribulation. 20 Behold, saith God, I will call together all the kings of the earth to reverence me, which are from the rising of the sun, from the south, from the east, and Libanus; to turn themselves one against another, and repay the things that they have done to them. 21 Like as they do yet this day unto my chosen, so will I do also, and recompense in their bosom. Thus saith the Lord God, 22 My right hand shall not spare the sinners, and my sword shall not cease over them that shed innocent blood upon the earth. 23 The fire is gone forth from his wrath, and hath consumed the foundations of the earth, and the sinners, like the straw that is kindled. 24 Wo to them that sin, and keep not my commandments! saith the Lord: 25 I will not spare them: go your way, ye children, from the power, defile not my sanctuary. 26 For the Lord knoweth all them that sin against him, and therefore delivereth he them unto death and destruction. 27 For now are the plagues come upon the whole earth, and ye shall remain in them: for God shall not deliver you, because ye have sinned against him. (2 Esdras 15:5–27)
Comment	The connection between Ellen White's statement and this passage is less sure when we see that "famine" and "sword" are commonly used together in the Old Testament. For example, see Job 5:20; Isa. 51:19; Jer. 29:18; and Ezek. 7:10–19.	
5. V46.	The wicked thought that we had brought the judgments down on them. They rose up and took counsel to **rid the earth of us**, thinking that then the evil would be stayed.[n] {WLF 19}	68 For behold, the burning wrath of a great multitude is kindled over you, and they shall take away certain of you, and feed you, being idle, with things offered unto idols. 69 And they that consent unto them shall be had in derision and in reproach, and trodden under foot. 70 For there shall be in every place, and in the next cities, a great insurrection upon those that fear the Lord. 71 They shall be like mad men, sparing none, but still spoiling and **destroying those that fear the Lord.** 72 For they shall waste and take away their goods, and cast them out of their houses. 73 Then shall they be known who are my chosen; and they shall he tried as the gold in the fire. 74 Hear, O ye my beloved, saith the Lord: behold, the days of trouble are at hand, but I will deliver you from the same. 75 Be ye not afraid, neither doubt; for God is your guide, (2 Esdras 16:68–75)
Comment	Though referenced by James White, there are no verbatim words linking the passages, and they do not run very closely in parallel. Moreover, 2 Esdras does not describe the motivation for destroying those that fear the Lord.	
6. V46.	The **streams ceased to flow.**[t] {WLF 19}	At that time shall friends fight one against another like enemies, and the earth shall stand in fear with those that dwell therein, **the springs of the fountains shall stand still**, and in three hours they shall not run. (2 Esdras 6:24)
Comment	In this example, there is a similar description of the stopping of the flowing of water but no verbatim parallels.	
7. V46.	Dark heavy **clouds** came up, and **clashed against each other.**[u] {WLF 19}	34 Behold **clouds** from the east and from the north unto the south, and they are very horrible to look upon, full of wrath and storm. 35 They shall **smite one upon another**, and they shall smite down a great multitude of stars upon the earth, even their own star; and blood shall be from the sword unto the belly, (2 Esdras 15:34, 35)
Comment	Here there is a similar description of angry clouds in collision (with "clouds" being the only verbatim word). Though the clouds in 2 Esdras are symbols of war. Second Esdras asserts that the clouds will	

	"smite down" stars (often a symbol, in Bible prophecy, for angels or saints), while Ellen White describes the delivery of God's people by the voice from the cloud, which takes place under the last plague.	
8. V1.	Jesus raised his mighty glorious arm, laid hold of the pearly gate and swung it back on its glittering hinges, and said to us, You have washed your robes in my blood, **stood stifly** [*sic*] **for** my **truth**, enter in. *(y)* {WLF 15; Isa. 26:2 is referenced, not 2 Esdras 2:47}	So he answered and said unto me, It is the Son of God, whom they have confessed in the world. Then began I greatly to commend them that **stood** so **stiffly for** the name of the Lord. (2 Esdras 2:47)
Comment	Following Ellen White, other Adventists used "stood stiffly for" with the "truth." Phebe Harp, of Troy, New York, also linked the phrase with 2 Esdras: "We mean to be of that company that Esdras saw who **stood stiffly for** the **truth.**"[685] Alexander Allen Marks, of Saline, Michigan, linked it with coming out of the world: "Oh, where will the sinner be then, and even those also who have professed the truth, but have coveted the friendship, of the ungodly, and have not come out from the world and **stood stiffly for** the **truth!**"[686] Isaac Sanborn, of Monroe, Wisconsin, linked it with making a covenant by sacrifice: "But I am satisfied that with proper care and labor there will be a large company raised up here around Monroe, who will make a covenant with God by sacrifice, and **stand stiffly for** the **truth.**"[687] Joseph Harvey Waggoner linked it with those "who have kept the commandments of God and the faith of Jesus, despite the rage of the Beast and False Prophet."[688] Harriet Maria Grant, of Three Rivers' Point (Clay), New York, linked it with the help of the Lord against the mighty: "I am determined to **stand stiffly for** the **truth**, and to come up to the help of the Lord against the mighty."[689]  Isaac Sanborn  J. H. Waggoner	
9. V46.	Their **countenances** were lighted up with the glory of God; and they shone with the glory as Moses' face did when he came down from Sinai. **The wicked could not look on them,** for the glory. *(bb)* {WLF 20}	[1] Then shall the righteous man stand in great boldness before the **face** of such as have afflicted him, and made no account of his labours. [2] **When they see it,** they shall be troubled with terrible fear, and shall be amazed at the strangeness of his salvation, so far beyond all that they looked for. [3] And they repenting and groaning for anguish of spirit shall say within themselves, This was he, whom we had sometimes in derision, and a proverb of reproach: [4] We fools accounted his life madness, and his end to be without honour. [5] How is he numbered among the children of God, and his lot is among the saints! (Wisdom of Solomon 5:1–5)
Comment	The most similar part of this comparison is verse 2: "When they see it, they shall be troubled with terrible fear." However, 2 Esdras does not mention the glory of God in the face of "the righteous man" as does Ellen White.	
10. V69.	I saw some who were not standing **stiffly for** present truth. {ExV 26.2}	Then began I greatly to commend them that **stood** so **stiffly for** the name of the Lord. (2 Esdras 2:47)
11. V138.	Those who profess the truth, and before they have learned its first principles, think they know it all, and are forward to take the place of teachers, and reprove those who for years have **stood stiffly for** the truth, plainly show that they have no understanding of the truth, and know none of its effects; for if they knew any of its sanctifying power, they would yield the peaceable fruits of righteousness, and be humbled under its sweet, powerful influence. {ExV54 39.3}	Then began I greatly to commend them that **stood** so **stiffly for** the name of the Lord. (2 Esdras 2:47)
Comment	These two instances apply the "stood stiffly" to standing "stiffly for the truth" and not "stiffly for the name of the Lord."	

The Adventist Adaptation of Wording from the Apocrypha

In the comparison above, we have identified, in Ellen White's earliest books, ten parallels to 2 Esdras and one possible parallel to the Wisdom of Solomon. In none of these instances does Ellen White borrow more than a few words of verbatim wording. The three instances in which she uses the verbatim phrase "stood stiffly for" were not linked by James White to 2 Esdras. In analyzing the usage of "stood stiffly for," we see that, while the usage of 2 Esdras was about standing "stiffly for the name of the Lord," the early Adventists adapted the phrase to express their unflinching commitment to the truth about obedience to God under pressure to abandon it. Of this same period, Ellen White bolstered the adapted term from 2 Esdras with biblical phrasing that expresses the same concept: "If we had not **stood stiffly** then, we should have made shipwreck of our faith. Some said we were stubborn; but we were obliged to set our faces as a flint, and turn not to the right hand nor to the left."[690] Thus, while the frequently used phrase likely originated in 2 Esdras, the early Adventists adapted it for their own usage.

*"Fear God, and give **glory** to him; for the hour of his judgment is come: and worship him that made heaven, and earth, and the sea, and the fountains of waters. . . . Here is the patience of the saints: here are they that keep the commandments of God, and the faith of Jesus."*[691]

Sizes of antiquarian Bibles, marking folio and quarto Bibles; inset, the Harmon family Bible, a King James Version folio Bible containing the Apocrypha

EXHIBIT-3. Miller and White's Accounts of the Second Coming Compared

William Miller

In response to allegations that Ellen White's first vision derived from William Miller's sermon on the Second Coming, the following exhibit compares the two. All verbatim parallel words are **boldfaced**. However, to distinguish between Scriptural parallel wording and Miller's, all scriptural words are colorized green.

Ellen G. White

William Miller *The Burlington Free Press*, Burlington, VT, Feb. 17, 1843	Ellen Harmon *The Day-Star*, Cincinnati, Ohio, Jan. 24, 1845
WILLIAM MILLER.	Letter from Sister Harmon. Portland, Me., Dec. 20, 1845
We re-publish the following from the Bennington Vt. *State Banner*. It is the latest news from this monomaniac and his whereabouts. His last fancy sketch will confirm his followers and amuse the curious. It seems the parson is gradually edging off his followers from indulging too high expectations of the month of *April*. "This gentleman arrived in this village, and commenced a course of lectures on his favorite and celebrated theme,—the Destruction of the World by Fire in A. D., 1843, on last Sunday week, the 22nd inst., which he continued through the week, delivering two lectures each day, generally to full audiences. During his first lecture he gave substantially the following description of the MANNER of the Second Advent. "A small bright spot will first **appear** in **the east**, which will gradually expand as it approaches the earth.[692] Bye and bye, **a small cloud** will appear before the luminous ball, and between it and the earth. **On** this **cloud** will be seen **the Son of Man**, standing erect, his figure plainly visible to the spectators on the earth.[693] At the **sound** of a **trumpet** (or some other signal,) the bright spot having	Bro. Jacobs:— [*Skipping the first part of the letter*] Soon our eyes were drawn to **the East**, for **a small** black **cloud** had **appear**ed about half as large as a man's hand, which we all knew was the Sign of **the Son of Man**.[698] We all in solemn silence gazed **on** the **cloud** as it drew nearer, lighter, and brighter, glorious, and still more glorious till it was a great white cloud.[699] The bottom appeared like fire, a rainbow was over it, around the cloud were ten thousand angels singing a most lovely song.[700] And on it sat the Son of Man, on his head were crowns, his hair was white and curly and lay on his shoulders.[701] His feet had the appearance of **fire**, in his right hand was a sharp sickle, in his left a **silver trumpet**.[702] His eyes were as a flame of fire, which searched his children through and through.[703] Then all faces gathered paleness, and those that God had rejected gathered blackness. Then we all cried out, who shall be able to stand?[704] Is my robe spotless?[705] Then the angels ceased to sing, and there was some time of awful silence, when Jesus spoke.[706] Those who have clean hands and a pure heart shall be able to stand, my grace is sufficient for you.[707] At this, our faces lighted up, and joy filled every heart. And the angels struck a note higher and sung again while the cloud drew still nearer the earth. Then Jesus' silver **trumpet sound**ed, as he descended on the cloud, wrapped in flames of fire.[708] He gazed on the graves of the sleeping saints, then raised his eyes and hands to heaven & cried out, Awake! Awake! Awake! ye that sleep in the dust, and **arise**.[709] Then there was a mighty earthquake.[710] The graves opened, and the dead came up **clothed** with **immortality**.[711] The 144,000 shouted, Hallelujah! as they recognized their friends who had been torn from them by death, and in the same moment we were **changed** and **caught up together** with them to **meet the** Lord **in the air**.[712] We all entered the cloud together, and were 7 days ascending to the sea of glass, when Jesus brought along the crowns and with his own right hand placed them on our heads.[713] He gave us harps of gold and palms of victory.[714] Here on the sea of glass the 144,000 stood in a perfect square.[715] Some of them had very bright crowns, others not so bright. Some crowns appeared hung with stars, while others had but few.[716] All were perfectly

gradually illuminated the whole heavens, the righteous dead shall **rise** from their resting places—and the risen and living saints shall **together** be **caught up** and **meet the** Saviour **in the air**, when they will instantly be **changed** and **clothed** with **immortality**.[694] The Saviour will then present them to the Father, whose presence is denoted by this luminous mass, perfect, without spot or wrinkle.[695] The Father will then give the Saints, by the marriage covenant, as a bride to the Son.[696] They will then be constituted the New Jerusalem, and, together with the Saviour, will descend to the earth, which during their absence has been purified by fire, and the wicked burned up, where the Saints will dwell with Christ forever.[697]

"The time of this phenomenon he maintains will be during the current year. Not having been very prompt in our attendance, we are unabled to give any general description of his lectures. Most are familiar with his method of reckoning time and of interpreting prophecies. His style is egotistical and dogmatical. These faults may result somewhat from old age.

"The Parson is a large, thick-set personage, something over 60, and stands on his leathers about five feet ten. He has a large head, and a large square full face, with small blue eyes, and small nose, light complexion, and light hair. He is earnest and vehement in his delivery and frequently intersperses his argument with episodes in which he sometimes puts in the "rich licks" against the clergy who oppose his system, and sometimes administers some very

satisfied with their crowns. And they were all clothed with a glorious white mantle from their shoulders to their feet.[717] Angels were all about us as we marched over the sea of glass to the gate of the City.[718] Jesus raised his mighty glorious arm, laid hold of the gate and swung it back on its golden hinges, and said to us, You have washed your robes in my blood, stood stiffly for my truth, enter in.[719] We all marched in and felt we had a perfect right in the City.[720] Here we saw the tree of life, & the throne of God.[721] Out of the throne came a pure river of water, and on either side of the river was the tree of life.[722] On one side of the river was a trunk of a tree and a trunk on the other side of the river, both of pure transparent gold.[723] At first I thought I see two trees. I looked again and see they were united at the top in one tree. So it was the tree of life, on either side of the river of life; its branches bowed to the place where we stood. And the fruit was glorious, which looked like gold mixed with silver.[724] We all went under the tree, and sat down to look at the glory of the place, when Bro. Fitch and Stockman, who had preached the gospel of the kingdom, whom God had laid in the grave to save them, came up to us and asked us what we had passed through while they were sleeping.[725] We tried to call up our greatest trials, but they looked so small compared with the far more exceeding and eternal weight of glory that surrounded us, that we could not speak them out, and we all cried out Hallelujah, heaven is cheap enough, and we touched our glorious harps and made heaven's arches ring.[726] And as we were gazing at the glories of the place, our eyes were attracted upwards to something that had the appearance of silver. I asked Jesus to let me see what was within there. In a moment we were winging our way upward, and entering in. Here we saw good old father Abraham, Isaac, Jacob, Noah, Daniel, and many like them. And I saw a veil with a heavy fringe of silver, and gold as a border on the bottom. It was very beautiful. I asked Jesus what was within the veil. He raised it with his own right arm, and bade me take heed. I saw there a glorious ark, overlaid with pure gold, and it had a glorious border, resembling Jesus' crowns. On it were two bright angels; their wings were spread over the ark as they sat on each end, with their faces turned towards each other and looking downward. In the ark, beneath where the angels wings were spread, was a golden pot of Manna, of a yellowish cast, and I saw a rod, which Jesus said was Aaron's, I saw it bud, blossom and bear fruit.— And I saw two long golden rods, on which hung silver wires, and on the wires most glorious grapes. One cluster was more than a man here can carry. And I saw Jesus step up and take of the manna, almonds, grapes, and pomegranates, and bear them down to the city, and place them on the supper table. I stepped up to see how much was taken away, and there was

wholesome exhortations to sinners and unbelievers, in general. He is afflicted with a shaking or trembling which is so considerable that the motion of his head and hands can be observed across the house. He seems to be vastly satisfied with the accuracy of his theory, although he failed to impress the same confidence upon us, and a large portion of the community. Still, that might not have been his fault. The old gentleman has a good fund of historical and biblical information, and a very retentive memory. The only fault which we should urge against it, is that he sometimes seemed to remember too much. However, we will not insist on that.

Deeming it our duty, as public chroniclers, to take some notice of the presence of so noted a personage as the parson, we have given above, what little we saw and heard of him as the fairest and most proper notice we could take of him.

just as much left; and we shouted Hallelujah. Amen. We all descended from this place down into the city, and with Jesus at our head we all descended from the city down to this earth, on a great and mighty mountain, which could not bear Jesus up, and it parted asunder, and there was a mighty plain.[727] Then we looked up and saw the great city with twelve foundations, twelve gates, three on each side, and an angel at each gate, and all cried out, the city, the great city, it's coming, it's coming down from God, out of heaven, and it came and settled on the place where we stood.[728] Then we began to look at the glorious things outside of the city. There I saw most glorious houses, that had the appearance of silver, supported by four pillars, set with pearls most glorious to behold, which were to be inhabited by the saints. In them was a golden shelf, I saw many of the saints go into the houses, take off their glittering crowns and lay them on the shelf, then go out into the field by the houses to do something with the earth; not as we have to do with the earth here; no, no.[729] A glorious light shone all about their heads, and they were continually shouting and offering praises to God. And I saw another field full of all kind of flowers, and as I plucked them, I cried out, well they will never fade. Next I saw a field of tall grass, most glorious to behold. It was living green, and had a reflection of silver and gold as it waived proudly to the glory of King Jesus. Then we entered a field full of all kinds of beasts; the lion, the lamb, the leopard and the wolf, altogether in perfect union.[730] We passed through the midst of them, and they followed on peaceably after. Then we entered a wood, not like the dark woods we have here, no, no; but light, and all over glorious. The branches of the trees waved to and fro, and we all cried out we will dwell safely in the wilderness and sleep in this woods.[731] We passed through the wood, for…

Similarities but Not the Same

Because the two accounts are built on a similar view of Scripture, it is not surprising that there would be similarities between their descriptions of the Second Coming. Yet, there are also differences. If the newspaper accurately reported Miller's teaching, Miller described Jesus returning to earth *standing*, while Harmon described Him as *sitting*—in keeping with several scriptural descriptions of Jesus' position in the clouds as He returns to earth. Also, Miller placed the New Jerusalem *descending* to earth directly after Christ receives the saints in the clouds, while Harmon (who has been called "Father Miller's daughter") broke with Miller and described the passage of seven days in the saints' *ascending* to the sea of glass, which is an obvious difference about where the saints go after the Second Coming.[732]

"And then shall they see the Son of man coming in a cloud with power and great. And when these things begin to come to pass, then look up, and lift up your heads; for your redemption draweth nigh." [733]

EXHIBIT-4. The Visions of William Ellis Foy

Responding to the suggestion that William Ellis Foy's visions were the basis for Ellen White's visions, this exhibit marks and comments on their similarities and dissimilarities. It begins with an interview in 1906 in which Ellen White described experiences with Foy.[734] Ellen White is speaking where we begin—

Then another time, there was Foy that had had visions. He had had four visions. He was in a large congregation, very large. He fell right to the floor. I do not know what they were doing in there, whether they were listening to preaching or not. But at any rate he fell to the floor. I do not know how long it was, about three-quarters of an hour, I think, and he had all these before I had them. They were written out and published, and it is queer that I cannot find them in any of my books. But we have moved so many times. He had four.

Did you ever have an interview with him?

I had an interview with him. He wanted to see me, and I talked with him a little. They had appointed for me to speak that night, and I did not know that he was there. I did not know at first that he was there. While I was talking I heard a shout. He is a great, tall man, and the roof was rather low, and he jumped right up and down, and, oh, he praised the Lord, praised the Lord! It was just what he had seen, just what he had seen. But they extolled him, so I think it hurt him, and I do not know what became of him.[735]

His wife was so anxious.[736] She sat looking at him, so that it disturbed him. "Now," said he, "you must not get where you can look at me when I am speaking." He had on an Episcopalian robe. His wife sat by the side of me. She kept moving about and putting her head behind me. "What does she keep moving about for?" [I wondered.] We found out when he came to his wife. "I did as you told me to," said she. "I hid myself. I did as you told me to." [It was] so that he should not see her face. She would be so anxious, repeating the words right after him with her lips. After the meeting was ended, and he came to look her up, she said to him, "I hid myself. You didn't see me." He was a very tall man, slightly colored. But it was remarkable testimonies that he bore.

(a) Casco Street Christian Church (pictured in inset), pastored by Lorenzo D. Fleming, where Ellen Harmon heard William Miller, (b) Beethoven Hall, where she heard Foy

I always sat right close by the stand. I know what I sat there for now. It hurt me to breathe, and with the breaths of all around me, I knew I could breathe easier right by the stand, so I always took my station.

Then you attended the lectures that Mr. Foy gave?

He came to give it right to the hall, in the great hall where we attended, Beethoven Hall. That was quite a little time after the visions.[737] It was in Portland, Maine. We went over to Cape Elizabeth to hear him lecture. Father always took me with him when we went. He would be going in a sleigh, and he would invite me to get in, and I would ride with them.[738] That was before I got any way acquainted with him.

Where did you see him first?

It was there, at Beethoven Hall. They lived near the bridge where we went over to Cape Elizabeth, the family did.[739]

Following is the complete text of Foy's book describing his first two visions, with each scene identified according to Delbert W. Baker's descriptions in *The Unknown Prophet*.[740]

THE

CHRISTIAN EXPERIENCE

OF

WILLIAM E. FOY

TOGETHER WITH THE

TWO VISIONS

HE RECEIVED IN THE MONTHS OF JAN. AND FEB. 1842

PORTLAND:

PUBLISHED BY J. AND C. H. PEARSON.

1845.

REMARKS.

It is often remarked, when a work of this character, is before the public, "I am no believer in dreams and visions." Very well; such are welcome to their own discerning incredulity. The object in publishing these visions, is not to benefit such as reject indiscriminately every thing of this kind; no such expectations are cherished. But an earnest desire to comfort, and encourage the dear saints of God in their weary pilgrimage, by a glimpse of the blessedness, awaiting the finally faithful, has prompted us to this step. And no doubt is entertained but that it will prove to them, a rich, and invigorating repast.

That God does manifest himself, in visions to his children, the records of every age, do abundantly testify. And on this point, the Bible is clear and positive. The Patriarchs and Prophets were shown the great and mighty events, that were yet in the distant future, by the agency of visions. But it is often asked, if the method of revealing the events, and scenes

4

of futurity, did not cease, when the dispensation of the spirit dawned. In reply, we would enquire, if this was the case, why then was the ushering in of the gospel age, so peculiarly marked by such manifestations? Revert to the scenes of Mount Tabor. The cloud of glory overshadowing the little band there assembled; how bright! how glorious! the appearance of the 'man of sorrows' as 'his face did shine as the sun,' and his raiment become 'white as the light'—how majestic![741] the appearance of Him who was carried to heaven in a fiery chariot, and Him whom "God buried," and the voice of Jehovah speaking from the cloud, saying, "This is my beloved son—how overpowering! Well might the disciples "fall on their faces, being sore afraid!"[742]

But why dwell upon a solitary case, when the Bible reader has so many before him?[743] Look at the case of a martyr Stephen, of a St. Paul, "caught up to the third heavens," of a John upon the isle of Patmos, and tell me if Jehovah has ceased to reveal himself in visions.[744]

God, has in every age, thus dealt with the church; especially in seasons of tribulation. This was one way, in which the martyrs, were sustained, in their unparalleled sufferings. It was during their martyrdom, that Perpetua and Felicitas saw a ladder studded with swords, daggers, and instruments of torture, reaching from earth to heaven, at top of which stood Je-

5

sus Christ encouraging them.[745]

William Tennent

Nor are we wanting in instances of this kind in our day; instances too, so clear and striking, as to be fully credited, by men of the greatest attainments, as well as the deepest piety. The extraordinary vision of Wm. Tennent, a Presbyterian Clergyman, in 1806; who, while he was conversing with his brother in Latin, fainted, and apparently died; and was only saved from burial, by the importunity of a friend; his own language; "I heard and saw things all unutterable," is familiar to many.[746]

Upon this subject the Bible is explicit; and those who truly have faith in the inspired word, are willing to let its testimony have full weight. Upon the day of Pentecost, when "the disciples were all filled with the Spirit, and, spake with other tongues," the multitude being amazed began to inquire; "What meaneth this?" And some said, "These men are filled with new wine."[747] But Peter explains the matter; saying, "This is that &c."[748] Now then, according to the prophecy of Joel as explained by St. Peter, the last days were to be peculiarly marked by these manifestations, so much so, as to become precursors of the great and notable day of God.[749]

The visions of our brother, are certainly very remarkable, and when related by him in public assemblies, have been blessed by God to

6

the awakening of sinners, reclaiming of backsliders, and the building up of the saints in the most holy faith. They are published as nearly as possible in his own language. There is a most beautiful resemblance in the views here given, with the visions of Ezekiel, Daniel and John. As for instance; the description of the "tall and mighty angel," and "the sea of glass."[750]

The view of the mighty angel having the trumpet of pure silver, and the announcement of the great and terrible voice, is exceedingly interesting and instructive.[751]

That the despised and humble few, who are patiently waiting for the appearing of their glorious King, may be refreshed and comforted, in this hour of trial, while perusing these two visions, is the fervent prayer of the Publishers.

CHRISTIAN EXPERIENCE AND VISIONS OF *WILLIAM E. FOY.*

In the year 1835, under the preaching of Elder Silas Curtis, I was led to inquire, what I should do to be saved.[752]

Christians, directed me to the Lamb of God, that taketh away the sins of the world.[753] I then began to pray earnestly to God to pardon my sins; but the more I prayed the more I beheld the sinfulness of my heart; and for many days I feared there was no mercy for me; but was led to see, that it would have been justice in God, to have cut me off, and sent me where hope or mercy could not have reached me. I then became willing to give up all; and in that moment Christ appeared the one altogether lovely, and the chiefest among ten thousands, and spake the life-giving word to my soul.[754] I then rejoiced in the God of my salvation; while all things around me appeared new, shining forth with the glory of God.[755] Then could my

Pastor Silas Curtis

8

heart unite in the song of the angels, "Glory to God in the highest, peace on earth, and good will towards men."[756] I then saw such a fulness in Christ, that I wanted to proclaim it to all the world. O the glory of God that filled my soul! Three months rolled away in which I enjoyed sweet communion with my God.[757] I was then thrown into a trial by those who should have been nursing fathers in Israel, and thus remained many days, struggling in prayer; but the Lord knows how to deliver the godly out of temptation."[758] A father in Israel whom I visited at this time, gave me instruction that proved a blessing to my soul. I then joined the Sabbath School, and was there instructed for the first time, to read the word of God, and soon became able to read my little Bible. Immediately the duty of baptism was impressed upon me; and after three months disobedience, I went before the church and related the dealings of God to my soul, and the day following was led down into the liquid stream by Bro. S. Curtis, and was buried with my Saviour in baptism. Then did I experience the fulfillment of the promise; "They that wait upon the Lord shall renew their strength; they shall mount up as on wings of eagles, run and not be weary, walk and not faint;"[759] and while coming up out of the water, it appeared to me the opening heavens around me shone; and I cried with a loud voice, saying: "Glory to God, and the

9

Lamb that sitteth upon the throne!"[760]

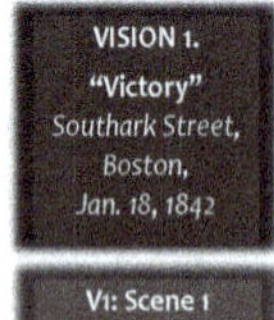

VISION 1.
"Victory"
Southark Street,
Boston,
Jan. 18, 1842
V1: Scene 1
Foy's angel guide

On the 18th of January, 1842, I met with the people of God in Southark St., Boston, where the christians were engaged in solemn prayer, and my soul was made happy in the love of God. I was immediately seized as in the agonies of death, and my breath left me; and it appeared to me that I was a spirit separate from this body.[761] I then beheld one arrayed in white raiment, whose countenance shone beyond the brightness of the stars, and a crown was upon his head which shone above the brightness of the sun.[762]

This shining one, took me by my right hand, and led me upon the bank of a river; in the midst, was a mount of pure water. Upon the bank, I beheld a multitude, both great and small; they were the living inhabitants of the earth.[763] Soon all moved towards the west, walking on the water, until we reached the mount. This became the separating line between the righteous and the wicked. The righteous crossed it, passed through three changes; 1st, their bodies were made glorious. 2d, they received pure and shining garments. 3d, bright crowns were given them.[764]

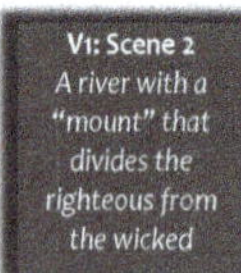

V1: Scene 2
A river with a
"mount" that
divides the
righteous from
the wicked

But when the wicked reached the spot where the righteous were changed, they cried for mercy, and sank beneath the mount.[765] The saints then passed on to a boundless plain, having the appearance like pure silver. Our guide then spake and said, *This is the plain of Paradise.*'[766]

10

This heavenly host was then divided into flocks, some, exceeding large in number, others, but small. In the middle of each was an angel. These angel's garments, were pure and white and unto each of them, was given a crown, shining with great brightness.[767] Their countenances were most lovely to behold; their wings like unto flaming fire, beneath which were the saints, both small and great.[768] The guide, then said, "*These angels are they that have preached the gospel on the earth.*"[769] I then beheld as it were a great gate before me. The gate was so tall, the height thereof I was unable to see. Before the gate stood a tall and mighty angel clothed in raiment pure and white; his eyes were like flaming fire, and he wore a crown upon his head, which lighted up this boundless plain.[770] The angel raised his right hand, and laid hold upon the gate, and opened it; and as it rolled upon its glittering hinges, he cried with a loud voice, to the heavenly host, you are all welcome!"[771] Then, the guardian angels, in the midst of the saints, struck a song of triumph, and the saints, both small and great sang with loud voices, and passed within the gate; and the guardian angels arose upon their glittering wings, and vanished from my sight.[772] The inside of the gate, appeared like glittering diamonds. Beneath our feet, was as the appearance of pure glass. I then beheld, countless millions of shining ones, coming with cards in

V1: Scene 3
The great gate and the mighty angel who opens the gate and welcomes them in

11

their hands. These shining ones become our guides. The cards they bore, shone above the brightness of the sun; and they placed them in our hands; but the names of them, I could not read.[773] These guides took us by the right hand, and led us to a boundless place. Then I lifted mine eyes, and looked above, no clouds, or skies appeared; but there, countless millions of bright angels, whose wings were like unto pure gold; and they sung with loud voices, while their wings cried "*Holy! Holy!*"[774] I then beheld an innumerable multitude, arrayed in white raiment, with cards upon their breasts; and unto each was given a crown of brightness. The guide spake, saying, "*These are they which have passed through death.*"

V1: Scene 4
Countless millions of angels who present cards to the redeemed who have passed through death

Explanation
This group has passed through death.

There was arrayed before me in the spirit, an innumerable multitude, which had not passed through death; their crowns were like the brightness of the stars; and in their right hands they held cards.[775] I then saw an individual, which had passed through death. Her brightness was beyond the expression of mortals, and at her right side stood a guardian angel; the angel's raiment was like pure gold, and his wings like flaming fire, and as she passed me, she cried with a lovely voice, "*I am going to the gate to meet my friends.*"[776] An angel then appeared flying through the midst of this boundless place, and came to the spirit of one of

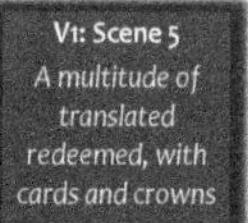

V1: Scene 6
An individual who had passed through death

12

those which had not passed through death, and cried with a loud voice, saying, "*This is my Mother.*"[777] He then became her guide. I then beheld in the midst, of this boundless place a high mountain like unto pure silver. It appeared perfectly round, and although I was unable to see through it, yet my vision extended around it. Around this mountain was a space in which stood no being. But after this vacant circle, stood as it appeared to be, a choir of angels, and as far as my sight could extend, throughout this boundless place, stood the countless millions of the righteous. And O! the singing no mortal can describe! It appeared to me, the angels next to the circle around about the mountain, with loud voices struck a lovely song, and then ceased. The saints next to them caught the strain, and with voices yet more loud, repeated it; and thus it echoed, and reechoed, until it had been sung by all the saints, and then it ceased: and then again the angels sang.

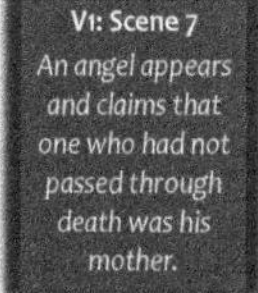

V1: Scene 8
A mountain like silver that Foy can see around

At the right side of the mountain, appeared a mighty angel, with raiment like unto burnished gold, his legs were like pillars of flaming fire, his countenance was like the lightning, and his crown gave light to this boundless place, and those that had not passed through death, could not look upon his countenance.[778] I then beheld upon the side of this mount, letters like pure

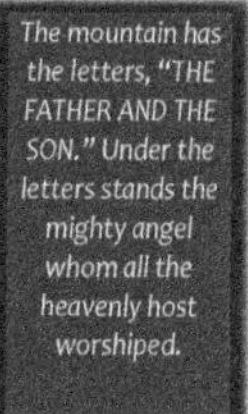

gold, which said, "*THE FATHER, AND*

13

THE SON." Directly under these letters stood the mighty angel, whose crown lighted up the place, and all the heavenly host worshiped at his feet, round about the mountain.[779] This mighty angel then raised his right hand, which appeared like a flaming sword, and all the multitude of those that had not passed through death, were caught up to the top of the mountain; and there was a large book opened, and their names came up out of the book in the form of cards, which were stamped upon their fore-heads.[780]

V1: Scene 9
Standing on the sea of glass, Foy is unable to see the being within the mountain.

We then stood again upon this pure sea of glass, before the mountain: and our bodies had become like transparent glass; but the being that was within the mountain, I was unable to behold. While I was gazing upon the glories before me, a great voice spake in the mountain, and the place was mightily shaken, and the countless multitudes of saints and angels, bowed at the feet of the mighty angel, and worshiped him crying with a loud voice "*Hallelujah*"![781] and then every voice was hushed, and the heavenly host remained bowed before the angel in solemn silence; and nought was heard save the trembling of the place caused by the voice of him who spake in the mount.

V1: Scene 10
Lower world wrapped in flames

I then beheld this lower world, wrapt as it were in rolling mountains of flame, and in this fire, I saw a countless multitude crying for mercy.[782] They appeared to be the aged and those

14

who had come to the years of understanding. Their cries came up before the mountain, while all the heavenly host were bowed in solemn stillness. The voice from the mountain, spake again, and all the saints and angels arose, and with loud voices cried "*AMEN.*"

Explanation
No mercy for those who have rejected the gospel and God's warnings

I then began to converse with my guide, and inquired, *why there was no mercy for those, whom I had seen in distress.* He answered, "*The gospel has been preached unto them, and the servants have warned them, but they would not believe; and when the great day of God's wrath comes, there will be no mercy for them.*"[783]

V1: Scene 11
A tree on a "boundless place" with small angels on its branches

I then beheld in the middle of this boundless place a tree, the body of which, was like unto transparent glass, and the limbs were like transparent gold, extending all over this boundless place. On every branch of the tree, were small angels standing.[784] There was an innumerable multitude of them, and they sung with loud voices, and such singing has not been heard this side of heaven. This tree was also clothed in light proceeding from the mighty angel. Beneath this tree standing on the sea of glass, were the countless millions of the righteous, arrayed in white raiment, with crowns on their heads, and cards upon their breasts; and in the multitude I saw some that I knew while they were living upon the earth, and they we all singing with loud voices and lifting up their glittering hands plucking fruit

15

from the tree; the fruit appeared like clusters of grapes in pictures of pure gold.[785] With a lovely voice, the guide then spoke to me and said "*Those that eat of the fruit of this tree, return to earth no more.*"[786] I raised my hand to partake of the heavenly fruit, that I might no more return to earth; but alas! I immediately found myself again, in this lonely vale of tears. The duty to declare the things which had thus been shown me, to my fellow creatures, and warn them to flee from the wrath to come, rested with great weight upon my mind; but I was disobedient, settling upon this point for an excuse, that my guide did not command me so to do; and I thereby, brought darkness, and death, upon my soul.[787] But I could find no peace or comfort. I began to doubt whether indeed my soul had ever been converted, and although I often met with the people of God, I obtained no relief, but felt distressed and lonely. I could get no access in prayer. At last in order to escape the cross of going and personally declaring it to the world, I decided to have it printed. Yet, in this I could find no relief. Besides after having an account of it printed, it was a very imperfect sketch; and indeed I was unable to relate it for that purpose. But the Lord in his mercy spared me to behold the evening of the 4th of Feb. 1842, when I met with the people of God in May St. A large congregation was gathered together, and

16

christians were engaged in exhortation and prayer.[788] But I enjoyed none of the sensible presence of God.

VISION 2. "Judgment"
African Methodist Episcopal Church, Beacon Hill, May Street, Boston, Feb. 4, 1842

In the last part of the evening, the house being much crowded, I gave my seat to a friend who had been standing through the evening. While I was thus standing, I began to reflect on my disobedience; and while thus engaged, suddenly I heard a voice, as it were, in the spirit, speaking unto me. I immediately fell to the floor, and knew nothing about this body, until twelve hours and a half, had passed away, as I was afterwards informed.

V2: Scene 1
Saw himself as a bodyless "spirit" standing alone on the earth

V2: Scene 2
A cloud darkens the sun; then a flaming bar comes from the heavens.

It appeared to me that I was a spirit separate from this body, standing upon the earth alone. No other being appeared to be with me. The earth had the appearance of a place perfectly level. The sun shone forth in its splendour, as it naturally does at noon day. I then beheld a cloud gently rising out of the west, which came up and covered the sun, so that it was darkened, and the whole heavens become like sackcloth; then something beyond the expression of mortal man, burst forth from the heavens, from the south even unto the north.[789] It was like a flaming bar of fire; and immediately after, something appeared, which it is impossible for me to describe. I then beheld innumerable multitudes coming from the four quarters of the earth and were assembled before this bar, and there stood in solemn silence, while paleness

V2: Scene 3
Large numbers assemble before the flaming bar.

17

gathered on all countenances.[790] Immediately they were caught up to this bar, and the bodies of the saints were changed, becoming like transparent gold; and they were clothed in light and shining garments, and crowns of brightness were placed upon their heads, and shining cards upon their breasts; and singing sweetly, they passed through the bar of fire. But the wicked were unable to pass. The world beneath appeared to be wrapt in darkness and fire; into this, the wicked sunk from my sight, crying for mercy. I beheld mothers with their infants in their arms come to the flaming bar; the bodies of the infants become like transparent gold, and on wings of flaming fire, they passed the bar, singing with lovely voices, and the unholy mothers, crying for mercy, would sink below.

I then beheld an innumerable multitude coming up from the waters, and an innumerable multitude, coming up out of the earth, arrayed in white raiment, with cards upon their breasts, and singing with loud voices, they passed this bar, and received crowns of glory upon their heads.[791]

V2: Scene 4
Innumerable multitude (the righteous dead) coming up out of water and earth

I then beheld, a multitude coming up out of the earth, and some of them I knew whose names were enrolled in the church books on earth, some of whom I had seen communing with the saints of different orders, and some which had profes-

V2: Scene 5
Multitude coming up out of the earth (the wicked dead), some of whose names were enrolled in the church books

18

sed to be preachers of the gospel.[792] Although they had high professions, yet they were not found worthy, but cried for mercy, and sunk with those who had blasphemed. As we passed the bar, we entered upon a boundless place which was lighted up with great brightness. Near the place through which we passed, I beheld a mighty angel clothed in pure white raiment, having a crown of brightness on his head.[793] He appeared to be gazing through the bar, and his eyes like lamps of fire were fixed with steadfastness upon the earth.[794] He stood with his right foot placed before him, as though walking; and his object appeared to be, to reach the earth. But three steps remained for him to take. Against his breast, and across his left hand, was as it were, a trumpet of pure silver; and a great and terrible voice came from the midst of the boundless place, saying, "*The sixth angel hath not yet done sounding*."[795] Behind the angel, I beheld countless millions of bright chariots, they had the appearance of pure gold, and were perfectly square. Each chariot had four wings like flaming fire. And while I was beholding, one of the chariots arose upon its wings of fire, and an angel followed after the chariot; and the wings of the chariot, and the wings of the angel, cried as with one loud voice, saying, "*Holy! Holy!*"[796] I watched the chariot, listening to the lovely sound of the wings. It passed towards the earth;

V2: Scene 6
The righteous have passed the bar and enter a "boundless place" (Paradise).

and there appeared a spirit,

19

arrayed in white raiment as it were, standing upon a mountain, and there was given him a crown of brightness; and he stepped into the chariot with the angel, and in a moment he was in this boundless place.[797] Although he shone with great brightness yet this individual I knew, it was the one referred to by the witness[798] who said, "I see the chariot coming!"[799] He departed this life, in just two weeks after I saw him in vision.

V2: Scene 7
A multitude of people the size of ten-year-old children form a perfect square and sing "a song which the saints and angels could not sing."

I then saw in the midst of the place, an innumerable multitude, arrayed in white raiment, standing in a perfect square, having, crowns of unfading glory upon their heads.[800] They were of the size of children ten years of age; and they sung a song, which the saints and angels could not sing. In the midst of this boundless place, there was a river of pure water, and on either side of the river, countless millions of angels stood, with crowns of brightness upon their heads; they had in their hands cups like pure gold, and were bowing down and partaking of the water of the river, singing with loud and lovely voices, and worshiping him, whose crown gave light, to this boundless place.[801]

V2: Scene 8
Foy's guide led him to a narrow door.

Then came one unto me clothed in white, whom I call my guide; —he led me to a place

20

like unto a narrow door. The first which I beheld, was a mighty angel, upon the right hand, having a large book open before him, also at the left, another with a book open before him.[802]

Explanation 1
Those who repent are moved from the book on the left to the one on the right.

My guide, then spake to me, saying, *They that repent of their sins on the earth, are blotted out of the book on the left, and recorded on the right.*"[803] I then beheld angels ascending and descending to and from the earth; they bore tidings to the recording angels.[804]

Explanation 2
Foy's spirit is to return to the world and warn his fellow creatures to flee the wrath to come.

My guide, now, informed me what I must do; saying, "*Thy spirit must return to yonder world, and thou must reveal those things which thou hast seen, and also warn thy fellow creatures, to flee from the wrath to come.*" I then answered him saying, "*How can I return to yonder world?*" He answered me; *I will go with thee, and support and help thee, to declare these things unto the world.*" Then, I answered the angel,— *I will go*.[805]

V2: Scene 9
The vail between the lower world and the "boundless place" is removed.

I then beheld this lower world. It seemed as though the vail which had separated it, from the boundless place in which I stood, was removed, and they had both become as one; and the saints and angels were continually passing from, and to, the earth.[806] The earth appeared like a calm sea of transparent gold; above no cloud or sky appeared, but the air was perfectly pure, and of a silvery brightness. I then heard all the saints, and angels, in heaven, and on the

21

earth, singing with loud voices. My guide then spread his wings, and brought my spirit gently to the earth, then soared away; and immediately I found myself in the body.

Notwithstanding the command of my guide, and my solemn promise to declare these things to the world; I was at first exceedingly unwilling so to do, and it was three days, before I revealed them in a public manner.

The message was so different—and the manner in which the command was given, so different from any I had ever heard of, and knowing the prejudice among the people against those of my color, it became very crossing.

These questions were continually arising. "Why should these things be given to me, to bear to the world, and not to the learned, or to one of a different condition from myself?[807] But no peace could I obtain in disobedience. "Woe is me if I declare not these things," rested heavily upon my soul.

On the 6th of Feb, the Pastor of the Broomfield St. Church, called upon me, and requested me to relate my visions in his house of worship. Several members of that church were present, and were anxious for me to comply. I consented; and the appointment was made for the next afternoon. After they had left me I regretted that such a step had been taken, and thought had the world been mine it would cheerfully be given, to have the appointment recalled.

22

The morning of the 7th, however, found my mind calm and peaceful; but as the hour for meeting drew nigh, temptations began sorely to afflict me. I feared lest my guide would not be with me, and I should be unable to tell the people, the things which had been shown me. A band of brethren, sympathising with me accompanied me to the meeting. Upon entering the house, I found a large congregation assembled, and each individual, seemed like a mountain. So much of the fear of man, rested upon me, that I asked the Pastor, to open the meeting with prayer; telling him, I thought they would be obliged to have a prayer meeting. But while he was addressing the throne of grace it seemed as though *I heard a voice, speaking unto me, and saying, "I am with thee; and I promised to be with thee!*" my heart then began to burn within me, the fear of man suddenly fled, and unspeakable glory filled my soul.[808] I then related with great freedom, the things shown me, while the congregation sat in perfect stillness. From this time I traveled three months delivering my message to crowded houses, enjoying continual peace of mind. But after this I began to fear my family would come to want, and so went to work laboring with my hands, and thus continued for three months. But I could find no rest day nor night, until again I consented to

23

do my duty.[809] Since then, I have traveled from place to place, and suffered some persecution, but the promise of my guide has never failed.[810] His supporting presence has been with me.

My object in publishing these visions, is to comfort the saints.[811] They have been a great consolation to me, in seasons of temptation and trial.

Often, in the silent hours of the night, I have seemed to hear again, the sweet song of the angels; and whenever my heart has felt sad and lonely, the things shown me by the angel, have lifted me up above the trying scenes of earth.

My desire is, that the children of God, may be blessed in the same manner. I am now waiting for my coming Lord. Although before the Lord was pleased to show me these heavenly things, I was opposed to the doctrine of Jesus' near approach, I am now looking for that event. I expect soon to see the tall and mighty angel.[812] "Then shall I be satisfied, when I awake in his likeness."

Ye saints of God, lift up your heads, for the glories of an earth made new, will soon be yours.

"Eye hath not seen, nor ear heard, neither have entered into the heart of man, the things which God hath prepared for them that love him." "But God hath revealed them unto us by his spirit; for the spirit searcheth all things, yea, the deep things of God."[813]

24

TESTIMONIALS.

We, the undersigned, inhabitants of Boston, were witnesses of the apparently inanimate condition into which our brother, Wm. Ellis Foy, was thrown from some unknown cause, on the 18th of January 1842, when he laid two hours and a half; and again February 4th, when he laid twelve hours and a half, during which, each time, he testifies that he experienced extraordinary visions of another world.[814]

Charles Tash.	Francis Sanders.
George Williams.	John Thomas.
David Williams.	Andrew Lewis.
Edward Williams.	George Harris.

Dr. Henry Cummings, testifies: "I was present with our brother at the time of his visions. I examined him, but could not find any appearance of life, except around the heart."[815]

Ann Foy testifies: "The first appearance of life I saw in him, was the raising of his right hand.[816] He then arose upon his knees, and made signs for water, which was given him. He dipped his hand into it, and wet his forehead, and his speech immediately came to him. We then wished him to tell us, what things he had seen, and he answered, as soon as I receive strength, I will reveal unto you, that which the Lord has revealed unto me."

Copy of certificate of church membership.

This certifies that Bro. Wm. E. Foy, is a regular member, of the first Freewill Baptist Church, in Augusta, in good standing. And as such, we commend him to the fellowship of the people of God, of every name, whenever he may chance to meet them.

DANIEL PALMER,
Church Clerk.[817]

Other Visions of William Foy

J. N. Loughborough

The comparison in this exhibit has included William Foy's two published visions, marking points of correlation to Ellen White's visions. Yet, in his online biographical sketch of William Foy, Benjamin Baker referenced a third vision and possibly an unrecorded fourth.[818] Baker's source for the third vision, with its four scenes, was Loughborough. Though Loughborough did not identify where he got it, certain details in his 1892 account correlate with what Ellen White told Loughborough about her meeting with Foy.[819] Here is how Loughborough described what Foy saw in the third vision:

> In this he was shown the pathway of the people of God through to the heavenly city. He saw a great platform, or step, on which multitudes of people gathered. Occasionally one would drop through this platform out of sight, and of such a one it was said to him, "Apostatized." Then he saw the people rise to a second step, or platform, and some there also dropped through the platform out of sight. Finally a third platform appeared, which extended to the gates of the holy city. A great company gathered with those who had advanced to this platform.[820]

Loughborough asserted that Foy could not explain what was intended by the three steps. However, Foy was present to hear Ellen Harmon describe a vision of similar import, which she *was* able to explain. The reason that she could do so is that—with other Sabbath-keeping Adventists—she had taken all three of the steps.

> I saw a company who stood well guarded and firm, and would give no countenance to those who would unsettle the established faith of the body. God looked upon them with approbation. I was shown three steps—one, two and three—the first, second and third angels' messages. Said the angel, Woe to him who shall move a block, or stir a pin in these messages. The true understanding of these messages is of vital importance. The destiny of souls hangs upon the manner in which they are received. I was again brought down through these messages, and saw how dearly the people of God had purchased their experience. It had been obtained through much suffering and severe conflict. Step by step had God brought them along, until he had placed them upon a solid, immovable platform. Then I saw individuals as they approached the platform, before stepping upon it examine the foundation. Some with rejoicing immediately stepped upon it. Others commenced to find fault with the laying of the foundation of the platform. They wished improvements made, and then the platform would be more perfect, and the people much happier. Some stepped off the platform and examined it, then found fault with it, declaring it to be laid wrong. I saw that nearly all stood firm upon the platform, and exhorted others who had stepped off to cease their complaints, for God was the master-builder, and they were fighting against him. They recounted the wonderful work of God, which had led them to the firm platform, and in union nearly all raised their eyes to heaven, and with a loud voice glorified God. This affected some of those who had complained, and left the platform, and again they with humble look stepped upon it.[821]

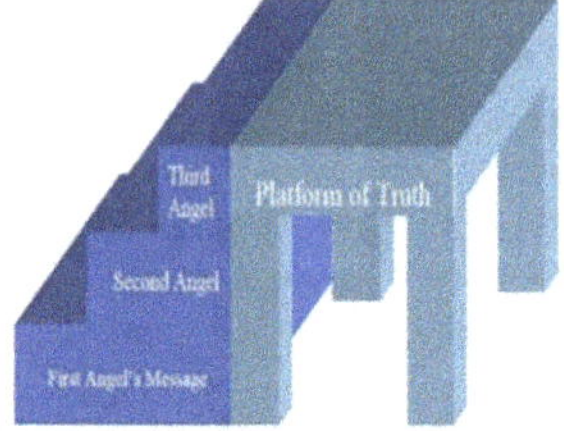

William Foy's grave, Sullivan, Maine

According to Loughborough, Foy described people losing their way at each of the steps. However, unlike Ellen White, Foy could not explain that there were biblical truths and a spiritual experience attached to each of the three steps. Ellen White explained that all three steps were essential to taking the Adventist people into the kingdom. Foy quit sharing the messages of his visions after 1844. Ellen White said that she did not know what happened to Foy. Loughborough assumed that he "sickened and died." However, Delbert and Benjamin Baker have traced Foy's labors as a Baptist minister, disconnected from Adventism, until the time of his death in 1893. According to Loughborough, another man, Hazen Little Foss, received this same vision but rejected God's calling to share it.[822]

Similarities and Differences between Foy and White's Visions

Tim Poirier, Vice-Director of the Ellen G. White Estate, summarized the similarities:

> While the parallels of the preceding pages show similar points between Foy's visions and Ellen White's, the context of those parallels is vastly different. Foy sees the living inhabitants of the earth as a great multitude walking on the water of a river until they reach a mount of pure water, where the righteous are separated from the wicked. There is no mention of the Second Advent. Ellen White sees the Advent people walking on a narrow path toward the New Jerusalem with a bright light behind them. She recounts the time of trouble up to the appearance of Christ in the clouds.
>
> Foy apparently interprets his vision in terms of his belief in the immortality of the soul. He sees an individual stepping into a heavenly chariot to be taken to paradise—an individual he recognizes as having died two weeks earlier. Obviously, no such concept appears in Ellen White's accounts, although she similarly describes seeing Fitch and Stockman who had recently died [but when she sees them, it is after Christ's return]. Perhaps this illustrates how a person's presuppositions can color his interpretations. Foy sees a great mountain on which was printed in gold letters, "The Father and the Son," and an apparent judgment scene with a large book opened. There is nothing similar to this scene in Ellen White's vision.
>
> The closest parallel is that regarding the tree of life. Both describe the fruit as gold-like, and both repeat the words that those who eat of the fruit will not return to the earth. Yet, even here, sharp differences appear. Foy saw the limbs of the tree extending all over the boundless place. He saw small angels standing on every branch. Ellen White sees two trunks uniting in one tree, and there is no mention of small angels in the tree.
>
> Foy's second vision is primarily a judgment scene, where countless multitudes appear before a "flaming bar of fire." This is entirely absent from Ellen White's vision. The "three steps" remaining for the mighty angel to take reach to the earth, but nothing is said about [the scene's] significance. Ellen White's later vision of the three steps or platforms was an extensive scene where individuals are examining the platform, suggesting improvements, etc. (EW 258–26). Foy sees an innumerable multitude standing in a perfect square, but they are of the size of children ten years of age, not the 144,000 Ellen White saw standing on the sea of glass.[823] Only a full reading of Foy's visions could bring out all the differences.
>
> If Foy's experience is accepted as genuine, the few specific parallels (e.g., the opening of the gate, the fruit of the tree of life, "cards" possessed by heavenly inhabitants) would be expected if two [people] were shown the same celestial city in heaven. But the overall contents of Foy's published visions do not parallel Ellen White's. According to Loughborough, it was Foy's third vision, one apparently never printed, that later was given to Ellen White. That is the vision where parallels would be expected to occur.[824]

While both visionaries speak of having to return to earth without eating the glorious repast set before them, Ellen White submitted to the instruction that only those who remain in glory can partake of the food that she saw, while Foy tried to sneak a bite of it before finding himself back on earth without getting any. Regarding the opening of the golden gates of the city, it is a "mighty angel" that opens the gates for Foy (and this same "mighty angel" is seen with people bowing in worship before him and light from his crown illuminates the place) while it is plainly Jesus for Ellen White. (Foy never refers directly to Jesus in any of the scenes.) Regarding the golden cards, Ellen White sees the cards solely in the possession of the angels, while Foy sees the angels giving the cards to the redeemed, who later use them.[825] Unlike Ellen White, Foy confuses the reader in not delineating where the scenes in his visions fall in line with the Second Coming. More importantly, Foy describes himself and other individuals in his visions as "spirits" and calls attention to an angel who identified a human as being his mother. These interpretations of what he saw may be indications of his Freewill Baptist leanings.

So, what are we to make of the similarities between the visions of Foy and White? These can be explained in at least two ways. Ellen White's critics would have us believe that Ellen White only *pretended* to have visions but *actually* took what she heard from Foy and reworked it into her own compositions. While plausible for some, such an explanation calls Ellen White's integrity as a Christian into question based on a naturalistic supposition that ignores the tangible evidence of the supernatural in her visions. Another explanation for their similarity could be that Ellen White and William Foy had glimpses of similar scenes, yet they interpreted those scenes differently through different theological lenses. This may also explain why Foy did not continue in a prophetic role in the Advent movement. Though racial prejudice would certainly have made it difficult for a fair-skinned Black man in the 19th century (the reason Foy gave for his hesitancy in sharing his first vision), the theological differences Foy had with White in reporting his first two visions and his puzzlement in interpreting the third show that Foy's theological background left him ill-equipped to properly interpret his visions or to nurture the largest church to come out of the Millerite movement with its biblical view of spirits, angels, and man's lack of awareness in death. Ellen White's biblical background, on the other hand, better equipped her to understand what was revealed to her in vision, making her descriptions more understandable and theologically accurate.

A final observation we might make concerns the marked difference in the lasting value of their visions. Though both Foy and White shared their visions publicly, the only published version of Foy's visions still in existence is in the small book published by the brothers Charles and John Pearson. White's first visions, on the other hand, have been published many times—from 1845 until the present—in periodicals, broadsides, and pamphlets, and in multiple editions of her vision book (*Experience and Views*) with its supplement. The facsimiles on the next page visibly contrast this fact.[826]

"But rejoice, inasmuch as ye are partakers of Christ's sufferings; that, when his glory shall be revealed, ye may be glad also with exceeding joy." [827]

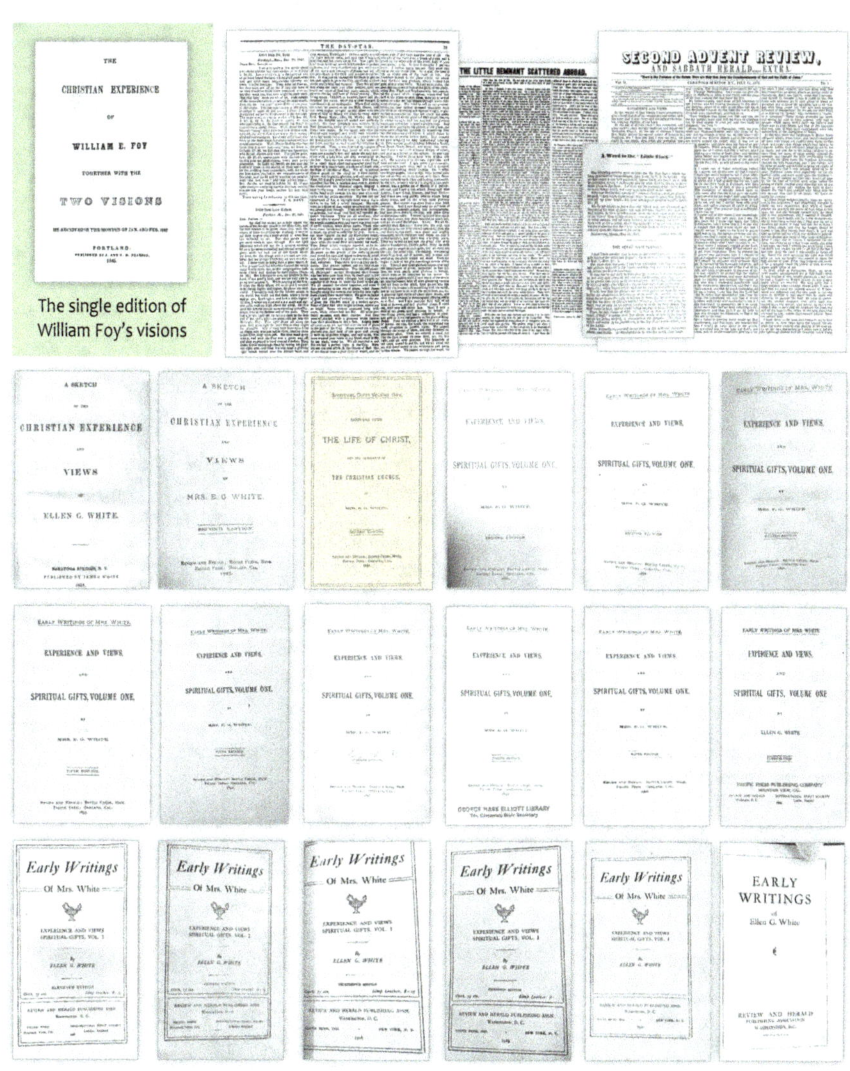

The single edition of Foy's vision, published by John Pearson, Jr. and Charles H. Pearson, compared to the various editions of Ellen White's first vision

EXHIBIT-5. Textual History of Ellen White's First Vision in Parallel

Seen below is a comparison of the various versions of Ellen White's V1 and V16, to show the omissions and changes (with differences in **2SG** in the footnotes). To simplify the notation, spelling and punctuation changes are not marked. Wording that varies or is omitted between versions has been highlighted. Text in green indicates scriptural wording; red colorization of text and the footnotes were added by the annotator.

The Day-Star, 24 Jan. 1846, Ellen G. Harmon	Broadside1, 6 April 1846; "A Word to the Little Flock," May 1847	*The Girdle of Truth and Advent Review*, 20 January 1848	*Second Advent Review and Sabbath Herald* Extra, 21 July 1851	*Experience and Views*, 1851, pp. 9-15	*Early Writings*, 1882, pp. 13-19
Portland, Me., December 20, 1845. Bro. Jacobs,	**To the Remnant Scattered Abroad**	(*The following Vision was published in 1845, '46 & '47.*) **To the Remnant scattered Abroad.**	**To the Remnant Scattered Abroad**	**To the Remnant scattered Abroad**	**My First Vision**
As God has shown me in holy vision the travels of the Advent people to the Holy City, and the rich reward to be given those who wait the return of their Lord from the wedding, it may be my duty to give you a short sketch of what God has revealed to me.[828] The dear saints have got many trials to pass through. But our light afflictions which are but for a moment worketh for us a far more exceeding and eternal weight of glory; while we look not at the things which are seen, for the things which are seen are temporal, but the things which are not seen are eternal. [2 Cor. 4:17, 18.] I have tried to bring back a good report, & a few	As God has shown me in holy vision the travels of the Advent people to the Holy City, and the rich reward to be given those who wait the return of their Lord from the wedding, it may be my duty to give you a short sketch of what God has revealed to me. The dear saints have got many trials to pass through. But our light afflictions, which are but for a moment, worketh for us a far more exceeding and eternal weight of glory—while we look not at the things which are seen, for the things which are seen are temporal, but the things which are not seen are eternal. I have tried to bring back a good report, and a few grapes	As God has shown me in holy vision the travels of the Advent people to the Holy City, **OMISSION-2** it may be my duty to give you a short sketch of what God has revealed to me. The dear saints have got many trials to pass through. But our light afflictions, which are but for a moment, worketh for us a far more exceeding and eternal weight of glory. **OMISSION-3** I have tried to bring back a good report, and a few grapes from	As God has shown me **OMISSION-1** the travels of the Advent people to the Holy City, and the rich reward to be given those who wait the return of their Lord from the wedding, it may be my duty to give you a short sketch of what God has revealed to me. The dear saints have got many trials to pass through. But our light afflictions, which are but for a moment, worketh for us a far more exceeding and eternal weight of glory—while we look not at the things which are seen, for the things which are seen are temporal, but the things which are not seen are eternal. I have tried to bring back a good report, and a few grapes	As God has shown me **OMISSION-1** the travels of the Advent people to the Holy City, and the rich reward to be given those who wait the return of their Lord from the wedding, it may be my duty to give you a short sketch of what God has revealed to me. The dear saints have got many trials to pass through. But our light afflictions, which are but for a moment, worketh for us a far more exceeding and eternal weight of glory—while we look not at the things which are seen, for the things which are seen are temporal, but the things which are not seen are eternal. I have tried to bring back a good report, and a few grapes	As God has shown me **OMISSION-1** the travels of the Advent [page] 14 people to the Holy City and the rich reward to be given those who wait the return of their Lord from the wedding, it may be my duty to give you a short sketch of what God has revealed to me. The dear saints have many trials to pass through. But our light afflictions, which are but for a moment, will work for us a far more exceeding and eternal weight of glory—while we look not at the things which are seen, for the things which are seen are temporal, but the things which are not seen are eternal. I have tried to bring back a good report and a few grapes

grapes from the heavenly Canaan, for which many would stone me, as the congregation bade stone Caleb and Joshua for their report, (Num. 14:10.) But I declare to you, my brother in the Lord, it is a goodly land, and we are well able to go up and possess it. While praying at the family altar the Holy Ghost fell on me and I seemed to be rising higher and higher, far above the dark world. I turned to look for the Advent people in the world, but could not find them, when a voice said to me, Look again, and look a little higher. At this, I raised my eyes and see a strait and narrow path, cast up high above the world. On this path the Advent people were traveling to the City, which was at the farther end of the path. They had a bright light set up behind them at the first end of the path, which an angel told me	from the heavenly Canaan, for which many would stone me, as the congregation bade stone Caleb and Joshua for their report, (Num. 14:10.) But I declare to you, my brethren and sisters in the Lord, it is a goodly land, and we are well able to go up and possess it. {WLF 14.1} While praying at the family altar, the Holy Ghost fell on me, and I seemed to be rising higher and higher, far above the dark world. I turned to look for the Advent people in the world, but could not find them— when a voice said to me, "Look again, and look a little higher." At this I raised my eyes and saw a straight and narrow path, *Mat. 7:14.* cast up high above the world. On this path the Advent people were travelling to the City, which was at the farther end of the path. They had a bright light set up behind them	the heavenly Canaan, for which many would stone me, as the congregation bade stone Caleb and Joshua for their report, (Numbers 14:10.) But I declare to you, my brethren and sisters in the Lord, it is a goodly land, and we are well able to go up and possess it. {GT 25.1} While praying at the family altar, the Holy Ghost fell on me, and I seemed to be rising higher and higher, far above the dark world. I turned to look for the Advent people in the world, but could not find them— when a voice said to me, "Look again, and look a little higher." At this I raised my eyes and saw a straight and narrow path, cast up high above the world. On this path the Advent people were traveling to the City, which was at the further end of the path. They had a bright light set up behind	from the heavenly Canaan, for which many would stone me, as the congregation bade stone Caleb and Joshua for their report, (Numbers 14:10.) But I declare to you, my brethren and sisters in the Lord, it is a goodly land, and we are well able to go up and possess it. {RH, July 21, 1851} While praying at the family altar, the Holy Ghost fell upon me, and I seemed to be rising higher and higher, far above the dark world. I turned to look for the Advent people in the world, but could not find them— when a voice said to me, "Look again, and look a little higher." At this I raised my eyes and saw a straight and narrow path, cast up high above the world. On this path the Advent people were traveling to the City, which was at the farther end of the path. They had a	from the heavenly Canaan, for which many would stone me, as the congregation bade stone Caleb and Joshua for their report, (Numbers 14:10.) But I declare to you, my brethren and sisters in the Lord, it is a goodly land, and we are well able to go up and possess it. {ExV 9.4} While praying at the family altar, the Holy Ghost fell upon me, and I seemed to be rising higher and higher, far above the dark world. I turned to look for the Advent people in the world, but could not find them— when a voice said to me, "Look again, and look a little higher." At this I raised my eyes and saw a straight and narrow path, cast up high above the world. On this path the Advent people were traveling to the City, which was at the farther end of the path.[841] They had a bright light set	from the heavenly Canaan, for which many would stone me, as the congregation bade stone Caleb and Joshua for their report. (Numbers 14:10.) But I declare to you, my brethren and sisters in the Lord, it is a goodly land, and we are well able to go up and possess it. {EW 13.3} While I was praying at the family altar, the Holy Ghost fell upon me, and I seemed to be rising higher and higher, far above the dark world. I turned to look for the Advent people in the world, but could not find them, when a voice said to me, "Look again, and look a little higher." At this I raised my eyes, and saw a straight and narrow path, cast up high above the world. On this path the Advent people were traveling to the city, which was at the farther end of the path. They had a bright light set

was the Midnight Cry.[829] This light shone all along the path and gave light for their feet so they might not stumble. And if they kept their eyes fixed on Jesus, who was just before them, leading them to the City, they were safe. But soon some grew weary, and said the City was a great way off, and they expected to have entered it before. Then Jesus would encourage them by raising his glorious right arm, and from his arm came a glorious light which waved over the Advent band, and they shouted, Hallelujah! Others rashly denied the light behind them, and said that it was not God that had led them out so far. The light behind them went out which left their feet in perfect darkness, and they stumbled and got their eyes off the mark and lost sight of Jesus, and fell off the path down in the dark and

at the first end of the path, which an angel told me was the Midnight Cry. *Mat. 25:6.* This light shone all along the path, and gave light for their feet so they might not stumble. And if they kept their eyes fixed on Jesus, who was just before them, leading them to the City, they were safe. But soon some grew weary, and they said the City was a great way off, and they expected to have entered it before. Then Jesus would encourage them by raising his glorious right arm, and from his arm came a glorious light which waved over the Advent band, and they shouted Hallelujah! Others rashly denied the light behind them, and said that it was not God that had led them out so far. The light behind them went out leaving their feet in perfect darkness, and they stumbled and got their eyes off the mark and lost sight of Jesus, and fell off the

them at the first end of the path, which an angel told me was the Midnight Cry. This light shone all along the path, and gave light for their feet so they might not stumble. And if they kept their eyes fixed on Jesus, who was just before them, leading them to the City, they were safe. But soon some grew weary, and they said the City was a great way off, and they expected to have entered it before. Then Jesus would encourage them by raising his glorious right arm, and from his arm came a glorious light which waved over the Advent band, and they shouted Hallelujah! Others rashly denied the light behind them, and said that it was not God that had led them out so far. The light behind them went out leaving their feet in perfect darkness, and they stumbled and got their eyes off the

bright light set up behind them at the first end of the path, which an angel told me was the Midnight Cry. This light shone all along the path, and gave light for their feet so they might not stumble. And if they kept their eyes fixed on Jesus, who was just before them, leading them to the City, they were safe. But soon some grew weary, and they said the City was a great way off, and they expected to have entered it before. Then Jesus would encourage them by raising his glorious right arm, and from his arm came a glorious light which waved over the Advent band, and they shouted Hallelujah! Others rashly denied the light behind them, and said that it was not God that had led them out so far. The light behind them went out leaving their feet in perfect darkness, and they stumbled and got their eyes off the mark, and lost

up behind them at the first end of the path, which an angel told me was the Midnight Cry. This light shone all along the path, and gave light for their feet so they might not stumble.[842] And if they kept their eyes fixed on Jesus, who was just before them, leading them to the City, they were safe. But soon some grew weary, and they said the City was a great way off, and they expected to have entered it before. Then Jesus would encourage them by raising his glorious right arm, and from his arm came a glorious light which waved over the Advent band, and they shouted Hallelujah![843] Others rashly denied the light behind them, and said that it was not God that had led them out so far. The light behind them went out leaving their feet in perfect darkness, and they stumbled and got their eyes off the mark, and lost sight of Jesus,

up behind them at the beginning of the path, which an angel told me was the midnight cry. This light shone all along the path and gave light for their feet so that they might not stumble. If they kept their eyes fixed on Jesus, who was just before them, leading them to the city, they were safe. But soon some grew weary, and said the city was a great way off, and they expected to have entered it before. Then Jesus would encourage [page] 15 them by raising His glorious right arm, and from His arm came a light which waved over the Advent band, and they shouted, "Alleluia!" Others rashly denied the light behind them and said that it was not God that had led them out so far. The light behind them went out, leaving their feet in perfect darkness, and they stumbled and lost sight of the mark and of Jesus, and fell off the path

wicked world below. It was just as impossible for them to get on the path again & go to the City, as all the wicked world which God had rejected. They fell all the way along the path one after another, until we heard the voice of God like many waters, which gave us the day and hour of Jesus' coming.[830] The living saints, 144,000, in number, know and understand the voice, while the wicked thought it was thunder & an earthquake. When God spake the time, he poured on us the Holy Ghost, and our faces began to light up and shine with the glory of God as Moses did when he came down from Mount Sinai, (Exod. 34:30-34.) By this time the 144,000 were all sealed and perfectly united. On their foreheads was written, God, New Jerusalem, and	path down in the dark and wicked world below. It was just as impossible for them to get on the path again and go to the City, as all the wicked world which God had rejected.[834] They fell all the way along the path one after another, until we heard the voice of God like many waters, *Eze. 43:2. Joel 3:16. Rev. 16:17.* which gave us the day and hour of Jesus' coming. *Ezek. 12:25; Mark 13:32.* The living saints, 144,000 in number, knew and understood the voice, while the wicked thought it was thunder and an earthquake. *John 12:29.* When God spake the time, he poured on us the Holy Ghost, and our faces began to light up and shine with the glory of God as Moses' did when he came down from Mount Sinai. *Isa. 10:27.*[835] {WLF 14.2} By this time the 144,000 were all sealed and perfectly united. On their foreheads was	mark and lost sight of Jesus, and fell off the path down into the dark and wicked world below. **OMISSION-4** They fell all the way along the path one after another, until we heard the voice of God like many waters, which gave us the day and hour of Jesus' coming. The living saints, 144,000 in number, knew and understood the voice, while the wicked thought it was thunder and an earthquake. When God spake the time, he poured on us the Holy Ghost, and our faces began to light up and shine with the glory of God as Moses' did when he came down from Mount Sinai. {GT 25.2} By this time the 144,000 were all sealed and perfectly united. On their foreheads was written, God, New Jerusalem, and a glorious Star containing Jesus' new	sight of Jesus, and fell off the path down in the dark and wicked world below. **OMISSION-4** **OMISSION-5** Soon we heard the voice of God like many waters, which gave us the day and hour of Jesus' coming. The living saints, 144,000, in number, knew and understood the voice, while the wicked thought it was thunder and an earthquake. When God spake the time, he poured on us the Holy Ghost, and our faces began to light up and shine with the glory of God as Moses' did when he came down from Mount Sinai. {RH, July 21, 1851} The 144,000 were all sealed and perfectly united. On their foreheads was written, God, New Jerusalem, and a glorious Star containing Jesus' new name. At our happy, holy	and fell off the path down in the dark and wicked world below.[844] **OMISSION-4** **OMISSION-5** Soon we heard the voice of God like many waters, which gave us the day and hour of Jesus' coming. The living saints, 144,000, in number, knew and understood the voice, while the wicked thought it was thunder and an earthquake.[845] When God spake the time, he poured on us the Holy Ghost, and our faces began to light up and shine with the glory of God as Moses' did when he came down from Mount Sinai.[846] {ExV 10.1} The 144,000 were all sealed and perfectly united. On their foreheads was written, God, New Jerusalem, and a glorious Star containing Jesus' new name. At our happy, holy	down into the dark and wicked world below. **OMISSION-4**[862] **OMISSION-5** Soon we heard the voice of God like many waters, which gave us the day and hour of Jesus' coming. The living saints, 144,000 in number, knew and understood the voice, while the wicked thought it was thunder and an earthquake. When God spoke the time, He poured upon us the Holy Ghost, and our faces began to light up and shine with the glory of God, as Moses' did when he came down from Mount Sinai. {EW 14.1} The 144,000 were all sealed and perfectly united. On their foreheads was written, God, New Jerusalem, and a glorious star containing Jesus' new name. At our happy, holy

a glorious Star containing Jesus' new name. At our happy, holy state the wicked were enraged, and would rush violently up to lay hands on us to thrust us in prison, when we would stretch forth the hand in the name of the Lord, and the wicked would fall helpless to the ground.[831] Then it was that the synagogue of Satan knew that God had loved us who could wash one another's feet, and salute the holy brethren with a holy kiss, and they worshipped at our feet.[832] Soon our eyes were drawn to the East, for a small black cloud had appeared about half as large as a man's hand, which we all knew was the Sign of the Son of Man. We all in solemn silence gazed on the cloud as it drew nearer, lighter, and brighter, glorious, and still more glorious, till it was a great

written, God, New Jerusalem, and a glorious Star containing Jesus' new name. *Rev.* 3:12. At our happy, holy state the wicked [page] 15 were enraged, and would rush violently up to lay hands on us to thrust us in prison, when we would stretch forth the hand in the name of the Lord, and the wicked would fall helpless to the ground. Then it was that the synagogue of Satan knew that God had loved us who could wash one another's feet, and salute the holy brethren with a holy kiss, and they worshipped at our feet. *Rev.* 3:9. Soon our eyes were drawn to the East, for a small black cloud had appeared about half as large as a man's hand, which we all knew was the Sign of the Son of Man. *Mat.* 24:30. We all in solemn silence gazed on the cloud as it drew nearer, lighter, and brighter, glorious, and still more glorious, till it was a great white cloud. *Rev.* 14:14. The

name. At our happy, holy state the wicked were enraged and would rush violently up to lay hands on us to thrust us in prison, when we would stretch forth the hand in the name of the Lord, and the wicked would fall helpless [page] 26 to the ground.

OMISSION-6[836]

Soon our eyes were drawn to the East, for a small black cloud had appeared about half as large as a man's hand, which we all knew was the Sign of the Son of Man. We all in solemn silence gazed on the cloud as it drew nearer, lighter, and brighter, glorious, and still more glorious, till it was a great

state the wicked were enraged, and would rush violently up to lay hands on us to thrust us in prison, when we would stretch forth the hand in the name of the Lord, and the wicked would fall helpless to the ground. Then it was that the synagogue of Satan knew that God had loved us who could wash one another's feet, and salute the holy brethren with a holy kiss, and they worshipped at our feet.

Soon our eyes were drawn to the East, for a small black cloud had appeared about half as large as a man's hand, which we all knew was the Sign of the Son of Man. We all in solemn silence gazed on the cloud as it drew nearer, and became lighter, glorious, and still more glorious, till it was a great white cloud. The bottom appeared like fire, a rainbow was over it,

state the wicked were enraged, and would rush violently up to lay hands on us to thrust us in prison, when we would stretch forth the hand in the name of the Lord, and the wicked would fall helpless to the ground. Then it was that the synagogue of Satan knew that God had loved us who could wash one another's feet, and salute the holy brethren with a holy kiss, and they worshipped at our feet.[847]

Soon our eyes were drawn to the East, for a small black cloud had appeared about half as large as a man's hand, which we all knew was the Sign of the Son of Man. We all in solemn silence gazed on the cloud as it drew nearer, and became lighter, glorious, and still more glorious, till it was a great white cloud. The bottom appeared like fire, a rainbow was over it,

state the wicked were enraged, and would rush violently up to lay hands on us to thrust us into prison, when we would stretch forth the hand in the name of the Lord, and they would fall helpless to the ground. Then it was that the synagogue of Satan knew that God had loved us who could wash one another's feet and salute the brethren with a holy kiss, and they worshiped at our feet. {EW 15.1}

Soon our eyes were drawn to the east, for a small black cloud had appeared, about half as large as a man's hand, which we all knew was the sign of the Son of man. We all in solemn silence gazed on the cloud as it drew nearer and became lighter, glorious, and still more glorious, till it was a great white cloud. The bottom appeared like fire; a rainbow was over the

white cloud. The bottom appeared like fire, a rainbow was over it, around the cloud were ten thousand angels singing a most lovely song. And on it sat the Son of Man, on his head were crowns, his hair was white and curly and lay on his shoulders. His feet had the appearance of fire, in his right hand was a sharp sickle, in his left a silver trumpet. His eyes were as a flame of fire, which searched his children through and through. Then all faces gathered paleness, and those that God had rejected gathered blackness. Then we all cried out, who shall be able to stand? Is my robe spotless? Then the angels ceased to sing, and there was some time of awful silence, when Jesus spoke, Those who have clean hands and a pure heart shall be able to stand,	bottom appeared like fire, a rainbow was over it, around the cloud were ten thousand angels singing a most lovely song. And on it sat the Son of Man, *Luke 21:27.* on his head were crowns, *Rev. 19:12.* his hair was white and curly and lay on his shoulders. *Rev. 1:14.* His feet had the appearance of fire, *Rev. 1:15.* in his right hand was a sharp sickle, *Rev. 14:14.* in his left a silver trumpet. *1 Thess. 4:16.* His eyes were as a flame of fire, *Rev. 1:14.* which searched his children through and through. Then all faces gathered paleness, and those that God had rejected gathered blackness. Then we all cried out, who shall be able to stand? Is my robe spotless? Then the angels ceased to sing, and there was some time of awful silence, *Rev. 8:1.* when Jesus spoke. Those who have clean hands and a pure heart shall be able to stand, my grace is sufficient for	white cloud. The bottom appeared like fire, a rainbow was over it, around the cloud were ten thousand angels singing a most lovely song. And on it sat the Son of Man, on his head were crowns, (a crown within a crown,) his hair was white and curly and lay on his shoulders. His feet had the appearance of fire, in his right hand was a sharp sickle, in his left a silver trumpet. His eyes were as a flame of fire, which searched his children through and through. Then all faces gathered paleness, and those that God had rejected, gathered blackness. Then we all cried out, who shall be able to stand? Is my robe spotless? Then the angels ceased to sing, and there was some time of awful silence, when Jesus spoke. Those who have clean hands and a pure heart shall be able to	around the cloud were ten thousand angels singing a most lovely song. And on it sat the Son of Man, on his head were crowns, his hair was white and curly and lay on his shoulders. His feet had the appearance of fire, in his right hand was a sharp sickle, in his left a silver trumpet. His eyes were as a flame of fire, which searched his children through and through. Then all faces gathered paleness, and those that God had rejected gathered blackness. Then we all cried out, who shall be able to stand? Is my robe spotless? Then the angels ceased to sing, and there was some time of awful silence, when Jesus spoke. Those who have clean hands and a pure heart shall be able to stand, My grace is sufficient for you. At this, our faces lighted up, and joy	around the cloud were ten thousand angels singing a most lovely song.[848] And on it sat the Son of Man, on his head were crowns, his hair was white and curly and lay on his shoulders. His feet had the appearance of fire, in his right hand was a sharp sickle, in his left a silver trumpet. His eyes were as a flame of fire, which searched his children through and through. Then all faces gathered paleness, and those that God had rejected gathered blackness. Then we all cried out, who shall be able to stand? Is my robe spotless? Then the angels ceased to sing, and there was some time of awful silence, when Jesus spoke. Those who have clean hands and a pure heart shall be able to stand, my grace is sufficient for you. At this, our faces lighted up, and joy filled every	cloud, while around it were ten thousand angels, [page] 16 singing a most lovely song; and upon it sat the Son of man. His hair was white and curly and lay on His shoulders; and upon His head were many crowns. His feet had the appearance of fire; in His right hand was a sharp sickle; in His left, a silver trumpet. His eyes were as a flame of fire, which searched His children through and through. Then all faces gathered paleness, and those that God had rejected gathered blackness. Then we all cried out, "Who shall be able to stand? Is my robe spotless?" Then the angels ceased to sing, and there was some time of awful silence, when Jesus spoke: "Those who have clean hands and pure hearts shall be able to stand; My grace is sufficient for you." At this our faces lighted up, and joy filled every heart.

my grace is sufficient for you. At this, our faces lighted up, and joy filled every heart. And the angels struck a note higher and sung again while the cloud drew still nearer the earth. Then Jesus' silver trumpet sounded, as he descended on the cloud, wrapped in flames of fire. He gazed on the graves of the sleeping saints then raised his eyes and hands to heaven & cried out, Awake! Awake! Awake! ye that sleep in the dust, and arise. Then there was a mighty earthquake. The graves opened, and the dead came up clothed with immortality. The 144,000 shouted, Hallelujah! as they recognized their friends who had been torn from them by death, and in the same moment we were changed and caught up together with them to meet the Lord in the

---

you. At this, our faces lighted up, and joy filled every heart. And the angels struck a note higher and sung again while the cloud drew still nearer the earth. Then Jesus' silver trumpet sounded, as he descended on the cloud, wrapped in flames of fire *2 Thess. 1:7, 8.* He gazed on the graves of the sleeping saints, then raised his eyes and hands to heaven and cried out, *John 5:25.* Awake! Awake! Awake! ye that sleep in the dust, and arise. Then there was a mighty earthquake. The graves opened, and the dead came up clothed with immortality. The 144,000 shouted, Hallelujah! as they recognized their friends who had been torn from them by death, and in the same moment we were changed and caught up together with them to meet the Lord in the air. *1 Thess. 4:17.* We all entered the cloud together, and were seven days ascending to the sea of glass,

---

stand, my grace is sufficient for you. At this, our faces lighted up, and joy filled every heart. And the angels struck a note higher and sung again while the cloud drew still nearer the earth. Then Jesus' silver trumpet sounded, as he descended on the cloud, wrapped in flames of fire. He gazed on the graves of the sleeping saints, then raised his eyes and hands to heaven and cried out, Awake! Awake! Awake! ye that sleep in the dust, and arise. Then there was a mighty earthquake. The graves opened, and the dead came up clothed with immortality. The 144,000 shouted, Hallelujah! as they recognized their friends who had been torn from them by death, and in the same moment we were changed and caught up together with them to meet the Lord in the air. We all

---

filled every heart. And the angels struck a note higher and sung again while the cloud drew still nearer the earth. Then Jesus' silver trumpet sounded, as he descended on the cloud, wrapped in flames of fire. He gazed on the graves of the sleeping saints, then raised his eyes and hands to heaven and cried, Awake! Awake! Awake! ye that sleep in the dust and arise. Then there was a mighty earthquake. The graves opened, and the dead came up clothed with immortality. The 144,000 shouted, Hallelujah! as they recognized their friends who had been torn from them by death, and in the same moment we were changed and caught up together with them to meet the Lord in the air. We all entered the cloud together, and were seven days ascending to

---

heart. And the angels struck a note higher and sung again while the cloud drew still nearer the earth. Then Jesus' silver trumpet sounded, as he descended on the cloud, wrapped in flames of fire. He gazed on the graves of the sleeping saints, then raised his eyes and hands to heaven and cried, Awake! Awake! Awake! ye that sleep in the dust and arise. Then there was a mighty earthquake. The graves opened, and the dead came up clothed with immortality. The 144,000 shouted, Hallelujah! as they recognized their friends who had been torn from them by death, and in the same moment we were changed and caught up together with them to meet the Lord in the air. We all entered the cloud together, and were seven days ascending to the sea of glass, when

---

And the angels struck a note higher and sang again, while the cloud drew still nearer the earth. {EW 15.2}

Then Jesus' silver trumpet sounded, as He descended on the cloud, wrapped in flames of fire. He gazed on the graves of the sleeping saints, then raised His eyes and hands to heaven, and cried, "Awake! awake! awake! ye that sleep in the dust, and arise." Then there was a mighty earthquake. The graves opened, and the dead came up clothed with immortality. The 144,000 shouted, "Alleluia!" as they recognized their friends who had been torn from them by death, and in the same moment we were changed and caught up together with them to meet the Lord in the air. {EW 16.1}

We all entered the cloud together, and were seven days ascending to the sea of glass, when Jesus brought

air. We all entered the cloud together, and were 7 days ascending to the sea of glass, when Jesus brought along the crowns and with his own right hand placed them on our heads. He gave us harps of gold and palms of victory. Here on the sea of glass the 144,000 stood in a perfect square. Some of them had very bright crowns, others not so bright. Some crowns appeared hung with stars, while others had but few.[833] All were perfectly satisfied with their crowns. And they were all clothed with a glorious white mantle from their shoulders to their feet. Angels were all about us as we marched over the sea of glass to the gate of the City. Jesus raised his mighty glorious arm, laid hold of the gate and swung it back on its golden

when Jesus brought along the crowns and with his own right hand placed them on our heads. *2 Esdras 2:43.* He gave us harps of gold and palms of victory. *Rev. 15:2. Rev. 7:9.* Here on the sea of glass the 144,000 stood in a perfect square. Some of them had very bright crowns, others not so bright. Some crowns appeared heavy with stars, while others had but few. All were perfectly satisfied with their crowns. And they were all clothed with a glorious white mantle from their shoulders to their feet. *Rev. 7:9.* Angels were all about us as we marched over the sea of glass to the gate of the City. Jesus raised his mighty glorious arm, laid hold of the gate and swung it back on its golden hinges, and said to us, You have washed your robes in my blood, stood stifly for my truth, enter in. *Isa. 26:2.* We all marched in and felt we had a perfect right in the City. Here

entered the cloud together, and were seven days ascending to the sea of glass, when Jesus brought along the crowns and with his own right hand placed them on our heads. He gave us harps of gold and palms of victory. Here on the sea of glass the 144,000 stood in a perfect square. Some of them had very bright crowns, others not so bright. Some crown[s] appeared heavy with stars, while others had but few. All were perfectly satisfied with their crowns. And they were all clothed with a glorious white mantle from their shoulders to their feet. Angels were all about us as we marched over the sea of glass to the gate of the City. Jesus raised his mighty glorious arm, laid hold of the gate and swung it back on its golden hinges, and said to us, You have washed

the sea of glass, when Jesus brought along the crowns and with his own right hand placed them on our heads. He gave us harps of gold and palms of victory. Here on the sea of glass the 144,000 stood in a perfect square. Some of them had very bright crowns, others not so bright. Some crowns appeared heavy with stars, while others had but few. All were perfectly satisfied with their crowns. And they were all clothed with a glorious white mantle from their shoulders to their feet. Angels were all about us as we marched over the sea of glass to the gate of the City. Jesus raised his mighty glorious arm, laid hold of the pearly gate and swung it back on its glittering hinges, and said to us, You have washed your robes in My blood, stood stiffly for My truth, enter

Jesus brought along the crowns and with his own right hand placed them on our heads. He gave us harps of gold and palms of victory. Here on the sea of glass the 144,000 stood in a perfect square. Some of them had very bright crowns, others not so bright. Some crowns appeared heavy with stars, while others had but few. All were perfectly satisfied with their crowns. And they were all clothed with a glorious white mantle from their shoulders to their feet. Angels were all about us as we marched over the sea of glass to the gate of the City. Jesus raised his mighty glorious arm, laid hold of the pearly gate and swung it back on its glittering hinges, and said to us, You have washed your robes in my blood, stood stiffly for my truth, enter in. We all marched in and

the crowns, and with His own right hand placed them on our heads. He gave us harps of gold and palms of victory. Here on the sea of glass the 144,000 stood in a perfect square. Some of them had very bright crowns, others not so bright. Some crowns appeared heavy with stars, while others had but few. All were perfectly satisfied with their crowns. And they were all [page] 17 clothed with a glorious white mantle from their shoulders to their feet. Angels were all about us as we marched over the sea of glass to the gate of the city. Jesus raised His mighty, glorious arm, laid hold of the pearly gate, swung it back on its glittering hinges, and said to us, "You have washed your robes in My blood, stood stiffly for My truth, enter in." We all marched in and felt that we

hinges, and said to us, You have washed your robes in my blood, stood stiffly for my truth, enter in. We all marched in and felt we had a perfect right in the City. Here we see the tree of life, & the throne of God. Out of the throne came a pure river of water, and on either side of the river was the tree of life. On one side of the river was a trunk of a tree and a trunk on the other side of the river, both of pure transparent gold. At first I thought I see two trees. I looked again and see they were united at the top in one tree. So it was the tree of life on either side of the river of life. Its branches bowed to the place where we stood. And the fruit was glorious, which looked like gold mixed with silver. We all went under the tree, and sat down to look at the glory of the place, when Bro. Fitch, and Stockman, who had preached

we saw the tree of life, and the throne of God. Out of the throne came a pure river of water, and on either side of the river was the tree of life. *Rev.* 22:1, 2. On one side of the river was a trunk of a tree and a trunk on the other side of the river, both of pure transparent gold. {WLF 14.3} [page] 16

At first I thought I saw two trees. I looked again and saw they were united at the top in one tree. So it was the tree of life, on either side of the river of life; its branches bowed to the place where we stood; and the fruit was glorious, which looked like gold mixed with silver. We all went under the tree, and sat down to look at the glory of the place, when brothers Fitch and Stockman, who had preached the gospel of the kingdom, and whom God had laid in the grave to save them, came up to us and asked us what we had passed through while they were

your robes in my blood, stood stiffly for my truth, enter in. We all marched in and felt we had a perfect right in the City. Here we saw the tree of life, and the throne of God. Out of the throne came a pure river of water, and on either side of the river was the tree of life. On one side of the river was a trunk of a tree and a trunk on the other side of the river, both of pure transparent gold. {GT 25.3}

At first I thought I saw two trees. I looked again and saw they were united at the top in one tree. So it was the tree of life, on either side of the river of life; its branches bowed to the place where we stood; and the fruit was glorious, which looked like gold mixed with silver. We all went under the tree, and sat down to look at the glory of the place, when brothers Fitch and Stockman, who had preached the gospel of the kingdom, and

in. We all marched in and felt we had a perfect right in the City. Here we saw the tree of life and the throne of God. Out of the throne came a pure river of water, and on either side of the river was the tree of life. On one side of the river was a trunk of a tree, and a trunk on the other side of the river, both of pure transparent gold. {RH, July 21, 1851}

At first I thought I saw two trees. I looked again and saw they were united at the top in one tree.—So it was the tree of life, on either side of the river of life. Its branches bowed to the place where we stood; and the fruit was glorious, which looked like gold mixed with silver. We all went under the tree, and sat down to look at the glory of the place, when brothers Fitch and Stockman, who had preached the gospel of the kingdom, and whom God had laid in the grave to save them,

felt we had a perfect right in the City. Here we saw the tree of life and the throne of God. Out of the throne came a pure river of water, and on either side of the river was the tree of life. On one side of the river was a trunk of a tree, and a trunk on the other side of the river, both of pure transparent gold.[849] {ExV 11.1}

At first I thought I saw two trees. I looked again and saw they were united at the top in one tree.—So it was the tree of life, on either side of the river of life. Its branches bowed to the place where we stood; and the fruit was glorious, which looked like gold mixed with silver. We all went under the tree, and sat down to look at the glory of the place, when brothers Fitch and Stockman, who had preached the gospel of the kingdom, and whom God had laid in the grave to save them,

had a perfect right in the city. {EW 16.2}

Here we saw the tree of life and the throne of God. Out of the throne came a pure river of water, and on either side of the river was the tree of life. On one side of the river was a trunk of a tree, and a trunk on the other side of the river, both of pure, transparent gold. At first I thought I saw two trees. I looked again, and saw that they were united at the top in one tree. So it was the tree of life on either side of the river of life. Its branches bowed to the place where we stood, and the fruit was glorious; it looked like gold mixed with silver. {EW 17.1}

We all went under the tree and sat down to look at the glory of the place, when Brethren Fitch and Stockman, who had preached the gospel of the kingdom, and whom God had laid in the grave to save them,

the gospel of the kingdom, whom God had laid in the grave to save them, came up to us and asked us what we had passed through while they were sleeping. We tried to call up our greatest trials, but they looked so small compared with the far more exceeding and eternal weight of glory that surrounded us, that we could not speak them out, and we all cried out Hallelujah, heaven is cheap enough, and we touched our glorious harps and made heaven's arches ring. And as we were gazing at the glories of the place, our eyes were attracted upwards to something that had the appearance of silver. I asked Jesus to let me see what was within there. In a moment we were winging our way upward and entering in. Here we saw good old father Abraham, Isaac, and Jacob, Noah,	sleeping. We tried to call up our greatest trials, but they looked so small compared with the far more exceeding and eternal weight of glory *2 Cor. 4:17.* that surrounded us, that we could not speak them out, *Isa. 65:17.* and we all cried out Hallelujah, heaven is cheap enough, and we touched our glorious harps and made heaven's arches ring. And as we were gazing at the glories of the place our eyes were attracted upwards to something that had the appearance of silver. I asked Jesus to let me see what was within there. In a moment we were winging our way upward, and entering in; here we saw good old father Abraham, Isaac, Jacob, Noah, Daniel, and many like them. And I saw a vail with a heavy fringe of silver and gold, as a border on the bottom; it was very beautiful. I asked Jesus what was within the vail.	whom God had laid in the grave to save them, came up to us and asked us what we had passed through while they were sleeping. We tried to call up our greatest trials, but they looked so small compared with the far more exceeding and eternal weight of glory that surrounded us, that we could not speak them out, and we all cried out, Hallelujah, heaven is cheap enough, and we touched our glorious harps and made heaven's arches ring. And as we were gazing at the glories of the place our eyes were attracted upwards to something that had the appearance of silver. I asked Jesus to let me see what was within there. In a moment we were winging our way upward, and entering in; here we saw good old father Abraham, Isaac, Jacob, Noah, Daniel, and many like them. And I saw a vail with a heavy fringe	came up to us and asked us what we had passed through while they were sleeping. We tried to call up our greatest trials, but they looked so small compared with the far more exceeding and eternal weight of glory that surrounded us, that we could not speak them out, and we all cried out Alleluia, heaven is cheap enough, and we touched our glorious harps and made heaven's arches ring. {RH, July 21, 1851}	came up to us and asked us what we had passed through while they were sleeping.[850] We tried to call up our greatest trials, but they looked so small compared with the far more exceeding and eternal weight of glory that surrounded us, that we could not speak them out, and we all cried out Alleluia, heaven is cheap enough, and we touched our glorious harps and made heaven's arches ring.[851] {ExV 13.1}	came up to us and asked us what we had passed through while they were sleeping. We tried to call up our greatest trials, but they looked so small compared with the far more exceeding and eternal weight of glory that surrounded us that we could not speak them out, and we all cried out, "Alleluia, heaven is cheap enough!" and we touched our glorious harps and made heaven's arches ring. {EW 17.2}
			OMISSION-7[837]	**OMISSION-7**	**OMISSION-7**

Daniel, and many like them. And I saw a veil with a heavy fringe of silver, and gold as a border on the bottom. It was very beautiful. I asked Jesus what was within the veil. He raised it with his own right arm, and bade me take heed. I saw there a glorious ark, overlaid with pure gold, and it had a glorious border resembling Jesus’ crowns. On it were two bright angels; their wings were spread over the ark as they sat on each end, with their faces turned towards each other and looking downward. In the ark, beneath where the angels wings were spread, was a golden pot of Manna of a yellowish cast, and I saw a rod, which Jesus said was Aaron’s, I saw it bud, blossom, and bear fruit.—And I saw two long golden rods on which hung silver wires, and on the wires most glorious	He raised it with his own right arm, and bade me take heed. I saw there a glorious ark, overlaid with pure gold, and it had a glorious border, resembling Jesus’ crowns; and on it were two bright angels—their wings were spread over the ark as they sat on each end, with their faces turned towards each other and looking downward. *Exod. 25:18, 20. Heb. 9:3-5.* In the ark, beneath where the angels’ wings were spread, was a golden pot of Manna, of a yellowish cast; and I saw a rod, which Jesus said was Aaron’s; I saw it bud, blossom and bear fruit. *Num. 17:8.* And I saw two long golden rods, on which hung silver wires, and on the wires most glorious grapes; one cluster was more than a man here could carry. And I saw Jesus step up and take of the manna, almonds, grapes and pomegranates, and bear them down to the	of silver and gold, as a border on the bottom; it was very beautiful. I asked Jesus what was within the vail. He raised it with his own right arm, and bade me take heed. I saw there a glorious ark, overlaid with pure gold, and it had a glorious border, resembling Jesus’ crowns; and on it were two bright angels—their wings were spread over the ark as they sat on each end, with their faces turned towards each other and looking downwards. In the ark, beneath where the angels’ wings were spread, was a golden pot of Manna, of a yellowish cast; and I saw a rod, which Jesus said was Aaron’s; I saw it bud, blossom and bear fruit. And I saw two long golden rods, on which hung silver wires, and on the wires most glorious grapes; one cluster was more than a man here could			

grapes. One cluster was more than a man here can carry. And I saw Jesus step up and take of the manna, almonds, grapes, and pomegranates, and bear them down to the city, and place them on the supper table. I stepped up to see how much was taken away, and there was just as much left, and we shouted Hallelujah. Amen. [V16.] We all descended from this place down into the city, and with Jesus at our head we all descended from the city down to this earth, on a great and mighty mountain, which could not bear Jesus up, and it parted asunder, and there was a mighty plain. Then we looked up and saw the great city with twelve foundations, twelve gates, three on each side, and an angel at each gate, and all cried out the	city, and place them on the supper table. I stepped up to see how much was taken away, and there was just as much left; and we shouted Hallelujah—Amen. [V16.] We all descended from this place down into the city, and with Jesus at our head we all descended from the city down to this earth, on a great and mighty mountain, which could not bear Jesus up, and it parted asunder, and there was a mighty plain. *Zech. 14:4.* Then we looked up and saw the great city, with twelve foundations, twelve gates, three on each side, and an angel at each gate, and all cried out, "the city, the great city, it's coming, it's coming down from God, out of heaven;" *Rev. 21:10-13.* and it came and settled on the place where we stood. Then we began to look	carry. And I saw Jesus step up and take of the manna, almonds, grapes and pomegranates, and bear them down to the city, and place them on the supper table. I stepped up to see how much was taken away, and there was just as much left; and we shouted Hallelujah—Amen. [V16.] We all descended from this place down into the city, and with Jesus at our head we all descended from the city down to this earth, on a great and mighty mountain, which could not bear Jesus up, and it parted asunder, and there was a mighty plain. Then we looked up and saw the great city, with twelve foundations, twelve gates, three on each side, and an angel at each gate, and all cried out, "the city, the great city, it's coming, it's	[V16.] With Jesus at our head we all descended from the City down to this earth, on a great and mighty mountain, which could not bear Jesus up, and it parted asunder, and there was a mighty plain. Then we looked up and saw the Great City, with twelve foundations, twelve gates, three on each side, and an angel at each gate. We all cried out "The City, the Great City, it's coming, it's	[V16.] With Jesus at our head we all descended from the City down to this earth, on a great and mighty mountain, which could not bear Jesus up, and it parted asunder, and there was a mighty plain. Then we looked up and saw the Great City, with twelve foundations, twelve gates, three on each side, and an angel at each gate. We all cried out "The City, the Great City, it's coming, it's	[V16.] With Jesus at our head we all descended from the city down to this earth, on a great and mighty mountain, which could not bear Jesus up, and it parted asunder, and there was a mighty plain. Then we looked up [page] 18 and saw the great city, with twelve foundations, and twelve gates, three on each side, and an angel at each gate. We all cried out, "The city, the great city, it's

city, the great city, it's coming, it's coming down from God, out of heaven, and it came and settled on the place where we stood. Then we began to look at the glorious things outside of the city. There I saw most glorious houses, that had the appearance of silver, supported by four pillars, set with pearls most glorious to behold, which were to be inhabited by the saints. In them was a golden shelf, I saw many of the saints go into the houses, take off their glittering crowns and lay them on the shelf, then go out into the field by the houses to do something with the earth, not as we have to do with the earth here; no, no. A glorious light shone all about their heads, and they were continually shouting and offering praises to God. And I saw another field full of all

at the glorious things outside of the city. There I saw most glorious houses, that had the appearance of silver, supported by four pillars, set with pearls, most glorious to behold, which were to be inhabited by the saints; *Isa.* 65:21. in them was a golden shelf; I saw many of the saints go into the houses, take off their glittering crowns and lay them on the shelf, then go out into the field by the houses to do something with the earth; *Isa.* 65:21. not as we have to do with the earth here; no, no. A glorious light shone all about their heads, and they were continually shouting and offering praises to God. {WLF 16.1}

[page] 17

And I saw another field full of all kinds of flowers, and as I plucked them, I cried out, well they will never fade. Next I saw a field of tall grass, most glorious to

coming down from God, out of heaven;" and it came and settled on the place where we stood. Then we began to look at the glorious things outside of the city. There I saw most glorious houses, that had the appearance of silver, supported by four columns, set with pearls, most glorious to behold, which were to be inhabited by the saints; in them was a golden shelf; I saw many of the saints go into the houses, take off their glittering crowns and lay them on the shelf, then go out into the field by the houses to do something with the earth; not as we have to do with the earth here; no, no. A glorious light shone all about their heads, and they were continually shouting and offering praises to God. {GT 26.1}

And I saw another field full of all kinds of flowers, and

coming down from God out of heaven;" and it came and settled on the place where we stood. Then we began to look at the glorious things outside of the City. There I saw most glorious houses, that had the appearance of silver, supported by four pillars, set with pearls, most glorious to behold, which were to be inhabited by the saints, and in them was a golden shelf. I saw many of the saints go into the houses, take off their glittering crowns and lay them on the shelf, then go out into the field by the houses to do something with the earth; not as we have to do with the earth here; no, no. A glorious light shone all about their heads and they were continually shouting and offering praises to God. {RH, July 21, 1851}

And I saw another field full of all kinds of flowers, and

coming down from God out of heaven;" and it came and settled on the place where we stood. Then we began to look at the glorious things outside of the City. There I saw most glorious houses, that had the appearance of silver, supported by four pillars, set with pearls, most glorious to behold, which were to be inhabited by the saints, and in them was a golden shelf.[852] I saw many of the saints go into the houses, take off their glittering crowns and lay them on the shelf, then go out into the field by the houses to do something with the earth; not as we have to do with the earth here; no, no.[853] A glorious light shone all about their heads and they were continually shouting and offering praises to God.[854] {ExV 13.2}

coming, it's coming down from God out of heaven," and it came and settled on the place where we stood. Then we began to look at the glorious things outside of the city. There I saw most glorious houses, that had the appearance of silver, supported by four pillars set with pearls most glorious to behold. These were to be inhabited by the saints. In each was a golden shelf. I saw many of the saints go into the houses, take off their glittering crowns and lay them on the shelf, then go out into the field by the houses to do something with the earth; not as we have to do with the earth here; no, no. A glorious light shone all about their heads, and they were continually shouting and offering praises to God. {EW 17.3}

I saw another field

kinds of flowers, and as I plucked them, I cried out, well they will never fade. Next I saw a field of tall grass, most glorious to behold. It was living green, and had a reflection of silver and gold as it waved proudly to the glory of King Jesus. Then we entered a field full of all kinds of beasts; the lion, the lamb, the leopard and the wolf, altogether in perfect union. We passed through the midst of them, and they followed on peaceably after. Then we entered a wood, not like the dark woods we have here, no, no; but light, and all over glorious. The branches of the trees waved to and fro, and we all cried out, we will dwell safely in the wilderness and sleep in this woods. We passed through the wood, for we were on our way to Mount Zion, as we were traveling along we met a	behold; it was living green, and had a reflection of silver and gold, as it waved proudly to the glory of King Jesus. Then we entered a field full of all kinds of beasts—the lion, the lamb, the leopard and the wolf, altogether in perfect union; *Isa. 11:6-9*. we passed through the midst of them, and they followed on peaceably after. Then we entered a wood, not like the dark woods we have here, no, no; but light, and all over glorious; the branches of the trees waved to and fro, and we all cried out, "we will dwell safely in the wilderness and sleep in this woods." *Ezek. 34:25*. We passed through the woods, for we were on our way to Mount Zion. As we were travelling along, we met a company who were also gazing at the glories of the place. I noticed red as a border	as I plucked them, I cried out, well they will never fade. Next I saw a field of tall grass, most glorious to behold; it was living green, and had a reflection of silver and gold, as it waved proudly to the glory of King Jesus. Then we entered a field full of all kinds of beasts—the lion, the lamb, the leopard and the wolf, altogether in perfect union; we passed through the midst of them, and they followed on peaceably after. Then we entered a wood, not like the dark woods we have here, no, no; but light, and all over glorious; the branches of the trees waved to and fro, and we all cried out, "we will dwell safely in the wilderness and sleep in the woods[.]" We passed through the woods, for we were on our way to Mount Zion. As we were traveling along, we met a company	as I plucked them, I cried out, They will never fade. Next I saw a field of tall grass, most glorious to behold; it was living green, and had a reflection of silver and gold, as it waved proudly to the glory of King Jesus. Then we entered a field full of all kinds of beasts—the lion, the lamb, the leopard and the wolf, altogether in perfect union. We passed through the midst of them, and they followed on peaceably after. Then we entered a wood, not like the dark woods we have here, no, no; but light, and all over glorious; the branches of the trees waved to and fro, and we all cried out, "We will dwell safely in the wilderness and sleep in the woods." We passed through the woods, for we were on our way to Mount Zion. As we were traveling	And I saw another field full of all kinds of flowers, and as I plucked them, I cried out, They will never fade. Next I saw a field of tall grass, most glorious to behold; it was living green, and had a reflection of silver and gold, as it waved proudly to the glory of King Jesus. Then we entered a field full of all kinds of beasts—the lion, the lamb, the leopard and the wolf, altogether in perfect union. We passed through the midst of them, and they followed on peaceably after. Then we entered a wood, not like the dark woods we have here, no, no; but light, and all over glorious;[855] the branches of the trees waved to and fro, and we all cried out, "We will dwell safely in the wilderness and sleep in the woods." We passed through the woods, for we were on our	full of all kinds of flowers, and as I plucked them, I cried out, "They will never fade." Next I saw a field of tall grass, most glorious to behold; it was living green and had a reflection of silver and gold, as it waved proudly to the glory of King Jesus. Then we entered a field full of all kinds of beasts—the lion, the lamb, the leopard, and the wolf, all together in perfect union. We passed through the midst of them, and they followed on peaceably after. Then we entered a wood, not like the dark woods we have here; no, no; but light, and all over glorious; the branches of the trees moved to and fro, and we all cried out, "We will dwell safely in the wilderness and sleep in the woods." We passed through the woods, for we were on our way to Mount Zion. {EW 18.1}

company who were also gazing at the glories of the place: I noticed red as a border on their garments. Their crowns were brilliant—their robes were pure white. As we greeted them, I asked Jesus who they were? He said they were martyrs that had been slain for him. With them was an innumerable company of little ones, they had a hem of red on their garments also. Mount Zion was just before us, and on the Mount sat a glorious temple, and about it were seven other mountains, on which grew roses and lilies, and I saw the little ones climb, or if they chose use their little wings and fly to the top of the mountains, and pluck the never fading flowers. There were all kinds of trees around the temple to beautify the place. The box, the pine, the fir, the oil, the myrtle, the pomegranate and the fig tree, bowed	on their garments; their crowns were brilliant; their robes were pure white. As we greeted them, I asked Jesus who they were? He said they were martyrs that had been slain for him. With them was an innumerable company of little ones; they had a hem of red on their garments also. *Jer. 31:15-17; Matt. 2:18.* Mount Zion was just before us, and on the Mount sat a glorious temple, and about it were seven other mountains, on which grew roses and lilies, *2 Esdras 2:19.* and I saw the little ones climb, or if they chose, use their little wings and fly to the top of the mountains, and pluck the never fading flowers. There were all kinds of trees around the temple to beautify the place; the box, the pine, the fir, the oil, the myrtle, the pomegranate, and the fig tree bowed down with the weight of its timely figs, that	who were also gazing at the glories of the place. I noticed red as a border on their garments; their crowns were brilliant; their robes were pure white. As we greeted them, I asked Jesus who they were? He said they were martyrs that had been slain for him. With them was an innumerable company of little ones; they had a hem of red on their garments also. Mount Zion was just before us, and on the Mount sat a glorious temple, and about it were seven other mountains, on which grew roses and lillies, and I saw the little ones climb, or if they chose, use their little wings and fly to the top of the mountains, and pluck the never fading flowers. There were all kinds of trees around the temple to beautify the place; the box, the pine, the fir, the olive, the myrtle, the pomegranate, and the fig tree bowed down with the	along, we met a company who were also gazing at the glories of the place. I noticed red as a border on their garments; their crowns were brilliant; their robes were pure white. As we greeted them, I asked Jesus who they were. He said they were martyrs that had been slain for him. With them was an innumerable company of little ones; they had a hem of red on their garments also. Mount Zion was just before us, and on the Mount was a glorious temple, and about it were seven other mountains, on which grew roses and lilies. And I saw the little ones climb, or if they chose, use their little wings and fly to the top of the mountains, and pluck the never fading flowers.— There were all kinds of trees around the temple to beautify the place; the box, the pine, the fir, the oil, the	way to Mount Zion. As we were traveling along, we met a company who were also gazing at the glories of the place. I noticed red as a border on their garments; their crowns were brilliant; their robes were pure white. As we greeted them, I asked Jesus who they were. He said they were martyrs that had been slain for him. With them was an innumerable company of little ones; they had a hem of red on their garments also. Mount Zion was just before us, and on the Mount was a glorious temple, and about it were seven other mountains, on which grew roses and lilies.[856] And I saw the little ones climb, or if they chose, use their little wings and fly to the top of the mountains, and pluck the never fading flowers.— There were all kinds of trees around the temple to beautify the	As we were traveling along, we met a company who also were gazing at the glories of the place. I noticed red as a border on their garments; their crowns were brilliant; their robes were pure white. As we greeted [page] 19 them, I asked Jesus who they were. He said they were martyrs that had been slain for Him. With them was an innumerable company of little ones; they also had a hem of red on their garments. Mount Zion was just before us, and on the mount was a glorious temple, and about it were seven other mountains, on which grew roses and lilies. And I saw the little ones climb, or, if they chose, use their little wings and fly, to the top of the mountains and pluck the never-fading flowers. There were all kinds of trees around the temple to beautify the place: the box, the pine, the fir,

down with the weight of its timely figs that made the place look all over glorious. And as we were about to enter the holy temple, Jesus raised his lovely voice and said, only the 144,000 enter this place, and we shouted Hallelujah. Well bless the Lord, Bro. Jacobs, it is an extra meeting for those who have the seal of the living God. This temple was supported by seven pillars, all of transparent gold, set with pearls most glorious. The glorious things I saw there, I cannot begin to describe. O, that I could talk in the language of Canaan, then could I tell a little of the glory of the upper world; but if faithful you soon will know all about it. I saw there the tables of stone in which the names of the 144,000, were engraved in letters of gold.—After we had beheld the glory of the temple, we went out. Then

made the place look all over glorious. *Isa. 60:13; 41:19.* And as we were about to enter the holy temple, Jesus raised his lovely voice and said, only the 144,000 enter this place, and we shouted Hallelujah. {WLF 17.1}

Well, bless the Lord, dear brethren and sisters, it is an extra meeting for those who have the seal of the living God *Rev. 14:3.* This temple was supported by seven pillars, all of transparent gold, set with pearls most glorious. The glorious things I saw there, I cannot describe to you. O, that I could talk in the language of Canaan, then could I tell a little of the glory of the upper world; but, if faithful, you soon will know all about it. I saw there the tables of stone in which the names of the 144,000 were engraved in letters of gold; after we had beheld the glory of the temple, we went out. Then

weight of its timely figs, that made the place look all over glorious. And as we were about to enter the holy temple, Jesus raised his lovely voice and said, only the 144,000 enter this place, and we shouted Hallelujah. {GT 26.2}

Well, bless the Lord, dear brethren and sisters, it is an extra meeting for those who have the seal of the living God. This temple was supported by seven pillars, all of transparent gold, set with pearls most glorious. The glorious things I saw there, I cannot describe to you. Oh, that I could talk in the language of Canaan, then could I tell a little of the glory of the upper world; but, if faithful, you soon will know all about it. I saw there the tables of stone in which the names of the 144,000 were engraved in letters of gold; after we had beheld the glory of the

myrtle, the pomegranate and the fig tree bowed down with the weight of its timely figs, that made the place all over glorious. And as we were about to enter the holy temple, Jesus raised his lovely voice and said, Only the 144,000 enter this place, and we shouted Alleluia. {RH, July 21, 1851}

OMISSION-8[838]

This temple was supported by seven pillars, all of transparent gold, set with pearls most glorious. The glorious things I saw there, I cannot describe. Oh, that I could talk in the language of Canaan, then could I tell a little of the glory of the better world.

OMISSION-9[839]

I saw there tables of stone in which the names of the 144,000 were engraved in letters of gold. After we beheld the glory of the temple, we went out, and

place; the box, the pine, the fir, the oil, the myrtle, the pomegranate and the fig tree bowed down with the weight of its timely figs, that made the place all over glorious.[857] And as we were about to enter the holy temple, Jesus raised his lovely voice and said, Only the 144,000 enter this place, and we shouted Alleluia. {ExV 14.1}

OMISSION-8

This temple was supported by seven pillars, all of transparent gold, set with pearls most glorious.[858] The glorious things I saw there, I cannot describe.[859] Oh, that I could talk in the language of Canaan, then could I tell a little of the glory of the better world.

OMISSION-9

I saw there tables of stone in which the names of the 144,000 were engraved in letters of gold.[860] After we beheld the glory of the temple, we

the oil, the myrtle, the pomegranate, and the fig tree bowed down with the weight of its timely figs—these made the place all over glorious. And as we were about to enter the holy temple, Jesus raised His lovely voice and said, "Only the 144,000 enter this place," and we shouted, "Alleluia." {EW 18.2}

OMISSION-8

This temple was supported by seven pillars, all of transparent gold, set with pearls most glorious. The wonderful things I there saw I cannot describe. Oh, that I could talk in the language of Canaan, then could I tell a little of the glory of the better world.

OMISSION-9

I saw there tables of stone in which the names of the 144,000 were engraved in letters of gold. After we beheld the glory of the temple, we went out, and Jesus left us

Jesus left us and went to the city. Soon we heard his lovely voice again, saying: Come my people; you have come out of great tribulation, and done my will, suffered for me; come in to supper, for I will gird myself, and serve you. We shouted Hallelujah, glory, and entered into the city, and I saw a table of pure silver, it was many miles in length, yet our eyes could extend over it. And I saw the fruit of the tree of life, the manna, almonds, figs, pomegranates, grapes, and many other kinds of fruit. We all reclined at the table. I asked Jesus to let me eat of the fruit. He said, not now. Those who eat of the fruit of this land, go back to earth no more. But in a little while if faithful, you shall both eat of the fruit of the tree of life, and drink of the water of the fountain, and he said, you must go back to the	Jesus left us, and went to the city; soon, we heard his lovely voice again, saying—"Come my people, you have come out of great tribulation, and done my will; suffered for me; come in to supper, for I will gird myself, and serve you." *Luke 12:37*. We shouted Hallelujah, glory, and entered into the city …….. ……. And I saw a table of pure silver, it was many miles in length, yet our eyes could extend over it. And I saw the fruit of the tree of life, the manna, almonds, figs, pomegranates, grapes, and many other kinds of fruit. We all reclined at the table. I asked Jesus to let me eat of the fruit. He said, not now. Those who eat of the fruit of this land, go back to earth no more. But in a little while, if faithful, you shall both eat of the fruit of the tree of life, and drink of the water of the fountain; and he said, you must go	temple, we went out. Then Jesus left us, and went to the city; soon we heard his lovely voice again, saying—"Come my people, you have come out of great tribulation, and done my will; suffered for me, come in to supper, for I will gird myself, and serve you," We shouted Hallelujah, glory, and entered into the city ... And I saw a table of pure silver, it was many miles in length,, [*sic*] yet our eyes could extend over it. And I saw the fruit of the tree of life, the manna, almonds, figs, pomegranates, grapes, and many other kinds of fruit. We all reclined at the table. I asked Jesus to let me eat of the fruit. He said, not now. Those who eat of the fruit of this land, go back to earth no more. But in a little while, if faithful, you shall both eat of the fruit of the tree of life, and drink of the water of the fountain,;	Jesus left us, and went to the City. Soon we heard his lovely voice again, saying, "Come, my people, you have come out of great tribulation, and done my will; suffered for me; come in to supper, for I will gird myself, and serve you." We shouted Alleluia, glory, and entered into the City. And I saw a table of pure silver, it was many miles in length, yet our eyes could extend over it. I saw the fruit of the tree of life, the manna, almonds, figs, pomegranates, grapes, and many other kinds of fruit. **OMISSION-10**[840] I asked Jesus to let me eat of the fruit. He said, Not now. Those who eat of the fruit of this land, go back to earth no more. But in a little while, if faithful, you shall both eat of the fruit of the tree of life, and drink of the water of the fountain. And he said, You must go back to the earth again,	went out, and Jesus left us, and went to the City. Soon we heard his lovely voice again, saying, "Come, my people, you have come out of great tribulation, and done my will; suffered for me; come in to supper, for I will gird myself, and serve you." We shouted Alleluia, glory, and entered into the City. And I saw a table of pure silver, it was many miles in length, yet our eyes could extend over it. I saw the fruit of the tree of life, the manna, almonds, figs, pomegranates, grapes, and many other kinds of fruit. **OMISSION-10** I asked Jesus to let me eat of the fruit. He said, Not now. Those who eat of the fruit of this land, go back to earth no more. But in a little while, if faithful, you shall both eat of the fruit of the tree of life, and drink of the water of the fountain. And he said, You must go back to the earth again,	and went to the city. Soon we heard His lovely voice again, saying, "Come, My people, you have come out of great tribulation, and done My will; suffered for Me; come in to supper, for I will gird Myself, and serve you." We shouted, "Alleluia! glory!" and entered into the city. And I saw a table of pure silver; it was many miles in length, yet our eyes could extend over it. I saw the fruit of the tree of life, the manna, almonds, figs, pomegranates, grapes, and many other kinds of fruit. **OMISSION-10** I asked Jesus to let me eat of the fruit. He said, "Not now. Those who eat of the fruit of this [page] 20 land go back to earth no more. But in a little while, if faithful, you shall both eat of the fruit of the tree of life and drink of the water of the fountain." And He said, "You must go back to the earth again and relate to

earth again, and relate to others, what I have revealed to you. Then an angel bore me gently down to this dark world. Sometimes I think I cannot stay here any longer, all things of earth look so dreary. I feel very lonely here, for I have seen a better land. O, that I had wings like a dove, then would I fly away, and be at rest. Ellen G. Harmon. N.B. This was not written for publication; but for the encouragement of all who may see it, and be encouraged by it. {DS January 24, 1846, par. 1} E. G. H.	back to the earth again, and relate to others, what I have revealed to you. Then an angel bore me gently down to this dark [page] 18 world. Sometimes I think I cannot stay here any longer, all things of earth look so dreary—I feel very lonely here, for I have seen a better land. O, that I had wings like a dove, then would I fly away, and be at rest. {WLF 17.2}	[*sic*] and he said, you must go back to the earth again, and relate to others, what I have revealed to you. Then an angel bore me gently down to this dark world. Sometimes I think I cannot stay here any longer, all things of earth look so dreary—I feel very lonely here, for I have seen a better land. Oh, that I had wings like a dove, then would I fly away, and be at rest. {GT 26.3}	and relate to others what I have revealed to you. Then an angel bore me gently down to this dark world. Sometimes I think I can stay here no longer, all things of earth look so dreary. I feel very lonely here, for I have seen a better land. Oh, that I had wings like a dove, then would I fly away and be at rest. {RH, July 21, 1851}	and relate to others what I have revealed to you. Then an angel bore me gently down to this dark world.[861] Sometimes I think I can stay here no longer, all things of earth look so dreary. I feel very lonely here, for I have seen a better land. Oh, that I had wings like a dove, then would I fly away and be at rest. {ExV 15.1}	others what I have revealed to you." Then an angel bore me gently down to this dark world. Sometimes I think I can stay here no longer; all things of earth look so dreary. I feel very lonely here, for I have seen a better land. Oh, that I had wings like a dove, then would I fly away and be at rest! {EW 19.1}

Editorial Changes and Their Effect

In comparing the first two columns of this exhibit, we see that James White made several minor editorial changes before the second publication of V1 and V16. He adjusted the target audience from "brother in the Lord" and "Bro. Jacobs" to "brethren and sisters." He corrected punctuation and tenses. In the third column, James White added scriptural references, which he did not carry over into later versions of the two visions. Then, from 1851 on, we see that he left out "in holy vision" (**OMISSION-1**), an expression Ellen White continued to use in other contexts concerning prophetic visions in the Bible.

In the final column, we see that the 1882 revision known as *Early Writings* made many other changes in capitalization, punctuation, and word choice. For example, it has changed the inconsistent "Hallelujah" and "Alleluia" to "Alleluia" and capitalized "He," "His," and "Him" when referring to God. Such changes were supported by Ellen White. In 1883, when some Adventists were resistant about revising the *Testimonies for the Church* because they believed inspired writings should not be revised, Ellen White wrote: "I cannot see the matter as my brethren see it. I think the changes made will improve the book. If our enemies handle it, let them do so" (Lt. 11, 1884).

In column 3, we see that, when Eli Curtis published V1 and V16 in *The Girdle of Truth*, he did not include **OMISSION-2**, "and the rich reward to be given those who wait the return of their Lord from the wedding," perhaps because he did not subscribe to Ellen White's view of the bridegroom. He also uniquely added an explanation about the crown on Jesus' head at His coming as being "a crown within a crown," which is a phrase that Ellen White herself would use in Ms. 4, 1850 (for V87) and Ms. 14, 1850 (for V97). Curtis also did not include **OMISSION-3**, "while we look not at the things which are seen, for the things which are seen are temporal, but the things which are not seen are eternal." It is puzzling why he would omit this verse when it follows a verse that he did include. The next two omissions may be easier to understand. **OMISSION-4** says, "It was just as impossible for them to get on the path again and go to the City, as all the wicked world which God had rejected," and **OMISSION-6** says, "Then it was that the synagogue of Satan knew that God had loved us who could wash one another's feet, and salute the holy brethren with a holy kiss, and they worshipped at our feet." To omit these would make sense if he rejected the light of the Midnight Cry and Jesus' admonition about foot-washing and Peter and Paul's admonition about using the holy kiss. Ellen White later noted that Curtis altered other of her visions in publishing them, and she requested that he cease from further publishing of her visions (see PrT, May 1, 1850; Ms. 4, 1883). Like Curtis, James White did not include **OMISSION-4** in other later versions of the visions, but he did include **OMISSION-6**. On the other hand, while Curtis retained **OMISSION-5**, "They fell all the way along the path one after another, until," James replaced it, in the other later versions of the visions, with the word "Soon."

The differences in omissions indicate that James White's editorial changes were not dependent on Curtis but were his own choices—*to avoid misunderstanding among the readers of the visions.* As we see, critics claim that **OMISSION-4** taught that probation for sinners had closed and that Ellen White's omission of the phrase in 1851 (column 4) was because she had abandoned belief in the close of probation. Actually, it would seem that she omitted it for just the opposite reason. It was that she did not believe, from her first writing of the vision, that probation had closed, yet the phrase would be *interpreted* as meaning that she did. Ellen White wrote: "It is claimed that these expressions prove the shut-door doctrine, and that this is the reason for their omission in later editions. But in fact they teach only that which has been and is still held by us as a people, as I shall show. For a time after the disappointment in 1844, I did hold in common with the advent body that the door of mercy was then forever closed to the world. This position was taken *before my first vision was given me*. It was the light given me of God that corrected our *error* and enabled us to see the true position. I am still a believer in the shut-door theory, but not in the sense in which we at first employed the term or in which it is employed by my opponents." Referencing a later vision, she added: "I was shown in vision, and I still believe, that there was a shut door in 1844. All who saw the light of the first and second angel's messages and rejected that light were left in darkness. And those who accepted it and received the Holy Spirit which attended the proclamation of the message from heaven and who afterward renounced their faith and pronounced their experience a delusion, thereby rejected the Spirit of God, and it no longer pleaded with them. Those who did not see the light, had not the guilt of its rejection. *It was only the class who had despised the light from heaven that the Spirit of God could not reach*" (Ms. 4, 1883, emphasis added). Add to this the testimony of Marion Crawford, née Stowell, who had asked Ellen in 1845 about a girl whose father had kept her from attending the Adventists' meetings, to which Ellen responded: "God never has shown me that there is no salvation for such persons. It is only those who have had the light of truth presented to them and knowingly rejected it" (Marion Crawford, Aug. 17, 1875).

We see also that the later versions of the visions did not include **OMISSION-7**, with (1) Ellen's mention of some of the "glories of the place," which is uncontroversial, and (2) her mention of Abraham, Isaac, Jacob, Noah, and Daniel, which is also uncontroversial since Jesus declared that the redeemed will sit down and eat with these personages after the resurrection (Matt. 8:11); (3) her first of three mentions of a temple, which does not use "temple," "ark *of the covenant*," or the tables of stone, though it does describe a veil that was lifted and an ark with angels on top of it and the golden pot of manna and Aaron's rod that budded and bore fruit inside it (all found in Rev. 11:19 and Heb. 9:4); (4) her description of grapes *hanging* from silver wires (which critics misconstrued as *growing* out of the wires, see Ms. 4, 1883) and (5) her description of Jesus' taking some of the almonds and grapes and serving them with manna, figs, and pomegranates at the supper table, which is also uncontroversial since it is mentioned in Rev. 19:9 and the fruits are elsewhere mentioned in this and every version of the vision. The difference between this vision of a temple and the later ones is a matter of emphasis. This *first* mention of a temple (**V1**) places the spotlight on the fruit inside and outside of the ark and not on the covenant. The *second* mention of a temple (**V16**) places the spotlight on the 144,000 and their privilege of entering the holy temple (but Ellen did not enter) and their names being engraved in letters of gold in tables of stone. The larger number of 144,000 living saints expands the original 50,000 Advent believers by more than double, thereby rebutting the assertion that the "shut door" meant that the vision taught that probation had closed for anyone but Adventists. In the *third* mention of the temple (**V46**), with items described in Hebrews 9, including the ark of the covenant, the spotlight is on the holiness of God's law and of the Sabbath in particular. (Joseph Bates indicated that Ellen's vision **V45** had a similar focus.[863])

The other omissions seem to be matters of editorial taste. **OMISSION-8**—"Well, bless the Lord, dear brethren and sisters, it is an extra meeting for those who have the seal of the living God"—revels in the gathering of the saints in sacred meeting; **OMISSION-9**—"but, if faithful, you soon will know all about it"—is a call to faithfulness right after the phrase, "the glory of the *upper* world," which becomes "the glory of the *better* world"; and **OMISSION-10**—"We all reclined at the table"—is reminiscent of the last supper, when John ate reclining on the bosom of Jesus.[864]

Thus we see that there was no nefarious motivation for the omissions in the refinement of Ellen White's first vision. The early visions did not teach that probation was closed but, rather, that the larger portion of the "living saints" had not yet responded to the Advent call. Clearly, the door of mercy was still open![865]

"A Lamb stood on the mount Sion, and with him an hundred forty and four thousand . . . And I saw another angel . . . saying with a loud voice, Fear God, and give glory to him . . ."[866]

EXHIBIT-6. Duplication and Expansion in *Early Writings*

The following exhibit compares *Experience and Views* and *Supplement* with *Spiritual Gifts*, as edited in *Early Writings*, revealing, to our surprise, that Ellen White used material from her two earliest books in describing the great controversy in *Spiritual Gifts* (1858). So, it wasn't all from her 1858 vision.

ExV/ExV54	*Experience and Views* in *Early Writings*	*Spiritual Gifts*, vol. 1, in *Early Writings*	1SG
ExV 13.2, first part **V16.** New Earth Vision, 1845	With Jesus at our head we all descended from the city down to this earth, on a great and mighty mountain, which could not bear Jesus up, and it parted asunder, and there was a mighty plain. Then we looked up [18] and saw the great city, with twelve foundations, and twelve gates, three on each side, and an angel at each gate. We all cried out, "The city, the great city, it's coming, it's coming down from God out of heaven," and it came and settled on the place where we stood. {EW 17.3, first part}	After the judgment of the wicked dead had been finished, at the end of the one thousand years, Jesus left the city, and the saints and a train of the angelic host followed Him. Jesus descended upon a great mountain, which as soon as His feet touched it, parted asunder and became a mighty plain. Then we looked up and saw the great and beautiful city, with twelve foundations, and twelve gates, three on each side, and an angel at each gate. We cried out, "The city! The great city! It is coming down from God out of heaven!" And it came down in all its splendor and dazzling glory and settled in the mighty plain which Jesus had prepared for it.[867] {EW 291.1}	1SG 213.1
ExV 17.3, first part **V46.** Sabbath Halo Vision, April 3, 1847 ExV 17.3, second part	In the time of trouble we all fled from the cities and villages, but were pursued by the wicked, who entered the houses of the saints with a sword. They raised the sword to kill us, but it broke, and fell as powerless as a straw. Then we all cried day and night for deliverance, and the cry came up before God. The sun came up, and the moon stood still. The streams ceased to flow. Dark, heavy clouds came up and clashed against each other. But there was one clear place of settled glory, whence came the voice of God like many waters, which shook the heavens and the earth. The sky opened and shut and was in commotion. The mountains shook like a reed in the wind, and cast out ragged rocks all around. The sea boiled like a pot and cast out stones upon the land. And as God spoke the day and the hour of Jesus' coming and delivered the everlasting covenant to His people, He spoke one sentence, and then paused, while the words were rolling through the earth. The Israel of God stood with their eyes fixed upward, listening to the words as they came from the mouth of Jehovah, and rolled through the earth like peals of loudest thunder. It was awfully solemn. And at the end of every sentence the saints shouted, "Glory! Alleluia!" Their countenances were lighted up with the glory of God; and they shone with the glory, as did the face of Moses when he came down from Sinai. The wicked could not look on them for the glory. And when the never-ending blessing was pronounced on those who had honored God in keeping His Sabbath holy, there was a mighty shout of victory over the beast and over his image. {EW 34.1}	As the saints left the cities and villages, they were pursued by the wicked, who sought to slay them. But [285] the swords that were raised to kill God's people broke and fell as powerless as a straw. Angels of God shielded the saints. As they cried day and night for deliverance, their cry came up before the Lord. {EW 284.2} It was at midnight that God chose to deliver His people. As the wicked were mocking around them, suddenly the sun appeared, shining in his strength, and the moon stood still. The wicked looked upon the scene with amazement, while the saints beheld with solemn joy the tokens of their deliverance. Signs and wonders followed in quick succession. Everything seemed turned out of its natural course. The streams ceased to flow. Dark, heavy clouds came up and clashed against each other. But there was one clear place of settled glory, whence came the voice of God like many waters, shaking the heavens and the earth. There was a mighty earthquake. The graves were opened, and those who had died in faith under the third angel's message, keeping the Sabbath, came forth from their dusty beds, glorified, to hear the covenant of peace that God was to make with those who had kept His law. {EW 285.1} The sky opened and shut and was in commotion. The mountains shook like a reed in the wind and cast out ragged rocks all around. The sea boiled like a pot and cast out stones upon the land. And as God spoke the day and the hour of Jesus' coming and delivered the everlasting covenant to His people, He spoke one sentence, and then paused, while the words were rolling through the earth. The Israel of God stood with their eyes fixed upward, listening to [286] the words as they came from the mouth of Jehovah and rolled through the earth like peals of loudest thunder. It was awfully solemn. At the end of every sentence the saints shouted, "Glory! Hallelujah!" Their countenances were lighted up with the glory of God, and they shone with glory as did the face of Moses when he came down from Sinai. The wicked could not look upon them for the glory. And when the	1SG 204.1 1SG 205.1 1SG 205.2 1SG 205.3

		never-ending blessing was pronounced on those who had honored God in keeping His Sabbath holy, there was a mighty shout of victory over the beast and over his image. {EW 285.2}	
ExV 18.1, first part	Then commenced the jubilee, when the land should rest. I saw the pious slave rise in triumph and victory and shake off the chains that bound him, while his wicked master was in confusion and knew not what to do; for the wicked could not understand the words of the voice of God. {EW 35.1, first part}	Then commenced the jubilee, when the land should rest. I saw the pious slave rise in victory and triumph, and shake off the chains that bound him, while his wicked master was in confusion and knew not what to do; for the wicked could not understand the words of the voice of God. {EW 286.1}	1SG 206.1
ExV 18.1, second part	Soon appeared the great white cloud. It looked more lovely than ever before. On it sat the Son of man. At first we did not see Jesus on the cloud, but as it drew near the earth we could behold His lovely person. {EW 35.1, second part}	Soon appeared the great white cloud, upon which sat the Son of man. When it first appeared in the distance, this cloud looked very small. The angel said that it was the sign of the Son of man. As it drew nearer the earth, we could behold the excellent glory and majesty of Jesus as He rode forth to conquer. {EW 286.2, first part}	1SG 206.1
ExV 18.1, third part	This cloud, when it first appeared, was the sign of the Son of man in heaven. The voice of the Son of God called forth the sleeping saints, clothed with glorious immortality. The living saints were changed in a moment and were caught up with them into the cloudy chariot. It looked all over glorious as it rolled upward. {EW 35.1, third part}	The earth mightily shook as the voice of the Son of God called forth the sleeping saints. They responded to the call and came forth clothed with glorious immortality, crying, "Victory, victory, over death and the grave! O death, where is thy sting? O grave, where is thy victory?" Then the living saints and the risen ones raised their voices in a long, transporting shout of victory. Those bodies that had gone down into the grave bearing the marks of disease and death came up in immortal health and vigor. The living saints are changed in a moment, in the twinkling of an eye, and caught up with the risen ones, and together they meet their Lord in the air. Oh, what a glorious meeting! Friends whom death had separated were united, never more to part. {EW 287.1}	1SG 207.1
ExV 18.1, fourth part	On either side of the chariot were wings, and beneath it wheels. And as the chariot rolled upward, the wheels cried, "Holy," and the wings, as they moved, cried, "Holy," and the retinue of holy angels around the cloud cried, "Holy, holy, holy, Lord God Almighty!" And the saints in the cloud cried, "Glory! Alleluia!" And the chariot rolled upward to the Holy City. Jesus threw open the gates of the golden city and led us in. Here we were made welcome, for we had kept the "commandments of God," and had a "right to the tree of life." {EW 35.1, fourth part}	On each side of the cloudy chariot were wings, and beneath it were living wheels; and as the chariot rolled upward, the wheels cried, "Holy," and the wings, as they moved, cried, "Holy," and the retinue of holy [288] angels around the cloud cried, "Holy, holy, holy, Lord God Almighty!" And the saints in the cloud cried, "Glory! Alleluia!" And the chariot rolled upward to the Holy City. Before entering the city, the saints were arranged in a perfect square, with Jesus in the midst. He stood head and shoulders above the saints and above the angels. His majestic form and lovely countenance could be seen by all in the square. {EW 287.2}	1SG 208.1
ExV 32.4 **V87.** *Perishing Souls Vision, Jan. 26, 1850*	I was pointed to Adam and Eve in Eden. They partook of the forbidden tree and were driven from the garden, and then the flaming sword was placed around the tree of life, lest they should partake of its fruit and be immortal sinners. The tree of life was to perpetuate immortality. I heard an angel ask, "Who of the family of Adam have passed the flaming sword and have partaken of the tree of life?" I heard another angel answer, "Not one of Adam's family has passed that flaming sword and partaken of that tree; therefore there is not an immortal sinner. The soul that sinneth it shall die an everlasting death—a death that will last forever, from which there will be no hope of a resurrection; and then the wrath of God will be appeased. {EW 51.2}	I was pointed to Adam and Eve in Eden. They partook of the forbidden tree, and then the flaming sword was placed around the tree of life, and they were driven from the garden, lest they should partake of the tree of life, and be immortal sinners. The fruit of this tree was to perpetuate immortality. I heard an angel ask, "Who of the family of Adam have passed that flaming sword, and have partaken of the tree of life?" I heard another angel answer, "Not one of the family of Adam has passed that flaming sword, and partaken of that tree; therefore there is not an immortal sinner." The soul that sinneth, it shall die an everlasting death—a death from which there will be no hope of resurrection; and then the wrath of God will be appeased. {EW 218.1}	1SG 113.2

ExV54 5.4 V95. Mysterious Rapping Vision, Aug. 24, 1850	I saw the rapping delusion—what progress it was making, and that if it were possible it would deceive the very elect. Satan will have power to bring before us the appearance of forms purporting to be our relatives or friends now sleeping in Jesus. It will be made to appear as if these friends were present; the words that they uttered while here, with which we were familiar, will be spoken, and the same tone of voice that they had while living will fall upon the ear. All this is to deceive the saints and ensnare them into the belief of this delusion. {EW 87.1}	The rapping delusion was presented before me, and I saw that Satan has power to bring before us the appearance of forms purporting to be our relatives or friends who sleep in Jesus. It will be made to appear as if these friends were actually present, the words they uttered while here, with which we were familiar, will be spoken, and the same tone of voice that they had while living will fall upon the ear. All this is to deceive the world and ensnare them into the belief of this delusion. {EW 262.1}	1SG 173.1
ExV54 6.1	I saw that the saints must get a thorough understanding of present truth, which they will be obliged to maintain from the Scriptures. They must understand the state of the dead; for the spirits of devils will yet appear to them, professing to be beloved friends and relatives, who will declare to them that the Sabbath has been changed, also other unscriptural doctrines. They will do all in their power to excite sympathy and will work miracles before them to confirm what they declare. The people of God must be prepared to withstand these spirits with the Bible truth that the dead know not anything, and that they who appear to them are the spirits of devils. {EW 87.2, first part}	I saw that the saints must have a thorough understanding of present truth, which they will be obliged to maintain from the Scriptures. They must understand the state of the dead; for the spirits of devils will yet appear to them, professing to be beloved relatives or friends, who will declare to them unscriptural doctrines. They will do all in their power to excite sympathy and will work miracles before them to confirm what they declare. The people of God must be prepared to withstand these spirits with the Bible truth that the dead know not anything, and that they who thus appear are the spirits of devils. {EW 262.2}	1SG 173.2
ExV54 6.2	We must examine well the foundation of our hope, for we shall have to give a reason for it from the Scriptures. This delusion will spread, and we shall have to contend with it face to face; and unless we are prepared for it, we shall be ensnared and overcome. But if we do what we can on our part to be ready for the conflict that is just before us, God will do His part, and His all-powerful arm will protect us. He would sooner send every angel out of glory to the relief of faithful souls, to make a hedge about them, than have them deceived and led away by the lying wonders of Satan. {EW 88.1}	We must examine well the foundation of our hope; for we shall have to give a reason for it from the Scriptures. This delusion will spread, and we shall have to contend with it face to face; and unless we are prepared for it, we shall be ensnared and overcome. But if we do what we can on our part to be ready for the conflict that is just before us, God will do His part, and His all-powerful arm will protect us. He would sooner send every angel out of glory to make a hedge about faithful souls, than have them deceived and led away by the lying wonders of Satan. {EW 262.3}	1SG 174.1
ExV54 6.3, first part	I saw the rapidity with which this delusion was spreading. A train of cars was shown me, going with the speed of lightning. The angel bade me look carefully. I fixed my eyes upon the train. It seemed that the whole world was on board, that there could not be one left. Said the angel, "They are binding in bundles ready to burn." Then he showed me the conductor, who appeared like a stately, fair person, whom all the passengers looked up to and reverenced. I was perplexed and asked my attending angel who it was. He said, "It is Satan. He is the conductor in the form of an angel of light. He has taken the world captive. They are given over to strong delusions, to believe a lie, that they may be damned. This agent, the next highest in order to him, is the engineer, and other of his agents are employed in different offices as he may need them, and they are all going with lightning speed to perdition." {EW 88.2}	I saw the rapidity with which this delusion was spreading. A train of cars was shown me, going with the speed of lightning. The angel bade me look carefully. I fixed my eyes upon the train. It seemed that the whole world was on board. Then he showed me the conductor, a fair, stately person, whom all the passengers looked up to and reverenced. I was perplexed and asked my attending angel who it was. He said, "It is Satan. He is the conductor, in the form of an angel of light. He has taken the world captive. They are given over to strong delusions, to believe a lie that they may be damned. His agent, the highest in order next to him, is the engineer, and others of his agents are employed in different offices as he may need them, and they are all going with lightning speed to perdition." {EW 263.1}	1SG 174.2
ExV54 6.3, second part–7.1	I asked the angel if there were none left. He bade me look in an opposite direction, and I saw a little company traveling a narrow pathway. All seemed to be firmly united, bound together by the truth, in [89] bundles, or companies. Said the angel, "The third angel is binding, or sealing, them in bundles for the heavenly garner." This little company looked careworn, as if they had passed through severe trials and conflicts. And it appeared as if the sun had just risen from	I asked the angel if there were none left. He bade me look in the opposite direction, and I saw a little company traveling a narrow pathway. All seemed to be firmly united by the truth. This little company looked careworn, as if they had passed through severe trials and conflicts. And it appeared as if the sun had just arisen from behind a cloud and shone upon their countenances, causing them to look	1SG 174.2–175.1

	behind a cloud and shone upon their countenances, causing them to look triumphant, as if their victories were nearly won. {EW 88.3}	triumphant as if their victories were nearly won. {EW 263.2}	
ExV54 7.2–8.1	I saw that the Lord has given the world opportunity to discover the snare. This one thing is evidence enough for the Christian, if there were no other; namely, that there is no difference made between the precious and the vile. Thomas Paine, whose body has now moldered to dust and who is to be called forth at the end of the one thousand years, at the second resurrection, to receive his reward and suffer the second death, is represented by Satan as being in heaven, and highly exalted there. Satan used him on earth as long as he could, and now he is carrying on the same work through pretensions of having Thomas Paine so much exalted and honored in heaven; as he taught here, Satan would make it appear that he is teaching in heaven. There are some who have looked with horror at his life and death, and his corrupt teachings while living, but who now submit to be taught by him, one of the vilest and most corrupt of men, one who despised God and His law. {EW 89.1}	I saw that the Lord has given the world opportunity to discover the snare. This one thing is evidence enough for the Christian if there were no other; there is no difference made between the precious and the vile. Thomas Paine, whose body has now moldered to dust and who is to be called forth at the end of the one thousand years, at the second resurrection, to receive his reward, and suffer the second death, is represented by Satan as being in heaven, and highly exalted there. Satan used him on earth as long as he could, and now he is carrying on the same work [264] through pretensions of having Thomas Paine so much exalted and honored in heaven; and as he taught here, Satan would make it appear that he is teaching there. And some who have looked with horror at his life and death, and his corrupt teachings while living, now submit to be taught by him—one of the vilest and most corrupt of men, one who despised God and His law. {EW 263.3}	1SG 175.2–175.3
ExV54 8.2	He who is the father of lies, blinds and deceives the world by sending forth his angels to speak for the apostles, and to make it appear that they contradict what they wrote by the dictation of the Holy Ghost when on earth. These lying angels make the apostles to corrupt their own teachings and to declare them to be adulterated. By so doing Satan delights to throw professed Christians and all the world into uncertainty about the Word of God. That holy Book cuts directly across his track and thwarts his plans; therefore he leads them to doubt its divine origin. Then he sets up the infidel, Thomas Paine, as if he were ushered into heaven when he died, and now, united with the holy apostles whom he hated on earth, were engaged in teaching the world. {EW 90.1}	He who is the father of lies, blinds and deceives the world by sending forth his angels to speak for the apostles, and to make it appear that they contradict what they wrote by the dictation of the Holy Ghost when on earth. These lying angels make the apostles to corrupt their own teachings and to declare them to be adulterated. By so doing, Satan delights to throw professed Christians and all the world into uncertainty about the Word of God. That holy Book cuts directly across his track and thwarts his plans; therefore he leads men to doubt the divine origin of the Bible. Then he sets up the infidel Thomas Paine, as if when he died he were ushered into heaven, and now, united with the holy apostles whom he hated on earth, were engaged in teaching the world. {EW 264.1}	1SG 176.1
ExV54 9.1	Satan assigns to each of his angels a part to act. He enjoins upon them all to be sly, artful, cunning. He instructs some of them to act the part of the apostles and to speak for them, while others are to act the part of infidels and wicked men who died cursing God, but now appear to be very religious. There is no difference made between the most holy apostles and the vilest infidel. They are both made to teach the same thing. It matters not whom Satan makes to speak, if his object is only accomplished. He was so intimately connected with Paine upon the earth, aiding him in his work, that it is an easy thing for him to know the very words Paine used and the very handwriting of one who served him so faithfully and accomplished his purposes so well. Satan dictated much of his writings, and it is an easy thing for him to dictate sentiments through his angels now and make it appear [91] that they come through Thomas Paine, who, while living, was a devoted servant of the evil one. This is the masterpiece of Satan. All this teaching, purporting to be from apostles and saints and wicked men who have	Satan assigns to each of his angels a part to act. He enjoins upon them all to be sly, artful, cunning. He instructs some of them to act the part of the apostles and to speak for them, while others are to act the part of infidels and wicked men who died cursing God, but now appear to be very religious. There is no difference made between the most holy apostles and the vilest infidels. They are both made to teach the same thing. It matters not whom Satan makes to speak, if his object is only accomplished. He was intimately connected with Paine upon earth, aiding him in his work, and it is an easy thing for him to know the very words and the handwriting of one who [265] served him so faithfully and accomplished his purposes so well. Satan dictated much of Paine's writings, and it is an easy thing for him to dictate sentiments through his angels now, and make it appear that they come through Thomas Paine. This is the masterpiece of Satan. All this teaching, purporting to be from apostles and saints and wicked men who have died,	1SG 176.2

	died, comes directly from his satanic majesty. {EW 90.2}	comes directly from his satanic majesty. {EW 264.2}	
ExV54 9.2	The fact that Satan claims that one whom he loved so well, and who hated God so perfectly, is now with the holy apostles and angels in glory, should be enough to remove the veil from all minds and discover to them the dark, mysterious works of Satan. He virtually says to the world and to infidels, No matter how wicked you are, no matter whether you believe or disbelieve in God or the Bible, live as you please, heaven is your home; for all know that if Thomas Paine is in heaven, and so exalted, they will surely get there. This error is so glaring that all may see if they will. Satan is now doing through persons like Thomas Paine what he has been trying to do since his fall. He is, through his power and lying wonders, tearing away the foundation of the Christian's hope and putting out the sun that is to light them in the narrow way to heaven. He is making the world believe that the Bible is uninspired, no better than a storybook, while he holds out something to take its place; namely, spiritual manifestations! {EW 91.1}	The fact that Satan claims that one whom he loved so well, and who hated God so perfectly, is now with the holy apostles and angels in glory, should be enough to remove the veil from all minds and discover to them the dark, mysterious works of Satan. He virtually says to the world and to infidels, "No matter how wicked you are, no matter whether you believe or disbelieve in God or the Bible, live as you please, heaven is your home; for all know that if Thomas Paine is in heaven, and so exalted, they will surely get there." This is so glaring that all may see if they will. Satan is now doing, through individuals like Thomas Paine, what he has been trying to do since his fall. He is, through his power and lying wonders, tearing away the foundation of the Christian's hope and putting out the sun that is to light the narrow way to heaven. He is making the world believe that the Bible is uninspired, no better than a storybook, while he holds out something to take its place; namely, spiritual manifestations. {EW 265.1}	1SG 177.1
ExV54 10.1, 2	Here is a channel wholly devoted to himself and under his control, and he can make the world believe what he will. The Book that is to judge him and his followers he puts back in the shade, just where he wants it. The Saviour of the world he makes to be no more than a common man; and as the Roman guard that watched the tomb of Jesus spread the lying report that the chief priests and elders put into their mouths, so will the poor, deluded followers of these pretended spiritual manifestations repeat and try to make it [92] appear that there is nothing miraculous about our Saviour's birth, death, and resurrection. After putting Jesus in the background, they attract the attention of the world to themselves and to their miracles and lying wonders, which, they declare, far exceed the works of Christ. Thus the world is taken in the snare and lulled into a feeling of security, not to find out their awful deception until the seven last plagues are poured out. Satan laughs as he sees his plan succeed so well and the whole world taken in the snare. {EW 91.2}	Here is a channel wholly devoted to himself, under his control, and he can make the world believe what he will. The book that is to judge him and his followers, he puts back into the shade, just where he wants it. The Saviour of the world he makes to be no more than a common man; and as the Roman guard that watched the tomb of Jesus spread the lying report that the chief priests and elders put into their [266] mouths, so will the poor, deluded followers of these pretended spiritual manifestations repeat and try to make it appear that there is nothing miraculous about our Saviour's birth, death, and resurrection. After putting Jesus in the background, they attract the attention of the world to themselves and to their miracles and lying wonders, which, they declare, far exceed the works of Christ. Thus the world is taken in the snare and lulled to a feeling of security, not to find out their awful deception until the seven last plagues shall be poured out. Satan laughs as he sees his plan succeed so well and the whole world taken in the snare. {EW 265.2}	1SG 178.1
	The Fall of Satan		
	Satan was once an honored angel in heaven, next to Christ. His countenance, like those of the other angels, was mild and expressive of happiness. His forehead was high and broad, showing great intelligence. His form was perfect; his bearing noble and majestic. But when God said to His Son, "Let us make man in our image," Satan was jealous of Jesus.[868] He wished to be consulted concerning the formation of man, and because he was not, he was filled with envy, jealousy, and hatred. He desired to receive the highest honors in heaven next to God. {EW 145.1}		1SG 17.1
	Until this time all heaven had been in order, harmony, and perfect subjection to the government of God. It was the highest sin to rebel against His order and will. All heaven seemed in commotion. The angels were marshaled in companies, each division with a higher commanding angel at its head. Satan, ambitious to exalt himself, and unwilling to submit to the authority of Jesus, was insinuating against the government of God. Some of the angels sympathized with Satan in his rebellion, and others strongly contended for the honor and wisdom of God in giving authority to His Son. There was contention among the angels. Satan and his sympathizers were striving to reform the government of God. They wished to look into His unsearchable wisdom, and ascertain His purpose in exalting Jesus and endowing Him with such unlimited [146] power and command. They rebelled against the authority of the Son. All the heavenly host were summoned to appear before the Father to have each case decided. It was there determined that Satan should be expelled from heaven, with all the angels who had joined him in the rebellion. Then there was war in heaven.[869] Angels were engaged in the battle; Satan wished to conquer the		1SG 17.2

<table>
<tr><td></td><td colspan="2">Son of God and those who were submissive to His will. But the good and true angels prevailed, and Satan, with his followers, was driven from heaven. {EW 145.2}

After Satan and those who fell with him were shut out of heaven, and he realized that he had forever lost all its purity and glory, he repented, and wished to be reinstated in heaven. He was willing to take his proper place, or any position that might be assigned him. But no; heaven must not be placed in jeopardy. All heaven might be marred should he be taken back; for sin originated with him, and the seeds of rebellion were within him. Both he and his followers wept, and implored to be taken back into the favor of God. But their sin—their hatred, their envy and jealousy—had been so great that God could not blot it out. It must remain to receive its final punishment. {EW 146.1}

When Satan became fully conscious that there was no possibility of his being brought again into favor with God, his malice and hatred began to be manifest. He consulted with his angels, and a plan was laid to still work against God's government. When Adam and Eve were placed in the beautiful garden, Satan was laying plans to destroy them. In no way could this happy couple be deprived of their happiness if they obeyed God. Satan could not exercise his power upon them unless they should first disobey God and forfeit His favor. Some plan must therefore be devised to lead them to disobedience that they might incur God's [147] frown and be brought under the more direct influence of Satan and his angels. It was decided that Satan should assume another form and manifest an interest for man. He must insinuate against God's truthfulness and create doubt whether God did mean just what He said; next, he must excite their curiosity, and lead them to pry into the unsearchable plans of God—the very sin of which Satan had been guilty—and reason as to the cause of His restrictions in regard to the tree of knowledge.[870] {EW 146.2}</td><td>1SG 18.1

1SG 19.1</td></tr>
<tr><td>ExV54 46.2

ExV54 46.3</td><td colspan="2">I have been shown the great love and condescension of God in giving His Son to die that man might find pardon and live. I was shown Adam and Eve, who were privileged to behold the beauty and loveliness of the Garden of Eden and were permitted to eat of all the trees in the garden except one.[871] But the serpent tempted Eve, and she tempted her husband, and they both ate of the forbidden tree. They broke God's command, and became sinners. {EW 125.2}</td><td></td></tr>
<tr><td></td><td colspan="2">The Fall of Man
Holy angels often visited the garden, and gave instruction to Adam and Eve concerning their employment and also taught them concerning the rebellion and fall of Satan. The angels warned them of Satan and cautioned them not to separate from each other in their employment, for they might be brought in contact with this fallen foe. The angels also enjoined upon them to follow closely the directions God had given them, for in perfect obedience only were they safe. Then this fallen foe could have no power over them. {EW 147.1}</td><td>1SG 20.1</td></tr>
<tr><td></td><td colspan="2">Satan commenced his work with Eve, to cause her to disobey. She first erred in wandering from her husband, next in lingering around the forbidden tree, and next in listening to the voice of the tempter, and even daring to doubt what God had said, "In the day that thou eatest thereof thou shalt surely die."[872] She thought that perhaps the Lord did not mean just what He said, and venturing, she put forth her hand, took of the fruit and ate. It was pleasing to the eye and pleasant to the taste. Then she was jealous that God had withheld from them what was really for their good, and she [148] offered the fruit to her husband, thereby tempting him.[873] She related to Adam all that the serpent had said and expressed her astonishment that he had the power of speech. {EW 147.2}</td><td>1SG 20.2</td></tr>
<tr><td></td><td colspan="2">I saw a sadness come over Adam's countenance. He appeared afraid and astonished. A struggle seemed to be going on in his mind. He felt sure that this was the foe against whom they had been warned, and that his wife must die. They must be separated. His love for Eve was strong, and in utter discouragement he resolved to share her fate. He seized the fruit and quickly ate it. Then Satan exulted. He had rebelled in heaven, and had gained sympathizers who loved him and followed him in his rebellion. He had fallen and caused others to fall with him. And he had now tempted the woman to distrust God, to inquire into His wisdom, and to seek to penetrate His all-wise plans. Satan knew that the woman would not fall alone. Adam, through his love for Eve, disobeyed the command of God, and fell with her. {EW 148.1}</td><td>1SG 21.1</td></tr>
<tr><td>ExV54 46.4

V142. Love of God in Giving His Son</td><td>The news spread through heaven, and every harp was hushed. The angels sorrowed, and feared lest Adam and Eve would again put forth the hand and eat of the tree of life and be immortal sinners. But God said that He would drive the [126] transgressors from the garden, and by cherubim and a flaming sword would guard the way of the tree of life, so that man could not approach unto it and eat of its fruit, which perpetuates immortality. {EW 125.2, second part}</td><td>The news of man's fall spread through heaven. Every harp was hushed. The angels cast their crowns from their heads in sorrow. All heaven was in agitation. A council was held to decide what must be done with the guilty pair. The angels feared that they would put forth the hand, and eat of the tree of life, and become immortal sinners. But God said that He would drive the transgressors from the garden. Angels were immediately commissioned to guard the way of the tree of life. {EW 148.2, first part}</td><td>1SG 21.2, first part

3SG 44, 45</td></tr>
<tr><td></td><td colspan="2">It had been Satan's studied plan that Adam and Eve should disobey God, receive His frown, and then partake of the tree of life, that they might live forever in sin and disobedience, and thus sin be immortalized. But holy angels were sent to drive them out of the garden, and</td><td>1SG 21.2,</td></tr>
</table>

<table>
<tr><td></td><td colspan="2">to bar their way to the tree of life.[874] Each of these mighty angels had in his right hand [149] something which had the appearance of a glittering sword. {EW 148.2, second part}
Then Satan triumphed. He had made others suffer by his fall. He had been shut out of heaven, they out of Paradise.[875] {EW 149.1}</td><td>second part; 22.1</td></tr>
<tr><td></td><td colspan="2">The Plan of Salvation</td><td></td></tr>
<tr><td>ExV54 47.1, first part

V142. Love of God in Giving His Son</td><td>Sorrow filled heaven as it was realized that man was lost and that the world which God had created was to be filled with mortals doomed to misery, sickness, and death, and that there was no way of escape for the offender. The whole family of Adam must die. I then saw the lovely Jesus and beheld an expression of sympathy and sorrow upon His countenance. Soon I saw Him approach the exceeding bright light which enshrouded the Father. Said my accompanying angel, "He is in close converse with His Father." The anxiety of the angels seemed to be intense while Jesus was communing with His Father. Three times He was shut in by the glorious light about the Father, and the third time He came from the Father we could see His person. His countenance was calm, free from all perplexity and trouble, and shone with a loveliness which words cannot describe. He then made known to the angelic choir that a way of escape had been made for lost man; that He had been pleading with His Father, and had obtained permission to give His own life as a ransom for the race, to bear their sins, and take the sentence of death upon Himself, thus opening a way whereby they might, through the merits of His blood, find pardon for past transgressions, and by obedience be brought back to the garden from which they were driven. Then they could again have access to the glorious, immortal fruit of the tree of life to which they had now forfeited all right. {EW 126.1}</td><td>Sorrow filled heaven, as it was realized that man was lost, and that world which God had created was to be filled with mortals doomed to misery, sickness, and death, and there was no way of escape for the offender. The whole family of Adam must die. I saw the lovely Jesus and beheld an expression of sympathy and sorrow upon His countenance. Soon I saw Him approach the exceeding bright light which enshrouded the Father. Said my accompanying angel, He is in close converse with His Father. The anxiety of the angels seemed to be intense while Jesus was communing with His Father. Three times He was shut in by the glorious light about the Father, and the third time He came from the Father, His person could be seen. His countenance was calm, free from all perplexity and doubt, and shone with benevolence and loveliness, such as words cannot express. He then made known to the angelic host that a way of escape had been made for lost man. He told them that He had been pleading with His Father, and had offered to give His life a ransom, to take the sentence of death upon Himself, that through Him man might find pardon; that through the merits of His blood, and obedience to the law of God, they could have the favor of God, and be brought into the beautiful garden, and eat of the fruit of the tree of life. {EW 149.2}</td><td>1SG 22.2</td></tr>
<tr><td></td><td colspan="2">At first the angels could not rejoice; for their Commander concealed nothing from them, but opened [150] before them the plan of salvation. Jesus told them that He would stand between the wrath of His Father and guilty man, that He would bear iniquity and scorn, and but few would receive Him as the Son of God. Nearly all would hate and reject Him. He would leave all His glory in heaven, appear upon earth as a man, humble Himself as a man, become acquainted by His own experience with the various temptations with which man would be beset, that He might know how to succor those who should be tempted; and that finally, after His mission as a teacher would be accomplished, He would be delivered into the hands of men, and endure almost every cruelty and suffering that Satan and his angels could inspire wicked men to inflict; that He would die the cruelest of deaths, hung up between the heavens and the earth as a guilty sinner; that He would suffer dreadful hours of agony, which even angels could not look upon, but would veil their faces from the sight.[876] Not merely agony of body would He suffer, but mental agony, that with which bodily suffering could in no wise be compared. The weight of the sins of the whole world would be upon Him.[877] He told them He would die and rise again the third day, and would ascend to His Father to intercede for wayward, guilty man.[878] {EW 149.3}</td><td>1SG 23.1</td></tr>
<tr><td></td><td colspan="2">The angels prostrated themselves before Him. They offered their lives. Jesus said to them that He would by His death save many, that the life of an angel could not pay the debt. His life alone could be accepted of His Father as a ransom for man.[879] Jesus also told them that they would have a part to act, to be with Him and at different times strengthen Him; that He would take man's fallen nature, and His strength would not be even equal with theirs; that they would be witnesses of His humiliation and great sufferings; and that as they would witness His sufferings, and the [151] hatred of men toward Him, they would be stirred with the deepest emotion, and through their love for Him would wish to rescue and deliver Him from His murderers; but that they must not interfere to prevent anything they should behold; and that they should act a part in His resurrection; that the plan of salvation was devised, and His Father had accepted the plan.[880] {EW 150.1}</td><td>1SG 24.1

1SG 25.1</td></tr>
<tr><td></td><td colspan="2">With a holy sadness Jesus comforted and cheered the angels and informed them that hereafter those whom He should redeem would be with Him, and that by His death He should ransom many and destroy him who had the power of death. And His Father would give Him the kingdom and the greatness of the kingdom under the whole heaven, and He would possess it forever and ever. Satan and sinners would be destroyed, nevermore to disturb heaven or the</td><td>1SG 25.2</td></tr>
</table>

	purified new earth. Jesus bade the heavenly host be reconciled to the plan that His Father had accepted and rejoice that through His death fallen man could again be exalted to obtain favor with God and enjoy heaven. {EW 151.1}		
ExV54 47.1 V142. Love of God in Giving His Son	Then joy, inexpressible joy, filled heaven, and the heavenly choir sang a song of praise and adoration. They touched their harps and sang a note higher than they had done before, because of the great mercy and [127] condescension of God in yielding up His dearly Beloved to die for a race of rebels. Then praise and adoration was poured forth for the self-denial and sacrifice of Jesus, in consenting to leave the bosom of His Father, and choosing a life of suffering and anguish, and an ignominious death, that He might give life to others. {EW 126.2}	Then joy, inexpressible joy, filled heaven. And the heavenly host sang a song of praise and adoration. They touched their harps and sang a note higher than they had done before, for the great mercy and condescension of God in yielding up His dearly Beloved to die for a race of rebels. Praise and adoration were poured forth for the self-denial and sacrifice of Jesus; that He would consent to leave the bosom of His Father, and choose a life of suffering and anguish, and die an ignominious death to give life to others. {EW 151.2}	1SG 26.1
ExV54 48.1 V142. Love of God in Giving His Son	Said the angel, "Think ye that the Father yielded up His dearly beloved Son without a struggle? No, no." It was even a struggle with the God of heaven, whether to let guilty man perish, or to give His darling Son to die for them. Angels were so interested for man's salvation that there could be found among them those who would yield their glory and give their life for perishing man. "But," said my accompanying angel, "that would avail nothing." The transgression was so great that an angel's life would not pay the debt. Nothing but the death and intercession of God's Son would pay the debt and save lost man from hopeless sorrow and misery. {EW 127.1}	Said the angel, "Think ye that the Father yielded up His dearly beloved Son without a struggle? No, no. It was even a struggle with the God of heaven, whether to let guilty man perish, or to give His beloved Son to die for him." Angels were so interested for man's [152] salvation that there could be found among them those who would yield their glory and give their life for perishing man, "But," said my accompanying angel, "that would avail nothing. The transgression was so great that an angel's life would not pay the debt. Nothing but the death and intercessions of His son would pay the debt and save lost man from hopeless sorrow and misery." {EW 151.3}	1SG 26.2
ExV54 48.2 V142. Love of God in Giving His Son	But the work which was assigned the angels was to ascend and descend with strengthening balm from glory to soothe the Son of God in His life of suffering. They administered unto Jesus. Also, their work was to guard and keep the subjects of grace from the evil angels and from the darkness which was constantly thrown around them by Satan. I saw that it was impossible for God to change His law in order to save lost, perishing man; therefore He suffered His darling Son to die for man's transgressions. {EW 127.2}	But the work of the angels was assigned them, to ascend and descend with strengthening balm from glory to soothe the Son of God in His sufferings, and minister unto Him. Also, their work would be to guard and keep the subjects of grace from the evil angels and the darkness constantly thrown around them by Satan. I saw that it was impossible for God to alter or change His law to save lost, perishing man; therefore He suffered His beloved Son to die for man's transgression. {EW 152.1}	1SG 26.3
	Satan again rejoiced with his angels that he could, by causing man's fall, pull down the Son of God from His exalted position. He told his angels that when Jesus should take fallen man's nature, he could overpower Him and hinder the accomplishment of the plan of salvation. {EW 152.2}		1SG 27.1
	I was shown Satan as he once was, a happy, exalted angel. Then I was shown him as he now is. He still bears a kingly form. His features are still noble, for he is an angel fallen. But the expression of his countenance is full of anxiety, care, unhappiness, malice, hate, mischief, deceit, and every evil. That brow which was once so noble, I particularly noticed. His forehead commenced from his eyes to recede. I saw that he had so long bent himself to evil that every good quality was debased, and every evil trait was developed. His eyes were cunning, sly, and showed great penetration. His frame was large, but the flesh hung loosely about his [153] hands and face. As I beheld him, his chin was resting upon his left hand. He appeared to be in deep thought. A smile was upon his countenance, which made me tremble, it was so full of evil and satanic slyness. This smile is the one he wears just before he makes sure of his victim, and as he fastens the victim in his snare, this smile grows horrible. {EW 152.3}		1SG 27.2

The Developing Great Controversy Theme

Regarding her 1858 "Great Controversy Vision" (~V189), Ellen White wrote: "In this vision at Lovett's Grove, most of the matter of the Great Controversy which I had seen ***ten years before, was repeated,*** and I was shown that I must write it out" (2SG 270.1, emphasis added). Evidence that the 1858 vision was an expansion of the earlier vision has here been illustrated by highlighting parallel verbatim wording between Ellen White's first two books (1851, 1853) and *Spiritual Gifts*, volume 1 (1858). The beginning scene in *Spiritual Gifts* (1SG 20.1–27.1, 2) expands on the last vision (V142) recorded in the second book (which was published in late 1853), regarding the council between the Father and the Son (ExV54 47.1). "The Fall of Satan" (1SG 17.1–19.1) is an addition. "The Fall of Man" (1SG 20.1–21.1) expands on the description of the Fall (ExV54 46.3), adding a description of the results of Adam and Eve's sin (1SG 21.2b–21.2). "The Plan of Salvation" (1SG 22.2–27.2) adds the angels' response to their fall (1SG 23.1–25.2), Satan's glee in causing humankind's downfall (1SG 27.1), and Satan's physical deterioration because of sin (1SG 27.2). There are other passages we have found adapted from the two first books for *Spiritual Gifts*, touching on several other visions (V16, V46, V87, V95).[881] Thus, we recognize that, from the very start of her ministry, Ellen White began rewriting what she had earlier written and that she continued to develop these early themes over the years.

Nonetheless, in 1898 Ellen White published a statement that some might *interpret* as indicating that she had abandoned her earlier description of the council between the Father and the Son: "The plan for our redemption was not an afterthought, a plan formulated after the fall of Adam. It was a revelation of 'the mystery which hath been kept in silence through times eternal.' "[882] But did she really abandon her early view of the council? A careful review of her writings demonstrates that she recognized *both* to be true. In 1886 and again in 1890, for example, she described, in more general terms, the heavenly council that took place after man's sin.

> When the race fell through Adam, there was no hope. Man was cut off from God. But Christ consented to take upon Himself the work of restoration, and offered Himself as a substitute in order that the race may be brought back into the favor of His Father.[883]
>
> The Son of God, heaven's glorious Commander, was touched with pity for the fallen race. His heart was moved with infinite compassion as the woes of the lost world rose up before Him. . . . Before the Father He pleaded in the sinner's behalf, while the host of heaven awaited the result with an intensity of interest that words cannot express. Long continued was that mysterious communing—"the counsel of peace" (Zechariah 6:13) for the fallen sons of men. The plan of salvation had been laid before the creation of the earth; for Christ is "the Lamb slain from the foundation of the world" (Revelation 13:8); yet it was a struggle, even with the King of the universe, to yield up His Son to die for the guilty race. But "God so loved the world, that He gave His only-begotten Son, that whosoever believeth in Him should not perish, but have everlasting life." John 3:16. Oh, the mystery of redemption! the love of God for a world that did not love Him! Who can know the depths of that love which "passeth knowledge"? Through endless ages immortal minds, seeking to comprehend the mystery of that incomprehensible love, will wonder and adore.[884]

Ellen White's declaration of adoration echoes the thought in the hymn penned by Charles Wesley just after his conversion:

> And can it be that I should gain
> An interest in the Savior's blood?
> Died He for me, who caused His pain?
> For me, who Him to death pursued?
> Amazing love! how can it be
> That Thou, my God, should die for me?
> Amazing love! how can it be
> That Thou, my God, should die for me!

The reality of Christ's offering of Himself as man's sacrifice persists in Ellen White's expositions and is expanded in the manuscripts she wrote while preparing *The Desire of Ages*.

> In the work of creation Christ was with God. He was one with God, equal with Him. . . . He alone, the Creator of man, could be his Saviour. No angel of heaven could reveal the Father to the sinner, and win him back to allegiance to God. . . . Christ proposed to reach to the depths of man's degradation and woe, and restore the repenting, believing soul to harmony with God. Christ, the Lamb slain from the foundation of the world, offered Himself as a sacrifice and substitute for the fallen sons of Adam.[885]
>
> Christ was not compelled to endure this cruel treatment. The yoke of obligation was not laid upon Him to undertake the work of redemption. Voluntarily He offered Himself, a willing, spotless sacrifice. He was equal with God, infinite and omnipotent. He was above all finite requirements. He was Himself the law in character. Of the highest angels it could not be said that they had never borne a yoke. The angels all bear the yoke of dependence, the yoke of obedience. They are the appointed messengers of Him who is Commander of all heaven.
>
> No one of the angels could become a substitute and *surety* for the human race, for their life is God's; they could not surrender it. On Christ alone the human family depended for their existence. He is the eternal, self-existent Son, on whom no yoke had come. When God asked, "Whom shall I send, and who will go for Us?" Christ alone of the angelic host could reply, "Here am I; send Me." He alone had covenanted before the foundation of the world to become a surety for man. He could say that which not the highest angel could say—"I have power over my own life. I have power to lay it down, and I have power to take it again."[886]

Then, in 1902, she described the Father's acceptance of the Son's voluntary sacrifice on behalf of humankind.

> When Adam fell, God's attributes of holiness, justice, and truth could not be changed. And yet He desired to reconcile man with heaven's immutable law. Yearning to save fallen humanity, He sought to devise a plan whereby the sinner need not perish, but might gain everlasting life. Christ, the Eternal Truth, the Light, the Life, the Sovereign of heaven, offered to clothe His divinity with humanity, and give His life as a ransom for the fallen race. God in His wisdom accepted the plan proposed by Christ for the accomplishment of His purpose.[887]

Thus Ellen White indicates that the plan of redemption was *not* an afterthought, though it was kept in silence *until* the angels needed to understand what God had always understood. Then, once man had sinned, the council between the Father and the Son visibly signaled to the heavenly host that the Son willingly gave Himself to the mission of redemption for humankind, and the Father agreed to the Son's willing sacrifice.[888]

The Work of the Godhead in Salvation

Lest some misunderstand from this literary picture that only the Father and Son were involved in planning for humankind's redemption, Ellen White later laid out all who were involved in the "councils of the Godhead."

> By Christ the work upon which the fulfillment of God's purpose rests was accomplished. This was the agreement in the councils of the Godhead. The Father purposed in counsel with His Son that the human family should be tested and proved to see whether they would be allured by the temptations of Satan, or whether they would make Christ their righteousness, keeping God's commandments, and live. God gave to His Son all who would be true and loyal. Christ covenanted to redeem them from the power of Satan, at the price of His own life. We have the condition of this covenant. "Yet it pleased the Lord to bruise him; he hath put him to grief. When thou shalt make his soul an offering for sin, he shall see his seed, he shall prolong his days, and the pleasure of the Lord shall prosper in his hand. He shall see of the travail of his soul, and shall be satisfied. By his knowledge shall my righteous servant justify many: for he shall bear their iniquities."[889]

For Ellen White, the term "*Godhead*" included the "three greatest powers in heaven" who alone can rightly be "called God" and "*worshipped*."[890] She clarified, in several statements, that, by the "Godhead," she meant the three powers of the Father, the Son, *and the Holy Spirit*.

> *The* **Godhead** was stirred with pity for the race, and **the Father, the Son, and the Holy Spirit** gave **themselves** to the working out of the plan of redemption. In order to fully carry out this plan, it was decided that Christ, the only begotten Son of God, should give Himself an offering for sin. What line can measure the depth of this love?[891]
>
> **The Father, the Son, and the Holy Ghost, the eternal** Godhead is involved in the action required to make assurance to the human agent to unite all heaven to contribute to the exercise of human faculties to reach and embrace the fulness of the threefold powers to unite in the great work appointed, confederating the heavenly powers with the human, that men may become, through heavenly efficiency, partakers of the divine nature and workers together with Christ.[892]
>
> Those who have by baptism given to God a pledge of their faith in Christ, and their death to the old life of sin, have entered into covenant relation with God. **The three powers of the** Godhead, **the Father, Son, and Holy Spirit**, are pledged to be their strength and their efficiency in their new life in Christ Jesus.[893]

In these statements we see how Ellen White developed biblical concepts over the course of her literary career, causing the truths of Scripture to come into sharper focus over time. And when we grasp these concepts, they have an effect on us as readers and our appreciation of God's wonderful plan of salvation.

"But we all, with open face beholding as in a glass the glory of the Lord, are changed into the same image from glory to glory, even as by the Spirit of the Lord."[894]

CHART-2.		Timeline of Events in Ellen White's Early Life
1827	Nov 26	Twins Ellen and Elizabeth Harmon are born to Robert and Eunice Harmon in Gorham, ME.
1836	late	Ellen abandons school after an accident nearly ended her life and weakened her lungs.
1840	Mar 11–23	Ellen hears William Miller present the Advent message in Portland, ME.
1841	Sep	Ellen is converted at a Methodist Camp Meeting, in Buxton, ME (2SG 12).
1842	Jun 26	Ellen is baptized in Casco Bay and accepted as a member of the Chestnut Street Methodist Episcopal Church.
	fall ?	Ellen attempts to return to school at the Westbrook Seminary for women.
	?	Ellen shares dreams with her mother and Levi Stockman, who encourages her that God has a purpose for her.
1843	Sep 2	The Harmon family is disfellowshipped from the Chestnut Street Methodist Episcopal Church for "long absence" and "breach of discipline."
1844	Oct 22	With other Adventists, Ellen experiences the Great Disappointment when Jesus did not return as they hoped.
	Dec	Ellen has her first vision (V1) in Portland, ME, at Elizabeth Haines' home and shares its message first with Joseph Turner and then with the believers at her father's house.
1845	Jan	A week later, Ellen has her second vision (V2), with the command, "Go and give the message." Later, John Pearson, Sr., witnesses the "Ball of Fire Vision" (V3), when Ellen holds up the "Big Bible."
	late Jan	The next day, Samuel Foss (Ellen's brother-in-law) arrives and takes Ellen to Poland, ME, where she shares her first three visions for the first time outside of Portland (date from Otis Nichols to William Miller, April 20, 1846).
	Feb-Mar	Ellen travels with her sister Sarah to the scattered Adventists in Orrington (where she meets James White), Garland, Exeter (receives V5), Atkinson (where she is warned of a coming trial, V6, and Israel Dammon is arrested), and Topsham, ME (receives V8); Corinth, VT (receives V10); Claremont (receives V11), Grantham (receives V12), and Springfield, NH; Portland (where she has the "New Earth Vision," V16) and Poland, ME.
	summer	Ellen relates her visions in Boston, Roxbury, Dorchester, Randolph, New Bedford, Carver, and Fairhaven, MA.
	Aug 19	James White describes Ellen Harmon's first vision in a letter published in *The Day-Star*, Sept. 6, 1845.
	Oct	At Carver, MA, Ellen receives the "Time of Trouble Vision" (V29), condemning time setting for Christ's return.
	Dec 20	Ellen writes out her first vision, which is published in *The Day-Star* of January 24, 1846.
1846	spring	Ellen has the "Randolph Vision" (V32) at the home of Zaccheus Thayer as she holds a quarto Bible in vision.
	Aug 30	James White and Ellen Harmon are married in Portland, ME.
	autumn	James and Ellen White accept the seventh-day Sabbath.
	Nov	Ellen receives the "Opening Heavens Vision" (V42), convicting Joseph Bates of the visions' authenticity.
1847	3 Apr 3	Ellen has the "Sabbath Halo Vision" (V46) with the halo of light around the fourth commandment.
	Aug 26	Henry Nichols White, first child of James and Ellen White, is born.
1848	Apr-Oct	James and Ellen attend Sabbath conferences in Rocky Hill, Bristol, CT; Port Gibson, Brooklyn, Volney, and Hannibal, NY; Topsham, ME; and Dorchester, MA.
	Oct	James and Ellen leave Henry to be raised by Frances Howland in Topsham, ME, until November 1853.
	autumn	Ellen receives "Filthy Weed Vision" (V55), instructing God's people to give up tobacco, tea, and coffee.
	Nov 18	Ellen receives the "Like the Rising of the Sun Vision" (V57), encouraging James to begin publishing.
1849	Jul	James White begins publishing *The Present Truth*, in Middletown, CT, to share the Sabbath truth.
	Jul 28	James Edson White, second child of James and Ellen White, is born.
	Aug	James and Ellen move to Centerport, NY, with William and Lydia Harris to publish *The Advent Review*.
	Nov	James and Ellen move to Oswego, NY, where James continues printing *The Present Truth* in December.
1850	Nov	James and Ellen move to Paris, ME, and begin publishing *The Second Advent Review and Sabbath Herald*.
1851	Aug 5	James and Ellen move to Saratoga Springs, NY, where Ellen's sister Sarah marries Stephen Belden.
	Sep	Ellen White's first book, *A Sketch of the Christian Experience and Views of Ellen G. White*, is published.
	Oct 23-Nov 18	Conferences in Medford, MA; Washington, NH; East Bethel, Johnson, and Vergennes, VT (see CHART-3)
	Dec 22-Feb 13	James and Ellen attend conferences in Camden, Oswego, Lincklaen, and Bath, NY.
1852	Mar 12-15	James and Ellen attend an organizing conference in Ballston Spa, NY.
	Apr	James and Ellen move to Rochester, NY.
1853	Jun	Case and Russell rebel against Ellen White's reproof from a vision and become disaffected.
1853	Dec	Ellen White's second book, *A Supplement to the Christian Experience and Views of Ellen G. White*, is published.
1854	Aug	William Clarence White, third child of James and Ellen White, is born. Disaffected Adventists first publish *The Messenger of Truth*, which ceases publication by the end of 1857.

In 1857 *A Sketch of the Christian Experience and Views of Ellen G. White* (1851) was bound and sold with *Supplement to the Christian Experience and Views of Ellen G. White* (1854). The volume pictured above, measuring $3\frac{5}{8}$ x $5\frac{7}{8}$ inches, was purchased by George W. Newman the same month it was advertised in *Review and Herald*, March 5, 1857. It included Testimony for the Church, Nos. 1 and 2, which had been published in 1856 as a single pamphlet with consecutive page numbering.

NOTES

[1] "Mrs. White's Dreams" and "William Miller's Dream" are in an appendix to *The Christian Experience and Views of Mrs. E.G. White* in *Early Writings* (1882), though Ellen White had mentioned her two early dreams in ExV 4 and first published them in 1860 in 2SG 16–20. Chronologically, Mrs. White placed the dreams after her baptism (2SG 14), which took place on June 26, 1842 (1BIO 372).

[2] See **EXHIBIT-1**, nos. 5, 15, 29, 32, 40; *online* **EXHIBIT-7**, no. 104. Many of that era used this exclamation; see Ron Graybill, " 'Glory! Glory! Glory!' When Adventists Shouted for Joy," *Adventist Review*, Oct. 1, 1987, pp. 12, 13.

[3] See Kevin Morgan, https://www.academia.edu/96259375/Dialogue_Regarding_Ellen_Whites_Visions_and_Literary_Sources.

[4] Supporters of this view cite general similarities between her visions and the writings of William Foy, William Miller, and John Milton. See **EXHIBIT-3** and **4**. Some cite Denis Fortin's surprise at finding similarities between the "Great Controversy Vision" (**~V189**) and Milton, but Denis Fortin clarified that he was "comparing 1SP [1870] and *Paradise Lost*" (Fortin, email Aug. 7, 2024). The similarities weren't verbatim quotations because the style of *The Spirit of Prophecy*, vol. 1 [1SP] is simple prose and the style of *Paradise Lost* is Old English poetry.

[5] D. T. Bourdeau, RH, Nov. 10, 1885, p. 700. For Ellen White's testimony to Jules-Etienne Dietschy, foreman of the Basel press, see LS 282, 283; EGWEurope 50. Jules-Etienne Dietschy, Albert Vuilleumier, and Jules-Henri Guenin requested, in a November 1872 letter, that the Seventh-day Adventists send an American missionary to Switzerland (GC Archives, Record Group 72, Box 13721D, folder "Albert Vuilleumier original letters"). They sent John N. Andrews, whose son, Charles Melville Andrews, married Dietschy's daughter Marie Ann.

[6] To the charge that James White controlled her visions, she responded that she had visions when he was not present (Lt. 2, 1874). Notable examples were her "Randolph Vision" (**V32**) and her "Protection in Storm Vision" (**V34**).

[7] Merritt G. Kellogg, M.D., Battle Creek, MI, Dec. 28, 1890, in J. N. Loughborough, RP 95; see **EXHIBIT-1**, no. 18, for the rest of this eyewitness account. Francis Pinkney Drummond, who had preached the Advent with Merritt E. Cornell (see AHBA, April 7, 1849, p. 127; AHBA, June 2, 1849, p. 191), became a physician and moved to Livingston County where he married Maria Van Drummond, née Leuven (see *History of Livingston County*, 1880, p. 407). Joseph Turner, who practiced mesmerism (hypnotism), claimed he could mesmerize her but, when given the opportunity, was unable to do so (2SG 62.1; Ms. 131, 1906; LSMS 142.2, 4). Later, Turner became a self-proclaimed homeopathic and hydropathic physician. His advertisement in the 1860 Hartford, Connecticut, City Directory declared: "The only Diploma he exhibits is his uniform success" (see *online* **EXHIBIT-7**, p. 284, (b)). For more regarding the use of hypnotism, see Theodore E. Wade, *Spirit Possession: The Counterfeit with Many Faces*, pp. 50–52, at https://archive.org/details/spiritpossession0000wade. Regarding her enthusiastic shouts of "glory" and the shouting of others in their services, see Graybill, "Enthusiasm in Early Adventist Worship," *Ministry*, Oct. 1991, pp. 10–12.

[8] George I. Butler, RH, June 9, 1874, p. 201. For the eyewitnesses from whom he summarized these facts, see **EXHIBIT-1**. Butler never saw her in vision (G. I. Butler, "The Early Visions of Mrs. E. G. White," RH, Aug. 17, 1916, p. 9), and though he was wounded by an open rebuke from her pen for failing to act decisively as General Conference president, to his credit, he never lost faith in her divine calling.

[9] See J. N. Loughborough, "Remarkable Fulfillments of the Visions," RH, Dec. 25, 1866, p. 30; GSAM 204. Transcriptions of Ellen's spoken words in vision are found in Ms. 1, 1848 (**V56**); Ms. 6, 1849 (**V74**); Ms. 5, 1849 (**V77**); Ms. 10, 1850 (**V100**); and Ms. 1, 1852 and Ms. 2, 1852 (**V120**).

[10] Marion Concordia Crawford (née Stowell) to Ellen G. White, Oct. 9, 1908, at https://ellenwhite.org/correspondence/236643. Marion

shared a pamphlet on the Sabbath with John N. Andrews in the spring of 1844 (*Advent Pioneers Biographical Sketches and Pictures*, 4.6).

[11] Sarah B. Harmon to Polly Davis Lawrence, July 29, 1850, at https://ellenwhite.org/correspondence/261019, emphasis added.

[12] Lt. 8, 1851, Nov. 12, from Waterbury, VT. "I saw *that*" usually involves the interpretation of what a visionary experience meant.

[13] Among these are James White's references in "A Word to the 'Little Flock,'" which are in *italics* in the notes. Included in these are references to 2 Esdras and Wisdom of Solomon, two books of the Apocrypha published in some Protestant Bibles and considered Scripture because of their spiritual and prophetic insights. The Harmon family Bible, which was an 1822 Joseph Teal Columbian Family and Pulpit Bible, included the Apocrypha. Other editions of the Teal Bible did not include it. Ezra L'Hommedieu Chamberlain advertised copies of the Apocrypha in RH, June 2, 1851, p. 96; RH, Aug. 5, 1851, p. 8.

[14] Minor editorial changes from the earlier wording have not been noted. For variations in the early printings of Ellen White's first vision, see EXHIBIT-5. See also Ron Graybill, "Visions and Revisions—part 1," *Ministry*, February 1994, p. 12, and "Visions and Revisions—part 2," *Ministry*, April 1994, p. 8. Every book of Ellen White has been compiled from her previous writing. The difference is that, from her midlife on, she had assistance in editing her book manuscripts for smoothness, and after her death, the compilations of her writings didn't have her mind to review them, so they tend to be gatherings of distinct quotations with added headings. For *Steps to Christ*, see "The Story of Steps to Christ" at https://www.academia.edu/36288932/The_Story_of_Steps_to_Christ.

[15] 1SG 6.1, emphasis added; Roswell Fenner Cottrell.

[16] Account adapted from Merlin Burt, "'My Burden Left Me' Ellen White's Conversion Story," *Adventist Review*, Oct. 25, 2001, pp. 8–12. Ellen White wrote of these events in YI, Dec. 1852, pp. 20–22.

[17] LS 9, 17, 50; ST, Jan. 6, 1876. The public common may have been the Park Street Common between Park and State Streets, bounded on the north and south by Spring and Gray Streets. "Ellen and her sister may have been returning from visiting the downtown area, where their father operated his hat shop, or maybe they were just playing in the park" (Merlin Burt, *Adventist Pioneer Places*, pp. 35, 37).

[18] A rod is equal to five and a half yards. It was a common term in measuring distance in the 19th century.

[19] *Life Sketches* (1880), p. 131.

[20] ST, Jan. 6, 1876.

[21] ST, Jan. 13, 1876; Life Sketches manuscript (unpublished), pp. 4, 5; *Life Sketches* (1880), pp. 132, 133.

[22] *Life Sketches* (1880), p. 132.

[23] Harlowe Harris, *The Portland Directory, for the Year 1841*, Portland: Arthur Shirley & Son, which includes a list of private schools.

[24] 1T 13.

[25] ST, Jan. 13, 1876; *Life Sketches* (1880), p. 135.

[26] LS 21, 22.

[27] LSMS 12; see also *Life Sketches* (1880), p. 136; ST, Jan. 13, 1876.

[28] *Catalogue of Books in the Sunday School Library of the Methodist Episcopal Church, Chestnut Street, Portland, Maine*, Staples & Lunt, Printers, Portland, 1854.

[29] LSMS 22; see also *Life Sketches* (1880), pp. 146, 147; ST, Feb. 3, 1876.

[30] LS 20, 21. Zoltán Szallós-Farkas contrasts the intellectual focus of Miller's meetings with the more emotion-charged Methodist meetings (*A Search for God*, p. 52). In her 1909 biographical information blank, Ellen White supplied "Probably in March, 1840" as the date of her conversion. See the facsimile of her biographical information blank accompanying *online* EXHIBIT-7, p. 396.

[31] ST, Jan. 20, 1876; 1T 16.

[32] ST, Jan. 20, 1876; LS 22.

[33] *Life Sketches* (1880), pp. 139, 140; LS 23.

[34] LSMS 21, 22; see also ST, Jan. 27, 1876; 1T 17, 18.

[35] YI, Dec. 1852, p. 21. How "The Old Baptising Shore" was described: "Another of the old landmarks that has been obliterated by the march of modern improvements is the old baptizing beach in the eastern part of the city in a locality known as 'Joppa.' It was a good beach, free from rocks and was well adapted for the performance of that ordinance. Here was where Elder Brown of the Christian chapel on Temple street and Elder Fleming of the Casco Street Church and sometimes other religious denominations baptized their converts. It was 'going down Jordan's banks' to many a sin-sick soul. . . . And then there was the large mansion opposite the shore, surrounded by a large field, where lived Artemus Prentice, and in his house the candidates clothed themselves in baptismal robes and proceeded to the beach" ("The Old Baptising Shore," Portland *Evening Express*, April 11, 1891, p. 1, at https://www.newspapers.com/image/851486503). "Pastor Brown" is Samuel E. Brown, of Portland. The date of the baptism is verified by Portland Chestnut Street Methodist Episcopal Church records, at https://whiteestate.org/about/issues/egw-records. See summary of records at https://archive.org/details/MerlinD.BurtcompiledByRecordsPertainingToTheRobertHarmonFamily. Artemus Prentiss lived on Fore Street between 1834 and 1841 (see https://digitalcommons.usm.maine.edu/por_directories/3; https://www.ancestry.com/imageviewer/collections/2469/images/14318418?pId=889870720).

[36] ST, Jan. 27, 1876; *Life Sketches* (1880), p. 145; first described in YI, Dec. 1852, p. 21; *A Statistical History of the Maine Conference of the Methodist Episcopal Church From 1793 to 1893*, collected and arranged by Daniel Boddy Randall, Portland: Lakeside Press, 1893, p. 119. For the church records on Ellen Harmon's baptism, acceptance into full membership, and disfellowshipping, see and https://adventistdigitallibrary.org/islandora/object/adl%3A22251104.

[37] ST, Feb. 3, 1876; LS 26.

[38] See https://archive.org/details/FrederickHoytWeLiftedUpOurVoicesLikeATrumpetMilleritesInPortland for more on Beethoven Hall.

[39] ST, Feb. 3, 1876; LS 27–2.

[40] LSMS 32; LS 29, 30; Ms. 80, 1903.

[41] ST, Feb. 10, 1876; LSMS 35; LS 32; ExV 4.1.

[42] ST, Feb. 10, 1876; LSMS 39; LS 35. The dreams are given in 2SG 16–20; comments on their significance in Szallós-Farkas, p. 55–59.

[43] ST, Feb. 24, 1876; LSMS 39; LS 36, emphasis added. Advent Christian Luther Boutelle described visiting Levi Stockman during his last sickness (Luther Boutelle, *Sketch of the Life and Religious Experience of Eld. Luther Boutelle*, p. 80, at https://archive.org/details/sketchlifeandreooboutgoog). Donald Casebolt compared Ellen White's dreams to the visionary experiences of Caleb Rich, the founder of

American Universalism, and Richard Randel (actually Benjamin Odger Randall), a founder of the Freewill Baptists: "Because they were convicted that they had received such doctrines during personal visionary experiences with Christ, they were certain that these doctrines were eternal truths" (Casebolt, *Child of the Apocalypse*, p. 56). Yet, Ellen White's dreams were encouragements, not the basis for doctrines.

[44] ST, Feb. 24, 1876; LSMS 43; LS 39.

[45] LS 38, 39; ExV 4. Many Methodists believed sanctification to be an instantaneous work of grace, sometimes called the "second blessing." For them it was not a state of sinless perfection, but rather one of perfect love and right intentions. After her visit with Stockman, Ellen attended a meeting at her uncle's house and, while kneeling in prayer, felt a complete relief from her despair. "I praised God from the depths of my heart," she wrote. "The Spirit of God rested upon me with such power that I was unable to go home that night" (LS 38). The uncle was likely Russell Wright, married to Dorcas Wright, née Gould, the sister of Ellen White's mother, Eunice Harmon, née Gould. The Wrights appear on the 1840 US Census in Portland, ME, and her Aunt Dorcas signed two witness statements, affirming that Ellen had not engaged in the fanaticism of the "no-work theory." Neither had she crept like a baby in "voluntary humility," nor promoted the view that the Second Advent had occurred spiritually, nor had she supported "spiritual union," which led to immorality (3SG 301, 302).

[46] See "Leader's Meeting Minutes of the Chestnut Street Methodist Episcopal Church in Portland, Maine," at https://adl.b2.adventistdigitallibrary.org/concern/published_works/22251104_millerism_and_methodists_in_maine_1830s_and_1840s, pp. 76, 77; https://adventistdigitallibrary.org/adl-366730/records-leaders-meetings-chestnut-street-methodist-church-photocopy, pp. 129, 140, 143, 166, 173, 183, for more information regarding the Harmon family.

[47] 1T 32, referencing Phil. 4:7.

[48] ST, Feb. 24, 1876; LSMS 45; LS 41, 42. Casebolt assumes that the "pretty miss" who spoke in meeting in Beethoven Hall in Portland was Ellen Harmon (Casebolt, p. 35). The description is by Matthew Franklin Whittier: "No sooner had this vindictive 'Son of Thunder' ceased, than he was succeeded by a pretty Miss of 'sweet sixteen,' or thereabouts, who, commencing in a very low, soft voice, gradually rose to the most peircing [*sic*] treble, as she descanted upon a sort of vision she had had the night before, in which she had seen the awful scenes of the judgment enacted. She was rather pretty and had a very benevolent and mild cast of countenance, which contrasted strangely with the fiendish exultation with which she described the coming agonies of her unbelieving friends and acquaintances" (*Portland Transcript*, Nov. 1, 1845, pp. 228, 229, at https://books.google.com/books?id=2OOcJfVYLjYC&pg=PA225). However, Ellen was not that pretty and was "rather dark," according to her own appraisal. Also, she affirmed that she did not have a vision until the winter of 1844/1845 (2SG 69.1).

[49] YI, Nov. 3, 1908; LSMS 46; LS 42. Casebolt sees this as the beginning of her being "God's messenger" (Casebolt, p. 34). He also takes a statement of James White as meaning that she acted as a public exhorter in different churches: "'Her experience was so rich and her testimony so powerful that ministers and leading men of different churches sought her labors as an exhorter in their several congregations'" (Casebolt, p. 49, quoting LS80 126). However, Casebolt omits the next sentence, which changes the sense of the one he quoted: "But at that time she was very timid, and little thought that she was to be brought before the public to speak to thousands." That James was speaking of her addressing thousands *in the future* is clarified by Ellen White's description of these earlier meetings, before she had her first vision, as "our little meetings" (Casebolt, p. 59; ST, Feb. 24, 1876; LS80 163; LS 41).

[50] ST, March 30, 1876; LSMS 75; 1T 54.

[51] Ms. 190, 1903.

[52] Ellen White described the two reactions to the disappointment among Advent believers: some renounced their faith in the former reckoning of the prophetic periods and others looked to the symbolism of the two phases of heavenly ministry in the biblical sanctuary as applying to the ministry of Christ in heaven (4SP 271, 272). Hiram Edson, in Port Gibson, NY, issued his own 16-page appraisal, in September 1850, stating: "It is highly necessary that we also 'remember,' and confess 'all the way' the Lord our God has led us in our Advent experience, which brings us to the keeping of his commandments under the voice of the third angel. . . . Then I repeat it, let us 'remember ALL the way the Lord' our God 'led' us through the proclamation of the hour (or time) of his judgment, the fall of Babylon, and the midnight cry. These messages brought us to the shut door, and an open door, which brought the commandments of God to our view" (*The Advent Review* Extra, Sept. 1850, p. 2). He also addressed the doctrine that seemingly replaced belief in the fulfilment of the tenth day of the seventh month—the "Age to Come" doctrine, quoting Rev. 22:11, 12: "We can have no faith in the new doctrine, now being taught, of probation in the age to come, after the second Advent. Before Christ comes in the clouds of heaven to raise the dead and change the living saints, the great plan and work of salvation by his blood, will be finished. Before our Great High Priest leaves the Sanctuary in heaven, the sins of all Israel will be blotted out, and put upon the head of the scape-goat, and by him borne into the land of separation, or forgetfulness. Then 'He that is UNJUST, let him be UNJUST STILL; and he which is FILTHY, let him be FILTHY STILL; and he that is righteous, let him be righteous still; and he that is holy, let him be holy still. - And behold, I come quickly; and my reward is with me, to GIVE EVERY MAN according as his work shall be.' Rev. xxii, 11, 12" (*The Advent Review* Extra, p. 14).

[53] Loughborough reasoned: "To relieve the mother, who had quite a family to care for, the sisters would wheel Ellen to their house for a day or two to relieve the mother. It was thus that she was at the home of Sister Haines, when she had her first vision" (GSAM 535.3). Ellen White said her mother was not well (Ms. 131, 1906). Douglass mistakenly took this to mean in a wheelchair (MOL 63). Three Mills siblings had attended the third "General Conference of Christians Expecting the Advent of the Lord" at the Casco Street Christian church in Portland, Oct. 12–14, 1841: Elizabeth, her sister Orinda (Berry) (Haines) Nash, née Mills (the widow of the brother of Elizabeth's husband Benjamin), and their brother Jacob Mills, Jr. Elizabeth had older children with her first husband, Richard I. Libby, who had died in 1833. Elizabeth married John Pearson, Sr., in 1864, after his second wife Nancy Pearson, née Lydston, had died in 1863 and Benjamin had died in 1858. John's son by his first wife, Harriet Poor Pearson, née Carlton, had traveled and preached the Advent with James White.

[54] GSAM 535. The earliest dating of the vision as being in December 1844 was from James White, WLF 22 (May 30, 1847) and then from Ellen White, Lt. 3, 1847 (July 13); RH, July 21, 1851, art. A; ExV 5.3 (1851). In 1874, she had forgotten exactly when she had the vision: "But I had no vision until about January or February, I cannot now state definitely which" (Lt. 2c, 1874, Aug. 24). From 1880 to 1888, she wrote that she "had no vision until 1845" (LS80 221; 1T 72.3; LS88 221). For the house location for the first vision, see "The Hunt for Elizabeth Haines' House, Where Ellen White Had Her First Vision," at https://documents.adventistarchives.org/Resources/Encyclopedia%20of%20Seventh-Day%20Adventists/Haines,%20E%20-%20Hunt_for_Elizabeth_Haines_House.pdf.

[55] Heb. 13:5.

[56] The "Midnight Cry" is from Matt. 25:6. Joseph Turner and Apollos Hale published Turner's view of the "Midnight Cry" and the pre-Advent judgment in the single issue of the *Advent Mirror*, Boston, January 1845 (https://encyclopedia.adventist.org/article?id=B8SY; https://archive.org/details/A.haleJ.turnerHasNotTheSaviorComeAsTheBridegroom1845). For more on the contents of Turner and Hale's paper and on the historical development of the "Shut Door" teaching, the movement built on acceptance of the validity of the "Midnight Cry," see Merlin Burt, "The Historical Background, Interconnected Development, and Integration of the Doctrines of the Sanctuary, the Sabbath, and Ellen White's Role in Sabbatarian Adventism from 1844 to 1849," Doctoral Dissertation, 2002, at https://digitalcommons.andrews.edu/dissertations/19, particularly pages 77-82. For the Miller-Himes dialogue on the Shut Door, see Burt, pp. 88–90. Turner wrote from South Paris, ME, on Jan. 23, 1845: "In every place I visited I found a goodly number, I think quite a majority, who were and are now believing that our work is all done for this world, and that the atonement was completed on the tenth day of the seventh month. Nearly all who heard me gladly received the message" (*Hope of Israel*, in HSAM 398).

[57] Elizabeth Haines' house was two stories tall. "Up chamber" meant going upstairs to a room on the upper level.

[58] "In what I should cut across his track" means "to avoid contradicting the view that he was teaching."

[59] Turner was residing temporarily in Portland with other Adventists and later in Poland (AHBA, Nov. 30, 1847, p. 177). By 1850, he was in Hartford, CT (US Census). From Portland he went to Dorchester, MA, staying with Freeman Greenwood Brown. While there in January, he and Hale published his new bridegroom views in Boston. He also went to Lowell, MA; Hartford, CT; and Worcester, MA (HSAM 398). Then he went to New York City (Turner to William Miller, Feb. 7, 1845), where he presented his bridegroom view to Samuel Sheffield Snow in four discourses on Feb. 10, in Franklin Hall (Burt, 115, n2; *Voice of Truth*, April 16, 1845, p. 20; HSAM 398). Snow accepted the view, promoting it in *The Jubilee Standard*, which was published from March 18 to August 7, 1845. Ellen's first vision preceded the publication of the *Advent Mirror*, despite the allegation that it was based upon Turner's view (Steve Daily, *Ellen G. White: A Psychobiography*, p. 52; http://www.truthorfables.com/Five_Loves_no_Fish.htm). The unread paper that Ellen described being in the house was the *Hope of Israel Extra*, published Dec. 20, 1844. The *Extra* (of which no copy is known to still exist) could not have included Turner's new view since he reported to young Ellen that he had just shared his *new* view the night before, and William Miller did not cite it as the source of the new view, when responding in Joseph Marsh's paper, *The Voice of Truth*, Feb. 19, 1845 (available at https://coggc.org/wp-content/uploads/2023/07/1844-Voice-of-Truth-vols-1-3-1844-J-Marsh.pdf), but rather cited Hale and Turner's *Advent Mirror* (see AR, Aug. 1850, p. 10). Snow himself also cited the *Advent Mirror* (see https://adventistdigitallibrary.org/adl-424773/book-judgment-delivered-israel-elijah-messenger-everlasting-covenant, pp. 83–105).

[60] About sixty in Portland accepted the vision and through it regained their confidence in the fulfillment of prophecy concerning October 22, 1844 (WLF 22). Noah Lunt was among those who first heard it (EGWE 458). Since seating at Robert Harmon's house was limited, arrangements must have been made for a larger meeting place for Ellen to relate her views (see Ms. 131, 1906).

[61] Allusion to 2 Cor. 12:9. In 5T 655–657, she describes, in greater detail, her trepidation about sharing the vision.

[62] "Father" was a term of respect for older Adventists, such as John Pearson, Sr., Edward Andrews, Henry Emmons, and Stephen Pierce.

[63] Ellen White recalled another incident that illustrated his affliction. "Old Father Pearson stood out pretty strong, but one morning Father went down there—he always had to pass where old Deacon Pearson lived, it was about a mile from our house. Father Pearson had rheumatism, and used to rub alcohol into his limbs. ([My father] was a hatter and he had to use alcohol in his business.) Father went to leave him a bottle of alcohol, and every single member of the family had no strength in them. The power of God was upon them, and they were the ones that had had the greatest trouble about it. They prayed. Father found he could not do anything there, so he took his bottle and went to his office" (Ms. 131, 1906).

[64] For responses to the charge that the Ellen G. White Estate no longer believes the "Big Bible" part of the "Ball of Fire Vision" (V3), see Arthur Lacey White, at https://ellenwhite.org/media/document/2475, and Tim Poirier, at https://ellenwhite.org/media/document/1686.

[65] Allusions to Rev. 21:27; 22:14; and 21:6.

[66] It is called "Megquier's Hill" (spelled "Macquires" in Lt. 37, 1890) because of the Megquier family who lived there. John Megquier was the most interested in the Advent message. He later moved from West Poland to Saco, ME. The first issue of *The Hope of Israel*, printed July 19, 1844, and edited by Joseph Turner and John Pearson, Jr., describes an early Millerite conference held at Megquier's Hill (see HST, Aug. 7, 1844, p. 5; https://adventist.news/news/recently-discovered-document-sheds-light-on-adventisms-origins).

[67] *Daily Eastern Argus*, April 28, 1845, p. 4, repeated the story of the arrest of Joseph Turner and Ellen Harmon at John Megquier's house, Wednesday, April 23, 1845. Otis Nichols referenced an attempted arrest (see https://ellenwhite.org/correspondence/269221).

[68] William M. Jordan and his sister Sarah Merrill Jordan lived in West Poland (see http://archive.org/details/sketchlifeandreo0boutgood, pp. 78, 79). Their father was a patriarchal leader among the Adventists (see *Life Sketches*, 1880, p. 89; *Sketch of the Life and Religious Experience of Luther Boutelle*, p. 79). The Jordans withdrew their membership from the Free-Will Baptist Church in 1844 (Bruce Weaver, unpublished manuscript on the Millerites in Maine, chapter 4). Sarah married Peter Staples, in 1848, after the death of his first wife in 1846.

[69] James recalled meeting Ellen nearly two years earlier in Portland (*Life Sketches*, 1880, p. 126). It may have slipped her mind that they had previously met, but she later recalled, "I was introduced to James White by the Pearsons in Portland" (DF 733c, Dec. 12, 1906). No source explains what he was doing in Orrington. Virgil Robinson conjectured that James had walked 20 miles from Palmyra (*James White*, p. 34). Ellen's mention of "Brother W." on her return trip to Orrington suggests James was living and working in Orrington at that time.

[70] Ellen White mentioned Louisa A. Brackett, née Foss, the sister of her brother-in-law, as her "constant and faithful companion at this time" (ST, May 4, 1876), and Sarah Jordan, who travelled with her to Orrington. However, pointing out that she had female chaperones would not have remedied the situation. She felt that only by going home to Portland could she refute the "lying reports" (2SG 39.1).

[71] These fanatical persons included Joseph Turner, an itinerate Adventist leader who, at first, accepted Ellen Harmon's prophetic gift, and John Howell, another early Adventist leader, who accepted the "Bridegroom" shut door teaching at first but then rejected Ellen White's prophetic role, working against her, as did his wife Lucinda S. Howell (later Burdick), née Armstrong, and aligned with the Advent Christians (https://m.egwwritings.org/en/book/12667.5328).

[72] By "blaze it out" she meant to spread it like wildfire.

[73] Sister Dearborn was Mary "Polly" Dearborn, née Wiggin, of Corinna, ME (see map page 28). The "shut door" was concerning Christ's entering the Most Holy Place. We see the attitude toward those excluded by the door being shut in contributors to *The Jubilee Standard*, using the phrase, "Remember Lot's wife," to encourage Adventists to not look back with sympathy on rejectors of the message of mercy.

[74] For the "Bridegroom Vision" (V5), see ExV 43.1. Ellen White identifies this vision as helping her understand "the parable of the Bridegroom's coming and shutting the door." "The Lord showed me the travail of the Advent band and midnight cry in December, but He did not show me the Bridegroom's coming until February following" (Lt. 3, 1847). James later wrote: "I think it is more safe to acknowledge that we may have been mistaken in what constituted the coming of the Bridegroom, and the shut door" (RH, Feb. 1851, p. 47).

[75] The *Piscataquis Farmer* attributes the ten stanzas of the hymn to John Craig, an Irish-born shoemaker, carpenter, and preacher who lived in Clinton and Natick, MA. In the fall of 1842 and spring of 1844, Craig preached in Halifax, Nova Scotia. March 9, 1851 he preached in North Abington, MA; March 12 and 13, 1851, in Haverhill, MA; March 16, 1851, in Newburyport, MA (AHSTR, March 8, 1851, p. 32); and May 25 and June 15, 1851, in Feltonville, MA (AHSTR, May 17, 1851, p. 112; May 24, 1851, p. 120; June 14, 1851, p. 144). Five of his children came down with typhus fever (AHSTR, Nov. 2, 1850, p. 317). Craig's infant daughter, Esther Ann, died Sept. 4, 1851, and his wife Elizabeth died Nov. 22, 1851 (AHSTR, Dec. 6, 1851, p. 342). Craig defended Joshua V. Himes against slander (AHSTR, Jan. 18, 1851, p. 412; HST, Jan. 3, 1844, p. 164; April 3, 1844, p. 72). Maintaining contact with the Sabbatarian Adventists, Craig reported his son George Franklin missing in RH, Feb. 2, 1860, p. 86.

[76] Dammon's arrest was on February 16 at the home of James Ayer, Jr., a farmer of Atkinson, ME. (Ayer's father signed a testimonial in 2SG 302.) The arresting officer was Joseph Moulton (John Shepley, *Reports of Cases Determined in the Supreme Judicial Court of the State of Maine*, vol. 15, Maine Reports, vol. 28, 1850, p. 505, available at https://books.google.com/books?id=9XooAQAAMAAJ&pg=PA505). Judge Moses Swett and Moulton were brothers-in-law through Moulton's sister, Mary. Ellen White's description of "the power of God" in the room witnessed by their singing and shouts of glory parallels Moulton's description of the meeting as "one continued shout." Ellen White insisted that the group did not resist arrest. William T. Hannaford; Hester A. Ring, née Hannaford; Dorcas Somes Hannaford, née Ayer; and James Ayer, Sr. affirmed the truthfulness of Ellen White's account (2SG 302). Ruth W. Wood, née Ayer, whose name was also attached to the affirmation, denied the account in 1888. Joseph Moulton testified: "A number of women jumped on to him [Dammon]—he clung to them, and they to him. So great was the resistance, that I with three assistants, could not get him out" (https://archive.org/details/TrailOfElderI.Dammon1845). The plausibility of his explanation diminishes as one wonders how four men, holding onto Dammon's arms and legs, which were the only handholds, could not overpower the women to remove Dammon, if that was what really happened. However, manhandling the women was apparently not a concern, for Moulton says he returned with more men and "overpowered" the women. The explanation reminds one of the testimony of the soldiers guarding the tomb of Jesus diminishing the supernatural nature of what happened by declaring that the disciples came and stole Jesus' body while they slept.

[77] Attorney Joseph Darling Brown, who worked for James Stuart Holmes, substantiated many points in Ellen White's account: "I well remember a remarkable scene in the year 1843 [1845], in which he [Holmes] was an active participant. The Adventists or followers of William Miller were numerous in the neighboring town of Atkinson. Their preaching of the second coming of Christ was deemed a heresy by leading citizens and members of other churches. Some of these citizens who opposed the Millerites went to Dover and instituted legal proceedings against Israel Damon and several others who were preachers and leaders in the Miller faith, under the vagrant act. In the old church on the hill they were arraigned before Moses Scott [*sic*], a justice of the peace. Without pecuniary compensation Mr. Holmes volunteered his services for the defense. For four days the courtroom was crowded with people. During the whole time there was a succession of praying, singing of hymns, plaintive and exhilarating, as only the old-style Millerites could sing, shouting, jeers, groans and applause, but above all these occasional distracting sounds could be heard Mr. Holmes' eloquent argument for religious freedom and toleration, and the right of every person to worship God according to the dictates of his own conscience, under his own vine and fig tree. At the close of the trial the prisoners were promptly discharged. … I remember it as one of the grandest defenses of religious toleration and freedom that it has ever been my pleasure to listen to or read of" (Letter by Joseph D. Brown of Foxcroft, quoted by John Francis Sprague, *Piscataquis Biography and Fragments*, Bangor, Maine: Charles Glass, 1899, pp. 9, 10; "The Millerites in Maine," *Sprague's Journal of Maine History*, January, February, March, 1922, p. 4, available at https://archive.org/details/spraguesjournal013spra; "James Stewart Holmes: The Pioneer Lawyer of Piscataquis County. Read before the Maine Historical Society May 20, 1886," *Collections and Proceedings of the Maine Historical Society*, Second Series, vol. IV, Portland, ME, 1893, p. 86, available at https://books.google.com/books?id=7Hk9AQAAMAAJ&pg=PA86). Joseph D. Brown was 22 years old and unmarried in February 1845. The errors of "1843" (1845) and "Moses Scott" (Moses Swett) could be faulty transcriptions of Brown's handwritten letter, or there may have been a fading of his memory. It is possible that he was thinking of the whole event—from the meeting and arrest to Dammon's acquittal—as being four days.

[78] Allusion to Matt. 24:30. The hymn is quoted in its entirety in RH, June 19, 1856, p. 63; RH, Feb. 18, 1868, p. 154 (including "They call us now a noisy crew"); in RH, June 26, 1860, p. 46, "noisy crew" became "silly crew" among other changes.

[79] Israel Dammon married Lydia B. Rich in 1838, so, by 1845, they had been married six years, and they had three children: Mary J. Bean, née Dammon (b. 1839), Lizzie C. (b. 1842), and Israel Allen (b. 1844).

[80] Due to their misinterpretation of the "holy kiss" and of men and women sitting on the floor for lack of chairs, several newspapers spread the false allegations that the Millerites engaged in immoral practices. "Warning to Adventists," *Christian Secretary*, April 4, 1845, p. 2, linked Israel Dammon, John Greenleaf Moody, and Dorinda Baker together (from AHSTR March 26, 1845, p. 8) and repeated the false charge that Dammon was "convicted in Maine of the grossest improprieties." There is evidence that the Baptists of Atkinson were dissatisfied with the verdict. "ATROCIOUS CONDUCT. The *Piscataquis Farmer* states that a band of men disguised as Indians, a few days since, forced the doors of a 'Miller' meeting in Atkinson and seized and carried off several persons not supposed to belong to the town and threatened to tar and feather the Adventists if they held any more meetings" (*The Bangor Courier*, April 1, 1845, p. 2).

[81] The ten stanzas published in the *Piscataquis Farmer*, March 7, 1845, are titled, "COME OUT OF HER, MY PEOPLE," and attributed to John Craig. It was "The Jubilee Hymn," at https://archive.org/details/ThingsNewandOldmagazine/THaO_04/page/n59, that provided the keywords to find other hymns with the tune, based on an overlapping stanza beginning, "A little longer here below." The other form of the hymn begins, "I never shall forget the day" and was first published, without music, in *Hymns: Designed for the Use of the Second Advent Band* (1843) by Henry Burchstead Skinner, a Boston publisher, and Norman Stevens, a farmer and Free Baptist minister in Compton, Canada East (see *History of Compton County*, 1896, p. 169; AHSTR, July 8, 1854, p. 215; July 3, 1858, p. 216). The tune for the hymn first appears in J. V. Himes' *Millennial Harp* (1846), at https://hymnary.org/hymn/MHDM1846/B14, but the fuller accompaniment (used on page 32) is found in *Salvation Army Music*, at https://hymnary.org/hymn/SAM1880/251. Craig apparently wrote his own lyrics to the tune. In publishing an

abbreviated version of the hymn, which included only four stanzas—corresponding to stanzas 1, 6, 8, and 9, in the version published in the *Piscataquis Farmer*— James White omitted a verse with the words, "This year's the jubilee" (stanza 3) and altered another to say instead, "And sound the Jubilee." He also changed the words in the overlapping stanza, "Hallelujah, I am free from all sectarian prejudice" to "Hallelujah now I see, that we soon shall be with Jesus" (see *Hymns for God's Peculiar People that Keep the Commandments of God, and the Faith of Jesus*, 1849, at https://adventistdigitallibrary.org/islandora/object/adl%3A22250161 and https://archive.org/details/HymnsForGodsPeculiarPeopleThatKeepTheCommandmentsOfGodAndThe; see the publication notice in PrT, March 1850, p. 56). At the 1899 General Conference, two pioneers sang the first three stanzas with rejoicing and shouts of victory in response (GCDB, March 6, 1899, p. 153). The third stanza had the altered ending, "That the Lord we soon shall see."

[82] Frances Lunt, née Howland, was a daughter of Stockbridge Howland and Louisa Howland, née Morse. She cared for James and Ellen's firstborn, Henry, when they decided it was best for the little one not to travel with them. She later married Noah Norton Lunt, who was likely the last surviving witness of the 60 who heard Ellen White relate her first vision in Portland and was an early witness to Ellen White's "Ball of Fire Vision" (V3) (RH, Jan. 28, 1902, p. 63; 2SG 302; WLF 22). Noah Lunt's first wife was Rebecca E. Lunt, née Chamberlain, and his second wife was Sarah Howland Lunt, née Chamberlain, who were daughters of John C. Chamberlain and Phebe Ripley Chamberlain, née Haskins. Frances provided a witness statement regarding Ellen White in vision (see EXHIBIT-1, no. 13). "For his sturdy defense of truth and his ready succor to the needs of the cause," Stockbridge Howland's house "was called Fort Howland" (*Footprints of the Pioneers*, p. 85).

[83] Witnesses (2SG 302) said that it was not James White who baptized her, as reported in 2SG 44.

[84] "Miss Ayres" could have been Ruth W. Ayer, who was single at the time, though she married Newel N. Wood sometime about 1848; see LS 75, 76.

[85] "Brother Patten" could have been William Wilson Patten who lived in Topsham and frequently appears as an Adventist believer in the *Advent Herald* (e.g., https://archive.org/details/AdventHerald1863V24N14-26).

[86] Louisa A. Brackett, née Foss (c. 1825–1861), married Benjamin F. Brackett in 1851. Louisa was the sister of Samuel Hoyt Foss, who married Ellen White's sister, Mary Plummer Foss, née Harmon.

[87] This was Stephen Files and Eunice B. Files, née Freeman. She later described these same travels: "But we went up to Vermont, and went to New Hampshire, and went all through where there had been the strongest influence in 1843 and 1844. But these families went with us. There was one family, Brother Files and his wife in one sleigh, and [Ralph] Haskins and his relatives—his niece went also—and so we had a little company, so that no reports could be made that I was traveling with an unmarried man. And I had my sister's husband's sister with me. My sister could not go because she had to take care of my mother, who was not well. So I had a great, tall, noble-looking woman, and I have thought what a help she would be to the cause if she was alive now. But she died. My sister's husband's sister came and went with me wherever I went, and there would be perhaps one or two women that would go with us as we traveled" (Ms. 131, 1906).

[88] "Spiritual magnetism" was related to mesmerism. See ST, May 11, 1876; ST, May 16, 1878, p. 146; Adelma von Vay de Vaya, *Spirit Power and Matter*, pp. 123, 124, at https://archive.org/details/in.ernet.dli.2015.227059.

[89] Allusion to Matt. 5:10.

[90] Springfield, according to 2SG 48.1. Grantham is between Claremont and Springfield, NH, but closer and slightly northwest of Springfield.

[91] At the end of 1845, John Howell wrote from West Poland, Maine (DS, Dec. 13, 1845, p. 45). By January, he had abandoned the Midnight Cry (DS, Jan. 31, 1846, p. 34).

[92] On this second trip, William and Sarah Jordan and Ellen Harmon "went from Portland to Orrington, Garland, and Exeter" (GSAM 532.3).

[93] This was Joseph Turner's second wife, Jane Barnard Turner, née Knapp; his first wife, Rebekah Turner, née Strout, had died in 1838.

[94] Her two married sisters in Poland, Maine, were Harriet Gould McCann, née Harmon, and Mary Plummer Foss, née Harmon.

[95] "Brother S." could have been Thomas Smith, a Methodist turned Adventist minister and agent of *The Advent Herald* in Orrington, ME (AHSTR, April 29, 1846, p. 96), who was married to Abigail Smith, née Coan. He is mentioned in Orrington in connection with Israel Dammon (AHSTR, July 22, 1848, p. 199; AHSTR, July 29, 1848, p. 207). In the 1860 US Census, Smith (in dwelling 274) is a neighbor of William Hannaford (in dwelling 278) in Brewer, ME (see https://www.familysearch.org/ark:/61903/3:1:33SQ-GBSS-S85). Hannaford was a witness of the arrest of Israel Dammon (2SG 303). There was an Advent chapel in Orrington, where Thomas Smith preached (AHSTR, Oct. 3, 1857, p. 320).

[96] Allusion to Heb. 6:6.

[97] If "Brother S." was Thomas Smith, then "Sister S." would have been his wife, Abigail Smith, née Coan. Ellen White used initials either because the individual was so well-known that an abbreviation was sufficient or because she wished to protect the person's identity.

[98] "Brother Brown" was George W. Brown, who lived in Orrington and was one of the Adventists who was arrested (*Daily Eastern Argus*, April 28, 1845, at https://archive.org/details/Millerism.-EasternArgusPortlandMe.1845Vol.11April24; *New York Journal of Commerce*, April 30, 1845, p. 2; *New York Tribune*, May 2, 1845, p. 1; *Republican Farmer*, Bridgeport, CT, May 6, 1845, p. 2; *Vermont Watchman and State Journal*, May 16, 1845, p. 1; *Northern Christian Advocate*, May 28, 1845, p. 35; all quoting the *Norway Advertiser*).

[99] Allusion to Eph. 6:6.

[100] Gerald Wheeler identifies "Brother W." as James White (*James White: Innovator and Overcomer*, p. 39). What James was doing in Orrington is unknown.

[101] Allusion to Ps. 55:14.

[102] "Sister Foss" was Louisa Brackett, née Foss. Phebe Gleason Kittredge, née Knapp, was the sister of Joseph Turner's wife Jane.

[103] Allusion to Matt. 26:64.

[104] Allusions to 1 Thess. 4:16; John 5:28, 29.

[105] Allusion to Matt. 24:30, 27.

[106] Though Gerald Wheeler adds James White into the story about the horsewhipping and being dragged to jail (Wheeler, p. 39, from *Ellen G. White, Her Friends and Fellow Workers*, p. 13; cf. James White to Enoch Jacobs, Sept. 6, 1845), James was likely simply reporting.

[107] Ellen used Scripture to show that the resurrection of the dead and the ascension of the living occur in a single event.

[108] The connection with Dammon would place the baptisms near Exeter. However, there are no "Ayres" or "Ayers" in the 1840 US Census for Exeter or Corinna, ME. There are, however, "Ayers" in Atkinson, ME. The baptizing "Mrs. Ayers" may be the "Mrs. Ayres" who is mentioned in Ms. 131a, 1906 in connection with William Henry Hyde and Sister Frances Howland in Topsham, of whom Ellen White must

have had some pity: "One woman—she was holy, tall, dignified, but she was one of the fanatical ones—would go right into a vision and tell them what they must do. They sent for me and I came up. Said I, 'What is it?' They said what she was doing. She was in vision, and she said they must do so and so. The poor woman did not know what spirit she was of. 'But, Sister Howland,' said I, as though I was whispering, 'get a pitcher of cold water, good cold water, and throw it right in her face; that will bring her out of it the quickest of anything you can do.' She started to get the water, but before she got there, [the woman] had come out. She was deceiving them in this way" (Ms. 131a, 1906). Burt and Nix have suggested that the tall, dignified woman could have been Dorinda Baker (Burt, Dissertation, p. 148) or Mary Hamlin (Nix, "Another look at Israel Dammon," note 57), but Dorinda's actions don't seem very dignified, and Mary Whiting, née Hamlin, was then but a "young girl" (Marion Stowell Crawford to EGW, Oct. 9, 1908, p. 4).

109 Ellen White later wrote: "Elder Dammon had the most positive evidences that the visions were of God. He became my enemy only because I bore a testimony reproving his wrongs and his fanatical course, which wounded the cause of God" (Lt. 2, 1874). Dudley M. Canright wrote: "I was personally acquainted with Eld. Dammon, and knew him to be a notorious fanatic. While preaching, he would halloo, and jump about, even over the desk into the congregation. He was a leader of a band of fanatics in Maine in 1845 who held that the dead had arisen and gone up. The visions condemned him for his fanaticism, which caused him to turn against them. He was associated with one Simeon Hall, who disturbed my meetings to that degree that I had to have him arrested to keep the peace" (*Advent Review and Herald of the Sabbath* Extra, April 14, 1874, p. 3). See the description of the trial of Simeon Hall in the Bangor Daily Whig and Courier, Feb. 3, 1846, p. 2, at https://www.newspapers.com/image/663003309/?match=1&terms=Simeon%20Hall.

110 After these two weeks, John Howell got Elizabeth Haines to sign a statement regarding what Ellen said in her delirium; Elizabeth regretted doing so (2SG 69).

111 The manuscript ends here, without describing Ellen White's "New Earth Vision" (**V16**), which is in ExV 13.2–15.1; 2SG 52.1–54.1.

112 Sadly, while setting type for *The Hope of Israel* (Portland, ME), edited by Joseph Turner and John Pearson, Jr., William Henry Hyde came to question and abandon the Adventist view of the coming of the Bridegroom to the marriage in heaven and the shut door (see DS, Oct. 11, 1845, pp. 46). Pictured on page 34 in his military uniform, Hyde served during the Civil War in Co. E, 10th Regiment, Maine Infantry as an army private. Before and after the war, Hyde was a bookseller (see https://www.familysearch.org/ark:/61903/3:1:S3HT-DZZ9-PPV?i=75), a businessman, and then, in 1882, a news agent. He was a Congregationalist (*The Republican Journal*, Belfast, ME, April 22, 1915, p. 2). The poem was published on the back of the March 1853 update of Ellen White's first book and is hymn no. 9 in James White's *Hymns for God's Peculiar People*, published by Richard John Oliphant in 1849 in Oswego. James White later noted that the hymn had also "been published in two or three Second Advent papers, Smith's collection of hymns, and that it finally made its way into the 'Advent Harp,' published by J. V. Himes in 1849." White wryly responded to Himes' dismissal of Ellen White's visions, writing: "Let those who 'despise prophesyings,' and reject the fulfillment of God's word in visions of the 'LAST DAYS,' remember when they sing this hymn, that it was composed from a vision"—a vision giving a foretaste of the glory of God that shall be revealed! ("SWINE'S FLESH," PrT, Nov. 1850, p. 88). It is in *The Seventh-day Adventist Hymnal* as "We Have Heard." For more on Oliphant, search on "Richard Oliphant," at https://adventistdigitallibrary.org.

113 In recounting, in *A Sketch of the Christian Experience and Views of Ellen G. White* (1851) and in *Spiritual Gifts*, vol. 2, *My Christian Experience, Views and Labors in Connection with the Rise and Progress of the Third Angel's Message* (1860), how she shared her first vision with others, Ellen White omitted how she first spoke with Joseph Turner, though she described their conversations in her July 13, 1847, letter to Joseph Bates. It should not come as a surprise that she would omit his involvement since, by the time she published her first book, Turner had become an avowed opponent to her for rebuking his fanaticism.

114 Turner would later give public exhibitions of his ability to control spirit mediums. See "Turner on Spirits," *Hartford Courant* (Hartford, Connecticut), Jan. 5, 1857, p. 2, at https://www.newspapers.com/image/369130490, a facsimile of which is in *online* **EXHIBIT-7**, p. 284, (b).

115 She also quoted herself saying: "Another angel, Lord! Another angel!" and being "taken off in vision right there" (Ms. 131, 1906).

116 Stevens was a Methodist minister who accepted the Advent message and was prone to fanaticism (see *online* **EXHIBIT-7**, no. 130).

117 "Bro. C" in Paris, ME, is likely "Brother Chase"—which was either Methodist minister and farmer Sibley Chase, whose son Peter later married Corinna Claramon Chase, née Stowell—even though there is no record of Sibley becoming an Adventist; or it was more likely farmer Thomas W. Chase, who had become a sabbath-keeping Adventist by 1845 (RH, Aug. 22, 1854, p. 16; RH, Nov. 13, 1856, p. 15). The obituary of his 14-year old daughter, Martha M. Chase, who was keeping the Sabbath at the time of her death, was published in RH, Dec. 27, 1853, p. 200. Sibley and Thomas Chase are on the same page of the 1850 US Census, in dwellings 219 and 217.

118 In LSMS 102.5, Ellen White chose not to identify the "talented minister" as Joseph Turner, but did so in Ms. 131, 1906. This incident, which is linked in Ms. 131, 1906, is out of chronological order there, but linked here because of the connection with Paris, Maine.

119 Some of Turner's fanatical views were "that Christ had come, that the marriage referred to in the parable in Matthew twenty-five had taken place, ... that ... those who had not gone in with him were lost, ... that the six thousand years of the earth's history were ended, ... that Adventists ought not to do any more work" (LSMS 126.2, 3). Joshua V. Himes concluded that Turner was a major promoter of Advent believers not working (AHSTR, June 18, 1845, p. 150).

120 Mary Ann Haskins, née Soren, died in 1850 while Thomas Waldo Haskins was serving a two-year sentence for the affair with his "spiritual wife," Rebecca Love Eaton, who served an eighteen-month sentence in the same house of corrections. Haskins and Eaton married on July 12, 1851, after they both were out of confinement.

121 In LSMS 128.2, Ellen White used the term "young sister" to describe 23-year-old Sarah Jordan, who was under the sway of Joseph Turner. So, who was the "young sister" in this case? Though we do not know with whom Ellen "tarried," one possibility of the "young sister" is the 22-year-old daughter of Adventists Tillson Pratt and Elizabeth Pratt, née Thomas (HST, July 15, 1841; HST, July 27, 1842, p. 136)—Elizabeth Tillson Stetson, née Pratt. Ellen's "Time of Trouble Vision" (**V29**), in Carver, averted disappointment when "many were expecting the Lord to come at the seventh month, 1845" (J. White, WLF 22).

122 Clorinda Fosdick Minor, née Strong, claimed to have had visions, believed in the "Age to Come," and died in Israel, pursuing her belief.

123 Isa. 50:7; 1 Tim. 1:19; Num. 20:17. 2 Esdras 2:47 has "stood so stiffly for the name of the Lord." 2SG 74.1 has "stood stiffly then."

124 Otis Nichols' account, at https://whiteestate.org/legacy/vault-otis_text-asp, identifies Sargent as "G. Sargent"; while HST, Dec. 13, 1843, p. 144, gives his name as "George." George Sargent had traveled from east to west with John D. Poor, proclaiming the soon return of Christ. Many newspapers (e.g., *Portland Press Herald*, Jan. 12, 1843, p. 2; *The Columbia Democrat* [Bloomsburg, PA], Jan. 28, 1843, p. 3) linked George

Sargent with Haverhill, where there was a group of seven Adventist women (RH, Jan. 12, 1864, p. 52), among whom were George's mother, Sarah "Sally" Sargent, née George; George's sister Elizabeth Dubois, née Sargent, and her daughter, Caroline Dubois; and Lucy Ann Sargent, née Hammond, the wife of George's brother Lorenzo Sargent (RH, Dec. 24, 1857, p. 55; RH, Sept. 17, 1861, p. 127; RH, Sept. 24, 1861, p. 135; RH, March 22, 1864, p. 136; RH, April 27, 1876, p. 2). The death of Caroline's father Henry Louis Dubois and of her sister Emily Dubois are listed in RH, Aug. 21, 1860, p. 111. "L. H. Dubois" is referenced in the *Review and Herald* from 1853–1859. Polly D. Lawrence mentioned "Sister Sargent" in her May 1, 1851, letter to Ruth Coggeshall. Lucy Sargent was the one who sent literature about the Sabbath to Larkin Patterson Hodges in Watauga County, North Carolina, leading him to embrace the Sabbath and become the "first Seventh-day Adventist pastor of North Carolina" (see RH, Feb. 27, 1894, p. 143).

125 Nichols described Ellen's visit to Randolph in August 1845 when Joseph Turner, John Howell, and Thomas Haskins undermined the band's belief in the visions and persuaded them that Ellen's visions came through James' mesmerizing. To respond to this assertion, she returned to Randolph without James in early 1846 (see *online* **EXHIBIT-7,** no. 20). Loughborough described the conversation about not going to Boston: "Mr. Nichols related this to me at his own house, in Dorchester, in 1858. He said that he had made all his calculations to go to Boston on Sabbath morning with his carriage to take Miss Harmon to the proposed meeting. That evening, during family prayers, she was taken off in vision. After coming out of it, she said, 'Brother Nichols, I am not going to Boston to-morrow; the Lord has shown me that I must go to Randolph. He has a work for me to do there.' Mr. Nichols had a great regard for his word. He had promised to take her to Boston the next day, and he anxiously inquired, 'What shall I do with my word to Sargent and Robbins?' 'Never mind that,' said Miss Harmon, 'the Lord has bidden me go the other way.' 'Well,' said Mr. Nichols, 'I do not understand it.' 'The Lord showed me that we would understand it when we get there,' said Miss Harmon. 'Well,' said Mr. Nichols, 'there is no way for you to get there unless we go and take you, but I do not know how I will explain matters to the brethren in Boston.' (RP 116, 117).

126 "Z. Thayer" was living in Randolph (JUBST, Aug. 7, 1845, p. 168). In 1843, Thayer was chairman of a conference in Stetson Hall in Randolph (HST, Nov. 4, 1843, p. 104).

127 Allusion to Ps. 27:5.

128 Stephen N. Haskell recounted the story as told him by John Belden: "Brother Ralph and I had taken a field of grass to mow, and Brother White thought of working with us to secure funds for printing the paper. We had the horse at the door ready to drive to Middletown to get a scythe for Brother White when Sister White fainted. We prayed for her. She was taken off in vision and shown that we should not wait to mow the field of grass, but should print the paper at once. Our house was small, and in order to have quiet Brother White took his Bible to my corn barn and there wrote the first paper" (RH, July 31, 1919, p. 16).

129 **V108**, "Not to Return to Paris Vision." Horace Cushman held extreme views of Jesus' teaching, "Sell that ye have, and give alms" (Luke 12:33) and used it to take advantage of Saul Samuel Strong, a generous Adventist who died from a stroke after the Whites moved to Rochester (see 2SG 153–159; Lt. 4, 1851, July 21; Lt. 3, 1851, Aug. 11). Cushman and Strong were neighbors, occupying dwellings 129 and 132 in the 1850 US Census (https://www.familysearch.org/ark:/61903/3:1:S3HT-6WL9-DVF?i=15).

130 For the encouragement of the brethren, see 2SG 151.1.

131 LS 125. Based on James White's own introductory statement, George R. Knight asserted that it was the publication of "A Word to the Little Flock" (May 30, 1847) that began the move toward establishing their own periodical. The pamphlet's contents were written as letters, but there had been a parting of ways with the editor of *The Day-Star* (see *Earliest Seventh-day Adventist Periodicals*, 2005, p. xiv).

132 James and Ellen had accepted the Sabbath in the fall of 1846 from the biblical evidence. Before this, Ellen had not felt the seventh-day Sabbath's importance, thinking that Joseph Bates "erred in dwelling upon the fourth commandment more than upon the other nine" (2SG 82.1). Her "Sabbath Halo Vision" (**V46**), the next year, confirmed what they had learned from Bible study (see Lt. 2, 1874).

133 Ellen G. White, Ms. 2, 1850, Jan. 9. James' words at the time were: "I gave it up forever" (James White to L. Hastings, Jan. 10, 1850).

134 Yet, James White does refer to the "Angels with Rods Vision" (**V74**) and the "Bible Applied Vision" (**V77**) with the months and years in which Ellen White received them in the first of four numbers of *The Advent Review* published in Auburn, NY (AR, Aug. 1850, p. 16).

135 James White understatedly wrote: "Our two dear boys were from us, and six hundred miles from each other. This was a sacrifice" (RH, Jan. 14, 1858, p. 77). Henry Nichols White (born in 1847) stayed with Stockbridge and Louisa Howland at Topsham, ME. James Edson White (born in 1849) stayed with Ira Abbey and Rhoda Bickford Abbey, née Rhodes, at Brookfield, NY, and was cared for by Clarissa Matilda Bonfoey. The Abbeys' daughter Lucinda M. Hall, née Abbey, who married William Hall between 1861 and 1862, became a close friend of Ellen White. The Abbeys, their children, Rhoda's mother, Stephen Belden, Sarah Harmon, Clarissa ("Clara") Bonfoey, and Edson White are listed in the same household in the 1850 US Census for Brookfield, NY, at https://www.familysearch.org/ark:/61903/3:1:S3HT-6917-H4. James and Ellen did not appear on any census in 1850.

136 Jesse Thompson was a "minister" (HST, Dec. 1, 1841, p. 131), an "elder" (*Christian Journal*, March 28, 1844, p. 2), a wedding officiant (*Saratoga Sentinel*, Feb. 5, 1828, p. 3), and an attendee of an 1840 Adventist conference (HST, Nov. 1, 1840, p. 120). See also "J. Tompson," 1855 New York State Census, at https://www.familysearch.org/ark:/61903/3:1:33S7-LBP2-4SB?i=13&cc=1937366.

137 See Ellen G. White, Lt. 1, 1851; Lt. 3, 1851; Lt. 4, 1851; Lt. 7, 1851.

138 "To the Little Remnant Scattered Abroad," Broadside1, April 6, 1846; "A Vision," Broadside3, April 7, 1847; "To Those Who Are Receiving the Seal of the Living God," Broadside2, Jan. 31, 1849 (see facsimiles in 1EGWLM 108, 110, 111).

139 Ellen G. White, Lt. 4, 1851, July 21.

140 In 1857, he would publish two visions; one vision in 1858; one article in 1859; six articles in 1861; ten in 1862; three in 1863; one in 1864; two in 1866; two in 1867; six in 1868; four in 1869; seven in 1870; ten in 1871; and five in 1872. In *The Youth's Instructor*, he published three of her articles in 1852; one in 1853; three in 1854; one in 1855; seven in 1856; two in 1857; one in 1858; two in 1859; one in 1871; two in 1872; seven in 1873; and three in 1874. James White omitted the "1" in "1 Thessalonians." He had published three of Ellen's letters in 1849; four, in 1850; the Extra and Ellen's notice about Eli Curtis' misuse of her visions in 1851; one letter in 1852 (part in ExV54); three in 1853 (also in ExV54); two articles in 1854; one article and a notice in 1855; and two letters and two notices in 1856.

141 James White, *Second Advent Review and Sabbath Herald* Extra, July 21, 1851, p. 4. Funding for the book came short of the $100 printing cost, with donations only totaling $82.90. The last donors listed were Annie R. Smith; Nabby Maria Thompson, née Gilbert, wife of Jesse Thompson; Mary S. Thompson [Mary Susan Seelye, née Thompson]; and Jesse Thompson's youngest daughter (RH, March 23, 1852, p. 112; RH, May 6, 1852, p. 8). The banner used the title of vol. 1 with the typestyle of vol. 2 (Aug. 5–March 23, 1852).

[142] James invited traveling Adventists to call on them "at the corner of Circular and Phila Streets" (RH, Nov. 25, 1851, p. 56). All four corners were rental property. George Young, Jr., purchased the *northwest* corner house on Oct. 12, 1850; Beekman Huling purchased the *southwest* corner house on Aug. 18, 1851; Lewis P. Close purchased the large *northeast* corner house on Oct. 22, 1844; Peter V. Wiggins purchased the *southeast* corner house on July 2, 1849. It is not known which house they lived in, and no original house is still standing. For the location of the post office, see *The Keene New Hampshire Sentinel*, 2 Dec. 1847; *Boyd's Saratoga Springs Directory, 1868–1869*; Cornelius E. Durkee, *Reminiscences of Saratoga and Ballston*, p. 9, at https://www.familysearch.org/library/books/viewer/51225. Loughborough wrote: "Here Mr. Thompson furnished Elder White and his wife house room free" (GSAM 312.2), which may refer to their previous stay in his house.

[143] For Stephen and Sarah Belden and Clarissa Bonfoey, see 2SG 152.1, 2. Stephen worked decades for the Review and Herald Publishing Association. Sarah died of consumption at age 45, leaving Stephen and their five children, ages 6 to 11. For John Nevins Andrews, see RH, Sep. 2, 1851. For Annie R. Smith, see Lt. 9, 1851. Annie accepted the Sabbath on July 26 or 27, 1851 (RH, Aug. 19, 1851, p. 14), and James invited her immediately to Saratoga Springs to work in publishing. For "Aunt Rachel," see EGW, Lt. 1, 1851; Lt. 8, 1851. She was Rachel D. Waterman, née Cushing, who stayed with the Whites in October and November of 1851. A note in Lt. 1, 1851, identified her last name as "Cushing." She attended the 1841 Portland Adventist Conference, withdrew her membership from the Chestnut Street Methodist Episcopal Church, Sept. 23, 1844 (https://archive.org/details/MerlinD.BurtcompiledByRecordsPertainingToTheRobertHarmonFamily, p. 4, compare full record at https://adventistdigitallibrary.org/adl-366730/records-leaders-meetings-chestnut-street-methodist-church-photocopy, p. 215), and is listed in RH, May 2, 1854, as "R. D. Cushing." On Oct. 20, 1856, she married Ebenezer Waterman and was afterward called "R. D. Waterman" (2SG 301; RH, May 7, 1857, p. 8; RH, Nov. 21, 1865, p. 200; RH, Jan. 7, 1873, p. 32; RH Extra, April 14, 1874, p. 3). For Marion Stowell, see letter Marion Concordia Crawford, née Stowell, to Ellen G. White, Oct. 9, 1908, at https://ellenwhite.org/correspondence/236643; James White, "Our Tour West," RH, Feb. 17, 1852, p. 94. Marion came from Volney, New York, arriving in Saratoga Springs, Feb. 13, 1852, and shared a room with Annie Smith. She went back to live with David and Lucretia Arnold (https://www.familysearch.org/ark:/61903/3:1:S3HY-6GTS-36X).

[144] Lt. 3, 1851, Aug. 11, to Harriet Arabella Hastings (born c. 1833), the oldest daughter of Leonard and Elvira Hastings.

[145] Fifteen of its 64 pages had been published in the "Extra." James wrote: "The Pamphlet, 'Experience and Views,' of 64 pages, will be ready in a few days" (RH, Sept. 16, 1851, p. 32). From 1851 to 1853, it was called a "pamphlet" (RH, Aug. 19, 1851, p. 16; RH, July 21, 1853, p. 4). Then, from 1855 to 1859, it was called a "book" (see RH, March 6, 1855, p. 192; RH, Feb. 10, 1859, p. 96). Ellen White referred to the 1851 and 1853 publications as "books containing my visions" (2SG iii). Gideon Miner Davison had published *The Saratoga Sentinel* (1818–1842), as well as books on travel and history (Nathaniel Bartlett Sylvester, *History of Saratoga County, New York*, 1878, p. 103). His printing office was on "Long Alley," which ran parallel to Broadway. For biographies of Davison, see William Leete Stone, *Reminiscences of Saratoga and Ballston*, 1875, pp. 313–320, at https://archive.org/details/reminiscencesofs01ston, and Sylvester Nathaniel Bartlett, *History of Saratoga County, New York*, 1871, pp. 197, 198, at https://archive.org/details/cu31924028833064/page/n269.

[146] Ira Allen Wyman was from Panton, VT (RH, May 6, 1852, p. 7), and would be eventually disfellowshipped (RH, July 4, 1854, p. 173) and join the Messenger party; Hiram Edson had a farm in Port Gibson, NY; Ezra Abell Poole was from Lincklaen, NY (RH, March 2, 1852, p. 103); Lebbeus Drew was from Pultney, NY (RH, May 5, 1851, p. 80); Washington Morse was from Royalton, VT. Marion C. Crawford described a conference she remembered being in the house in Saratoga Springs, NY (letter to E. G. White, Oct. 9, 1908). She may have meant the meeting at Jesse Thompson's commodious house.

[147] "The Conference," RH, March 23, 1852, p. 108. James gave four reasons for having their own press (RH, March 2, 1852, p. 104).

[148] GSAM 285; Arthur W. Spalding, *Footprints of the Pioneers*, 1947, p. 121. Ellen White wrote: "The office hands boarded with us, and our family numbered from fifteen to twenty" (2SG 191.3). Loughborough reported that Masten offered his services to James White (RH, July 31, 1919, p. 14). "Luman Maston" boarded with "Martin L Hulbert" in Saratoga Springs in the 1850 US Census at https://www.familysearch.org/ark:/61903/3:1:S3HY-DCB7-859?i=35&cc=1401638. He described his conversion to Adventism in RH, May 6, 1852, p. 3; Nov. 25, 1852, p. 109. For the arrival of the press, see RH, May 6, 1852, p. 8.

[149] See RH, Jan. 10, 1854, p. 208; RH, Jan. 24, 1854, p. 8. Ellen White described it as containing "more recent views" (ExV54 3.1). *Experience and Views* was advertised from July 1851 until February 1859, and the *Supplement*, from January 1854 to December 1857. In 1857, *Experience and Views*, *Supplement*, and "Testimony for the Church," Nos. 1 and 2, were sold by Mrs. White bound together in one small book, marked "Christian Experience" on the spine (see RH, March 5, 1857, p. 144), with "Testimony for the Church," Nos. 1 and 2, which were by that time sold together as a single pamphlet with consecutive paging from start to finish. See the facsimile of *The Christian Experience and Views of Ellen G. White*, from Hiram Edson's library, at https://adventistdigitallibrary.org/adl-366537/sketch-christian-experience-and-views-ellen-g-white and, from Ellen White's library, at https://adventistdigitallibrary.org/islandora/object/adl%3A22251200, as well as the facsimile of the *Supplement* from Ellen White's office library, at https://adventistdigitallibrary.org/islandora/object/adl%3A22251199.

[150] *Ellen G. White: Messenger to the Remnant*, p. 63. These would be no. 2, 1856; nos. 3 and 4, 1857; no. 5, 1859; no. 6, 1861; nos. 7 and 8, 1862; no. 9, 1863; no. 10, 1864; nos. 11–13, 1867; no. 14, 1868.

[151] See William Rufus Hyde Avery's eyewitness view of the "Great Controversy Vision" (~V189), at Lovett's Grove, March 14, 1858, in **EXHIBIT-1**, no. 30. See also "Duplication and Expansion in *Early Writings*" in **EXHIBIT-6**. A facsimile of *Spiritual Gifts: The Great Controversy Between Christ and His Angels, and Satan and His Angels* is found at https://adventistdigitallibrary.org/islandora/object/adl%3A22250390. Volume 1 was first advertised as "Spiritual Gifts, or The Great Controversy, between Christ and his angels, and Satan and his angels" (RH, Sept. 30, 1858, p. 152); however, it did not become "Spiritual Gifts Vol. 1" until 1860 (RH, Nov. 20, 1860, p. 8). Volume 2 was likewise, at first, without a number. That these four volumes had different content would indicate that they were not planned to be a series. In 1868, Ellen White anticipated a fifth volume (2T 112.1) but shifted her focus to writing out her "Rebuking One, He Designs to Correct Many Vision" (~V259), she received on June 12, 1868, in Battle Creek.

[152] See RH, July 26, 1864, p. 72. Listings in the *Review and Herald*, from Dec. 18, 1866, to Aug. 4, 1868, describe *Spiritual Gifts*, vols. 1 and 3 (predecessors to the Spirit of Prophecy and Conflict of the Ages series) with the words, "as shown in vision." The Spirit of Prophecy series and the Conflict of the Ages series do not make this claim since they also utilize more background material from historical sources.

[153] Benjamin Franklin Snook and William H. Brinkerhoff were Adventist ministers who left the church and became key leaders of the Marion Party (later becoming Universalists). Uriah Smith responded to Snook and Brinkerhoff's book, *The Visions of E. G. White Not of God* (1866), at https://archive.org/details/B.F.SnookWm.H.BrinkerhoffTheVisionsOfE.g.WhiteNotOfGod1866, in *The Visions of Mrs. E. G. White, a*

Manifestation of Spiritual Gifts According to Scripture (1868), at https://archive.org/details/UriahSmithTheVisionsOfMrs.E.G.White1868. In an 1874 statement, J. N. Andrews, who had known Ellen White since 1844, along with six other early Adventists from Paris and Portland, ME, testified: "At a later point while many of the advent people were still firm in the belief that there was no salvation for sinners, she [Ellen White] was shown with respect to the open and shut door of Rev. 3 in which the whole subject was explained in the light of the heavenly sanctuary. Thus instead of the visions leading them to adopt this view, it corrected them upon this point while they were holding it." See also James White, RH, April 14, 1853, p. 188; and William S. Ingraham, RH, June 9, 1853, p. 10.

[154] The decision was made in fall 1882 (Ms. 4, 1883). The announcement of the book's publication says: "The first book written by sister White, entitled 'Experience and Views,' was small, but of exceeding great interest to all who early embraced the faith of the third angel's message. It was published in 1851, and has been out of print for a number of years. It has now been republished and this fact will be learned with pleasure by all the friends of this cause" ("Publisher's Department," RH, Dec. 12, 1882, p. 784). Thus, in 1882, an edited version of *Experience and Views* and the *Supplement* was published as a second edition. The preface indicates that nothing from "the original work" was omitted in it, which would not cover the early articles and manuscripts that had not been published in the first edition. Also, a volume combining all three books, paged separately, was published as *Early Writings*. The 1882 and 1884 printings of the three-in-one volume carry the designation "second edition" (https://adventistdigitallibrary.org/islandora/object/adl%3A22250191). A 154-page edition was printed in Australia in 1888. The 1891 printing was designated the fourth edition; the 1893 printing, the fifth; the 1894 printing, the sixth; the 1898 printing, the seventh; the 1899 printing, the eighth; the 1900 printing, the ninth; the 1906 printing, the tenth; the 1907 printing, the eleventh; the 1912 printing, the twelfth; the 1916 printing, the thirteenth; the 1918 printing, the fourteenth; and the 1919 printing, the fifteenth. The 1920 printing does not have an edition number. The online edition counts the 1906 printing, which introduced consecutive paging for the whole book, as the "third edition" (https://m.egwwritings.org/ro/book/28.2). The 1945 printing, which reset type but had the same paging, was designated the "fourth edition." The "fifth edition" added new introductory material. Arthur L. White wrote a six-part series on the background of *Early Writings* (RH, Sept. 18, 25; Oct. 2, 23, 30; Nov. 20, 1947). (For title pages of the various printings, see p. 191.)

[155] Published May 30, 1847, "A Word to the 'Little Flock'" was meant as an epistle to Advent believers who were still open to seeing significance in the 1844 fulfillment of Daniel 8:14. With the change of views of *The Day-Star*'s editor and the discontinuance of *The Day-Dawn*, James White published this pamphlet of expositions on prophecy separately, in "A Word to the 'Little Flock,'" with three letters from Ellen White—one to Eli Curtis, April 21, 1847, occupying half of page 11 and all of page 12; a second to Enoch Jacobs, Dec. 20, 1845, published in Cincinnati, Ohio, in DS, Jan. 24, 1846, and as Broadside1, April 6, 1846, with James White contributing the biblical references (included in this book), occupying pages 14 through 17, and part of page 18; and a third written to Joseph Bates, April 7, 1847, which was published by Bates with his comments as Broadside3. Joseph Bates' comments are also included.

[156] For Joseph Harvey Waggoner, see RH, Sept. 3, 1889, p. 558. The advertisement is in RH, Aug. 28, 1883, p. 560.

[157] "Advent Experience," RH, Feb. 10, 1885, p. 89; Feb. 17, 1885, pp. 105, 106; Feb. 24, 1885, pp. 121, 122; March 3, 1885, p. 137; March 10, 1885, pp. 153, 154; March 17, 1885, p. 169; March 24, 1885, pp. 184, 185; March 31, 1885, pp. 201, 202; April 7, 1885, pp. 216, 217; April 14, 1885, pp. 232, 233.

[158] RH, March 3, 1885, p. 137; Miller's letter is from AHSTR, Dec. 11, 1844. George William Needham was a minister first with the Congregational Church, then with the Advent Christians (AHBA, Oct. 26, 1847, p. 143), and then with the Union Congregational Church. John Ball Cook was from New Bedford, MA.

[159] The figure 50,000 is mentioned in James White, ed., *The Early Life and Later Experience and Labors of Elder Joseph Bates*, p. 297.

[160] *Advent Review* Extra, Dec. 1887, p. 14, at https://documents.adventistarchives.org/Periodicals/RH/RH18871231-V64-50e.pdf. Ira Abbey lived in Camden, NY (RH, Aug. 19, 1851, p. 16), where the Dec. 25, 1851, General Conference was held (RH, Dec. 9, 1851, p. 64).

[161] This was Heman Allen Churchill (see AR, Aug. 1850, p. 15; J. H. Waggoner, "'Suppression' and 'The Shut Door,'" *Review and Herald Supplement*, Aug. 14, 1883, p. 2, at https://documents.adventistarchives.org/Periodicals/RH/RH18830814-V60-33s.pdf). Regarding a girl kept from attending meetings by her father, Ellen had told her friend Marion: "God never has shown me that there is no salvation for such persons. It is only those who have had the light of truth presented to them and knowingly rejected it" (Marion Truesdail, Aug. 17, 1875, in RP 119; RH, April 7, 1885, p. 217). "Another occasion worthy of mention was a vision given in 1846 [V36], in Paris, ME. Miss Harmon was shown that when Satan could not prevent the honest hearted from doing their whole duty, he would exert his skill in pushing them beyond duty. One good sister had been telling the churches that God had rejected them because they had rejected the message sent from heaven to save them. Sister Harmon was shown that there was no truth in her message, as there were many in the churches who would yet embrace the truth; that the good angels would leave her (this sister) at the door of the church if she went there upon such an errand" (letter Marion Truesdail, Jan. 27, 1891, in RP 119). Ira Abbey wrote: "Never do I remember of hearing Sr. White say that there was no hopes of the unconverted; but there were hopes of the backslidden and those that had not rejected the truth" (AR *Extra*, Dec. 1887, p. 14). Regarding her April 3, 1847, vision (V46), Ellen White wrote: "I saw that God had children who do not see and keep the Sabbath" (RP 147).

[162] Ellen G. White, "The 'Shut Door' Defined," Ms. 4, 1883. See James White on her change of views with her first vision (WLF 22.5).

[163] Further research may refine the list, improving the dates and locating other visions. See the General Index for mentions in this book. A partial list of her early visions is at https://www.askanadventistfriend.com/ellen-white/a-comprehensive-list-of-ellen-whites-visions.

[164] W. C. White wrote Sarah Elizabeth Peck, an educational pioneer who organized Ellen White's letters and manuscripts and compiled *Education*: "My folks told the story to me." Sarah Belden told Loughborough that her sister held the Bible open and either she or "some other person present, looked at every text to which [Ellen's] finger pointed and saw clearly that in every instance she was repeating the scripture upon which her finger was resting" (GSAM 237). Ellen's mother told Loughborough that Ellen "was unable, for lack of strength, to lift that heavy Bible from the bureau; but in the vision she held it as easily, apparently, as though it were only a pocket Testament" (GSAM 237). Loughborough reported that about sixty believers saw her in this vision (RH, Nov. 5, 1914, p. 5). W. C. White wrote that the part "about her holding it open may be all right, but I never heard it from Father" (https://ellenwhite.org/media/document/2475).

[165] "R. Curtis" is Robert G. Curtis. In Ms. 167, 1904, Ellen White recalled a conversation between Howland and Curtis (listed as a fisherman in the 1880 US Census).

[166] Ellen White later wrote that, instead of being discouraged, Washington Morse "should have rejoiced that the world was granted a reprieve" (LSMS 106.2; LS 78.2).

[167] "Charles Collier" is Charles Sterne Collier, Sr., or "C. S. Collier" in AHSTR, Feb. 26, 1848, p. 31.

[168] John Garnsey Bennett and Albert Merritt Billings were both from Claremont, NH. Bennett was a Methodist minister turned Adventist,

and Billings was the sheriff from 1835 to 1846. In 1844 the two traveled together, proclaiming Christ's soon return (see AHSTR, July 24, 1844, p. 199; July 31, 1844, p. 205; Aug. 7, 1844, p. 8; Aug. 28, 1844, p. 32). After October 22, 1844, Bennett and Billings did not deny their past experience yet became involved in fanaticism (see Ms. 10, 1859; Lt. 15, 1857; Ms. 46, 1904). Ellen White described their behavior as "darkness and iniquity covered up with a pious garb" (Ms. 10, 1859). Billings went on to abandon his Advent faith and earn a fortune, financing the overhead rail system in New York City. Bennett engaged with Adventist believers in Claremont but was censured on Feb. 10, 1848, for "propagating, privately, the doctrine of spiritual wifery, or the coupling together of the sexes, not man and wife" (AHSTR, Jan. 1, 1848, p. 176; Feb. 26, 1848, p. 31; Dec. 9, 1848, p. 151). After the censure, he moved to Dummerston, VT, where he served as a Baptist minister (see "J G Bennett baptist," https://archive.org/details/vermontyearbookz184753ches/page/n631), then, in 1850, to Hartland, VT, where he served as a Methodist minister (see https://www.familysearch.org/ark:/61903/3:1:S3HY-67S9-GBT?i=42&cc=1401638), then, in 1853, to Hinsdale, NH, where he served as a Calvinist Baptist minister and, in 1860, as an Adventist clergyman (see https://www.familysearch.org/ark:/61903/3:1:33S7-9BS4-LFR?i=21&cc=1473181), then, in 1862, to Burlington, WI, where he served as a Methodist minister (see https://www.familysearch.org/ark:/61903/3:1:S3HY-6Q47-R5V?i=43&cc=1438024). He returned, in 1874, to Hinsdale, NH, to serve as a Baptist minister (https://archive.org/details/newhampshireregо2unkngoog/page/n143). Two other misleading ministers were farmer John Bayles Libbey, of Johnson, VT, and Elder Noah Bailey (PrT, Aug. 1850, p. 15; RH, Feb. 1851, p. 46; 2SG 131, 132).

169 The date is predicated on the name of the location given; she passed through "Garland" in spring 1845. RP 106 has Garland near Exeter, and Loughborough has Ellen White, after meeting Joseph Turner in Garland, where he told her that he was going to Portland, telling him: "You are not wanted in Portland, and the Lord has shown me that if you go to Portland, your character will be manifest there" (DPF 81). Turner moved to Hartford, CT, and the 1850 US Census and city directories from 1851-1862 list his occupations as "minister," "Second Advent," "circuit preacher," and, lastly, "homeopathic" physician.

170 In Lt. 2, 1874, she wrote that she "would rather die than have a vision," yet she knew she had a duty to deliver God's messages.

171 Ellen White's older sisters, Harriet Gould McCann, née Harmon, wife of Samuel F. McCann, a Methodist pastor, and Mary Plummer Foss, née Harmon, wife of Samuel Hoyt Foss, lived in West Poland.

172 John Megquier was a farmer in West Poland, ME, at whose house Ellen Harmon met with other Adventists to relate her first vision. The *Daily Eastern Argus*, April 28, 1845, reported that Ellen Harmon was arrested at Megquier's house on April 23, 1845. The names "J. Megguire" (John Megquier), "S. Foss" (Samuel Foss), and "W. McAnn" (William H. McCann, Samuel F. McCann's brother) appear on a map of West Poland, around Tripp Pond (see p. 26). By 1858, when the map was produced, Samuel F. McCann had moved to Sanford, ME, but other members of the McCann family remained in West Poland (see https://www.loc.gov/resource/g3733a.la000265/?r=0.259,0.614,0.064,0.032,0).

173 Loughborough connected the no-work and no-more-mercy doctrines to Joseph Turner, citing Himes' June 6, 1845 report in the *Morning Watch* (GSAM 220). "Bro. C" in Paris, ME, is likely "Brother Chase"—which was either Sibley Chase or Thomas W. Chase.

174 Marion Truesdail, née Stowell, to J. N. Loughborough, Jan. 27, 1891, in GCDB, Jan. 29, 30, 1893, p. 35.

175 James White wrote: "At our conference in Topsham, Maine, last Nov., Ellen had a vision of the handy works of God. She was guided to the planets Jupiter, Saturn, and *I think one more*" (WLF 22, emphasis added). Though Loughborough may have described what he imagined having taken place, describing Ellen as relating what she saw *while still in vision*, James and Ellen described her as relating what she saw *after* she came out of vision (WLF 22; SG 83.1). Loughborough also gave specific numbers of moons (RH, Nov. 30, 1886, p. 745; RP 127; GSAM 258; not in GCDB, March 18, 1891, p. 145). James and Ellen gave no numbers. Ultimately, it was not the description of the planets but of the "opening heavens" that impressed Bates since that was the subject of his book *The Opening Heavens* (1846), printed at the Press of Benjamin Lindsey, where he also published *A Vindication of the Seventh-day Sabbath and the Commandments* (1848). Marion Stowell mistakenly conflated a vision in 1849 in which Ellen White saw Enoch and "majestic beings" on a planet (V64) with the 1846 vision (V42) (see Kevin Morgan, https://www.academia.edu/34934231/Ellen_Whites_Amazing_View_of_Jupiter_and_Saturn).

176 "Leonard Hastings" is Leonard Wood Hastings.

177 "Brother and Sister Ralph" are Richard Ralph and Abby Minerva Ralph, née Kilby, of Berlin, Connecticut.

178 George and Polly Penfield, lived in Portland, CT, near Charlotte Selina Hurlbut, née Welch, with the Penfields in dwelling 331 and Hurlbut in dwelling 330 (https://www.familysearch.org/ark:/61903/3:1:S3HY-6SFQ-QP8; see also RH, April 9, 1857; RH, March 17, 1859).

179 Centerport was two miles from Port Byron, NY, the location of Hiram Edson's farm. The Whites would stay August to October 1850 at William Harris's home while publishing *The Advent Review* at nearby Auburn, NY (2SG 136–140; *Footprints of the Pioneers*, p. 112).

180 As corroboration of their residence in Oswego, James White directed that mail be sent to him in care of Luman Carpenter, of Oswego (PrT, Dec. 1849, p. 40; Dec. 1849, p. 48; March 1850, p. 56; March 1850, p. 64; April 1850, p. 72). Ellen White referenced a conference in Oswego on Nov. 3, 1849 (2SG 119) and to their renting a house in Oswego afterward (2SG 122; CET 131); James published *The Present Truth* in Oswego from March to May 1850. However, "Bro. M" remains unidentified, despite his being called a "brother" and Loughborough's saying that he "had rejected the truth," which could both imply that he had been an Adventist (see https://documents.adventistarchives.org/Periodicals/RH/RH18850224-V62-08.pdf). Loughborough also called him a treasurer, relying on the oral history of Elias Goodwin (GSAM 230), who mistakenly referred to Sarah as Hiram's fiancé when they were already married (June 12, 1841, marriage record in Cuyahoga, Ohio, at https://www.familysearch.org/ark:/61903/1:1:XDK6-H4Z). Ellen White only mentioned the man's misuse of public funds and his being held in the "black hole" (2SG 123), which was the county jail (*Thirteenth Publication of the Oswego Historical Society*, p. 22, at https://nyheritage.contentdm.oclc.org/digital/collection/p16694coll19/id/15377/rec/6). She also wrote that, after the man's arrest, "his Methodist brethren were left to carry on the revival" (2SG 123). That his wife hid the money in the snow indicates that it was winter. There is evidence of an 1850 revival in Oswego: "A powerful revival of religion is in progress at Oswego. The first Methodist Church has had an addition of nearly 200 within a few weeks.—The Baptist and Presbyterian churches have also had large accessions. Prof. Smith, of the Auburn Theological Seminary, has been laboring there, and Rev. Mr. Burchard is expected" (*The Rochester Daily American*, March 28, 1850, p. 2). These two ministers—Professor Joseph Few Smith and Rev. Samuel Dickinson Burchard—were Presbyterians, so they cannot be the unidentified "Bro. M."

181 The hypocritical woman was Emma Loretta (Pauling) Payne, née Prior, the sister of Edward Prior. Later there would be a vision about the lack of judgment regarding Georgianna Prior's obtaining medical aid (V151, "Georgianna Prior Vision," Aug. 1854; 2SG 134).

[182] This is Henry Lillis, Jr., of Oswego, NY. See a regrettable episode involving Lillis in RH, Aug. 19, 1851, p. 11, and GSAM 325.2, and Ellen White's warning of his rashness.

[183] "Bro. Gorsline" is Richard Gorsline, a farmer of Oswego. "Bro. Chapin" is Roderick R. Chapin, a peddler and farmer in Rochester, NY, who moved, in 1850, to Greece, NY (see https://www.familysearch.org/ark:/61903/3:1:S3HY-DRN9-WQX?i=79). He died between 1862, when he sold some property (see https://www.familysearch.org/ark:/61903/3:1:3QS7-89WR-FVC9?i=724), and 1865, when his wife, Desdemona Chapin, née Graham, was listed as the head of household in the 1865 New York Census (see https://www.familysearch.org/ark:/61903/1:1:QVNN-BKGP). Rescued from his delusion, Chapin worked for a time encouraging the brethren but ultimately rejected the brethren's concern and the visions (RH, Jan. 10, 1854, p. 207; RH, Aug. 15, 1854, p. 6), joining the Messenger party and writing several letters to the periodical. Gorsline, on the other hand, embraced the testimony given him (Ms. 5, 1850) and ultimately willed the remainder of his estate to the Seventh-day Adventist publishing association. His will reads: "Lastly I give and bequeath unto Elder James White of Battle Creek in the State of Michigan all the rest and residue of my estate after the same shall be converted into money as hereinafter directed in trust to be used and expended by him for paying the debts and forwarding the objects of 'The seventh day adventist publishing association' by whom the 'Advent review and Sabbath Herald' is now published." Elias Goodwin was the executor of the will.

[184] For all three extant issues, see https://cdm.llu.edu/digital/collection/bftmm/id/72; https://cdm.llu.edu/digital/collection/bftmm/id/77; and https://www.nonsda.org/egw/messenger_party.shtml.

[185] Clorinda was not alone in propagating the Age to Come. Silas Hawley, a Congregational pastor of Groton, MA, and editor of the *Church Reformer* did so also (*Goshen Democrat*, Goshen, IN, May 15, 1845, p. 4).

[186] For Orrin [Oren] Hewitt, see AHSTR, May 8, 1847, p. 111; *Bible Advocate*, April 24, 1847, p. 11; RH, Dec. 1850, p. 16; June 24, 1852, p. 32; May 1, 1855, p. 222.

[187] "Sally Chase" is Sarah Chase, of Fairhaven, MA. Though disfellowshipped in 1850, she was reinstated and went on to contribute generously to the mission of the Seventh-day Adventists (RH, Dec. 2, 1873, p. 200; ST, May 6, 1875, p. 208; RH, June 13, 1878, p. 191).

[188] "C. Preston" is Chandler Bristol Preston. The vision (V106) was copied on June 29 by Abram A. Dodge. There is a spurious "Camden Vision" with the dateline "Camden, N. Y. June 29, 1851" (see Grant, *The True Sabbath*, p. 91), a date she was not in Camden, so some suggest that maybe this is referring to the earlier vision in Camden (V90). However, James White indicated that the visit to Camden was in May 1850 (PrT, May 1850, p. 80). A second handwritten copy of the spurious "Camden Vision" has the dateline "June 24, 1851" and no mention of Camden, lending no support to the earlier date. It is possible that the preparer of the spurious vision used the copying date from the *true* vision, adapting the 1850 vision to apply to all sinners. The vision is marked as transcribed by R. R. Chapin and supposedly initialed by E. G. White, though handwriting analysis shows it is someone attempting to copy her writing (see https://ellenwhite.org/media/document/838).

[189] Almira Matilda Preston, née Barnes, was married to John Stiles Preston, brother of Chandler Bristol Preston. Initially opposed to his wife's faith (2SG 150.2), John ultimately died in the hope of the resurrection, as witnessed by his obituary in RH, Oct. 30, 1879, p. 151.

[190] Ellen White mistook "Mrs. C." for Mary Burritt, Francis Mary Bragg's mother (age 61). "Mrs. C." may have been Mary Crane, née Taplin (age 53), of Vergennes, VT, wife of Milton Crane, who lived on Water Street in Vergennes near Stephen Bragg and Francis Mary Bragg (see "M. Crane" on inset Vergennes map at https://www.loc.gov/resource/g3753a.la001181a/?r=0.768,0.241,0.107,0.042,0).

[191] Paul Folsom lived in West Medford, MA, then in Somerville, MA, near the foot of Winter Hill (RH, Dec. 18, 1856, p. 56).

[192] Allen preached in Vergennes, VT (AHSTR, March 6, 1844, p. 40) with Stephen Smith (JUBST, April 3, 1845, p. 31) but later taught the no-Sabbath heresy (RH, Nov. 15, 1853, p. 149). Disfellowshipped and taken back at least twice only to leave again in the 1850s, Smith returned a changed man in 1885 (1EGWLM 310, n11).

[193] John Stowell was a farmer who lost three wives through death before the Adventists met on his property in Washington, NH.

[194] John Carrington Bowles, of Jackson, MI, was a Millerite preacher who accepted the Sabbath from Joseph Bates in 1849. He traveled with other ministers in Michigan, preaching the Adventist message. He died of typhus in 1853 ("From Bro. Whitmore," RH, Oct. 4, 1853, p. 103). Whitmore is John H. Whitmore.

[195] John Byington, of Buck's Bridge, NY, was named the first Seventh-day Adventist General Conference president in 1863.

[196] Samuel Benson was the husband of Betsey Benson, née Barrow, who is mentioned in Lt. 8, 1851. Previously a Methodist, he had died by the time Ellen White published 2SG (RH, March 22, 1860, p. 143). The Bensons lived in Irasburg, VT.

[197] Almira Pierce, née Tarbell, was the wife of Stephen Pierce. They were Adventists in Vermont who embraced the Sabbath in 1852. Out of respect for his age, Ellen White called Stephen Pierce "Father Pierce" (Lt. 253, 1903). He became a Seventh-day Adventist minister.

[198] This was the first of Ellen White's visions that Loughborough ever witnessed. He wrote that he would see her in vision over 40 times (GSAM 6.2; 204.1). Christopher Riggs is referenced in AHBA, Nov. 18, 1848, p. 175; Nov. 25, 1848, p. 183; RH, March 3, 1853, p. 168; April 14, 1853, p. 192; Aug. 11, 1853, p. 56.

[199] F. C. Gilbert, *Divine Predictions of Mrs. Ellen G. White Fulfilled*, p. 26.

[200] Though Loughborough says that had a manuscript for this vision (eight pages of foolscap paper, GCCP 61.3), written by Ellen White on June 2 (RH, May 6, 1884, p. 299), he is the only source for the vision's contents. "Mrs. Alcott" was Elizabeth Hanna Olcott, née Stevens (born in 1820), who had married widower Philander Wilcox Olcott (born in 1793) in 1844. Aligning with Loughborough's description, Philander turned 60 in 1853 and was thus an "old man." Philander did indeed have a son by a previous marriage—Horace L. Olcott (born in 1816)—who lived in Lansing, which was within driving distance of Elder Walter White ("Remarkable Fulfillments of the Visions. No. 2," RH, Jan. 15, 1867, pp. 62, 63; GSAM 322–325; https://www.familysearch.org/tree/person/details/L5RW-51Q). Merritt E. Cornell corroborated Loughborough's description of the event, declaring that he found it "correct in every particular, as nearly as I can remember" (RH, Jan. 15, 1867, p. 63). Also corroborating Loughborough's description of Mrs. Alcott's response were Ira Gardner, of Orleans, MI (son of William Gardner, who was the "Bro. G." in Loughborough's account that embraced the Adventist message), Betsey Wilson, née Temple, Phidelia Ann Maynard, née Wilson, and Amelia A. Wilson, née Butler, of Greenville, MI ("Fulfillments of the Visions," RH, Feb. 5, 1867, p. 104). Mrs. Olcott's companion, Nathaniel Pease (b. 1824), is designated a "Second Advent preacher" and living in Michigan (https://archive.org/details/genealogicalhistoopeas/page/328; "Western Tour," RH, July 7, 1853, p. 28). "Bro. Pease, from Vergennes" had held meetings in North Plains, MI, in March 1853 (see https://archive.org/details/1853-advent-harbinger-apr-2-9-16-30/page/n11, p. 347). Philander Wilcox Olcott lived within walking distance of Nathaniel's uncle, Pliny Pease, where Nathaniel could have stayed. For Pliny Pease's

property location, see "P. Peace" in sect. 6 of the map at http://www.migenweb.org/kent/platmaps/1855/grattan.html; for Philander W. Olcott's property location, see "P. W. Alcott" in District 8 of the same map; for Walter White's property location, see "W. White" in Districts 1 and 10 of the map at http://www.migenweb.org/kent/platmaps/1855/vergennes.html. In late 1853, Joseph B. Frisbie paid a missionary visit to Horace Olcott, in Lansing, because he was a subscriber to *The Advent Review and Sabbath Herald* though he hadn't accepted the Sabbath (RH, Oct. 18, 1853, p. 119). Bates reported that "Mrs. Olcott" later interrupted meetings in Greenville, MI, with "an unusual howling and groaning" (RH, July 16, 1861, p. 56). M. E. Cornell also confirmed Ellen White's gift by interviewing long-standing Sabbatarian Adventists in the East. He wrote: "Most of my labor during the two and a half years that I have been in the eastern mission, has been in the vicinity where Bro. and sister White spent the days of their youth, and where they have been known from the commencement of their labors. I have conversed with both friends and foes in regard to them. And now I must say, that having inquired out all the particulars of the scenes and circumstances of their first experiences and labors, and having traced out evil reports to their origin, I am perfectly settled in the conviction that God has been with them from the beginning. It is the motive as manifest by the general tenor of the life and the fruits we should judge by. I have watched for years, to see what was the fruit of Sr. White's visions. I have been over the ground in some fourteen different States, have become acquainted with many who have believed the visions the longest and the strongest; and if they are not the humble devoted children of God, I doubt whether any can be found on earth" (RH, April 3, 1866, p. 140).

201 Daniel R. Palmer, a blacksmith in Jackson, MI, was the husband of Abigail Palmer, née Wilmarth.

202 "C. Smith" is Cyrenius Smith, who was a farmer turned stationery merchant.

203 Charles P. Russell is best known for being one of the founders of the Messenger party, which survived until about 1857. Having joined Millerite Adventism in 1843 (Jackson, MI *Citizen Patriot*, Dec. 5, 1879, p. 2), Russell accepted the Sabbath from Joseph Bates in 1849 but broke with the church in the summer of 1853 over what he called "those vain visions" (MT, Oct. 19, 1854, p. 2), after he and Hiram S. Case were rebuked by a vision (V134) for their severity in a church discipline case involving Abigail Palmer, who was accused by Case's daughter Savilla of calling a neighbor an abusive name that she contested that she had not used, though she did call her a "witch" when the lady threw her dirty mop water on Palmer's sheets drying on the line (Strayer, *J. N. Loughborough*, p. 81). Palmer apologized for her angry reaction to the neighbor's actions. Part of a collection of extracts with its own date of July 1853, Ms. 5, 1853 is likely a part of the July 2 vision.

204 Future study of her prayers during this period would be instructive, calling attention to what she prayed about and the results. See CHART-1 for the visions that addressed time setting, i.e. V19, V29, V86, and V106.

205 2 Timothy 3:8 refers to the magicians in Exodus 7, who are unnamed there. In 2 Timothy 3:8, Paul used the traditional names given them, though not attributing to them the legends in the apocryphal works. Paul used their example as an illustration of active rejection of the truth in the last days. James White used it as an illustration of rejection of the truth through false miracles. In his introduction to the 1847 pamphlet, "A Word to the 'Little Flock,'" (p. 13), James White articulated his understanding of the relationship of the visions to the Bible: "True visions are given to lead us to God, and his written word; but those that are given for a new rule of faith and practice, separate from the bible, cannot be from God, and should be rejected." Answers to objections to the visions can be found in RH, July 3, 1866, p. 33.

206 Sadly, without ever witnessing Ellen White in vision or considering the content of her messages, Joshua V. Himes accepted and repeated the appraisal of his associates who likewise had never witnessed Ellen White in vision. Himes wrote, in response to Matthew Lane Clark's letter of complaint about the evangelistic efforts of the Sabbatarian Adventists Joseph Bates, James and Ellen White, David Arnold, George W. Holt, and Samuel W. Rhodes, in Melbourne, Canada East (now Québec): "As to ELLEN WHITE'S visions, they are known, where she is known, to be the result of mesmeric operations—a miserable deception and humbug" ("Note," AHSTR, May 4, 1850, p. 111, at https://archive.org/details/AdventHerald1850V5N14-26). Mesmerism was that era's name for hypnotism, suggesting that Ellen White's visions were from an altered state of consciousness under someone else's control or by her own self-hypnosis. Many who were present at public meetings during which she had a vision put this hypothesis to the test without being able to induce nor to terminate a vision. Thus, the false claim of "mesmeric operations" was a careless dismissal of the visions without careful study of the evidence about how the visions were given or what they communicated. Himes part also uncritically accepted the false report that Israel Dammon had a "spiritual wife" who had visions (J. V. Himes to Bro. Miller, March 27, 1845, p. 2). At his trial in Atkinson, ME, Dammon had the opportunity to set the record straight about his "spiritual wife," telling the court that "he had a lawful wife, and he could thank God that she had been a very spiritual woman ever since his acquaintance with her" (2SG 42). See the response to Matthew Lane Clark in AR, August 1850, p. 13.

207 Levi S. Stockman, a Methodist minister respected by his denomination, accepted and preached the Advent message. In 1842, at the time of his conversation with young Ellen, he was about 30 years old. On June 25, 1844, he died of consumption (tuberculosis, a wasting disease). For other descriptions of Ellen White regarding her other interactions with Levi Stockman, see ST, March 23, 1876.

208 Ledgers of church membership only mark five of the Harmons as being disfellowshipped from the Chestnut Street Methodist Episcopal Church in August and September 1843: Robert Harmon, Sr., Eunice Harmon, Sarah B. Harmon, Robert Harmon, Jr., and Ellen Harmon (see https://whiteestate.org/vault/portland2.asp and https://whiteestate.org/vault/portland3.asp). Mary Plummer Foss, née Harmon, had married in 1842 and moved away, though there is no record of a transfer. Elizabeth N. Harmon's acceptance into membership was not recorded in the church books. It is probable that, with the family's dismissal, Elizabeth also stopped attending. However, church trial notes refer to "the cases of Robert Harmon & those of his family who are a members of the M. E. Church in this City, all of whom having violated the rules of our Discipline in their long absence from our Church & ordinances & supporting an Anti Methodist doctrine & congregation Viz. Millerism &c" ("Records of Stewards and Leaders of Chestnut Street Methodist Episcopal Church of Portland, Maine," in F. D. Nichol, *The Midnight Cry*, p. 457; https://adventistdigitallibrary.org/adl-366730/records-leaders-meetings-chestnut-street-methodist-church-photocopy, p. 183). Ellen's father knew that other church members had been out of attendance much longer than they had without being disfellowshipped (2SG 24.1). A spokesperson for the church said that the "anti-Methodist doctrine" they were spreading was "the views of William Miller's time setting" (http://truthorfables.com/Methodist_Church_Letter.htm). He ignores the fact that Miller had set no specific date for Christ's return at the time of their dismissal—but only some time between the spring of 1843 and of 1844. And he also ignores the fact that Ellen White stated: "We made no secret of our new belief, although we did not urge it upon others on inappropriate occasions, or manifest any antagonism toward our church" (ST, March 9, 1876; ST, April 25, 1878, p. 123).

209 The original has "exciteing" rather than "exciting." For the traveling of "the Advent people," see the facsimile of DS, Jan. 24, 1846, p. 17 (1EGWLM 94). Ludwig Richard Conradi assumed, in *The Founders of the Seventh Day Adventist Denomination*, p. 11, that she had this vision

(V1) on Dec. 22, 1844, precisely two months after the disappointment. However, Ellen White never placed a precise date on the vision, though she did refer specifically to the place where she received it.

[210] 2 Cor. 12:9. For details of the "Midnight Cry Vision" (V1), see ExV 10–13.

[211] In Ms. 16, 1894, she reported, "When my breath came again to my body," "I could not hear anything," and "everything was dark."

[212] At first she was reticent to share what she saw in the vision because, like herself, the believers meeting at her father's house had moved on from the Midnight Cry, which is what made it so remarkable to her, when she shared the vision with Joseph Turner at his urging, that they accepted it (Lt. 3, 1847).

[213] Allusion to 2 Cor. 12:9.

[214] James White wrote: "When she had her first vision, she was an emaciated invalid, given up by her friends and physicians to die of consumption" (LI 273).

[215] Rev. 22:2, 1. For a physical description of the "Ball of Fire Vision" (V3), see 2SG 37.1 and Ms. 131, 1906, Aug. 13.

[216] Perhaps this was during the "Fifty Texts Vision" (V20) when she let herself entertain the thought that her visions were mesmerism (see ExV 7.2). The hypnotizing physician may have thought her visions were the result of hyper-suggestibility. But the evidence says otherwise.

[217] Luke 11:11, 12.

[218] Ellen White was gallingly accused of participating in the very thing she combatted in these early days—fanaticism. Many people who knew her countered this accusation. For example, Abram Barnes, on Sept. 18, 1874: "I have been connected with the Advent people since 1844, was personally acquainted with those that was [*sic*] led into fanaticism. I was also acquainted with Sr. White and her father's family in Portland. I have seen her have a number of visions, have heard her relate them. I have compared them with the word of God, have found them to be in harmony with the Bible. I have perfect confidence in them. I knew Sr. White at that time to labor faithfully from place to place with a pointed testimony to those that had gone into fanaticism, showing them their wrong course and pointing out the errors that they had fallen into." Samuel W. Flanders, also of Hartland, ME, affirmed his statement. (See also 2SG 301.)

[219] Dan. 12:1. A testimony in 2SG 301, 302, signed by N. N. Lunt, S. H. Lunt, Jacob Mills, Jr., Thomas Worcester, Dorcas Wright, Phebe A. Gammon, Elizabeth Haines, and Isaiah Libby, rebuts the charge that James and Ellen White engaged in fanaticism. For descriptions of other types of fanaticism she had to confront, see *Ellen G. White: Messenger to the Remnant*, pp. 32, 33; Ms. 9, 1859; Ms. 10, 1859; 2SG 45, 49; Lt. 2, 1874; ST, May 4, 1876; RH, Nov. 20, 1883; GCDB, April 23, 1901, Art. A, par. 13; Ms. 131, 1906; Ms. 97, 1909; LS 83–88.

[220] Matt. 24:48. The expression "I was charged with being with the evil servant" means that they thought she was delaying Christ's return.

[221] See ExV 35.2–42.13. This is a general statement about the number of texts. In 2SG 59.2, she lists the references without a number.

[222] Ps. 149:6. Here she skips over her 1845 travels. This is likely the same Bible she lifted up during the "Ball of Fire Vision" (V3).

[223] "Sister A." is Melora Atwood Ashley, née Crapo, the identification coming from an 1896 letter that "Brother G.," or Heman Stetson Gurney, wrote to his son, Charles. The family to visit on West Island was that of James M. Hall. About her companions, she wrote: "I am accused of traveling with Elder James White before our marriage. He did sometimes accompany us to appointments, always accompanied by my elder sister or my twin sister" (Lt. 2, 1874). These would be Sarah B. Belden, née Harmon, and Elizabeth N. Bangs, née Harmon. "We had a little company, so that no reports could be made that I was traveling with an unmarried man" (Ms. 131, 1906; cf. 2SG 46.1). She also mentioned traveling in 1845 with her brother-in-law's sister, Louisa A. Brackett, née Foss; Stephen Files and his wife, Eunice B. Files, née Freeman; or Ralph Thurston Haskins, brother of Charlotte Farnham Cleveland, née Haskins (see Ms. 10, 1859; 2SG 46.1; ST, May 4, 1876, p. 165; Ms. 131, 1906; LS 77.1). Originally owned by Stephen West, West Island was *southeast* of Fairhaven.

[224] See Joshua V. Himes, responding to a letter from Matthew Lane Clark, of Melbourne, Canada East [Quebec], in AHSTR, May 4, 1850, p. 111.

[225] Notices in the *New Bedford Mercury* and *The Evening Standard* (1848–1869) for the sale of the 250-acre south side farm list Jabez Taber as the seller. The names on an 1855 map are R. Anthony and J. Taber. These men did not live on West Island. "J. Taber" lived in New Bedford in district VIII and R. Anthony likely lived in Wilbur's Point, Sconticut Neck, Fairhaven, Massachusetts. James M. Hall and the other family on the island must have been renters of the farms.

[226] Thus, she indicates that she would be omitting certain repetitions. The inclusion of the "Open and Shut Door Vision" (V69) refutes the notion of Dudley Marvin Canright that they were left out because Adventists had renounced the "shut door" (LEGW 145).

[227] Luke 12:36, "return from the wedding." For "the return of their Lord from the wedding," see DS, Sept. 6, 1845, p. 17.

[228] Adapted from 2 Cor. 4:17, 18.

[229] Deut. 3:25; Num. 13:30. From 1848–1851, Eli Curtis published *The Girdle of Truth and Advent Review*; Barnet Matthias was the periodical's editor. Ellen White wrote: "It is well known by many of the brethren, that Eli Curtis has published many of my visions. . . . I feel it my duty to say to the brethren that I have no faith in his course; and that he has published my visions contrary to my wishes, even after I had requested him not to publish them" (PrT, May 1, 1850). Eli Curtis was at one time a Sabbatarian Adventist, defending the Sabbath in *The Sabbath Advocate* and in *The Girdle of Truth* (see https://archive.org/details/GirdleOfTruthAndAdventReview1848Jan20V1N6). Yet, he was also fascinated with supernatural phenomena, and he published, in 1850, *Wonderful phenomena, wonders of the age: a thrilling narrative of the facts relating to the Dixboro Ghost* (see RH, April 7, 1851). Then, in 1851, he published the broadside "The Sharp Sword with Two Edges! Truth from heaven!" which contains messages purporting to be from spirits (see the review and warning at https://books.google.com/books?id=rjsbAAAAYAAJ&pg=PA347). In 1861, he published *The Millennial Messenger* and *Address to the True Church Militant*. His article "Mediums' Home" was published in the spiritualist *Banner of Light*, Sept. 28, 1867, p. 2. Curtis died in March of 1872, age 76, and his cause of death was listed as "Spiritualism" (see https://www.familysearch.org/ark:/61903/3:1:S3HT-DZZ9-4LV?i=1207).

[230] *Matt.* 7:14, "strait . . . narrow."

[231] *Matt.* 25:6. For one discussion of the "midnight cry," see DS, Sept. 6, 1845, p. 17.

[232] For omitted words that are in DS, Jan. 24, 1846; Broadside1 1846; and WLF 14.2, see EXHIBIT-5. The context for Ellen White's "wicked world" statement "takes the reader to a particular time in the future, after the Mark of the Beast test, right before Jesus returns" (@carltonmouzon9547, YouTube).

[233] *Ezek.* 43:2; Rev. 1:15. For descriptions of the concept of deliverance by the voice of God, see *Joel* 3:16 (cf. AR, Sept 1850, p. 8); *Rev.* 16:17; *Ezek.* 12:25; *Mark* 13:32; Jer. 25:30. For "the day and hour of Jesus' coming" (cf. Rev. 3:3), see DS, Nov. 29, 1845, p. 35, at https://documents.adventistarchives.org/AdvRelated/WMC/WMC18451129-V08-09.pdf.

[234] Rev. 14:1; *John 12:29*. With the number of Adventists being far below 144,000 (the highest estimate is about 50,000), this prophecy assumes that there was evangelistic work yet to be accomplished before Jesus' return.

[235] 2 Cor. 3:7; *Isa 10:27 [actually Exod. 34:29]*. For Moses' face shining "when he came down from" Sinai, see DS, Sept. 6, 1845, p. 17.

[236] *Rev. 3:12*; 14:1; 22:4.

[237] For a further description of "the wicked" falling "to the ground," see DS, Sept. 6, 1845, p. 17.

[238] John 13:14, "wash one another's feet"; "salute" with a "holy kiss," Rom. 16:16; 1 Cor. 16:20; 2 Cor. 13:12; 1 Thess. 5:26; 1 Peter 5:14; "the holy brethren," 1 Thess. 5:27; "worshipped at our feet," *Rev. 3:9*. James White included this scene in the latter part of his 1845 description of the "Midnight Cry Vision" (**V1**). For "who could wash 'one another's feet,'" see DS, Sept. 6, 1845, p. 17. Ellen White did not countenance a man's washing of a woman's feet (ExV54 37.2).

[239] *Matt. 24:30*. For the "east," see Matt. 24:27.

[240] *Rev. 14:14*. Thus, James White connects the "*Sign of the Son of Man*," with the "great white cloud" (DS, Sept. 6, 1845, p. 17). That the cloud would be small at first makes sense and aligns with 1 Kings 18:44. See also William Miller's statement in "William Miller," *The Burlington Free Press*, Feb. 17, 1843, p. 1, col. 5, at https://archive.org/details/WilliamMiller.-BurlingtonFreePress1843/mode/1up.

[241] Rev. 4:3; 5:11; Matt. 25:31.

[242] *Luke 21:27; Rev. 19:12; 1:14*. William Ellis Foy also described the Son of Man as wearing "a crown upon his head" (Foy, p. 10). That His hair was curly may be suggested from "the hair of his head like the pure wool" (Dan. 7:9).

[243] Matt. 24:31; 1 Cor. 15:52. Foy describes Jesus as having legs "like pillars of flaming fire" and "a trumpet of pure silver," but Rev. 10:1 has "His feet as pillars of fire."

[244] *Rev. 1:15; 14:14; 1 Thess. 4:16; Rev. 1:14*.

[245] Rev. 7:14; 6:17; 2 Peter 3:14, "without spot."

[246] *Rev. 8:1*.

[247] Ps. 24:4; Rev. 6:17; 2 Cor. 12:9.

[248] 1 Thess. 4:16; *2 Thess. 1:7, 8*.

[249] Ps. 17:15; Eph. 5:14; Job 7:21; Dan. 12:2.

[250] Joel 2:10.

[251] Matt. 27:52; 2 Cor. 5:2; 1 Cor. 15:53.

[252] Rev. 19:6.

[253] 1 Cor. 15:52; *1 Thess. 4:17*; see John 5:25 for the voice of the Son of God.

[254] *2 Esdras 2:43*, 46, 47: "And in the midst of them there was a young man of a high stature, taller than all the rest, and upon every one of their heads he sets crowns, and more exalted which I marvelled greatly. . . . Then said I to the angel, What young person is it that crowneth them, and giveth them palms in their hands? So he answered and said unto me, It is the Son of God, whom they have confessed in the world." This view is supported by John and Paul. Rev. 2:10: ". . . be thou faithful unto death, and I will give thee a crown of life." Rev. 3:11: "Behold, I come quickly: hold that fast which thou hast, that no man take thy crown." 2 Tim. 4:8: "Henceforth there is laid up for me a crown of righteousness, which the Lord, the righteous judge, shall give me at that day: and not to me only, but unto all them also that love his appearing."

[255] *Rev. 15:2; 7:9*.

[256] Rev. 15:2. William Foy has "an innumerable multitude, arrayed in white raiment, standing in a perfect square" (Foy, p. 19).

[257] Rev. 7:9. Ellen White's mention of a "white mantle" and Foy's mention of "white raiment" are based on Rev. 7:9, 13.

[258] Rev. 15:2.

[259] 2 Esdras 2:47: "Then began I greatly to commend them that stood so stiffly for the name of the Lord"; other wording from Rev. 21:21; 7:14; 22:14; Matt. 25:21; *Isa. 26:2*. "Standing stiffly" for truth was a common expression among early Adventists (see **EXHIBIT-2**). In Foy's vision, an angel opens the gate with "its glittering hinges" (Foy, p. 10). The original wording in Ellen White's letter to Enoch Jacobs was "laid hold of the gate and swung it back on its golden hinges."

[260] Rev. 22:14, 3.

[261] *Rev. 22:1, 2*.

[262] Rev. 22:2. Though Foy didn't mention a divided trunk, he does describe the tree as looking like transparent gold (Foy, p. 14). Neither Revelation nor Ellen White has the sea of glass directly beside the tree as Foy does.

[263] Rev. 22:1, 2.

[264] Matt. 4:23; etc. "Brothers Fitch and Stockman" are Charles Fitch and Levi S. Stockman, who both died the year they expected Christ to return—Stockman on June 25 and Fitch on October 14. Fitch is known for applying the second angel's message to the papacy and to Protestant churches rejecting the Advent message; Stockman is known for giving young Ellen sage advice in her Christian experience about God's purpose for her life. In his 1842 vision, William Foy described seeing people he knew on earth, but he does not mention Stockman and Fitch and he placed the righteous "beneath this tree standing on the sea of glass" (Foy, pp. 14, 15), not beside the river of life.

[265] *2 Cor. 4:17; Isa. 65:17*. In 2SG 52, Ellen White distinguished her "New Earth Vision" (**V16**), given her in the spring of 1845, from her "Midnight Cry Vision" (**V1**), though she does not separate the two in her account published in DS, Jan. 24, 1846.

[266] *Zech. 14:4*. The omitted part, which comes before this, would seem to be a part of the "New Earth Vision" (**V16**).

[267] Rev. 21:14, 12; Rev. 21:2; *Rev. 21:10–13*.

[268] *Isa. 65:21*.

[269] Comparing the text of *Experience and Views* and its *Supplement* with *Spiritual Gifts*, vol. 1, we notice that *Spiritual Gifts* duplicated and revised material from the earlier books, showing that there were earlier "great controversy" scenes that predated Ellen White's 1858 "Great Controversy Vision." The reader will note references to "1SG" where such duplication occurs.

[270] *Isa. 11:6–9*; see also Isa. 65:25.

[271] *Ezek. 34:25*.

[272] From *Jer. 31:15–17; Matt. 2:18.* "These," said Christ, "are children who were murdered for my sake and for the faith of their parents" (LS80 217.2).

[273] 2 *Esdras 2:19:* "I Esdras saw upon the mount Sion a great people, whom I could not number . . . And as many fountains flowing with milk and honey, and seven mighty mountains, whereupon there grows roses and lilies, whereby I will fill thy children with joy."

[274] *Isa. 60:13; 41:19.*

[275] GT, Extra, Jan. 20, 1848; WLF 17.2; DS, Jan. 24, 1846; Broadside1 April 6, 1846. All have "Well, bless the Lord, dear brethren and sisters, it is an extra meeting for those who have the seal of the living God." Allusions in this exclamation are from *Rev. 14:3*. Significantly, she does not enter this temple.

[276] Rev. 7:14; *Luke 12:37.*

[277] Rev. 22:2. Each of these foods have been alluded to in the vision.

[278] Rev. 22:2; 21:6. Foy described a similar caution; however, he attempted to eat the fruit so he wouldn't have to return, while Ellen Harmon heard and obeyed. "With a lovely voice, the guide then spoke to me and said, 'Those that eat of the fruit of this tree return to earth no more.' I raised my hand to partake of the heavenly fruit, that I might no more return to earth; but alas! I immediately found myself again in this lonely vale of tears. The duty to declare the things which had thus been shown me, to my fellow creatures, and warn them to flee from the wrath to come, rested with great weight upon my mind; but I was disobedient, settling upon this point for an excuse, that my guide did not command me so to do . . ." (Foy, p. 15, parallel words highlighted in gray).

[279] 2 Esdras 2:42: "then the angel said unto me, Go thy way, and tell my people what manner of things, and how great wonders of the Lord thy God, thou hast seen."

[280] *Heb. 9:1–24.*

[281] That is, on April 3, 1847; it was published in Broadside3, April 7, 1847, four days later (see WLF 18.1). *The Girdle of Truth*, Extra, Jan. 20, 1848, also contains Ellen White's description of the vision she had four months after the first one, the "Bridegroom Vision" (**V5**), as in DS, March 14, 1846, and Broadside1, April 6, 1846, beginning with the words, "About four months since, I had a vision of events all in the future" and ending with the words, "the synagogue of Satan worshipped at the saint's feet" (Rev. 3:9). The editor of *The Girdle of Truth*, Barnet Matthias professed to believe in the visions, though he rejected the Sabbath, arguing against it in Rocky Hill, CT, on Sabbath, April 22, 1848 (see James White, letter to Brother and Sister Hastings, April 27, 1848, at https://ellenwhite.org/correspondence/179852). It should come as no surprise that he did not include the "Sabbath Halo Vision" (**V46**) in his paper.

[282] Rev. 21:2, "the holy city." Rev. 7:15; 11:19, "temple." Rev. 3:8; 4:1, "door." Exod. 30:1, 6; Heb. 9:4, "incense." Heb. 9:2, "candlestick." Exod. 25:37; Rev. 4:5, "seven lamps." Exod. 25:30; Heb. 9:2, "table" and "shewbread." Heb. 9:3, and "the second vail." Ellen White uses both "vail" and "veil." In Lt. 2, 1847, Ellen White refers to a vision supporting the view of "two literal resurrections, 1000 years apart." That she used many of the terms as in Lt. 1, 1847—"the Holy of Holies," "the time of trouble," "the cloudy chariot," "Jesus on the cloud," the saints crying "day and night," and "the voice of the Son of God"—may indicate that she is describing the same vision (**V46**). However, because the message is unique enough, it may represent a separate vision, the "Millennium Vision" (**V47**). It is significant that, in describing what she saw, in Lt. 2, 1847, she repeatedly wrote "I saw *that*," which is an indication that she is interpreting rather than reporting what she saw.

[283] *Exod. 25:18–22;* Rev. 11:19; Heb. 9:4.

[284] *Exod. 25:20–22.*

[285] *Rev. 8:3, 4.*

[286] *Heb. 9:4;* cf. Num. 17:10; 1 Kings 8:9.

[287] *Exod. 31:18;* Deut. 9:10.

[288] *Isa. 58:13, 14.*

[289] *Mal. 3:6.*

[290] *Dan. 7:25.*

[291] *Rev. 11:19;* Exod. 31:18; Deut. 9:10; *Exod. 20:10.*

[292] *Experience and Views* omits a sentence that is in the original: "And if one believed, and kept the Sabbath, and received the blessing attending it, and then gave it up, and broke the holy commandment, they would shut the gates of the Holy City against themselves, as sure as there was a God that rules in heaven above." Explaining this omission in Ms. 4, 1883 (in 1SM 66.5), Ellen White affirmed: "Those who have clearly seen and fully accepted the truth upon the fourth commandment, and have received the blessing attending obedience, but have since renounced their faith, and dared to violate the law of God, will find, if they persist in this path of disobedience, the gates of the city of God closed against them." The difference is "if they persist."

[293] Dan. 12:1; Luke 1:67; *Hosea 6:2, 3.* This is in 1847, when critics said that she believed other Christians were unsavable.

[294] *Ezek. 7:10–19; 2 Esdras 15:5:* "Behold, saith the Lord, I will bring plagues upon the world; the sword, famine, death, and destruction."

[295] 2 *Esdras 16:68–74* (no significant verbatim parallel wording). ExV omits: "I saw all that 'would not receive the mark of the Beast, and of his Image, in their foreheads or in their hands,' could not buy or sell. I saw that the number (666) of the Image Beast was made up; and that it was the Beast that changed the Sabbath, and the Image Beast had followed on after, and kept the Pope's, and not God's Sabbath. And all we were required to do, was to give up God's Sabbath, and keep the Pope's, and then we should have the mark of the Beast, and of his image" (WLF 19.1). Green wording from *Rev. 13:15–18.*

[296] Dan. 12:1; *Ezek. 7:15, 16; Luke 17:30–36.*

[297] Rev. 13:10.

[298] *Luke 18:7, 8.*

[299] *Hab. 3:11.*

[300] *2 Esdras 6:24.*

[301] *2 Esdras 15:34, 35:* "Behold clouds from the east and from the north unto the south, and they are very horrible to look upon, full of wrath and storm. They shall smite one upon another . . ."

[302] Deut. 4:33; Rev. 14:2; *Joel 3:16; Heb. 12:25–27.* "*Voice of God*" is used in Ezek. 10:5. Notice the contrast of this place of glory to the previous darkness.

[303] *Rev. 6:14; Matt. 24:29.*

[304] Job 41:31; *Hab.* 3:8–10; *Isa.* 2:19–21.

[305] *Ezek.* 12:25; *Mark* 13:32; *Ezek.* 20:37; *Heb.* 12:22–25; *Jer.* 25:30, 31.

[306] Gal. 6:16.

[307] Exod. 34:29; Moses' face shining was in DS, Sept. 6, 1845, p. 17.

[308] *Wisdom of Solomon* 5:1–5. The most similar part is verse 2, "When they see it, they shall be troubled with terrible fear."

[309] Rev. 15:2.

[310] Lev. 25; *Dan.* 12:10; Ezek. 10:5.

[311] *Rev.* 14:14.

[312] *Luke* 21:27.

[313] *Matt.* 24:30.

[314] *John* 5:25–28; 1 Thess. 4:14; 1 Cor. 15:54.

[315] *1 Thess.* 4:17; 1 Cor. 15:51, 52.

[316] Ezek. 1:19, 23; Rev. 4:8. Foy described the "four wings" of the "chariot and the wings of the angel," as crying, "Holy! Holy!" (Foy, p. 18).

[317] Rev. 21:2.

[318] Rev. 21:12; *Isa.* 26:2.

[319] *Rev.* 22:14.

[320] "Bro. Belden" is Albert C. Belden, the father of Stephen T. Belden who married Sarah B. Harmon.

[321] Exod. 39:26. The "Sealing Vision" (V59) described the sealing of 144,000 saints at a time that many of the original 50,000 Adventists had abandoned their faith in the Advent. The obvious discrepancy indicated that many more were to join them. In publishing this vision, Joseph Bates remarked: "I do not publish the above vision thinking to add or diminish from the 'sure word of prophecy.' That will stand the test of men and wreck of worlds! 'It is written that man shall not live by bread alone, but by every word of God.' Amen" (WLF 21).

[322] Dan. 12:1.

[323] Rev. 10:7; Isa. 59:17; Rev. 15:1.

[324] Rev. 7:1; 15:1. Several visions dealt with the four angels holding the four winds (V59, V60, V74, V94, V120).

[325] Jer. 30:7.

[326] Dan. 5:27.

[327] Ezek. 34:18; Isa. 58:12; Dan. 5:27.

[328] Rev. 7:1, 2; 9:14, 15. That more than one angel presents a golden card suggests that the card is not for identification but is a record of their missions to Earth.

[329] Luke 4:23; Ps. 103:3; James 5:14.

[330] Luke 22:20; "Father" is from Luke 23:34; Rev. 3:5.

[331] Rev. 7:1, 3; 9:15.

[332] The original in ExV 21.1; 53.2; PrT, Aug. 1849; and Broadside2 has "plead with him"; EW 38.2 changes "plead" to "pleaded."

[333] Rev. 7:2, 3; the phrase "seal of the living God" is in DS, Nov. 29, 1845, p. 35.

[334] Matt. 7:14, "strait . . . wide."

[335] Here the golden card is for angels going to earth, so it is quite possibly a record of their visits to Earth. William Foy mentions seeing cards in his visions, but they have different purposes (see EXHIBIT-4).

[336] This may be one of the "number of interesting visions of late which she has written," which James White referred to in his letter of Jan. 25, 1849, to Brother and Sister Hastings, since it is grouped with the "Shaking of the Powers of Heaven Vision" (V58) that he mentioned.

[337] Rev. 12:17; 14:12.

[338] Heb. 11:5.

[339] Matt. 24:29. For the shaking of "the powers of the heavens," see DS, Nov. 29, 1845, p. 35.

[340] Luke 21:26; Rev. 6:14.

[341] Rev. 6:14, based on Isa. 34:4.

[342] Rev. 21:2.

[343] Matt. 24:29.

[344] Heb. 12:22. The "Open and Shut Door Vision" (V69) portrayed Jesus' entrance into the Most Holy Place, illustrating the link between the commandments and the shut door. Ellen White's view of the "shut door" was interpreted one of two major ways. Eyewitnesses James White, Marion C. Truesdail, Ira Abbey, and John Yale Wilcox affirmed that she did not hold to the extreme shut-door view after the Bridegroom vision of Feb. 1845 (Loughborough, RH, Sept. 25, 1866, p. 134; GSAM 222–224; G. I. Butler, RH, April 7, 1885, p. 217). I. C. Wellcome, Israel Dammon, John Megquier, Lucinda S. Burdick, and O. R. L. Crosier held that, from 1845-1848, Ellen White advocated the view that the door of mercy was forever closed to sinners, whether or not they rejected truth. See Miles Grant, *True Sabbath*, pp. 69–75; Wellcome, *Second Advent Message*, p. 397; D. M. Canright, *Seventh-Day Adventism Renounced*, 1889, pp. 143, 144; L. R. Conradi, *Ist Frau E. G. White die Prophetin der Endgemeinde?*, p. 29 (Pieter Gerard Damsteegt, *Foundations of the Seventh-day Adventist Message and Mission*, p. 149, n1). The latter interpretation is based on the assumption that there was only one shut-door concept, and other shut-door believers did see probation as having been closed. In 1874, Lucinda also claimed that Ellen had had a vision that Christ would return in June of 1845 and that the prophecy was discussed in all the churches and in a "shut-door paper in Portland." The same year, J. N. Andrews, said he never heard such a thing and that it wasn't published. Marion Stowell Truesdail confirmed.

[345] Rev. 12:17. For the "shut door" doctrine not teaching "there was no more salvation for sinners," see William S. Ingraham, RH, June 9, 1853, p. 10, par. 6; and George I. Butler, "The Shut Door," AR Extra, Dec. 1887, pp. 14, 15, at https://documents.adventistarchives.org/Periodicals/RH/RH18871231-V64-50e.pdf.

[346] Luke 13:25; Rev. 11:19.

[347] The reference in brackets—Rev. 3:7, 8—is in the original published text.

[348] Matt. 25:6. This was a concept that gave the Adventists great hope. The clause, "The midnight cry was finished" is also used in DS, Jan.

24, 1846, p. 25, at https://documents.adventistarchives.org/AdvRelated/WMC/WMC18460124-V09-07,08.pdf.

[349] 2 Peter 1:12; 2 Cor. 3:3. The sense of "the present truth" (Greek *tē parousē alētheia*) is the truth that has come, or is present [with you].

[350] 2 Peter 1:12; Dan. 12:1.

[351] 2 Thess. 2:11, 12.

[352] 2 Peter 1:12.

[353] Ps. 50:21.

[354] 2 Esdras 2:47: "Then began I greatly to commend them that stood so stiffly for the name of the Lord."

[355] Rev. 15:1.

[356] The original had "sighs and wonders" instead of "signs and wonders."

[357] "The writer of these words did not understand them as teaching that the time for the salvation of all sinners was past. At the very time when these things were written she herself was laboring for the salvation of sinners, as her writings have been doing ever since. Her understanding of the matter as it has been presented to her is given in the following paragraphs, the first published in 1854 [ExV54 4.2], and the second in 1888 [adapting GC88, based on 4SP 270.2]: 'The "false reformations" here referred to are yet to be more fully seen. The view relates more particularly to those who have heard and rejected the light of the advent doctrine. They are given over to strong delusions. Such will not have "the travail of soul for sinners" as formerly. Having rejected the advent, and being given over to the delusions of Satan, "the time for their salvation is past." **This does not, however, relate to those who have not heard and rejected the doctrine of the second advent.**' 'It is a fearful thing to treat lightly the truth which has convinced our understanding and touched our hearts. We cannot with impunity reject the warnings which God in mercy sends us. A message was sent from heaven to the world in Noah's day, and the salvation of men depended upon the manner in which they treated that message. Because they rejected the warning, the Spirit of God was withdrawn from the sinful race, and they perished in the waters of the flood. In the time of Abraham, mercy ceased to plead with the guilty inhabitants of Sodom, and all but Lot with his wife and two daughters were consumed by the fire sent down from heaven. So in the days of Christ. The Son of God declared to the unbelieving Jews of that generation, "Your house is left unto you desolate." Looking down to the last days, the same infinite power declares, concerning those who "received not the love of the truth, that they might be saved," "For this cause God shall send them strong delusion, that they should believe a lie: that they all might be damned who believed not the truth, but had pleasure in unrighteousness." As they reject the teachings of His Word, God withdraws His Spirit, and leaves them to the deceptions which they love'" (fn. *Early Writings*, 1945 ed.).

[358] Gen. 49:24; Ps. 132:2, 5.

[359] 1 Peter 1:7.

[360] Luke 10:19.

[361] 2 Peter 1:12.

[362] Ps. 11:4.

[363] Prov. 1:27 has "destruction," "cometh" and "whirlwind." William Miller's dream was recorded in his letter of Dec. 3, 1847, and published in AHSTR, Jan. 8, 1848, p. 182, at https://archive.org/details/LetterFromBro.Wm.MillerADream1848. It was published in Oswego, NY, in May 1850 by James White in PrT, May 1850, pp. 73–75, and as a separate 11-page pamphlet entitled, "BROTHER MILLER'S DREAM, WITH NOTES," a facsimile of which is found at https://adventistdigitallibrary.org/islandora/object/adl%3A22250342.

[364] 2 Peter 1:12.

[365] Matt. 19:22; the bracketed reference is in the original published text.

[366] 1 Peter 3:18.

[367] John 19:5, etc.; 1 John 2:2.

[368] 2 Peter 1:12.

[369] Matt. 13:44.

[370] Rev. 14:12; 22:14. For their entering the city because they had the "right to the tree of life," see DS, Jan. 24, 1846, p. 25.

[371] Gen. 3:24.

[372] Ezek. 18:20. The closing quotation mark was omitted in the original published text.

[373] Rev. 5:10; 20:4, 6; Zech. 14:4; Rev. 2:7.

[374] Rev. 20:9; Mal. 4:1. Ellen White had described seeing this concept in Lt. 2, 1847, April 21, to Eli Curtis (see WLF 11, 12).

[375] 1 Peter 1:7. Ellen White received her first vision on the millennium, the "Millennium Vision" (V47) before writing Eli Curtis, editor of *The Day-Dawn*, on April 21, 1847: "I beg leave to state to you, and the scattered flock of God, what I have seen in vision relative to these things on which you have written. I fully agree with you, that there will be two literal resurrections, 1000 years apart. I also agree with you that the new heavens and the new earth, (Rev. 21:1, Isa. 65:17, 2 Pet. 3:13.) will not appear till after the wicked dead are raised, and destroyed, at the end of the 1000 years. I saw that Satan was 'loosed out of his prison,' at the end of the 1000 years, just at the time the wicked dead were raised; and that Satan deceived them by making them believe that they could take the Holy City from the saints. The wicked all marched up around the 'camp of the saints,' with Satan at their head; and when they were ready to make an effort to take the city, the Almighty breathed from his high throne, on the city, a breath of devouring fire, which came down on them, and burnt them up, 'root and branch'" (Lt. 2, 1847). The first number of *The Day-Dawn*, issued March 1845, carried O. R. L. Crosier's view of the change in Christ's heavenly sanctuary ministry (see Merlin D. Burt, at https://digitalcommons.andrews.edu/cgi/viewcontent.cgi?article=2964&context=auss). James White's article on the thousand-year judgment is in the 1847 pamphlet, "A Word to the Little Flock," p. 24. (See also RH, July 21, 1851, p. 4.) In an "Extra" of the paper in 1850 in responding to the "Age to Come" doctrine, James referred to the unique point in the "Sutton Vision" (V97) of September 1850: "But where will the saints reign with Christ through the one thousand years, if the earth lies desolate? We would here say that the doctrine, that the saints will dwell on the earth through the seventh thousand years, is without foundation in the word of God. It is true that the saints will finally inherit, and dwell on the earth, but not till after the seventh thousand years. Not till the new heaven and the new earth are created" ("The Age to Come," *The Advent Review* Extra, pp. 15). Egbert Ralph Pinney, of Seneca Falls, NY, "held as early as 1844, that the Kingdom of God would not be established on the earth till the close of the seventh millennium. The Editor of the Review has taught the same since 1845, five years before Mrs. W. had a view of this subject—that the saints would go to heaven at Christ's second advent [John vii, 33; xiii, 33, 36; xiv, 1–3, 28; 1 Pet. i, 3–8; Rev. v, 10], that the 1000 years' reign of the saints in judgment [Rev. xx, 4; Matt. xix,

28] would be in the 'Father's house' above—New Jerusalem—which Jesus has gone to prepare for his followers, while the earth remained desolate, [Jer. iv, 19–26; xxv, 15–33; Isa. xxviii, 21, 22; Zeph. i, 2–18; iii, 6–8; Isa. xiii, 9–11; xxiv, 1–6; 2 Thess. i, 7–9; ii, 8–12,] and that at the end of the 1000 years, Jesus would return to the earth with his SAINTS, [Zech. xiv, 5; Jude 14, 15,] to execute judgment upon ALL, from Cain to the latest ungodly sinner, which cannot be until the second resurrection, when all ungodly sinners will be raised" (James White, "A Test," RH, Oct. 16, 1855, p. 61; see "What is E. R. Pinney's full name?" at https://askthecenter.freshdesk.com/support/solutions/articles/15140-what-is-e-r-pinney-s-full-name-, and "Death of Elder E. R. Pinney," AHSTR, June 30, 1855, pp. 206, 207, at https://archive.org/details/AdventHerald1855V15N14-26). With Joseph Turner, John C. Bywater, John J. Porter, Alva Noyes Seymour, and Joshua V. Himes, Pinney continued writing for Joseph Marsh's *Advent Harbinger and Bible Advocate*.

[376] 2 Peter 1:12; Rev. 15:1; 21:9. The conference in Sutton, VT, lasted from September 26 to 29.

[377] Rev. 14:10.

[378] Song of Solomon 6:10; Rev. 15:1.

[379] 1 Cor. 15:54; 1 Thess. 4:17.

[380] Rev. 20:12.

[381] Rev. 2:7.

[382] Matt. 25:34.

[383] Rev. 21:19.

[384] Ellen White's "Sutton Vision" (V97) on the events of the millennium confirmed what Bible study had already revealed. James White wrote on the saints' role in heaven during the thousand years: "In the City of the Living God, which has not yet descended from God out of heaven, reigning with Christ kings and priests, one thousand years, while the earth remains desolate, waste, without inhabitant" ("The Day of Judgment," AR, Sept. 1850, p. 51, at https://documents.adventistarchives.org/Periodicals/PT-AR/PT-AR-Part2-04.pdf). This was prior to Ellen White's vision on the millennium, which she received during the Sutton conference, because the announcement of that conference is in this very issue: "There will be a General Conference of the Brethren, at the house of Bro. Harvey Childs, in Sutton, Vt., to commence Sept. 26, 9 o'clock A. M., and hold over the Sabbath. The scattered brethren and sisters are invited to attend the meeting. 'He that hath an ear to hear, let him' come and 'hear' " (AR, Sept. 1850, p. 64). For a more complete study of this history, see Miguel Patiño's summary paper on this subject, "Doctrinal Development of the Millennium in Adventism Between 1831-1850," Jan. 6, 2014.

[385] Although somewhat arbitrary, the numbering of the texts comes from *Christian Experience and Teachings of Ellen G. White*, p. 77.

[386] Heb. 1:3. God's person comes up again in ExV 64.1. Alva Noyes Seymour thought he saw a contradiction in Ellen White's statements that the Father's person was covered with a cloud while she saw Him rising from the throne (AHBA, March 26, 1853, p. 323, at https://archive.org/details/1853-advent-harbinger-mar-5-12-19-26/page/n15). It is not hard to reconcile the two descriptions.

[387] Luke 19:12; Rev. 3:4; John 20:22; 14:3.

[388] Ps. 104:3; Ezek. 1:16; Dan. 7:9. The "Bridegroom Vision" (V5) described Christ's entering the chamber with the Father to receive the kingdom before coming to earth. It explained the delay, but it did not condemn those who had not willfully rejected the fulfillment of Daniel 8:14 or the third angel's message.

[389] See Dan. 7:13. Foy used the phrase, "he stepped into the chariot," but he was not describing Christ's traveling to the Most Holy Place in heaven (Foy, p. 19).

[390] Acts 7:56; Heb. 4:14.

[391] Exod. 39:26; 28:34.

[392] Luke 11:13.

[393] John 21:19.

[394] DS, March 14, 1846 adds: "I saw one after another leave the company who were praying to Jesus in the Holiest and go and join those before the throne, and they at once received the unholy influence of Satan." Additional material is in Broadside1, April 6, 1846.

[395] Dan. 12:1.

[396] 2 Peter 1:12.

[397] 1 Kings 18:38.

[398] Luke 12:33.

[399] Hosea 8:3; 2 Peter 1:12.

[400] Ps. 24:4.

[401] 1 Thess. 4:15.

[402] 2 Peter 1:12; Rev. 7:2, 3.

[403] Rev. 12:17.

[404] Matt. 24:39.

[405] Rev. 7:1.

[406] The original text has "August 4th," which was corrected in EW 59.1.

[407] Isa. 8:19; Eccl. 9:5; the bracketed reference is in the original published text.

[408] Heb. 3:12; Eccl. 9:5.

[409] "When this view was given, spiritualism had but just arisen and was small; there were but few mediums. Since that time it has spread all over the world and counts its adherents by many millions. As a general thing, spiritualists have denied the Bible and derided Christianity. Individuals have, at different times, deplored this and protested against it, but they were so few that no attention was paid to them. Now spiritualists are changing their method, and many call themselves 'Christian spiritualists,' declaring that it will not answer to ignore religion, and affirming that they have the true Christian faith. Bearing in mind, also, that many prominent clergymen are in sympathy with spiritualism, we now see the way open for the complete fulfillment of this prediction, given in 1850. Read also remarks by the author on page 86 [ExV54 4.4–5.4: "4. *Spirit Manifestations*."]" (fn. *Early Writings*, 1945 ed.).

[410] Isa. 59:19.

[411] 1 Chron. 5:20.

[412] Prov. 10:24.
[413] Eph. 6:16.
[414] See Rev. 10:6. The evidence suggests she is referring to setting a date for Christ's return. This is particularly significant in 1851 because Joseph Bates had set a new date for Christ's return in that year. He interpreted the "seven *times*" of the day of atonement, in Lev. 16:14, 19, as predicting a seven-*year* delay for Christ's return from October 1844 to October 1851. He wrote: "The seven spots of blood on the Golden Altar and before the Mercy Seat, I fully believe represents the duration of the judicial proceedings on the living saints in the Most Holy, all of which time they will be in their affliction, even *seven years*, God by his voice will deliver them. 'For it is the blood that maketh atonement for the soul'" ("An Explanation of the Typical and Anti-typical Sanctuary by the Scriptures with a Chart," 1850, pp. 10, 11, emphasis added). Even with the vision's warning, when the time in 1851 passed, it left Ezra P. Butler in discouragement (see Ellen G. White, Lt. 8, 1851). However, Ellen White's June 21st vision had saved them from another disappointment. For a facsimile of Ellen White's "Time Never Again a Test Vision" or "Camden Vision" (**V106**), as hand copied by "A. A. D." (Abram A. Dodge) at Milton, NY, on June 29, 1851, with Ellen White's own handwritten affirmation on the envelope, "Testimony given in regard to the setting of time June 21, 1851. Preserve carefully," see *Ministry*, June 1941, p. 17; and Arthur L. White, *Ellen G. White: Messenger to the Remnant*, p. 42. Ellen White came across the envelope again (as pictured above) before leaving for Australia (RH, March 22, 1892, p. 178).
[415] The subject of the qualifications of the "messengers," or the traveling ministers who preached to the scattered bands of Adventists, was of keen interest at this point in the developing church. "I have been writing out the visions for publication and expected them to be out sooner and then you could have them in print; but as the first paper is delayed and you will be anxious to learn something of our calculations, I will wait no longer" (Lt. 4, 1851). Since this was written July 21, 1851, the very day that the "Extra" was published, she may be describing visions in *Experience and Views* that had not been previously published.
[416] Mal. 3:17; 2 Peter 1:12. George W. Holt wrote: "Precious souls are hungry for the present truth, and will perish unless they are fed with it. Mere impressions, feelings and exercises will not feed, and save them; but they must see, and understand our past experience, and our present position from the word of God. Then the 'rubbish' will be swept away, and the 'jewels' will be gathered" (PrT, March 1850, p. 64).
[417] 2 Peter 1:12; Heb. 13:17.
[418] Dan. 12:3.
[419] Rev. 7:14. Loughborough attaches this paragraph to "a vision of Aug. 24, 1850" (GSAM 498.1), the "Mysterious Rapping vision" (**V95**).
[420] 2 Peter 1:12.
[421] Isa. 52:11.
[422] 2 Cor. 2:16.
[423] 1 Peter 5:2.
[424] 2 Peter 1:12; Acts 8:21.
[425] Eph. 6:16.
[426] 2 Peter 1:12.
[427] 2 Peter 1:12.
[428] Dan. 8:14; Rev. 14:12. Ellen White's vision was not the basis for the cleansing of the sanctuary being in heaven (RH, Dec. 22, 1874, p. 204).
[429] Matt. 8:20.
[430] Rev. 15:1.
[431] Rev. 14:9.
[432] Exod. 20:11; 34:21; Dan. 7:25; Heb. 4:4, 9, 10.
[433] Isa. 58:12.
[434] Rom. 7:12.
[435] 2 Cor. 4:17 has "a far more exceeding and eternal weight of glory."
[436] 1 John 5:2.
[437] Rev. 15:1.
[438] Phil. 1:29.
[439] Isa. 13:9; cf. Zeph. 2:2; 1 Thess. 5:2.
[440] Rev. 7:2; Dan. 12:1; Isa. 33:17.
[441] Key parallel verbatim phrasing with Ms. 5, 1881, May 18, shows that she received the "Holiness of God Vision" (**V105**) on May 14, 1851.
[442] Exod. 20:10; Lev. 23:3; Deut. 5:14.
[443] Eph. 4:13.
[444] Exod. 20:10.
[445] Rom. 8:7.
[446] 2 Peter 3:16; Isa. 58:12, 13.
[447] Ezek. 13:5.
[448] 2 Peter 1:12; Mal. 3:17.
[449] Exod. 20:10; Lev. 23:3; Deut. 5:14.
[450] Isa. 11:11; Exod. 15:1.
[451] Rom. 14:16.
[452] Neh. 1:5. "Passed," in the previous sentence, was "past" in the original.
[453] 2 Peter 3:10.
[454] Ezek. 13:5; 1 Peter 1:22.
[455] Rev. 22:11.
[456] Ezek. 13:5.
[457] Mark 11:24.
[458] The opening quotation mark was omitted in the original published text.
[459] Matt. 6:6.

[460] John 15:5.

[461] The original had "I asked the angel why their."

[462] 1 Kings 18:43, 44.

[463] Isa. 53:1; John 12:38; James 5:17; Eph. 6:16. See Lt. 8, 1850, Aug. 4; RH, Aug. 19, 1851, p. 11, about the "Enchanted Ground Vision" (V94).

[464] The original had "If the Enemy can get the disponding" instead of "If the Enemy can get the desponding."

[465] Isa. 11:11. The mistaken date of September was first included in PrT, Nov. 1850, and then republished in the *Second Advent Review and Sabbath Herald* Extra, July 21, 1851; EW 74.1; and 1BIO 187.4. Her first use of the biblical phrase, "God has stretched out His hand the second time to recover the remnant of His people" was in Ms. 5, 1850, regarding the "Enchanted Ground Vision" (V94). For the October date, see Ms. 15, 1850 (Theodore James Turner, "A LETTER TO THE E. G. WHITE ESTATES [*sic*] REGARDING EARLY WRITINGS PAGE 74-75," at https://www.academia.edu/49512865/A_Letter_to_the_E_G_White_Estates_Regarding_Early_Writings_page_74_).

[466] "This applies to the chart used during the 1843 movement, and has special reference to the calculation of the prophetic periods as it appeared on that chart. The next sentence explains that there was an inaccuracy which in the providence of God was suffered to exist. But this does not preclude the publication of a chart subsequently which would correct the mistake, after the 1843 movement was past, and the calculation as then made had served its purpose" (fn. *Early Writings*, 1945 ed.).

[467] Dan. 8:13; in the KJV, the word "sacrifice," though in green, was supplied by the translators because they believed that it should have been included.

[468] Rev. 10:6.

[469] This was the "Age to Come" doctrine. She was right: modern Jerusalem is not Old Jerusalem restored. The temple is still in ruins, and Israel is not a religious state. See Julia Neuffer, "The Gathering of Israel: A Historical Study of *Early Writings*, pp. 74-76," at https://whiteestate.org/legacy/issues-gather-html.

[470] 2 Peter 1:12.

[471] Rev. 14:12.

[472] "The children of the Lord," Deut. 14:1; "the day of the Lord," Isa. 2:12; 13:6, 9. The point she is making is that conversion of Israel to Christ, as in the "Age to Come" doctrine, was a wrong-headed goal. Much better was to evangelize those within one's reach. Eventually, the expanding Advent message went to Europe and the Southern United States and Asia and South America and the islands of the Pacific as well as to the Jewish people. Regarding the building up of Old Jerusalem, J. H. Waggoner wrote of James Martin Stephenson and Dwight P. Hall: "Elds. Stephenson and Hall both expressed themselves as being convinced that the Testimonies were from the Lord. [See RH, Aug. 7, 1856, p. 110, for Stephenson's opinion of a vision related on June 8, 1853.] But they soon discovered something in the book, 'Experience and Views,' which directly crossed the track of the age to come. It was to the teaching of this book that they first took exception, not professing to doubt the message, but affirming that the Testimonies were not a part of the message, nor necessary to the message. But they soon took the next step, a step which we expected they would take. They found that the whole theory of the message,—the doctrine of the Sanctuary, the Judgment, the seven last plagues before the advent, the great day of the wrath of the Lamb, and the desolation of the earth,—was in harmony with the 'Experience and Views,' but could not be harmonized with the age to come. They took their stand on the age to come, and rejected the message. They could not retain both" (RH, March 13, 1883, p. 170). Stephenson and Hall joined the dissident Messenger party. Stephenson also referred to Christ as a "created being" (https://asitreads.com/jm-stephenson).

[473] The engraving "Our Saviour," by John Sartain, has been identified as the image of Jesus that W. C. White described to Fred Harvey as what Ellen G. White considered "the most nearly correct of any picture she had seen," to what she had seen of Jesus in vision, though he associated it with the picture above that is found in Edson White's book, *The Coming King*, copyright 1898, 1905, 1907, and 1911 (Letter, April 25, 1935, at https://ellenwhite.org/correspondence/183865).

[474] Rev. 6:16.

[475] Rev. 22:2; 21:6; 22:1.

[476] Heb. 1:3. The closing quotation mark was omitted in the original. One instance of seeing the lovely Jesus was on May 14, 1851, in the "Holiness of God Vision" (V105). Ellen White wrote: "I saw the beauty and loveliness of Jesus, and it seemed as though I could never bear to be parted from His lovely presence" (Ms. 5, 1851, May 18). However, in 1846, Enoch Jacobs joined the Shakers. He wrote: "O what an ocean of contradictory theories is that upon which the multitudes have been floating for the last 18 months" (DS, May 23, 1846, p. 51). Later he added: "We thought the fault was all without—sad mistake!! It was within. This out of doors salvation has always been a precarious thing" (DS, June 13, 1846, p. 9). Thus, the "Personhood of God Vision" (V30) would have been in 1846. The statement in ExV 64.1 contrasts with the creedal statement, "There is but one living and true God, everlasting, *without body or parts*, of infinite power, wisdom, and goodness: the maker and preserver of all things, visible and invisible. And in unity of this Godhead, there are three persons, *of one substance*, power, and eternity;—the Father, the Son, and the Holy Ghost" (Robert R. Roberts, *The Doctrines and Discipline of the Methodist Episcopal Church*, 1840, p. 9). Early Adventists frequently expressed concern that the creedal statements taught "that God is without form or parts" (Uriah Smith, "Communications," RH, July 10, 1856, p. 87), when Exod. 33:11, 20, 22, 23 refer to His form and parts. James White insisted that "God is a *person*" (DS, vol. 9, no. 7, Jan. 24, 1846, p. 25), and Ellen White agreed with him. Nothing in her visions implied that Christ was less than eternal. Full divinity requires it. In describing His sonship, she repeatedly called Him the "*eternal* Son" (RH, Aug. 8, 1878, Art. A; Lt. 6, 1880; Lt. 37, 1887; YI, Aug. 31, 1887; Ms. 58, 1897; Ms. 99, 1897; RH, Feb. 8, 1898; ST, Jan. 4, 1899; Lt. 232, 1903; RH, April 5, 1906), and she quoted: "Strong in the strength which God supplies through His eternal Son" from Charles Wesley's hymn, "Soldiers of Christ, Arise" (see ST, Jan. 4, 1883; Lt. 3, 1893; Lt. 16, 1896; Lt. 150, 1897; and Lt. 69, 1903). In a passage using language from Proverbs 8 to describe Christ's pre-existence, she wrote: "Christ was God *essentially*, and *in the highest sense*. He *was with God from all eternity, God over all*, blessed forevermore. The Lord Jesus Christ, the divine Son of God, *existed from eternity*, a distinct person, yet one with the Father" (RH, April 5, 1906; ST, April 26, 1899, emphasis added). Again, in another passage using language from Proverbs 8 for the same purpose, she wrote: "Christ is the pre-existent, self-existent Son of God. . . . In speaking of His *pre-existence*, Christ carries the mind back through dateless ages. He assures us that there *never was a time when He was not in close fellowship with the eternal God*. He to whose voice the Jews were then listening had been with God *as one brought up with Him*" (ST, Aug. 29, 1900, emphasis added). Describing Christ's reception into glory, she wrote: "As soon as this ceremony was completed, the Holy Spirit descended upon the disciples in rich currents, and Christ was indeed glorified, even with the glory which He had with the Father *from all eternity*" (AA 38.3, emphasis added). For God to pass on His divinity in the way that humans

pass on their humanity would contradict the eternal nature of divinity.

[477] The phrase "last days" was used of the apostles' time (see Acts 2:17; Heb. 1:2; James 5:3), but it was also used of a time future to the apostles (2 Tim. 3:1; 2 Peter 3:3). The promise of visions in the last days is found in Acts 2:17, 18, which is the fulfilment of Joel 2:28, 29. The gift of prophecy is given for "edification, and exhortation, and comfort" (1 Cor. 14:3)—just what we find in the ministry of Ellen G. White.

[478] Rom. 8:5.

[479] Isa. 4:5.

[480] In 1853, James White wrote: "We have on hand a quantity of the Pamphlet, entitled, 'A Sketch of the Christian Experience and Views of Ellen G. White.' The author has recently added a few notes of explanation, which make the little work of more interest. As it was not fully paid for by donations, we conclude to sell it at ten cents a copy" (RH, March 31, 1853, p. 184). Thus, in 1853, Ellen White prefaced the "Notes of Explanation" with the comment: "In looking over this little work, I have thought it my duty to refer to, and explain some points." Then she gave five points of explanation, four of which are virtually the same as points 1 through 4 carried over into the 1854 "Supplement." The omitted point, number "4" in the additional "Notes of Explanation," says: "Also see the second paragraph of page 57, and compare that view, given Sept. 7th, 1851, with the bitter, slanderous remarks of those who have opposed the Sabbath since that time, especially for the past year." Point number 5, regarding "Spirit Manifestations," occurred for the first time in the January 1854 "Supplement" and was not included in the 1853 "Notes of Explanation." A facsimile of the first page is found in *The Ellen G. White Letters and Manuscripts with Annotations*, vol. 1, p. 304.

[481] Dan. 12:1.

[482] Acts 3:19; Ezek. 13:5; Rev. 18:1–4; 15:1.

[483] Ellen White listed this as a separate view; otherwise, we likely would judge it a part of the "Open and Shut Door Vision" (**V69**).

[484] Isa. 11:11.

[485] Ellen White listed this as a separate view, otherwise we would consider it part of the "Open and Shut Door Vision" (**V69**).

[486] James White referred to "mysterious rappings" in ExV 2.1, though headed "Mysterious Rapping."

[487] Rev. 13:13.

[488] Matt. 24:24.

[489] ExV54 5.4–10.2 (which corresponds to EW 87.1–91.2) was used in the chapter "Spiritualism," in 1SG 173.1–178.1 (which corresponds to EW 262.1–265.2).

[490] 2 Peter 1:12.

[491] Rev. 16:14.

[492] Rev. 16:14.

[493] 2 Peter 1:12; 1 Peter 3:15.

[494] Rev. 16:14; Matt. 13:30.

[495] 2 Cor. 11:14.

[496] 2 Thess. 2:11, 12.

[497] Matt. 13:30.

[498] Matt. 7:14.

[499] The closing quotation mark was omitted in the original published text.

[500] Jer. 15:19.

[501] Rev. 21:8. Thomas Paine, the English-born American political theorist, authored *Common Sense* (1776) and *The American Crisis* (1776–1783), which inspired patriots, in 1776, to declare independence from Great Britain. In ridiculing Christianity, he lost many friends and only had six people attending his funeral when he died at nearly 73 years of age (Poughkeepsie *Political Barometer*, June 21, 1809).

[502] "To appreciate the force of these remarks the reader needs to understand that a work was published through the mediumship of 'Rev. C. Hammond,' entitled *Pilgrimage of Thomas Paine in the Spirit World*, in which Paine is represented as an exalted spirit in the Seventh Sphere. And in the 'Investigating Class in New York,' it was said that Christ himself had conversed with a medium and revealed that he was in the Sixth Sphere. The disparity will be understood when it is remembered that they represent the spirits as progressing in the spirit world, and that Christ, after more than 1800 years of progress, has reached the sixth sphere, while Paine, in about 100 years, has reached the seventh! A further explanation of this may be found in the statement of doctor Hare, that his spirit sister said her progress had been retarded by her belief in the atonement of Christ. Thus does spiritualism exalt infidels and infidelity. See also appendix [in *Early Writings*]" (fn. *Early Writings*, 1945 ed.). The non-capitalization of "Satan" was common among Adventists at this time, as one can see here and in several other instances in the text. Also "Christian," when referring to an individual, was frequently left uncapitalized.

[503] John 8:44.

[504] Rev. 3:1.

[505] John 8:44.

[506] 2 Thess. 2:9.

[507] 1 John 4:14; 2 Thess. 2:9.

[508] Rev. 15:1; 16:14.

[509] This should have been point number 6.

[510] 2 Peter 1:12.

[511] Continuing the quotation from Ms. 1, 1853, a quotation mark should have begun and ended this paragraph in the original published text, which would have changed the other quotation marks for "woe" and "There are others who … The paper will be supported without my help" into single quotation marks, as in EW 93.3.

[512] Hosea 8:3. Quotation marks within the quotation should have been single quotes, as follows: "… 'loaves and fishes.' Such had much better have been at home laboring with their hands, 'the thing that is good,' …" This is distinguished as a separate view in ExV54 13.1, otherwise we would consider it part of the "Sutton Vision" (**V97**), given sometime on Sep. 26–29, 1850.

[513] Eph. 4:28.

[514] 2 Peter 1:12.

[515] "Gospel order" means "church organization." See https://documents.adventistarchives.org/Books/OrgCPPD1938.pdf. The rapidly growing young church required organization and discipline. "The Adventists were of all churches, and at first they had no idea of forming another church. After 1844 there was great confusion, and the majority were strongly opposed to any organization, holding that it was inconsistent with the perfect liberty of the gospel. The testimony and labors of Mrs. White have always been opposed to fanaticism, and in the instruction given through her, organization in some form was early insisted upon, as necessary to prevent confusion" (fn. *Early Writings*, 1945 ed.). "Gospel Order" was a major bone of contention for those who aligned with the Messenger party.

[516] Eph. 4:13.

[517] 2 Peter 1:12.

[518] 2 Peter 1:12.

[519] 2 Peter 1:12.

[520] Acts 20:27.

[521] Mal. 3:17.

[522] Mal. 3:17.

[523] Eph. 4:13.

[524] 2 Tim. 1:7.

[525] Rev. 16:14.

[526] Josh. 24:19; cf. Exod. 20:5; 34:14; Deut. 4:24; 5:9; 6:15.

[527] Eph. 5:27.

[528] Mal. 3:6.

[529] The original text did not have an apostrophe in "other's."

[530] 2 Peter 1:12.

[531] Ezek. 45:4.

[532] John 17:19.

[533] James 5:15.

[534] Ezra 3:12.

[535] Isa. 53:3.

[536] Matt. 8:20; Luke 9:58.

[537] Luke 8:17.

[538] Mark 12:13; Luke 23:21.

[539] Luke 19:37–40.

[540] Luke 19:40.

[541] Acts 1:11.

[542] Isa. 25:9.

[543] 1 Cor. 15:52; Dan. 12:2; 1 Cor. 15:54.

[544] 1 Cor. 15:52; 1 Thess. 4:17.

[545] Heb. 6:5.

[546] Titus 2:13; Phil. 3:21.

[547] Phil. 3:20.

[548] 1 Peter 1:7 (previous sentence); Phil. 1:29; Rom. 5:3.

[549] Isa. 53:5; Matt. 12:36; Gen. 16:3.

[550] Isa. 57:15.

[551] Heb. 12:2, 3; Isa. 53:4.

[552] This explanation seems to be a direct response to "Delusion.—E. White's Visions," AHBA, March 26, 1853, p. 323, written by Alva Noyes Seymour, of Plymouth, MI, who had acted deceptively toward the Adventists (Samuel W. Rhodes, AR, Sept. 1850, p. 48) and would oppose them about the Sabbath.

[553] Rev. 12:11.

[554] She originally had written, "I saw that they did not come together to sit still, and look at each other" (Ms. 3, 1853).

[555] In Lt. 9, 1853, she identified the vision as having been received "at our last conference," at New Haven, VT, Oct. 28 and 29, 1853.

[556] Rev. 4:8.

[557] "Wash . . . feet," John 13:14; "Lord's supper," 1 Cor. 11:20; "example," "do as," and "done," John 13:15.

[558] Luke 7:44.

[559] For the "*holy kiss*," see Rom. 16:16; 1 Cor. 16:20; 2 Cor. 13:12; 1 Thess. 5:26. Peter calls it the "kiss of charity" (1 Peter 5:14).

[560] Allusions are from Matt. 13:29, 39.

[561] Rev. 3:17.

[562] 2 Esdras 2:47: "Then began I greatly to commend them that stood so stiffly for the name of the Lord." Her concern is similar to what she wrote in Lt. 11, 1853, from the "To Those of Little Experience Vision" (**V138**): "About some being too fast and some too slow, I saw that some have run into the field to labor before they were sent, and traveled extensively. I might mention individual cases. Brother Lothrop is one that was shown me. His influence has been bad in many places. He has thought too much of himself, when he had but little judgment. Towle and Eastman were others whom God had never sent, and who were only a curse to the cause." "Brother Lothrop" is Howard Lothrop. Towle and Eastman are identified in RH, Nov. 15, 1853, p. 148, as "J. R. Towle" and "Ezra Eastman," which were John R. Towle, of West Canaan, NH, who took the discipline well (see Towle's "Confession of Faults" in RH, Dec. 11, 1856, p. 46), and Ezra Stowell Eastman, who was living with family on his mother's side in Hatley, Canada East, in the early 1850s (RH, Feb. 3, 1852, p. 88; cf. RH, July 22, 1852, p. 148; cf. RH, Oct. 28, 1852, p. 104; RH, Feb. 17, 1853; RH, March 31, 1853, p. 184; RH, July 7, 1853, p. 32; RH, Oct. 18, 1853, p. 120), and who left Adventism after he was not recognized as an Adventist preacher (RH, Nov. 15, 1853, p. 148). A very large man of over 300 pounds and a

height of 6' 7" (*Manchester Daily Mirror*, Sept. 7, 1863, p. 4), he became a Baptist minister (*The Story of Sunapee*, 1941, p. 62).

563 "Stupidity" is highlighted because earlier she wrote: "A dream the Lord gave me August 22. . . . Many I saw sleeping. I said as I saw those poor souls, they have heard of Jesus' coming and that great day of God's wrath just upon them, but as time went on a little longer then they expected it would, they have lost their interest. Stupidity has crept over them and now they slumber never to awake. They ought to have watched and then they would have seen the angels. This dream has made quite an impression upon my mind" (Ms. 6, 1850, Aug. 22). Describing this dream in a letter, she wrote: "I looked around and saw some sleeping. O how I felt as I saw some who now profess to be with us asleep as I saw them. I said, 'Poor souls. They have heard of Jesus' coming and that the day of His wrath was very soon to come, but as time went on a little longer than they expected it would, they have lost their interest. Stupidity has crept over them and now they slumber never to awake again. They ought to have watched and then they would have seen the angels.' This dream has made a great impression on my mind. I hope it will cause me to double my diligence and to make my calling and election sure" (Lt. 14, 1850, Sept. 1, key parallel word highlighted).

564 Jer. 25:37.

565 Ps. 65:5.

566 Rev. 15:1.

567 Ellen White wrote on Dec. 14, 1851: "I have seen in vision that *tobacco* was a *filthy weed*, and that it must be laid *aside* or given up. Said my accompanying angel, 'If it is an idol it is high time it was given up, and unless it is given up the frown of God will be upon the one that uses it and he cannot be sealed with the seal of the living God. *If it is used as a medicine*, Go to God, He is the great Physician and those that use the *filthy weed* for medicine greatly dishonor God.' There is a 'balm in Gilead'; there is a 'physician there.' [Jeremiah 8:22.] 'Be ye clean that bear the vessels of the Lord.' 'Be ye clean that bear the vessels of the Lord' [Isaiah 52:11]" (Lt. 5, 1851, emphasis added).

568 Rev. 20:13; Matt. 16:27; see also Rom. 2:6.

569 1 Tim. 6:16; Exod. 33:20.

570 Isa. 29:9.

571 Ezek. 13:5. She had used this phrase in Ms. 5, 1850: "Said the angel, Can ye stand in the battle in the day of the Lord?"

572 Isa. 29:9.

573 Isa. 10:4; Rev. 3:9. For "that God has loved them," see DS, Nov. 29, 1845, p. 35.

574 Rev. 9:5; Isa. 5:25; 9:17; John 10:12, 13; Gen. 7:23.

575 Mark 7:7.

576 Gal. 5:1.

577 2 Peter 1:12; 1 Peter 3:15.

578 Ezek. 13:5.

579 Gen. 3:22, 24. Ellen White later used ExV54 46.2–48.2 in writing 1SG 21.2–22.2; and 26.1–26.3, which she used in writing 1SP 45.1, 47.2–48.2 (see EXHIBIT-6). Ellen White described the same scene of ExV54 46.3, 4 in PrT, April 1850, using the verbatim phrase, "of the tree of life, and be immortal sinners."

580 Matt. 26:44, parallel to the three times in the garden. She does not mention the Holy Spirit here, but she would later describe the involvement of all three members of the Godhead (see Lt. 12, 1901 and Ms. 45, 1904).

581 Matt. 20:28. At least six scriptures support Ellen White's view of the Son's willingly offering Himself as our sacrifice. "Who gave himself for our sins, that he might deliver us from this present evil world, according to the will of God and our Father" (Gal. 1:4). "I am crucified with Christ: nevertheless I live; yet not I, but Christ liveth in me: and the life which I now live in the flesh I live by the faith of the Son of God, who loved me, and gave himself for me" (Gal. 2:20). "Husbands, love your wives, even as Christ also loved the church, and gave himself for it" (Eph. 5:25). "Who gave himself a ransom for all, to be testified in due time" (1 Tim. 2:6). "Who gave himself for us, that he might redeem us from all iniquity, and purify unto himself a peculiar people, zealous of good works" (Titus 2:14). "How much more shall the blood of Christ, who through the eternal Spirit offered himself without spot to God, purge your conscience from dead works to serve the living God?" (Heb. 9:14).

582 A scripture that supports Ellen White's view that it was not without a struggle that the Father gave the Son is John 3:16: "For God so loved the world, that he gave his only begotten Son . . ." So very much is packed into that little word "so"!

583 Heb. 6:18.

584 Uriah Smith was born in New Hampshire and took part in the Advent movement as a boy. He was baptized a Sabbatarian Adventist in 1852 and is well-known for editing the *Review and Herald* for many years and for writing several books on Daniel and Revelation.

585 See RH, Nov. 25, 1851, p. 52.

586 In 1868, James White published the words and the music in *The Seventh-day Adventist Hymn and Tune Book*, and the hymn later appeared in other hymnals, such as https://ia800501.us.archive.org/27/items/hymnsofadventoobark/hymnsofadventoobark_bw.pdf; http://www.archive.org/details/hymnsofmorningdeoobark; https://hymnary.org/hymn/SDAH1886/page/401. To bring a spiritual truth home to the heart of the reader, Ellen White loved to sing hymns and frequently quoted from a hymn in a letter or an article. For more on her use of hymns, see Kevin Morgan, "Hymns Loved and Sung by Ellen White," at https://www.academia.edu/43684888/Hymns_Loved_and_Sung_by_Ellen_White, and Kevin Morgan, "Anonymous No Longer, Poetry in Ellen White's Writings," at https://www.academia.edu/43607204/Anonymous_No_Longer_Poetry_in_Ellen_Whites_Writings.

587 Rom. 8:18.

588 Marion C. Truesdail, Jan. 27, 1891, in GSAM 238.4. Supernatural feats alone are not a test of the gift of prophecy since Satan can perform miracles, except when those feats are backed by a noble character and messages that lead to greater faithfulness to God (see A. G. Daniells, *The Abiding Gift of Prophecy*, p. 271).

589 Mercy A. Curtis, née Barnes, wife of Robert G. Curtis, who is listed as a fisherman in the 1880 US Census.

590 Frances Lunt, née Howland, wrote from Oakland, CA, Jan. 19, 1890, in GSAM 238.1; cf. GSAM 245.2.

591 Ellen G. White Record Book 2, p. 18, Ellen G. White Estate, no date, but other testimonials in the book are dated to 1874, quoted in 15MR 66.3. Loughborough says it was a Teal Bible (GCDB, March 18, 1891, p. 145). Rebekah E. Lunt, née Chamberlain, is "Rebecca" on her tombstone but "Rebekah" in RH, May 30, 1918, p. 23. Both this vision and V77, in 1849, were at Topsham, Maine. No one else mentioned

the Apocrypha in relation to the 1845 vision, but they did mention it in relation to V77. Denford Ntini points out how Ellen White elevated the "Word of God" while observing that the "hidden book" was "not there." She did not say that "parts of the Word of God were missing, but showed a distinction between the Bible and the hidden book" ("Article on Ellen White, Adventism and the Apocrypha," p. 8).

592 Ellen G. White Record Book 2, p. 16, Ellen G. White Estate, Sept. 18, 1874.

593 See DF 105f, https://whiteestate.org/legacy/vault-otis_text-asp, which was edited and included in 2SG 77.2–79.1; LS80 233.

594 Sargent, Robbins, and French were Adventist leaders in the Boston area. French is possibly John French, Sr., who lived near Thayer.

595 Zaccheus Thayer (d. 1852) is listed in Randolph, MA, in the 1840 US Census (https://www.familysearch.org/ark:/61903/1:1:XHYQ-QG1).

596 RH, Sept. 5, 1899, p. 566: "This I have stated as related to me by Elders Bates and White" (PGGC 56). Reuel Stinson Webber, residing in Battle Creek on Feb. 9, 1891, corroborated the story, saying that, about twenty years before, Dammon had described the same event and his account agreed precisely with Loughborough's (RP 130; GSAM 262.5). In 1873, Webber held meetings in Penobscot County, ME, where Dammon resided (GDB Nov. 4, 1889, p. 132; RH, Aug. 5, 1873, p. 63). W. C. White heard the story many times from his father (W. C. White to Mabel Workman, July 23, 1937, *online* **EXHIBIT-7,** no. 36, and at https://ellenwhite.org/correspondence/297097).

597 The original has the spelling "Damon," which is also spelled "Dammon" and "Damman." Dammon quit traveling with the Whites as a result of "an old grudge against Bro. White for a letter he wrote him in 1845 or '46" (U. Smith, *Defense of Eld. James White and Wife*, p. 109).

598 Joseph Bates, writing from Fairhaven, MA, in the pamphlet "A Word to the Little Flock," 1847, p. 21.

599 James White, "A Sketch of the Rise and Progress of the Present Truth," RH, Dec. 31, 1857, p. 61; see 2SG 95–99.

600 The "Empire State," in the United States of America, is New York.

601 Alexander Ross, oral report, Roosevelt, NY, Jan. 4, 1884, in RP 138; GSAM 269.2. Ross was one of 35 present at David Arnold's carriage house (GSAM 268.1).

602 See https://ellenwhite.org/correspondence/179857, handwritten, excerpted in 2SG 64. In this letter to Leonard and Elvira Hastings, dated Aug. 26, 1848, is the first mention of Ellen White's breathlessness—"she did not breathe at all."

603 Ellen G. White Record Book 2 (unpublished), p. 18, Ellen G. White Estate, no date given, but other testimonials in the book are dated to 1874. The signers were "Mrs. S. Howland" (Louisa Howland, wife of Stockbridge Howland), Rebekah Howland Winslow, and Frances Howland Lunt. Rebekah married Henry Clay Winslow in 1857, and Frances married Noah Lunt in 1869, so this testimonial had to have been written after 1869.

604 Marion Truesdail, née Stowell, GSAM 245.1. The date "April, 1847" that Loughborough inserted in brackets was not in the original.

605 Frances Lunt, née Howland, oral testimony, Jan. 19, 1890, in GSAM 244.3. Loughborough reported: "In a letter from Mrs. Frances Lunt, she gives the names of three persons who were present on this occasion, and on whom the Bibles were laid while Mrs. White talked to them on the text for each, and among the names was that of Mrs. Truesdail." (RP 134; GSAM 245.2).

606 Augusta Stowell is Harriet Augusta Barton, née Stowell.

607 Ms. 5, 1849, Sept. 23. The vision's reporter is unknown. According to Louisa Howland, the vision took place at her house. The report in the memory statement, "the hidden book was not there," sounds remarkably similar to "Hidden book, it is cast out."

608 Washington Morse, "Items of Advent Experience during the Past Fifty Years.—No. 5," RH, Oct. 23, 1888, p. 658.

609 Washington Morse is describing another vision that Ellen White had that weekend, the "Feed the Sheep Not the Dogs Vision" (**V115**).

610 Martha D. Amadon, née Byington, written from St. Joseph, MI, on Nov. 24, 1925, in "Mrs. E. G. White in Vision," *Notebook Leaflets From the Elmshaven Library*, DF 105c (1930), at https://ellenwhite.org/media/document/8010, and RH, May 18, 1944, pp. 7, 8. This was the 65th anniversary of her marriage to George Washington Amadon. Brian Strayer lists her middle name as "Dorner."

611 Taken from the hymn written by William Henry Hyde after he heard Ellen White relate her "New Earth Vision" (**V16**), which is published in PrT, Nov. 1850.

612 If "cataleptic," as some claim, she would have been stiff and not moving about with fluid movements, as described by witnesses (see https://documents.adventistarchives.org/Periodicals/RH/RH18871231-V64-50e.pdf, p. 11).

613 1 Peter 1:23.

614 See RH, Aug. 19, 1852, p. 64. Conferences were held in Vermont, New York, and Michigan (RH, Oct. 13, 1859, p. 164). One was at Buck's Bridge, NY, on Oct. 19, 1859 (RH, Sept. 22, 1859, p. 144; RH, Dec. 1, 1859, p. 12). A later meeting at Buck's Bridge was on Aug. 17 and 18, 1861 (RH, Sep. 3, 1861, p. 108). Regarding this meeting, James Henry Curtis, of North Stockholm, NY, testified: "I have been slow to learn, too apt to reject truth before investigating the matter. I have been skeptical in regard to spiritual gifts; but when I heard sister White's exhortation last Summer at Buck's Bridge, I began to get my eyes open to the truth, and thanks be to God! I now see the beauty of the doctrine of the gifts of the Spirit" (RH, July 22, 1862, p. 63). John Byington, who had broken with the Methodist Episcopal Church over its views of slavery, would become the first president of the Seventh-day Adventists.

615 J. N. Loughborough, "THE STUDY OF THE TESTIMONIES.—No. 2," GCB, Jan. 29 and 30, 1893, pp. 19, 20; earlier in "Recollections of the Past.—No. 4," RH, March 4, 1884, p. 154; also in PUR, Aug. 12, 1915, p. 1. In 1866, Loughborough recounted how Ellen White was shown that a "Sr. R.," who "boarded much of her time in the city," was "nightly tormented by the Devil, who would appear to her as soon as she retired in the form of an old woman dressed in black" (RH, Dec. 25, 1866, p. 30), threatening to choke her to death if she told anyone. "Sr. R" was Elizabeth Riggs, née Hunt, of Parma, NY, who had attended several seances (RP 173; https://documents.adventistarchives.org/Periodicals/PUR/PUR19090722-V08-51.pdf). After relating these facts to Sr. Riggs, Mrs. White encouraged her to rebuke the devil in the name of the Lord, and Sr. Riggs acknowledged the correctness of the vision and immediately appeared to be choking. Through the prayers of William S. Ingraham and others at the home of Jonathan and Caroline Orton, Riggs rebuked the devil, recovered, and was no longer tormented. In the same vision, Ellen White also received a message for Riggs' husband, Christopher Dean Riggs, revealing that he had violated the seventh commandment (see RH, Dec. 25, 1866, p. 30; RH, March 4, 1884, p. 154). His property is located at https://www.loc.gov/resource/g3803m.la000518/?r=0.222,0.245,0.102,0.051,0.

616 In 1866, he used "about fifty visions"; in 1905, "over forty different times" (GSAM 488); in 1911, "nearly fifty times" (PGGC 14). He didn't leave a detailed list.

617 Compare Daniel's description while in vision: "there remained no strength in me, neither is there breath left in me" (Dan. 10:17).

618 F. C. Castle, "Thoughts of the Past," RH, March 30, 1897, p. 197. The vision links to Ms. 2, 1853, March 1. Franklin Chauncey Castle was

born in Edwards, St. Lawrence County, NY, and lived in the county much of his early life. His oldest son, Herbert Alfred Castle, was born in Royalton, VT. Castle moved to Battle Creek in 1870 and later to Cedar Edge, Colorado, engaging in evangelism wherever he went. Tragically, he died in a wagon accident.

[619] Nathaniel White died May 6, 1853; Anna White, Nov. 30, 1854. They are buried at Mt. Hope Cemetery, Rochester, NY.

[620] Merritt G. Kellogg's Dec. 28, 1890, statement is in RP 95, 96; cf. RH, May 6, 1884, p. 299; PGGC 45.2. This was Ellen White's first vision in Michigan. On June 3, 1906, Kellogg wrote J. H. Kellogg: "I have seen Mrs. White in vision quite a number of times between 1852 and 1859 . . . every vital function was reduced to the lowest point compatible with life; pulse almost stopped and very infrequent breathing so slight as to be imperceptible." Dr. Francis Pinkney Drummond examined her in vision and verified that she did not breathe. George Orlando States placed this vision in a new barn [William Dawson's] in Sylvan, MI, in the summer of 1853: "My mother explained to me about Sister White's visions, that she was for some time without breathing while her eyes were open, the same as were the prophets in Bible times. Although I was only a child, these things made impressions which are still very vivid upon my mind" (RH, Aug. 2, 1906, p. 10).

[621] RH, July 22, 1884, pp. 472, 473; cf. RP 188, 189; GSAM 322.3. George States remembered this vision (RH, Sept. 2, 1915, p. 17).

[622] Ellen White described the June 3 visions in 2SG 181.1; Cyrenius Smith confirmed seeing her in vision (MT, Oct. 19, 1854, p. 3).

[623] Ms. 1, 1853; Hiram's daughter, Savilla A. Case, said what Abigail Palmer called her neighbor rhymed with "witch" (MT Nov. 30, 1854, p. 4).

[624] With some other articles, the "main purpose of the paper . . . was to speak against Ellen White's visions, to oppose James White's work and leadership, and to accuse Sabbatarians of an un-Christian spirit against those who did not agree with them" (Theodore N. Levterov, "The Development of the Seventh-day Adventist Understanding of Ellen G. White's Prophetic Gift, 1844-1889," p. 82).

[625] Castle's statement, first in RP 96, was written when he was living in Gunnison Valley, Colorado (see RH, Jan. 24, 1888, p. 60; RH, March 30, 1897, p. 197). At the time of the Stowe conference, he was living in Edwards, St. Lawrence County, NY, and was able to attend the conferences there and in Stowe, VT, a short distance away (see RH, Aug. 11, 1853, p. 56). Many from New York attended the Stowe conference (RH, Oct. 4, 1853, p. 104). Loughborough wrote: "On another occasion, in 1853, a physician seeing her recover her breath on coming out of vision, said: 'The action is precisely like that of the new-born infant drawing its first breath, and is *positive proof* that while in vision she has not been breathing" (RH, Aug. 8, 1899, p. 502). Mary Abigail Morton, née Sanford, who received the Advent message from Joseph Bates in 1852, wrote: "I was present when Sister White was in vision, as early as 1854, and can corroborate what Elder Loughborough has written in his book concerning the visions. It was truly wonderful to see and hear her while in open vision" (RH, July 7, 1927, p. 2).

[626] Loughborough called on David Henry Lamson to give his eyewitness account at the General Conference at Battle Creek, Feb. 8, 1893 (see https://documents.adventistarchives.org/Periodicals/GCSessionBulletins/GCB1893-03.pdf; GSAM 207, 208). Lamson was introduced to Adventism in 1853 by J. N. Loughborough during meetings in Clarkson, NY (RH, Sept. 27, 1853). The two physicians were Dr. Lorenzo Dow Fleming, who had practiced medicine at the Lake-View Water Cure Institution since 1853, and Dr. David Abeel Baldwin, who practiced with him (*Water-Cure Journal*, Dec. 1853, p. 138). Fleming, who pastored the Casco Street Christian church, invited William Miller to Portland, ME, March 11–23, 1840 (see *Advent Review*, Sept. 1850, p. 53; RH, Nov. 25, 1884; Ms. 186, 1905). When his speaking voice failed, Fleming resigned his ministerial post in March 1841 and became a doctor in Canandaigua, NY; New Bedford, MA; and Rochester, NY, using homeopathic methods to regain his voice (Evan William Humphreys, *Memoirs of Deceased Christian Ministers*, 1880, pp. 129–131). Ellen White apparently had a public vision in July or August of 1854 during meetings in Hastings, MI (RH, Aug. 29, 1854, p. 24) because Dr. Aaron Whitney Nichols (see RH, July 4, 1854, p. 176; RH, Aug. 15, 1854, p. 8) attended meetings in Hastings and told others "he saw Sister White in vision and this had a deep and lasting impression on his mind" (RH, March 21, 1907, p. 23). By now, the Whites had moved from Mount Hope Street to Monroe Street in Rochester. When Jonathan Orton was beaten to death in 1866, Dr. Fleming performed the autopsy (*New York Times*, March 11, 1866; GSAM 381.3). Joseph Bradley Lamson, cousin to David Henry Lamson, married Drusilla Orton, who lived in Rochester, NY. In September 1852, she and her parents, Jonathan Orton and Caroline Orton, née Kerr, accepted the seventh-day Sabbath at the same time as J. N. Loughborough. Loughborough listed this vision, in RH, Aug. 8, 1899, p. 502, as occurring June 24, 1854.

[627] Her March 9, 1893, statement at Clifton Springs, NY (where she served as the matron of the sanitarium), is in GSAM 208.

[628] Seeley's Aug. 20, 1897, statement, written in Fayette, Iowa, is in GSAM 208. "At the time of this vision at Rochester, the Messenger party was doing its work, and the church was just on the verge of the defection of Stephenson and Hall, of Wisconsin" (1BIO 304.2).

[629] Loughborough worded it slightly differently in RH, Aug. 8, 1899, p. 502: "That settles it! There is not a particle of breath in that woman's body!" In this same article he listed additional tests that were applied to her while in vision: "The closest tests applied to Mrs. White while in vision have led the most skeptical to decide that she was oblivious to all her surroundings. *Pricking the hands with needles* would not occasion the slightest resistance. *A lighted candle* brought suddenly so near her eyes as to singe her eyebrows, or even *the tip end of the finger touched to the pupil of the eye*, failed in causing her to flinch, or to produce the least resistance. Those thus experimenting have exclaimed, 'She does not know anything of what is taking place around her' " (RH, Aug. 8, 1899, p. 502, emphasis added).

[630] Louisa M. Morton, "An Appeal to the Brethren in Wisconsin, and All Others Who Have Forsaken the Third Angel's Message," RH, March 19, 1857, p. 157. Morton had attended Randolph Academy and Ladies Seminary, in Randolph, NY, in 1851-1852 and 1852-1853 (https://books.google.com/books?id=XtQlzOoJfrQC), and Fredonia Academy, in Fredonia, Chautauqua, NY, in 1853-1854 (https://books.google.com/books?id=XtQlzOoJfrQC&pg=PA13). It was in Fredonia that she heard and accepted the Sabbath (RH, May 2, 1854, p. 120). She lived in Friendship, Allegany, NY (RH, May 23, 1854, p. 141); taught in Nile, Allegany, NY (RH, Aug. 1, 1854, p. 205) and in Warren County, PA (RH, Jan. 9, 1855, p. 159). She is listed, in 1855 and 1856, as a teacher in Johnstown Centre, Rock County, WI, and Fort Atkinson, Jefferson County, WI (https://books.google.com/books?id=RxowAQAAMAAJ&pg=PA437; RH, May 15, 1855, p. 232). In 1857, she visited Battle Creek, MI, and "started a school in the second church building nearly as soon as its erection in 1857; but she continued it for only one year" (Spalding, *Captain of the Host*, p. 442). In writing the 1857 letter, Morton reveals that she had joined others, while in Wisconsin, in the "great error" of "forsaking the Third Angel's Message" and receiving the doctrine of "the future age" of Stephenson and Hall. Her letter is an attempt to persuade believers in Wisconsin to leave the "Age to Come" doctrine and return to the third angel's message. From March 3, 1859 to March 8, 1860, she corresponded with *The Advent Review and Sabbath Herald* from "N. Y."—conceivably from Randolph (search on "Sister Morton" and "L. M. Morton"). Charles Clark Lewis affirmed that he visited Morton in the Battle Creek "Old People's Home" in the summer of 1907 (RH, Dec. 9, 1909, p. 17; confirmed in *R. L. Polk & Co.'s Battle Creek City Directory*, 1908, p. 188). Sometime between 1875 and 1880, she married George Divoll, 32 years her senior, in Randolph, New York. (He was not married in the 1875 NY State

census but was married to Louisa in the 1880 US Census.) In the 1889 *Battle Creek City Directory*, she is listed as the widow of George Divoll, who could have died just before the move. George's son, George W. Divoll, with whom the father was living in 1875, was a Baptist minister.

[631] Mal. 3:7; Jer. 3:22.

[632] Written Jan. 1, 1891 (in RP 96), by Archibald Franklin Fowler and Phedima Fowler, née Doty. Fowler was a carpenter in Hillsdale, MI, who accepted the Sabbath in 1856 under the preaching of Joseph H. Waggoner and Merritt E. Cornell. "Dr. Lord" is David H. Lord, M.D., a Freewill Baptist minister who served as pastor from 1833–1877 and 1884–1888 (https://archive.org/details/nativeministryofoocartrich/page/678) but graduated from the Medical School of Bowdoin College in 1849 (https://archive.org/details/bub_gb_v8RBAAAAIAAJ/page/540) and served as the Ransom, Hillsdale County, postmaster from 1854–1855 and as a trustee of Hillsdale College from 1857 to 1862, 1865 to 1866, and 1870 to 1871.

[633] In RP 96, written in Battle Creek, Mich., Jan. 19, 1891. Charles Smith Glover was the one ridiculed in *The Messenger of Truth*, Nov. 30, 1854, p. 1, as "a vision lover." Yet, he "was not ashamed of the visions, nor to own that he loved them" (RH, Feb. 11, 1862, p. 85). Glover is recorded as seeing her in vision on several occasions (EGWEnc 389).

[634] RP 96, written Aug. 30, 1896, by William Rodham Carpenter and Eliza C. Carpenter, née Carpenter, who lived in Noblesville, IN. Eliza later married Noble Nordyke.

[635] In RP 97, written in Battle Creek, MI, Feb. 4, 1891. The date or the place is wrong. The meeting at Buck's Bridge was held on June 21, 1857 (1BIO 357.8; "Eastern Tour," RH, July 16, 1857, p. 88). The one held on the 28th was at Parish, NY, at the farm of Squire Joseph Howard (RH, June 18, 1857, p. 56). Bourdeau would not have performed this test without James White's approval.

[636] RH, Feb. 24, 1859, p. 110, the *second* published mention of Ellen's not breathing in vision. "Mrs. Parker" was Alvira P. Parker, née Ferrin. Her family is not on the 1859 map at https://www.loc.gov/resource/g37530.la001189/?r=0.191,0.529,0.075,0.045,0, of Morristown, VT, because they were in Bakersfield, VT, so her husband, Elisha H. Parker, could sell his late father's property (see "Elisha Parker's Estate," *St. Albans Messenger*, May 16, 1850, p. 3). Bakersfield adjoins Enosburgh to the south. They returned to Morristown by 1860 (see https://www.familysearch.org/ark:/61903/3:1:33SQ-GBS6-9SXT). When their daughter Julia died of typhus fever at Alvira's twin sister's house, April 7, 1863, Elisha quoted the line: "The maid's not dead, but sleepeth" (*Lamoille Newsdealer*, April 16, 1863, p. 4).

[637] Heb. 10:29; Rev. 14:12.

[638] Matt. 11:29; Acts 26:19.

[639] Eccl. 9:5; 1 Thess. 5:3; Matt. 13:30; 2 Peter 3:7.

[640] John 16:8; Eph. 4:13; 6:10; 1 Tim. 6:12; Matt. 3:7.

[641] J. White, "Report of Meetings!" RH, Oct. 22, 1857, p. 196; "He Went Away Sorrowful, for He Had Great Possessions," RH, Nov. 26, 1857, p. 18; RH, Nov. 30, 1911, pp. 3, 4; RH, Jan. 23, 1919, p. 22; Lt. 2, 6, 9, 1857; 2SG 238.1ff; T04 21.2ff; 1T 170.4ff; PH016 25.1ff.

[642] "George Lay" is George Talbot Lay, a wealthy landowner and businessman of Monterey, MI (see 1EGWLM 859).

[643] William Rufus Hyde Avery (of Bowling Green, Ohio), "Former Days," *The Welcome Visitor* (Columbia Union) Feb. 22, 1905, p. 3, at https://documents.adventistarchives.org/Periodicals/CUV/CUV19050222-V09-08.pdf, written from Wood, Ohio. See also 2SG 270.1; LS 162.1; 1BIO 366.1. William Rufus Hyde Avery was a farmer in Plain, Ohio, two miles north of Bowling Green. An earlier eight-minute vision at Otsego, MI, on Jan. 8, 1858, addressed the secret use of tobacco of Gilbert W. Cranmer, of Comstock, MI, and Joseph J. Perkins, of Otsego, MI, and gave messages of comfort to other desponding ones. Cranmer, at first, claimed to accept the correction, but he never gave up tobacco, and he complained that the Adventists would not issue him a license to preach (Loughborough, "Recollections of the Past.—No. 17," RH, Feb. 1, 1887, p. 74, at https://documents.adventistarchives.org/Periodicals/RH/RH18870201-V64-05.pdf). Perkins wrote a letter, attested by Seth Newton and Anna Maria Newton, née Berry, alleging falsely that Ellen White had a revelation that all must believe her visions or be lost (RH, Sept. 9, 1858, p. 132).

[644] "G. W. Holdt" is George W. Holt, of Oswego, NY, who was the first to link the third angel and the mark of the beast to the lamblike image to the beast in Rev. 13:11–18 ("Letter From Bro. Holt," PrT, March 1850, p. 64). Before this meeting, about 40 people decided for the Sabbath (RH, March 25, 1858, p. 149).

[645] Compare 2SG 265.1. From a record book of Mildred A. Arnbruster in the Bowling Green Public Library, Merlin Burt identified the boy as John M. Avery (Feb. 6, 1857- March 13, 1858), the son of William and Betsey Avery, who died the day before the vision.

[646] J. N. Loughborough, RH, Dec. 25, 1866, p. 30; cf. RH, Nov. 14, 1899, p. 730; PCCG 79; PUR March 7, 1912, p. 1; W. C. White, RH, Nov. 26, 1936, p. 6. Ellen White confirmed that she had a vision in Parkville (Lt. 2, 1861). George Orlando States, born in 1848 near Danville, MI, heard how the "Civil War Vision" prepared Adventists for the coming crisis: "In the spring of 1861, when the war broke out in this country, President Lincoln called for seventy-five thousand men for three months. Few believed the war would last that long. Those who believed what had been shown Sister White in Parkville, Mich., Jan. 12, 1861, knew something serious was before this nation. 'We knew that a most terrible war was before us, which would cause great distress and anguish.' As the war progressed, the North was confident of final victory, not realizing how well the South was prepared for the conflict" (RH, Oct. 18, 1906, p. 8). Martha Virginia Ensign, née Beck, a non-Adventist living in Lockport, MI (1860 US Census), heard from her neighbors about Ellen White's vision and prediction (GSAM 338). Parkville elder Harvey G. Keeney remembered the prediction (see RP 239).

[647] Loughborough's 1866 identification of the examiner as "a noted Spiritualist and mesmerizer" became, in 1892, "Dr. Brown, a hale, strong man physically, who was a Spiritualist medium" (RP 97; cf. RH, Aug. 29, 1899, p. 550), a description virtually unchanged in GCDB, Jan. 31, 1893, p. 60; RH, Aug. 29, 1899, p. 550; GSAM 210 (1905); PUR, March 7, 1912, pp. 1, 2; and "Sketches of the Past—No. 122," PUR, March 14, 1912, p. 2. Ellen White endorsed Loughborough's 1892 book, and her son reiterated her approval, though she wished that she had not figured so prominently in the book (WCW to J. N. Loughborough, Nov. 20, 1899). Ron Graybill found the name "J. S. Brown," a spiritualist lecturer, living in Albion, Calhoun County (the county where Battle Creek is), Michigan, in the *Spiritualist Register* for 1861, at http://iapsop.com/spirithistory/1861_spiritualist_register.html. Brown had supported his family as a "Tanner & Currier" of leather (https://www.loc.gov/resource/g4113c.la000323/?r=0.59,0.335,0.111,0.055,0). By 1860, he had moved to the adjacent town of Sheridon (https://www.familysearch.org/ark:/61903/3:1:33SQ-GBSQ-PLM). His second wife, Marie Brown, née Green, was a spiritualist, and J. S. Brown was a doctor in Albion (https://archive.org/details/IAPSOP-humanitarian_review_v7_aug_1908-jul_1909/page/404). When Marie died, John married Electa (Moulton) Brown, née Squier, in Otsego, MI. They moved to Kendallville, IN, where John is listed as a doctor (see

https://www.familysearch.org/ark:/61903/3:1:S3HY-67W9-SDQ?i=19; https://archive.org/details/IAPSOP-rpj_may_1873/page/n5; *Cincinnati Daily Gazette*, May 22, 1873, p. 3) and a clairvoyant spiritualist lecturer (see http://iapsop.com/archive/materials/religio-philosophical_journal/rpj_nov_1872.pdf, p. 3; http://iapsop.com/archive/materials/religio-philosophical_journal/rpj_dec_1872.pdf, p. 11). The graves of John and Electa Brown, in Kendallville, are unmarked. "Elders J. S. Brown and W. F. Jamison, of Albion, Calhoun Co., Mich.," are advertised in *The Spiritual Age*, Nov. 26, 1859, to Jan. 7, 1860, as answering "calls to lecture on Spiritualism" in Michigan and parts of Illinois, Wisconsin, and Indiana. William F. Jamieson was the Canada-born spiritualist who debated Moses Hull in October 1862 in Paw Paw, Michigan, leading to Hull's becoming a Spiritualist (see https://archive.org/details/greatestdebatew00jamigoog; p. 64). Having attended Albion College in 1854, Jamieson dropped out due to his father's illness (https://books.google.com/books?id=_HCHWP2RqxcC&pg=PA999).

648 William C. White, "Sketches and Memories of James and Ellen G. White: A Comprehensive Vision—I," RH, Feb. 10, 1938, p. 6, from a 1905 talk in Takoma Hall, in https://documents.adventistarchives.org/Periodicals/ALUG/ALUG19170418-V16-16.pdf. For the vision's contents, see RH, Aug. 27, 1861; 1T 264.2; 266.3; 270.3; 272.1; 326.1; 1BIO 449. Martha D. Amadon, née Byington, remembered another foreshadowing of bloodshed. In summer 1858, before she and her husband left Buck's Bridge, she saw Ellen White walking up and down in a tent and lamenting, "This country is to be deluged with blood"—a very memorable image (RH, May 19, 1859, p. 206; https://ellenwhite.org/media/document/8010).

649 For the last vision W. C. White witnessed, "A World Work Vision" (~V272), see **EXHIBIT-1**, no. 40.

650 J. N. Loughborough, GCDB, March 18, 1891, p. 145; see also EGW, Lt. 17, 1862; MML 58 describes Mr. Daigneau's tests in detail.

651 The original has "the autumn of 1863." In RP1892 247, Loughborough links the vision with 1T 426, which is dated Nov. 5, 1862, and identifies the stone mason as his next-door neighbor, "Mr. Daigneau," which was John Magloire Daigneau, who was well-known to the people of Battle Creek. Notice of Daigneau's death was published in the Battle Creek *Enquirer*, May 27, 1922, p. 1.

652 Martha D. Amadon, née Byington, RH, May 18, 1944, pp. 7–9, written at St. Joseph, Michigan, Nov. 24, 1925; cf. RH, Oct. 8, 1863.

653 RH, Oct. 8, 1867, p. 260. Aaron Hilliard began keeping the Sabbath in 1852 while living in Buck's Bridge, NY. He moved to Otsego, MI, in 1859. Aaron's uncle was John Byington. His mother, Lucy Hilliard, née Byington, was John's sister. "Sister White was asked to lead in prayer at family worship. She did so in a most wonderful manner. Elder White was kneeling a short distance from her. While praying, she moved over to him, and laying her hand on his shoulder continued praying for him until she was taken off in vision. She was in vision about forty-five minutes. It was at this time she was given instruction on the health question which soon after became such a matter of interest to our people. Those present at the time this vision was given will never forget the heavenly influence that filled the room. The cloud passed from the mind of Elder White, and he was full of praise to God" (Martha Amadon, *A Prophet Among You*, p. 227).

654 Edward Hilliard, "The Reminiscence of Early Days," RH, Dec. 15, 1932, pp. 1184–1185. Edward was the son of Aaron H. Hilliard.

655 "Monterey and Battle Creek," RH, June 16, 1868, p. 409, for the first paragraph; LI 271–273, from the second paragraph on. Ellen White described the beginning of the vision in the following words: "While speaking, the solemn and awful presence of God seemed to be in the meeting and I immediately fell to the floor and was shown in vision many things" (Ms. 6, 1868). About 120 pages of 2T are from this vision (RH, Jan. 20, 1949, p. 10; see 2T 112.1ff; 113.2ff; 116.2ff; 156.1ff; 165.3ff; 183.1ff; 5T 659.1ff; see also Lt. 16, 1868; Lt. 27, 1868; Ms. 3, 1868; Ms. 4, 1868; Ms. 5, 1868; Ms. 6, 1868; Ms. 3, 1869). Describing the vision in her diary as "terrible," meaning "awe-inspiring," Emma Webber, a young lady present on the occasion, decided to join the church the next day through baptism (Llewellyn E. Poll, "Emma Webber's Diary, Window into Early Battle Creek (1865-1874)," *Adventist Heritage*, vol. 7, no. 2, fall 1982, p. 57, at https://documents.adventistarchives.org/ScholarlyJournals/AH/AH19821001-V07-02.pdf).

656 A fairly accurate estimate. As we construct a vision chart beyond the one in this book, the actual count, for this period, is just about 260 visions. Totals of visions for these years are: 1844-1; 1845-26; 1846-14; 1847-5; 1848-9; 1849-24; 1850-19; 1851-17; 1852-11; 1853-14; 1854 to 1868-approximately 122 visions.

657 Uriah Smith, "A Token for Good," RH, June 16, 1868, p. 412; republished in William C. White, "Sketches and Memories of James and Ellen G. White, XLVI—Arduous Labors as God's Messenger," RH, Feb. 25, 1937, p. 5. The final paragraph here is from Smith's 1868 book, *The Visions of Mrs. E. G. White*, p. 6.

658 Isa. 55:9.

659 "Experience Related by Mrs. G. B. Starr of Observing Ellen White in Vision (June 12, 1868, in Battle Creek, MI)," reported through a stenographer by Arthur L. White and Frieda B. White, DF 496d, "Camp Meeting Talks," 1931, quoted in 2BIO 232-236. In 1863, Ellen "Nellie" Elizabeth Starr, née Sisley, immigrated from England with her parents, John Sisley and Susanna Sisley, née Gower. In 1883, she married George Burt Starr, who had worked as an evangelist with Dwight L. Moody. Nellie's sister, Maud Boyd, née Sisley, and Maud's husband, Charles L. Boyd, were missionaries to the U.S. Northwest, South Africa, and Australia.

660 These two men were identified in "Brief Statement by an Eye Witness," at https://ellenwhite.org/media/document/8861, as Jotham M. Aldrich, then president of the Review and Herald, and Harrison Sherwood Woolsey.

661 Report from Bordoville, VT, Dec. 13, 1871, by Augustin Cornelius Bourdeau and Daniel Toussaint Bourdeau, "Important Meetings in Vermont," RH, Dec. 26, 1871, p. 14, at https://documents.adventistarchives.org/Periodicals/RH/RH18711226-V39-02.pdf. For the content of the vision, linking health reform with the work of evangelism, see 3T 39.2ff; 48.1ff; 67.2ff; 161.1ff; 202.1ff; 212.1ff; 243.2ff; PH159 97.1ff; 171.1ff; LS 203.2ff.

662 "Sr. Hall" is Lucinda M. Hall, née Abbey, who married William Hall between 1861 and 1862 (see RH, Sept. 9, 1862, p. 120). Lucinda Hall told Merritt G. Kellogg that Ellen White's last open vision was in 1879 (DF 105k).

663 The original spelling is "promiscous." It meant "mingled" or "common" (Webster's, 1828). Here it is Adventists with non-Adventists.

664 Those identified are Alida Inez Leila Kellogg, daughter of George Washington Kellogg, of Richford, VT; John Saxby; Parmenas Francis Watts Saxby; Arthur John Saxby; and Parmenas' wife, Edna Charlotte Saxby, née Snow.

665 William C. White, "Sketches and Memories of James and Ellen G. White: A Comprehensive Vision—I," RH, Feb. 10, 1938, p. 6, adapted from a talk given in Takoma Hall, Dec. 17, 1905, at https://legacy.egwwritings.org/?ref=en_VisEGW.2.1¶=731.13; AUG, April 18, 1917, pp. 1–3; https://media2.ellenwhite.org/docs/4256/4256.pdf; and James White's note in 3T 570. For the contents of the vision, see LS 283.3; RH, Feb. 17, 1938, p. 9.

666 S. N. Haskell, UCR, July 28, 1899, Special No. 9, p. 12, at https://documents.adventistarchives.org/Periodicals/AAR/AAR18990728-V02-

06s09.pdf; GCB, April, 15, 1901, p. 232, at https://documents.adventistarchives.org/Periodicals/GCSessionBulletins/GCB1901-01ex11.pdf. Haskell associated this presentation with the meetings in 1874, which began in mid-December, even though Ellen White spoke on Jan. 4, 1875. George Orlando States, who was attending the school in Battle Creek, also described the occasion ("Lessons from Past Experience—No. 19," RH, Oct. 3, 1907, p. 10).

[667] 1860 text is from 2SG 292–294, adapted from Lt. 8, 1860, June 11, to J. N. Andrews; 1906 text is from Ms. 49, 1906, April 14; RH, June 14, 1906, p. 8. See James White, LS1880 335, 336, for an interpretation of Rev. 19:10 and the meaning of "the spirit of prophecy."

[668] This may suggest that they did not test her breathing every time or that cessation of breathing did not accompany every vision.

[669] W. C. White described one that came during a silent moment in prayer at an 1870 camp meeting (*Ellen G. White: Messenger to the Remnant*, p. 8).

[670] Witnesses described Ellen White's not breathing in several visions—"Large Bible in Hand Vision" (**V53**), "Thou Art the Man Vision" (**V127**), "Pretensions of Holiness Vision" (**V132**), "Jackson Vision" (**V133**), "To Those of Little Experience Vision" (**V138**), "Triumph of the Saints Vision" (**V149**), "Return Unto Me and I Will Return Unto You Vision" (**~V173**), "Buck's Bridge Vision" (**~V176**), "Great Distress Coming Vision," (**~V214**), "Slavery and the War Vision" (**~V217**), "Blessed Jesus Vision" (**~V254**), "Rebuking One, He Designs to Correct Many Vision" (**~V259**), and "A World Work Vision" (**~V272**). These include J. N. Loughborough (RH, Dec. 25, 1866, p. 30), Martha D. Amadon, née Byington (https://ellenwhite.org/media/document/8010), Thaddeus Moore Steward (Bible-Reading, No. 89, p. 167, at https://documents.adventistarchives.org/Books/BR1884.pdf, p. 167), and Merritt G. Kellogg (Letter to J. H. Kellogg, June 3, 1906). In 1883, nineteen people testified that they had seen her examined while in vision by a competent physician who then declared that she did not breathe (see https://documents.adventistarchives.org/Books/BR1884.pdf, p. 16). She herself described her breath returning after the "Midnight Cry Vision" (**V1**; Ms. 16, 1894) and the "Trying for Our Good Vision" (**V49**; 2SG 88.2). Thus, one might logically assume that this phenomena accompanied more of her visions, though not all of her visions were described. The earliest reports of her not breathing in vision are in a letter of James White to Leonard and Elvira Hastings (Aug. 26, 1848), two of James White's reports (RH, Dec. 31, 1857, p. 61; *Life Incidents*, 1868, p. 272), Daniel T. Bourdeau's description (RH, Feb. 24, 1859, p. 110), and Loughborough's 1866 report (RH, Dec. 25, 1866, p. 30). One of this book's reviewers noted: "That there were many eyewitnesses, even allowing for some bias, does strongly support the conclusion that she failed to breathe for periods of time longer than a normal human being could survive."

[671] "Shrill" had a slightly different sense in the Victorian age. It meant "piercing," as in the sound of "a *shrill* trumpet" (Webster's 1828 dictionary). His first mention of her "shrill voice" was replaced with "clear voice" in 2SG 77.2; LS80 232.3; LSMS 159.2. Pastor Clifford A. Russell described her usual speaking voice: "Her voice was low in pitch, and had wonderful carrying qualities. At the great 1909 General Conference held in Takoma Park, I purposely stepped to the outside of the great tent filled with thousands of listeners. At that distance and in spite of many people milling around I could hear distinctly every word" (*The Church Officers' Gazette*, Dec. 1944, p. 11, at https://documents.adventistarchives.org/Periodicals/TCOG/TCOG19441201-V31-12.pdf).

[672] In November 1851, previously skeptical **Ezra P. Butler** responded: "I believe them [the visions] to be of God, am a full believer in the visions" (Lt. 8, 1851). On this same occasion, **Joseph Baker** heartily accepted the visions: "Well, say you, what is Brother Baker going to do? *Believe the visions*" (Lt. 8, 1851). **Josiah Rice Hart**, who initially opposed the visions, also became "convinced that the visions were of God" (Lt. 8, 1851). Daniel Bourdeau's father, **Augustin Bourdeau**, had also been "naturally skeptical, and required a good reason for every doctrine proposed to him before receiving it. He was slow to believe that God now speaks to his people through visions, yet he was too prudent to oppose the manifestations and productions of the Spirit of prophecy among us. But this time he himself shared in the same gift. While his son was singing, heaven was opened to his view. He saw a company of angels in beautiful attire, with instruments on which they played, after a leading angel had struck the first note. And they sang while they played. . . . Father Bourdeau fell asleep on the Sabbath that he so dearly loved" ("In Memoriam [of Mrs. Sarah A. Bourdeau-Giguere]," pp. 9, 10, 11). **Edith Brownsberger, née Donaldson**, second wife of Professor Sidney S. Brownsberger, was a much later witness who described seeing a light rest upon Ellen White in the pulpit, strengthening her to speak (see "An Experience of Long Ago," DF 745, available at https://ellenwhite.org/media/document/2339). Nearing the end of her life, she wrote: "I often wonder why it is that the good Lord lengthens my life. Why am I kept alive so long? I have thought that maybe the Lord has something for me to do yet in bearing testimony concerning my life with Sister White. One thing I know beyond the shadow of a doubt, the Lord did speak through Sister White, and her writings are true. *I am naturally skeptical. But I saw and heard enough while I was in her home to convince me that her work was from God*" ("Confidence in Prophetic Gift," RH, March 9, 1967, p. 13, emphasis added). Ella R. Sanders, née King, was also an eyewitness of the strengthening of Mrs. White (also in DF 745). **Sarepta Myrenda Henry, née Irish**, described grasping Ellen White's role in relation to Scripture in an article entitled, "My Telescope," published in *The Gospel of Health*, Jan. 1898. **Horace Lorenzo Hastings** is a special case. "Elder Hastings and wife [Harriet Frances Hastings, née Barnett], the doctor and family, as also Elder Phineas Smith, who had been bitter against our people, listened with interest to the presentation of the truth of the messages in these meetings with the Rochester company. Elder Hastings presented no objections to what he heard, and was apparently convicted of the truth, for when questioned with reference thereto his only answer would be, 'Brethren, pray for me.' In one of these meetings *Sister White was in vision for nearly half an hour* (1858). He had opportunity to know for himself her condition in vision,' and to realize the evident presence of the Spirit of the Lord accompanying the manifestation. The next night after this he had an appointment away from the city. On returning the next day, he said to me, 'What subject do you suppose I spoke from last night?' I replied, 'I can not say.' 'Well,' said he, 'I spoke on the subject of the perpetuity of spiritual gifts.' It was evident to us all that he was strongly convicted on the truth of the three messages. I do not think he ever openly opposed the work. But he, like many others, failing to act according to convictions on time, seemed to settle down to a state of indifference to the importance of the message. It was reported, however, that for several months his wife refrained from labor on the Sabbath. But she never fully identified herself with the Seventh-day Adventists. While our Rochester meetings were a source of encouragement to that company, and also abated prejudice in some, there was no direct addition to their number as the result" (J. N. Loughborough, PUR, Aug. 17, 1911, p. 1). In 1849, Loughborough had traveled with Elder Phineas Atwater Smith, of Rochester, New York, to observe his methodology in preaching (see RH, Feb. 12, 1884, p. 106). Smith had a friendly debate over the Sabbath but did not accept it, remaining an Advent Christian minister.

[673] 1T 328.1. She described how she felt: "I anxiously watched the result, and if the individual reproved, rose up against it, and afterwards opposed the truth, these queries would arise in my mind. Did I deliver the message just as I should? Oh, God! could there not have been

some way to save them?" (2SG 60.2).

674 For Joshua V. Himes' blind acceptance of the appraisal of others, see AHSTR, May 4, 1850, p. 111. Years later, Himes sent a donation to aid Ellen White in the Adventist health work (Lt. 31a, 1895). Isaac Cummings Wellcome claimed in HSAM 397 and 402, which contain a number of erroneous assertions, that he had seen Ellen White in several visions and even caught her twice, but D. M. Canright countered that Wellcome admitted in a letter that he had "only learned what he reported by hearsay" (RH Extra, April 14, 1874, p. 3), a claim that Wellcome denied (HSAM 402, n. 1), but Wellcome said they didn't call Ellen's exercises visions when, from her December 20, 1845, letter to Enoch Jacobs, she began with the words, "As God has shown me in holy vision ..." Canright himself never saw her in vision but claimed that her visions were "merely the result of nervous disease, a complication of hysteria, catalepsy and ecstasy" (*Seventh-Day Adventism Renounced*, 1887, p. 49; 1889, p. 151). Loughborough responded: "People who never saw Sister White in vision, say they can explain all about it, that it is only the result of disease, hysterics, etc., but the testimony of skillful physicians who have examined her at such times is altogether different" (GCDB, Jan. 29, 1893, p. 20). Ellen White wrote: "Before 1844 I sometimes lost my strength under the blessing of God. I. C. Welcome may have confounded these exercises of the power of the Spirit of God upon me with the visions. I had no visions in the winter, near spring, after the time had passed [in early 1844]" (Lt. 2, 1874). She described one of these incidents when she lost her strength and "everything was shut out from me but Jesus and glory" (ExV 4). Neither these experiences nor the dreams she had between the autumn of 1843 and April 1844 were outright visions. She points out when her first vision came: "It was not long after the passing of the time in 1844 that my first vision was given me" (1T 58.4). She added, "And I had no vision until 1845" (1T 72.3). However, both she and James placed the vision in December 1844 (see WLF 22, May 30, 1847; Lt. 3, 1847, July 13; RH, July 21, 1851, art. A; and ExV 5.3, 1851).

675 Joseph Bates was not the "beloved brother" who wrote, "I cannot endorse sister Ellen's visions as being of divine inspiration" (WLF 22.4), after he had seen Ellen White in vision "several times," as Donald Casebolt assumes (https://www.academia.edu/36890562/Casebolt_Spectrum). James White did not indicate who the "beloved brother" was, and Bates wrote: "I once was slow to believe that this sister's visions were of God. *I did not oppose them*, for the word of the Lord is positively clear that spiritual visions will be given to his people in the last days. More than two years are now past since I proved them true. Therefore I profess myself a firm believer in her visions so far as I have witnessed, and I have seen her have many" (*A Seal of the Living God* 1849, p. 31). Bates also indicated that it was seeing her in vision that contributed to his acceptance of her gift (WLF 21.3, April 7, 1847). Sargent and Robbins denounced Ellen's visions as from the devil even while seeing the supernatural nature of the visions because they showed their errors, (2SG 75.1). Sargent persisted in disbelief even though members of his family became Seventh-day Adventists. John Megquier, who believed that Ellen had some of her first visions at his house in Poland, alleged that she taught from a vision that the door of mercy had closed for the world and that she made acceptance of her visions a test for being saved (Grant, *The True Sabbath*, p. 70). Ransom Hicks confessed: "As concerning Ellen G. White's *visions*, I have heretofore known but little about them. I once saw her have one [in 1853—MT, Nov. 2, 1854, p. 4], and I once saw a table tip over and then tip back again of its own accord so far as I could discern. Neither the phenomenon of the vision, nor of the table-tipping did I understand. I have read her published visions, but only with a passing notice, having vital truths to occupy my mind which I considered of vast more consequence." Then he described what he considered "vital truth"—the supposedly "self-evident" "Geometric Diagram which chronologically establishes every period in Daniel's vision to a mathematical demonstration" (MT, Oct. 19, 1854, p. 3). Few, if any, would affirm Hick's view of what was "vital truth." Hicks relied on J. B. Bezzo's appraisal of Ellen White without his own scrutiny.

676 Concerning Hiram Case, see Lt. 2, 1852; Ms. 1, 1853; Lt. 3, 1853; Lt. 6, 1853; Lt. 9, 1853; https://www.nonsda.org/egw/MOT4.pdf. In her letter to the church of Jackson, MI, Ellen White wrote a personal appeal to Case: "Dear Brother Case, make thorough work. Dig deep and confess from the bottom and then the bars will be put up behind you and you will not be so likely to go astray again. What shall I say more dear friends? Make straight paths for your feet lest that which is lame be turned out of the way. Do be humble, be watchful, prayerful, in understanding, men, but in malice children. Look at the troubled, confused state you have been in and then acknowledge the teaching of God, which He has given to set you right. I have written this in great haste by lamp light, excuse all mistakes. In love from your sister" (Lt. 3, 1853, June 29). For Charles P. Russell see *n203*. Israel Dammon explained his rejection of the visions: "We were formerly acquainted with Mr. and Mrs. White, and for a time had confidence in her visions, but for a good many years have had none at all. When we saw they contradicted one with another, we renounced them altogether, and betook ourselves to the word of the Lord" (*The True Sabbath*, p. 68). Ellen White explained: "We were sent to Garland, Maine, where we met Elder Dammon and many others in meeting and bore our testimony, that they were in error and delusion in believing that the dead had been raised. . . . Our testimony was rejected, and they clung tenaciously to their errors. . . . Elder Dammon had the most positive evidences that the visions were of God. He became my enemy only because I bore a testimony reproving his wrongs and his fanatical course, which wounded the cause of God" (Lt. 2, 1874). The visit was in the summer of 1845. Regarding supposed contradictions in the "High and Holy Path Vision" (V41), Ellen White wrote: "After I came out of vision, Elders Dammon and Reed enquired if I saw them upon that high and holy path. I told them I recollected their countenances with many others, [and] at the same time gave them a warning not to become exalted, lest they lose the crowns it was their privilege to gain through humility and faithfulness" (Ms. 7, 1876). "I have never seen any persons crowned in the kingdom of God, only on conditions if they were faithful they would receive the crown of immortal life in the kingdom of glory" (Lt. 2, 1874). "Elder Reed" was Nicholas Gilman Reed, of Orrington, ME, who was previously a Methodist (AHSTR, May 31, 1851, p. 127). Dammon held a grudge against James White for writing a letter he thought unjustly "censured him to the wrath of God." In a second letter, White addressed Dammon as "Dear Bro. Dammon" and agreed "his first letter to him was too severe" and "apologized for it" (*Defense of Elder James White and Wife*, 1870, pp. 148, 150). Neither letter is extant. For Elias Willets Shortridge see the next note.

677 Henry Edward Carver, who never observed Ellen White in vision, joined the Sabbatarian Adventists with doubts about the prophetic gift and reacted to the disciplinary actions against the rebellion of Benjamin Franklin Snook (Robert Coulter, *The Journey: A History of the Church of God (Seventh Day)*, Broomfield, CO, 2014, pp. 92, 93). He described his disappointment that Ellen White didn't predict specific losses and victories in the Civil War (Grant, *The True Sabbath*, p. 82). William Sheldon had a different interpretation of prophecy (RH, Sept. 25, 1866, p. 132). Abraham Cauffman Long accepted the Sabbath and preached it but also had different views of prophecy and, after purchasing many books from the Adventists (RH, Aug. 1, 1871, p. 56; RH, March 2, 1876, p. 72) published a critical tract against Ellen White for supposedly suppressing some of her early writings, "Comparison of the Early Writings of Mrs. White with Later Publications" (1883) in *The Advent and Sabbath Advocate* of Marion, IA, and as a standalone tract (RH, May 1, 1883, p. 280; RH, Aug. 14, 1883, p. 528; RH Supplement, Aug. 14, 1883).

Ellen White said that Joseph Turner rejected her visions "because I had faithfully told them what had been shown me concerning his fanatical course" (Ms. 9, 1859). For Jesse Stevens, see LS 86.4. For Gilbert Cranmer, who had accepted the Sabbath in 1852 (Coulter, p. 53) and confirmed that Ellen White did not breathe in a vision he witnessed (RH, Feb. 1, 1887, p. 74), it was the tobacco habit that he chose not to quit (GSAM 564; RH, Sept. 9, 1858, p. 132; RH, Jan. 17, 1865, p. 60; https://nonegw.org/cranmer.shtml). John Howell, of West Poland, ME, who identified with the "Shut Door" Adventists at first, became in 1845 an opponent of Ellen White and her visions. Benjamin Franklin Snook and William Henry Brinkerhoff left because of their independent view of the church and unique view of certain doctrines. Henry C. Blanchard, of Avilla, Missouri, and Elias Willets Shortridge also left "because of the visions," with Blanchard giving up preaching and Shortridge embracing spiritualism and immortality (RH Supplement, Aug. 14, 1883, pp. 6, 12). Moses Hull ignored Ellen White's warnings and left the church embracing Spiritualism (see his struggle in RH, Jan. 21, 1863, p. 69). D. M. Canright spread distortions about Ellen White having never seen her in vision (GCDB, Jan. 31, 1893, p. 59). Out of ill feelings toward her, he glibly dismissed her visions as "wholly the fruit of her own imagination" and added, "I dislike her very much indeed" (letter, Dec. 8, 1883, in *I Was Canright's Secretary*, p. 65; cf. RH, Oct. 7, 1884, p. 92), leaving the church with the pledge that he would "give himself to revival and Christian work ... to labor for the salvation of souls" (RH Extra, Dec. 1887, p. 1), while he actually became the father of Ellen G. White critics and showing up "the poor Adventists" became "his principal stock trade" and "his principal means of livelihood." Significantly, his last words about her at her funeral were: "There is a noble Christian woman gone" (W. A. Spicer, *The Spirit of Prophecy in the Advent Movement*, p. 127). George I. Butler then wrote: "But we have no fears in regard to the effect of this *apostasy* upon our people and work in general" (RH, March 1, 1887, p. 138, emphasis added). According Norman F. Douty, Canright's apologist, it was calling his departure "apostasy" that triggered Canright's attack (Norman Douty, *The Case of D. M. Canright*, pp. 93–98). Butler responded: "How little the poor man could realize the spirit of an apostate till he commenced to play the role! We have the charity to believe that he himself never realized the nature of the spirit which would possess him" (RH Extra, Dec. 1887, p. 2). Elmer Ellsworth Franke reported on a Spiritualist medium who shut herself away when she wished to have a vision, since Satan works in darkness, and on Spiritualist lectures "*Religious* Spiritualism," "Spirits in Open Gaslight," etc. (ST, Nov. 6, 1893, p. 12). Never seeing Ellen White in vision, Franke dismissed her counsels as being fed her by others, then left the church, claiming he would keep to the high road of preaching the gospel but ended up picking trifles in public with Ellen White about health, dress, and falsely claimed that she had been threatened with a lawsuit over *Sketches from the Life of Paul* (https://encyclopedia.adventist.org/article?id=79BK&highlight=Franke). Ludwig Richard Conradi translated for Ellen White while she was in Switzerland and Germany in 1886/1887, becoming an evangelist and administrator in Europe. Sadly, personal alienation and doctrinal differences led him to break with Adventism in 1932, when he joined the Seventh Day Baptists and became an outspoken critic of Ellen G. White's prophetic ministry.

[678] The three extant issues of *The Messenger of Truth* at https://www.nonsda.org/egw/messenger_party.shtml have some positive articles about obedience to the law of God, but they also rehearse supposed errors in the visions and perceived slights from supporters of Ellen White's visions (RH, Nov. 29, 1853, p. 168; Aug. 7, 1856, p. 110). See transcription by Kevin Morgan at https://www.academia.edu/120890217/Reflections_on_The_Messenger_of_Truth_a_short_lived_rival_to_The_Advent_Review_and_Sabbath_Herald. By January 1858, James White listed seven of 18 former "messengers" who had ceased lecturing: (1) Ira Allen Wyman was "rejected by his party for crime, and a town charge"; (2) John Baptiste Bezzo, "their editor," was fined $25 for presenting a pistol, and threatening to shoot a scholar in school"; (3) Hiram S. Case was "run out as a preacher, and fishing on the lakes"; (4) Roderick R. Chapin was running "a clothing store"; (5) Henry Lillis, Jr., had become "a Spiritualist"; (6) Charles P. Russell and (7) Ransom Hicks "had denounced Bezzo and the publishers of their sheet hypocrites, and were standing alone" (RH, Jan. 14, 1858, p. 77). The rest of the eighteen may have included the original publishing committee of *The Messenger of Truth*—besides Case, Russell, and Bezzo—(8) William J. Lusk, of Goodrich, MI (see RH, April 11, 1854, p. 95); (9) Hiram Charles Drew, of Sylvan, MI, who boasted, "You go ahead and shake the bush, and we will follow up and catch all the birds" (PGGC 82); (10) Ephraim Picket, of Jackson County, MI; and (11) Erastus Clark, of Kent County, MI, whose offense seems to be that James White did not publish his study of Revelation 13 in which he identified England as the head of the church that received a deadly wound that was healed (see *Messenger of Truth*, Nov. 2, 1854, p. 1, at https://cdm.llu.edu/digital/collection/bftmm/id/73). In 1855, (12) James M. Stephenson and (13) Dwight P. Hall, of Wisconsin, joined the Messenger party, bringing with them the "Age to Come" doctrine (RH, Dec. 4, 1855, p. 80). Another possible messenger, (14) Hiram Vaughn Reed, of Rosendale, WI, of "the Age-to-Come persuasion" (BECOG 120), may have believed the Sabbath but gave it up in 1857 (RH, May 28, 1857, p. 28; RH, June 2, 1863, p. 8), and persuaded Stephenson to do the same. Loughborough alleged that Hall and Stephenson suffered mental problems at the end of their lives (GSAM 332, 333), yet Hall preached until 1863 and Stephenson until 1888 (BECOG 253, 120, 121). The last four messengers could have been (15) Titus Ives Giddings, of Allegany County, NY, and Plum River, IL (RH, Sept. 27, 1853, p. 95); (16) Howard Lothrop, of Eaton, Canada East (RH, Aug. 27, 1861, p. 100); (17) Henry J. Barringer, of Troy, NY (RH, Feb. 14, 1856, p. 160; MT, Nov. 30, 1854, p. 1); and (18) Aaron Foster Servis (RH, Dec. 1853, p. 1891; MT, Nov. 2, 1854, p. 4). Canright listed many of these men in *Seventh-day Adventism Renounced*, 1889, pp. 62, 63. Other publications critical of Seventh-day Adventists and Ellen White were *The Advent and Sabbath Advocate*, of Marion, IA, at https://www.friendsofsabbath.org/ABC/CG7/cog7.htm, and *The Gathering Call*, edited first by Albion Fox Ballenger and then his brother Edward Stroud Ballenger (see https://archive.org/details/TheGatheringCallDevotedToDeathOfAlbionF.Ballenger1921; EGWEnc 303).

[679] Miles Grant accused Ellen White of engaging in fanaticism with Israel Dammon and believing that anyone outside of shut door Adventism was lost. Seventh-day Adventists rebutted the accusation in a *Review and Herald* Extra, April 14, 1874. In 1877, Grant published *The True Sabbath: Which Day Shall We Keep? An Examination of Mrs. Ellen White's Visions*, with the erroneous testimony of Lucinda S. Burdick, whose first husband was John Howell. Burdick claimed that Ellen White had confessed that she could "throw herself into vision when she chose" (p. 72), though Ellen White declared that she had no control over when she had a vision (Lt. 2, 1874) and that those who attempted to put her into a vision through mesmerism or who attempted to bring her out of one had been unsuccessful. John N. Andrews and several other witnesses corroborated this view (see *online* EXHIBIT-7, no. 8). In 1885, Grant followed Ellen White to Europe. "After a month in England, he traveled to Torre Pellice, in northern Italy, where he rented the same hall that Ellen White and other pastors were using to hold meetings. . . . Ellen White went right on with her meetings without reference to Grant, hoping to reach the hearts of the few who came to hear her" (Denis Fortin, "Grant, Miles (1819–1911)," at https://encyclopedia.adventist.org/article?id=C9DI; see *Historical Sketches of the*

Foreign Missions of the Seventh-day Adventists, pp. 236, 237; Campbell, https://www.adventistbiblicalresearch.org/wp-content/uploads/Michael-Campbells-article.pdf).

680 Thankfully, many broke ties with the Messenger party. John C. Day, of Massachusetts, confessed, "Instead of putting the best construction upon what the brethren had done, I would put the worst. This I feel was all wrong, and feel heartily sorry for it" (RH, Oct. 9, 1856, p. 184). Nonetheless, further exhortation was needed, and Mrs. White received a message of reproof for Day's "cruel, crooked, and wicked" course (~V198, "State of Things in the East Vision"). Yet, she wrote that, if he "made thorough work he could still be of some use (Ms. 2, 1858, Dec. 27). Solomon Myers, of Plum River, IL, wrote the Whites, "It is a cause of grief to us that we have added to your pangs and wounds, when we realize how many you have suffered to get the truth before an indifferent public, who are evidently not aware of the danger they are in; and we have no doubt your faithful, persevering labors will be rewarded at the coming of the Lord"(RH, Sept. 30, 1858, p. 148). Stephen Smith, of Unity, NH, testified: "I received a testimony myself twenty-eight years ago, and I took it home and locked it up in my trunk, and I never read it until last Thursday. I was mad all the time, nearly. Brethren, every word of the testimony for me is true, and I accept it, and I have come to that place where I firmly believe they are all of God. And if I had heeded the one God sent to me, as well as the rest, it would have changed the whole course of my life, and I should have been a very different man. . . . I'm too old to undo what I've done. I'm too feeble to get out to our large meetings, but I want you to tell our people everywhere that *another rebel has surrendered*" (Eugene William Farnsworth to Ellen G. White, July 15, 1885, at https://ellenwhite.org/correspondence/262069; RH, Feb. 19, 1857, p. 126). He died in Unity, NH. Farnsworth's letter refers to "W. H. Ball" (Worcester H. Ball), who wrote a pamphlet against the visions. Ellen White sent him a testimony (Ms. 2, 1868), and Ball wrote a confession published in RH, July 7, 1868, p. 42; cf. RH, May 6, 1862, p. 179; and *The Visions of Mrs. E. G. White*, pp. 130–137. Unfortunately, in 1872, Ball resumed his attacks. Ellen White "wrote to him to no avail (Letter 28, 1872) and two years later responded to false charges made against her from some who claimed that she had predicted a specific time for the second coming of Christ (Letter 53, 1874). After this latest disaffection, Ball became a supporter of B. F. Snook and W. H. Brinkerhoff" (EGWEnc 301). The negativity of Smith and Ball had an effect on Rachel Oakes Preston who "became cold in religion, and prejudiced to some extent against the Testimonies, having never seen Bro. and Sr. White," yet, after reading Testimony No. 13, sent her by an unknown friend, which addressed the harsh spirit against James White during his illness (1T 572) but also included a testimony of reproof for him, "Rachel Preston changed her mind about James and Ellen White. Shortly before her death she also heard of the 1867 Christmastime revival in Washington, New Hampshire, and rejoiced" (EGWEnc 301; RH, Dec. 28, 1939, p. 12). Waterman Phelps, of Hebron, Wisconsin, wrote: "I believe many of us were honest, but deceived. . . . I desire to confess all my errors, and be found without fault before the throne of God. Rev. xiv,5" (RH, Nov. 11, 1858, p. 199). Elmore W. Waters, of Norwich, NY, confessed: "And to all the wounded ones by me, from the slanderous sheet or otherwise, I do not feel that I have even approached the merits of my just deserts. All that I can ask at your hands is, that you will ask for me a spirit of heart-felt repentance, and then it may be I shall be prepared to seek your pardon" (RH, Dec. 30, 1858, p. 46; cf. 2SG 134.1). Edwin R. Seaman, of Rochester, NY, wrote: "I have been deceived by liars that have told them with such a grace, and such enormity of expression, that I thought there must be some truth. . . Am willing to do anything to undo the evil I have caused against the truth" (RH, July 24, 1856, p. 92). Thaddeus Moore Steward wrote: "Dear brother and sister White, I have felt prejudiced against you, and said wrong things of you. I pray you to forgive me this wrong" (RH, June 9, 1859, p. 23); "O, when shall I be able to counteract the influence of my past course!" (RH, April 1, 1862, p. 143). Dr. William Russell, who had written, "Mrs. White's visions were the result of a diseased organization or condition of the brain or nervous system," changed his mind, and wrote a letter of confession to the Whites (see RH, April 25, 1871, p. 152; see also https://documents.adventistarchives.org/Periodicals/RH/RH18700315-V35-13s.pdf). Philip Strong, also of Michigan, linked up with dissidents for a time but returned to ministerial labors (RH, Feb. 26, 1867, p. 144). Later, after he left ministerial labors, Ellen White visited to bring him back into service (see RH, Dec. 2, 1884, p. 762). His son, Earl J. Strong died in a tragic accident in Battle Creek in 1889.

681 LeRoy Froom explained James' references to apocryphal books, stating "expressions in Sister White's message reminded Brother White of certain expressions he had read in the Apocrypha" (Froom, "Mrs. White and the Apocrypha," Estate File: 31-C-2, in Ntini, p. 13). Though one might see his conclusions as exceeding the evidence, Matthew J. Korpman's study, "Forgotten Scriptures: Allusions and Quotations by Ellen White to the Apocrypha," *Spes Christiana* 31.2 (2020), pp. 109–146, at https://www.academia.edu/41558577/Forgotten_Scriptures_Allusions_and_Quotations_by_Ellen_White_to_the_Apocrypha_Spes_Christiana_31_2_2020_109_146, is the most exhaustive on the subject. Korpman follows Ronald D. Graybill, "Under the Triple Eagle: Early Adventist Use of the Apocrypha," in *Adventist Heritage*, Winter 1987 (12:1), 25–32, and Denis Fortin, "Ellen G. White and the Apocrypha," June 1998, at https://digitalcommons.andrews.edu/cgi/viewcontent.cgi?article=1012&context=theology-christian-philosophy-pubs. A counterbalance to Korpman's conclusions about Ellen White's use of the Apocrypha is the point-by-point rebuttal of Denford Ntini at https://www.academia.edu/67801859/Article_on_Ellen_White_Adventism_and_the_Apocrypha.

682 Ms. 4, 1850, emphasis added, part of the "Perishing Souls Vision" (V87).

683 Ms. 5, 1849, emphasis added.

684 We notice that Otis Nichols also referred to 2 Esdras in his letter to William Miller, April 20, 1846. *The Day-Star*, March 4, 1845, p. 10. To Delia Gove (Kendall) Needham, née Prescott, second wife of Norman Gardner Needham, the editors of the *Review and Herald* responded: "Concerning the Apocrypha, we regard portions of it as containing much light and instruction. If we were asked to specify, we should mention 2 Esdras, Wisdom of Solomon, and 1 Maccabees. . . ." ("To Correspondents OLD STYLE AND NEW," RH, Aug. 5, 1858, p. 96). Joseph Bates wrote: "The 2nd book of Esdras, contains very important truths" (*A Seal of the Living God*, 1849, p. 66). There are references to 2 Esdras in his article in DS, Sept. 6, 1845. Regarding the historical value of the Apocrypha, see George Washington Morse, "Scripture Questions," RH, Feb. 2, 1886, p. 75.

685 RH, April 24, 1856, p. 15, referencing 2 Esdras 2:47.

686 RH, Aug. 21, 1856, p. 126, referencing 1 Cor. 5:10: "for then must ye needs go out of the world."

687 RH, March 31, 1859, p. 148, referencing Ps. 50:5: "those that have made a covenant with me by sacrifice."

688 RH, Feb. 23, 1860, p. 106, referencing Rev. 4:12; 16:13.

689 RH, April 22, 1862, p. 167, referencing Judges 5:23: ". . . because they came not to the help of the LORD, to the help of the LORD against the mighty."

690 2SG 74.1; 1 Tim. 1:19 (previous sentence); allusion to Isa. 50:7; Num. 20:17.

691 Rev. 14:7.

692 For "the east," see Matt. 24:27.

693 Miller pictured Jesus as *standing*, whereas Ellen Harmon pictured Him as sitting, based on Matt. 26:64 and Mark 14:62, which describe Him as "sitting on the right hand of power, and coming in the clouds of heaven," and Matt. 25:31, which says that he will "sit on the throne of his glory." See also Rev. 14:14, which says, "And I looked, and behold a white cloud, and upon the cloud *one sat* like unto the Son of man, having on his head a golden crown, and in his hand a sharp sickle."

694 1 Cor. 15:52, 53: "In a moment, in the twinkling of an eye, at the last trump: for the trumpet shall sound, and the dead shall be raised incorruptible, and we shall be changed. For this corruptible must put on incorruption, and this mortal *must* put on immortality"; 1 Thess. 4:16, 17: "For the Lord himself shall descend from heaven with a shout, with the voice of the archangel, and with the trump of God: and the dead in Christ shall rise first: Then we which are alive *and* remain shall be caught up together with them in the clouds, to meet the Lord in the air: and so shall we ever be with the Lord"; 2 Cor. 5:2, 3, "clothed."

695 Eph. 5:27: "That he might present it to himself a glorious church, not having spot, or wrinkle, or any such thing; but that it should be holy and without blemish."

696 Rev. 21:2: "And I John saw the holy city, new Jerusalem, coming down from God out of heaven, prepared as a bride adorned for her husband." See also Luke 12:36: "And ye yourselves like unto men that wait for their lord, when he will return from the wedding; that when he cometh and knocketh, they may open unto him immediately."

697 "New Jerusalem" is from Rev. 21:2. Miller has the Second Coming function something like a woman dusting her table, lifting up an object to be able to wipe the table and then setting the object back down, with the New Jerusalem holding the saints until the earth is purged by fire and then bringing them back down to the earth's surface. Miller's link between the Second Coming and the saints immediately descending to the purified earth. Ellen Harmon does not so link the Second Coming with an immediate return to a fire-purified earth and has the redeemed taking seven days to ascend to the sea of glass. Her timeline works well with her later descriptions of the millennium (see Ellen White, ExV 32.5; PrT, April 1850; see also James White, AR, Sept. 1850, p. 51). "Burned up" is from 2 Peter 3:10: "But the day of the Lord will come as a thief in the night; in the which the heavens shall pass away with a great noise, and the elements shall melt with fervent heat, the earth also and the works that are therein shall be burned up" and from Mal. 4:1: "For, behold, the day cometh, that shall burn as an oven; and all the proud, yea, and all that do wickedly, shall be stubble: and the day that cometh shall burn them up, saith the LORD of hosts, that it shall leave them neither root nor branch." To "dwell" with "the Lord forever" comes from Ps. 23:6: "Surely goodness and mercy shall follow me all the days of my life: and I will dwell in the house of the LORD for ever."

698 For the appearing of "the sign of the Son of Man," see Matt. 24:30 and DS, Sept. 6, 1845, p. 17. For "the east," see Matt. 24:27. For a "cloud" the size of "a man's hand," see 1 Kings 18:44.

699 The "white cloud" is from Rev. 14:14. That He is on the cloud comes from Luke 21:27.

700 The number "ten thousand" comes from Rev. 5:11; and the "angels" accompanying Him, from Matt. 25:31.

701 That He has many "crowns" upon "His head" is from Rev. 19:12; William Ellis Foy describes the Son of Man's wearing "a *crown* upon his head" (Foy, p. 10). That His "hair" is "white" is from Rev. 1:14.

702 Rev. 1:15 describes "his feet like unto fine brass, as if they burned in a furnace." The "sharp sickle" comes from Rev. 14:14. The "trumpet" comes from Matt. 24:31; 1 Cor. 15:52; and 1 Thess. 4:16. Foy describes legs "like pillars of flaming fire" (Foy, p. 12) and Jesus as having "a trumpet of pure **silver**" (Foy, p. 18); "pillars of fire" is from Rev. 10:1.

703 Rev. 1:14 describes His eyes "as a flame of fire."

704 The statement comes from Rev. 6:17.

705 Having "spotless robes" derives from Eph. 5:27, "That he might present it to himself a glorious church, not having spot, or wrinkle, or any such thing."

706 The "silence" in heaven is from Rev. 8:1.

707 "Clean hands and a pure heart" comes from Ps. 24:4; "shall be able to stand" comes Rev. 6:17; and "my grace is sufficient for you" is from 2 Cor. 12:9.

708 The "trumpet" is from 1 Thess. 4:16 and 1 Cor. 15:52; "Flames of fire" comes from Isa. 66:15 and is applied in 2 Thess. 1:7, 8.

709 "Awake" is from Ps. 17:15: "As for me, I will behold thy face in righteousness: I shall be satisfied, when I awake, with thy likeness." "Sleep in the dust" is from Job 7:21: "And why dost thou not pardon my transgression, and take away mine iniquity? for now shall I sleep in the dust; and thou shalt seek me in the morning, but I *shall* not *be*." "Sleep in the dust" and "awake" are both used in Dan. 12:2. The command to "awake" is from Eph. 5:14.

710 Joel 2:10.

711 Matt. 27:52; 1 Cor. 15:53.

712 Rev. 19:6 has the Greek for "hallelujah": "And I heard as it were the voice of a great multitude, and as the voice of many waters, and as the voice of mighty thunderings, saying, Alleluia: for the Lord God omnipotent reigneth." The "change" in a "moment," at Christ's return, is found in 1 Cor. 15:52. Most is from 1 Thess. 4:17: "Then we which are alive *and* remain shall be caught up together with them in the clouds, to meet the Lord in the air: and so shall we ever be with the Lord." See John 5:25 for the voice of the Son of God.

713 2 Esdras 2:43, 46, 47: "And in the midst of them there was a young man of a high stature, taller than all the rest, and upon every one of their heads he set crowns, and more exalted which I marvelled at greatly. . . . Then said I to the angel, What young person is it that crowneth them, and giveth them palms in their hands? So he answered and said unto me, It is the Son of God, whom they have confessed in the world." Rev. 2:10: "be thou faithful unto death, and I will give thee a crown of life." Rev. 3:11: "Behold, I come quickly: hold that fast which thou hast, that no man take thy crown."

714 The "harps" and "victory" come from Rev. 15:2: "And I saw as it were a sea of glass mingled with fire: and them that had gotten the victory over the beast, and over his image, and over his mark, *and* over the number of his name, stand on the sea of glass, having the harps of God." The "palms" are from Rev. 7:9: "After this I beheld, and, lo, a great multitude, which no man could number, of all nations, and kindreds, and people, and tongues, stood before the throne, and before the Lamb, clothed with white robes, and palms in their hands."

715 Their standing "on the sea of glass" is from Rev. 15:2. William Foy has "an innumerable multitude, arrayed in white raiment, standing in

a perfect square" (Foy, p. 19).

[716] The word "hung" in the statement, "Some crowns appeared hung with stars," is a word picture of fruit tree branches so laden with fruit that they hang down. Hence, the word means "heavy" with stars.

[717] That they are clothed in "white robes" is in Rev. 7:9. Harmon describes their dress as a "white mantle" and Foy, as "white raiment."

[718] The "sea of glass" is from Rev. 15:2.

[719] 2 Esdras 2:47: "Then began I greatly to commend them that stood so stiffly for the name of the Lord." Rev. 21:21 describes twelve gates. Rev. 7:14 has "washed their robes." Matt. 25:21: "His lord said unto him, Well done, thou good and faithful servant: thou hast been faithful over a few things, I will make thee ruler over many things: enter thou into the joy of thy lord." Isa. 26:2 has "Open ye the gates, that the righteous nation which keepeth the truth may enter in." Early Adventists often spoke of standing "stiffly" for truth.

[720] Rev. 22:14, "Blessed *are* they that do his commandments, that they may have right to the tree of life, and may enter in through the gates into the city."

[721] Rev. 22:14, 3.

[722] Rev. 22:1, 2.

[723] Rev. 22:2. Though Foy didn't mention a divided trunk, he described the tree looking like transparent gold: "Then I beheld in the boundless place a tree, the body of which, was like unto transparent gold, and the limbs were like transparent gold" (Foy, p. 14). Neither Scripture nor Ellen White has the sea beside the tree.

[724] Rev. 22:1, 2.

[725] Matt. 4:23; etc. "Brothers Fitch and Stockman" are Charles Fitch and Levi. S. Stockman, who both died the year they expected Christ to come. Fitch is known for applying the second angel's message to the papacy and to Protestant churches rejecting the Advent message; Stockman is known for giving young Ellen sage advice in her Christian experience. William Foy saw people he knew on earth, but doesn't mention Stockman and Fitch, and he placed the righteous "beneath this tree, standing on the sea of glass" (Foy, pp. 14, 15).

[726] 2 Cor. 4:17: "For our light affliction, which is but for a moment, worketh for us a far more exceeding and eternal weight of glory." Isa. 65:17 describes not being able to bring past trials to memory: "For, behold, I create new heavens and a new earth: and the former shall not be remembered, nor come into mind." Her first book, *A Sketch of the Christian Experience and Views of Ellen G. White* (1851), omits the description of the ark and temple, with wording from Exod. 25:18, 20; Heb. 9:3–5; Num. 17:8, beginning with, "And as we were gazing at the glories of the place" and ending with, "We all descended from this place down into the city, and" (though it is published in WLF 16.1; Broadside1 April 6, 1846; DS, Jan. 24, 1846).

[727] The description of the "mountain" parting asunder, creating a plain or a valley, comes from Zech. 14:4: "And his feet shall stand in that day upon the mount of Olives, which *is* before Jerusalem on the east, and the mount of Olives shall cleave in the midst thereof toward the east and toward the west, *and there shall be* a very great valley; and half of the mountain shall remove toward the north, and half of it toward the south." 2SG 52.1 separates this from the "Midnight Cry Vision" (**V1**) and designates it as the "New Earth Vision" (**V16**).

[728] The description of the descent of the "great city" comes from Rev. 21:2, 10–13: "And I John saw the holy city, new Jerusalem, coming down from God out of heaven, prepared as a bride adorned for her husband. … And he carried me away in the spirit to a great and high mountain, and shewed me that great city, the holy Jerusalem, descending out of heaven from God, Having the glory of God: and her light *was* like unto a stone most precious, even like a jasper stone, clear as crystal; and had a wall great and high, *and* had twelve gates, and at the gates twelve angels, and names written thereon, which are *the names* of the twelve tribes of the children of Israel: On the east three gates; on the north three gates; on the south three gates; and on the west three gates." The "twelve foundations" comes from Rev. 21:14: "And the wall of the city had twelve foundations, and in them the names of the twelve apostles of the Lamb."

[729] The idea that the redeemed will have "houses" comes from Isa. 65:21: "And they shall build houses, and inhabit *them*; and they shall plant vineyards, and eat the fruit of them."

[730] The peaceful co-existence of the animals comes from Isa. 11:6–9 and Isa. 65:25: "The wolf also shall dwell with the lamb, and the leopard shall lie down with the kid; and the calf and the young lion and the fatling together; and a little child shall lead them. And the cow and the bear shall feed; their young ones shall lie down together: and the lion shall eat straw like the ox. And the sucking child shall play on the hole of the asp, and the weaned child shall put his hand on the cockatrice' den. They shall not hurt nor destroy in all my holy mountain: for the earth shall be full of the knowledge of the LORD, as the waters cover the sea." "The wolf and the lamb shall feed together, and the lion shall eat straw like the bullock: and dust *shall be* the serpent's meat. They shall not hurt nor destroy in all my holy mountain, saith the LORD."

[731] Safety in the woods parallels the text quoted, Ezek. 34:25: "And I will make with them a covenant of peace, and will cause the evil beasts to cease out of the land: and they shall dwell safely in the wilderness, and sleep in the woods."

[732] See Donald Edward Casebolt, *Father Miller's Daughter*.

[733] Luke 21:27, 28.

[734] Ms. 131, 1906, Aug. 3. The location of Beethoven Hall is given in an 1891 article: "Beethoven Hall . . . was in the third story of a building on the eastern side of Congress street, near the head of Center street" ("The Second Adventists," *Evening Express*, Portland, ME, June 13, 1891, p. 1, at https://www.newspapers.com/clip/110228923/describes-the-location-of-beethoven; for the building's final demolition, see "Beethoven Hall: Another Old Landmark to Give Way to Progress," *The Portland Daily Press*, May 11, 1894, p. 7).

[735] Enthusiastic outbursts were common. So, by "extolled him," she is likely saying that they "exalted [him] in commendation; praised; magnified" ("extol," *Webster's International Dictionary*, 1900) for his visions, which, she believed, ended up hurting him, and she did not know what happened to him thereafter.

[736] Nothing else is known of his wife Ann Foy except that she married Foy in 1837 and that they had a daughter named Amelia.

[737] His visions were given in January and February of 1842, so his recounting of them would have been some time later. There is a "Notice" in the *Portland Advertiser*, Feb. 27, 1844, p. 2, that Foy would be holding meetings at the Casco Street Christian church in Portland, Maine (Burt, "Historical Background," p. 16), designated a Freewill Baptist on the 1836 map (see https://oshermaps.org/map/11753.0001).

[738] That she traveled there in a sleigh indicates that she made the trip in snowy weather. His residing near the Portland bridge would have been of short duration since he is not listed in the 1840 or 1850 censuses of Portland, ME.

[739] Ms. 131, 1906, Aug. 3.

[740] Book facsimile found at https://archive.org/details/FoyWilliam.TheChristianExperienceOfWilliamE.FoyTogetherWithTheTwo.

[741] Isa. 53:3; Matt. 17:2.

[742] Mark 9:7. The original has "appearence" for "appearance." The original is missing a quotation mark before "God buried."

[743] In two instances, the original has "bible."

[744] 2 Cor. 12:2; Matt. 17:6.

[745] The original has "Perpetia" for "Perpetua" and "encourageing" for "encouraging," and it is missing the final period.

[746] The original has "buriel" for "burial" and "whenuse" for "his."

[747] Acts 2:4, 12, 13. In "Perpetuity of Spiritual Gifts," ST, May 20, 1875, pp. 217, 218, J. H. Waggoner recounts visions of a Mr. Tennent, an Elder J. B. Finley, and a Dr. Bond.

[748] Acts 2:16.

[749] Acts 2:20. The original has "precursers" and "notaable."

[750] Rev. 10:1, "mighty angel"; Rev. 4:6; 15:2, "sea of glass."

[751] Neh. 1:5.

[752] Silas Curtis was a Baptist pastor in Augusta, ME.

[753] John 1:29.

[754] Song of Solomon 5:16; 5:10.

[755] Ps. 25:5.

[756] Luke 2:14.

[757] "Sweet communion" is an expression used by Millerites; see ExV54 31.5.

[758] 2 Peter 2:9.

[759] Isa. 40:31. The original of this paragraph has "bible."

[760] Mark 1:10; Luke 2:14; Rev. 5:13.

[761] Unlike Ellen White, Foy describes his visionary experience as being "seized as in the agonies of death" and in the form of a "spirit" apart from his body, likely reflecting the Baptist view of death.

[762] Acts 26:13.

[763] "multitude," Rev. 7:9; 19:6; "both small and great," Rev. 11:18. It is unclear what the "mount" is; it was somehow over the river. The original has "inhabitance" for "inhabitants."

[764] The original has "appearence." For the three changes, see 1 Cor. 15:52; Rev. 3:4; Rev. 4:4, 10. ExV 11.1 has "bright crowns" and "glorious white mantle."

[765] Foy sees the wicked on earth near this "mount."

[766] The original has "appearence." Foy repeatedly uses "boundless."

[767] Similar to Jesus' clothing, Rev. 1:13; one clothed in white linen, Dan. 10:5; the clothing of the redeemed, ExV 11.1.

[768] "both small and great," Rev. 11:18.

[769] Angels preaching the gospel on earth seems odd, though the angel of Rev. 14:6 is said to declare it.

[770] Dan. 10:6; Rev. 10:1; 15:6; 1:14. See also ExV 11.1. For the crown on his head, see Rev. 14:14; ExV 11.1; and 1SG 199.1.

[771] Rev. 10:4; 19:2. In Ellen White's first vision (V1), it is Jesus who raises "His mighty glorious arm," swings back the gate on "its glittering hinges," (her original description has "its golden hinges"), and welcomes the saints, saying, "You have washed your robes in My blood, stood stiffly for My truth, enter in" (ExV 11.1). See Rev. 7:14; 22:14; Matt. 25:21; Isa. 26:2.

[772] "both small and great," Rev. 11:18.

[773] The golden cards with names are similar to the white stones of Rev. 2:17. These cards, which seem to be a form of identification, are mentioned by Foy several times. (1) They are given at their arrival to the city. (2) The cards are glorious and have something written that Foy cannot read. (3) Cards are given to the resurrected redeemed along with white raiment and bright crowns. (4) The redeemed themselves bear the cards in heaven. Ellen White's golden cards are in the "Sealing Vision" (V59) and "God's Love for His People Vision" (V63) in 1849.

[774] Zech. 5:1; Isa. 6:3.

[775] These would have been alive to meet Jesus without dying and parallel the 144,000 of Rev. 14:3. The original has "the held cards."

[776] The original does not have a period at the end of this sentence.

[777] Rev. 8:13. Here are three possible interpretations: either the one saying, *"This is my mother,"* is using the term figuratively, or Foy misinterpreted what he saw, or Foy meant that the "spirit" spoke and believed that people on earth become angels at death.

[778] Matt. 28:3; Rev. 10:1; 1:15; esp. Dan. 10:6. See also ExV 11.1.

[779] Rev. 10:1. Is this "mighty angel" that is worshiped Jesus?

[780] Rev. 10:5: "And the angel which I saw stand upon the sea and upon the earth lifted up his hand to heaven"; Rev. 14:1: "a Lamb stood on the mount Sion, and with him an hundred and forty and four thousand . . . Father's name written in their forehead." See also Rev. 14:4, for following the Lamb.

[781] "I heard a voice from heaven, as the voice of many waters, and . . . of a great thunder," paralleling the "great thunder" of Rev. 14:2.

[782] Flames parallel "fire and brimstone" of Rev. 14:11.

[783] There is no closing quotation mark in the original. Compare: "Then I saw that Satan, and all the wicked host, were consumed, and the justice of God was satisfied; and all the angelic host, and all the redeemed saints, with a loud voice said, Amen!" (1SG 217.1).

[784] Ellen White "saw the little ones climb, or if they chose, use their little wings and fly to the top of the mountains, and pluck the never fading flowers" (ExV 14.1) as part of the "New Earth Vision" (V16). Foy may have interpreted little children with wings in the branches of the trees as angels. In her "Midnight Cry Vision" (V1), White saw the two-trunked tree of life like "transparent gold" (ExV 11.1).

[785] Allusions, Rev. 22:2; 15:2. Similar wording to Prov. 25:11. Also, notice that the redeemed have "cards upon their breasts."

[786] The highlighted words are parallel to words in the "New Earth Vision" (V16) in ExV 15.1.

[787] Luke 3:7.

[788] The original has "evnmg" and "exortation."

789 The original has "barst."
790 Rev. 20:8.
791 Rev. 13:11.
792 The original has "enroled."
793 The original has a period after "passed."
794 Dan. 10:6. The original has "appeard."
795 Rev. 4:1; 9:13; the original did not have a period after "done sounding." Compare the "Three Steps Vision" (V4) in 1SG 168.
796 Isa. 6:3.
797 ExV 43.1 has "he stepped into the chariot" to travel to the Most Holy Place. This is part of the "Bridegroom Vision" (V5), Feb. 1845.
798 [Original note] Mary Black, the wife of the deceased Eld. George Black (the individual seen in the vision) testifies, "These are his dying words, 'I see the chariots coming to waft my spirit home.' He then left the world with a shout." [Freewill Baptists believed that a conscious spirit can exist apart from the body.]
799 The original has "too and from."
800 From V1, Ellen describes the 144,000 "in a perfect square. Some of them with very bright crowns, others not so bright" (ExV 11.1).
801 Rev. 22:2. Significantly, the tree of life is not described as being on both sides of the river.
802 Rev. 10:1.
803 Ps. 69:28. The original does not capitalize the word "my."
804 Gen. 28:12. The original has "refered."
805 Acts 26:16; Matt. 3:7. In V2, Ellen was told, "The grace of God is sufficient for you; He will hold you up" (ExV 5.4).
806 The original has "continuilly." This depiction was perhaps to illustrate the close interaction between heaven and earth.
807 The original has "to to bear to the world." In V2, Ellen begged God to lay the burden on someone else (ExV 6.1).
808 Acts 26:14; 18:10.
809 Rev. 14:11.
810 The original has "Since then. I," with a period after then.
811 1 Cor. 14:3. James White alluded to "comfort the saints" in ExV 2.6.
812 Rev. 10:1.
813 1 Cor. 2:9, 10.
814 The original has "Febuary" and "inhabitance" for "inhabitants."
815 With little information besides their names, that they were "inhabitants of Boston," and that they were likely Black or mulatto, it is difficult to identify the witnesses in this list. However, some identifications are more certain than others. "Charles Tash" was Charles G. Tash, who cut and styled African American hair in Charlestown, MA, a neighborhood of Boston (see https://www.familysearch.org/ark:/61903/3:1:S3HY-6QN3-CWH?i=375&cc=1401638), and served in a Massachusetts regiment during the Civil War (email Kevin Burton, June 15, 2023). George Williams and John Thomas, who both signed a petition for Black sailors' rights, may be listed as mariners in the 1843 Boston City Directory (https://archive.org/details/bd-1843/page/522 and https://archive.org/details/bd-1843/page/478). Edward Williams may have been a mulatto laborer who appeared in the US Census of 1850, 1860, and 1880. Dr. Henry Cummings was a mulatto botanic physician living in Charlestown (see https://www.familysearch.org/ark:/61903/3:1:3QS7-99QB-L369?i=51&cc=2061550 and https://www.familysearch.org/ark:/61903/3:1:S3HY-69B9-TCT?i=44&cc=1401638). From newspaper marriage records, we can infer that Tash and Cummings worshipped at the church of Jehiel Chappell Beman, an African Methodist Episcopal minister known as an abolitionist and temperance advocate. His church, the First African Methodist Episcopal Zion Church of Boston, was founded in 1838 on West Centre Street (*The Liberator*, Nov. 16, 1838; Aug. 25, 1843, p. 135; Aug. 19, 1842, p. 131).
816 The original has "appearence." Ann Foy was William Foy's wife whom he married in 1837. Nothing more is known of her except what Ellen White mentioned about her in Ms. 131, 1906.
817 "Daniel Palmer" could have been Daniel Carleton Palmer, a lumberman and surveyor of Augusta, ME, then mayor of Gardiner, ME.
818 Benjamin Baker, "Foy, William Ellis (1818–1893)," at https://encyclopedia.adventist.org/article?id=9CEN. That there was a fourth is based on Ellen White's statement, which she repeated in the interview that is transcribed in Ms. 131, 1906.
819 Although Loughborough's 1905 account says that Foy was preparing to take holy orders as an Episcopal minister, Foy actually remained a Freewill Baptist. That conclusion may have come from Ellen White's describing Foy as wearing an Episcopalian robe (Ms. 131, 1906). Yet, many Black churches in America have embraced the formality of special robes for the clergy.
820 GSAM 146; see also Loughborough's earlier mention of Foy in "The Prophetic Gift," RH, July 18, 1899, p. 454.
821 1SG 168, 169. Loughborough reported that it was this third vision, given in 1844, that Foy could not understand and that he heard Ellen Harmon relate in 1845 (GSAM 146.2; see also Ms. 131, 1906) and that he refused to share with others (GSAM 182.1; 212.2). 1SG gives no date for the vision, but it comes after Ellen White's recounting of the three angels' messages.
822 For Hazen Little Foss, see RH, June 12, 1866, p. 10; GSAM 182.1; and Lt. 37, 1890, Dec. 22, to Mary Foss, sister-in-law of Hazen Foss.
823 Delbert Baker lists similarities to the 144,000, though the number is not mentioned (*The Unknown Prophet*, p. 101). They are (a) translated saints (p. 11); (b) companions with Jesus (p. 13); (c) placed on the holy mount (p. 13); (d) have a name on their forehead (p. 13); (e) hear God speak (p. 13); (f) saved by believing (p. 14).
824 Tim Poirier, "The Visions of William Foy and Hazen Foss: An Examination of the Historical Sources," May 1982; cf. Lt. 37, 1890.
825 For Ellen White's use of golden cards, see ExV 19.1; 22.1. For Foy's use of "cards," see Foy, pp. 11, 13, 14, and 17.
826 Not shown is James White's condensed version of the first vision (V1), published in DS of Sept. 6, 1845. James' recounting of the main points of the vision could be an indication he heard her rehearse the vision sufficiently to tell it from memory. A facsimile of the book is available online at https://archive.org/details/FoyWilliam.TheChristianExperienceOfWilliamE.FoyTogetherWithTheTwo, and a rare copy of Foy's book is in the Huntington Library in San Marino, California.
827 1 Peter 4:13.
828 The concept of "the wedding" came from the "Bridegroom Vision" (V5), which she received in February 1845.
829 The "Midnight Cry" was the "powerful proclamation during the late summer and autumn of 1844 announcing the second coming of

Christ on October 22" (1EGWLM 86, n6). Many Adventists abandoned any significance to this development, but Ellen White saw its value in stirring interest in Christ's return.

830 Ellen White did not claim to know the day and hour of Jesus' coming, writing: "I have not the slightest knowledge as to the time spoken by the voice of God. I heard the hour proclaimed, but had no remembrance of that hour after I came out of vision" (Lt. 38, 1888).

831 Because Millerite expositors (e.g., Josiah Litch, Apollos Hale, Enoch Jacobs, and Clorinda S. Minor) viewed the seven last plagues as poured out *after* the Second Coming, James White included a section in WLF about the plagues falling *before* the Second Coming, in keeping and in support of Ellen's view.

832 "Wash one another's feet" is from John 13:14; "Salute" "with" a "holy kiss" is from Rom. 16:16; 1 Cor. 16:20; 2 Cor. 13:12; 1 Thess. 5:26; 1 Peter 5:14; "the holy brethren" is from 1 Thess. 5:27; and "worshipped at our feet" is from Rev. 3:9.

833 The colloquial usage of "hung," which is imagery from tree branches hanging down with a burden of fruit, was replaced by the better understood "heavy."

834 Ellen White later identified who these two groups were. "These two classes are brought to view in the vision—those who declared the light which they had followed a delusion and the wicked of the world who, having rejected the light, had been rejected of God. No reference is made to those who had not seen the light and therefore were not guilty of its rejection" (Ms. 4, 1883).

835 WLF 14 has "Isa. 10:27," but the reference should be Exod. 34:30–34.

836 The omission may indicate his rejection of footwashing and the "holy kiss."

837 In the omitted portion, she described seeing "Abraham, Isaac, Jacob, Noah, Daniel, and many like them." That she had also described seeing Fitch and Stockman before indicates that this scene will take place *after* the Second Coming. Without the scene beginning, "And as we were gazing at the glories of the place," the "also" in the later "we met a company who were *also* gazing at the glories of the place" makes less sense. This scene is not included in *Spiritual Gifts*, vol. 2.

838 **2SG 54.1** also omits this brief interjection.

839 Omits "but, if faithful, you soon will know all about it," though Ellen White's sense of the nearness of Christ's return never wavered.

840 Omits the sentence, "We all reclined at the table." Reclining at table was how Jesus ate in John 21:20; John 13:23, ESV.

841 **2SG 30.2** has "*further*" rather than "farther." Other differences from *Experience and Views* and *Early Writings* are noted below.

842 **2SG 30.2** has "This shone" instead of "This light shone" and "*that* they might not stumble" instead of "so they might not stumble."

843 **2SG 30.2** has "a *bright* light" rather than "a glorious light" and "Advent *people*" rather than "Advent band."

844 **2SG 30.2** has "*into* the dark and wicked world" instead of "in the dark and wicked world."

845 **2SG 30.2** omits "144,000, in number."

846 **2SG 30.2** has "Holy *Spirit*" instead of "Holy Ghost."

847 **2SG 30.2** omits "who could wash one another's feet, and salute the holy brethren with a holy kiss."

848 **2SG 32.1** adds "*and*" before "around the cloud were ten thousand angels."

849 **2SG 32.1** has "both *like* pure, transparent gold," not "both of pure transparent gold," clarifying that they appeared to be of gold.

850 **2SG 34.1** has "Brn." instead of "brothers."

851 **2SG 34.1** has "*golden* harps" instead of "glorious harps," which is more explicit about what made them "glorious."

852 **2SG 52.1** has "*beautiful* houses" instead of "glorious houses," which explains what she meant by "glorious."

853 **2SG 52.1** does not have "no, no."

854 **2SG 52.1** omits the words "shouting and" in "continually shouting and offering praises to God."

855 **2SG 53.1** has "but light and *beautiful*" instead of "no, no; but light, and all over glorious."

856 **2SG 53.1** (54) has "*a building which looked to me like* a temple" instead of "a glorious temple." In this second mention of a temple, she emphasizes the right of the 144,000 to enter, calling attention to tables of stone with their names inscribed in them.

857 **2SG 53.1** omits "around the temple."

858 **2SG 54.1** has "*The* temple" instead of "This temple."

859 **2SG 54.1** has "The things" instead of "The glorious things."

860 **2SG 54.1** has "the names of 144,000" rather than "the names of the 144,000."

861 **2SG 54.1** ends with "Then an angel bore me gently down to this dark world," omitting the last three sentences.

862 In his August 10, 1845, letter, which predates Ellen's first writing, James White expressed the same thought as the omitted words: "In her vision [V1] she heard the 'Midnight Cry'—she saw a mighty host start at the point where the cry was made, (finished)—soon she saw many denying the light *set behind them*, (which was the midnight cry.) *By this time they were in darkness, and began to stumble and fall off from the strait and narrow path, down into the dark world below to rise no more.* She saw them continually falling till the voice of God was heard as recorded in Ezek. 12:25, which was a number of days before the 'Sign of the Son of Man' appeared—which was the great white cloud, Rev. 14:14" (DS, Sept. 6, 1845, emphasis added). The omitted part may have seemed unnecessary since one could reasonably assume that those who fell off the pathway would climb back on. Ellen White commented, "No reference is made to those who had not seen the light, and therefore were not guilty of its rejection" (Ms. 4, 1883). Very early on, people who had not heard and rejected the message of Christ's return joined the movement, such as John Yale Wilcox; Hiram and Sarah Ann Patch; Heman Allen Churchill; and Luman V. Masten (see RP1892 136, 137, 152; RH, Aug. 1850, p. 15; "Experience of Bro. Masten," RH, Sept. 30, 1852, p. 86). Sarah's mother, Lucy Benson, became a Sabbath-keeper in Oswego (RH, Feb. 9, 1886, p. 94). Heman Churchill was married to Betsey Barrows Benson, "a daughter of Sr. Benson, a '44 Adventist," on May 1, 1844 (RH, April 7, 1885, p. 217) by Baptist minister Jared L. Green, yet he did not become an Adventist until *after* 1844 (see PrT, Nov. 1850, p. 88). Ellen White's long-time friend Marion C. Stowell did not become a Christian or embrace the Advent message until *after* she heard Ellen White in 1845 (Crawford to Ellen White, Oct. 9, 1908, at https://ellenwhite.org/correspondence/236643).

863 WLF 21. Thanks to David J. Conklin for the insight about "spotlighting" and to Daniel Winters for his scrutiny of the exhibit.

864 See John 21:20 and Ellen White's comment in DA 653.1: "In harmony with the rest that had been given them, the people then partook of the Passover supper in a reclining position."

865 For another review of these changes, see Ron Graybill, "Visions and Revisions-part 1," *Ministry*, Feb. 1994, p. 10 –13, 28.

866 Rev. 14:1, 6, 7.

867 Scriptural references are omitted for allusions that were already marked in the text of *Experience and Views* and the *Supplement*.

868 Gen. 1:26.

869 Rev. 12:7.

870 Gen. 2:9.

871 Ezek. 36:35; Gen. 3:2. Ellen White's view of Adam and Eve in the garden goes back to her "Perishing Souls Vision" (V87) at Oswego, NY, Jan. 26, 1850 (see Ms. 4, 1850, Jan. 28; PrT April 1850).

872 Gen. 2:17.

873 Gen. 3:6.

874 Gen. 3:24.

875 Luke 10:18; Gen. 3:23; Rev. 2:7.

876 Luke 9:44.

877 1 John 2:2.

878 Matt. 16:21; John 20:17.

879 Matt. 20:28; Mark 10:45; 1 Tim. 2:6.

880 Matt. 4:11; Mark 1:13; Luke 22:43.

881 When first published, the book was advertised as "*Spiritual Gifts, or The Great Controversy, between Christ and his angels, and Satan and his angels*" (RH, Sept. 30, 1858, p. 152); it did not become "Spiritual Gifts Vol. 1" until 1860 (RH, Nov. 20, 1860, p. 8).

882 DA 22.2 quotes Rom. 16:25, English Revised Version. For other authors who described the plan of redemption as not "an afterthought," see https://www.academia.edu/93556769/The_Desire_of_Ages_Chapter_1_God_With_Us_A_Biblical_Essay_on_the_Incarnation, note 65. In 1877, Ellen White repeatedly referred to Christ's equality with the Father (2SP 10.2; 11.1; 38.2; 91.2; 167.2) and to the voluntary nature of His sacrifice (2SP 10.1, 4). In the 1890s, Ellen White also wrote: "But known unto God are all his works, and from eternal ages the covenant of grace (unmerited favor) existed in the mind of God. It is called the everlasting covenant; for the plan of salvation was not conceived after the fall of man, but it was that which was 'kept in silence through times eternal, but now is manifested and by the Scriptures of the prophets according to the commandment of the eternal God, is made known unto all the nations unto obedience of faith' " (ST, Feb. 13, 1893). "God is love, God is life. It is the prerogative of God to redeem, reconstruct, and restore. Before the foundation of the world the Son of God was given to die, and redemption is the mystery that was "kept in silence from times eternal" (ST, Feb. 26, 1895). ST, March 25, 1897, links the phrasing in Colossians 1:26 with that of Romans 16:25, ASV, ERV. Her earliest statement that hints at this understanding is in 3SG 37.3: "Satan unblushingly makes known to all the heavenly family, his discontent, that Christ should be preferred before him, to be in such close conference with God, and he be uninformed as to the result of their frequent consultations. God informs Satan that this he can never know. That to his Son will he reveal his secret purposes, and that all the family of Heaven, Satan not excepted, were required to yield implicit obedience."

883 Ms. 48, 1886; allusions, Heb. 9:14.

884 *Patriarch and Prophets*, p. 63.

885 ST, Feb. 13, 1893; allusions, John 1:1; 10:30; 17:11, 21; 5:18; Phil. 2:6; Rev. 13:8; Heb. 9:14.

886 Ms. 101, 1897; allusions, Heb. 9:14; John 5:18; Phil. 2:6; Heb. 7:22; Isa. 6:8; John 17:24; Eph. 1:4; 1 Peter 1:20; Heb. 7:22; John 10:18.

887 ST, May 14, 1902.

888 Five times we find Christ "gave Himself" (Gal. 1:4; 2:20; Eph. 5:25; 1 Tim. 2:6; Titus 2:14); once, He "offered Himself" (Heb. 9:14).

889 Lt. 126, 1898, allusion, Acts 26:18; quoting Isa. 53:10, 11. Biblically, the term "Godhead" comes from three related Greek words: STRONG's G2304, θεῖος *theios* (Acts 17:29), an adjective that means "divine" or "god-like"; STRONG's G2305, θεῖος *theios* (Rom. 1:20), a noun that means "divinity" (abstractly); and STRONG's G2320, θεότης *theotes* (Col. 2:9), a noun that also means "divinity" (abstractly).

890 Acts 17:29; Rom. 1:20; Col. 2:9; 2 Thess. 2:4. Ellen White's descriptions of the *threeness* of the Godhead are many: "There are three living persons of the heavenly trio ... these three great powers" (Ms. 21, 1906; SpTB07 63.2; BTS, March 1, 1906); "the three persons—the Father, the Son, and the Holy Spirit" (Ms. 57, 1900); "The three powers of the Godhead" (RH, July 18, 1907; and Ms. 141, 1907; AUCR, Oct. 7, 1907); "these three highest powers of heaven" (Ms. 158, 1904); "the three highest powers in/of heaven/in the heavenly courts/in the universe" (Ms. 27a, 1900; Lt. 253a, 1903; Lt. 53, 1904; Ms. 106, 1904; Ms. 108, 1904; Ms. 50, 1904; RH, May 26, 1904, Art. A; Ms. 191, 1905; ST, Aug. 16, 1905; SpTB07 51.1, 1905; Ms. 180, 1907; Ms. 61, 1907; Ms. 67, 1908; PUR, July 2, 1908; SW, Dec. 15, 1908; RH, Aug. 12, 1909); "these three great/greatest powers" (Ms. 31, 1901; RH, June 22, 1905; and GCB, April 14, 1901; Ms. 78, 1905; Lt. 32, 1907; Ms. 183, 1907; Ms. 21, 1906; Lt. 131, 1902; Ms. 57, 1900; Ms. 190, 1903, July 11; Ms. 182, 1907; Ms. 37, 1908; Ms. 11, 1901; ST, June 19, 1901; ST, Feb. 12, 1902; Ms. 30, 1902; Ms. 118, 1902; Ms. 136, 1903; ST, March 11, 1903; RH, May 5, 1903; Lt. 102, 1903; Lt. 129, 1903; Lt. 129, 1903; Lt. 1, 1904; 8T 254.1, 1904; Lt. 53, 1904; SW, Feb. 23, 1904; Ms. 181, 1905; Ms. 187, 1905; ST, May 10, 1905; Ms. 54, 1905; RH, June 15, 1905; Ms. 191, 1905; ST, Aug. 16, 1905; ST, May 10, 1910; Ms. 159, 1904); "the three great heavenly Powers" (Ms. 130, 1902; Ms. 192, 1903; Ms. 147, 1906; Ms. 186, 1907); "these three great, infinite powers" (Ms. 144, 1901; GCB, April 4, 1901, Art. A); "the three great personal powers, the authorities of heaven" (Lt. 205, 1901); "the three great authorities of heaven" (Ms. 177, 1907); "the three heavenly authorities" (Lt. 396, 1906); "the three highest authorities of the heavenly courts—the Father, the Son, and the Holy Ghost" (Ms. 87, 1902); "these three representatives/greatest representatives of heavenly authority" (Lt. 174, 1909; Ms. 57, 1902); "the three highest authorities in the universe" (Ms. 129, 1907); "these three great agencies/individual Agencies" (Ms. 67, 1907; Ms. 68, 1900); "three distinct agencies, the Father, the Son, and the Holy Ghost, work together for human beings" (Ms. 27a, 1900); "the Father, the Son, and the Holy Ghost are heaven's loving, powerful agencies for the accomplishment of the work of representing God in the world" (Lt. 93, 1900); "the three great and glorious heavenly characters" (Ms. 45, 1904); "the three dignitaries and powers of heaven" (Ms. 85, 1901); "the three great personal dignitaries of heaven" (Ms. 92, 1901); "the three holy dignitaries of heaven" (Ms. 92, 1901); "the eternal heavenly dignitaries—God, and Christ, and the Holy Spirit" (Ms. 130, 1901); "the three great Instrumentalities of heaven" (Ms. 11, 1901); "the three great Worthies" (Ms. 95, 1906; Ms. 139, 1906; Ms. 95, 1906; Ms. 145, 1906); "the threefold name of the Father, the Son, and the Holy Ghost/Spirit" (Ms. 27a, 1900; 6T 91.3); "the threefold powers/power" (Ms. 45, 1904; Ms. 229, 1902; Ms. 11, 1901; ST, June 19, 1901); "the three holiest beings in heaven" (Ms. 95, 1906).

891 Lt. 12, 1901, with allusions to Acts 17:29; John 3:18. The phrase "gave themselves" is reminiscent of Christ's giving Himself.

892 Ms. 45, 1904, with allusions to Eph. 3:19; 2 Peter 1:4.

893 Ms. 141, 1907.

894 2 Cor. 3:18.

INDEXES

The portraits on the following page are individuals mentioned in endnotes whose portrait was discovered during research for the Biographical Index. They can be cross referenced to the names in the indexes.

Charles Andrews | Marie Andrews | J. N. Andrews | Jehiel Beman | Charles L. Boyd | Maud Boyd

Electa Brown | Samuel Brown | Sidney Brownsberger | Samuel D. Burchard | Phebe Chamberlain | John Ball Cook

Eli Curtis | John Daigneau | Israel Allen Dammon | J. E. Dietschy | Martha Ensign | Jules-Henri Guenin

Harriet F. Hastings | Squire Howard | W. F. Jamieson | Charles C. Lewis | Mary Loughborough | Noah Lunt

Harriet McCann | Mary Morton | Noble Nordyke | Richard Oliphant | Caroline Orton | Jonathan Orton

Sarah Peck | Stephen Pierce | John Stiles Preston | John Sisley | S. S. Snow | Peter Staples

George States | Albert Vuilleumier | Walter White | Matthew Whittier | Henry Winslow | Rebecca Winslow

Illustrations Index

Most of the graphics have been colorized and enhanced.

Ellen White writing, https://ellenwhite.org/media/image/2112 cover
Daniel T. Bourdeau, https://ellenwhite.org/media/image/103 6
Merritt Gardner Kellogg, https://www.centerforadventistresearch.org/photos/special-collections/L.%20T.%20Nicola%20Album/b17479514_k0001.jpg 6
George I. Butler, https://media1.ellenwhite.org/img/125.4/125.4.jpg 7
Ellen G. White looking up, krea.ai 8
Roswell F. Cotrell 10
Typical School Scene 1901, by W. L. Taylor, via Brown Brothers, *Journal True Education*, June 1953, cover 12
Angry girl throws stone at Ellen, Harry Baerg, *His Messenger*, frontispiece 12
Bird's-eye view of Portland, 1876, https://www.mainememory.net/record/71166, insets Middle Street, Portland, ME, ca. 1850, https://www.mainememory.net/record/4153; "Tom (Piggy) Huston, Market Square, Portland, 1869," www.mainememory.net/item/23436; carrying Ellen, adapted Marcus Mashburn, *Vision in the Storm,* 24; Harmon house, Spruce St., 1909, https://centrowhite.org.br/downloads/imagens/pessoas/white-estate-cd-13 12
Ellen in bed with bandage, krea.ai 13
Westbrook Seminary, https://www.mainememory.net/record/29225 13
William Miller, 1841, https://aurora.edu/academics/library/jenks-collection/jenks-writings/denomination-founding.html 14
Esther before the King, Providence Lithograph Co., ©1899 14
Methodist Camp Meeting, Charles Henry Granger, https://pixels.com/featured/1-methodist-camp-meeting-granger.html 15
"Father and Mother Took the Whole Family to Camp Meeting in a Wagon," *Sister White*, 11, by Kreigh Collins 15
The "Old Baptising Shore," from 1876 Bird's eye map, https://www.mainememory.net/record/71166 16
Baptism, adapted from Rachel Barrett by Honor Him Publishers 16
Believers seeking sanctification, 19th century tent revival, https://unusualkentucky.blogspot.com/2010/08 17
Bleeding lamb, https://depositphotos.com/photos/blood-lamb.html 17
Girl following angel up stairway, krea.ai 17
Jesus, by Heinrich Hofmann, https://pixels.com/featured/portrait-head-of-jesus-christ-heinrich-hofmann.html 18
Chestnut Street Methodist Episcopal Church, Portland, Maine, 1836, https://oshermaps.org/map/11753.0001 18
Victorian doctor and young woman, https://archive.org/details/aib.punchvolume980000unse.98/page/130, krei.ai 19
Location of Robert Harmon's house and Elizabeth Haines' house on 1857 Map of Portland Maine, inset "Map of Cumberland County, Maine," at https://www.loc.gov/resource/g3733c.la000266/?r=0.677,0.276,0.195,0.117,0 20
The Advent Mirror, https://archive.org/details/A.haleJ.turnerHasNotTheSaviorComeAsTheBridegroom1845 21
Winter scene near Portland, ca. 1848 Maine Historical Society, https://www.mainememory.net/record/6891 22
"The church gathered to pray for her," *Pioneer Stories*, 193 24
Samuel Hoyt Foss, https://ellenwhite.org/media/image/296 25
"Portland Cutter" one-horse open sleigh 25
Mary Plummer Foss, https://ellenwhite.org/media/image/311 ... 25
Hazen Foss, https://ellenwhite.org/media/image/250 26
Map West Poland with properties of J. Meggire, W. McAnn, and S. Foss, https://www.loc.gov/resource/g3733a.la000265/?r=0.259,0.614,0.064,0.032,0 26
Norway Advertiser, 25 Apr 1845, arrest Turner and Harmon 27
James White, https://ellenwhite.org/media/image/2163 27
1859 map of Corinna-Exeter, Maine, marked for Mrs. Dearborn and I. Dammon, https://www.loc.gov/resource/g3733p.la000272a/?r=0.139,0.673,0.056,0.022,0 28
Israel Dammon, courtesy Jim Nix 28
Ellen Harmon's early 1845 vision-sharing tour, Google maps 29
Aerial view of James Ayer's property, Google maps 30
Israel Dammon, courtesy Jim Nix 31
Charles P. Chandler, Dover-Foxcroft Historical Society 31
James Stuart Holmes, via Ian.Kent, ancestry.com, 4 Sep 2013 31
William C. Crosby, Esq., via Erin Ortiz, ancestry.com, 25 Apr 2017 31
Joel Doore, Jr. *The Iowa Recorder*, 23 Nov 1904 31
Piscataquis County Courthouse, Dover, Maine, built in 1844, http://courthousehistory.com/gallery/states/maine/counties/piscataquis 31
Sound the Jubilee, https://hymnary.org/hymn/MHDM1846/B14 32
"Fort Howland," Topsham, Maine, *Footsteps*, 44 33
William Henry Hyde, via Shirley_York_Anderson, ancestry.com, 13 Sep 2012 34
Crawling adult 35
Albert M. Billings, https://www.findagrave.com/memorial/76567415/albert-merritt-billings 37
Elizabeth Haines' house, *His Messenger* (1939), 36 39
Small boat to Belfast, Kevin Morgan 44
Man looking through his fingers, krea.ai 47
Aerial view of Boston, taken from a balloon, 13 Oct 1860, by James Wallace Black, https://en.wikipedia.org/wiki/James_Wallace_Black 50
Otis R. Nichols, https://ellenwhite.org/media/image/596; Mary Bird Nichols, https://ellenwhite.org/media/image/586 51
Map of Massachusetts with towns Ellen Harmon visited 51
The Advent Message to the Daughters of Zion, edited by Clorinda S. Minor, https://encyclopedia.adventist.org/article?id=99SX 53
Joseph Bates, https://ellenwhite.org/media/image/65 58
August 16, 1846, intention of marriage for James S. White, of Palmyra, and Miss Ellen G. Harmon, of Portland 58
Planets, NASA, via https://www.sas.rochester.edu/planetary-science 59
James and Ellen White, c. 1857, restored by Kevin Morgan, https://ellenwhite.org/media/image/2163 60
Map of Ballston Spa marked for Jesse Thompson's home, https://www.loc.gov/resource/g3803s.la000557/?r=0.363,0.902,0.178,0.113,0 and two views of Jesse Thompson's house, taken in 1975 https://ellenwhite.org/media/image/1814 and https://ellenwhite.org/media/image/1813 61
"Saratoga Springs," 1850s, hand-colored lithograph by Currier and Ives, 158 Nassau Street, New York, https://digitalcoll.skidmore.edu/record/2329 62
Stephen Belden, https://ellenwhite.org/media/image/90; Sarah Belden https://encyclopedia.adventist.org/article?id=7C9D .. 62
1856 map of Saratoga Springs Samuel Geil survey at https://www.loc.gov/resource/g3803s.la000557/?r=0.855,1.259,0.086,0.051,0; Gideon M. Davison, from Nathaniel Bartlett Sylvester, *History of Saratoga County, New York* (1878), 198, https://archive.org/details/cu31924028833064/page/n269; John Bevan map, https://digitalcollections.nypl.org/items/19398e40-5978-0133-99c2-00505686a51c 63
124 Mount Hope Avenue, Bird's Eye View of Rochester, New York 1880, at https://www.loc.gov/resource/g3804r.pm006250/?r=0.208,0.464,0.18,0.108,0 64
Washington hand press used in Rochester, https://www.adventist.org/who-are-seventh-day-adventists/publishing-work-was-central-to-early-adventist-church 64
Spiritual Gifts, volumes 1, 2, 3, and 4 64
B. F. Snook, https://encyclopedia.adventist.org/article?id=AA6M 64
James White, 1859, https://ellenwhite.org/media/image/830 76
Robert Harmon, Ellen White's father 78
Ellen White's first vision at Elizabeth Haines' home, by Clyde Provonsha, *The Story of Our Church*, 190 78
Lay the burden on someone else, https://www.youtube.com/watch?v=I5bmBR1PRGA 79
Sarah Harmon Belden, Ellen's older sister, age regressed via FaceApp, https://ellenwhite.org/media/image/5592; Ellen Harmon, age regressed via FaceApp, https://ellenwhite.org/media/image/2156 80
1855 map of Fairhaven and West Island, Massachusetts, by Henry F. Walling, Andrew S. Mowry, showing landowners, not residents, https://collections.leventhalmap.org/search/commonwealth:1257bc97r 81
Advent people on the path to the heavenly city, Harry Anderson, adapted, at https://www.ellenwhite.info/books/ellen-g-white-book-early-writings-ew-02.htm 82
Jesus crowning a saint with his heavenly reward, https://fbnw.wordpress.com/2015/02/23/a-comment-on-awards-should-christians-be-honored 83
Jesus opening heaven's gates, https://www.pinterest.ph/pin/350858627213054863 83
Tree of Life, Elfred Lee, adapted 84
Millerite preacher Charles Fitch, https://adventistdigitallibrary.org/adl-364874/charles-fitch 84

"Peace," painted by William Strutt, 1896 85
Sabbath commandment with halo of glory, https://www.slideshare.net/machopolo/christ-in-the-midst-of-the-hebrew-sanctuary-6700021 86
Jesus' appearing, with sky rolling up like a scroll 88
Angels ascending and descending on ladder, https://eliakashifofficial.medium.com/the-nine-orders-of-angels-in-christian-angelology-weird-stuff-global-bizarre-632668db38cb 89
Inhabitants of unfallen world of different sizes 90
The open space in Orion Nebula, M42/M43, NGC 1976, https://noirlab.edu/public/images/noao-02677 91
Birthplace of modern Spiritualism, Hydesville (Arcadia), NY 93
Ellen G. White, photographer G. W. Loring of Battle Creek, 1864, https://ellenwhite.org/media/image/803 94
"The Rich Young Man," by Harold Copping 96
"The Expulsion from the Garden," by Gustave Doré 97
Final destruction of Satan after the millennium 98
EVENTS OF THE MILLENNIUM BEFORE AND AFTER 99
Father on throne with the Son and the redeemed 105
June 21, 1851 envelope marked "Preserve carefully" 108
The Three Angels, by Joe Maniscalco, courtesy LLT Production 110
The Augsburg Confession regarding the papacy's claim of the change of the Sabbath 112
Jesus welcoming the redeemed, https://blesseddad.wordpress.com/2011/07/27/the-one-who-loved-jesus 112
The 1843 prophecy chart, downloaded from https://www.truthseeker.church/the-prophetic-chart-of-1843 117
Jesus, frontispiece of *The Coming King*, https://ia802508.us.archive.org/27/items/comingking00whit/comingking00whit.pdf, krei.ai 119
Ellen White holding up a Bible in vision, https://www.pinterest.cl/pin/124060164726287709 120
Train of cars at lightning speed, https://www.openpr.com/news/2111687/high-speed-trains-market-to-enjoy-explosive-growth-to-2025 124
Thomas Paine, painted by Auguste Millière, 1888, https://is.wikipedia.org/wiki/Thomas_Paine 125
Header *Advent Review and Sabbath Herald*, 23 Jun 1853 128
Foot washing, https://www.itf.edu.br/institucional/noticias-exibe/128703834/as+multiplas+dimensoes+do+lavapes.htm 141
"Cigares de Joy Cure Asthma," *Truth*, 21 Nov 1895, https://archive.org/details/truth38unse/page/1286/mode/2up 144
Weeping angel, https://wallpapersafari.com/w/orFxNe 146
"Agony in the Garden," by Franz Schwartz, 1898, https://fineartamerica.com/featured/agony-in-the-garden-1898-frans-schwartz.html 147
Annie Rebekah Smith, self-portrait, https://ellenwhite.org/media/image/678 148
When a Colt Bowed Its Head, *Stories of Little Ellen and the Message*, 43 150
Frances H. Lunt, https://www.centerforadventistresearch.org/photos/special-collections/L.%20T.%20Nicola%20Album/b17485307_k0001.jpg 150
Bible over head, "Historic Adventist Village Stories - Ellen White," at https://www.youtube.com/watch?v=FH2aMRMEkh0&t=5s 151
Joseph Bates, https://encyclopedia.adventist.org/article?id=88Y2 152
Israel Dammon, courtesy Jim Nix 152
A wild colt tamed, Harry Baerg, *His Messenger* (revised), 60 152
James White cutting hay, RH 4 Apr 1935, 4 153
Hiram Edson, https://www.youtube.com/watch?v=jHJq-viYnIU 153
Louisa Howland, https://ellenwhite.org/media/image/408 154
Washington Morse, https://encyclopedia.adventist.org/article?id=89TR 155
George and Martha D. Amadon, 1865, G. W. Loring, photographer, https://adventistdigitallibrary.org/adl-364930/george-and-martha-amadon 155
John Byington, https://en.wikipedia.org/wiki/John_Byington 156
J. N. Loughborough, by Adams and Stillard, https://ellenwhite.org/media/image/520 156
Franklin Chauncey Castle, via Danielle Elizalde, ancestry.com, 23 Jan 2015 157
Daniel Palmer's house, Jackson, MI, *Footprints of the Pioneers*, 142 158
Daniel R. Palmer, https://ellenwhite.org/media/image/612 158
Abigail Palmer, https://ellenwhite.org/media/image/613 158
Cyrenius Smith, https://encyclopedia.adventist.org/article?id=BA6C 158
David Henry Lamson, https://www.centerforadventistresearch.org/photos/special-collections/L.%20T.%20Nicola%20Album/b1748666x_k0001.jpg 159
Victorian antique brass hand mirror, https://www.etsy.com 159
Drusilla Orton Lamson, https://www.findagrave.com/memorial/59110555/drusilla-lamson/photo 159
Victorian candle, https://www.freeimages.com/photo/candle-1183068 159
Charles S. Glover, https://ellenwhite.org/media/image/337 160
Daniel T. Bourdeau, https://ellenwhite.org/media/image/97 160
Mrs. Alvira P. Parker, from the collection of Michael Ayn Gray, https://www.judyandconradproductions.net/terrill/images/c2008-04-15-006-px.jpg 161
Ellen G. White, 1859, https://ellenwhite.org/media/image/831 161
Lovett's Grove schoolhouse, location of the Great Controversy Vision, https://ellenwhite.org/media/image/1910 162
The Parkville meetinghouse, ... 162
"John S. Brown," advertisement, Fort Wayne Directory, 1874–1875, https://archive.org/details/fortwayneindiana00rlpo_7/page/306 162
Locations of the SDA Church and James White's house in Battle Creek (1858 map), https://www.loc.gov/resource/g4113c.la000323/?r=0.011,0.198,0.093,0.046,0; SDA Church, https://ellenwhite.org/media/image/1153; James White's house, https://ellenwhite.org/media/image/4273 163
Martha D. Amadon, née Byington, RH 25 Mar 1937, 23 163
Otsego Vision, from painting by Vernon Nye, using Krea.ai 163
Aaron Hilliard, https://encyclopedia.adventist.org/article?id=F9HA 164
Edward Hilliard, https://encyclopedia.adventist.org/article?id=A7XE 164
Aaron Hilliard's house in Otsego, Michigan, photographed in 1938 https://encyclopedia.adventist.org/article?id=F9HA 164
James White, https://ellenwhite.org/media/image/2163 165
Uriah Smith, c. 1860, https://ellenwhite.org/media/image/689 .. 166
Nellie Sisley Starr, via starrjeff55, ancestry.com, 11 Sep 2017 . 167
Jotham M. Aldrich, https://ellenwhite.org/media/image/4560 167
Harrison Sherwood Woolsey, https://www.findagrave.com/memorial/15332067/harrison-s-woolsey 167
Rochester lamp, https://www.invaluable.com/auction-lot/the-rochester-victorian-oil-lamp-73-c-1b1436da46 167
Lucinda Hall, https://ellenwhite.org/media/image/354 168
Daniel T. Bourdeau, https://ellenwhite.org/media/image/100 168
Parmenas Saxby and Edna Snow Saxby, via MAN273842, ancestry.com, 10 Jun 2013 169
Augustin Cornelius Bourdeau, https://encyclopedia.adventist.org/article?id=790F 169
William C. White, https://ellenwhite.org/media/image/880 169
S. N. Haskell, https://encyclopedia.adventist.org/article?id=69G2 . 170
Ellen White writing, "Ellen White's Visions" by Journey Films, https://www.youtube.com/watch?v=3DOwUIftNlo 170
Heman Gurney, https://ellenwhite.org/media/image/348; Joseph Bates, https://ellenwhite.org/media/image/64; Ezra P. Butler https://ellenwhite.org/media/image/121; J. N. Loughborough, https://www.centerforadventistresearch.org/photos/photographs/b1747/b17483852_k0001.jpg; Daniel T. Bourdeau, https://ellenwhite.org/media/image/100; Nellie Sisley Starr, https://www.centerforadventistresearch.org/photos/photographs/b1747/b17485447_k0001.jpg; silhouettes; S. M. I. Henry, https://encyclopedia.adventist.org/article?id=89GU; Edith Brownsberger, via gpcarlson1, ancestry.com, 11 Nov 2016; *H. L. Hastings*, via JasenPowell, ancestry.com, 15 Feb 2020; Rachel Preston, https://ellenwhite.org/media/image/55; Worcester Ball, https://ellenwhite.org/media/image/55; John C. Day, via Bonnie Cox, ancestry.com, 6 Oct 2023; Solomon Myers, via llh14018, ancestry.com, 5 Apr 2020; Stephen Smith, https://ellenwhite.org/media/image/683; T. M. Steward, https://scholarsrepository.llu.edu/cgi/viewcontent.cgi?article=1022&context=advent-heritage; Philip Strong, https://www.familysearch.org/tree/person/memories/KHYQ-B34, via RobertShultz7, 22 Jan 2018; Joshua V. Himes, Isaac C. Wellcome, Miles Grant, https://archive.org/details/HistoryOfTheSecondAdventMessage, 589; John Megquier, in H. A. and G. W. Poole, *History of Poland* (1890), 21, https://archive.org/details/historyofpolande00pool/page/20/mode/2up; Israel Dammon, via Jim Nix; B. F. Snook, https://www.centerforadventistresearch.org/photos/photographs/b2900/b29281234_k0001.jpg; W. H. Brinkerhoff, https://www.centerforadventistresearch.org/photos/

photographs/b2900/b29281234_k0001.jpg; John B. Bezzo, https://www.wikitree.com/wiki/Bezzo-18; Erastus Clark, https://www.findagrave.com/memorial/13061973/erastus-clark; James M. Stephenson, *Adventist Heritage*, v 9, no 2, 32; and Hiram V. Reed, https://www.academia.edu/44110676/Biographical_Encyclopedia_of_Church_of_God_AF, 248, 120; A. C. Long, https://www.findagrave.com/memorial/20780378/abraham-cauffman-long; Gilbert W. Cranmer, https://en.wikipedia.org/wiki/Church_of_God_(Seventh-Day); Henry C. Blanchard, via katemblanchard, ancestry.com, 25 Mar 2013; Moses Hull, https://upload.wikimedia.org/wikipedia/commons/2/25/Moses_Hull_circa_1902.png; D. M. Canright, https://ellenwhite.org/media/image/140; Albion Fox Ballenger and Edward Ballenger, via Lisa Arnett, ancestry.com, 9 Apr 2019; Elmer E. Franke, via LindaKAllen, ancestry.com, 3 Mar 2016; Ludwig R. Conradi, https://adventistdigitallibrary.org/adl-365025/richard-conradi ... 172

2 Esdras, https://www.kingjamesbibleonline.org/2-Esdras_1_1611 ... 173

Isaac Sanborn, https://ellenwhite.org/media/image/672 ... 175

Joseph H. Waggoner, https://ellenwhite.org/media/image/742 175

Antiquarian Bibles, (Inset) boy holding Harmon family Bible https://ellenwhite.org/media/image/2002 ... 176

William Miller, https://ellenwhite.org/media/image/555 ... 177

Ellen White, c. 1878, https://ellenwhite.org/media/image/193 .. 177

Grapes in Ontario on trellis wire, posted by Agne27 on 27 Dec 2010, https://commons.wikimedia.org/wiki/File:Wine_grapes_nearing_harvest_in_Ontario-also_example_of_trellis_wire.jpg ... 178

"Map of Cumberland County, Maine," Casco Street Christian Church and Beethoven Hall, Portland, https://www.loc.gov/resource/g3733c.la000266/?r=0.778,0.296,0.073,0.044,0; inset, https://oshermaps.org/map/11753.0001 ... 180

William Tennent, https://www.wikitree.com/photo/jpg/Tennent-163 181

Silas Curtis, https://encyclopedia.adventist.org/article?id=9CEN .. 182

African Methodist Episcopal Church, on Beacon Hill, https://encyclopedia.adventist.org/article?id=9CEN ... 185

J. N. Loughborough, via Marcia Tangwell, ancestry.com, 17 Oct 2018 ... 191

Platforms of the three steps, Antonio Bernard ... 191

Foy's gravesite, Sullivan, Maine, courtesy of Jim Nix ... 191

The Christian Experience of William E. Foy Together with the Two Visions He Received in the Months of January and February 1842 (1845); *The Day-Star*, 24 Jan 1846, with Ellen Harmon's letter, "To the Little Remnant Scattered Abroad," "A Word to the 'Little Flock,'" *Second Advent Review and Sabbath Herald* Extra (21 Jul 1851); *A Sketch of the Christian Experience and Views of Ellen G. White* (1851); *A Sketch of the Christian Experience and Views of Ellen G. White*, 2nd edition (1882, 1884); *Spiritual Gifts Volume One: Sketches from the Life of Christ, and the Experience of the Christian Church* (1882); *Early Writings of Mrs. White Experience and Views and Spiritual Gifts*, Volume One, 2nd ed. (1882, 1884), 4th ed. (1891); 5th ed. (1893), 6th ed. (1894), 7th ed. (1898), 8th ed. (1899), 9th ed. (1900), 10th ed. (1906), 11th ed. (1907), 12th ed. (1912), 13th ed. (1916), 15th ed. (1919); *Early Writings of Mrs. White Experience and Views and Spiritual Gifts, Volume One* (1920); *Early Writings of Ellen G. White* (1945) ... 194

Ellen White's handwriting, Ada K. Morgan ... 212

The crucifixion, engraving by Richard Brend'Amour (1831–1915), https://www.flickr.com/photos/britishlibrary/11174983695 220

1857 combined *Experience and Views of Ellen G. White, Supplement*, courtesy Ruthie Karr; *Testimonies*, Nos. 1 and 2, Center for Adventist Research ... 223

Charles Andrews, https://adventistdigitallibrary.org/adl-364894/charles-m-andrews; John N. Andrews, https://adventistdigitallibrary.org/adl-421890/john-n-andrews; Marie Andrews, https://adl.b2.adventistdigitallibrary.org/concern/images/p007099_marie_ann; Jehiel Beman, https://www.wikitree.com/photo.php/thumb/5/5e/Beman-132.jpg/500px-Beman-132.jpg; Charles Boyd, https://encyclopedia.adventist.org/article?id=AAZ0; Maud Boyd, https://encyclopedia.adventist.org/article?id=AAZ0; Electa Brown, via Brekke Shulthise, ancestry.com, 26 Apr 2020; Samuel Brown, via MaureenReuter213, ancestry.com, 5 Mar 2022; Sidney Brownsberger, https://encyclopedia.adventist.org/article?id=G91J; Samuel D. Burchard, via Sherral72, ancestry.com, 23 May 2015; Phebe Chamberlain, https://adventistdigitallibrary.org/adl-364910/phebe-r-chamberlain; Eli Curtis, via GeneBetit, ancestry.com, 16 Jul 2014; John Daigneau, https://www.centerforadventistresearch.org/photos/photographs/b1750/b1750529x_k0001.jpg; Israel Allen Dammon, MROUETTE74, ancestry.com, 18 Feb 2010; Jules-Etienne Dietschy, https://cdm.llu.edu/digital/collection/wephotos/id/628/rec/2; Martha Ensign, https://www.familysearch.org/tree/person/timeline/KN6C-JQD; Jules-Henri Guenin, https://documents.adventistarchives.org/Periodicals/LM/LM19211101-XXV-21.pdf; Harriet F. Hastings, *Pebbles from the Path of a Pilgrim*, frontispiece; Squire Howard, via Jean Hutchins, ancestry.com, 26 Oct 2012; Moses Hull, https://www.centerforadventistresearch.org/photos/photographs/b2900/b29281234_k0001.jpg; William F. Jamieson, via gober1901, ancestry.com, 16 Jul 2016; Charles C. Lewis, via Amy Fritsch nee Hull nee Brinton, ancestry.com, 25 Apr 2018; Noah Lunt, Noah Norton Lunt, via Cynthia Logan, ancestry.com, 18 Jul 2011; Harriet McCann, https://commons.wikimedia.org/wiki/File:Harriet_McCann.jpg; Mary Morton, née Sanford, https://ancestors.familysearch.org/en/L4SK-MJ2/mary-abigail-sanford-1840-1932; Noble Nordyke, https://www.wikitree.com/photo/jpg/Nordyke-138; Richard Oliphant, publisher https://archive.org/details/historyofoswegoc00john/page/n221; Caroline and Jonathan Orton, https://www.findagrave.com/memorial/41077208/jonathan-trumbull-orton; Sarah Peck, https://encyclopedia.adventist.org/article?id=AJI9; Stephen Pierce, https://ellenwhite.org/media/image/5700; John Stiles Preston, via shelleybrown76, ancestry.com, 26 Nov 2015 (from Eva Alice Robbins, step granddaughter); Rachel Preston, Review and Herald Publishing Assn.; John Sisley, via mws1551, ancestry.com, 8 Jun 2011; S. S. Snow, *The Voice of Elias; Or Prophecy Restored*; Peter Staples, via Julie Leslie, ancestry.com, 13 Feb 2022; George States, via skellyglenn, ancestry.com, 25 Jan 2013; Albert Vuilleimier, https://ellenwhite.org/media/image/34; Walter White, via JamesAnible, ancestry.com, 7 May 2014; Matthew F. Whittier, *Mathew Franklin Whittier in His Own Words*; Henry Winslow, https://www.centerforadventistresearch.org/photos/special-collections/L.%20T.%20Nicola%20Album/b1748456x_k0001.jpg; Rebecca Winslow, https://www.centerforadventistresearch.org/photos/special-collections/L.%20T.%20Nicola%20Album/17484571_k0001.jpg ... 262

Biographical Index

Birth and death dates have links to biographical summaries; credit for contributors is in parentheses; an asterisk (*) marks portraits.

ABBEY, Diana, née Risley (1815–1886) *m. Alonzo Abbey* https://www.findagrave.com/memorial/209733870/diana-abbey

ABBEY, Ira Asa (c. 1816–1894) 2SG 101, 102, 143, 150, 303; EGWE 289; 2EGWLM 996; RH 11 Dec 1894, 783

ABBEY, Rhoda Bickford, née Rhodes (c. 1813–1895) *m. Ira Asa Abbey* 2SG 101, 102, 303; EGWE 289; RH 10 Sep 1895, 591; 2EGWLM 996

ALCOTT, Mrs., *see OLCOTT, Elizabeth Hanna*

ALDRICH, Jotham M. (1826–1870) EGWE 290; RH 27 Sep 1870, 120; https://www.findagrave.com/memorial/15332930/jotham-m-aldrich *167

ALLEN, Henry (?–?) 2SG 157, 159

AMADON, George Washington (1832–1913) RH 20 Mar 1913, 279; 2SG 299, 304; 1EGWLM 780; EGWE 291; 10SDAC 58; https://encyclopedia.adventist.org/article?id=F8V3 (Brian Eugene Strayer) *155

AMADON, Martha D., née Byington (1834–1937) ("Dorner," according to Brian Strayer) *m. George W. Amadon* 1EGWLM 780; EGWE 291; 10SDAC 58; RH 21 Jan 1937, 24; RH 4 Feb 1937, 21; https://encyclopedia.adventist.org/article?id=58V5 (Brian E. Strayer) *155, 163

ANDREWS, Charles Melville (1857–1927) RH 18 Aug 1927, 22; https://www.findagrave.com/memorial/167917727/charles-melville-andrews *262

ANDREWS, Edward (1798–1865) 2SG 143, 301, 303; 1EGWLM 781; EGWE 293; RH 2 May 1865, 175

ANDREWS, John Nevins (1829–1883) 2SG 117, 144, 221, 299, 300; 1EGWLM 781; EGWE 294; 10SDAC 68; RH 30 Oct 1883, 680; https://encyclopedia.adventist.org/article?id=C8VX (Gilbert M. Valentine); https://documents.adventistarchives.org/Books/JNA-TMTM-1984.pdf (Harry Leonard, ed.); *J. N. Andrews: Mission Pioneer, Evangelist, and Thought Leader* (Gilbert M. Valentine); see also the bibliography at https://library.puc.edu/heritage/bib-jnandrw.html *262

ANDREWS, Marie Ann, née Dietschy (1864–1958) *m. Charles Melville Andrews* https://www.findagrave.com/memorial/167917768/marie-ann_d.-andrews; RH 26 Feb 1959, 26 *262

ANTHONY, R. *owner of northern farm on West Island*

ARNOLD, David (1805–1889) 2SG 97, 98, 149; 1EGWLM 783; https://encyclopedia.adventist.org/article?id=18WA (Michael W. Campbell); EGWE 297; 10SDAC 116; RH 23 Jul 1889, 479

ARNOLD, Lucretia Susestice, née Root (1812–1899) *m. David Arnold* 2SG 149; 1EGWLM 783

ASHLEY, Melora Atwood, née Crapo (1820–1904) *m. Josiah Leonard Ashley* 2SG 303; 1EGWLM 784; RH 24 Mar 1904, 23

AVERY, Betsey Hannah, née Meeker (1832–1911) *m. William Rufus Hyde Avery*

AVERY, John Mason (1857–1858)

AVERY, William Rufus Hyde (1827–1916) RH 9 Mar 1916, 21; https://www.findagrave.com/memorial/135333455/william-rufus_hyde-avery

AYER, James, Jr. (1806–1891) https://www.findagrave.com/memorial/54892924/james-ayer

AYER, James, Sr. (1773–after 1860) https://www.familysearch.org/ark:/61903/1:1:M6V7-LPM

BAILEY, Noah (1818–1870) https://www.familysearch.org/tree/person/details/KCTQ-WT3; https://www.findagrave.com/memorial/23618276/noah-bailey; 2SG 131, 132

BAKER, Dorinda, *see MANSELL, Dorinda*

BAKER, Joseph (1800–1862) 2SG 145; 1EGWLM 785; 10SDAC 155; https://encyclopedia.adventist.org/article?id=98XB (Kevin M. Burton)

BAKER, Mary, née Austin (1797–1876) *m. Joseph Baker*

BALDWIN, David Abeel, Dr. (1827–1905) https://www.findagrave.com/memorial/197063174/david-abeel-baldwin

BALLENGER, Albion Fox (1861–1921) EGWE 161; 302; 10SDAC 156; https://www.findagrave.com/memorial/147173223/albion-fox-ballenger *172

BALLENGER, Edward Stroud (1864–1955) EGWE 303; https://www.findagrave.com/memorial/136177485/edward-stroud-ballenger *172

BALL, Worcester H. (1825–1902). https://www.findagrave.com/memorial/27390204/worcester-h-ball; EGWE 301, though confusing with William H. Ball (1823–1872) *172

BANGS, Elizabeth N., née Harmon (1827–1891) *m. Reuben Bangs* https://www.findagrave.com/memorial/129109835/elizabeth-n-bangs; 1EGWLM 786; EGWE 304

BARNES, Abram (1822–1894) 2SG 301, 302; RH 11 Dec 1894, 783

BARR, Eri L. (1814–1864) https://encyclopedia.adventist.org/article?id=8CDT (Benjamin Baker); 1EGWLM 787; RH 15 Dec 1864, 23

BARRINGER, Henry J. (1811–1891) https://www.findagrave.com/memorial/119446064/henry-barringer

BARTON, Harriet Augusta, née Stowell (1832–1914) *m. Major Barton* https://www.findagrave.com/memorial/53415082/harriet-augusta-barton; EGWE 788

BATES, Joseph, Jr. (1792–1872) https://www.findagrave.com/memorial/42355160/joseph-bates; 2SG 82, 83, 92, 93, 97-101, 104, 116; 1EGWLM 789; EGWE 305; 10SDAC 170; RH 16 Apr 1872, 140; https://encyclopedia.adventist.org/article?id=88Y2 (Douglas Morgan); *The Autobiography of Elder Joseph Bates*; *The Early Life and Later Experience and Labors of Elder Joseph Bates* (James White); *Outrider of the Apocalypse: Life and Times of Joseph Bates* (Godfrey T. Anderson); *Joseph Bates: The Real Founder of Seventh-day Adventism* (George Knight) *58, 152, 172, 284

BEAN, Henry C. Bean (1839–1916) https://www.findagrave.com/memorial/44134240/henry-c.-bean

BEAN, Mary J., née Dammon (1839–?) *m. Henry C. Bean* https://www.familysearch.org/ark:/61903/1:1:F4DT-QZY

BELDEN, Albert C. (1800–1893) 2SG 93, 113, 149; 1EGWLM 790; https://www.findagrave.com/memorial/172529512/albert-belden; EGWE 307; RH 14 Nov 1893, 723

BELDEN, John (1824–1900) https://www.findagrave.com/memorial/41477832/john-belden; 2EGWLM 1002

BELDEN, Sarah B., née Harmon (1822–1868) *m. Stephen Treat Belden* 2SG 65, 73, 75, 138, 143, 152, 301, 304; 1EGWLM 791; EGWE 311; RH 22 Dec 1868, 286

BELDEN, Stephen Treat (1829–1906) 2SG 152, 304; 1EGWLM 791; EGWE 311; https://ellenwhite.org/people/19457; https://encyclopedia.adventist.org/article?id=7C9D (Milton Hook); *Union Conference Record*, 3 Dec 1906, 8

BEMAN, Jehiel Chappell (c. 1791–1858) https://en.wikipedia.org/wiki/Jehiel_Beman (has wrong birth year) *262

BENNETT, John Garnsey (1812–1893) 2SG 46, 47; https://www.findagrave.com/memorial/132484000/john-garnsey-bennett

BENSON, Betsey, née Barrows (1795–1865) *m. Samuel Benson* https://www.findagrave.com/memorial/149311714/betsey-benson; RH 6 Feb 1866, 79

BENSON, Lucy, née Chappell (1794–1886) *m. Orrin David Benson* https://www.findagrave.com/memorial/71606855/lucy-benson; RH 9 Feb 1886, 94

BENSON, Samuel (1795–1860) 2SG 168; RH 22 Mar 1860, 143; https://adventistdigitallibrary.org/islandora/object/adl%3A22250540, 13

BEVAN, John (1817–1884) https://www.geographicus.com/P/ctgy&Category_Code=bevanjohn

BEZZO, John Baptiste (1828–1877) https://www.findagrave.com/memorial/57363203/john-baptiste-bezzo; https://archive.org/details/1854-messenger-of-truth-jackson-mi-1854-oct-19-v-1-n-3 *172

BILLINGS, Albert Merritt (1814–1897) 2SG 46, 47; https://archive.org/details/cu31924020334813; https://en.wikisource.org/wiki/The_Cyclop%C3%A6dia_of_American_Biography/Billings,_Albert_Merritt *37

BLANCHARD, Henry C. (1833–1920) https://www.findagrave.com/memorial/57131073/henry-c.-blanchard; https://www.kancoll.org/books/cutler/labette/labette-co-p26.html; EGWE 155 *172

BONFOEY, Clarissa Matilda (1821–1856) 2SG 96, 104, 113, 127, 133-135, 139, 140, 143, 152, 191, 208-210; 1EGWLM 793; https://encyclopedia.adventist.org/article?id=I907 (Theodore N. Levterov); EGWE 318; 10SDAC 217; RH 12 Jun 1856, 55

BOURDEAU, Augustin (1809–1875) https://www.findagrave.com/memorial/43223600/augustin-bourdeau

BOURDEAU, Augustin Cornelius (1834–1916) 1EGWLM 794; EGWE 318; https://encyclopedia.adventist.org/article?id=790F (Denis Fortin); 10SDAC 224; LUH 30 Aug 1915, 7 *168

BOURDEAU, Daniel Toussaint (1835–1905) RH 13 Jul 1905, 17; https://encyclopedia.adventist.org/article?id=C90G (Denis Fortin); 1EGWLM 795; EGWE 319; 10SDAC 224 *6, 160, 168, 172

BOUTELLE, Luther (1806–1898) https://encyclopedia.adventist.org/article?id=890H (Douglas Morgan); *Sketch of the Life and Religious Experience of Eld. Luther Boutelle*

BOWLES, John Carrington (1800–1853) 1EGWLM 796; RH 4 Oct 1853, 103

BOYD, Charles L. (1843–1898) EGWE 321; RH 12 Jul 1898, 452 *262

BOYD, Mary "Maud," née Sisley (1851–1937) *m. Charles L. Boyd* https://encyclopedia.adventist.org/article?id=AAZ0 (Michael W. Campbell); EGWE 321; 10SDAC 225; AAR 7 Jun 1937, 1; RH 19 Aug 1937, 22 *262

BRACKETT, Benjamin F. (1821–1882) https://www.findagrave.com/memorial/208806523/benjamin-brackett

BRACKETT, Louisa A., née Foss (c. 1825–1861) *half-sister of Samuel Hoyt Foss and Hazen Little Foss; m. Benjamin F. Brackett* 2SG 46, 48; 1EGWLM 797; EGWE 322

BRAGG, Frances Mary, née Burritt (1826–1896) 2SG 157-159; RH 28 Apr 1896, 271; 2EGWLM 1007

BRAGG, Stephen Anson (1821–1907) *The West Michigan Herald*, 20 Feb 1907, 4; 2EGWLM 1007

BRINKERHOFF [Brinckerhoff, Brinkerhoof], William Henry (1837–1903) 10SDAC 247; EGWE 153 *172

BROWN, Electa Squier, née Moulton (1824–1894) *m. John S. Brown* https://www.ancestry.com/genealogy/records/electa-squier-24-1wkm8b *262

BROWN, Freeman Greenwood (1813–1878) 10SDAC 253; https://www.findagrave.com/memorial/127089599/freeman-greenwood-brown

BROWN, George W. (1834–1890) https://www.findagrave.com/memorial/153257482/george-w-brown

BROWN, John S. (1815–1884)

BROWN, Joseph Darling (1823–1898) https://www.findagrave.com/memorial/250524289/joseph-darling-brown

BROWN, Marie, née Green (c. 1828–c. 1861) *m. John S. Brown*

BROWN, Samuel E. (1806–1862) https://www.findagrave.com/memorial/19487096/samuel-e.-brown *262

BROWNSBERGER, Edith, née Donaldson (1862–1948) *m. Sidney S. Brownsberger Southern Tidings*, 18 Aug 1948, 15 *172

BROWNSBERGER, Sidney S. (1845–1830) https://encyclopedia.adventist.org/article?id=G91J; https://www.findagrave.com/memorial/60194915/sidney-brownsberger; 10SDAC 253

BURCHARD, Samuel Dickinson (1812–1891) https://www.findagrave.com/memorial/28048572/samuel-dickinson-burchard *262

BURDICK, Lucinda S. (Howell), née Armstrong (1827–1914) *half-sister Sophia Elizabeth Reed, née Armstrong; m. John Howell; m. (unknown) Burdick* https://www.findagrave.com/memorial/142823085/lucinda-s.-burdick; EGWE 328

BURRITT, Mary, née Brown (1790–1861) *mother of Mary Francis Bragg* https://books.google.com/books?id=ZHBXGuZ7KQMC&pg=PA142

BUTLER, Ezra Pitt (1796–1875) 1EGWLM 800; EGWE 330; RH 9 Dec 1875, 183 *172

BUTLER, George Ide (1834–1918) 1EGWLM 801; EGWE 331; https://encyclopedia.adventist.org/article?id=7925 (Denis Fortin); RH 29 Aug 1918, 14; 10SDAC 265; *G. I. Butler: An Honest but Misunderstood Church Leader* (Denis Fortin) *7

BYINGTON, John (1798–1887) 1EGWLM 802; EGWE 333; https://encyclopedia.adventist.org/article?id=H92D (Brian E. Strayer); *John Byington: First General Conference President, Circuit-Riding Preacher, and Radical Reformer* (Brian E. Strayer); 10SDAC 266; RH 25 Jan 1887, 57 *156

BYWATER, John C. (1814–1876) https://www.academia.edu/44110676/Biographical_Encyclopedia_of_Church_of_God_AF, 46

CANRIGHT, Dudley Marvin (1840–1919) EGWE 159, 336; 10SDAC 289; *I Was Canright's Secretary* (Carrie Johnson); *The Case of D. M. Canright* (Norman Douty) *172

CARPENTER, Eliza C., née Carpenter, *see NORDYKE, Eliza C.*

CARPENTER, Luman (1812–1880) RH 9 Dec 1880, 382

CARPENTER, William Rodham (1822–1895) RH 14 May 1895, 319; 2EGWLM 1013

CARVER, Henry Edward (1820–1895) EGWE 154; https://encyclopedia.adventist.org/article?id=493C (Denis Kaiser); https://www.friendsofsabbath.org/Further_Research/History%20of%20the%20Sabbatarian%20Movement/historysdcog/history6.html; https://www.familysearch.org/tree/person/details/LK3W-TVS; https://www.findagrave.com/memorial/109943263/henry-e-carver

CASE, Hiram S. (1814–1882) 2SG 181, 182; 1EGWLM 805; 10SDAC 301

CASE, Savilla A. (1836–1869) *d. Hiram S. Case* https://www.findagrave.com/memorial/83470476/savilla-a.-case

CASTLE, Franklin Chauncey (1835–1906) RH 18 Jan 1906, 23 *157

CASTLE, Herbert Alfred (1855–1901) RH 12 Mar 1901, 174

CHAMBERLAIN, Ezra L'Hommedieu (1798–1855) 2SG 91, 96, 98, 116; 1EGWLM 806; EGWE 340; 10SDAC 319; RH 24 Jan 1856, 134; https://encyclopedia.adventist.org/article?id=E93X (Brian E. Strayer)

CHAMBERLAIN, John C. (1792–1856) https://www.findagrave.com/memorial/192208229/john-c-chamberlain

CHAMBERLAIN, Phebe Ripley, née Haskins (1803–1898) *m. John C. Chamberlain* https://www.findagrave.com/memorial/192208074/phebe-ripley-chamberlain *262

CHANDLER, Charles Parsons, Esq. (1801–1857) *31 https://www.wikitree.com/wiki/Chandler-4068

CHAPIN, Desdemona, née Graham (c. 1811–1891) https://www.findagrave.com/memorial/33820668/desdemona-chapin

CHAPIN, Roderick R. (1816–1868) 1EGWLM 807

CHASE, Corinna Claramon, née Stowell (1834–1920) *m. Peter Farmington Chase* RH 21 Oct 1920, 31

CHASE, David (1797–1867) RH 31 Dec 1867, 46

CHASE, Martha M. (1839–1853) https://www.findagrave.com/memorial/239766401/martha-chase; RH 27 Dec 1853, 200

CHASE, Sarah "Sally" (c. 1794–1878) RH 13 Jun 1878, 191

CHASE, Sibley (1803–1859) https://www.findagrave.com/memorial/94662423/sibley-chase

CHASE, Thomas W. (1803–1872) https://www.findagrave.com/memorial/239766379/thomas-w.-chas

CHILDS, Harvey (1796–1868) https://www.findagrave.com/memorial/28852805/harvey-childs

CHURCHILL, Heman Allen (1816–1883) https://www.findagrave.com/memorial/6314713/heman-allen-churchill; ST 3 Apr 1879, 112 (last mention)

CLARK, Erastus (1803–1880) https://www.findagrave.com/memorial/13061973/erastus-clark *172

CLARK, Matthew Lane (1794–1875) https://www.findagrave.com/memorial/80177398/mathew-lane-clark

CLEVELAND, Charlotte Farnham, née Haskins (1823–1914) *m. Charles Cleveland; m. William Cleveland* https://www.findagrave.com/memorial/175419359/charlotte-farnam-cleveland

CLOSE, Lewis P., *resident of Saratoga Springs*

COGGESHALL [COGGSHALL], Ruth Russell, née Handy (1819–1888) *m. Richard Henry Coggeshall* RH 7 Aug 1888, 511

COLLIER, Charles Sterne, Sr. (1803–1856) 2SG 47, 48, 64 https://www.familysearch.org/ark:/61903/3:1:33SQ-GYY1-FR1

COLLINS, Philip (1809–1859) 2SG 108; 1EGWLM 811; EGWE 345; https://www.findagrave.com/memorial/61718972/philip-collins; RH 23 Jun 1859, 39

CONRADI, Carl Ludwig [Charles Louis] Richard (1856–1939) https://en.wikipedia.org/wiki/Ludwig_R._Conradi; EGWE 346; 10SDAC 406 *172

COOK, John Ball (1803–1888) https://encyclopedia.adventist.org/article?id=A95W (Michael W. Campbell); 10SDAC 409

COON, Roger Wooldridge (1927–2011) CUV Sep 2011, 46; https://www.findagrave.com/memorial/256103981/roger-wooldridge-coon

CORNELL, Merritt Eaton (1827–1893) 1EGWLM 812; EGWE 350; https://archive.org/details/michiganhistoric26michuoft/page/52; https://encyclopedia.adventist.org/article?id=4962 (Brian E. Strayer); 10SDAC 410; RH 23 Jan 1894, 63

COTTRELL, Roswell Fenner (1814–1892) RH 19 Apr 1892, 253; https://en.wikipedia.org/wiki/Roswell_F._Cottrell; 1EGWLM 814; EGWE 351; 10SDAC 414 *10

CRAIG, Elizabeth (1814–1851) *m. John Craig* https://archive.org/details/AdventHerald1851V8N17-20

CRAIG, Esther Ann (1850–1851) *d. John D. Craig*

CRAIG, George Franklin (1847–1908) https://www.familysearch.org/tree/person/details/M7BQ-15M

CRAIG, John D. (1809–1883) https://www.familysearch.org/tree/person/sources/G8QT-51M

CRANE, Mary, née Taplin (1798–1869) https://www.findagrave.com/memorial/114272705/mary-crane

CRANE, Milton (1791–1875) https://www.findagrave.com/memorial/114272769/milton_crane

CRANMER, Gilbert W. (1814–1903) 2EGWLM 1017; https://encyclopedia.adventist.org/article?id=G96G (Denis Kaiser) *172

CRAWFORD, Marion Concordia (Truesdail), née Stowell (1829–1913) *m. Delos La Grange Truesdail; m. Franklin A. Crawford* 2SG 301; https://www.findagrave.com/memorial/128378302/marion-crawford; 1EGWLM 817; EGWE 353; RH 18 Dec 1913, 230

CROSBY, William Chase, Esq. (1806–1880) https://www.findagrave.com/memorial/57723939/william-chase-crosby

CROSIER [CROZIER], Owen Russell Loomis (1820–1912) 10SDAC 420; EGWE 354; 2EGWLM 1023; https://www.academia.edu/44110676/Biographical_Encyclopedia_of_Church_of_God_AF, 78

CUMMINGS, Henry (1811–1884) https://www.findagrave.com/memorial/200212158/henry-cummings

CURTIS, Eli (1794–1872) EGWE 355; https://encyclopedia.adventist.org/article?id=A96U (Michael W. Campbell); 10SDAC 424 *262

CURTIS, James Henry (1831–1899) https://www.familysearch.org/tree/person/details/MDVY-5HC

CURTIS, Mercy A., née Barnes (1818–1907) *m. Robert G. Curtis* https://www.findagrave.com/memorial/208031190/mercy-a-curtis; 2SG 43; 1EGWLM 818; RH 12 Dec 1907, 31

CURTIS, Robert G. (1811–1899) https://www.findagrave.com/memorial/208031185/robert-g-curtis; 2SG 83; 1EGWLM 818

CURTIS, Silas (1804–1893) https://www.findagrave.com/memorial/67781475/silas-curtis *182

CUSHMAN, Horace, Sr. (1796–1870) 2SG 153-155; 1EGWLM 818; https://www.findagrave.com/memorial/20926572/horace-cushman

DAIGNEAU, John Magloire (1832–1922) 2EGWLM 1025; EGWE 357; https://www.findagrave.com/memorial/5088295/john-magloire-daigneau *262

DAILY, Steven Gerald https://whiteestate.org/about/issues/psychobiography

DAMMON, Elizabeth C. (1842–?)

DAMMON, Israel (1811–1886) 2SG 40-43; EGWE 358 *28, 172

DAMMON, Israel Allen (1844–1926) https://www.findagrave.com/memorial/179955145/allen-damon *262

DAMMON, Lydia B., née Rich (1821–1893) *m. Israel Dammon* https://www.findagrave.com/memorial/66252652/lydia-damon
DAMMON, Mary J., *see BEAN, Mary J.*
DAVISON, Gideon Miner (1791–1869) https://archive.org/details/cu31924028833064/page/n269
DAWSON, William (1808–1889) *History of Livingston County, Michigan*, 393, 394, 410, at https://archive.org/details/bad0972.0001.001.umich.edu/page/n529
DAY, John Carter (1810–1895) https://ellenwhite.org/people/19458; https://www.findagrave.com/memorial/231496183/john-c-day; 1EGWLM 820 *172
DEARBORN, Mary "Polly," née Wiggin (1778–1866) https://www.findagrave.com/memorial/60054912/polly-dearborn
DELAFIELD, Dwight Arthur Parce (1913–2003) RH 11 Dec 2003, 20; https://www.findagrave.com/memorial/69920911/dwight-arthur-delafield
DIETSCHY, Jules-Etienne (c. 1832–1907) *father of Marie Ann Andrews née Dietschy* *262
DIVOLL, George (1800–before 1889) https://www.familysearch.org/ark:/61903/1:1:VNVL-34
DIVOLL, George W. (1825–19) https://www.findagrave.com/memorial/10936379/george-w-divoll
DIVOLL, Mary Louise [Louisa M.], née Morton (1832–1928) *m. George Divoll* RH 2 May 1854, 120; LUH 8 Jul 1914, 6
DODGE, Abram A. (1817–1892) 2SG 304; RH 31 May 1892, 351; https://www.findagrave.com/memorial/8474060/abram-a-dodge; 1EGWLM 822; EGWE 365
DOORE, Joel, Jr. (1813–1907) https://www.findagrave.com/memorial/132915970/joel-doore
DREW, Hiram Charles (c. 1809–c. 1892) 1EGWLM 823
DREW, Lebbeus (1808–1898) https://www.findagrave.com/memorial/22412771/lebbeus-drew
DRUMMOND, Francis Pinkney, Dr. (1822–1898) https://ancestors.familysearch.org/en/KZQY-DWP/dr.-francis-p-drummond-1822-1898; https://www.findagrave.com/memorial/134407013/francis-p-drummond
DRUMMOND, Maria, née Van Leuven (1831–1860) https://www.findagrave.com/memorial/192496876/maria-drummond
DUBOIS, Caroline Francis (1854–?)
DUBOIS, Elizabeth, née Sargent (1814–?) *m. Henry Louis Dubois* https://www.familysearch.org/tree/person/details/K81W-BN1
DUBOIS, Emily (1859–1860) https://www.findagrave.com/memorial/95258914/emily-dubois
DUBOIS, Henry Louis (c. 1814–1859) RH 21 Aug 1860, 111
DURKEE, Cornelius Emerson (1837–1933) *historian Saratoga Springs* https://www.findagrave.com/memorial/51565381/cornelius-emerson-durkee
EASTMAN, Ezra Stowell (1821–1874) https://www.findagrave.com/memorial/57146925/ezra-stowell-eastman
EDSON, Hiram (1806–1882) 2SG 94, 98, 99, 136; 1EGWLM 823; EGWE 366; 10SDAC 493; *Hiram Edson: The Man and the Myth* (Brian E. Strayer); https://encyclopedia.adventist.org/article?id=BJIN (Brian E. Strayer); RH 21 Feb 1882, 126 *153
EMMONS, Henry Ware (1808–1899) https://www.findagrave.com/memorial/45645502/henry-ware-emmons
ENSIGN, Martha Virginia, née Beck (1833–1930) *m. Lucius Bird Ensign* https://www.findagrave.com/memorial/17123843/martha-virginia-ensign *262
EVERTS, Elon E. (1807–1858) 2SG 157, 217-219; 1EGWLM 824; https://encyclopedia.adventist.org/article?id=G99V (Michael W. Campbell); https://www.findagrave.com/memorial/52463405/elon-everts; RH 11 Mar 1858, 135
FARNSWORTH, Eugene William (1847–1935) EGWE 374; https://encyclopedia.adventist.org/article?id=49A0 (Samuel Gomide); RH 19 Feb 1889, 12; 10SDAE 540
FASSETT, Oel Ray Fassett (1816–1899) 10SDAC 542; https://www.findagrave.com/memorial/65464164/oel-ray-fassett; HSAM 332
FILES, Eunice B., née Freeman (1808–1885) *m. Stephen Files* 2SG 46 https://www.findagrave.com/memorial/121447165/eunice-b-files
FILES, Stephen (1800–1882) https://www.findagrave.com/memorial/121447102/stephen_files; 2SG 46
FITCH, Charles (1804–1844) EGWE 377; 10SDAC 551; https://www.findagrave.com/memorial/76871153/charles-fitch; https://encyclopedia.adventist.org/article?id=A9AJ (Samuel Gomide, Douglas Morgan)
FITCH, Lemon Elisha (1811–1889) https://www.findagrave.com/memorial/150750244/l.-fitch
FLANDERS, Samuel Whitmore (1822–1888) 2SG 301, 302; https://www.findagrave.com/memorial/61180270/samuel-whitmore-flanders; 1EGWLM 827; RH 28 Aug 1888, 559
FLEMING, Lorenzo Dow, Dr. (1808–1867) https://archive.org/details/memoirsofdecease00hump/page/129; 10SDAC 552; https://encyclopedia.adventist.org/article?id=I9AO (Milton Hook); HSAM 171
FOLSOM, Paul (c. 1817–1870) EGWE 377
FOSS, Hazen Little (1819–1893) https://www.findagrave.com/memorial/57470490/hazen-little-foss; 10SDAC 562 *26
FOSS, Louisa A., *see BRACKETT, Louisa A.*
FOSS, Mary Plummer, née Harmon (1821–1912) *m. Samuel Hoyt Foss* EGWE 379 https://www.findagrave.com/memorial/36719631/mary-plummer-foss *25
FOSS, Samuel Hoyt (1817–1888) EGWE 379
FOWLER, Archibald Franklin (1821–1893) RH 27 Jul 1893, 479; https://www.findagrave.com/memorial/109845649/archibald-franklin-fowler
FOWLER, Phedima, née Doty (1829–1919) RH 7 Aug 1919, 29; https://www.findagrave.com/memorial/109947406/phedima-fowler
FOY, Amelia (1837–?)
FOY, Ann (?–?) *m. William Ellis Foy*
FOY, William Ellis (c. 1819–1893) 10SDAC 563; EGWE 379; https://encyclopedia.adventist.org/article?id=9CEN (Benjamin Baker); "Black Forerunner to Ellen White: William E. Foy," *Spectrum*, vol 17, no 5 (1987), 23–28 (Tim Poirier); *The Unknown Prophet* (Delbert W. Baker)
FRANKE, Elmer Ellsworth (1861–1946) https://encyclopedia.adventist.org/article?id=79BK (Douglas Morgan); EGWE 381 *172
FRENCH, John, Sr. (1790–1849) *possible identification of leader in Boston area* https://www.findagrave.com/memorial/209759427/john-french; 2SG 77, 79
GAMMON, Phebe Ann, née Chamberlain (1823–1913) *m. William Whitney Gammon* 2SG 301, 302; RH 5 Mar 1914, 22
GARDNER, Ira (1826–1889) https://www.findagrave.com/memorial/140632298/ira-gardner; RH 9 Apr 1889, 239
GARDNER, William (1797–1862) https://www.findagrave.com/memorial/71554870/william-gardner; RH 11 Nov 1862, 191
GEIL, Samuel Fretz (1825–1909) https://www.findagrave.com/memorial/70799703/samuel-fretz-geil
GIDDINGS, Titus Ives (1817–1886) https://www.findagrave.com/memorial/61964906/titus-i_ives-giddings
GILBERT, Frederick Carnes (1867–1946) 10SDAC 610; EGWE 387; https://encyclopedia.adventist.org/article?id=CAUZ
GLOVER, Charles Smith (1814–1898) https://www.findagrave.com/memorial/79289774/charles-s-glover; 1EGWLM 831; EGWE 388; RH 24 May 1898, 339 *160
GOODWIN, Elias (c. 1818–c. 1872) 2SG 135
GORSLINE, Richard (1806–1864) https://www.findagrave.com/memorial/117932865/richard-gorsline; RH 19 Jul 1864, 63; 1EGWLM 833
GRANT, Harriet Maria, née Hall (1817–1900) https://www.familysearch.org/ark:/61903/1:1:FH18-2LR
GRANT, Miles (1819–1911) EGWE 155, 391; 10SDAC 624; https://archive.org/details/lifeandlaborsmi00pipegoog; https://encyclopedia.adventist.org/article?id=C9DI (Denis Fortin); *Injustice of Eld. Miles Grant, Editor of the "World's Crisis," Toward Seventh-day Adventists* (J. N. Andrews), at https://documents.adventistarchives.org/Periodicals/RH/RH18740414-V43-18e.pdf; HSAM 589 *172
GUENIN, Jules-Henri (1836–1918) *Le Messager, 15 Feb 1918, 19;* https://documents.adventistarchives.org/Periodicals/RA/RA19720401-04.pdf *262
GURNEY, Charles Herbert (1856–1945) https://www.findagrave.com/memorial/141021336/charles-h.-gurney; RH 20 Dec 1945, 23
GURNEY, Heman Stetson (1818–1896) RH 8 Sep 1896, 577; https://encyclopedia.adventist.org/article?id=B9E9 (Michael W. Campbell); 1EGWLM 836; EGWE 393; 2SG 93, 97, 98, 104 *172, 284
HAINES, Benjamin (1812–1859) "Deaths," *Portland Weekly Advertiser*, 27 Apr 1858, 9
HAINES, Elizabeth, née Mills, *see PEARSON, Elizabeth*

HAINES, Orinda, née Mills, *see NASH, Orinda*

HALE, Apollos (1807–1898) https://encyclopedia.adventist.org/article?id=7INS (Milton Hook); https://www.findagrave.com/memorial/159377998/apollos-hale; 10SDAC 657

HALL, Dwight Philander (c. 1828–1894) 10SDAC 658; https://www.academia.edu/44110676/Biographical_Encyclopedia_of_Church_of_God_AF, 120 (listed incorrectly as "David P. Hall"; birth information is also incorrect)

HALL, James M. (1806–1875) https://www.familysearch.org/ark:/61903/1:1:N7PT-HH6; *Whaleman's Shipping List*, 21 Dec 1875, 2; RH 23 Mar 1876, 95; 2EGWLM 1039

HALL, Lucinda M., née Abbey (1838–1929) *m. William Hall* EGWE 394; RH 19 Sep 1929, 29; 2EGWLM 1039 *168

HALL, Simeon (c. 1806–1857) https://www.findagrave.com/memorial/173415504/simeon-hall

HALL, William (1837–1865) https://www.findagrave.com/memorial/32900408/william-hall; RH 18 Apr 1865, 160

HANNAFORD, Dorcas Somes, née Ayer (1804–1881) *m. William T. Hannford* https://www.findagrave.com/memorial/80259779/dorcas-s.-hanaford

HANNAFORD, William T. (1801–1881) https://www.findagrave.com/memorial/80259768/william-t.-hanaford; 2SG 303

HARMON, Eunice, née Gould (1786–1863) *m. Robert F. Harmon, Sr.* https://www.findagrave.com/memorial/57335751/eunice-harmon; 2SG 80, 81, 119, 161, 174, 182; 1EGWLM 839; EGWE 399; RH 26 Jan 1864, 71

HARMON, Robert F., Jr. (1825–1853) https://www.findagrave.com/memorial/71742337/robert-f-harmon; 2SG 82, 161-164, 174; EGWE 400; RH 14 Apr 1853, 192

HARMON, Robert F., Sr. (1786–1866) https://www.findagrave.com/memorial/57335226/robert_harmon; 2SG 85, 163, 174, 182; 1EGWLM 839; EGWE 399

HARP, Phebe (c. 1813–after 1875) https://www.familysearch.org/ark:/61903/1:1:MC1C-YRB

HARRIS, George, *witness of William Foy*

HARRIS, Lydia M., née Jordan (c. 1808–after 1875) *m. William Harris* 2SG 100, 136, 138, 161 (?), 303; 1EGWLM 840

HARRIS, William (1803–1873) 2SG 100, 136, 138, 140, 303; 1EGWLM 840; RH 22 Apr 1873, 151

HART, Josiah Rice (1817–1858) 1EGWLM 840; EGWE 402; https://encyclopedia.adventist.org/article?id=7JK2 (Rachel Middaugh); RH 2 Sep 1858, 127

HASKELL, Stephen Nelson (1833–1922) 1EGWLM 841; EGWE 403; 10SDAC 669; *S. N. Haskell: Man of Action* (Ella M. Robinson); https://encyclopedia.adventist.org/article?id=69G2 (Gerald Wheeler); RH 14 Dec 1922, 7 *169

HASKINS, Mary Ann, née Soren (1798–1850) *m. Thomas Waldo Haskins* https://www.findagrave.com/memorial/150430083/mary-a.-haskins

HASKINS, Ralph Thurston (1808–1890) https://www.findagrave.com/memorial/236567200/ralph-thurston-haskins

HASKINS, Rebecca Love, née Eaton (c. 1810–c. 1882) *m. Thomas Waldo Haskins*

HASKINS, Thomas Waldo (1801–c. 1880) 2SG 67, 68; https://www.familysearch.org/ark:/61903/1:1:MZD6-LRX

HASTINGS, Elvira, née Burrows (1807–1850) 2SG 109-112; 1EGWLM 843; EGWE 405; PrT Aug 1850, 14-16

HASTINGS, Harriet Arabella (c. 1833–1854) 1EGWLM 842; RH 5 Sep 1854, 31; https://www.findagrave.com/memorial/63067483/harriet-a-hastings

HASTINGS, Harriet Frances, née Barnett (1829–1913) *m. Horace Lorenzo Hastings* https://www.ancestry.com/search/collections/60525/records/45942178 *262

HASTINGS, Horace Lorenzo (1831–1899) https://encyclopedia.adventist.org/article?id=GG0H; https://www.findagrave.com/memorial/66407064/horace-lorenzo-hastings *172

HASTINGS, Leonard Wood (1803–1883) 2SG 112; 1EGWLM 843; https://encyclopedia.adventist.org/article?id=D9G3 (Michael W. Campbell); EGWE 405; 10SDAC 670; RH 5 Jun 1883, 367

HAWLEY, Silas (1815–1888) https://www.findagrave.com/memorial/9777948/silas-hawley; https://encyclopedia.adventist.org/article?id=BJKZ (Michael W. Campbell)

HENRY, Sarepta Myrenda, née Irish (1839–1900) EGWE 408; https://encyclopedia.adventist.org/article?id=89GU; 10SDAC 691; https://en.wikipedia.org/wiki/S._M._I._Henry; https://www.findagrave.com/memorial/135708720/sarepta-myrenda-henry *172

HEWITT, Orrin [Oren] (1807–1855) RH 1 May 1855, 222 (Oren Hewett); https://www.findagrave.com/memorial/40511845/orrin-hewitt

HICKERSON, Stanley D. (1952–2016) https://www.findagrave.com/memorial/181474522/stanley-d-hickerson; LUH Apr 2016, 26; RH 1 Mar 2016, 11

HICKS, Ransom (1802–1872) https://www.findagrave.com/memorial/178921227/ransom-hicks; RH 22 Oct 1872, 151

HILLIARD, Aaron Henderson (c. 1820–1875) RH 2 Sep 1875, 71; https://encyclopedia.adventist.org/article?id=F9HA (Brian E. Strayer) *164

HILLIARD, Edward (1851–1936) RH 24 Dec 1936, 21, 22; https://encyclopedia.adventist.org/article?id=A7XE (Shirley Tarburton) *164

HILLIARD, Lucy, née Byington (1790–1854) *m. Clark Hilliard* https://www.findagrave.com/memorial/57111015/lucy-hilliard

HIMES, Joshua Vaughan (1805–1895) EGWE 411; 10SDAC 694; https://encyclopedia.adventist.org/article?id=49HD (Douglas Morgan); 2EGWLM 1041; HSAM 89 *172

HODGES, Larkin Patterson (1851–1894) RH 27 Feb 1894, 143; https://www.findagrave.com/memorial/76251456/larkin-patterson-hodges

HOLLIS, Nelson A. (1806–1885) https://www.findagrave.com/memorial/150786454/nelson-a-hollis; 2SG 145; 1EGWLM 846 RH 14 Apr 1885, 239

HOLMES, James Stuart (1792–1879) https://www.findagrave.com/memorial/24860624/james-s-holmes *31

HOLT, George W. (1812–1877) 2SG 133; 1EGWLM 847; RH 21 Feb 1878, 63; https://encyclopedia.adventist.org/article?id=A9HU (Jonathan Gomide)

HOWARD, Squire Joseph (1832–1903) https://www.findagrave.com/memorial/69753251/squire-joseph-howard (wrong birth date) *262

HOWELL, John (c. 1820–1861) 2SG 49, 50, 71; 1EGWLM 848; EGWE 414; *The World's Crisis*, 8 Jan 1862, 66

HOWELL, Lucinda S., née Armstrong, *see BURDICK, Lucinda S.*

HOWLAND, Louisa, née Morse (1806–1897). *m. Stockbridge Howland* https://www.findagrave.com/memorial/15333170/louise-howland; 2SG 87, 199, 301, 302; 1EGWLM 848; EGWE 415; RH 9 Mar 1897, 160 *154

HOWLAND, Stockbridge (1801–1883) 2SG 42, 43, 87, 93, 94, 107, 108, 117, 121, 149, 152, 160, 214, 301, 302; 1EGWLM 848; https://encyclopedia.adventist.org/article?id=D9IK (Brian E. Strayer); EGWE 415; 10SDAC 716; RH 17 Apr 1883, 254

HULING, Beekman (1794–1864) https://www.findagrave.com/memorial/22272047/beekman-huling

HULL, Moses (1836–1907) 2EGWLM 1046; EGWE 417; 10SDAC 718; https://www.findagrave.com/memorial/256150621/moses-hull; http://iapsop.com/ssoc/1907__hull___moses_hull.pdf *172, 262

HUNGERFORD, Sealey (1811–1867) 1EGWLM 850

HURLBUT, Charlotte Selina, née Welch (1813–1862) *m. Alanson Ames Hurlbut* https://www.findagrave.com/memorial/101897563/charlotte-selina-hurlbut; RH 8 Apr 1862, 151

HYDE, William Henry (1828–1915) 2SG 44, 45, 55; EGWE 420; 10SDAC 732; https://encyclopedia.adventist.org/article?id=G9J7 (Michael W. Campbell) *34

INGRAHAM, William S. (1823–1874) https://www.familysearch.org/ark:/61903/1:1:FDWY-8H2; EGWE 421; RH 26 May 1874, 192; 2EGWLM 1049

JACOBS, Enoch (1809–1894) https://www.findagrave.com/memorial/14212034/enoch-jacobs; EGWE 427; 10SDAC 815

JAMIESON, William F. (1837–1928) https://books.google.com/books?id=_HCHWP2RqxcC&pg=PA999 *262

JORDAN, Sarah, *see STAPLES, Sarah Merrill "Sally"*

JORDAN, William M. (1815–1870) https://www.findagrave.com/memorial/34010358/william-m-jordan; EGWE 433

KEENEY, Harvey G. (1804–1884) RH 21 Oct 1884, 671

KELLOGG, Alida Inez Leila (1850–1872) RH 13 Feb 1872, 71

KELLOGG, George Washington (1814–1876) https://www.findagrave.com/memorial/210468475/george-washington-kellogg

KELLOGG, John Harvey (1852–1943) 10SDAC 851; RH 30 Dec 1943, 24; https://encyclopedia.adventist.org/article?id=89LQ (James L. Hayward)

KELLOGG, Merritt Gardner (1832–1921) 10SDAC 853; RH 9 Feb 1922, 22; https://encyclopedia.adventist.org/article?id=A9LS (Milton Hook); 2EGWLM 1052 *6

KITTREDGE, Phebe Gleason, née Knapp (1824–1870) https://www.findagrave.com/memorial/147385745/phebe-kittredge

KNAPP, Phebe, *see KITTREDGE, Phebe Gleason*

LAMSON, David Henry (1835–1897) 1EGWLM 857; EGWE 445; https://www.findagrave.com/memorial/215980109/david-henry-lamson; RH 26 Oct 1897, 687 *159

LAMSON, Drusilla, née Orton (1831–1919) *m. Joseph Bradley Lamson* https://www.familysearch.org/ark:/61903/1:1:QV2H-HW2D; 2SG 304; https://encyclopedia.adventist.org/article?id=89ND (Michael W. Campbell); EGWE 446; https://www.findagrave.com/memorial/59110555/drusilla_lamson; 1EGWLM 858 *159

LAMSON, Joseph Bradley (c. 1828–1870) 1EGWLM 858; RH 15 Feb 1870, 71; https://www.findagrave.com/memorial/32090535/joseph-bradley-lamson

LAWRENCE, Polly Davis, née Robinson (1794–1882) RH 17 Apr 1883, 254; https://www.findagrave.com/memorial/77796127/polly-d-lawrence; https://encyclopedia.adventist.org/article?id=GJID (Kevin L. Morgan)

LAY, George Talbot (1822–1901) https://www.findagrave.com/memorial/104177475/george-talbot-lay; 2SG 238

LEWIS, Andrew, *witness of William Foy*

LEWIS, Charles Clark (1857–1924) https://www.findagrave.com/memorial/139631928/charles-clarke-lewis

LIBBEY, John Bayles (1820–1872) https://www.findagrave.com/memorial/48405443/john-b-libbey; 2SG 131

LIBBY, Elizabeth, née Mills, *see PEARSON, Elizabeth*

LIBBY, Isaiah (1799–1873) https://www.findagrave.com/memorial/215878389/isaiah-libby

LIBBY, Richard (1782–1833) https://www.findagrave.com/memorial/108505062/richard-libby

LILLIS, Henry, Jr. (1807–1862) https://www.findagrave.com/memorial/162312917/henry-lillis; 1EGWLM 862

LITCH, Josiah Lincoln (1809–1886) https://encyclopedia.adventist.org/article?id=59OZ (Jonathan Gomide); 10SDAC 930; EGWE 452; HSAM 69

LONG, Abraham Cauffman (1846–1900) https://www.friendsofsabbath.org/Further_Research/History%20of%20the%20Sabbatarian%20Movement/historysdcog/history6.html; https://www.findagrave.com/memorial/20780378/abraham-cauffman-long *172

LORD, David H., Dr. (1814–1889) https://www.findagrave.com/memorial/53848356/david-h-lord

LOTHROP, Howard (1804–1883) 1EGWLM 864

LOUGHBOROUGH, John Norton (1832–1924) 2SG 182, 183, 221, 222, 296, 300, 304; 1EGWLM 864; EGWE 456; 10SDAC 960; https://encyclopedia.adventist.org/article?id=99PK (Brian E. Strayer); *J. N. Loughborough: The Last of the Adventist Pioneers* (Brian E. Strayer); GSAM 567; RH 17 Apr 1924, 24; PUR 19 Jun 1924, 6 *156, 172

LOUGHBOROUGH, Mary Jane, née Walker (1832–1867) https://www.findagrave.com/memorial/15334245/mary-jane-loughborough; RH 2 Jul 1867, 40

LOVELAND, Belinda, née Boutwell (1812–1906) *m. Reuben Loveland* 1EGWLM 865; EGWE 457; RH 22 Mar 1906, 23

LOVELAND, Reuben (1807–1897) 1EGWLM 865; EGWE 457

LUNT, Frances, née Howland (1829–1917) *m. Noah Norton Lunt* (third wife) https://www.findagrave.com/memorial/15333178/frances-lunt; 2SG 42, 43, 90, 301, 302; 1EGWLM 866; EGWE 415 *150

LUNT, Noah Norton (1821–1902) https://www.findagrave.com/memorial/158085891/noah_norton_lunt; 2SG 301, 302; 1EGWLM 866; EGWE 458; RH 28 Jan 1902, 63 *262

LUNT, Rebecca E., née Chamberlain (1827–1851) *m. Noah Norton Lunt* (first wife) https://www.findagrave.com/memorial/99350210/rebecca_e_lunt

LUNT, Sarah Howland, née Chamberlain (1834–1868) *m. Noah Norton Lunt* (second wife) https://www.findagrave.com/memorial/15333177/sarah_howland_lunt; 2SG 301, 302; 1EGWLM 866; RH 2 Jun 1868, 382

LUSK, William John (c. 1817–1894) https://www.familysearch.org/ark:/61903/3:1:S3HY-6359-DKF

MANSELL, Dorinda, née Baker (1817–after 1859) *m. Ira Mansell*

MARKS, Alexander Allen (1826–1897) https://www.findagrave.com/memorial/34846113/alexander-a.-marks; 2EGWLM 1065

MARSH, Joseph Arnold (1802–1863) https://www.academia.edu/44110676/Biographical_Encyclopedia_of_Church_of_God_AF, 169; https://www.findagrave.com/memorial/146831165/joseph-arnold-marsh; 11SDAC 37; https://en.wikipedia.org/wiki/Joseph_Marsh_(Adventist); https://encyclopedia.adventist.org/article?id=1JQB

MASTEN [MASTON], Luman V. (c. 1828–1854) 2SG 171-173; 1EGWLM 868; RH 14 Mar 1854, 63; *Memories of the Dead*, 77

MATTHIAS, Barnet (1797–1873) https://www.findagrave.com/memorial/19032918/barnet-mathias

MAYNARD, Augustus W. (1822–1906) 2EGWLM 1066

MAYNARD, Phidelia Ann, née Wilson (1830–1873) *m. Augustus W. Maynard* RH 15 Apr 1873, 153

McCANN, Harriet Gould, née Harmon (1813–1876) *m. Samuel F. McCann* https://www.findagrave.com/memorial/232223291/harriet-gould-mccann; 1EGWLM 868; EGWE 463 *262

McCANN, Samuel F. (1812–1872) https://www.findagrave.com/memorial/232223230/samuel_f_mccann; 1EGWLM 868

MCCANN, William H. (1804–1878)

MEARS, Oliver (1820–1913) https://encyclopedia.adventist.org/article?id=39RS (Brian E. Strayer); RH 4 Sep 1913, 862

MEGQUIER, John (c. 1795–1880) https://www.familysearch.org/ark:/61903/3:1:3QS7-89FQ-H9QK-L?i=622&cc=2241461 *172

MILLER, William (1782–1849) https://www.findagrave.com/memorial/60532213/william-miller; EGWE 468; 11SDAC 73; *A Brief History of William Miller the Great Pioneer in Adventual Faith* (Advent Christian Pub.); *Sketches of the Christian Life and Public Labors of William Miller* (James White) *14, 177

MILLS, Jacob, Jr. (1806–1878) https://www.findagrave.com/memorial/101618563/jacob-mills

MINOR, Clorinda Fosdick, née Strong (1807–1855) *m. William P. Minor* http://en.wikipedia.org/wiki/Clorinda_S._Minor; https://encyclopedia.adventist.org/article?id=99SX (Richard Elofer); https://www.findagrave.com/memorial/68708167/clorinda-fosdick-minor; 2SG 72, 73; 11SDAC 91; *William Miller and the Rise of Adventism* (George R. Knight)

MOODY, Dorcas, *see WILCOX, Dorcas*

MOODY, Dwight Lyman (1837–1899) https://en.wikipedia.org/wiki/Dwight_L._Moody; https://www.findagrave.com/memorial/2493/dwight-lyman-moody

MOODY, John Greenleaf (1830–1914) https://www.findagrave.com/memorial/90952856/john-g-moody

MOODY, Mary Rogers (c. 1784–1868) *m. Samuel Moody*

MOODY, Samuel (c. 1775–1848) 2SG 97, 103; https://www.familysearch.org/ark:/61903/1:1:2WPT-C3Q

MORSE, Washington (1816–1909) EGWE 473; 11SDAC 123; https://encyclopedia.adventist.org/article?id=89TR (Jonathan Gomide); 2EGWLM 1068; RH 25 Nov 1909, 24; RH 23 Dec 1909, 17 *155

MORTON, Louisa M., *see DIVOLL, Mary Louise*

MORTON, Mary Abigail, née Sanford (1840–1932) *m. Asa Carder Morton* PUR 1 Sep 1932, 6; https://www.findagrave.com/memorial/41789346/mary-abbie-morton *262

MOULTON, Joseph (1797–1880) https://www.findagrave.com/memorial/140080947/joseph-moulton

MYERS, Solomon (1819–1898) https://www.findagrave.com/memorial/117565826/solomon-myers *172

NASH, Orinda (Berry) (Haines), née Mills (1797–1856) https://www.findagrave.com/memorial/19367835/orinda-nash

NEEDHAM, Delia Gove (Kendall), née Prescott (1831–1882) https://www.findagrave.com/memorial/70142301/delia_gove_needham

NEEDHAM, George William (1805–1870) https://jrm.phys.ksu.edu/Genealogy/Needham/d0004/I41.html

NEEDHAM, Norman Gardner (1808–1887) https://www.findagrave.com/memorial/40903999/norman-g-needham

NEWTON, Anna Maria, née Berry (1832–1929) *m. Seth Newton* RH 28 Nov 1929, 29; 2EGWLM 1069

NEWTON, Seth (1822–1907) https://www.findagrave.com/memorial/15635909/seth-newton; 2EGWLM 1069

NICHOLS, Aaron Whitney (1816–1906) RH 21 Mar 1907, 23

NICHOLS, Mary E., née Bird (1800–1868) *m. Otis R. Nichols* 2SG 75-79, 84, 91; RH 11 Feb 1868, 142; 1EGWLM 873; EGWE 476; https://encyclopedia.adventist.org/article?id=DIPQ (Michael W. Campbell)

NICHOLS, Otis R. (1798–1876) 2SG 71, 73, 75-80, 84, 91, 106, 108, 109; 1EGWLM 873; EGWE 476; 11SDAC 179; RH 27 Jul 1876, 40; https://encyclopedia.adventist.org/article?id=DIPQ (Michael W. Campbell) *51

NORDYKE, Eliza C. (Carpenter), née Carpenter (1833–1919) *m. William Rodham Carpenter; m. Noble Nordyke* RH 16 Oct 1919, 30; 2EGWLM 1013; https://www.findagrave.com/memorial/105741945/eliza-nordyke

NORDYKE, Noble (1832–1912) https://www.findagrave.com/memorial/8471055/noble-nordyke; RH 12 Sep 1912, 23 *262

OLCOTT [ALCOTT], Elizabeth Hanna, née Stevens (1820–1914) *m. Philander Wilcox Olcott* https://www.findagrave.com/memorial/91064834/elizabeth_h_olcott

OLCOTT, Horace L. (1816–1877) https://www.findagrave.com/memorial/60466144/horace-l-olcott

OLCOTT, Philander Wilcox (1793–1874) https://www.findagrave.com/memorial/83186484/philander-w-olcott

OLIPHANT, Richard John (1801–1862) https://archive.org/details/historyofoswegoc00john/page/n221; https://www.findagrave.com/memorial/30362975/richard-oliphant *262

ORTON, Caroline, née Kerr (c. 1812–1873) 1EGWLM 874; https://www.findagrave.com/memorial/41077205/caroline-orton; *262

ORTON, Jonathan Trumbull (c. 1810–1866) 1EGWLM 874; https://www.findagrave.com/memorial/41077208/jonathan-trumbull-orton; https://encyclopedia.adventist.org/article?id=A9X3 (Ron Graybill); "The Murder of Jonathan Orton," *Insight*, 5 Dec 1978 (Ron Graybill); EGWE 484 *262

PAINE, Thomas (1736–1809) https://en.wikipedia.org/wiki/Thomas_Paine *125

PALMER, Abigail, née Wilmarth (1823–1902) *m. Daniel R. Palmer* https://www.findagrave.com/memorial/29915216/abigail-palmer; 2SG 181, 188, 271, 304; 1EGWLM 875; RH 23 Dec 1902, 23 *158

PALMER, Daniel Carleton (1820–1893) https://www.findagrave.com/memorial/94089806/daniel-carleton-palmer

PALMER, Daniel R. (1817–1897) https://www.findagrave.com/memorial/29915160/daniel_r_palmer; 2SG 189, 271, 304; 1EGWLM 875; https://encyclopedia.adventist.org/article?id=A9XM (Brian E. Strayer); EGWE 485; RH 18 Sep 1894, 607 *157

PARKER, Alvira P., née Ferrin (1826–1907) *m. Elisha H. Parker* https://www.familysearch.org/tree/person/details/K88T-ZBB *161

PARKER, Elisha H. (1818–1891) https://www.findagrave.com/memorial/70578745/elisha-h-parker

PARKER, Julia A. (1848–1863) *Lamoille Newsdealer*, 16 April 1863, 4

PATCH, Hiram (1821–1886) https://www.findagrave.com/memorial/173700343/hiram-patch; RH 23 Mar 1886, 190

PATCH, Sarah Ann, née Benson (1826–1890) *m. Hiram Patch* https://www.findagrave.com/memorial/173700655/sarah_m_patch; RH 13 Jan 1891, 30

PATTEN, William Wilson (1805–1888) https://www.findagrave.com/memorial/176166551/william-wilson-patten

PAYNE, Emma Loretta (Pauling), née Prior (1817–1883) *m. William Henry Payne, IV* https://www.findagrave.com/memorial/206660680/emma-payne; 2SG 125, 126

PAYNE, William Henry, IV (1809–c. 1858) https://www.findagrave.com/memorial/249113331/william-payne

PEARSON, Charles Henry (1824–1906) https://www.findagrave.com/memorial/18893377/charles-h.-pearson

PEARSON, Elizabeth (Libby) (Haines), née Mills (1801–1879) *m. Richard Libby; m. Benjamin Haines; m. John Pearson, Sr.* https://www.findagrave.com/memorial/226415599/elizabeth-c-pearson; https://encyclopedia.adventist.org/article?id=5J9B (Kevin L. Morgan); 2SG 49, 302; EGWE 393

PEARSON, Harriet Poor, née Carlton (c. 1790–1830) *m. John Pearson, Sr.*

PEARSON, John, Jr. (1813–1900) https://www.findagrave.com/memorial/226415738/john-pearson; 11SDAC 309

PEARSON, John, Sr. (1788–1878) https://www.findagrave.com/memorial/226415585/john-pearson; EGWE 489; 11SDAC 309

PEARSON, Nancy, née Lydston (c. 1785–1863) *m. John Pearson, Sr.* https://www.findagrave.com/memorial/226415561/nancy-pearson

PEASE, Nathaniel (1824–after 1903) https://www.familysearch.org/tree/person/sources/LZ63-KBH

PEASE, Pliny (1787–1861) https://www.findagrave.com/memorial/14097689/pliny-pease

PECK, Sarah Elizabeth (1868–1968) 11SDAC 309; RH 8 Aug 1968, 27; https://www.findagrave.com/memorial/48243506/sarah-elizabeth-peck; https://encyclopedia.adventist.org/article?id=AJI9 (Jim Wibberding) *262

PENFIELD, George (1823–1896) https://www.findagrave.com/memorial/89202465/george-penfield

PENFIELD, Polly Post (1824–1912) https://www.findagrave.com/memorial/89208577/polly_p_penfield

PERKINS, Joseph J. (c. 1813–1887) https://www.findagrave.com/memorial/25867717/joseph-j-perkins

PHELPS, Waterman (1814–1874) https://www.findagrave.com/memorial/105612590/waterman-phelps

PICKET, Ephraim (c. 1819–1898) https://www.familysearch.org/tree/person/sources/LDJN-WJC

PIERCE, Almira, née Tarbell (1806–1875) 2SG 168-171; RH 13 Jan 1876, 15

PIERCE, Stephen (1804–1883) 2SG 168-171; EGWE 490; 11SDAC 351; RH 9 Oct 1883, 637 *262

PINNEY, Egbert Ralph (1808–1855) https://www.academia.edu/44110676/Biographical_Encyclopedia_of_Church_of_God_AF, 214; 11SDAC 353

POOLE, Ezra Abell (1807–1894) https://www.findagrave.com/memorial/47220330/ezra-abell-poole; RH 3 Apr 1894, 223; 1EGWLM 879

POOR, John D. (c. 1810–1859) https://www.familysearch.org/tree/person/sources/LCF6-RJ1

PORTER, John Jermain (1821–1901) https://www.findagrave.com/memorial/106976914/j-jermain-porter

PRATT, Elizabeth, née Thomas (1785–1864) *m. Tillson Pratt* https://www.findagrave.com/memorial/26500793/elizabeth-pratt

PRATT, Tillson (1790–1858) https://www.findagrave.com/memorial/26500792/tillson-pratt

PRENTISS, Artemus (1783–1868) https://www.findagrave.com/memorial/101709036/artemus-prentiss

PRESTON, Almira [Elmira] Matilda, née Barnes (1811–1888) *m. John Stiles Preston* https://www.findagrave.com/memorial/27221637/almira-matilda-preston; 2SG 150; 1EGWLM 879; RH 17 Jul 1888, 463

PRESTON, Chandler Bristol (1806–1891) 2SG 127, 134, 150, 303; 1EGWLM 880; EGWE 495; RH 17 Nov 1891, 719

PRESTON, John Stiles (1804–1879) https://www.findagrave.com/memorial/229986032/john_stiles_preston; 1EGWLM 879; RH 30 Oct 1879, 151

PRESTON, Rachel Delight (Oakes), née Harris (1809–1868) *m. Emery Oakes; m. Nathan T. Preston* EGWE 480; 11SDAC 382; https://encyclopedia.adventist.org/article?id=AIQ1 (Denis Kaiser); RH 3 Mar 1868, 190 *172

PRIOR, Edward (c. 1815–pre-1860) 1EGWLM 880

PRIOR, Georgianna, née Paul (1819–1853) 2SG 134; https://www.familysearch.org/ark:/61903/3:1:S3HY-67YS-F36

RALPH, Abby Minerva, née Kilby (c. 1815–1854) *m. Richard Ralph* https://www.familysearch.org/search/linker?ark=/ark:/61903/1:1:F7DB-7M8&id=LBQN-QJK; 1EGWLM 881; RH 17 Oct 1854, 79

RALPH, Richard (1812–1897) https://www.findagrave.com/memorial/133586130/richard-ralph; 2SG 116; 1EGWLM 881; RH 5 Oct 1897, 639

RANDALL, Benjamin Odger (1749–1808) *Life and Influence of the Rev. Benjamin Randall: Founder of the Free Baptist* (Frederick Levi Wiley); https://www.wikitree.com/wiki/Randall-7858

RANDALL, Daniel Boody (1807–1899) https://www.findagrave.com/memorial/128735190/daniel-b.-randall

REED, Hiram Vaughn (1836–1920) https://www.academia.edu/44110676/Biographical_Encyclopedia_of_Church_of_God_AF 223; https://www.findagrave.com/memorial/155679447/hiram-vaughn-reed *172

REED, Nicholas Gilman (1808–1889) https://www.findagrave.com/memorial/260392056/nicholas-reed

RHODES, Lydia, née Ward (1764–pre-1855) *m. Silas Rhodes* https://www.familysearch.org/ark:/61903/3:1:S3HT-6917-H4

RHODES, Samuel W. (1810–1883) 2SG 133, 134, 136, 137, 144; 1EGWLM 882; EGWE 497; 11SDAC 450

RICHARDS, John Thomas (1953–2022)

RICH, Caleb (1750–1821) https://www.wikitree.com/wiki/Rich-1111

RIGGS, Christopher D. (c. 1800–1860) https://www.familysearch.org/ark:/61903/1:1:MCBS-718

RIGGS, Elizabeth "Betsey," née Hunt (1802–1881) *m. Christopher D. Riggs* https://www.findagrave.com/memorial/134658489/elizabeth-riggs

RING, Hester A., née Hannaford (1828–1900) *m. Peletiah H. Ring* https://www.findagrave.com/memorial/157707453/hester-a.-ring

ROBBINS, "Bro." *a church leader in the Boston area* 2SG 75-79

ROSS, Alexander (1810–1888) 1EGWLM 884; EGWE 501; RH 12 Jun 1888, 383; https://www.findagrave.com/memorial/22242214/alexander-ross

RUSSELL, Charles P. (1810–1879) 2SG 181, 182; 11SDAC 476; https://www.familysearch.org/ark:/61903/3:1:S3HT-DCB3-21F; 1EGWLM 885; EGWE 504; "Messenger Party," 11SDAC 51; *Messenger of Truth*, 19 Oct 1854, 2

RUSSELL, Clifford A. (1870–1954) https://www.findagrave.com/memorial/77054715/clifford-a.-russell; RH 18 Mar 1954; LUH 9 Feb 1954

RUSSELL, William (1832–1910) https://www.findagrave.com/memorial/124996446/william-russell

SANBORN, Isaac (1822–1913) EGWE 507; 11SDAC 532; RH 19 Jun 1913, 597; https://encyclopedia.adventist.org/article?id=7IR4 (Douglas Morgan); 2EGWLM 1081 *175

SANDERS, Charles Norton (1862 –1945) https://www.findagrave.com/memorial/248152909/charles-n-sanders

SANDERS, Ella R., née King (1858–1950) *m. Charles Norton Sanders* https://www.findagrave.com/memorial/248152917/ella-king-sanders

SANDERS, Francis, *witness of William Foy*

SARGENT, George (1810–1848) 2SG 75-79; EGWE 508

SARGENT, Lorenzo (1825–1859) https://www.familysearch.org/tree/person/memories/KC4L-X37

SARGENT, Lucy Ann, née Hammond (1825–1920) *m. Lorenzo Sargent* https://www.findagrave.com/memorial/165940571/lucy-ann-sargent

SARGENT, Sarah "Sally," née George (1790–1875) *m. Phineas Sargent* RH 11 Mar 1875, 87

SAXBY, Arthur John (1851–1922) https://www.findagrave.com/memorial/68766749/arthur-john-saxby; RH 20 Jul 1922, 22

SAXBY, Edna Charlotte, née Snow (1852–1925) *m. Parmenas Francis Watts Saxby* RH 30 Jul 1925, 22 *168

SAXBY, John (1793–1874) https://www.findagrave.com/memorial/15720107/john-saxby; RH 24 Nov 1874, 175

SAXBY, Parmenas Francis Watts (1844–1929) *168

SEAMAN, Edwin R. (c. 1820–1858) https://www.findagrave.com/memorial/7652758/edwin-r.-seaman; RH 28 Jan 1858, 95

SEELYE, Mary Susan, née Thompson (1839–1925) *m. Nathan Alson Seelye* https://www.findagrave.com/memorial/117110803/mary-s.-seelye

SERVIS, Aaron Foster (1825–1894) https://www.newspapers.com/article/detroit-free-press/21777195

SEYMOUR, Alva Noyes (1818–1895) https://www.academia.edu/44110676/Biographical_Encyclopedia_of_Church_of_God_AF, 235

SHIPMAN, Isaiah Hatch (1810–1882) https://www.findagrave.com/memorial/65865409/sh

SHORTRIDGE, Elias Willets (1826–1890) 2EGWLM 1085; RH 27 Nov 1860, 15; https://www.findagrave.com/memorial/104422904/elias-willets-shortridge; https://www.friendsofsabbath.org/ABC/CG7/john_kiesz/History%20of%20the%20CoG7_Kiesz.pdf; RH 11 Dec 1860, 31; EGWE 510

SISLEY, John, Sr. (1805–1859) https://www.familysearch.org/ark:/61903/1:1:2NFP-DHB *262

SISLEY, Susanna, née Gower (1820–1910) *m. John Sisley* RH 9 Jun 1910, 23

SKINNER, Henry Burchstead (1812–1856) https://www.findagrave.com/memorial/38136445/henry-burchstead-skinner

SMITH, Abigail, née Coan (1798–1884) *m. Thomas Smith*

SMITH, Annie Rebekah (1828–1855) 2SG 152, 164, 178; 2EGWLM 1087; https://en.wikipedia.org/wiki/Annie_R._Smith; EGWE 512; https://www.findagrave.com/memorial/85105230/annie-rebekah-smith; 11SDAC 617; RH 21 Aug 1855, 31; *148

SMITH, Cyrenius (1804–1874) 2SG 181, 191, 206, 299, 304; https://encyclopedia.adventist.org/article?id=BA6C (Michael W. Campbell); https://www.findagrave.com/memorial/15330830/cyrenius_smith; 1EGWLM 889; EGWE 513; RH 30 Jun 1874, 23 *158

SMITH, Joseph (1805–1844) https://en.wikipedia.org/wiki/Joseph_Smith

SMITH, Joseph Few, D. D. (1816–1888) https://en.wikipedia.org/wiki/Joseph_FewSmith

SMITH, Phineas Atwater (c. 1815–1895) https://www.findagrave.com/memorial/145457216/phineas-atwater-smith

SMITH, Stephen (1806–1889) 2SG 144; 1EGWLM 890; https://www.findagrave.com/memorial/176982040/stephen-smith; EGWE 514; RH 28 Jan 1890, 63 *172

SMITH, Thomas (1792–1874) *History of the Second Advent Message* (I. C. Wellcome), 291

SMITH, Uriah (1832–1903) 2SG 304; 1EGWLM 890; EGWE 515; 11SDAC 618; RH 10 Mar 1903, 3; *Yours in the Blessed Hope, Uriah Smith* (Eugene F. Durand) *166

SNOOK, Benjamin Franklin (1835–1902) EGWE 153; 11SDAC 620; https://encyclopedia.adventist.org/article?id=AA6M (Denis Kaiser); https://www.findagrave.com/memorial/108426994/benjamin-franklin-snook; 2EGWLM 1089 *64, 172

SNOW, Isaac Cook (1819–1894) https://www.findagrave.com/memorial/104429737/isaac-cook-snow; RH 10 Apr 1894, 239

SNOW, Samuel Sheffield (1806–1870) https://www.findagrave.com/memorial/85595584/samuel-sheffield-snow; 11SDAE 620; https://encyclopedia.adventist.org/article?id=9A6O (Kevin Vinicius Felix Oliveira, and Clodoaldo Tavares) *262

SPICER, William Ambrose (1865–1952) https://www.findagrave.com/memorial/163405104/william-ambrose-spicer; RH 13 Nov 1952, 14; 11SDAC 690

STAPLES, Peter (1795–1897) https://www.findagrave.com/memorial/65196351/peter-elder-staples *262

STAPLES, Sarah Merrill "Sally," née Jordan (1821–1886) *m. Peter Staples* https://www.findagrave.com/memorial/65688635/sarah-merrill-staples; https://www.familysearch.org/tree/person/details/GM31-JCH; EGWE 433

STARR, Ellen "Nellie" Elizabeth, née Sisley (1854–1934) *m. George Burt Starr* RH 15 Mar 1934, 22 *166, 172

STARR, George Burt (1854–1944) EGWE 519; 11SDAC 702; RH 20 Apr 1944, 20

STATES, George Orlando (1848–1917) RH 29 Nov 1917, 22; https://documents.adventistarchives.org/Periodicals/PUR/PUR19171206-V17-18.pdf, 7; https://www.findagrave.com/memorial/27932336/george-orlando-states; https://archive.org/details/genealogyofstaat00instaa/page/n363 *262

STEPHENSON, James Martin (1822–1888) 2SG 273, 295; 11SDAC 704; LeRoy E. Froom, *Movement of Destiny*, 152; https://www.academia.edu/44110676/Biographical_Encyclopedia_of_Church_of_God_AF, 248 *172

STETSON, Elizabeth Tillson, née Pratt (1823–1875) *m. Kimball W. Stetson* https://www.findagrave.com/memorial/198638452/lizzie-t.-stetson

STEVENS, Cyprian (1795–1858) 2SG 215, 301; 1EGWLM 892; https://www.findagrave.com/memorial/22396128/cyprian-stevens; EGWE 521; RH 28 Oct 1858, 183

STEVENS, Jesse Harlow (1802–1847) https://www.findagrave.com/memorial/153461264/jessie-harlow-stevens; 2EGWLM 1091

STEVENS, Norman (c. 1813–c. 1875) https://archive.org/details/historyofcompton00chanuoft/page/168; https://www.findagrave.com/memorial/225045805/elder-norman-stevens

STEWARD, Thaddeus Moore (1827–1907) 2EGWLM 1092; EGWE 522; https://www.findagrave.com/memorial/234223797/t-m-steward; https://encyclopedia.adventist.org/article?id=BA8C (Theodore N. Levterov) *172

STOCKMAN, Levi S. (c. 1812–1844) 2SG 20, 21; EGWE 523; https://encyclopedia.adventist.org/article?id=5A8F (Kevin L. Morgan); https://www.findagrave.com/memorial/116681400/levi-stockman; 11SDAC 706

STORRS, Bezalell C. (1803–1868) https://www.familysearch.org/tree/person/sources/K2DV-QDY

STOWELL, Corinna Claramon, *see CHASE, Corinna Claramon*

STOWELL, Harriet Augusta, *see BARTON, Harriet Augusta*

STOWELL, John (1803–1870) https://www.findagrave.com/memorial/33681245/john_stowell

STOWELL, Lewis Oswald (1828–1918) 2SG 301; 1EGWLM 895; https://www.findagrave.com/memorial/150285951/louis-oswald-stowell; EGWE 524; RH 17 Oct 1918, 12
STOWELL, Marion Concordia, *see CRAWFORD, Marion Concordia*
STRONG, Earl J. (c. 1872–1889) https://www.findagrave.com/memorial/15428273/earl-j-strong
STRONG, Philip (1835–1891) *Kalamazoo Gazette*, 2 Dec 1891 *172
STRONG, Saul Samuel (1802–1852) https://www.findagrave.com/memorial/199600216/saul-strong; 2SG 153-156
SWETT, Mary, née Moulton (1805–1836) *m. Moses Swett* https://www.findagrave.com/memorial/24874246/mary-swett
SWETT, Moses (1804–1847) https://www.findagrave.com/memorial/24874248/moses-swett
TABER, Jabez (c. 1774–1870) https://www.findagrave.com/memorial/273304280/jabez-taber
TASH, Charles G. (c. 1823–1867) *witness of William Foy*
TENNENT, William, Sr. (1673–1746) https://www.findagrave.com/memorial/19255738/william-tennent; *The Vision That Changed A Nation: The Legacy of William Tennent* (John F. Hansen)
THAYER, Zaccheus (1795–1852) https://www.findagrave.com/memorial/17564577/zaccheus-thayer; 2SG 78; https://www.familysearch.org/ark:/61903/1:1:XHYQ-QG1
THOMAS, John, *witness of William Foy*
THOMAS, Mary A. (c. 1813–1875) https://www.findagrave.com/memorial/135682984/mary-a-thomas
THOMPSON [TOMPSON], Jesse (1795–1858) 1EGWLM 898; https://www.findagrave.com/memorial/16206391/jesse-thompson
THOMPSON, Nabby Maria, née Gilbert (1805–1866) 1EGWLM 898; https://www.findagrave.com/memorial/16206375/maria-maria-thompson
TOWLE, John R. (1812–1896) https://www.findagrave.com/memorial/117249770/john-r-towle
TRUESDAIL, Marion Concordia, née Stowell, *see CRAWFORD, Marion Concordia*
TURNER, Jane Barnard, née Knapp (1815–1901) *m. Joseph Turner* https://www.findagrave.com/memorial/144298780/jane-barnard-turner
TURNER, Joseph (1807–1862) 2SG 49-51, 62, 63, 67, 68; 11SDAC 802; EGWE 530; https://www.findagrave.com/memorial/146218070/joseph-turner
TURNER, Rebekah, née Strout (1809–1838) https://www.findagrave.com/memorial/66132522/rebekah-turner
VUILLEUMIER, Albert Frédéric (1835–1923) EGWE 533; 11SDAC 847 *262
WAGGONER, Joseph Harvey (1820–1889) 2SG 273; 1EGWLM 900; https://encyclopedia.adventist.org/article?id=9ACI (Brian E. Strayer); https://www.findagrave.com/memorial/16915216/joseph-harvey-waggoner; EGWE 537; 11SDAC 849; RH 3 Sep 1889, 558 *175
WATERMAN, Ebenezer (1795–1863) https://www.findagrave.com/memorial/101524835/ebenezer-waterman
WATERMAN, Rachel D., née Cushing ("Aunt Rachel") (1796–1875) *m. Ebenezer Waterman* https://www.findagrave.com/memorial/101524836/rachel-d-waterman; 2SG 301; RH 3 Jun 1875, 183
WATERS, Elmore [Elmer] W. (c. 1806–1877?) 2SG 134; 2EGWLM 1097
WEAVER, Bruce (1952–2024) https://www.triadfuneralservice.com/obituaries/Bruce-Weaver?obId=33265714
WEBBER, Emma A. (1845 –1912) RH, 20 Feb 1913, 189; https://www.findagrave.com/memorial/229035608/emma-a-webber; *Adventist Heritage*, fall 1982, 53-61
WEBBER, Reuel Stinson (1837–1899) https://www.findagrave.com/memorial/73130141/reuel-s-webber; RH 16 Jan 1900, 48
WELLCOME, Isaac Cummings (1818–1895) 11SDAC 864; https://encyclopedia.adventist.org/article?id=DADN (Milton Hook); HSAM 567 *172
WENDELL, Jonas (1815–1873) https://www.findagrave.com/memorial/5760441/jonas-wendell
WESLEY, Charles (1707–1788) https://en.wikipedia.org/wiki/Charles_Wesley
WESTON, Jacob (1803–after 1870) https://www.familysearch.org/tree/person/sources/MNRF-KPL
WEST, Stephen (1654–1748) https://www.whalingmuseum.org/research/research-resources/manuscripts/mss-38
WHEELER, Frederick Meriam (1811–1910) 1EGWLM 902; 2SG 155, 156; https://encyclopedia.adventist.org/article?id=8AE3 (Samuel Gomide); https://www.findagrave.com/memorial/54241955/frederick-wheeler; EGWE 546; 11SDAC 871; RH Nov 1910, 15
WHITE, Anna (1829–1854) 2SG 173, 175, 188, 191, 193-195; 1EGWLM 904; EGWE 547; RH 12 Dec 1854, 135
WHITE, Arthur Lacey (1907–1991) https://www.findagrave.com/memorial/48336782/arthur-lacey-white; EGWE 547; 11SDAC 871; https://encyclopedia.adventist.org/article?id=DHMN (Norma Collins)
WHITE, Ellen Gould, née Harmon (1827–1915) [EGW] *m. James Springer White* 1EGWLM 906; EGWE 398, 549; 11SDAC 873; RH 22 Jul 1915, 24 *8, 60, 161, 177, 285
WHITE, Henry Nichols (1847–1863) 2SG 211; 1EGWLM 904; https://www.findagrave.com/memorial/15331021/henry-nichols-white; https://encyclopedia.adventist.org/article?id=AB5D (Kathy Lewis); EGWE 398, 553; 11SDAC 888; RH 29 Dec 1863, 39
WHITE, James Edson (1849–1928) 2SG 116, 123, 127, 136, 139, 152, 165-167, 211; https://www.findagrave.com/memorial/15331015/james-edson-white; 1EGWLM 905; EGWE 554; 11SDAC 889; RH 21 Jun 1928, 24 *27
WHITE, James Springer (1821–1881) 1EGWLM 906; EGWE 556; https://www.familysearch.org/ark:/61903/3:1:3QS7-99NW-3HYN; 11SDAC 890; RH 16 Aug 1881, 121; *James White* (Virgil Robinson); *Life Incidents* (James White); *James White Innovator and Overcomer* (Gerald Wheeler) *60, 165
WHITE, Nathaniel (1831–1853) 2SG 173-179, 194, 195; RH 26 May 1853, 8
WHITE, Walter (1809–1882) https://www.findagrave.com/memorial/14089395/walter-white *262
WHITE, William Clarence (1854–1937) 2SG 192, 207, 208, 295; https://www.findagrave.com/memorial/15331018/william-clarence-white; 1EGWLM 910; EGWE 564; 11SDAC 897 *169
WHITING, Mary, née Hamlin (1827–1884) https://www.findagrave.com/memorial/81666507/mary-whiting
WHITMORE, John H. (1837–1927) https://www.findagrave.com/memorial/130057407/john-h-whitmore
WHITTIER, Matthew Franklin (1812–1883) *The Life and Works of Matthew Franklin Whittier* (Lloyd Wilfred Griffin); https://ancestors.familysearch.org/en/K8Y8-YJY/matthew-franklin-whittier-1812-1883; https://www.findagrave.com/memorial/140228831/matthew-franklin-whittier
WIGGINS, Peter V., *resident of Saratoga Springs*
WILCOX, Dorcas, née Moody (1821–1875) *m. John A. Wilcox*
WILCOX, John Yale (1834–1910) https://www.findagrave.com/memorial/33740562/john-y-wilcox; 1EGWLM 911; RH 13 May 1910, 23
WILLIAMS, David and George, *witnesses of William Foy*
WILLIAMS, Edward (1819–?), *witness of William Foy*
WILSON, Amelia A., née Butler (1844–1909) *m. William J. Wilson* RH 14 Oct 1909, 22
WILSON, Betsey, née Temple (1800–1885) *m. Daniel Wilson* RH 5 May 1885, 287
WINSLOW, Henry Clay (1836–1915) RH 25 Mar 1915, 22 *262
WINSLOW, Rebecca [Rebekah] D., née Howland (1836–1918) *m. Henry Clay Winslow* 2SG 301, 302; RH 30 May 1918, 23 *262
WOOD, Newel N. (1826–1902) https://www.findagrave.com/memorial/216392023/newel_n_wood
WOOD, Ruth W., née Ayer (1818–1899) *m. Newel N. Wood* https://www.findagrave.com/memorial/216392022/ruth-w.-wood
WOOLSEY, Harrison Sherwood (1841–1874) https://www.familysearch.org/ark:/61903/3:1:S3HY-6QR9-RD7?i=494 *167
WORCESTER, Thomas (1809–1869) https://www.findagrave.com/memorial/211076276/thomas-worcester
WRIGHT, Dorcas L., née Gould (c. 1792–1860) *m. Russell Wright* https://www.findagrave.com/memorial/117480607/dorcas-l-wright
WRIGHT, John S. (1823–1897) https://www.findagrave.com/memorial/97066057/john-s.-wright
WRIGHT, Russell (c. 1788–1864) https://www.findagrave.com/memorial/117475214/russell-wright
WYMAN, Ira Allen (1807–1885) https://www.familysearch.org/tree/person/sources/KNW9-8DP
YOUNG, George, Jr., *resident of Saratoga Springs*

Scripture Index

*Scripture references are **boldfaced**; endnote numbers are italicized.*

General Index

Names in ALL CAPS are in the ***Biographical Index****; an asterisk (*) marks portraits.*

Other books and resources by the author on related topics

SABBATH REST: Is there something missing in your busy life?
(TEACH Services, Inc., 2002)
Validates the call to worship on the seventh day through history and scripture, stuffed with statements by historians and church leaders about the Sabbath and the rationales for observing Sunday

SACRED TIME UNREMEMBERED: How the Original Sabbath Was Lost and Why It Matters (Torchlight Intelligence Publishing, 2014)
Co-researched with Daniel Knauft, the book responds from history to the question: Why is it necessary to abandon the seventh day which honors God as the Creator?

MORE THAN WORDS: A Study of Inspiration and Ellen White's Use of Sources in The Desire of Ages (Honor Him Publishers, 2010)
Co-written with E. Marcella Anderson King, the book recounts the story behind the writing of one of the most loved and best selling of Ellen White's works—the devotional classic on the life of Christ, The Desire of Ages *with comparative exhibits with other authors*

THE POWER OF HUMILITY: What to do when you are "right"
(Weimar College Press, 2011, available from the editor, Kevin Morgan)
Leroy Moore unpacks the experience of Jones and Waggoner in a new light. Through these stories, he reveals the secret of helping others see truth—through humility

WHITE LIE SOAP: For removal of lingering stains on Ellen White's integrity as an inspired writer (Honor Him Publishers, 2013)
Specially formulated to lift the lingering stains and leave a fresh appreciation of God's prophetic guidance in the Seventh-day Adventist Church

JOURNEYING TO THE SAME HEAVEN: Ellen G. White, the Civil War, and the Goal of Post-Racialism (TEACH Services, Inc., 2015)
Contextualizes from history Ellen White's view of the Black race, slavery, the Civil War, and ministry to the freedmen after the abolition of slavery

LITERARY BEAUTY OF ELLEN G. WHITE'S WRITINGS: Explore the Conflict of the Ages series in a new way! (Honor Him Publishers, 2018)
Annotated edition of Gladys King-Taylor's largely forgotten study of the elements of Mrs. White's writings that have charmed readers for over one hundred years

See other research by the author available on academia.edu
at https://southern.academia.edu/KevinMorgan

and videos by the author about Ellen White and her literary ministry on the YouTube channel **ELLEN WHITE RECONSIDERED**
at https://www.youtube.com/@kevinmorgan_truth

www.ingramcontent.com/pod-product-compliance
Lightning Source LLC
Chambersburg PA
CBHW070240230426
43664CB00014B/2368

* 9 7 8 1 4 7 9 6 1 8 1 5 6 *